OECD-FAO
Agricultural Outlook
2014-2023

BETTER POLICIES FOR BETTER LIVES

FOOD AND AGRICULTURE ORGANIZATION
OF THE UNITED NATIONS

This work is published under the responsibility of the Secretary-General of the OECD. The opinions expressed and arguments employed herein do not necessarily reflect the official views of OECD member countries.

This document and any map included herein are without prejudice to the status of or sovereignty over any territory, to the delimitation of international frontiers and boundaries and to the name of any territory, city or area.

Please cite this publication as:
OECD/Food and Agriculture Organization of the United Nations (2014), *OECD-FAO Agricultural Outlook 2014*, OECD Publishing.
http://dx.doi.org/10.1787/agr_outlook-2014-en

ISBN 978-9264-21089-9 (print)
ISBN 978-92642-1174-2 (PDF)

Annual: OECD-FAO Agricultural Outlook:
ISSN 1563-0447 (print)
ISSN 1999-1142 (online)

FAO:
ISBN 978-92-5-108397-0 (print)
E-ISBN 978-92-5-108398-7 (PDF)

The statistical data for Israel are supplied by and under the responsibility of the relevant Israeli authorities. The use of such data by the OECD is without prejudice to the status of the Golan Heights, East Jerusalem and Israeli settlements in the West Bank under the terms of international law.

The position of the United Nations on the question of Jerusalem is contained in General Assembly Resolution 181(II) of 29 November 1947, and subsequent resolutions of the General Assembly and the Security Council concerning this question.

Photo credits: Cover © withGod/Shutterstock.com; © D. Donovan; © Ekkachai/Shutterstock.com; © baibaz/Shutterstuck.com; © Tukaram Karve/Shutterstock.com; © monticello/Shutterstock.com; © simpleman/Shutterstock.com.

Foreword

The Agricultural Outlook, 2014-2023, is a collaborative effort of the Organisation for Economic Co-operation and Development (OECD) and the Food and Agriculture Organization (FAO) of the United Nations. It brings together the commodity, policy and country expertise of both organisations and input from collaborating member countries to provide an annual assessment of prospects for the coming decade of national, regional and global agricultural commodity markets. The special feature on India has been prepared in collaboration with analysts associated with the National Council of Applied Economic Research (NCAER), the Department of Agriculture and Cooperation, the Ministry of Agriculture of the Government of India and the FAO Representation in India. However, OECD and FAO are responsible for the information and projections contained in this document, and the views expressed do not necessarily reflect those of Indian institutions.

The baseline projection is not a forecast about the future, but rather a plausible scenario based on specific assumptions regarding the macroeconomic conditions, the agriculture and trade policy settings, weather conditions, longer term productivity trends and international market developments. The projections of production, consumption, stocks, trade and prices for the different agricultural products described and analysed in this report cover the years 2014 to 2023. The evolution of markets over the outlook period is typically described using annual growth rates or percentage changes for the final year 2023 relative to a three-year base period of 2011-13.

The individual commodity projections are subject to critical examination by experts from national institutions in collaborating countries and international commodity organisations prior to their finalisation and publication in this report. The risks and uncertainties around the baseline projections are examined through a number of possible alternative scenarios and stochastic analysis, which illustrate how market outcomes may differ from the deterministic baseline projections.

The fully documented outlook database, including historical data and projections, is available through the OECD-FAO joint internet site www.agri-outlook.org.

Acknowledgements

This *Agricultural Outlook* is jointly prepared by the OECD and FAO Secretariats.

At the OECD, the baseline projections and *Outlook* report were prepared by members of the Agro-Food Trade and Markets Division of the Trade and Agriculture Directorate: Annelies Deuss, Armelle Elasri (publication coordinator), Hubertus Gay, Céline Giner, Gaëlle Gouarin, Yukako Inamura, Wayne Jones (Division Head), Pete Liapis, Ira Matuschke, Claude Nenert, Koki Okawa, Ignacio Pérez Domínguez, Graham Pilgrim, Raed Safadi (Deputy Director), Garry Smith and Grégoire Tallard (Outlook coordinator). The OECD Secretariat is grateful for the contributions provided by consultants Pierre Charlebois and Merritt Cluff, staff loans Xu Lei (China), Yunus Poyraz (Turkey), and Stephen MacDonald (United States Department of Agriculture), Michel Prud'Homme from the International Fertilizer Association and Antonio Carlos Kfouri Aidar and Felipe Serigati from Fundação Getulio Vargas (FGV). Additional materials were contributed by Jonathan Brooks, Mitsuhiro Inamura, Andrzej Kwiecinski, and Ronald Steenblik (OECD). Meetings organisation and document preparation were provided by Christine Cameron. Technical assistance in the preparation of the Outlook database was provided by Eric Espinasse and Frano Ilicic. Many other colleagues in the OECD Secretariat and member country delegations furnished useful comments on earlier drafts of the report. The report has benefited from an in-depth review by Ken Ash (Director) and Carmel Cahill (Senior Counsellor).

At the FAO, the team of economists and commodity officers from the Trade and Markets Division contributing to this edition consisted of Abdolreza Abbassian, ElMamoun Amrouk, Pedro Arias, Boubaker BenBelhassen (EST Principal Officer), Franck Cachia, Concepcion Calpe, Emily Carroll (publication coordinator), Marco Colangeli, Cheng Fang, Michael Griffin, Yasmine Iqbal, David Hallam (EST Division Director), Hideki Kanamaru, Tatsuji Koizumi, Holger Matthey (Team Leader), Jamie Morrison, Shirley Mustafa, Masato Nakane, Jean *Senahoun,* Shangnan Shui, Timothy Sulser and Peter Thoenes. Marcel Adenäuer from Bonn University and Tracy Davids from the Bureau for Food and Agricultural Policy at the University of Pretoria joined the team as consultants. Audun Lem and Stefania Vannuccini contributed from the Fisheries and Aquaculture Department, with technical support from Pierre Charlebois. Research assistance and database preparation were provided by Claudio Cerquiglini, Barbara Ferraioli, Berardina Forzinetti, Emanuele Marocco, Patrizia Masciana, and Marco Milo. Several other colleagues from FAO and member country institutions improved this report through valuable details and comments. From FAO's Publishing Group, Rachel Tucker and Yongdong Fu provided invaluable assistance.

Chapter 2 of the *Outlook* "Feeding India: Prospects and challenges in the next decade" was written in close collaboration between Indian colleagues and the Secretariats at OECD and FAO with support from Merritt Cluff and Ira Matuschke. From the FAO Permanent

Representation in India, Bhaskar Goswami provided extensive input and assistance in drafting the chapter, and Peter Kenmore provided valuable guidance. Their contribution was facilitated by an on-going cooperation with the Department for International Development (DFID) in the United Kingdom. Shashanka Bhide and Ayyapasore Govindan from the National Council of Applied Economic Research contributed extensive input and assistance with data and advice. Badri Singh Bhandari from the Department of Economics and Statistics of the Ministry of Agriculture, and Parmod Kumar from the Institute for Social and Economic Change devoted a week in Paris to assist in forming the projections and commenting on the analysis. Drafts from Satish Chander, Director General, and Tapan Kumar Chanda of the Fertilizer Association of India formed the basis for Box 2.4 on the fertiliser industry of India. Ashima Goya of the Indira Gandhi Institute of Development Research in Mumbai contributed drafts for input to Box 2.3 on macroeconomic challenges, which were supplemented with assistance by Isabelle Joumard of OECDs Economics Department. The work benefited from the support of Sanjeev Chopra, Joint Secretary at the Ministry of Agriculture.

The European Commission provided the stochastic analysis of the baseline results. This work was performed by the Agrilife Unit of the Joint Research Centre (JRC-IPTS in Seville). The contributors to this section were Sergio René Araujo-Enciso and Marco Artavia, with inputs from Alison Burrell, Zebedee Nii-Naate and Fabien Santini.

Finally, the valuable information and feedback provided by the International Cotton Advisory Committee, International Dairy Federation, International Fishmeal and Fish Oil Organisation, International Grains Council, and International Sugar Organization is gratefully acknowledged.

Table of contents

Tables

Figures

Acronyms and abbreviations

ACP	African, Caribbean and Pacific countries
AMIS	Agricultural Market Information System
ARS	Argentinean Peso
ABNJ	Areas beyond National Jurisdiction
ACEP	Agricultural Conservation Easement Program (United States)
ACRE	Average Crop Revenue Election (United States)
AMS	Aggregate Measurement of Support
ANP	National Agency of Petroleum, Natural Gas and Biofuels (Brazil)
APEDA	Agricultural and Processed Food Products Export Development Authority (India)
ARC	Agriculture Risk Coverage
ASEAN	Association of South East Asian Nations
ASF	African Swine Fever
AUD	Australian Dollars
AY	Attainable Yield
BCM2	Bergen Climate Model Version 2
BDT	Bangladeshi Taka
bln	Billion
bln L	Billion litres
bln t	Billion tonnes
BRIC	Emerging economies of Brazil, Russian Federation, India and China
BRICS	Emerging economies of Brazil, Russian Federation, India, China and South Africa
BRL	Brazilian Real
Bt	Bacillius thuringiensis
CAD	Canadian Dollar
CAP	Common Agricultural Policy (European Union)
CCC	Commodity Credit Corporation
CET	Common Exterior Tariff
CFA	Communauté Financière Africaine
CFP	Common Fisheries Policy (European Union)
c.f.r.	Cost and freight
CIS	Commonwealth of Independent States
CLP	Chilean Peso
CNY	Chinese Yuan
CMO	Common Market Organisation for sugar (European Union)
CO$_2$	Carbon dioxide
CPI	Consumer Price Index
CPIF	Consumer Price Index for Food
CRP	Conservation Reserve Program (United States)

CSP	Conservation Stewardship Program (United States)
cts/lb	Cents per pound
CV	Coefficient of variation
c.w.e.	Carcass weight equivalent
DDA	Doha Development Agenda
DDG	Dried Distiller's Grains
DPDP	Dairy Product Donation Program (United States)
dw	Dressed weight
DZD	Algerian Dinar
EBA	Everything-But-Arms Initiative (European Union)
EGP	Egyptian Pound
EISA Act	Energy Independence and Security Act of 2007 (United States)
EMFF	European Maritime and Fisheries Fund
El Niño	Climatic condition associated with the temperature of major sea currents
EPA	US Environmental Protection Agency
EPAs	Economic Partnership Agreements (between EU and ACP countries)
ERS	Economic Research Service of the US Department for Agriculture
EQUIP	Environmental Quality Incentives Program (United States)
est	Estimate
E85	Blends of biofuel in transport fuel that represent 85% of the fuel volume
EU	European Union
E15	Fifteen member states that joined the European Union before 2004
E28	Twenty eight member states of the European Union (including Croatia)
EUR	Euro (Europe)
FAO	Food and Agriculture Organization of the United Nations
FCE Act	Food, Conservation and Energy Act of 2008 US Farm Bill
FDP	Fresh dairy products
FFV	Flex fuel Vehicles
f.o.b.	Free on board (export price)
FFP	Feedstock Flexibility Program (United States)
FMD	Foot and Mouth Disease
FPI	Food Price Index
FRP	Fair and Remunerative Price
FTA	Free Trade Agreement
FY	Farm Yield
GBEP	Global Bioenergy Partnership
GM	Genetically modified
GDP	Gross domestic product
GDPD	Gross domestic product deflator
Gt	Billion tonnes
ha	Hectares
HFCS	High fructose corn syrup
hl	Hectolitre
ICAR	Indian Council for Agricultural Research
IDR	Indonesian rupiah
IEA	International Energy Agency
IFA	International Fertiliser industry association

IFPRI	International Food Policy Research Institute
IGC	International Grains Council
IMC	Index of Market Connection
IMF	International Monetary Fund
IMPACT	International Model for Policy Analysis of Agricultural Commodities and Trade
INR	Indian Rupees
IPCA	Brazilian Consumer Price Index
IPCC	Intergovernmental Panel on Climate Change
IUU	Illegal, unreported and unregulated (fishing)
JPY	Japanese Yen
kg	Kilogrammes
kha	Thousand hectares
KRW	Korean Won
kt	Thousand tonnes
La Niña	Climatic condition associated with the temperature of major sea currents
LAC	Latin America and the Caribbean
lb	Pound
LDCs	Least Developed Countries
lw	Live weight
MBM	Meat and bone meal
MERCOSUR	Mercado Común del Sur/Common Market of South America
MFA	Multi-fibre Arrangement
Mha	Million hectares
MILC	Milk Income Loss Contract
Mn	Million
MPP	Margin Protection Program
MPS	Market Price Support
MRP	Maximum Retail Price
MSP	Minimum Support Prices
Mt	Million tonnes
MXN	Mexican peso
MYR	Malaysian Ringgit
N	Nitrogen
NAFTA	North American Free Trade Agreement
NBS	Nutrient Based Subsidy
NFSA	National Food Security Act (India)
NP	Nitrogen, phosphate
NPK	Nitrogen, phosphate, potassium
NZD	New Zealand Dollar
NPS	New Pricing Scheme
OECD	Organisation for Economic Cooperation and Development
OIE	World Organisation for Animal Health
P	Phosphorus
p.a.	Per annum
PAP	Processed animal protein
PCE	Private consumption expenditure
PDS	Public Distribution System

PECEGE	Programme of Continuing Education in Economics and Management (Brazil)
PEDv	Porcine Epidemic Diarrhoea virus
PKR	Pakistani Rupee
PLC	Price Loss Coverage
PPP	Purchasing power parity
PSE	Producer Support Estimate
PY	Potential Yield
RECC	Rice Economy Climate Change model
RED	Renewable Energy Directive in the EU
RFS2	Renewable Fuels Standard in the US, which is part of the Energy Policy Act
RIN	Renewable Identification Numbers prices
rse	Raw sugar equivalent
RSRP	Refined Sugar Re-export Program
RTA	Regional Trade Agreements
r.t.c.	Ready to cook
RUB	Russian Ruble
RUK	Russian Federation, Ukraine and Kazakhstan
RY	Realisable Yield
SAPS	Single area payment scheme (European Union)
SAR	Saudi Riyal
SCO	Supplemental Coverage Option
SMM	Special Safeguard Mechanism
SMP	Skim milk powder
SMP	Statutory Minimum Price
SNAP	Supplemental Nutrition Assistance Program (United States)
STAX	Stacked Income Protection Plan (United States)
SPS	Single payment scheme (European Union)
t	Tonnes
t/ha	Tonnes/hectare
THB	Thai Baht
TFP	Total Factor Productivity
TPP	Trans Pacific Partnership
TRL	Turkish Lira
TRQ	Tariff rate quota
TTIP	Transatlantic Trade and Investment Partnership
UAH	Ukrainian Grivna
UN	The United Nations
US	United States
USD	United States Dollar
USDA	United States Department of Agriculture
UYU	Uruguayan Peso
VHP	Very high polarization sugar
WMP	Whole milk powder
wse	White sugar equivalent
wv	White sugar value
WTO	World Trade Organisation
ZAR	South African Rand

Executive summary

The international prices of major crops have dropped significantly from their historical highs, largely in response to bumper crops in 2013/14. In contrast, meat and dairy product prices are at historically high levels, primarily because their supply fell short of expectations in 2013. World ethanol and biodiesel prices continued their declines from the historical peak levels they had reached in 2011 in a context of ample supply for both.

Demand for agricultural products is expected to remain firm although expanding at slower rates compared with the past decade. Cereals are still at the core of human diets, but growing incomes, urbanisation and changes in eating habits contribute to the transition of diets that are higher in protein, fats and sugar.

In the next decade, livestock and biofuel production are projected to grow at higher rates than crop production. This changing structure of global agricultural production prompts a relative shift toward coarse grains and oilseeds to meet demands for food, feed and biofuel, away from staple food crops like wheat and rice. The bulk of the additional production will originate in regions where determining factors, such as land and water availability, and policy regulations, are the least constraining.

Crop prices are expected to drop for one or two more years, before stabilising at levels that remain above the pre-2008 period, but significantly below recent peaks. Meat, dairy and fish prices are expected to rise. In real terms, however, prices for both crops and animal products are projected to decline over the medium term. The expected stock-to-use ratios for cereals improve significantly, which should ease concerns about their price volatility.

World fishery production will be driven primarily by gains in aquaculture in developing countries. Sustained high costs in a context of firm demand will keep fish prices well above their historical averages, holding back consumption growth in the coming decade.

Production growth will come mainly from developing countries in Asia and Latin America. Trade continues to grow, although at a slower pace compared with the previous decade. The Americas will strengthen their position as the dominant export region, both in value and volume terms, while Africa and Asia will increase their net imports to meet their growing demand.

Recent policy reforms in agriculture and fisheries markets have enabled demand and supply fundamentals to become more responsive to market signals; however, both remain influenced by policies such as producer support, public stockholding and biofuel mandates. Further policy changes are underway. The United States' Agricultural Act of 2014 and the 2013 reform of the Common Agricultural Policy in the European Union have been agreed upon during the last year; however, their provisions are not considered in the current projections because implementation details have not been completed/specified.

Global commodity highlights to 2023

Cereals: World prices of major grains will ease early in the outlook period, boosting world trade. Stocks are projected to rise with rice inventories in Asia reaching record high levels.

Oilseeds: The global share of cropland planted to oilseeds continues to increase albeit at a slower rate as sustained demand for vegetable oils pushes prices up.

Sugar: After weakening in late 2013, international sugar prices will recover, driven by strong global demand. Exports from Brazil, the world dominant sugar exporter, will be influenced by the ethanol market.

Meat: Firm import demand from Asia, as well as herd rebuilding in North America support stronger meat prices, with beef prices rising to record levels. Poultry overtakes pork to become the most consumed meat product over the outlook period.

Dairy: Prices fall slightly from their current high levels due to sustained productivity gains in the major producing countries and resumed growth in China. India overtakes the European Union to become the largest milk producer in the world, building considerable skimmed milk powder exports over the projection period.

Fisheries: The growth of aquaculture production will be concentrated in Asia. It remains one of the fastest-growing food sectors and surpasses capture fisheries for human consumption in 2014.

Biofuels: The consumption and production levels of biofuels are expected to increase by more than 50%, led by sugar-based ethanol and biodiesel. The ethanol price increases in line with crude oil price, while the biodiesel price follows more closely the path of the vegetable oil price.

Cotton: The expected release of accumulated global stocks will boost consumption on the back of lower prices, before prices recover by 2023.

Focus on India

This edition of the *Outlook* focuses on India, the world's second most populous country with the largest number of farmers and also the largest number of food-insecure people. The Outlook portrays a relatively optimistic scenario for India, which is projected to sustain production and consumption growth of food, led in particular by higher value added sectors.

The new National Food Security Act is the largest right to food programme of its kind ever attempted, allocating rations of subsidised cereals (about 90% below retail price) to more than 800 million people. Its implementation will be a major challenge.

Subsidies to encourage greater use of fertilisers, pesticides, seeds, water, electricity, and credit, as well as market support prices, have contributed to strong annual agricultural output growth in the last decade. These programmes continue to promote production growth enabling Indian agriculture to expand per capita supplies considerably, although rising resource pressures reduce absolute growth rates over the next decade.

While remaining largely vegetarian, Indian diets will diversify. Cereal consumption is expected to grow, but greater consumption of milk and dairy products, pulses, fruits and vegetables will contribute to improved intake of food nutrients. Fish will also provide an important and growing source of protein, while meat consumption will grow strongly, though still ranking among the lowest in the world.

Key uncertainties lie in India's macro performance, the sustainability of yield growth and the viability of government programmes.

Note on macroeconomic assumptions

The macroeconomic situation underlying this *Outlook* assumes an average GDP growth of 2.2% per year for OECD countries. Economic prospects for many emerging economies are robust but revised downward slightly compared to the last decade. Most African economies exhibit strong growth. A stronger US dollar will affect the competitiveness of numerous countries. The crude oil price is assumed to reach USD 147 per barrel by 2023.

Chapter 1

Overview of the OECD-FAO Outlook 2014-2023

Introduction

The *Agricultural Outlook* is a collaborative effort of the Organisation for Economic Co-operation and Development (OECD) and the Food and Agriculture Organization (FAO) of the United Nations. It combines the commodity, policy and country expertise of both organisations with inputs from collaborating member countries and international organisations to provide an annual assessment of medium-term projections of national, regional and global agricultural commodity markets. The projections cover production, consumption, stocks, trade and prices for 25 products for the period 2014 to 2023. These projections constitute a plausible scenario of how global agriculture would develop under a certain set of assumptions about its main drivers, productivity, macroeconomic and population trends as well as agricultural and trade policy settings of countries around the world. Given the uncertainties which surround agricultural markets, the final section of the Overview discusses important assumptions affecting the future evolution of agricultural markets and the sensitivity of the baseline projections to selected conditioning factors.

This year's edition contains a Chapter on India, the world's second most populous country, which is fed by the largest farming community in the world. India's agricultural sector has witnessed a considerable transformation in recent years, with significant gains in productivity and total production volume. With its predominantly vegetarian diet, large arable land base and slowly urbanising society, India presents unique opportunities and challenges. Most of the country's agricultural policies in the next decade will be focusing on food security and how to invigorate agriculture to promote growth and employment in populous rural communities.

The setting: Turbulent agricultural markets at the start of the outlook period

Global production of most agricultural commodities increased in 2013, after having been affected by adverse weather conditions in the previous year. Production increases were particularly pronounced for cereals, especially for wheat and maize which rose sharply to record levels due to good growing conditions in the main producing countries. Driven by soybeans, global oilseed production is setting a new record in 2013/14. Together with further expansion in Indonesian palm oil production, this resulted in surplus production of both vegetable meal and oil in the current season. The increased production levels allowed countries to rebuild stocks and increase trading activities. Global sugar markets also experienced a significant surplus in 2013. During the course of the 2013/14 marketing season, international prices of most crops remained under downward pressure, largely in response to positive supply situations.

While grains and oilseeds markets were characterised by significant production increases, meat production increased marginally in 2013. The profitability of meat production has been highly uncertain in recent years as the occurrence of animal diseases and higher feed costs worked their way through the meat complex, driving prices higher and slowing consumption growth.

Higher feed cost, in combination with a significant production shortfall in China, drove the firm rebound in milk and dairy prices in 2013, following a sharp decline in 2012. During the first half of 2013, the United States, European Union, New Zealand and Australia – all major players in global dairy markets – produced less milk than in 2012, further contributing to the price recovery.

Fish from aquaculture production has been growing rapidly, reaching more than 40% of total production in 2013. This expansion has been the main factor allowing markets to meet the increasing demand for fish and fish products. Despite these gains, prices for fish and fishery products have been volatile as they are influenced by inelastic supply due to catch quotas for captured fish and volatile conditions in the aquaculture sector stemming from disease outbreaks and fluctuation in feed costs.

Cotton prices reached a peak in 2010, but have been on a declining trend ever since, while the stock-to-use ratio has increased rapidly, reaching about 85% in 2013. These record stock levels were mainly driven by China, where the authorities have been purchasing large quantities of cotton for the official reserve since 2010.

In 2013, world ethanol and biodiesel prices continued their declines from the historical high levels of 2011 in a context of ample supply for both ethanol and biodiesel. The 2013 market environment for biofuels was strongly influenced by policies: blending requirements were increased in Brazil (ethanol), and in Argentina and Indonesia (biodiesel); the European Union put in place anti-dumping duties against Argentinean, US and Indonesian shipments of biodiesel; and there were proposals towards lower biofuel targets for 2020 in the European Renewable Energy Directive (RED) as well as towards lower mandates in the United States.

In addition to the above-cited market factors specific to each commodity, a number of other developments need to be considered for the projections. Among the major influences are the economic slowdown in many emerging markets, in particular China and India; high oil and energy prices; slower population growth rates; moderate inflation rates; and an appreciation of the US Dollar compared to the currencies of Brazil, India and South Africa by more than 40% for the period 2014-23. Box 1.1 discusses the main assumptions underlying the agricultural projections and Box 1.2 analyses recent food price movements.

Box 1.1. **Macroeconomic and policy assumptions**

The main assumptions underlying the baseline projection

The *Outlook* is presented as a baseline scenario that is considered plausible given a range of conditioning assumptions. These assumptions portray a specific macroeconomic and demographic environment which shapes the evolution of demand and supply for agricultural and fish products. These general factors are described below. The statistical tables, at the end of the publication, provide more detailed data for these assumptions.

Box 1.1. **Macroeconomic and policy assumptions** (cont.)

The global recovery is likely to remain modest and uneven

Growth since the 2008 global crisis has been uneven and hesitant, and continues to show divergence both between and within advanced and emerging economies. The global recovery remains modest, despite some moderate acceleration in the short term, and there are large downside risks. The growth slowdown in the emerging market economies leads to large negative spillover effects on the world economy as a whole via trade effects. Moreover, with the BRICS now accounting for about 28% of world GDP (at PPP rates), a slowdown in growth has larger effects on the global economy and OECD countries than in the past. In OECD countries, direct trade relations with non-OECD countries have grown substantially in importance over the past two decades.

Moreover, any slowdown in emerging economies is also likely to lower commodity prices, with adverse effects on the terms of trade of commodity exporters. Financial conditions have tightened significantly in some emerging economies, and financial linkages with OECD countries could increase the impact of a decelerating growth in the emerging economies. Similarly, as the links in the banking sectors of several developed and emerging economies have grown stronger since the financial crisis, tightening financial conditions in some emerging economies may also influence income growth of OECD countries.

In the Euro area, recovery is lagging and uneven. Unemployment remains very high, but inflationary pressures are subdued. Weakness in the banking system remains a major drag on growth in the Euro area. Still weak bank balance sheets, fragile public finances and the uncertain political situation in some vulnerable countries could unsettle financial markets.

The macroeconomic assumptions used in the *Agricultural Outlook* are based on the *OECD Economic Outlook* (November 2013) and the International Monetary Fund's, *World Economic Outlook* (October 2013).

Growth in the OECD area was moderately better than expected in 2013 at 2.2%, and it is assumed to be stronger in 2014 at 2.6%. Growth prospects for OECD countries in the medium-term are expected to be maintained at an average level of 2.2% p.a. After a slight recession in 2013, EU15 members as a group should show a positive growth of 1.3% in 2014, and for the remaining period, they are expected to recover gradually at an average growth rate of 1.75% p.a.

Among the OECD countries, Korea and Turkey are expected to exhibit the strongest growth during the next decade at 4.4% and 4.3% p.a., respectively. Australia and Mexico should continue to show a firm recovery at 3.5% p.a. The United States and Canada are expected to recover gradually; averaging 2.4 and 2.3% p.a., respectively, during the next ten years, and Japan should exhibit a slow growth of 1.1% p.a.

In the non-OECD area, medium-term prospects for emerging economies have been revised slightly downward. China and India are expected to grow on average 7% and 6.4% p.a., respectively, over the next ten years. Although impressive compared to developed economies, these rates are below the growth rates experienced during the previous ten years. Two other major emerging economies, Brazil and South Africa, will maintain average annual growth rates of 3.7% and 3.4% p.a., respectively, during the next decade.

Among developing countries, those in the African region show strong growth during the next decade, partly because the expected recovery in the European Union leads to increasing exports from those countries. Asian countries also maintain high growth rates, but the slowdown in China and India will curb growth rates in the region. Income growth in Latin American economies is assumed to be weaker compared to other emerging economies, but the resilient US economy is a positive factor for the region.

Population growth to slow

World population growth is expected to slow to 1.0% p.a. in the next decade. This is the case for all regions, even for India, whose population will nevertheless increase by 141 million people. An additional 776 million people will be living on the planet in 2023, half of them in the Asia and Pacific region, although the growth rate in this region is below the growth rate experienced during the last decade.

Box 1.1. **Macroeconomic and policy assumptions** (*cont.*)

Figure 1.1. **Korea and Turkey expected to exhibit the strongest GDP growth in OECD**
Average GDP growth rates 2004-13 and 2014-23

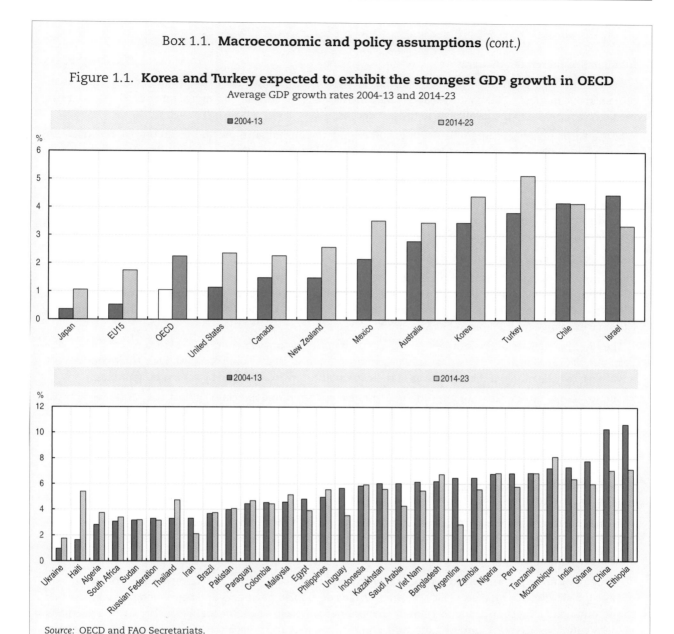

Source: OECD and FAO Secretariats.

StatLink ᵐˢᴸᵖ *http://dx.doi.org/10.1787/888933098649*

Among OECD countries, Japan's population is expected to decrease by nearly 3 million inhabitants during the next decade, and Europe should also expect a slightly negative growth of its population. The European Union however, continues to grow at a rate of 0.1% p.a. Australia, Turkey and Mexico have the highest projected population growth rates among the OECD countries.

The Russian Federation is another country where the population will be shrinking, with a drop of 4.5 million expected in the coming decade. World population growth is still driven by developing countries, and, among the developing countries, those in Africa are expected to show the fastest population growth at 2.4% p.a., which is nevertheless lower than in the last decade.

Box 1.1. **Macroeconomic and policy assumptions** *(cont.)*

Inflation should remain moderate

Inflation in OECD countries is measured by the Private Consumer Expenditure (PCE) deflator. It is expected to remain stable in most OECD countries and should increase only slightly at an average rate of 2.2% p.a. over the next ten years, close to the level of 2% in the last decade.

In the Euro area, where unemployment is still high, inflation remains low and deflation risk has risen. In Japan, where deflation is a concern, monetary policies should allow inflation to turn positive, with the inflation rate expected to reach 2.1% p.a. during the next decade.

Inflation pressures in developing countries (GDP deflator base) are expected to ease during the next decade. Capital inflows to emerging markets have been reduced, and countries which are exposed to inflation risk started to increase interest rates. Energy prices are estimated to increase, but their impact on inflation is expected to be limited.

A stronger US Dollar in the Outlook period

The nominal exchange rate for the period 2014-23 is mostly driven by the inflation differentials *vis-à-vis* the United States (small change in real terms). The assumptions on exchange rates during the next decade are characterised by a stronger US Dollar compared to other currencies in line with the recovery of the US economy. Nominal exchange rates adjust in line with inflation rates.

The projected depreciation of more than 40% of their currency for the period 2014-23 in some countries, like Brazil, India and South Africa, will stimulate export growth in these countries, although their competitive advantage may be muted if the currencies of their competitors also depreciate by similar magnitudes.

The exchange rates of developing countries are also expected to depreciate against the US Dollar in most countries. However, currencies of some, especially resource rich, countries will appreciate relative to the US Dollar.

Energy prices

The world oil price assumption used in the baseline until 2015 is from the short term update of the *OECD Economic Outlook No. 94* (November 2013), while oil prices during the projection period are from the *World Energy Outlook* (IEA, 2013).

In nominal terms, the price is expected to increase slowly over the outlook period from USD 109 per barrel in 2013 to USD 147 per barrel by 2023, an average annual growth rate of 2.8%.

Policy considerations

Policies play an important role in agricultural and fisheries markets, with policy reforms often contributing to change the structure of markets. Policy reforms such as decoupled payments and continued progress towards the elimination of direct price supports imply that policies will have a less direct effect on production decisions in many countries. However, import protection, domestic support and price intervention policies still loom large in many countries with the subsequent distorting effects on international markets and trade.

The projections for United States do not reflect the recently enacted Agricultural Act of 2014. Instead, the projections are based on the 2008 Farm Act which was assumed to be extended and remain in effect through the period.

This baseline does not take into account the proposal made by the US Environmental Protection Agency (EPA) to reduce the total, (i.e. the advanced and the cellulosic biofuel mandates) for 2014, as the final EPA decision is expected in June 2014 (or in the course of 2014).

Box 1.1. **Macroeconomic and policy assumptions** (*cont.*)

The agreement on the reform of the common agricultural policy (CAP) towards 2020 provides EU member states with implementation options which need to be decided by August 2014. Therefore, the baseline will reflect the CAP reform only in part: expiry of the milk quota as of 2015, expiry of the sugar quota system as of 2017, budget ceilings for decoupled single farm payment, coupled payments to stay at current level until August 2014 when each member state shall inform the Commission of their decision on the management and magnitude of coupled payments. The effects of "greening", in particular the requirements on permanent grassland and ecological focus area, are also taken into account to the extent possible.

Box 1.2. **Food price inflation**

Consumer food price inflation is slowing across the world

Global inflation of consumer food prices, as measured by year over year changes in the monthly global Consumer Price Index for Food (CPIF), is estimated at 6.4% in early 2014.[1] During the commodity price crisis of 2008, CPIF inflation peaked at 16.5% then fell below 5% in the weakness of the Great Recession in 2009. It fluctuated between 5% and 11% from 2009 to 2013, following the volatility of commodity prices and general domestic inflationary pressures. The roller coaster path of primary agricultural commodity prices had a different impact on consumer prices around the world. Less developed countries faced the highest inflation rates (Figure 1.2). In Africa, for example, food price inflation peaked at 23% in 2008, and again at 14% in 2011, but it fell to 6% at the start of 2014. At the other extreme, food price inflation in the OECD area peaked at 7% in 2008, but has fallen to 2.1% at the beginning of 2014. At the start of the outlook period, food price inflation at the consumer level appears lower and more stable for all regions than it has been in the turbulent years following the price crisis.

Figure 1.2. **Consumer food price inflation lower in developed countries**

Average annual food price inflation rates in per cent, 2008-14

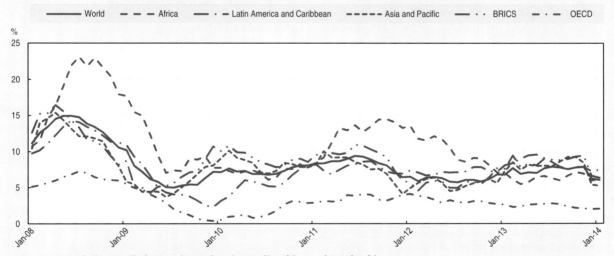

Note: BRICS includes Brazil, the Russian Federation, India, China and South Africa.
Source: OECD and FAO Secretariats.

StatLink *http://dx.doi.org/10.1787/888933098668*

Box 1.2. **Food price inflation** (*cont.*)

Regional data obscure the divergent experiences of individual countries. While those listed in Figure 1.3 follow the general global or regional trends, they exhibit variation that may also be the result of local factors such as exchange rate movements, higher domestic inflation or adverse weather events. For example, while food prices fell in the United States and Japan during the recession, India witnessed its highest inflation rate. Retail food price inflation in China has fallen from high to low levels in the past year. Food price inflation in Turkey has remained higher during the period relative to other OECD countries. Detailed information on a country basis is provided in Tables B.1 of the Statistical Annex.

Figure 1.3. **Consumer food price inflation: Selected countries**
Food price inflation per cent change

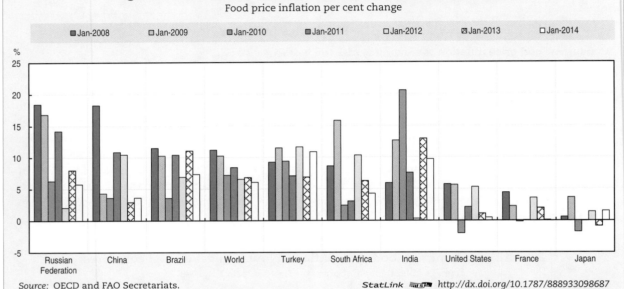

Source: OECD and FAO Secretariats.   *StatLink* ᴍ𝒮ᵖ *http://dx.doi.org/10.1787/888933098687*

Consumer prices for food follow primary agricultural commodity prices

In March 2014, the FAO's Food Price Index (FPI) of internationally traded primary food commodities reached the value of 212, relative to its base value in 2002-04 of 100. This level is thus over 100% higher in nominal terms, and 50% in real terms, than its level a decade ago. Primary commodity prices transmit to retail level, and data show that consumer prices follow agricultural commodity prices.[2] However, the degree of co-movement and the time-lag varies significantly across regions.[3] Levels of price pass-through from international commodity markets to domestic retail markets depend on the degree of market integration, import dependency and the presence of short value-chains. Figure 1.4 illustrates some regional differences in transmission from the international benchmark price, as represented by FPI, to the domestic retail price indicator (CPIF). The transmission is stronger, for example in Eastern Africa than for the world as a whole, given the strong reliance on primary commodities in final consumption and on imports. The transmission from the FPI to the CPIF in the OECD area appears particularly weak, due largely to the length of value added chains in final consumption.

Real food consumer prices are rising

Real food consumer prices measure the extent to which food prices are rising relative to the prices in the basket of all consumer goods in the economy. Real food price inflation is still a feature in most countries, but it is significantly higher and more volatile in developing countries than in OECD countries, as illustrated in Figure 1.5. One of the explanatory factors is a higher weight of food in the consumer basket of developing countries. Another factor is the higher integration in developed countries between food markets and other sectors of the economy, due to lengthier, more complex and diversified value-chains and market structures.

Box 1.2. **Food price inflation** (*cont.*)

Figure 1.4. **Consumer price inflation follows changes in primary commodity prices**

FAO Food Price Index and Consumer Price Index for Food (CPIF) per cent change

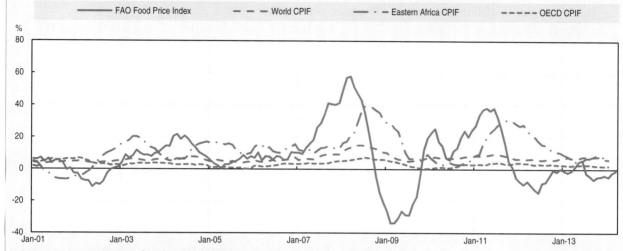

Source: FAO, ILO, UNSD and national websites; calculations by FAO Statistics Division.

StatLink ᵃˢᴸ *http://dx.doi.org/10.1787/888933098706*

Figure 1.5. **Real consumer prices are rising**

Real food price inflation per cent change

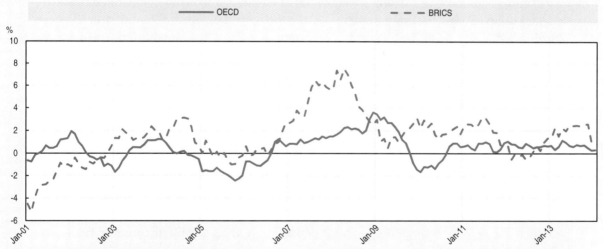

Note: Real food price inflation is the ratio of Food CPIs to all items CPIs. BRICS refers to Brazil, the Russian Federation, India, China and South Africa.

Source: FAO, ILO, UNSD and national websites; calculations by FAO Statistics Division.

StatLink ᵃˢᴸ *http://dx.doi.org/10.1787/888933098725*

1. See glossary part for a description of methodology used in the construction of the indices.
2. Agricultural commodity prices refer to international benchmark prices for the main raw agricultural commodities such as wheat, maize, etc. The FAO Food Price Index measures the change in the value of the trade basket of several agricultural commodities, including sugar, dairy products and meat. Food consumer prices refer mainly to derived products bought in retail markets by consumers. Food Consumer Price Indices measure the change in the value of an average basket of food products purchased by households.
3. For more details on this topic, see for example: FAO *Global and regional consumer food inflation monitoring*, January 2014, FAO, Rome.

Consumption: Global consumption continues to increase but at a slower rate

Having demonstrated its resilience in the past, the demand for agricultural products is expected to remain firm through the outlook period, even if the rate of growth is slower compared to the past decade. Rapidly growing Asian economies are expected to account for the greatest share of additional consumption, while saturated levels of per capita food consumption and declining population growth rates result in much slower consumption growth from regions like North America and Europe. Substantial population growth in Africa will drive significant increases in total consumption, however per capita consumption growth in the region remains marginal.

In addition to increasing consumption levels, growing incomes and urbanisation also result in shifts in lifestyle habits and dietary structure, typically from a traditional cereal-based diet to a more protein-rich, diversified diet. Consumption trends also tend toward processed and prepared foods, widening the spread between farm gate and retail prices of food items. Expansion of the livestock sector alters the demand for crops, resulting in a declining share of pure food crops, in favour of crops like coarse grains and oilseeds which are also used to feed livestock. The emergence of biofuel and other industrial uses adds a further important dimension to demand, which will remain significant in the future.

Growing diversity in the use of agricultural products

Cereals are still at the core of human nutrition, but their role has been shifting and will continue to do so in the coming decade. On a global scale, food remains the most important use of cereals: more than 1.2 billion tonnes (Bt) of food demand is projected for 2023, which is 150 million tonnes (Mt) more than in 2011-13 (Figure 1.6). Feed demand is the fastest growing sector, in line with shifting diet preferences. Almost 160 Mt additional feed will be needed by the end of the decade. After the rapid expansion in the previous decade, ethanol use currently accounts for 12% of global coarse grains consumption. However, a significant slow-down in the expansion of maize-based ethanol is expected as the blend wall in the United States is approached in the coming years.

Based on strong feed demand, coarse grain demand will grow by 20%. Wheat demand, mostly a food commodity, is projected to increase by 12% through the next decade, while rice consumption will grow marginally faster, increasing by 15% through the same period. Consumption of rice in Africa is expected to increase substantially, increasing its importance relative to other more traditional staple food crops, like roots and tubers. Supported by a strong demand for vegetable oils and protein meals, oilseeds consumption will increase by 26% through the ten-year period, more than any other commodity.

Growing incomes, urbanisation and a certain globalisation of eating habits all contribute to more food being consumed ready-made, increasing the consumption of vegetable oils and sugar. Both are important components in human diets and especially in many developing economies constitute a crucial source of energy. The annual per capita food consumption of vegetable oils in developing economies is expected to grow by 1.3% p.a. over the next decade, reaching a level of just over 20 kg per capita by 2023, compared to a level of 25 kg per capita in developed economies. Per capita consumption of vegetable oil in least developed economies is expected to reach only about 13 kg by 2023. Projections indicate that sugar consumption will grow on average by 2% p.a., with developing countries displaying the fastest growth. Sugar consumption is projected to show little or no growth in many developed countries due to saturated consumption levels in these markets. The increasing demand for biofuel will impact on the sugar, coarse grains and vegetable oil markets by providing a demand dimension that links food to energy markets and their political environment. Increased consumer spending power will elevate the demand for cotton products. India, the world's largest cotton producer, will be the leading beneficiary of additional cotton intake through the next decade. However, China is expected to retain the biggest share of global cotton use in 2023.

Figure 1.6. **Growing diversity of crop use**
Cereal consumption in developed and developing countries

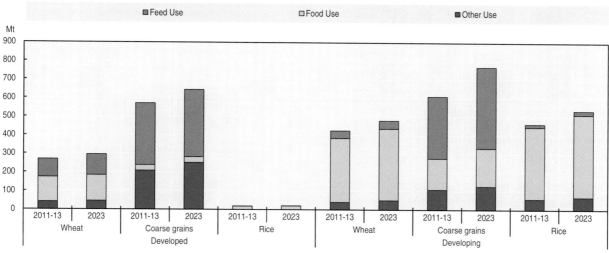

Source: OECD and FAO Secretariats.

StatLink ⌸⌸⌸ *http://dx.doi.org/10.1787/888933098744*

Food and fuel use of agricultural commodities continues to be regulated in many countries

The policy environment will continue to shape the consumption of agricultural commodities, both as food and biofuel. For example, the Indian National Food Security Act, adopted by the Indian Parliament in 2013, is expected to subsidise the consumption of rice and wheat for about two-thirds of the Indian population, resulting in higher levels of rice, wheat and coarse grain consumption in India over the outlook period.

The consumption level of bioethanol for fuel and biodiesel continues to depend mostly on the targets or mandates set by governments in both developed and developing economies. Those targets have been introduced over the past years to achieve higher levels of energy security, lower levels of carbon dioxide emissions and generate income opportunities. Most of these policies establish blending targets of renewable fuels in total transport fuels and changes in these target levels will impact the use of biofuels in the next decade.

Population growth and changing dietary preferences drive firm demand for meat and dairy products

The demand for meat and dairy products will increase substantially through the next decade, as higher income levels and increasing urbanisation in developing regions allow consumers to raise the level of protein intake in their diets relative to starches. Global meat consumption is projected to increase by 1.6% p.a. through the next decade, resulting in more than 58 Mt of additional meat consumed by 2023 (Figure 1.7). Consistent with the

Figure 1.7. **Most of the growth in meat and fish consumption will occur in developing countries**

Livestock consumption in developed and developing countries

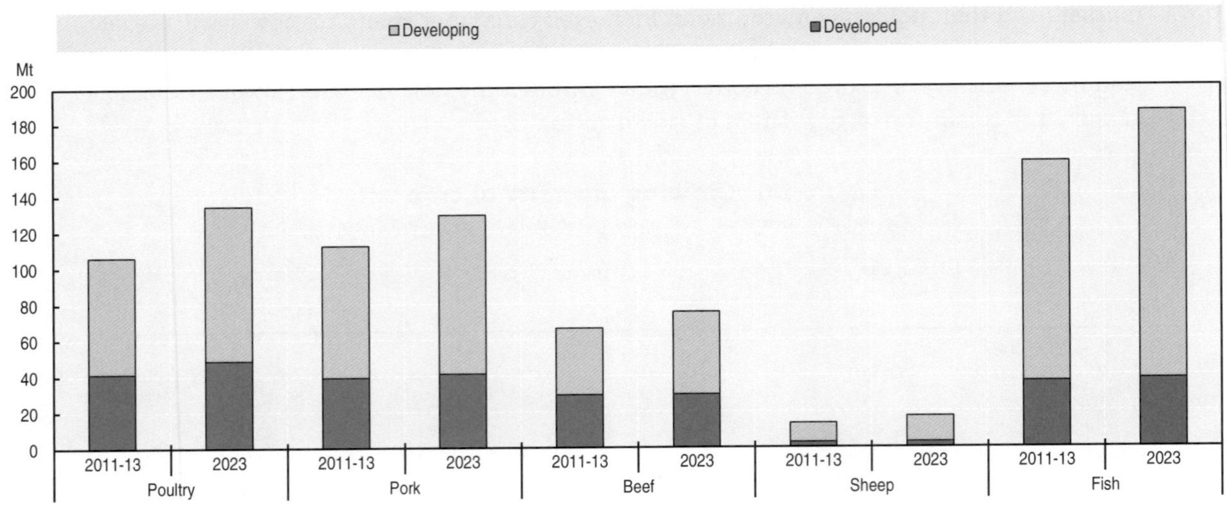

Source: OECD and FAO Secretariats.

StatLink ᵃᵇ *http://dx.doi.org/10.1787/888933098763*

trend through the past decade, developing countries will consume more than 80% of the additional meat, in part due to substantially higher population and income growth relative to developed countries, but also due to the fact that per capita meat consumption in developed regions is already high. In Canada for example, per capita meat consumption will stagnate through the next decade.

The choice between different meat products consumed is driven mostly by the relative prices of meat products, traditional tastes and preferences, as well as consumer sentiments related to health, the environment and convenience. Growth in global meat consumption will be led by poultry, which remains the cheapest and most accessible source of meat for lower income consumers, while its low share of saturated fats results in it being viewed as the healthiest meat choice. In addition, poultry faces few cultural barriers related to its consumption, resulting in robust consumption growth across geographical areas. This combination of factors results in poultry accounting for half of the additional meat consumed by 2023.

The second most popular meat is pork which is projected to account for nearly 30% of the additional meat consumed in the next decade. This increase is driven by Asia and the Pacific, notably Chinese consumers who will capture half of the global increase. Beef amounts to 15% of the additional meat consumed and sheep meat to the remaining 6%. Growth in demand for sheep meat is concentrated in Asia and the Pacific and the Middle East, while that for beef is concentrated in Latin America and the Caribbean.

Per capita fish consumption will also be rising on all continents except Africa where it will decline slightly. Average annual growth rates in fish consumption are expected to slow down in the second half of the outlook period, when fish prices will increase more than meat prices, and, as a consequence, consumers will substitute some fish dishes by meat dishes.

The demand for dairy products will continue to expand at a rapid rate through the next decade. Fresh dairy products constitute the bulk of consumption in developing regions, where India is expected to increase its consumption to 170 kg per capita by 2023.

Nevertheless, total consumption of dairy products in milk equivalent will remain considerably higher in developed than in developing countries. This difference stems from the per capita consumption of cheese which is more than tenfold higher in developed countries compared to developing ones. Per capita consumption of dairy products in developing countries is projected to increase by 1.9% p.a. for cheese and butter and at 1.2% p.a. for milk powder.

Production: The developing world remains the epicentre of most agricultural production growth

Rising income levels and a growing global population that is increasingly urbanising, especially in populous developing countries, together with increasing non-food use of agricultural products, will require a substantial expansion of production through the coming decade. While cereals remain a key dietary component, particularly in least developed countries, rising protein consumption in other developing regions will require an increased production of livestock and dairy products, which also implies greater demand for feed grains and oilseeds.

The rate of production growth is constrained by different factors, including increasing costs of production, limited expansion of agricultural land, environmental concerns and changes in the policy environment. These factors are particularly relevant in most developed countries and some highly populated developing countries, limiting expansion in these countries while presenting opportunities to regions that are less affected by these limiting factors. As in the past decade, projected production growth through the outlook period will be led by Latin America, Sub-Saharan Africa, Eastern Europe and parts of Asia, with production growth in Western Europe increasing only marginally. Developing regions will account for more than 75% of additional agricultural output over the next decade

Global cereal production is expected to increase by almost 370 Mt through the next decade, reflecting a growth of 15% by 2023, relative to the base period (Figure 1.8). Developing regions will account for 60% of additional production by 2023. Coarse grains remain the greatest driver of increased cereal production in terms of volume, while the rate of production growth for oilseeds, at 26% through the ten-year period, will exceed that of all other crops. Developed countries will account for almost 50% of the additional global coarse grain production, while developing countries will supply approximately 65% of additional oilseed production. The expansion of coarse grain and oilseed production will be driven by high demand for biofuels and other industrial uses in developed countries, as well as greater feed demand, particularly from developing regions.

In contrast to crops produced for multiple purposes, the expansion rates of cereals, produced mainly for food consumption, will be moderate through the outlook period. Wheat production will increase by around 12%, while rice production is projected to increase by 14% through the ten-year period, well below their growth rates through the past decade. While developed regions are expected to account for almost 50% of additional wheat produced globally by 2023, developing countries will produce more than 95% of the additional rice output, with China accounting for the greatest share of global production to meet the ambitious self-sufficiency targets set up by the Chinese government.

Sugar production is projected to increase by 20% through the coming decade, concentrated mainly in developing countries. Brazil remains the world's largest sugar producer and it is expected that its sugarcane producers will keep taking advantage of the

Figure 1.8. **Production of crops rising**
Additional crop production: volume and per cent 2023 relative to 2011-13

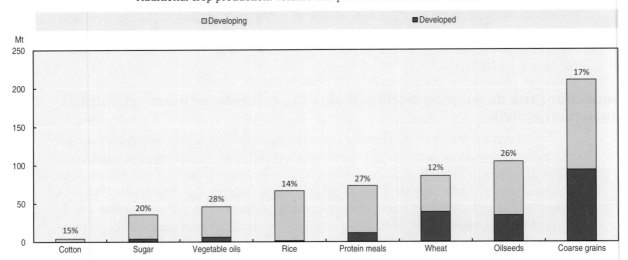

Source: OECD and FAO Secretariats.

StatLink ⬛ http://dx.doi.org/10.1787/888933098782

fact that they can supply for two competing markets: sugar and ethanol. This will allow for a continued expansion of sugar production in Brazil through the next decade.

Biofuel production will expand substantially, with both ethanol and biodiesel production increasing by more than 50% through the next decade. This represents a significant slowdown relative to the past decade, when production more than doubled through the ten year period from 2004 to 2013. It is anticipated that cellulosic biofuels will only contribute marginally to these figures and that traditional feedstock (i.e. sugar molasses, maize and vegetable oils) will remain the main feedstock for biofuel production in the next decade.

Poultry continues to dominate the livestock sector

Global meat production will increase by more than 58 Mt through the outlook period, concentrated in developing regions, which will account for 78% of the additional meat production, mainly from countries that produce surplus feed grains (Figure 1.9). Poultry continues to dominate the meat sector, as reflected in production growth of 27% by 2023 relative to the base period. This represents almost half of additional meat produced globally by 2023. A high feed conversion ratio, short production cycle and simple production process has made poultry the low cost alternative which consumers in developing countries demand first as their income level rises. Currently, pork accounts for the greatest share in world total meat production, however, a comparatively slower growth rate through the next decade will result in it being surpassed by poultry by 2020. Pork production is projected to increase by 17 Mt, by 2023, 15% higher compared to the base period. China continues to dominate the market and is expected to produce almost half of the additional pork.

The production of pork and poultry relies on the intensive use of feed grains. This increases the extent to which the supply response is conditioned by feed prices that remain relatively high through the outlook period compared to historic norms. The result is declining production growth rates through the projection period compared to the past decade. In contrast, beef production, which exhibits greater flexibility in terms of feeding regimes, is

Figure 1.9. **Higher livestock production**

Additional livestock production: volume and per cent 2023 relative to 2011-13

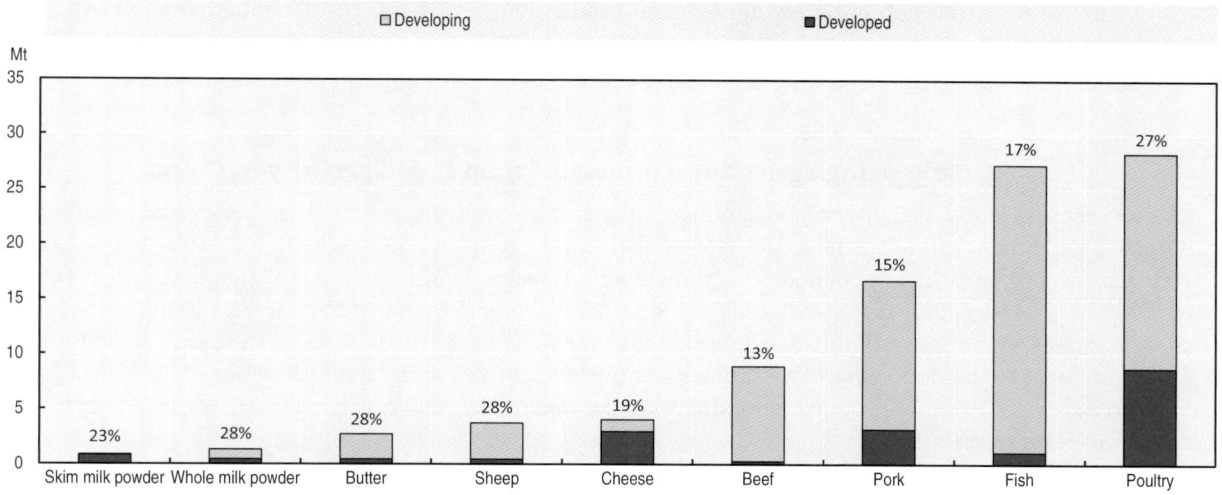

Source: OECD and FAO Secretariats.

StatLink ⟶ http://dx.doi.org/10.1787/888933098801

expected to grow faster in the coming decade compared to the last. Nevertheless, projected production growth through the outlook period is only 13%, as reduced herd numbers, environmental constraints and a longer production cycle limit the initial supply response to improved profitability. Brazil will account for the greatest share of additional beef produced through the next decade. Sheep meat production is also projected to grow faster in the coming decade than the last, driven by firm prices due to strong import demand from Asia and the European Union. An increase of 28% through the outlook period amounts to 3.8 Mt. Australia and New Zealand are expected to supply the bulk of this additional output. However, firm dairy prices, which imply greater competition for pasture from the dairy sector, result in much slower production growth in New Zealand compared to Australia.

India is expected to become the largest milk producer in the world through the next decade, thereby overtaking the European Union's leading position in the dairy sector. China's milk production prospects have been lowered in this *Outlook*, due to low production levels in 2012 and 2013, but it is expected that its dairy industry will return to a stronger growth path. Most of the production increases in cheese and skimmed milk powder (SMP) will occur in developed countries, while butter and whole milk powder (WMP) production will grow the strongest in developing countries.

Fish production is expected to expand by 17% over the next decade. This growth will be the result of increased aquaculture production, which is anticipated to surpass captured fish for human consumption in 2014. In 2023, 62% of the world aquaculture production will take place in China.

Yield increases will drive production growth of most crops

The main challenges that contribute to declining production growth rates through the outlook period are the rising costs of production, including higher prices of energy inputs, feed and labour. Further resource constraints, like land degradation, water scarcity and increasing environmental pressures, present additional limitations, particularly in regions where land availability for agricultural expansion is severely constrained. Continued investment in research and development, and extension services, remains critical to achieve much needed productivity gains, especially in developing countries. Box 1.3 lists different policy actions that can enhance agricultural productivity in China. The recent expansion of shale gas production in the United States could potentially reduce fertiliser prices in the United States, but this input price reduction is not expected to transfer to other countries (Box 1.4).

Box 1.3. **Enhancing agricultural productivity and food security in China**

Better access to and availability of food along with higher incomes in China have lifted 114 million people out of undernourishment (from 272 million in 1990-92 to 158 million in 2011-13, accounting for two-thirds of the worldwide drop). The incidence of undernourishment almost halved in China, falling to 11.4% of the population (FAOSTAT, 2014). Indeed, the past two decades have witnessed a more than five-fold increase in urban real per capita incomes and a more than three-fold increase for rural households. During the same period food availability per person doubled and protein supply per person was up by more than one-third. Currently, undernourishment in China is concentrated among the poorest in rural areas, often amongst members of small-scale farm households.

Improving agricultural productivity, while conserving natural resources, is an essential requirement to increase China's food supplies on a sustainable basis. Currently, China's agriculture is still dominated by small-scale farming that is intensive in terms of input use – fertilisers and pesticides – leading to high land productivity but at the cost of environmental degradation. With continued large-scale rural-urban migration, the number of farmers is falling, boosting the low level of labour productivity and raising incomes, but remaining farmers are ageing with negative implications for future productivity. Consolidation of smaller farms and greater mechanisation will be needed to ensure increases in production from a falling and ageing labour force. Overall, the old model of intensification with ever increasing inputs is no longer sustainable, and China's food system will need to "produce more from less" and to benefit from stronger integration with international markets. A number of policy actions can support transformation, including:

- *Completing the conversion of input subsidies into direct payments and, ultimately, into strategic public investments:* gradually replace input subsidies by direct payments paid at a flat rate per unit of land, with no requirement to purchase a given input or to produce a specific commodity.

- *Improving agricultural productivity via enhanced innovation:* further strengthen research and development, intellectual property rights, technology adoption and transfer, education, and farm training and advisory services; consider new seeds and applying better fertilisers.

- *Enhancing efficient water use:* adjust water pricing to cover water provision costs and to stimulate a move away from water-intensive crops.

- *Let the market mechanism play a more decisive role in the allocation of resources:* balance between market mechanism and government intervention; innovate markets regulation and strengthen credit availability and risk management.

- *Diversifying sources of food through stronger integration of domestic and international agro-food markets:* safeguard national grain security, ensuring 100% self-sufficiency in rice and wheat; promote the opening-up of agricultural markets and make timely and appropriate use of global resources and channels of international agricultural products market.

- *Enhancing the development of the land market:* improve the land rights of farmers, allowing them to buy, sell, lease and inherit land rights so improving prospects for larger farms and mechanisation; base the compensation paid when agricultural land is converted to other uses on market prices; allow farmers to sell land zoned as residential directly to developers.

Sources: OECD (2013), *Agricultural Policy Monitoring and Evaluation 2013: OECD Countries and Emerging Economies*, OECD Publishing *http://dx.doi.org/10.1787/agr_pol-2013-en;* OECD-ATPC/MOA Workshop on Policies to Enhance Agricultural Innovation and Productivity: Focus on China: *www.oecd.org/tad/agricultural-policies/innovation-productivity-china-workshop-2013.htm;* news report of *China's food security strategy summit.*

Box 1.4. **Feedstock issues and developments in the nitrogen fertiliser sector**

Natural gas currently accounts for two-thirds of global ammonia capacity (ammonia being one of key components of nitrogen fertiliser). Other feedstocks include coal, naphtha and petroleum fuel. Over the next decade, virtually all new ammonia projects will be based on natural gas. Feedstock supply for the manufacture of fertilisers has become a decisive factor in the competitiveness of large producing and exporting countries, in terms of relative costs and security of supply. Between 2008 and 2013, natural gas prices have been rising in the main ammonia producing and consuming regions, with the exception of North America. According to industry sources, natural gas prices are projected to increase in the Russian Federation and China within the next five years, while remaining relatively stable in Western Europe. Moderate increases are expected in Western Asia and Northern Africa.

The rapid emergence of shale gas production in the United States has resulted in a significant increase in domestic gas supply and lower natural gas prices than five years ago. The United States accounts for 88% of global unconventional gas[1] production (International Energy Agency, 2013). Shale gas accounted for 39% of the total US gas production in 2012, against 3% in 2002. Shale gas is expected to drive all incremental gas supply in the United States over the next decade. In 2035, shale gas production is projected to account for half US natural gas production (US Energy Information Administration, 2012). While many countries with potential shale gas resources wish to replicate the developments seen in the United States, no significant exploitation of shale gas is anticipated outside Northern America before the end of this decade.

Related to the development of shale gas, the most significant supply-related development in the global nitrogen fertiliser industry since 2011 has been the development of new ammonia capacity with ammonia capacity expanding in the United States for the first time since 1998.

Prospects of rising supplies of gas from unconventional sources and projections of moderate prices in the long term, have led several companies and organisations to announce plans for new greenfield capacity. Since June 2012, more than 25 projects have been announced in the United States (and some in Canada) for nitrogen-based capacity, including brownfield expansions, new stand-alone ammonia plants and fully integrated multi-production downstream complexes. These projects, if implemented, would add more than 10 Mt of new urea capacity in Northern America. Among the announced projects, only a few (between five to eight) are forecast to start operating before 2018, and already several (at least five) of these have been cancelled due to growing competition as well as regulatory and logistical issues. All new projects will have to comply with demanding regulatory processes and stringent environmental legislations.

Figure 1.10. **US ammonia capacity**

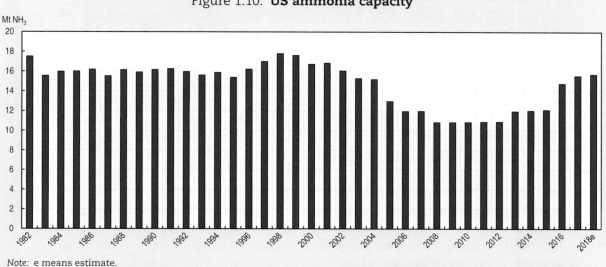

Note: e means estimate.
Source: IFA, 2014.

StatLink *http://dx.doi.org/10.1787/888933098820*

Box 1.4. **Feedstock issues and developments in the nitrogen fertiliser sector** *(cont.)*

The expansion of shale gas in the United States will significantly shift the production and trade balance of the US fertiliser industry. The United States is currently the world's fourth largest ammonia producing country (after China, India and the Russian Federation) although its capacity has been dwindling since 1998, when it was close to 18 Mt. Due to competitive pressures, high feedstock cost and industry restructuring, US ammonia capacity fell by 40% between 1998 and 2012, to less than 11 Mt. Lower domestic production led to a rise in ammonia imports. At the beginning of 2000, the United States was the world's largest importer of ammonia, accounting for nearly one-third of global ammonia trade (IFA).

With the new projects coming on stream, by 2017 US ammonia production is projected at around 16 Mt, 45% higher than 2012. Most new production plants are aiming to produce a wide range of downstream nitrogen products.

In the short term, access to ample supply of natural gas at competitive prices in the United States has improved the margins of nitrogen producers and allowed the US industry to improve its operational performance, increase production and operate at higher utilisation rates. In the near term, rising nitrogen capacity will mean that the United States will substitute some imports of ammonia and urea with domestic supplies. In very few cases, some projects may lead to the export of US nitrogen products, but overall the United States is not likely to become a large net exporter

1. The term unconventional gas refers to methods used to extract methane gas from underground shale rock and coal beds. *Sources:* International Fertilizer Association (IFA), Production and trade statistics, accessible at *www.fertilizer.org.* International Energy Agency (2013), Gas Medium-Term Market Report 2013, International Energy Agency. US Energy Information Administration (2012), Annual Energy Outlook 2012, US Energy Information Administration.

The limited availability of additional arable land will impact the expansion and concentration of additional crop production. Additional arable land is more readily available in Eastern Europe, Latin America and the Caribbean and Sub – Saharan Africa, while the allocation of limited land amongst different crops in most other regions will be derived from market conditions and the relative profitability of suitable crops.

Production increases in wheat, coarse grains and rice will be mostly based on yield growth (Figure 1.11). Even though the area increases for coarse grains are relatively small, in 2023 this crop will account for the greatest share of total area harvested (34%), followed by wheat (23%) and oilseeds (17%). Production increases in oilseeds, sugarcane and cotton, on the other hand, are a combination of growth in yield and area expansion. This is not surprising as these commodities are mostly grown in regions where additional land suitable for agricultural production is still available: 63% of oilseeds are grown in the Americas, most of the world's sugarcane is cultivated in Latin America and the Caribbean, while India is expected to become the world's largest producer of cotton, surpassing China. West Africa will realise the fastest yield growth in cotton, while in China less area will be cultivated with cotton as a result of the uncertainties surrounding its cotton policies.

Milk production will be driven by yield growth in developed countries and by increased herd numbers in developing countries. Greater livestock numbers will also be required in order to meet the demand for additional meat through the outlook period, resulting in growing environmental concerns. Significant scope remains for improved productivity in both meat and dairy production, particularly in developing regions, which will be key to the growth of a sustainable livestock sector. The cost of compliance to environmental regulations will also impact the regional concentration of livestock production.

Figure 1.11. **Growth in arable crop area and yield**

Per cent change 2023, relative to 2011-13

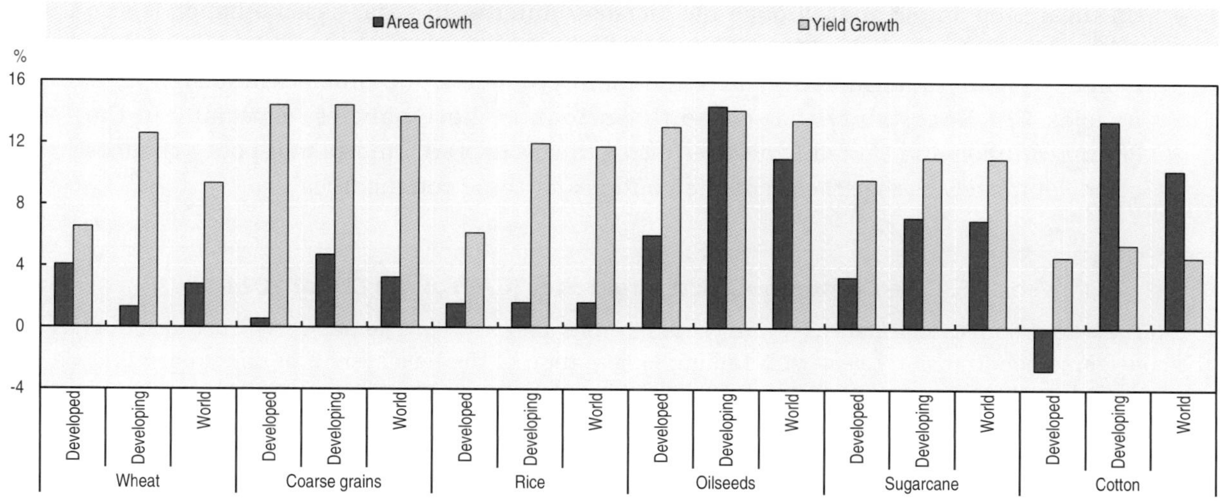

Source: OECD and FAO Secretariats.

StatLink ᕟᕟᕟ http://dx.doi.org/10.1787/888933098839

Growing influence of domestic policies on production decisions

Policies continue to shape production decisions in many countries. Although producer support has fallen over time, in 2013, about one-sixth of farm gross receipts in OECD countries are due to public policies that support farmers. This is indicated by the percentage Producer Support Estimate (%PSE) which, on average for the OECD area, fluctuated between 18% and 19% over the 2011-13 period. In value terms, the PSE in 2013 totalled USD 258 billion. The composition of support is arguably even more important than the level. Some countries continue to rely mostly on output-based support, which is potentially the most production and trade distorting. The majority of this support is generated through border protection and domestic price regulation. Other countries reoriented their policies away from market price support. The shift away from market price support and the introduction of payments decoupled to different degrees from commodity output increase the flexibility of producers in their choices of product mixes. Boxes 1.5, 1.6, and 1.7 give an overview of recent policy developments in the European Union, the United States and Japan.

Agriculture policies in the key emerging economies monitored by OECD (Brazil, China, Indonesia, Kazakhstan, Russian Federation, South Africa and Ukraine) demonstrate trends that differ from those observed in the OECD area. Recently, agricultural support levels in most of the emerging economies have tended to rise, in particular in China and Indonesia. This reflects increasing availability of budgetary resources, policy priorities turning more towards agricultural and rural development, and recently, a strengthened emphasis on food security concerns which these countries tend to view mostly from the self-sufficiency angle.

Government policies also influence the biofuel industry, where they are still expected to drive future developments. They subsequently also shape production of the feedstock commodities. In the United States, government mandates have played a major role in the fast growth of maize based ethanol production, while the EU biodiesel policy has led to strong increases in the cultivation of rapeseed for vegetable oil production. Palm oil production in Indonesia and Malaysia is also expected to expand as a result of changing biofuel policies. Sugar production is promoted by government support schemes such as the US sugar programme and, through the increased interest in sugar-based ethanol, is also affected by biofuel policies. The future of biofuel production and the associated feedstock is hence greatly determined by how the main producers of biofuels will design their policies. The uncertainty that currently surrounds these policies, especially in the European Union and United States (see also Biofuel Chapter), implies that policy changes could completely change the production outlook for these commodities.

Box 1.5. **The Common Agricultural Policy (CAP) of the EU for 2014-20**

The new Common Agricultural Policy (CAP) began to enter into force on 1 January 2014. The year 2014 has to be considered as a transitory year with full implementation of the new system of direct payments as of 1 January 2015. While the existing structure of policy instruments was broadly maintained, the reformed CAP provides greater emphasis on environmental issues, and more flexibility in the reallocation of funds between the two pillars (Pillar I: direct payments and market measures; Pillar II: rural development programmes) as well as on the implementation of its instruments at member state level.

The CAP has been allocated a total budget of EUR 408.3 billion for the period 2014-20, which represents 37.7% of all EU expenditure for the next multiannual financial framework. This constitutes a decrease in real terms in the total agricultural budget compared to the previous funding period.

The reformed CAP aims to maximise its effectiveness and efficiency in reaching its objectives, which includes a higher level of sustainability and an increase in competitiveness, through:

i)   Requiring member states to distribute 30% of first pillar direct payments subject to fulfilling certain practices beneficial for the environment and addressing climate change and to allocate at least 30% of each rural development programme (second pillar payments) to environment and climate related measures adapted to local needs.

ii) Limiting direct payments to beneficiaries who are actively engaged in agricultural activities, providing additional support for young farmers, and giving member states the option to offer a special scheme for small farmers, a supplement for farmers in areas with natural constraints and to increase product specific support to potentially vulnerable sectors (the so-called coupled support).

iii) Direct payments among countries and among farmers will progressively be reallocated based on convergence of basic direct payment levels across and within member states and on the degressivity of these payments; besides member states may implement a voluntary redistributive payment to rebalance payments towards smaller farms and introduce a capping for the basic payments.

iv) Dismantling all existing restrictions on production volumes and modernising commodity aid schemes.

v)   Offering more flexibility to implement exceptional measures and an improved risk management toolkit under the second pillar.

vi) Providing a reinforced framework for producer co-operation as tool for improving the functioning of the food chain.

vii) Establishing a common and coherent overall EU policy framework for all European Structural Investment funds, including rural development.

viii) Facilitating knowledge dissemination through the European Innovation Partnership and the Farm Advisory System.

As the agreement on the CAP reform provides member states the possibility to decide their respective implementation options for Pillar I by August 2014, with full implementation of the reformed CAP from 1 January 2015, it is premature at this time to provide a full assessment of the impact of the reform.

Government stockholding policies for various commodities in China, India, Thailand and Viet Nam have resulted in large inventories. The costs that these programmes may incur, especially if stocks have to be released at below acquisition prices, question their sustainability in the long run. Thailand's rice pledging scheme, which was re-instated in 2011, has accumulated large inventories and the manner in which they will eventually be released has important implications for rice producers. In China, virtually the entire increase in cotton stocks has been driven by state authorities purchasing China's official cotton reserves. Significant differences between world prices and domestic prices supported by policy resulted in substantial increases in imports, compounding the rising stock levels. Policy makers in China have indicated that the current level of cotton stocks is unsustainable and are reforming the policies that led to the increase. With such large stocks, any change in policy could have significant impacts on cotton prices, production and trade.

Box 1.6. **Japan's agricultural policy reform post-2014**

On 10 December 2013, Japan announced the *Plan to Create Vitality for Agricultural, Forestry and Fishery Industries and Local Communities*. The reform is the first major agricultural policy change since the introduction of income support payments in 2011. The Plan aims at doubling the incomes of agricultural industries and communities within a decade, doubling food exports up to JPY 1 trillion (USD 10.2 billion) by 2020, doubling the number of new entrants to agriculture (young farmers), concentrating 80% of farmland use to core (potentially viable) farmers and lowering the cost of rice production of core farmers by 40%. To achieve these goals, the Plan is based on four pillars: i) strengthening farms and production, ii) reforming agricultural subsidies with careful attention to the multifunctionality of agriculture, iii) establishing food value chains and iv) increasing demand for food and other agricultural products. This plan was developed against the backdrop of an increased need for supply-side structural reform in Japan. Over the past two decades, the agricultural sector experienced a decrease of nearly 30% of agricultural production (JPY 11.2 to 8.2 trillion), a drop in agricultural income of more than 40% (JPY 4.9 to 2.8 trillion), an increase in the average age of farmers by seven years (from 59 to 66 years) and a doubling of the size of abandoned farmland.

According to the Plan, the allocation of the rice production quota will be phased out by March 2019. The programme limits the supply of rice by allocating a production quota to rice farmers, and it keeps the price above the market equilibrium level. In spite of the production limits, the rice farming sector has experienced a price decrease of over 30% over the last two decades (1992-2011), driven by a decrease in consumption at an average rate of 80 000 tonnes annually. The government, agricultural organisations and farmers will work together in the next few years to create a situation where farmers plan rice production and shipment according to actual rice demand, without depending on the allocation of the rice production quota. In order to realise the situation, the government will provide more information on the forecast for supply and demand for rice and monthly data on selling and price situation by growing area to farmers. A number of changes have been planned for the payments for rice and upland crops. Starting in 2014, the direct payment for rice production, (under the income support payments), offered to rice farmers who met the quantitative target set by the government, will be reduced by half from the current JPY 15 000 (USD 154) per 0.1 ha to JPY 7 500 (USD 77) per 0.1 ha. This payment will be abolished in 2018. The price-contingent payment for rice will be eliminated in 2014. This payment, for which all farms with sales records are eligible, triggers when the average producer price of current crop year falls below the average price of the preceding three crop years.

Box 1.6. **Japan's agricultural policy reform post-2014** (cont.)

The direct payment under the income support payments for upland crops (wheat, barley, soybean, sugar beet, starch potato, buckwheat and rapeseed), for which all farms with sales records are eligible, will remain unchanged in 2014, but it will be made to core farmers regardless of their farm size from 2015 onwards. Also starting in 2015, the eligibility for the income-based payment (which is available to producers of rice, wheat, barley, soybean, sugar beet and starch potato) will be limited to core farmers, independent of their farm size. The income-based payment compensates 90% of the loss of income compared with the average income of the preceding three crop years (an average of three out of the previous five, leaving out the highest and lowest). If a farm is eligible for both the price contingent payment and the income-based payment, the income-based payment is made after subtracting the amount of the price contingent payment so as to avoid duplication of payment. A policy option to introduce income insurance will be considered in the medium-term. Incentives to diversify crops (e.g. rice for feed) will be reinforced by increasing the amount of payments as well as introducing a quantity based payment to support rice farmers who want to shift from rice production into other crops. In addition, a new multi-functional payment to local community activities to conserve and improve the quality of rural resources will be introduced in 2014 through reorganising the current financial support for infrastructure, such as irrigation and drainage facilities.

Discussions on related issues are also taking place in other fora. The Regulatory Reform Committee is responsible for the reform of the agricultural sector, including agricultural co-operatives and requirements for land ownership of private companies. The Council of Industrial Competitiveness deals with deliberating measures to increase added values of agricultural products and to double food exports. Based on these reforms, Japan will launch discussions to revise the Basic Plan on Food, Agriculture and Rural Areas in 2014. The Basic Plan is a national plan for implementing policies on food, agriculture and rural areas, which is revised every five years. The Basic Plan was previously revised in 2010. A key issue in the next revision will be to discuss whether the current food self-sufficiency target of 50% on a calorie supply basis and 70% on production value basis by 2020 is sufficient. This is in comparison to the former Basic Plan (revised in 2005), which targeted 45% on a calorie supply basis and 76% on a production value basis by 2015. The actual rates were reported at 39% and 68% in 2012 for calorie supply and production value, respectively.

Sources: Prime Minister of Japan and His Cabinet; Ministry of Agriculture, Forestry and Fisheries of Japan.

Box 1.7. **New US farm legislation in 2014**

A new farm law, the Agricultural Act of 2014, was signed on 7 February 2014, and will remain in force through 2018. The 2014 Farm Act makes major changes in commodity programmes, adds new crop insurance options, streamlines conservation programmes, modifies key provisions of the Supplemental Nutrition Assistance Program (SNAP, formerly known as food stamps) and expands programmes for specialty crops, organic farmers, bioenergy, rural development, and beginning farmers and ranchers. Total outlays for 2014-18 under the new Farm Act are projected to be USD 489 billion (nominal USD), of which 80% will be for programmes under the Nutrition title

The 2014 Farm Act makes major changes in commodity programmes, ending more than 15 years of crop programmes that made payments to producers based solely on historical production, removing upland cotton from coverage under Title I programmes and introducing a new dairy margin insurance programme. The legislation also renews the Supplemental Disaster Assistance programmes for livestock and orchards and nursery stock. The Congressional Budget Office projects these changes in Title 1 will reduce outlays by USD 6 billion (nominal USD), or 25%, over the projected costs of continuing current commodity programmes.

Box 1.7. **New US farm legislation in 2014** (*cont.*)

The Direct Payments, Countercyclical Payments and Average Crop Revenue Election (ACRE) programmes are repealed and replaced by the Price Loss Coverage (PLC) and Agriculture Risk Coverage (ARC) programmes. Producers of covered commodities (wheat, feed grains, rice, oilseeds, peanuts and pulses) may choose to participate in either, but not both programmes, for the life of the 2014 Farm Act. To receive payments under these programs producers must comply with applicable conservation requirements, which also apply to producers participating in conservation and crop insurance programmes. The marketing assistance loan programme continues unchanged, except that the loan rate for upland cotton, unlike the fixed rates set for other commodities, will be based on a moving average within a fixed range, with a maximum rate no higher than the rate set under previous legislation. The sugar price support programme also continues unchanged.

The Dairy Product Price Support Program and the Dairy Export Incentive Program are repealed and replaced by the Margin Protection Program (MPP) for dairy producers and the Dairy Product Donation Program (DPDP). MPP makes payments when the difference between milk prices and feed costs falls below a minimum level. Under the DPDP, the US Department of Agriculture will purchase dairy products for distribution to low-income Americans when milk margins fall below legislated triggers. The Milk Income Loss Contract (MILC) programme continues until MPP is operational, but is then repealed.

The Livestock Indemnity Program, Livestock Forage Disaster Program, Emergency Assistance for Livestock Honeybees, and Farm-Raised Fish Program and Tree Assistance Program are renewed with mandatory funding and made permanent and retroactive to cover losses in fiscal years 2012 and 2013, when many producers were impacted by severe weather.

The Stacked Income Protection Plan (STAX) provides premium subsidies to upland cotton producers to purchase revenue insurance policies in place of coverage for cotton under the new commodity programmes, seeking to address the WTO ruling that found US upland cotton subsidies distorted trade.

The Supplemental Coverage Option (SCO) offers producers additional area-based insurance coverage in combination with traditional crop insurance policies. Producers who elect to participate in the Agriculture Risk Coverage programme or the STAX programme are not eligible to purchase SCO coverage

The 2014 Farm Act maintains strong overall funding for USDA conservation programmes and through consolidation reduces the number of programmes from 23 to 13. The Congressional Budget Office estimates that between 2014 and 2018, mandatory spending on USDA conservation programmes will decline by USD 200 million – less than 1% of the USD 28 billion (nominal USD) that would have been spent if the 2008 Farm Act had continued through 2018. All major conservation programmes, with the exception of Conservation Technical Assistance, have mandatory funding. Among the major changes:

1. The Conservation Reserve Program (CRP) acreage cap is reduced to 24 million acres by 2017. Current enrolment has fallen to 25.6 million acres. Up to 2 million acres of grassland can be enrolled. Funding for the Environmental Quality Incentives Program (EQIP) and the Conservation Stewardship Program (CSP) is increased.

2. The Wildlife Habitat Incentives Program is repealed, although 5% of EQIP funds will be set aside for habitat-related practices.

3. The new Agricultural Conservation Easement Program (ACEP) consolidates the Wetland Reserve Program, Grassland Reserve Program and the Farmland Protection Program. Funding is just over half of what was provided for these three programmes in the 2008 Farm Act.

4. The Regional Conservation Partnership Program consolidates functions of existing regional programmes: Agricultural Water Enhancement Program, Chesapeake Bay Watershed Program, Co-operative Conservation Partnership Initiative and Great Lakes Basin Program.

Box 1.7. **New US farm legislation in 2014** (cont.)

The new Farm Act reauthorises the Market Access Program, Foreign Market Development Program and Technical Assistance for Specialty Crops Programs and maintains strong funding levels for these programmes. The new law reauthorises international food assistance programmes, including the McGovern-Dole Food for Education and Food for Progress programmes. It also authorises a new Local and Regional Purchase food aid programme. The Farm Act reduces the maximum repayment term under the export credit guarantee programme from three years to 24 months.

The new Farm Act reauthorises the Supplemental Nutrition Assistance Program (SNAP), the nation's largest food and nutrition assistance programme, maintaining the programme's basic eligibility guidelines while restricting access to an income deduction that boosted benefits for some households. It provides additional SNAP funding for enhanced employment and training activities, increased healthy food options, and expanded anti-fraud efforts.

Trade: The Americas dominate exports, while China drives import growth in Asia

In line with the reduced growth in production and consumption, trade will be growing at a slower pace when compared to the previous decade. Grains and meat trade, for example, are anticipated to grow by around 1.5% and 2.5% p.a. in volume-terms over the outlook period, which are only half the rates of the previous decade. Historic trade patterns are expected to continue; the leading export regions will maintain their positions and only a few newcomers are expected to enter the trade arena during the next decade.

The Americas will strengthen their position as the dominant export region, both in value and volume terms, as illustrated in Figure 1.12 and Table 1.1. Figure 1.12 shows the evolution of total net export values of all *Outlook* commodities from 2000 to 2023 in different regions, while Table 1.1 presents net exports by commodity from these regions in 2023. Net trade in value terms in Latin America and the Caribbean and in North America will grow more than 2% p.a. between 2011-13 and 2023 (Figure 1.12). This growth is mainly fuelled by increased exports of high-value commodities, such as meat, ethanol, sugar,

Figure 1.12. **Value of net-exports positive in Americas, Oceania and East Europe**

Real value of net-exports of agricultural commodities

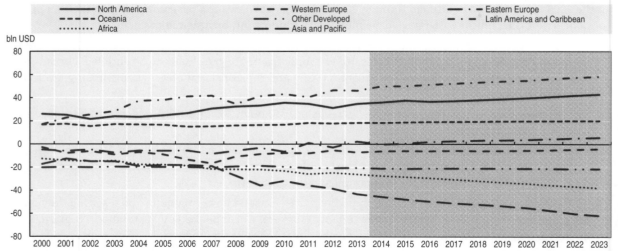

Note: Net exports are calculated by weighing exports and imports by the international reference prices for the period 2004-06 for the agricultural commodities included in this *Outlook*

Source: OECD and FAO Secretariats.

StatLink 🔗 *http://dx.doi.org/10.1787/888933098858*

oilseeds and cotton. In 2023, these two regions are expected to be the main net exporters in volume terms for most commodities (Table 1.1). Oceania is also anticipated to keep a positive trade balance in value terms, mainly because of the increased demand for sheep meat and dairy products from the expanding middle class in the Middle East and Asia.

Table 1.1. **The largest trade deficits in volume terms in 2023 will occur in Asia and Africa**

Volume of net-exports in 2023 ('000 tones)

	Africa	Asia and Pacific	Europe	Latin America and Caribbean	North America	Oceania Developed	Other Developed
Wheat	-44 987	-49 963	45 788	-7 074	46 206	18 329	-8 299
Rice	-18 052	21 083	-1 368	-1 192	2 419	299	-2 637
Coarse grains	-22 851	-63 999	30 402	21 795	53 574	4 154	-19 595
Oilseeds	-3 494	-98 449	-11 469	57 748	58 323	2 921	-5 185
Protein meals	-4 461	-27 206	-19 586	49 715	8 963	-2 669	-4 912
Beef	- 877	-2 105	-1 110	3 341	42	2 224	-1 147
Pork	- 714	-2 625	1 715	- 376	3 621	- 362	-1 280
Sheep	53	- 790	- 140	9	- 71	1 032	- 40
Poultry	-2 192	-5 234	877	3 677	4 710	57	-1 729
Fish	-3 323	9 625	-1 822	2 015	-3 406	- 220	-2 769
Fish meal	43	-1 418	- 7	1 398	125	- 28	- 112
Fish oil	56	- 124	- 189	296	4	- 12	- 30
Butter	- 161	- 413	80	- 22	98	476	- 39
Cheese	- 219	- 633	879	- 284	318	518	- 365
Skim milk powder	- 387	-1 241	640	- 367	826	642	- 95
Whole milk powder	- 618	-1 372	379	- 46	4	1 656	- 21
Vegetable oils	-8 775	5 447	-2 366	8 362	235	- 386	-2 279
Sugar	-11 684	-17 342	- 591	38 337	-4 511	3 636	-4 475
Cotton	1 620	-7 164	48	927	2 562	1 035	741

Note: For each commodity, the blue shaded areas indicate the regions with largest net exports, with the darkest blue shaded area representing the region with the largest net exports. Conversely, the grey shaded areas indicate the areas with the smallest net exports, with the darkest grey shaded area representing the region with the smallest net exports (largest net imports).
Source: OECD and FAO Secretariats.

StatLink ⟨⟩ http://dx.doi.org/10.1787/888933101043

Eastern Europe, which is projected to become a surplus region from 2013 onward, is anticipated to maintain a small positive trade balance by realising its export potential in cereals and oilseeds. Ukraine in particular will become a key player, as it is expected to become the leading exporter of grains and oilseeds in Europe, surpassing the European Union and staying ahead of the Russian Federation. It will also be the only country outside the Americas to maintain a positive trade balance for meat through the outlook period.

The positive overall trade balances in the Americas, Oceania and Eastern Europe are matched by overall trade deficits in the remaining regions. Western Europe will display on average a negative trade balance with flat exports due to low production growth, a stable domestic demand for high value products and a strong currency. The rapidly growing population and shift in diets in Africa result in increasing food imports (Box 1.8). The largest demand for imports is generated in Asia, which is expected to exhibit a trade deficit in 2023 for all commodities, except rice, vegetable oils and fish. This development is greatly influenced by China, which will import large quantities of most commodities. India will remain one of the leading exporters of cereals and rice and is also projected to become a major exporter of meat and cotton keeping it in an overall trade surplus situation for agricultural products. Agricultural trade will be affected by government policies, including those pertaining to public stockholding, an issue that forms part of the post-Bali WTO agenda (Box 1.9).

Box 1.8.   **Dealing with rising food imports: Policy options for West African countries**

Despite its vast agricultural potential, Africa has remained a net importer of agricultural products in the last three decades. In 1980, Africa had a balanced agricultural trade when both exports and imports were at about USD 14 billion, but by 2007 its agricultural imports exceeded exports by about USD 20 billion (FAOSTAT). The increase in agricultural and food imports has been particularly striking for basic foodstuffs such as dairy products, edible oils and fats, meat and meat products, sugars, and especially cereals, implying that food imports have been playing an increasingly important role in ensuring food security. For Low-Income Food-Deficit countries, persistently high and rising import bills can have serious macroeconomic and social impacts. Moreover, rising imports could reduce incentives to invest in increased food production.

Grain deficit is being increasingly filled by wheat and rice imports. For example, per capita wheat consumption in West Africa in 2007-09 was nearly double its average levels in 1994-96, while per capita demand increased by over 70% in Central Africa during the same period. Similarly, between 1961 and 2006, rice consumption in Sub-Saharan Africa increased at a rate of 4.5% p.a. while rice production grew at 3.2% p.a.[1] In West Africa, per capita rice consumption increased from about 30 kg in the early 1990s to about 45 kg in 2010, a 50% increase over 20 years.[2] Nigeria, South Africa, Ivory Coast and Senegal rank among the world's ten leading rice importing countries.

A recent FAO study entitled "*Why has Africa become a net food importer,*"[3] concluded that population growth along with low and stagnating productivity in food and agricultural production and policy distortions, poor infrastructure and weak institutional support, were the main reasons for the increase in the food-trade deficit in Africa.

A case study was carried out for Senegal, one of the leading cereal importing countries in West Africa. The study used annual import data (FAOSTAT data) covering the period 1960-2012 to determine endogenously the most important years when structural breaks occurred in wheat and rice imports. The test identified a break in total wheat imports and per capita wheat imports in 1997 and 1996, respectively, while 2001 and 2002 emerge as the most significant break-years for total rice imports and per capita rice imports, respectively. These years correspond to significant policy shifts in Senegal, starting with the devaluation of the local currency (the CFA Franc) in 1994. Policy measures adopted included a full liberalisation of import in 1996 (rice trade was highly regulated by the State and imports were subject to quotas until 1996) and the implementation of the regional Common Exterior Tariff (CET) in 2000, leading to a drop in rice import tariff from 38% to 10%. These reforms led to a significant increase in cereal imports.

The case study also provided projections of rice demand, supply and imports in Senegal under alternative scenarios for the period 2013-22 using the FAO-OECD Aglink-Cosimo model. Simulated policies included a 30% increase in rice and coarse grains yields (optimistic scenarios) as well as stagnant yields scenario (pessimistic). In addition, a doubling of the rice CET to 20% was simulated. The baseline scenario assumes that current production and consumption trends and policies are maintained. Rice imports are projected to expand by about 30% under the baseline scenario. The scenario with the biggest reduction in rice imports is a combined additional 30% increase in rice and coarse grains yields over the simulation period. Production of rice and coarse grains is expected to increase by 71% and 37%, respectively, compared to the base year levels.

Interestingly, doubling the rice import tariff to 20% has little impact on rice production and imports. Under this scenario, rice imports are projected to decline by 5% compared to the baseline scenario. A higher tariff rate is needed to have any significant effects on rice consumption and imports. The limited impact of the simulated tariff increase reflects the low price elasticity of rice demand due to its convenience of processing and preparation for the urban consumer. As underlined by several studies, the switch to rice consumption in West Africa is driven by long-run structural factors including employment patterns and urbanisation, although dramatic short term changes in relative prices can amplify the phenomenon.

1. Mason, N., T.S. Jayne, B. Shiferaw (2012), "Wheat Consumption in Sub-Saharan Africa: Trends, Drivers, and Policy Implications", *MSU International Development Working Paper* N°127.
2. Mendez del Villar, P., J.M. Bauer, (2013), "Le riz en Afrique de l'Ouest: dynamiques, politiques et perspectives", *Cahiers de l'agriculture*, Vol. 22 (5), pp. 1-9.
3. FAO (2011), Why has Africa become a net food importer?, FAO, Rome.

Box 1.9. **Public stockholding for food security**

Public procurement for the maintenance of food stocks proved to be a difficult issue to resolve at the 9th World Trade Organization (WTO) Ministerial Conference held in Bali in December 2013. A proposal submitted by the G33 group of developing countries had argued that procurement at administered (above market) prices from resource-poor, low-income farmers for the purpose of public stockholding with the objective of food security should not be subject to limitations imposed by the WTO Agreement on Agriculture. The main argument was that the existing flexibilities under the WTO Agreement, which allow developing countries to count the resulting producer support against their bound total Aggregate Measurement of Support (AMS) or *de minimis* limits, do not provide developing countries with sufficient "policy space" for addressing their food security concerns. At the same time, it was argued that the existing rules were asymmetric in their treatment of countries, with historically high levels of support in some countries having provided them with greater latitude to use trade-distorting domestic support. The proposal was opposed by some WTO members, who argued that such policies could distort global markets and negatively impact food security in other developing countries, and also needed to be considered in the overall context of the Doha mandate to substantially reduce trade distorting subsidies.

An interim mechanism was agreed at Bali whereby Members will refrain from challenging, through the WTO Dispute Settlement Mechanism, those developing countries with existing public stockholding programmes which breach their domestic support commitments, provided specific conditions are met. The agreed outcome was for this interim mechanism to exist until a permanent agreement is concluded, with a work programme set up with a view to producing such an agreement by the 11th WTO Ministerial Conference in 2017. A number of transparency obligations and safeguard provisions were introduced as part of the mechanism in an effort to limit potential negative effects on other members. These included additional information and reporting obligations and the requirement that countries operating such programmes ensure that they do not adversely affect the food security of other members.

Determining the market impacts of government food stockholding policies is complicated by the fact that schemes are designed in pursuit of different objectives and implemented using different instruments. In some cases, the objective may be to maintain an emergency reserve to protect against domestic supply shocks, reflecting a reluctance to rely entirely on international markets to ensure adequate food availability. Such emergency reserves generally involve purchases at market prices; food security programmes operated along these lines are not constrained under WTO rules. In other cases, stockholding policies involve purchases at prices higher than prevailing market prices, and in this case WTO limitations on domestic support do apply. Public stocks may be held as part of a domestic price stabilisation policy, or to stimulate production and incomes. Targeted distribution of stocks to urban and rural poor consumers in developing countries at below market prices is without restriction under WTO rules. The domestic implications of public stockholding schemes depend critically on the extent to which intervention prices on either the producer or consumer side differ from prevailing market prices, the volume of intervention, and on how responsive producers and consumers are to changes in price incentives.

The extent of the impact on external trade of government stockholding at administered prices depends, in part, on the size of the country's market and on the magnitude of the operation and, hence, the price distortion that is created by the procurement programme. Evidence from the national statistical authorities of India and the Philippines suggests that in India 33% of domestically produced rice will be procured for public stocks, while in the Philippines the share is likely to be only 2%. Where procurement is significant, a reduction in net exports could be observed during the procurement period as products that are otherwise destined for export are diverted to stocks. Equally, imports could be reduced if an increasing share of consumption is covered by products entering markets through the government food distribution programmes. The release of stocks can also have important implications. The scale and timing of release, especially if unpredictable and not factored into traders' decision making, can significantly influence price levels and volatility, both domestically, and, if the country is a significant trader, internationally.

Geographical separation of demand and supply spurs growth in trade

Relative to the 2011-13 base period, trade volumes of all commodities in the Outlook are projected to rise, but as Figure 1.13 shows, the growth rates vary widely across commodities. The traditional global grains export leaders will continue to dominate the market. The United States will remain the top wheat exporter despite a slight decline of its exports, while the Russian Federation is expected to increase exports by nearly 8 Mt to pass the European Union and Australia to become the world's third largest exporter by 2023. Egypt, the Middle East and Indonesia are anticipated to account for almost 25% of total wheat imports by the end of the outlook period. Coarse grain exports continue to be similarly concentrated, with the United States expanding its share to 30% by 2023. The most significant gains are anticipated in Ukraine which will position the country in fourth place closely behind Argentina and Brazil.

Figure 1.13. **Skim milk powder and poultry to show largest growth over the outlook period**

Growth in commodity trade in 2023 relative to the 2011-13 base period

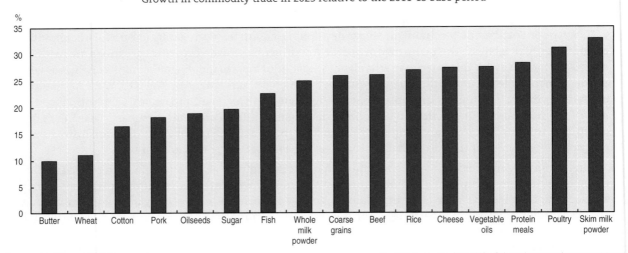

Source: OECD and FAO Secretariats.

StatLink 🔗 *http://dx.doi.org/10.1787/888933098877*

Imports will be dispersed around the globe without any emerging dominant importer. Rice trade will continue to expand relatively quickly in the next ten years, albeit at slower rates than the previous decade. Thailand is projected to regain its leadership from Viet Nam as the world's largest rice exporter. All other traditional exporters (Viet Nam, India, Pakistan and the United States) are also expected to increase their exports, while least developed Asian countries such as Cambodia and Myanmar are anticipated to become major rice exporters as well. Increased import demand will generally be generated in Africa, which is expected to remain a net importer of rice, as local producers are not expected to meet growing domestic demand.

Over 90% of oilseeds exports are generated in the Americas. The United States, Brazil and Argentina will remain the principal exporters, but Canada, Uruguay and Paraguay are expected to increase their role. Ukraine is projected to be the only country outside the Americas exporting large quantities of oilseeds. More than 60% of all vegetable oils exports continue to originate from Indonesia and Malaysia, as these two countries contribute significantly to an almost 30% growth of global vegetable oil trade over the outlook period. Imports of vegetable oils are much less concentrated, with the European Union, China and India leading the charts.

In the sugar market, exports will originate from a few countries while imports are fragmented over the world. Brazil will remain the largest exporter, supported by a falling currency, with Thailand in second place. Australia is projected to become a growing sugar exporting country, contingent on the projected investments in its sugarcane area. At the beginning of the outlook period, China and Indonesia are, after the European Union, the leading importers of sugar. However, over the projection period, Indonesia is expected to have the biggest deficit and become the leading sugar importer, followed by China and the United States. Sugar imports into the European Union and the United States are controlled by their domestic market regimes. The new EU sugar regime, in which sugar and isoglucose quotas are abolished, will result in lower EU imports as sugar beet production is expected to expand (Box 6.1 in the Sugar Chapter).

Global meat trade patterns will stay stable, with poultry expected to account for 42% of total meat trade, followed by beef (31%) and pork (22%). North and South America will dominate poultry exports, while the biggest importers are expected to be Africa, Asia and the Middle East. Asia will import by far the greatest share of beef, most of which is supplied by South America. India is expected to continue exporting beef to developing regions, notably low priced buffalo meat, and is projected to become the largest bovine meat exporter by the end of the projection period. For pork, the greatest share of additional import demand will come from Asia and Sub-Saharan Africa, while the bulk of exports will originate from North America and Europe. Interestingly, countries in Asia, as an aggregate, will not only be the largest producers of pig meat, but also the largest importers. The region will also import the greatest share of additional sheep meat, which is exported from Oceania.

The bulk of export growth in dairy originates in the United States, European Union, New Zealand and Australia. The European Union will remain the main cheese exporter, but its growth rate is slower than New Zealand's, the United States' and Australia's. The United States is the largest exporter of SMP, while India is expected to increase its exports considerably over the next decade. The main destinations for dairy products are developing countries, especially in Asia and Africa. In the case of cheese, the developed countries still dominate imports, but the developing countries are closing the gap. WMP imports by China, which skyrocketed in recent years, are expected to slow down.

Fish and fishery products are expected to be highly traded, with about 37%* (including intra-EU trade and 32% if excluding it) of world fishery production exported. Developed countries continue to be the main importers of fish for human consumption, with their share in world imports projected to remain above 50% in quantity terms. Developing countries represent two-thirds of world exports in fish for human consumption, with more than half of exports in 2023 originating from Asia. In terms of fishmeal, on the other hand, the developing countries will be the main importers, reflecting the high demand for fishmeal from aquaculture production.

Prices: Global supply and demand projections point to slowly declining real prices

The model underlying the *OECD-FAO Agricultural Outlook* simultaneously simulates the domestic markets for all its individual country modules and world markets for all commodities in which the national imports and exports are cleared by international reference prices. Since the *Outlook* price projections are predicated on the key assumption

---

* Including fish meal on a fish equivalent basis.

of normal production conditions and the absence of unforeseen market shocks, such as droughts and animal disease outbreaks, prices are a reflection of expected market fundamentals during the outlook period. Domestic and international prices are determined simultaneously, but the degree by which they are connected varies by country and commodity. Countries with dominant trade shares may be considered as price setters in a particular market, and thus their marginal cost of production plays an important role in the future course of global prices. Trade volumes of minor traders are assumed to influence international markets only slightly so international reference prices transmit the signals from the global level into their domestic markets. Countries with very small interactions with the global market are considered somewhat independent of international prices and vice versa. Their domestic market conditions are most relevant for setting prices paid by their producers and consumers. The *Outlook* focuses mostly on international prices, but for any analysis of individual country markets, their relationship with the global market should be carefully examined (Box 6.1 for a discussion on the determinants of food price movements). The following summary of developments in international reference prices highlights the important features of each global commodity market in the coming decade.

Near record prices in 2012 resulted in strong production responses around the world in 2013, creating surplus market conditions for the commodities covered in this *Outlook*. Most prices subsequently eased in 2013, hence *Outlook* price projections are taking off from a correction period which is expected to persist for one or two more years, depending on the commodity.

International prices of major cereals are projected to remain under downward pressure in 2014/15 (Figure 1.14). Wheat prices decrease further through the first three years of the outlook period, due to ample production prospects until 2016/17. This decline slows production growth over the second half of the projection period, and wheat prices will recover. This recovery is anticipated to stay below the projected inflation rate: In real terms wheat prices decrease in the coming decade by about 1% p.a., remaining around 13% below the average of the previous decade (Figure 1.15). For coarse grains, the production response to the high prices in recent years is expected to be especially strong in the United States, the Russian Federation and Argentina. Global demand will not be able to absorb this supply at current prices. Based on this expected surplus in international markets, coarse grains prices will experience considerable decreases in the early years of the outlook period, before rebounding to about USD 230/t from 2017/18 onward. Adjusted for inflation, the coarse grain price in 2023 is expected to be very close to the current level.

The international reference price for rice (Viet Nam) eased in 2013 as a result of the large supplies accumulated earlier this decade. These large inventories, which were accumulated by exporting countries through domestic support schemes, will keep the market in a surplus situation for several years and consequently weigh on international prices. The world price is predicted to recover in the second half of the projection period and reach about 400 USD/t in 2023. All grain prices decline in real terms, and they will fall below current levels at the end of the projection period (Figure 1.15).

The ease of substitution of land between coarse grains and oilseeds in the United States influences the price movements expected for oilseeds. Because of the significant fall in coarse grain prices described above, a shift in land to oilseeds is anticipated in 2014/15 which should contribute to further declines in the prices of oilseeds. Over the medium-term, market conditions of the two oilseeds products – meal and oil – are expected to differ, leading to

Figure 1.14. **Price trends in nominal terms for agricultural commodities to 2023**

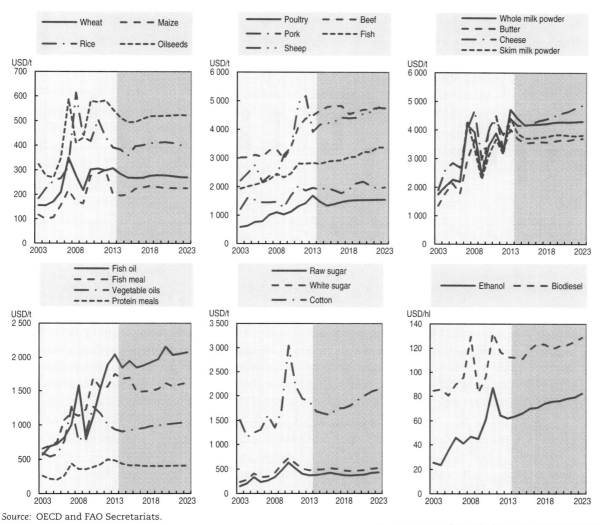

Source: OECD and FAO Secretariats.

StatLink 🔗 *http://dx.doi.org/10.1787/888933098896*

diverging price projections. In the oil sector, a strong demand for food and fuel will push the price to increase as of 2015/16. The price of protein meal will not increase as much, because of the joint nature of both products global meal supplies will be ample keeping prices flat. In real terms, all three prices are expected to fall compared to the very high levels of recent years.

World sugar prices are expected to follow a moderately upward trend, and they continue to follow a familiar "sugar cycle". Brazil's cost of production and the relative profitability between sugar and ethanol production determine the general level of world sugar prices over the outlook period, while the shape of the cycle is mostly driven by specific market conditions in sugar producing countries in Asia. Sugar prices are projected to stay far below their recent peaks, with nominal raw sugar price oscillating around USD 400/t. The white sugar premium is projected at nearly USD 100/t, yet narrowing over the decade.

Similar to the prices of their feedstock, world ethanol and biodiesel prices continued their decline in 2013. Real ethanol prices are expected to increase slightly over the outlook period as

Figure 1.15. In real terms, prices for livestock, dairy and ethanol are higher than in the previous decade

Per cent change in average real prices relative to different base periods 2011-13 and 2004-13

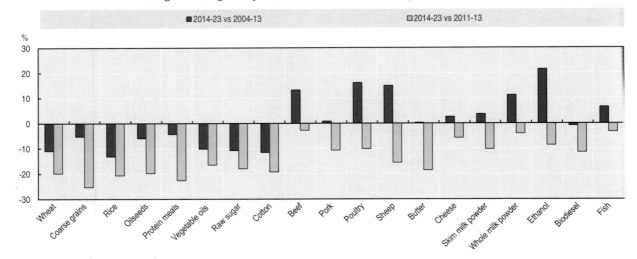

Source: OECD and FAO Secretariats.

StatLink 🔗 http://dx.doi.org/10.1787/888933098915

they will be influenced by market-driven demand, due to strong crude oil prices, and policies in place, especially in the United States and in Brazil. Profitability of the ethanol sector should improve slightly in the coming years, because the margin between feedstock and ethanol prices is expected to increase in real terms. With biodiesel demand being mostly policy and not market driven, biodiesel prices are expected to follow the evolution of vegetable oil prices.

Cotton prices are driven by macroeconomic developments, market policies, technological progress in the man-made fibre sector and preferences in textile demand. After a 2010 cotton price spike, driven by macroeconomic volatility and policy changes in key countries, prices have declined significantly in recent years but cotton prices are expected to remain relatively stable during 2014-23 as the assumptions regarding policy and macroeconomic stability do not indicate any future price run-ups. A certain cyclical price behaviour is caused by the projected production patterns of major producers, but by 2023, world cotton prices are expected to be lower than in 2011-13, in both real and nominal terms.

To properly reflect conditions in the global market for beef and pork, the Pacific and Atlantic market segments need to be considered separately. For each segment a market clearing price is projected. Prices follow similar projection paths, but they differ in level, with the Pacific price generally above the Atlantic, because of sanitary and phytosanitary measures that prevent beef from the Atlantic region to access the more lucrative markets in the Pacific region. Poultry and sheep meats are traded in single international markets. Prices of beef and sheep meat, which are produced more on pasture and are hence less feed grain dependent, increase from 2014 throughout the projection period, ending above current levels. Beef prices follow a customary cycle that reflects herd management in important producer countries. Prices of sheep meat, a relatively small sector, rise continuously nominally, but stay flat in real terms. By contrast, pork and poultry prices reflect the decline in feed prices in the near term. Nonetheless, meat-to-feed price margins are expected to improve compared to those experienced when feed costs reached their peak. Because of a strong meat demand, meat prices fall relatively less than feed prices, before stabilising along with them in two to three years. After accounting for general price inflation, real meat prices will average higher than in the previous decade, although they trend marginally down from their current highs.

The outlook for dairy product prices starts from a very different situation. Milk and dairy product prices increased strongly in 2013 due to reduced production in major countries from increasing feed costs. In the near term, prices of all dairy products are expected to decline sharply as production in the major dairy exporting countries expands in to the current high prices and feed costs decrease. Over the medium-term, production growth from increasing dairy herds and rising yields will be able to more than satisfy the continued growth in demand, especially in developing countries. Due to this broad production base, it is expected that real dairy product prices will decline slightly over the next ten years. Within the dairy sector, butter prices will be flat in nominal terms, while cheese prices are expected to continue on the growth trend of the previous years.

Higher prices and higher production costs are expected to prevail in the fisheries sector in the next ten years due to a strong demand for protein, high feed costs, limited production growth of captured fisheries and high prices of alternatives like meat and dairy products. Fish prices are differentiated between captured and aquaculture products. The average prices of wild fish for human consumption, which will remain under restrictive production quotas, are projected to increase twice as fast as the price for aquaculture fish during the outlook period. Future prices for individual fisheries commodities could significantly differ from one another due to supply swings caused by changes in catch quotas, disease outbreaks in the aquaculture sector as well as fluctuations in feed costs.

Box 1.10. **Macroeconomic factors influencing food prices**

The 2007-08 food price increase period generated a renewed interest in understanding food price behaviour, their determinants, dynamics and transmission across markets. A wealth of research has since been produced. The general consensus is that there was no single factor responsible for the price surge, but rather a set of various elements which collectively explained most of the increase. Where research diverges is on the contribution of each of these factors. Most cited drivers leading to the price surge include: unfavourable weather conditions that prevailed in some of the major grain producing countries/regions in 2006 and 2007, the rise in energy prices, increases in demand for biofuels, depreciation of the United States dollar, slower productivity growth, low grain stock levels and market speculation. Each of these factors has been researched in detail.[1] One characteristic of the price surge, was that it was broadly based across the commodity markets. Those factors associated with supply shocks are likely to be less correlated across food crops at world level, and as a result less likely to explain such common movements in food prices. Instead, factors that are common across commodities are more likely to explain the rise in aggregate food prices. Such common factors are likely to be demand related and macroeconomic in nature (Gilbert, 2010).[2]

In order to provide some empirical evidence linking demand related factors to food price movements, a set of pairwise Granger causality tests were applied using the FAO food price index (FFPI)[3] and a selection of cross cutting factors. These included, i) changes in the value of the United States dollar relative to a broad group of major currencies[4] (XR), ii) the United States money supply (M2), as a measure of world liquidity, iii) imports of goods and services into China (CHINAIMP), as a proxy for aggregate demand growth in emerging economies, and iv) crude oil prices[5] (OIL), as a measure of energy prices. The Granger causality test is an econometric tool that determines whether one time series is useful in predicting the value of another series. The analysis spans from January 1980 to November 2013.

Box 1.10. **Macroeconomic factors influencing food prices** *(cont.)*

Results showed that Granger causality was established for the FFPI, with respect to all four factors, meaning that XR, M2, CHINAIMP and OIL, caused changes in the food price index over the sample range. When the analysis was carried using maize prices or wheat prices instead of the food price index, a causal relationship was not established in several cases (Table 1.2). For example, the statistical tests could not detect a causal link between maize or wheat prices and the exchange rate. However, given that the exchange rate caused the overall food index (FFPI), it means that its effect is more pronounced on most of the food crops comprising the Food index, and less so on commodities such as wheat and maize. In the case of oil prices, a causal relationship was detected between West Texas Intermediate (WTI) and the Food price index, as well as between WTI and maize, and WTI and wheat prices. Oil prices impact food prices through production costs, but also through increased demand for food crops as biofuel feedstock.

Several implications can be drawn from this analysis. First, there is evidence that demand related factors such as rising demand from emerging markets, changes in United States exchange rate, the US money supply and oil prices (with their effect on demand for feedstock), help explain food prices movements. Second, appropriate policies to mitigate the impact of high food prices may require multilateral coordination, given the global nature of the determinants of food prices. Third, oil prices do have an impact on food prices, but the nature of that relationship has probably changed over recent years with the emergence of biofuels. Still, the extent to which biofuels impact food price remains a subject of discord amongst researchers. Finally, macroeconomic data is critical to an agricultural market outlook exercise, given their contribution to commodity prices.

Table 1.2. **Granger Causality tests**

Dependent variable	Common factor	X^{2}*	Prob**
FFPI			
	OIL	13.72	0.032
	XR	8.48	0.037
	M2	13.05	0.0015
	CHINAIMP	14.92	0.004
Maize			
	OIL	7.64	0.02
	XR	2.17	0.33
	M2	0.49	0.065
	CHINAIMP	26.04	0
Wheat			
	OIL	10.69	0.005
	XR	2.88	0.23
	M2	9.04	0.01
	CHINAIMP	38.66	0

* Khi 2.
** Value of p.

StatLink ⫘⫘ *http://dx.doi.org/10.1787/888933101062*

1. See for example Heady, D. and S. Fan (2008), "Anatomy of a crisis: The causes and consequences of surging food prices", *Agricultural Economics*, Vol. 39.
2. Gilbert, C. (2010), "How to understand high food prices", *Journal of Agricultural Economics*, Vol. 61, No. 2.
3. The FFPI index aggregates price changes of 23 traded agricultural commodities, including wheat (10 price quotations) and maize (1 price quotation).
4. Trade weighted US Dollar Index: Broad (TWEXBMTH), United States Federal Reserve.
5. West Texas Intermediate, WTI.

Uncertainty analysis

Rather than forecasting what will occur in the future, the baseline projects future outcomes conditional on a specific set of assumptions about the policies in place, the responsiveness of market participants and the future values of exogenous market drivers, such as weather conditions or the macroeconomic environment. As a complement to the baseline, uncertainty analysis (partial stochastic analysis) is undertaken. Stochastic analysis gives an indication of the range of possible outcomes around the baseline, given the variability observed in previous years for key agricultural and macroeconomic drivers. Partial stochastic analysis aims to identify such key risks and uncertainties most likely to affect the projection. It involves performing multiple simulations with different values of selected exogenous variables and studying their impact on selected endogenous variables like prices, production or trade. It also allows the policy maker to select specific sources of uncertainty and quantify the likely range of market variation that derives from these identifiable sources of uncertainty. This year, special efforts were made to identify the impact of uncertainties surrounding milk yields in Oceania (reflecting milk yield uncertainties from grass-fed livestock systems) on milk production and world dairy product markets.

Sources of uncertainty analysed

Major sources of systematic uncertainty in agricultural markets (i.e. macroeconomic conditions and yields) are treated stochastically, and their effects are analysed. The analysis is only partial in that it does not capture all the sources of variability that affected agricultural markets in the past. For example, uncertainty related to animal diseases is not captured. The selection of which variables to treat stochastically aims to cover the major sources of uncertainty for agricultural markets whilst keeping the analysis simple enough to be able to identify the main ones in each market.

- *Global macroeconomic drivers: Values of* 32 variables: real Gross Domestic Product (GDP), the Consumer Price Index (CPI) and the GDP Deflator in the United States, the European Union, China, Japan, Brazil, India, the Russian Federation and Canada; national currency-US Dollar exchange rates for the last seven of these countries or regions; and the world crude oil price are assumed uncertain.

- *Agricultural yields*: Uncertainty affecting the yields of 17 crops in 20 major producing countries is also analysed, giving a total of 78 product-country-specific uncertain yields (see *Methodology* for further explanation).

The uncertainty coming from macroeconomic conditions and crop yields is analysed jointly and separately. Three scenarios are presented: i) macroeconomic uncertainty, ii) yield uncertainty and iii) combined macroeconomic and yield uncertainty. Figure 1.16 illustrates for the world coarse grain price the corridor of future values based on the combined macroeconomic and yield uncertainty. The indicator used to represent and compare the impact of uncertainty on projected outcomes is the coefficient of variation (defined as the standard deviation divided by the mean) in the last projection year, 2023 (CV2023). The CV is calculated from values lying between the 10th and the 90th percentiles of the outcomes in 2023.

Figure 1.16. **Uncertainty around the world coarse grain price**

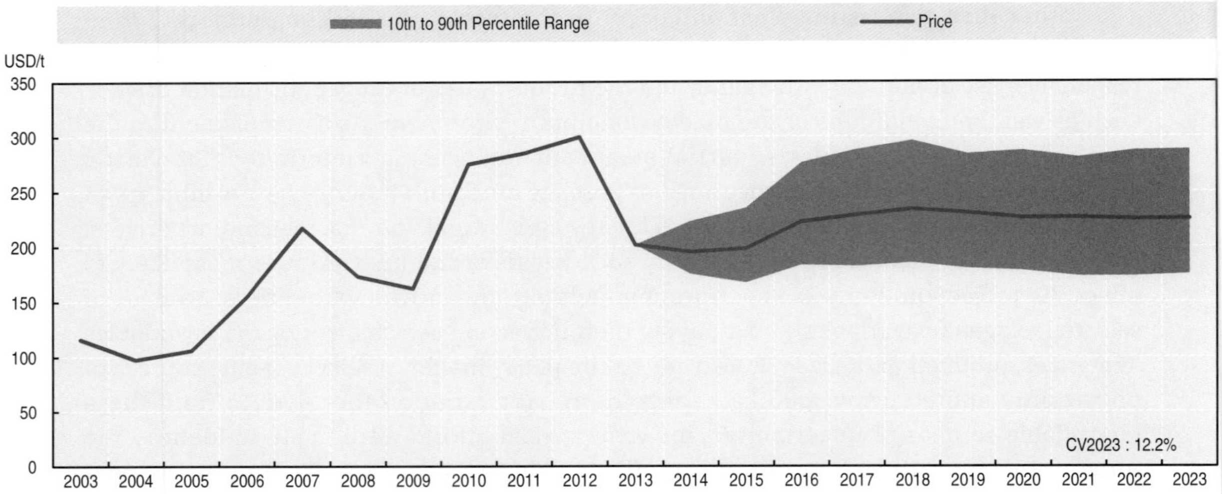

Source: JRC-IPTS, European Commission.

StatLink http://dx.doi.org/10.1787/888933098934

Relative impact of uncertainty on market outcomes, by commodity

Arable crops

For arable crops, the effect of yield uncertainty works through production and is transmitted to trade and prices (Figure 1.17). Macroeconomic uncertainty affects i) input costs (through the production cost, crude oil prices and the GDP deflator), ii) competitiveness (through exchange rate variation) and iii) consumption (from uncertainty in GDP growth and consumer price indices). Worldwide, arable crop production (cereals and oilseeds) is more affected by yield than by macroeconomic uncertainty for the last year of the projection period. For consumption, by contrast, the effect of macroeconomic uncertainty is slightly larger than that of yield uncertainty because consumption is directly affected by shocks to GDP and the consumer price index. Supply shocks are also not entirely transmitted to consumers for the following reasons: i) arable crop stocks serve as a buffer, and ii) there is substitution between the different coarse grains, wheat and oilseeds, especially for animal feed and, to a lesser extent, in biofuels. Concerning the uncertainty effect on trade, cereals (wheat, coarse grains and rice) are generally more affected by yield than by macroeconomic uncertainty, while oilseeds are more affected by macroeconomic uncertainty. The main sources of uncertainty affecting trade are yields and, to a lesser extent, exchange rates for exporting countries, while for importing countries they are exchange rates and demand conditions. The uncertainty in world market prices is transmitted from domestic markets via trade flows, and is determined by shocks to demand and supply, especially in important trading countries, and changing relative prices between domestic and world markets. Macroeconomic uncertainty has a greater effect on world market prices than yield uncertainty.

Protein meals and vegetable oils

Vegetable oils are more affected by macroeconomic and yield uncertainty than protein meals. Uncertainty in oilseeds yield has a direct effect on the quantities available for crushing, while macroeconomic uncertainty affects both demand and supply. Protein meal demand is subject to uncertainty coming from meat and dairy production, which are

Figure 1.17. **Uncertainty in the world wheat market in 2023 by scenario**

CV2023, in %

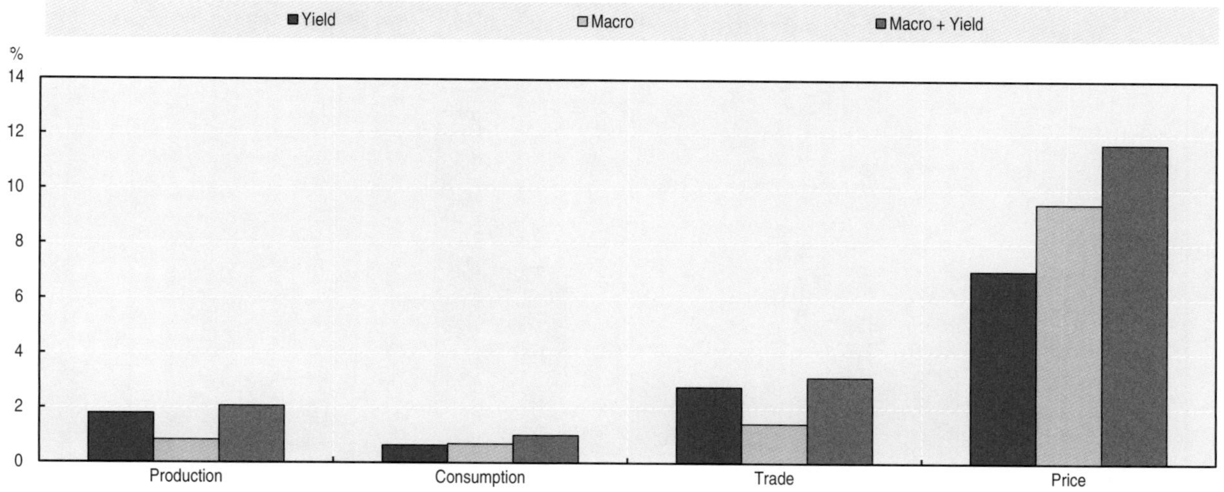

Source: JRC-IPTS, European Commission.

StatLink ⧉ http://dx.doi.org/10.1787/888933098953

affected by macroeconomic variables. Vegetable oil demand is closely linked to biodiesel production, which is less strongly affected by macroeconomic uncertainty since consumption is often dictated by mandates. Exchange rate uncertainty affects not only vegetable oil trade but also oilseeds trade. For both protein meals and vegetable oils, macroeconomic uncertainty affects trade via the exchange rate.

Biofuels and sugar

The development of the sugar market is closely linked to biofuels, in particular ethanol in Brazil. The production and use of ethanol and biodiesel are more responsive to macroeconomic uncertainty than to yield. Indeed, macroeconomic uncertainty directly affects both consumption and trade of biofuels because there is substitution between ethanol and biodiesel, the level of the substitution depends on the relative prices. Furthermore, mandates serve as a direct link between crude oil and biofuel consumption, such that uncertainties surrounding the world crude oil price are directly transmitted to the biofuels markets, and to the sugar markets. Additionally, the uncertainty coming from GDP growth affects demand for fossil fuels on which the mandates are based.

Meat and dairy

The effect of macroeconomic uncertainty on supply and demand for meat and dairy products is bigger than the effect of yield uncertainty. This is largely because i) meat and dairy product demand is more elastic than demand for crop products, leading to greater impacts from income and domestic price variations, and ii) macroeconomic uncertainty has an impact on feed costs, which are directly linked to production. For meat, uncertainty from macroeconomic variables affects traded volumes much more than yield uncertainty, particularly in the case of pork (Figure 1.18). Accordingly, the effect of yield uncertainty on world market prices is very low compared to macroeconomic uncertainty. In the case of dairy products, production costs are important for these manufactured goods, thus the cost of production index plays a significant role.

Figure 1.18. **Comparing uncertainty by commodities in world trade (exports) in 2023 by scenario**

CV2023, in %

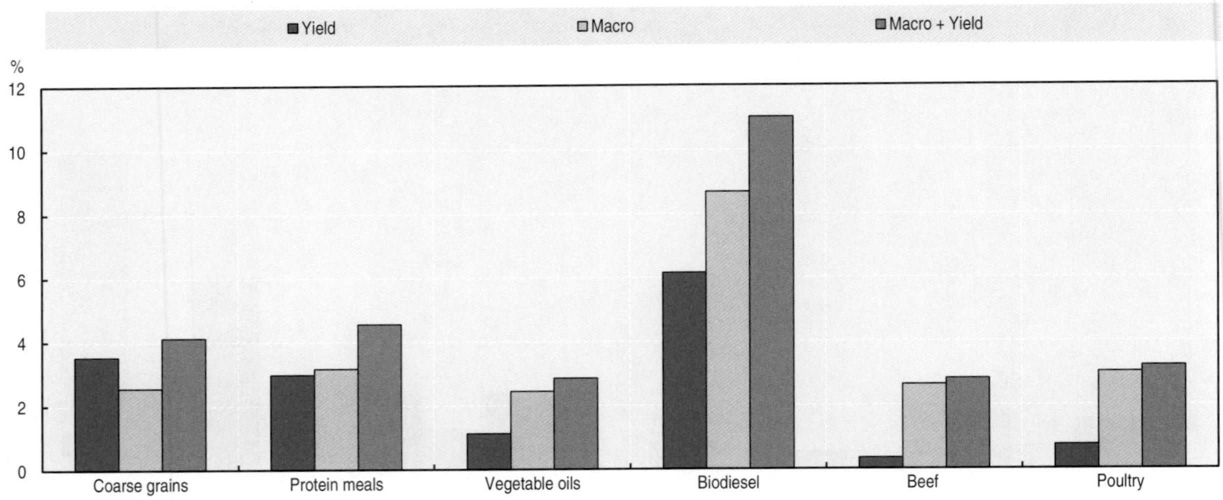

Source: JRC-IPTS, European Commission.

StatLink ⌗⌗⌗ http://dx.doi.org/10.1787/888933098972

Milk world market price uncertainty

The above analysis covers the impact of overall uncertainties on world markets. It is, however, also of interest to analyse specific types of uncertainty. This section focuses on dairy markets and in particular on two of the largest dairy exporting countries, New Zealand and Australia. In 2023, the shares of these two countries in world market exports are projected to be around 60% for butter and WMP, 29% for SMP and 17% for cheese. With such important shares of dairy exports, it is interesting to investigate the possible transmission of uncertainty surrounding milk production in these two countries to world dairy markets. Various factors can affect milk yield, including grass and fodder availability, feed composition, season of calving, frequency of milking and disease. As those factors are not modelled in Aglink-Cosimo, the approach is to use the historical milk yield variation as a measure of uncertainty in milk production.

Four scenarios are presented here: i) New Zealand and Australia milk yield uncertainty only, ii) all crop yield uncertainty (milk yield in Oceania excluded), iii) macroeconomic uncertainty and iv) joint milk yield, crop yield and macroeconomic uncertainty. Two new scenarios [i) and ii)] are introduced in order to see solely the effect of milk yield uncertainty without being offset by other sources of uncertainty, i.e. crop yield. As in the analysis for the overall uncertainties, the coefficient of variation in 2023 (CV2023) for the outcomes lying between the 10th and 90th percentiles is used to describe market uncertainty.

Milk yield uncertainty in Australia and New Zealand only has a significant effect on domestic milk production (2.6% and 1.5% respectively). Moreover, given the importance of Oceania in world dairy markets, this uncertainty also has an effect on world dairy trade and market prices. However, as shown in Figure 1.19, at the global level, milk production is more sensitive to macroeconomic uncertainty than to yield (crops or milk) uncertainty. This is due to the multiple effects of macroeconomic uncertainty on the dairy sector. In the first place, it affects feed costs, notably via exchange rate and crude oil price, as well as through other dairy production costs. In addition, GDP and CPI uncertainty affects demand. This is of particular interest in large importing countries such as China for milk

Figure 1.19. **Uncertainty in Australia, New Zealand and world milk production in 2023 by scenario**

CV2023, in %

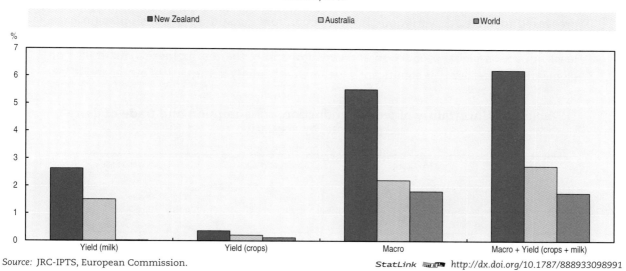

Source: JRC-IPTS, European Commission.

StatLink ⧉ *http://dx.doi.org/10.1787/888933098991*

powders or Russian Federation for cheese, the demand for which represents a considerable share of world market demand. Finally, macroeconomic uncertainty has an effect on relative prices (domestic/world market), thus directly affecting world imports and exports.

The consequences of macroeconomic uncertainty for world dairy prices are considerably greater than those of yield uncertainty (Figure 1.20). Milk yield uncertainty in Australia and New Zealand directly affects the export supply of these countries, resulting in variability of less than 1% in terms of CV2023 in the world market price for cheese and SMP and around 1.5% for that of butter and WMP. Crop yield uncertainty throughout the world also affects world dairy products prices by between 1.6% and 2.5%, through its impact on feed cost. Therefore, the impacts of both scenarios (i.e. milk yield uncertainty in

Figure 1.20. **Uncertainty of world market prices in 2023 by scenario**

CV2023, in %

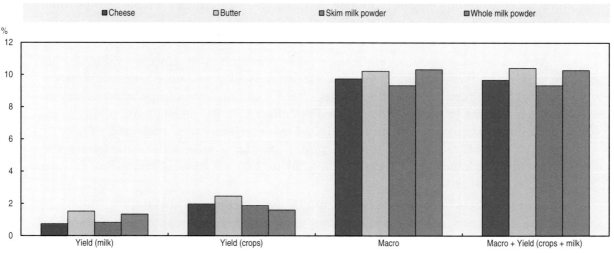

Source: JRC-IPTS, European Commission.

StatLink ⧉ *http://dx.doi.org/10.1787/888933099010*

New Zealand and Australia only and crop yield uncertainty worldwide) on world market prices are of a similar small magnitude.

Finally, the implications of uncertainty for world dairy product balance sheets are presented in Table 1.3. Variations in production and consumption are similar for each scenario and each dairy product. Although milk yield uncertainty in Oceania alone has the least impact on global production and consumption of the four scenarios, its impact on global trade uncertainty is significantly greater, particularly in the case of butter and WMP.

Table 1.3. **Uncertainty of world production, consumption and trade of dairy products, by scenario**

CV2023, in %

CV2023 (%)	World production				World consumption				World trade			
	Yield (milk)	Yield (crops)	Macro	Macro + Yield (crops + milk)	Yield (milk)	Yield (crops)	Macro	Macro + Yield (crops + milk)	Yield (milk)	Yield (crops)	Macro	Macro + Yield (crops + milk)
Cheese	0.0	0.1	0.9	0.9	0.0	0.1	0.9	0.9	0.3	0.6	2.5	2.6
Butter	0.0	0.2	2.4	2.3	0.0	0.2	2.4	2.3	0.7	0.4	2.8	3.0
Skim milk powder	0.1	0.3	0.6	0.6	0.1	0.3	0.6	0.7	0.2	0.4	1.0	1.1
Whole milk powder	0.2	0.2	1.8	1.8	0.2	0.2	1.8	1.8	0.9	0.5	3.8	4.0

Source: JRC-IPTS, European Commission.

StatLink ⧉ http://dx.doi.org/10.1787/888933101081

Conclusion

This analysis shows how partial stochastic analysis can be used to supplement the information provided by the deterministic baseline, by identifying which baseline variables are more affected by the uncertainty associated with a given set of exogenous variables. The results are based on the past pattern of variability in yields and macroeconomic drivers. For crop yields, variability observed over the last two decades has been used; it is greatest in Eurasia, South America and Australia and smallest in the European Union, the United States and China. Macroeconomic uncertainty, based on observed forecast errors, is greater in Brazil, Russian Federation, India and China (BRIC). However, it should be borne in mind that past trends may not continue in the future. For example, climate change could bring more yield variability, or economic growth patterns observed in recent past might change. This analysis does not capture these possible developments.

Overall, the consequences of the uncertainty coming from macroeconomic indicators are larger than those coming from yield variation. Yield uncertainty mainly affects the supply of agricultural commodities, but regional fluctuations may compensate each other. However, changes in macroeconomic variables affect both the demand and supply sides. Production and consumption are less affected by uncertainty than trade and prices. The commodities more exposed to uncertainty are those with more linkages to the macroeconomic indicators, e.g. meat (strong link to GDP) and biofuels (strong link to crude oil prices).

Dairy markets are principally affected by macroeconomic uncertainty. Important sources of uncertainty in these markets are economic developments in importing countries such as China and Russian Federation from the demand side, which are greater than yield uncertainty. Contrary to what might have been expected, uncertainty linked to production, even in major exporting countries such as New Zealand and Australia, has a marginal effect (one to two percentage points of variation) on the world market prices of dairy products.

References

FAO (2011), *Why has Africa become a net food importer?*, FAO, Rome.

Gilbert, C. (2010), "How to understand high food prices", Journal of Agricultural Economics, Vol. 61, No. 2.

Heady D., Fan S. (2008), "Anatomy of a Crisis: The Causes and Consequences of Surging Food Prices", *Agricultural Economics*, Vol. 39.

International Fertilizer Association (IFA), *Production and trade statistics*, accessible at *www.fertilizer.org*.

International Energy Agency (2013), *Gas Medium-Term Market Report 2013*, International Energy Agency.

Mason, N., T.S. Jayne, B. Shiferaw (2012), "Wheat Consumption in Sub-Saharan Africa: Trends, Drivers, and Policy Implications", *MSU International Development Working Paper*, No. 127.

Mendez del Villar, P., J.M. Bauer, (2013), "Le riz en Afrique de l'Ouest: dynamiques, politiques et perspectives", *Cahiers de l'agriculture*, Vol. 22 (5), pp. 1-9.

US Energy Information Administration (2012), *Annual Energy Outlook 2012*, US Energy Information Administration

Chapter 2

Feeding India: Prospects and challenges in the next decade

This chapter reviews the prospects and challenges facing India's agriculture and fish sectors in the next decade. It briefly reviews sector performance, outlines the current context for markets, provides detailed quantitative medium-term projections for the ten-year period 2014-23, and assesses key risks and uncertainties. India's main challenges in promoting sector growth and reducing its large number of food insecure people are discussed in the context of its various policies to address them, including minimum support prices, trade policy, input subsidies and its new National Food Security Act (NFSA). The chapter outlines a relatively positive scenario in which recent trends of higher production and consumption continue, offering India considerable potential to reduce the number of food insecure people over the next decade. The key risks to this scenario include India's macro performance, its ability to effectively implement NFSA and the sustainability of productivity growth.

Introduction

Last year, the *Outlook* focussed on the agricultural and food prospects facing the world's most populous country, China. This year the *Outlook* turns its attention to India, the country with the world's second largest population, and the largest in terms of number of farmers and rural population. Perhaps, most importantly, India currently has the largest number of food insecure people, about one-quarter of the world's total.[1] Like China, India's markets have witnessed considerable transformation in recent years, with huge gains in production and productivity. But unlike China, India has sustained a positive surplus in agriculture and food trade, and with its larger arable land base, its predominantly vegetarian diet and more slowly urbanising society, concerns that sustained economic development will draw heavily on world markets have been mute. Rather, major concerns have centred on food insecurity in the presence of trade surpluses, and how to invigorate agriculture to promote growth and employment in populous rural communities, where unlike the experience of most countries, the size of average land holdings continues to decline.

India's policy effort to support farmers, promote rural development, and at the same time address food insecurity has been, and is now, very significant. A range of supply side programmes such as input subsidies for fertilisers, irrigation, electricity and farm credit, coupled with investments in irrigation, are designed to encourage higher yields and production. A range of market support prices are set to cover costs and improve farmer returns. High food subsidies help poor consumers: in September 2013, India enacted a new National Food Security Act (NFSA), which is now implementing the most ambitious "right to food" programme yet to be applied in history, covering over 800 million people and providing 60 kg of food grain per person each year at prices that are about 10% of current retail prices for food grains. A major question facing the *Outlook* is how these policies will impact Indian and potentially international food markets, and how they will contribute to meet India's objectives of increasing production and reducing food insecurity.

In the last decade, India has experienced rapid economic growth, and while growth is anticipated to slow, it may stay high for some time. Agricultural growth has also risen in the past decade, supported by solid increases in crop yields, and with both increased cropping intensity and greater area devoted to food crops. Potential yield gaps remain, and concerns about the sustainability of growth in production are mounting. Rural labour costs are rising, water supplies are being depleted and smaller farm sizes due to fragmented land holdings potentially impede the capture of economies of scale. Yet, high production growth is anticipated. On the demand side, India remains largely vegetarian, and both calorie and protein consumption have remained low compared to levels in developed countries. How diets change in the next decade may have important implications for domestic and international commodity markets.

This chapter reviews the performance of India's agriculture over the past decades, noting its strong production growth and the reduction of food insecurity in the presence of sizable population growth. It describes projections for major agricultural commodities, set against anticipated macroeconomic, demographic and resource conditions. Finally, the chapter concludes with a review of important risks and uncertainties facing India's agriculture over the next decade, and what these may mean for both domestic and international markets.

The performance of India's agriculture

Agriculture has played an essential role in India's economic development, growing about three percent each year on average over the last forty years. Besides providing food to a growing population, agriculture has provided income to rural areas, released labour for downstream industry, provided savings for investment and has increased demand for industrial goods. It also is the source of raw material for a large number of domestic industries and has provided an important source of foreign exchange.

However, despite its growth, the role of agriculture in India's economy has been declining sharply as other sectors, particularly services, have grown more quickly. Primary agriculture accounted for about 14% of national gross domestic product (GDP) in 2012, down from close to 30% in 2000. But, while there has been a reduction in the share of agriculture in GDP, a commensurate reduction in its employment share has not taken place. Primary agriculture still employs around half of the Indian population, and it is the main driver of employment in rural areas, where 68% of the population live (Figure 2.1).

Figure 2.1. **Agriculture's share of national employment remains large in India**

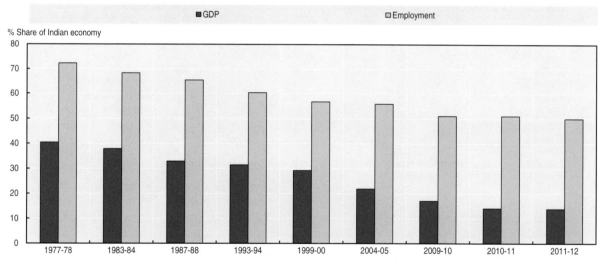

Sources: Employment share from 1977-78 to 1999-00 from Papola, T.S. (2006), *Employment Trends in India*, Institute for Studies in Industrial Development, New Delhi, India; Employment share for 2004-05; 2009-10 from World Bank (2014a), *World Development Indicators* (database). GDP share data from Government of India (2013a), *Economic Survey 2012-13*, Government of India, New Delhi.

StatLink ᴍ𝒮ᴾ *http://dx.doi.org/10.1787/888933099029*

This important role of agriculture was stressed in India's recent *Economic Survey for 2012-13*, which noted the fact that a declining share of the agriculture and allied sectors in a country's GDP is consistent with the normal development trajectory of any economy (Government of India, 2013a). But it stressed that fast agricultural growth remains vital for jobs, incomes and the food security of the population. The role of agriculture will remain significant in the medium-term, particularly owing to concerns over food security, employment and rural poverty. Agriculture will continue to be a major source of employment in the future, which challenges policy makers to raise the incomes of millions of Indian rural households. However, a key challenge to reducing poverty in rural areas will be to raise productivity in agriculture, which the data indicate is much lower than in the rest of the economy.

Growth in agricultural output has been strong

As measured by the FAO's agricultural production index, production growth, net of intermediate production of seed and feed, increased about four times over the last 50 years. In the years prior to the start of the Green Revolution in India (Box 2.1), which is considered to be in the late 1960s, per capita output was declining. Since then, the increase in aggregate terms has been one of the most significant globally, but in per capita terms growth has been much more modest. Crop production remains most significant in India, given its largely vegetarian diet, but livestock production has grown more quickly from its small base. It is noteworthy that per capita growth in agriculture has been most significant in the period after the year 2000, and especially after 2005-06. The reasons for increased growth have been ascribed to measures taken under the National Food Security Mission of 2007-08, the National Horticulture Mission and the Rashtriya Krishi Vikas Yojana (National Agricultural Development Scheme).[2]

Table 2.1. **Growth of agriculture in India increased in the last decade**
% p.a

	1961-70	1971-80	1981-90	1991-2000	2001-12	1971-2012
Total						
Agriculture	1.8	2.8	3.5	2.8	3.9	3.0
Crops	1.9	2.5	3.3	2.6	3.9	2.8
Livestock	1.3	3.6	4.2	3.6	3.9	3.8
Per capita						
Agriculture	-0.3	0.4	1.3	1.0	2.4	1.1
Crops	-0.2	0.2	1.1	0.8	2.4	0.9
Livestock	-0.9	1.3	2.0	1.8	2.4	1.9

Note: Based on net production indexes from FAOSTAT, compound annual rates.
Source: FAO (2014), FAOSTAT (database), *http://faostat.fao.org/*.

StatLink 🖼️ *http://dx.doi.org/10.1787/888933101100*

India is the top producer of milk, pulses and jute in the world. It ranks second in the production of rice, wheat, sugarcane, groundnut, vegetables, fruit and cotton. India also is a leading producer of spices, fish, poultry, livestock and plantation crops. Agricultural commodity production in India rose significantly over the past six decades: the production of food grains increased from around 50 Mt in 1950-51 to over 263 Mt during 2013-14, a five-fold increase in six decades. This phenomenal growth, however, was marked by phases of stagnation, such as the period from 1996-97 to 2004-05 when real prices fell, and periods of rapid growth, which have been experienced since that year. From 2004-05 to 2012-13, cereal production increased 24% and oilseed production increased 20%. Higher growth has been experienced in sectors which are·more market oriented, such as the production of pulses, fruits and vegetables which together have increased by 40%.

Figure 2.2. **Production of major agricultural products in India**

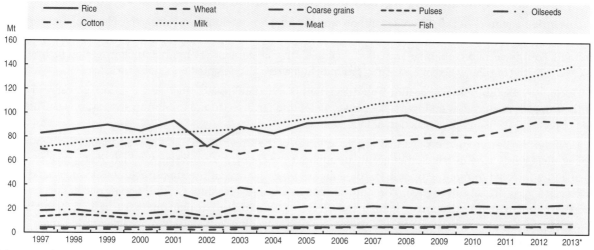

* Advance estimate.

Source: Government of India (2013b), *Agricultural Statistics at a Glance 2013*, Government of India, New Delhi.

StatLink ⫘⫘ http://dx.doi.org/10.1787/888933099048

Faster output growth is occurring in the higher value added sectors. As a predominantly vegetarian population, livestock production has remained relatively small, although it has been growing more rapidly than crop production, albeit from a small base. Milk production, from the buffalo and milk cow herd and from the goat herd, has grown rapidly since the initiation of the "Operation Flood" programme in the early 1970s. Milk production increased over six times, from 20.8 million tonnes in 1970, to 133 million tonnes in 2012. Production of beef from the buffalo herd has recently been undertaken for export shipments, putting India into the top three bovine meat exporters in the world (Box 7.2 in Chapter 7). As the second largest producer of fish in the world, India's production has grown almost four times since 1980, including a 12-fold increase in aquaculture production during this period.

Box 2.1. **Transforming Agriculture: India's Green and White Revolution**

India's agriculture has been transformed by two major events: The Green Revolution, which significantly increased yields of the country's major staple crops, wheat and rice, and the White Revolution that transformed the country's dairy sector. Both events are described below.

The Green Revolution began in India with the introduction of semi-dwarfed, high-yielding varieties of wheat in 1967 and rice in 1968. To ensure market support, the Food Corporation of India and the mechanism of market support prices were established in the mid-1960s. Favourable policies in the form of price and procurement support as well as input subsidies encouraged farmers to adopt the new varieties and to invest in their land. The Green Revolution spread largely in areas with favourable agro-climatic conditions, i.e. irrigated areas where wheat and paddy were mainly grown. The success of the Green Revolution was remarkable. From a net importer of food in the 1950s, India transformed itself during the last four decades: From a mere 82 Mt of food grain produced in 1960-61, India in 2013-14 produced a record 263.2 Mt of food grains, mainly attributed to the significant rise in rice and wheat output.

Box 2.1. **Transforming Agriculture: India's Green and White Revolution** (*cont.*)

One striking feature of the Green Revolution was the adoption of double-cropping, i.e. planting two crops or more per year on the same land. The earlier practice of one crop per year was dependent on the monsoon rainfall. For the second crop, huge irrigation facilities, such as dams, were built. Simple irrigation techniques, like the digging of tube wells for extracting groundwater, were also adopted on a massive scale.

During the 1990s, there was a shift from investments in capital assets, such as irrigation, power and rural infrastructure, to subsidies on inputs like power, water and fertiliser and to minimum support prices. This has led to regional shifts in the production of food grains.

However, higher production has had repercussions. As the Green Revolution spread mainly in favourable areas, yield gains were distributed unevenly throughout the country. In addition, the high yielding varieties of rice and wheat led to mono-cropping in some areas, which increased the susceptibility to biotic and abiotic stresses (e.g. pests and droughts). The natural resource base is eroding. Ground water, particularly in the northern Indian states of Haryana, Punjab and Western Uttar Pradesh, is depleting fast. In Punjab, the upper layer of groundwater is exhausted and farmers are now investing in installing more powerful pump-sets to extract water for irrigation. Various advisories have been issued against growing water intensive paddy in Punjab and Haryana. A comprehensive approach to food insecurity includes protecting the production base by sustaining the natural environment.

India's White Revolution transformed India's dairy sector. In the 1950s and 1960s, India relied heavily on milk imports, and the total per capita availability of milk was 113 g a day in 1968. Dairy farmers had only a few animals and were struggling to get their highly perishable product to the markets in the urban centres. Against this background, the Indian government decided to "flood India with milk" and launched Operation Flood in 1970. Operation Flood aimed to increase milk production, connect milk producers and consumers and raise the income of dairy farmers.

Operation Flood addressed three different levels: i) at the farm-level, dairy farmers were organised into co-operatives. Co-operatives were provided with advanced technologies, such as modern animal breeds that produced more milk. ii) At the district level, co-operative unions were formed, which owned and operated milk processing plants as well as storage and transport equipment. The unions also provided animal health services. iii) At the state level, state federations conducted and co-ordinated the nation-wide marketing of milk.

Operation Flood took place in three phases. In the first phase (1970-80), one million dairy farmers were covered and focus was on serving the market of the country's metropolis. In the second phase (1981-85) about ten million dairy farmers were part of the programme and all major cities of India were covered, and in the last phase of the operation (1985 to 1995) nearly seven million dairy farmers were targeted.

The results of the dairy policy were notable: From 1988-89 to 1995-96, milk production rose from 42 million litres to 67 million litres a day. Today, India is the largest producer of fresh buffalo and goat milk and the second largest producer of fresh cow milk in the world. Most of the milk produced is consumed within the country. Milk is an essential source of protein in the predominantly vegetarian diet of many Indians. Today, every Indian consumes about 250 g of milk per day.

Sources: Conway, G.R. and E.B. Barbier (1988), "After the Green Revolution. Sustainable and equitable agricultural development", *Futures*, Vol. 20. pp. 651-670. Cunningham, K. (2009), "Rural and urban linkages: Operation Flood's role in India's dairy development", *IFPRI Discussion Paper*, No. 00924, International Food Policy Research Institute, Washington, DC. FAO (2014), FAOSTAT (database), Food and Agriculture Organization, Rome.

Progress, but a large food insecurity problem remains

According to the 2011 census, the population of India was 1.21 billion people, an increase of 364 million people in the last two decades. FAO (Figure 2.3) estimates that the number of undernourished people in India dropped from a high of 262 million in 1993-95 to a low of 206 million in 1997-99. The number increased to 246 million in 2004-06, but higher agricultural production and stronger economic progress resulted in a reduction of about 33 million undernourished people to an estimated 213 million by 2010-12. This progress occurred despite the addition of some 94 million people to India's population during that time frame, indicating more rapid progress in reducing food insecurity. However, with about one-quarter of the world's food insecure people within India, improving its nutritional status remains a significant challenge. Undernourishment has a significant impact on child development, which in turn influences adult productivity and economic growth. UNICEF reports that, in 2005-06, 43% of Indian children under-five years were moderately and severely underweight, and 48% were stunted due to chronic undernourishment, down from 58% in 1992-93 (UNICEF, 2014). India is unlikely to meet the Millennium Development Goal target of reducing by half the percentage of undernourished people by 2015. The number of food insecure has remained high despite India's rising trade surplus in cereals.

Figure 2.3. **Undernourishment in India**

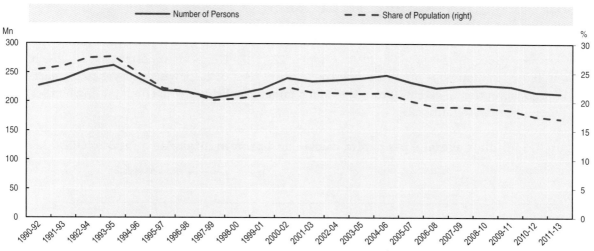

Source: FAO (2013), The State of Food Insecurity. The multiple dimensions of food security, Food and Agriculture Organization, Rome.

StatLink ⬛⬛ http://dx.doi.org/10.1787/888933099067

The average composition of diets in India is illustrated in Figure 2.4, which demonstrates the extent to which the population is vegetarian. The livestock and fish sectors provide only 9% of calories and 20% of protein intake. Cereals provide more than 50% of both calorie and protein intake in both rural and urban India, although survey data point to a declining contribution from cereals (NSSO, 2012). Those foods contributing to increased intake of calories are vegetable oils, fruits and vegetables. Sugars appear to represent a proportionately large component of calorie intake. Pulses are an increasing source of proteins, now accounting for almost 13% of protein intake.

The role of cereal consumption in food security is highlighted by dietary evidence. The Planning Commission of India has taken note of this issue in the 12th Five-Year Plan Document (2012-17), which expresses concern that falling cereal consumption per capita since the mid-1990s "is the main reason why per capita calorie intake has not increased despite rising income. Even poor people are reducing the share of income spent on all foods in order to meet other non-food needs. In such a situation, where there is a

Figure 2.4. **Estimated daily calorie and protein intake by food item in India, 2009**

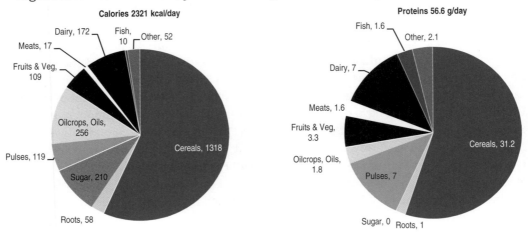

Source: FAO (2014), FAOSTAT (database), http://faostat.fao.org/.

StatLink ᴍ⫘ http://dx.doi.org/10.1787/888933099086

disjunction between such a basic requirement of human development as nutrition and other consumer demands, there is a need to ensure that minimum nutrition requirements are met" (Government of India, 2013c, Chapter 12, p. 17). This is an important aspect which underlies the rationale of India's new Food Security Act of 2013, which strives to increase the consumption of cereals (Box 2.5) through targeted subsidies while maintaining market support prices to farmers.

Figure 2.5. **India's average per capita calorie and protein intake as a ratio to OECD levels**

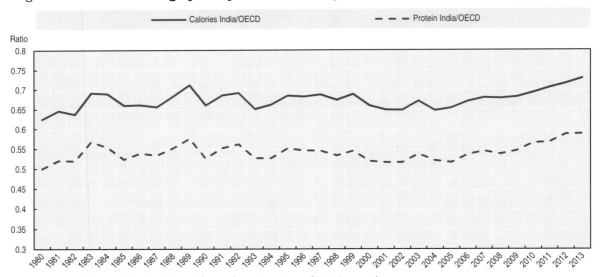

Source: FAO (2014), FAOSTAT (database), http://faostat.fao.org/; OECD and FAO Secretariats.

StatLink ᴍ⫘ http://dx.doi.org/10.1787/888933099105

In fact, progress in both calorie and protein intake has been slow. From 1970 to 2004, average daily calorie intake per capita has fluctuated in the range of 1 950 to 2 350 kcal. Protein intake also fluctuated but with a small trend increase over the range of 49 to 55 grams. But from 2005, calorie and protein intake have shown continuous improvement, increasing from 2 252 kcal and 54.1 grams respectively to an estimated 2 500 kcal and 61.5 grams by 2013.[3] Relative to OECD, or developed country averages, it has not changed much in the last three decades, as noted in Figure 2.5, but some increase has occurred in recent years. Average intake of calories in 1980 in India was about 63%, and by 2013 it was 73% of OECD levels.[4] For protein, intake was 50% of OECD levels in 1980 and 59% by 2013. While some progress is evident over time, the extent of the difference has not changed rapidly. However, there does appear to be an upward trend in this ratio since the middle of the last decade.

India's agricultural resources are large

Human resources

Labour in rural areas available to agriculture in India is large. India remains dominantly rural, with some 68% of its population residing in rural areas, as compared to the world average of 49% (2012). Long term world population projections indicate a cross over point for rural and urban populations around 2045. While the urban population is now growing at a faster rate than the rural population, as documented in the recent decennial census of 2011 (Government of India, 2014a), the rural population will be in the majority for a considerable time. The quality of India's labour is increasing, with over 97% of its youth finishing primary school. India expects to achieve 100% youth literacy by 2015 (Government of India, 2013d). This will help improve the effectiveness of India's extension services and programmes (Government of India, 2013e).

In 2011, cultivators (land owners and tenants) and agricultural labourers represented almost 55% of the Indian labour force: 50% for men and 65% for women. The share of cultivators is declining, while that for agricultural labour is rising (Table 2.2), indicating on-going change in land tenure.

Table 2.2. **Share of agricultural labour and cultivators in population in India**

	2001			2011		
	Total	Rural	Urban	Total	Rural	Urban
Cultivators (% of total workers)						
Persons	31.7	40.2	2.8	24.6	33.0	2.8
Male	31.1	42.0	2.5	24.9	35.2	2.7
Female	32.9	37.1	4.1	24.0	28.8	3.1
Agricultural labour (% of total workers)						
Persons	26.5	33.0	4.7	30.0	39.3	5.5
Male	20.8	27.5	3.4	24.9	34.4	4.6
Female	38.9	43.0	10.7	41.1	48.5	9.0

Note: Cultivators are landowners or tenants. Agricultural labourers work for wages in farms.
Source: Government of India (2014a), Census 2010-11, Government of India, New Delhi.

StatLink ⟶ http://dx.doi.org/10.1787/888933101119

Land

India has the largest area of arable and permanently cropped land in the world, estimated at 169.6 Mha in 2011 (FAO, 2014), marginally ahead of the United States at 162.7 Mha. The country also has the largest area of irrigated land, estimated at 63.2 Mha. While land resources are large, India's high population density means that land resource endowment on a per capita basis is actually less than the world average. Increasing urbanisation has limited the gross area under cultivation, with increasing pressure from demand for land for non-agricultural purposes. This means that higher aggregate production in the future will come from yield growth and increases in the cropping intensity rather than an expansion in agricultural area.

As a tropical country, India supports a diverse range of crops. Depending upon the availability of water, cropping activities continue year-round. The extent of multiple cropping in India is among the highest in the world. In general, there are two distinct cropping seasons: *Kharif* (July to October) and *Rabi* (October to March).

Data from the Agricultural Census indicate that there were about 138 million agricultural holdings in India in 2010-11, of which around 117 million were small and marginal farmers with holding sizes of less than 2 hectares. The average holding size has declined from 2.3 ha in 1970-71 to 1.33 ha in 2000-01, and 1.16 ha in 2010-11. Small and marginal farmers account for more than 80% of total farm households, but their share in operated area is around 44%. Large holdings (10 ha and above) account for 0.7% of the total household farms and 10.9% of the total operated area. There are therefore significant land inequalities in India. Access to land is affected by inheritance practices, limited legal literacy and attitudes towards women's ownership and control of land (OECD, 2014). Indian law guarantees equal access to land for women and men, but women own only 10.9% of agricultural land. Lower access to land has an impact on agricultural productivity, because it influences access to institutional credit, extension services and other agricultural inputs (Rao, 2011, Tara Satyavathi et al., 2010).

Water

India may have a large annual water supply, but water cannot be fully utilised due to topographical and other constraints, including high losses to evaporation and evapo-transpiration. Large temporal and spatial variations in rainfall limit water availability. Most of the water is available during the monsoon period, but it often results in floods. Lack of access to irrigation is a major problem for farmers trapped in poverty, and it will be a critical issue in the future. India has one of the world's largest irrigation systems but it also faces high levels of inefficiency, particularly for those relying on surface water sources, the efficiency for which is estimated at 35-40%, as opposed to ground sources, whose efficiency is estimated at 65-75%. More serious is the problem of ground water depletion, which is viewed to be in crisis as a result of excess extraction, due in part to the lack of regulated use and power subsidies which lower extraction costs (Government of India, 2013e, p.29).

Capital formation

Investment as a percentage of agricultural output was 20% in 2011-12, up from under 15% five years earlier, and an average of only 10% in the 1990s (Government of India, 2013e, p. 7, 17). Public sector investment has risen slowly in the last decade, falling from as much as 50% of total investment in the 1980s to less than 15% in recent years. Private investment has risen more rapidly, almost doubling over the period 2004 to 2011, and rising to over 17% of agricultural output. Part of the reason for this is the provision of credit schemes by the government at favourable interest rates. They have helped foster a tenfold increase in credit in the decade prior to 2011. However, growth of capital on farms is hampered by the trend decrease in the size of land holdings. Small and marginal farmers who cultivate most of India's land cannot afford to buy modern farm capital which requires a larger size to reach the economies of scale necessary to justify its acquisition. India's tractor density, at about 16 per 1 000 ha, is less than the global average of 19.

Productivity growth has been key to increased production

Estimates of total factor productivity (TFP) for Indian agriculture provide important insights into the nature and drivers of productivity growth, although results vary depending on the methodology and level of aggregation of the analysis (Kumar et al., 2013). Studies show that while technical progress has been the key driver of productivity change, productivity growth in India has not been consistent over time. Production efficiency improved in the 1980s, plateaued in the early 1990s, and then declined in the period from 1997 to 2003, likely due to weather shocks. This time pattern of productivity change is evident in changes in crop yields (a partial measure of productivity) over time, as noted in Figure 2.6. Yield growth has resumed after 2007.

Figure 2.6. **Annual change in yields of wheat and rice in India**

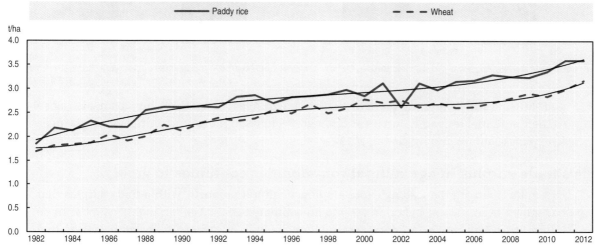

Note: Lines in black are smoothed curves fit to yield changes.
Source: Gautam M. and P.K Aggarwal (2013), "Yield Gaps in Cereals: Progress and Potential", Unpublished paper, World Bank, Washington, DC.
StatLink ᐧᐧᐧ http://dx.doi.org/10.1787/888933099124

A study by Gautam and Aggarwal (2013) analysed yield gaps in paddy and wheat. Using a crop model to simulate the potential for popular and established rice and wheat cultivars in different parts of India, the study generated three different yield scenarios: i) a biological potential yield (PY) based only on varietal characteristics without constraints in the growing environment, ii) an attainable yield (AY), which introduces water management into the simulation based on the current level of irrigation development in each state[5] and, iii) a "realisable" yield (RY), which is the research station or experimental yield recorded for a given cultivar in the official varietal release database. Realisable yields (RY) should be close to the AY, yet they should still reflect soil problems, pests, other management problems and local conditions, because some biotic and abiotic stresses cannot be controlled even on an experiment station. All of these yields can then be compared to actual or farm yields (FY) to establish the size of yield gaps. Figure 2.7 shows the all-India weighted (production weights) averages for RY, AY, and FY, providing an aggregate picture of yield gaps for rice and wheat and the potential to increase actual yield.

The study also found that yield gaps vary considerably across states, and some areas have little scope for further improvement. West Bengal – not a traditional wheat-growing area – is an outlier that has exceeded its expected performance. Maharashtra and Gujarat seem to have exhausted their potential with the current wheat technology, whereas Punjab

Figure 2.7. **Yield gaps for rice and wheat, all India**

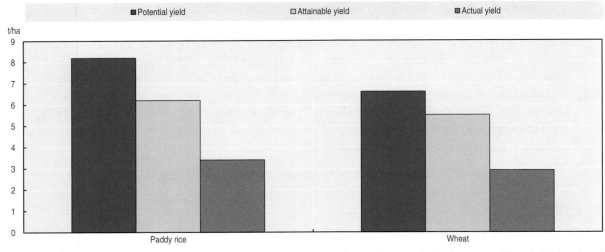

Source: Gautam M. and P.K Aggarwal (2013), "Yield Gaps in Cereals: Progress and Potential", Unpublished paper, World Bank, Washington, DC.
StatLink ᴹˢ⁴ *http://dx.doi.org/10.1787/888933099148*

and Haryana still have some room to increase yields. West Bengal and Punjab are also close to their potential for paddy, but most other states have significant potential yield advances to exploit (Gautam and Aggarwal, 2013).

India's trade surplus in agricultural commodities continues to grow

India is among the leading exporters of agricultural products, with a trade surplus that has grown from USD 3.6 billion in 2000 to an estimated USD 22 billion in 2013 (Global Trade Information Services, 2014).[6] Rice accounts for the bulk of exports, followed by cotton and fishery products. Exports of wheat and coarse grain vary, and have often reached high levels, and exports of protein meal are rising. Recently India has become one of the top bovine meat exporters (Box 7.2). On the other hand, India continues to be the largest importer of edible oils and pulses in the world and alternates as a major sugar importer or exporter.

Figure 2.8. **India's trade surplus in agricultural and fish products is rising**

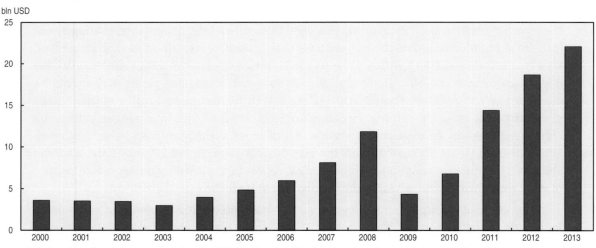

Source: Global Trade Information Services (2014), *Global Trade Atlas* (database), *www.gtis.com/gta/*. Data refer to Chapters 1-24 of the trade classification.
StatLink ᴹˢ⁴ *http://dx.doi.org/10.1787/888933099162*

Box 2.2. **Domestic and international market integration**

The degree to which prices in different markets move together is an indication of how efficiently trade occurs between them. Within India, Sekhar (2012) found that the commodity markets that do not face inter-state or inter-regional movement restrictions like pulses or vegetable oils appear well-integrated, while those that do have such restrictions, such as rice, do not show integration at the national level. With respect to domestic and international markets, as indicated in the graphs, and as tested using statistical methods, the interrelationship of markets is weak. Domestic prices illustrate lower volatility than international markets, a feature which is the result of India's market and trade policies, which include market support prices, tariffs and export restrictions. Statistical tests for causality indicate that Indian rice prices may impact those in international markets.

Figure 2.9. **Interrelationship of domestic and international markets in India**

Sugar (top left figure), Vegetable oil (top right figure), Wheat (bottom left panel) and Rice (bottom right panel)

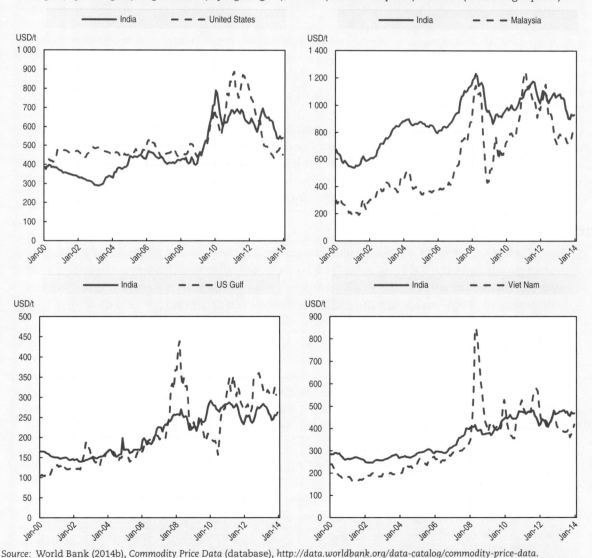

Source: World Bank (2014b), *Commodity Price Data* (database), *http://data.worldbank.org/data-catalog/commodity-price-data.*

StatLink ᴍᵴ᱑ *http://dx.doi.org/10.1787/888933099181*

Box 2.2. **Domestic and international market integration** (cont.)

Table 2.3. **Indexes of market connection (IMC)**

	Rice	Wheat	Sugar	Vegetable oil	Maize	Soybean
IMC	77*	21	39	36	30	5

Note: Estimations over the period 2000-13. Prices in India are wholesale prices converted to USD, and restricted least squares regression of relation PD= (1 + b1) * PD(-1) + b2 * (PI-PI(-1)) + (b3-b1) * PI(-1), yields coefficients such that IMC = (1 + b1)/(b3 - b1) provides an indicative measure of market connection. An IMC of 0 indicates highest connection between markets, and higher values lower connection (Timmer, 1984). In the case of rice, the estimated relationship is not statistically significant, meaning no market connection from international markets; Granger causality tests indicate an inverse connection from domestic to international markets may be noted.
Sources: OECD and FAO Secretariats. Sekhar, C.S.C. (2012), "Agricultural Market Integration in India", Food Policy, Vol. 37, pp. 309-322.

StatLink ╤╗╤╝ http://dx.doi.org/10.1787/888933101138

For a country as large and populous as India, changes in trade can be small in relation to domestic consumption/production, but large in the context of international markets. This raises the issue of market integration, and the degree to which prices of key commodities in India follow or cause price movements in international markets. The evidence presented in Box 2.2 suggests that for some commodities, such as rice, Indian markets impact on global markets, but for the most part the connection between the domestic and international markets is weak or non-existent. Weak connection between markets is due to policy structures in India, such as market support prices, intervention programmes, export restrictions and tariffs which sever market linkages (Gulati et al., 2013).

Agricultural policy

For almost 60 years, India's agricultural policy has been guided by Five-Year Plans, the latest of which is the 12th (2012-17). The Plan's broad vision is "Faster, Sustainable, and More Inclusive Growth", leading to broad-based improvement in the economic and social conditions of people and achieving inclusiveness by both delivering benefits directly to the poor and excluded groups, and increasing their ability to access employment and income opportunities (Government of India, 2013c). As per the Plan, the higher GDP growth of 8.2% assumed envisages 4% growth in the agriculture and allied sectors. Some of the key priorities are to improve the economic viability of farming with stable prices and a minimum income for farmers, to encourage diversification, increase investments, reduce environmental degradation, and enhance food security by further production diversification into oilseeds, pulses, livestock and fish. Importantly the 12th Five-Year Plan continued the important National Food Security Mission (NFSM), National Horticulture Mission and the Rastriya Krisha Vikas Yojana (RKVY) programmes, which have had a large impact on the agricultural sector, along with initiatives to increase farm support prices, investments, input subsidies for credit, fertilisers and food distribution.

There are four broad policy instruments which the Indian government has employed to achieve its diverse objectives. These are market support policies, trade policies, input subsidies and food distribution subsidies.

i) Market support policies

The Agricultural Prices Commission was set up in January 1965 to advise the Government on price policy for agricultural commodities. The basis for setting up the Commission was to develop a balanced and integrated price structure in the perspective of the overall needs of the economy and with due regard to the interests of the producer and the consumer. Currently the Commission (renamed Commission for Agricultural Costs and Prices) sets Minimum Support Prices (MSP) for 24 commodities and a Fair and Remunerative Price (FRP) for sugarcane. For most products, other than tariffs, there is no effective mechanism to ensure that prices do not fall below the MSP. Procurement is used for some products, rice and wheat in a few states such as Punjab, Haryana, Uttar Pradesh, Chhattisgarh, Andhra Pradesh, and to some extent in Madhya Pradesh and Rajasthan, and in a few other states for sugarcane, cotton and jute. Procurement has led to higher public stocks in recent years, creating challenges for stock management and for redistribution and the prevention of product waste.

Figure 2.10. **Minimum support price for key commodities in India**

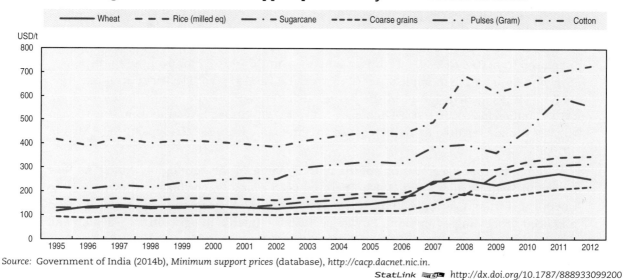

Source: Government of India (2014b), *Minimum support prices* (database), *http://cacp.dacnet.nic.in.*

StatLink 🔗 *http://dx.doi.org/10.1787/888933099200*

The MSPs for all commodities increased sharply after 2007-08. Prior to this year, the MSPs for all commodities were flat for over a decade. For food grains, the MSP for paddy and wheat was higher than that for coarse cereals and maize. For pulses, the MSPs were increased in 2008-09, at a rate higher than that for food grains. However, this has not translated into larger areas planted under pulses, because the risks associated with their cultivation are very high. In comparison, paddy cultivation does not involve substantial risks and farmers are also assured of procurement by government agencies, whereas this is not the case for pulses.

ii) Trade policy

The operation of MSPs may also rely on tariff/border measures. Tariffs for food grains range from 51% for wheat to 80% for rice. For vegetable oils, tariffs are low at 2.75%. Meat tariffs are 31%, while those for dairy products are 36%. Applied tariffs on a number of commodities were lowered during the prices spikes after 2008. However, export bans were also implemented for rice and wheat to assure stable domestic supplies. The impacts of these bans are evident in the charts of Box 2.2. They indicate a calibrated trade policy designed to stabilise prices in domestic Indian markets. In addition to these, some non-tariff barriers also exist, such as sanitary and phyto-sanitary measures which may affect India's trade.

India has been an active participant in the World Trade Organization (WTO), and a key member of both the G33 and G20 groups of negotiating countries. Its stance with respect to the agriculture negotiations reflects its objective to safeguard the livelihoods of its 650 million people who are reliant on a primarily smallholder based agricultural sector. In this context, it has been one of the main proponents of the introduction of an effective special safeguard mechanism (SSM), resistant to significant reductions in bound tariffs for key commodities and the main proponent in seeking dispensation to undertake commodity procurement at above market prices for food stockholding for the purposes of food security.

iii) Input market policies

Input policies play a very important role in India's agriculture. In particular, policies affecting seed distribution, fertilisers, electricity, water and farm credit have considerably increased input use in the last decade. From 2000 to 2011, annual seed distribution increased from 0.86 to 2.8 Mt. Fertiliser use rose from 16.7 to 27.7 Mt over the same period, implying an increase in application from 90 kg/ha to 144 kg/ha. Electricity use rose from 84.7 to 119.5 gigawatt hours in the period 2000-09. Agricultural credit increased from USD 12 billion in 2000 to USD 84 billion by 2011 (NCAER, 2013a). Investments in irrigation in the last decade resulted in an increase in irrigated area from 58 Mha in 2001 to 63 Mha in 2010 (FAO, 2014).

The Indian seed sector is one of the most dynamic in the developing world. The New Policy on Seed Development (1988) liberated seed markets, because it allowed for the import of seed and germplasm for research purposes and lowered import duties on seed and seed processing equipment. Private sector investments in agricultural research and development increased significantly in the aftermath of the reform. The Plant Varieties Protection and Farmers Rights Act (2001) allowed plant breeders of new varieties to capitalise on their research investments, while allowing farmers and researchers to use protected varieties for their purposes. Improvements have also been made in seed testing and certification, thereby increasing the quality of seed. Today, approximately 400 to 500 private seed companies are registered in India (Government of India, 2014c). The private sector generally focuses on high value, low volume crops, like hybrid varieties of cotton, sunflower, maize and vegetables, while the public sector dominates the production of high volume, low value crops, like wheat, rice and pulses (Rabobank, 2001). In recent years, the seed sector expanded further owing to the fast adoption of genetically modified cotton varieties.

Although India's seed industry underwent major changes in the past decades, the majority of farmers continue to rely on farm-saved seeds. However, seed replacement rates, i.e. the frequency with which farm-saved seed are replaced by quality seeds, are increasing. Seed replacement rates vary by crop and region. For example, the percentage of the area sown with quality seeds of wheat in the total wheat area sown in India increased from 13% in 2001 to 33% in 2011. The seed replacement rate for rice in India doubled from 19% to 40% over the same period (Government of India, 2014c). This increased use in quality seed can contribute to increases in agricultural productivity. This rate can be expected to increase further with rising yield differences between quality and farm-saved seed.

India is the world's second largest importer of fertiliser, importing over 40% of its domestic use. As a means of increasing crop yields, India has undertaken a programme to subsidise fertilisers on the basis of nutrients. Under the New Pricing Scheme (NPS) a maximum retail price (MRP) applies to nitrogen fertilisers (mainly urea), such that producers buy at the MRP, and sellers are refunded the difference between the estimated delivery cost and the MRP. Other components such as phosphate and potassium fertilisers as well as various composites, are covered under the Nutrient Based Subsidy (NBS) and per kilogramme subsidies apply based on market conditions. They are provided equally to both domestic and imported products. There has been a concern that with a fixed MRP for nitrogen, depending on market prices for the other components, the subsidy/support structure has affected the mix of fertilisers applied to crops, notably a relatively high application of nitrogen (NCAER, 2013a). As prices rose dramatically in recent years, market prices of nitrogen were held down by the support structure and market prices of other components rose. The fertiliser subsidy has accounted for about 37% of total subsidies that the government has provided to agriculture, and is anticipated to cost Indian Rupees (INR) 681 billion (USD 11.4 billion) in 2014-15 (Government of India, 2014d)

Figure 2.11. **Fertiliser subsidy in India**

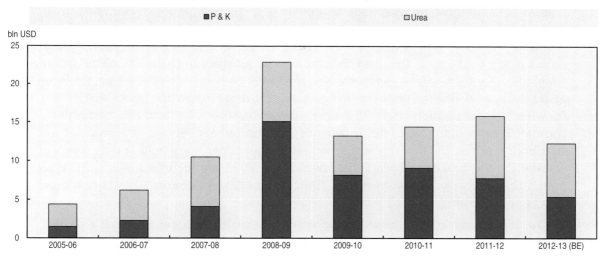

Note: BE -budget estimate, P&K – phosphorus and potassium.
Source: NCAER (2013b), *Agricultural Outlook and Situation Analysis Reports* (September 2013), National Council of Applied Economic Research, New Delhi.

StatLink ᵐˢᵖ *http://dx.doi.org/10.1787/888933099219*

Apart from the subsidy on fertilisers, power subsidies are another major component of agricultural policy. Electric power, which is used to provide energy for pump sets, is used extensively on Indian farms, and the state governments provide generous subsidies to farmers to irrigate their crops. Figure 2.12 shows the size of the power subsidy in agriculture in nominal terms.

Figure 2.12. **Electricity subsidy in agriculture in India**

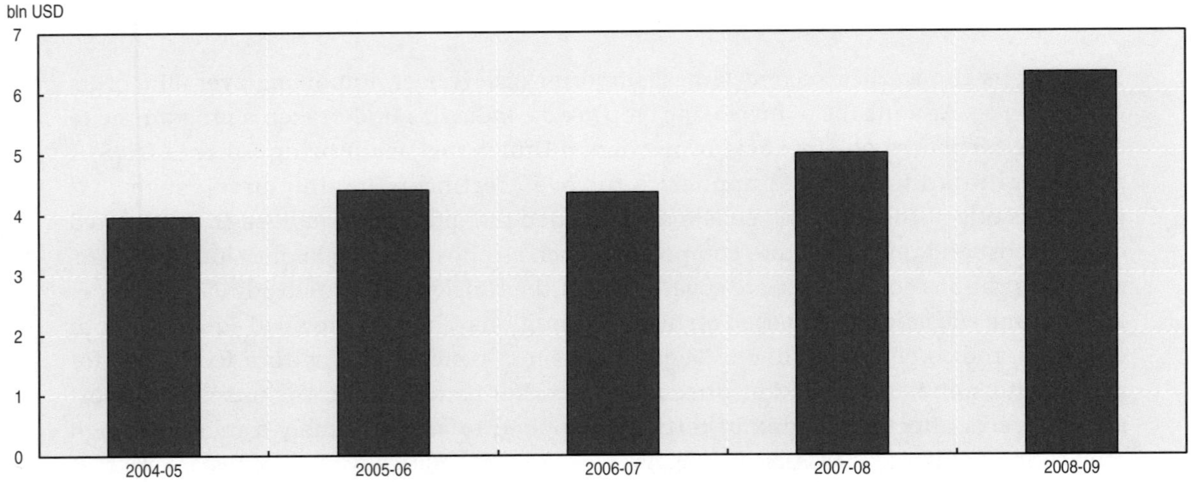

Source: Government of India (2010), *Agricultural Statistics at a Glance 2010*, Government of India, New Delhi.

StatLink ㎜므 *http://dx.doi.org/10.1787/888933099238*

iv) Food distribution

India has provided wheat and rice at favourable prices through its Public Distribution System (PDS) for food grain. This has involved the distribution of products that have been procured by the Department of Food and Public Distribution at minimum support prices. Prior to 2013, distribution was made separately to qualifying groups in rural and urban areas depending on their income status (over or under the poverty line) and if they belonged to severe poverty group of about 10 million persons, known as Antyodaya-Anna-Yojana (AAY). In the total, this food distribution was provided to about 30% of the Indian population. For those over the poverty line, rice could be bought for INR 8.3/kg, for those under the poverty line the price was INR 5.65, and for those in AAY the prices was INR 3.0. For wheat the distribution prices for these groups were INR 6.1, 4.15 and 2/kg, respectively. The effective cost of the food subsidy depends on the difference between procurement and distribution prices, the size of distribution entitlements per household and the costs of distribution. In the last ten years, the costs of the PDS have increased substantially as minimum support prices were raised, from about USD 5 billion in 2002-03 to almost USD 14 billion in 2012-13.

In September 2013, a new National Food Security Act was enacted that will substantially enlarge India's food distribution programme (Box 2.5). As of early 2014, the programme has been implemented in a number of states, and it remains to be implemented in others. The programme extends the previous distribution programme for wheat and rice. The NFSA now provides up to 5 kg per person per month for 67% of the population at prices of INR 3/kg for rice, INR 2/kg for wheat and INR 1/kg for coarse grain. This programme, if fully implemented, would be the largest food distribution programme ever to be undertaken. Further analysis of the programme is deferred to the next section of this chapter where policies are discussed as they may affect the *Outlook*.

The outlook for India's agricultural sector

The growth of India's agricultural production has more than enabled its food supply to keep pace with growing demand in recent decades. However, despite growing supply,

India's major challenge, recognised nationally and internationally, is the need to reduce food insecurity. With its National Food Security Mission of 2007-08, India has undertaken a number of substantive policy actions to further increase agricultural output and policies have been enhanced to promote its wider distribution. This section examines the prospects for India's commodity sectors over the next decade and attempts to provide a framework against which the various challenges may be examined. It first reviews the key factors and constraints which may affect the outlook for India, then looks at the prospects for each of its major commodity sectors.

Key factors and constraints underlying India's outlook

Any projection for any country's agricultural sector needs to rely on numerous hypotheses/assumptions concerning the environment surrounding the sector. These include macroeconomic conditions, the international sector, domestic social trends, and very importantly in the case of India, the policy environment.

Income growth lower, but maintains stimulus over the medium-term

A key factor underlying the outcomes for India's agricultural sector over the next decade is the performance of the economy at large. This includes economic growth, price inflation and exchange rate performance. In these domains, India's economy performed generally well in the last decade, alongside Brazil, Russian Federation and China in the BRIC group of emerging countries. In the last decade (2004-13), per capita real GDP grew at a compound rate of almost 6% p.a., and inflation was 7.3% p.a. India's real exchange rate – its nominal rate adjusted for inflation compared to that in the United States – appreciated substantially from 2000 to 2011, before depreciating in the past two years, as the economy cooled down. These conditions were very supportive of India's agricultural development, providing higher incomes to support consumption, a favourable investment climate and more resources for the government to undertake policies and programmes.

According to the International Monetary Fund projections of fall 2013, India's economic performance in the coming decade is anticipated to slow somewhat from that of the previous decade. This *Outlook* assumes that India's per capita output growth will average almost one full percentage point lower, at 5.2% p.a., which should still offer a stimulus to incomes and consumption over the next decade. This growth implies that average output per head will be over 50% higher at the end of the decade than it is now, providing considerably more resources for consumption and investment. The depreciation in its real exchange rate, which reduces the terms of trade, is anticipated to remain at current levels. Inflation in the nominal GDP price deflator is anticipated to fall to an average 6% p.a. in the next decade. A key risk for India is that economic growth, which has slowed down in the last two years, will not resume at higher rates into the medium-term. This risk and its implications are assessed further in the section of this chapter which discusses risks and uncertainties facing the outlook for India.

Slower population growth may provide a dividend

For many emerging economies, growth in population has fallen in the past decades and urbanisation has proceeded at a very fast pace. This was certainly true of China, Thailand and other Asian economies. India's population growth in the previous decade was 1.3% p.a., a rate which is still higher than the global average. However, population growth is anticipated to fall to just over 1% in the next decade. While this may reduce

Figure 2.13. **Macroeconomic indicators in India**

GDP Growth (left) and Real Exchange Rate (right)

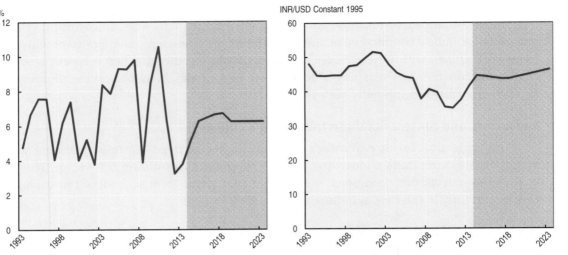

Source: IMF (2014), World Economic Outlook (database), extended by OECD and FAO Secretariat.

StatLink ⃞⃞⃞⃞ http://dx.doi.org/10.1787/888933099257

aggregate demand pressures, it may also provide dividends in the sense of proportionately more population in the workforce which may provide more resources on a household basis, and hence higher consumption growth. However, India's rural population remains large relative to the total population (68%), and as such this may mean less change in dietary composition than might be experienced in other countries. In most countries, the consumption profile of the rural population is quite different to that in urban areas, in terms of diet diversification, and less dynamic in terms of change toward more processed and diverse foods.

Will productivity growth overcome resource constraints?

Land available for cropping, which is arable land including permanent crops, peaked in 2000 at 171 Mha, and has declined since to 169.7 Mha in 2011. It is anticipated that agricultural land will continue to decline slowly over time. However, around 25-30 Mha may be left fallow each year. Consequently, while the land base continues to decline, management options for land may affect the quantity cropped in any given year. Without change in fallow land and cultivable waste, it appears that any further increase in crop production must come as a result of increased crop yields. While the number of crops per year could be increased further, India's cropping intensity is among the highest in the world.

According to the Indian Council for Agricultural Research (ICAR) and the National Academy for Agricultural Sciences, of the 141 Mha which are under cultivation in India, about 100 Mha are at risk of becoming increasingly difficult to farm owing to increasing cropping intensity on fragile soils, inappropriate application of fertilisers, inadequate application of manure, reduced organic carbon and severe nutrient deficiencies (ICAR, 2010). These effects are heavily felt in those states that benefited most from the Green Revolution, e.g. Punjab, Haryana, Uttar Pradesh and Bihar, which produce almost half of India's food grains.

Box 2.3. **Short-and long-term macroeconomic challenges for India**[*]

The important macroeconomic challenge for India over the next decade is to create more productive jobs for its almost 500 million workforce – especially the 10-12 million annual youthful entrants. This is a critical challenge since the agricultural sector still accounts for almost half of total employment and has been destroyed jobs as productivity is very low. Meanwhile net job creation in the manufacturing sector has slowed down.

From 2010 to 2013, the Indian Rupee (INR) depreciated by about 40% in nominal terms relative to the US Dollar, and about 17% in real terms. This has increased inflation and placed increased pressures on public and private finances. India's monetary policy framework has now assigned a higher weight toward containing inflation, but containing inflation will require reducing the public fiscal deficit and dealing with supply constraints that are limiting economic growth. These constraints impede the economy from responding to the boom in competitiveness provided by real depreciation. India has passed a new land acquisition law which may promote investment, but implementation of the new National Food Security Act will be fiscally costly and, along with the oil subsidy and other programmes, may keep the deficit high. Rupee devaluation has increased the costs of India's oil and fertiliser subsidy, given the large size of its imports, and how the programme is structured.

After growing by a large 7.8% annually from 2000 to 2010, India's economy slowed to an average growth rate of 5.2% from 2010 to 2013. Stronger agricultural growth and public sector consumption have failed to compensate for sluggish industrial production, investment and exports. This is a substantial slowdown compared to previous years, and the question is whether and when recovery will occur. Persistent high inflation and low productivity have contributed to a loss of competitiveness. High government transfers through social security schemes also raised wages, especially in rural areas; rural real wages that had been flat earlier showed a substantial rise after 2007 when high food inflation and rural employment programmes set in.

The economy is expected to recover in the medium-term and to achieve average growth of 6.3% p.a., which is lower than that of the previous decade. Real INR depreciation combined with a projected increase in external demand should increase exports. Higher investment should also stimulate growth as new government infrastructure programmes and the Land Acquisition Law reduce business uncertainty. Boosting growth and making it more inclusive will require addressing structural bottlenecks, in particular gaps in energy, transport and water infrastructure, overly stringent labour regulations and the shortage of skills. Tax reforms should raise more revenue, being less distortive for growth and redistributing more from the rich to the poor.

[*] Based on the OECD (2013), *OECD Economic Outlook*, Vol. 2013/2, OECD Publishing. doi: *http://dx.doi.org/10.1787/eco_outlook-v2013-2-en*, and input provided by Professor Ashima Goya, of Indira Gandhi Institute of Development Research, Mumbai.

Not just land, but water supply is also under stress. Loss of agricultural land for non-agricultural uses is prompting the adoption of more input-intensive farming practices. But this reduces the availability of irrigation water. As a result, the exploitation of ground water has reached critical levels in many parts across the country. Excessive and improper use of agro-chemicals is causing water pollution (Divja and Belagali, 2012). However, the per hectare use of agro-chemicals is much less in India than it is in many other countries.

India has traditionally had abundant rural labour. However, recently the population engaged in farming has declined, and labour has become more expensive (Chand and

Srivastava, 2014). After remaining stagnant for a long time, rural wages have been increasing since 2008-09 (Figure 2.14). The increase in wages has also been due to the MGNREGA[7] Scheme which is underpinning the labour market. Higher real wages have triggered capital investment in the economy, which in turn helped to increase labour productivity by some 50% from 2005 to 2011 Sustaining these changes will require extensive new investment, which the Planning Commission has described as unsustainable without further increases in the productivity of new capital.

Figure 2.14. **Real rural wages are rising in India**

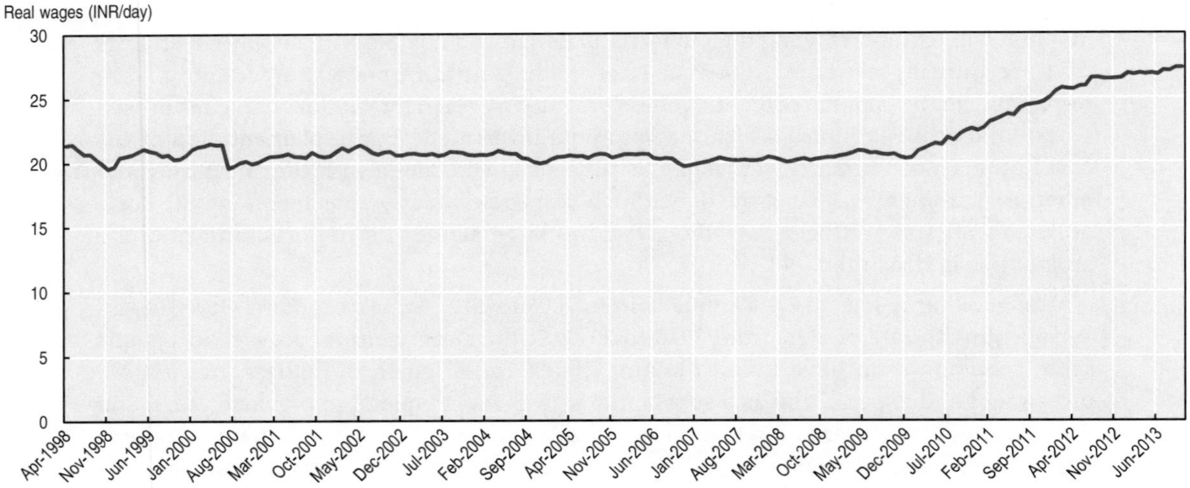

Real wages (INR/day)

Source: Government of India, *Indian Labour Journal* (various issues), *http://labourbureau.nic.in/main2.html.*
StatLink ⟡⟡⟡ *http://dx.doi.org/10.1787/888933099276*

Due to a number of factors, India's crop yields increased at a relatively fast pace in the last decade, and in particular from 2005. For example, during the period 2005 to 2013, national average yields for rice, wheat and coarse grains increased at 2.0%, 2.6% and 2.7% annually respectively. An important question is whether such a pace can be sustained over the next decade. The previous section noted that in some states, actual yields were not far from their potential, realisable level, while in other states a considerable gap remains. Further, some neighbouring countries have higher yields, and it appears that sustaining high yield growth may well be possible. This *Outlook* is optimistic in assuming the yield growth will remain robust over the next decade, particular if the current policy set remains in place (see discussion below).

One caveat to this optimistic scenario suggesting lower yield growth is associated with climate change which is beginning to show its impact. According to one study, climate change is projected to reduce timely sown, potential irrigated wheat yields by about 6% by 2020. In the case of late sown wheat, the projected decrease is 18%. Similarly, it is estimated that climate change may reduce potential irrigated rice yields by 4% and rain-fed rice yields by 6% by 2020. These projected impacts appear large over such a short time frame, but do point to factors which may aggravate yield fluctuations and thereby influence food security levels (Shetty et al. 2013).

Policies will play a critical role in market outcomes

Agriculture and food distribution policies will play a critical role in the next decade, if the current settings are maintained. This *Outlook* assumes that current legislation will remain in place, and it is appropriate to outline what influence they may have in affecting outcomes over the next decade. This policy set is diverse and pervasive, and following the experience of growth following the National Food Security Mission of 2007-08, the policy environment potentially stimulates both the demand and supply sides in certain sectors, particularly for food grains. Three important policy considerations concern i) market support prices , especially for rice and wheat, ii) input programmes, especially for fertiliser and iii) the new National Food Security Act of 2013. The *Outlook* assumes no change in India's trade policy.

i) Market support prices

Market support prices have been increased annually according to estimated changes to farm costs of production. Figure 2.15 below provides the projection for MSPs in USD, relative to the international reference prices projected in this *Outlook*. The interesting point to note is that under the assumptions/conditions of the projection, market support prices may provide support for wheat and rice which is broadly similar to price levels prevailing in international markets. This, however, depends on anticipated inflation rates, exchange rates and, of course, quality differences. The second point of interest is that MSPs remain at higher real levels compared to those prevailing prior to 2007, and therefore continue to stimulate higher production levels.

The MSP for the other 22 commodities are also assumed to increase according to increases in production costs.[8] However, since these programmes are not usually backed by an effective procurement mechanism as exists for rice and wheat, production preferences for the latter two are assumed to broadly sustain area allocation to these commodities.

Figure 2.15. **Market support prices in India and world prices for rice and wheat**

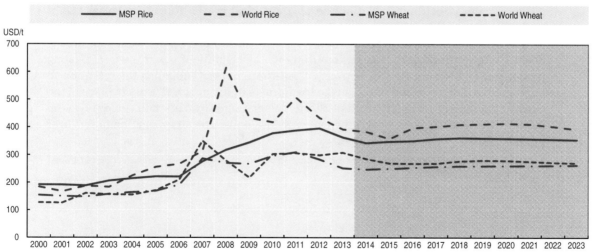

Note: Minimum Support Price (MSP) for paddy rice is adjusted to milled basis. Market margins of 15% are added to MSP. The world reference price for wheat is US Gulf HRW, and for rice is Viet Nam 5%.
Source: Government of India (2012), Agricultural Statistics at a Glance 2012, Government of India, New Delhi; OECD and FAO Secretariats.

StatLink ⟐ *http://dx.doi.org/10.1787/888933099295*

ii) Fertiliser

The fertiliser subsidy is assumed to continue in its current form, with constant MRP for nitrogen-based fertiliser and subsidies for the respective nutrients. This structure poses challenges for the fertiliser industry as noted in Box 2.4. Assumed high crude oil prices in this *Outlook* imply that related fertiliser prices will remain high in the coming decade.

Box 2.4. **The fertiliser industry in India: Its challenges and prospects in the next decade**[1]

Mineral fertilisers play a crucial role in Indian agriculture. Increasing use of fertiliser, coupled with high yielding seeds and irrigation has transformed Indian agriculture.

India is the second largest consumer of fertiliser in the world next to China, although on a per hectare basis, the use of fertiliser is still lower than in many countries. Indian fertiliser consumption recorded a phenomenal growth in India during the past decades, growing more than 12 times from 2.3 Mt in 1970-71 to 28.1 Mt in 2010-11. However, total nutrient consumption fell in the past two years, falling to 27.8 and 25.5 Mt in 2011-12 and 2012-13, respectively. Fertiliser use will need to expand in the future, to 30.5 Mt by 2021/22 and 37.4 Mt by 2031/32, partly reflecting the production requirements foreseen by the National Food Security Act.

Favourable policies led to substantial addition to domestic production capacity of nitrogenous and phosphatic fertilisers until the late 1990s. India became self-sufficient in urea production in early 2000. Since then, however, no brown field or green field projects have been commissioned. Policies focused more on containing the level of subsidy. Investment policy in 2008 for urea led to a small addition in existing capacity of about 2.5 Mt.

Rising consumption and stagnant/slow growth in indigenous fertiliser production has led to increasing dependence on imports. Currently, India imports about 17 Mt of finished fertilisers and 12 Mt of raw materials in nutrient equivalent terms.

Government policies will continue to play a critical role in future for better use of fertilisers. The fertiliser industry emphasises that full reform of the sector is necessary, so that prices of nutrients promote more balanced use. An investment policy for urea is needed to encourage new capacity, requiring the availability of gas to sustain existing production and to support new capacity. The Government of India has the intention to implement a direct transfer of subsidy to the farmers in the next few years in place of the current system of transfer through the fertiliser industry. This will encourage the industry to take independent commercial decisions and focus on innovation in fertiliser products and services to the farmers.

1. This box is based on inputs provided by the Fertilizer Association of India, under the direction of Director General Satish Chander.

The result of India's support/subsidy for fertiliser is a projection of sustained low fertiliser prices in the future which will continue to stimulate fertiliser application, including relatively high nitrogen application. The comparison of movements in fertiliser prices between India and global markets is noted in Figure 2.16.

Figure 2.16. **Movements in fertiliser prices, India vs World**

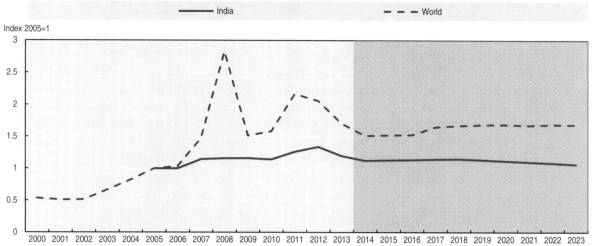

Note: Prices indexed to 1 in 2005, world fertiliser price index from the World Bank. India's fertiliser price is calculated from nitrogen, phosphate and potassium according to the same composition.
Source: OECD and FAO Secretariats.

StatLink ᵃˢᵖ *http://dx.doi.org/10.1787/888933099314*

iii) Food grain distribution

The NFSA (Box 2.5), is being implemented across India. This *Outlook* has assumed that the Act will remain in effect over the next decade, to 2023-24. Its implications need to be assessed for a clear understanding of its potential impact on markets. It should be noted that the NFSA extends an already large food distribution programme, which previously covered about 30% of India's population.

The NFSA may be examined from the point of view of both consumers and of government finances. For consumers, data on the consumption profile of the average recipient of NFSA food grain is not available. If it is assumed that the average recipient consumes 75 kg of rice, 62 kg of wheat and 21 kg of coarse grain (average per capita disappearance in 2013), then the programmes provision of 60 kg p.a. of food grain would cover about 38% of an individual's consumption. If no change in consumption mix is assumed, this means effective subsidisation of 28 kg of rice at a price of INR 3/kg (USD 0.047/kg), 24 kg of wheat at a price of INR 2/kg (USD 0.031/kg), and 8 kg of coarse grain at INR 1/kg (USD 0.015/kg).[9] At retail prices for rice, wheat and coarse grain of about INR 31.8 (USD 0.59/kg), INR 19.6 (USD 0.36/kg) and INR 24.2/kg (USD 0.38/kg) respectively, the net saving for the average recipient is about INR 1 674 (USD 26) per year in 2013. Assuming no change in the offer prices, in the rates of inflation and of the USD exchange rate, the effective subsidy in this projection rises to INR 3 076 (USD 29) p.a. per person by 2023.

An important question for the *Outlook* concerns the demand effects of the NFSA on food consumption in India which are not fully understood, yet, given that the programme started at the end of 2013. A detailed analysis of the NFSA is beyond the scope of this *Outlook*, but anticipating its overall impact on markets is nevertheless required. The approach adopted in performing the projection is to establish a base projection, using simplifying assumptions, and then examine the implications of an alternative approach to test sensitivity. This is reported in the last section of this chapter.

Impacts of a subsidy programme consist of price and income effects. As noted above, the offer prices are low, but since the coverage limit of 60 kg per person per year is well under the average consumption profile of most people in India, it means that at the margin the effect on cereal consumption with respect to these prices may be close to zero. This is because consumption beyond 60 kg still faces the full retail price.[10] Of course, the distribution of consumption around the average may imply that some people face the marginal price at the subsidised rate, such those in the AAY group which are entitled to a family subsidy limit of 35 kg/month. But overall, the impact on consumption for most people would be from the income saved by access to the cereals at the much lower prices and not to the price incentive to buy more at the margin. The question then is how consumers will allocate the additional net income provided by the programme.[11]

Accounting for the income effect of NFSA on consumption is also contentious. Some research on food consumption behaviour in India suggests that the marginal income expenditure elasticities for some goods such as cereals are negative (Kumar, 2013). This would imply that the programme effect may be to reduce cereal consumption and use the additional income to buy other goods. Against this perspective, the model used in the preparation of the *Outlook* employs a demand system with positive income effects. These elasticities vary by product, and in the case of cereals, the value is small at 0.13 in 2013. However, these model estimates are national in scope and refer to the "average" consumer, while the NFSA is targeted by income and location. With income inequality and with budget shares for commodities that differ significantly by income scale, using the model without adjustment may understate the impact of an income subsidy for consumption goods with a higher budget share for consumers in lower income brackets (such as cereals).[12]

In the context of this discussion some simplistic assumptions have been used in accounting for the impact of the NFSA. These assumptions specify shifting the demand functions of the projection model upward by a factor reflecting the percentage of additional product that is bought at current retail prices with the share of the income savings from the programme. The share used is determined by the food expenditure shares at the median income. This approach implies, for example, that a 25% share of the subsidy would buy about 14 kg of the average basket of cereals at 2013 prices.[13] As the NFSA extends previous programme benefits from about 30% to 67% of the population, the net effect in this example would be to raise per capita national average consumption by about 3%. The projections for the other commodities have been also adjusted in a similar way, and accordingly the demand functions for pulses, milk products, vegetable oil, sugar, meat products, and fruits and vegetables are shifted by 2%, 2%, 2%, 1%, 2% and 2% respectively. An alternative approach would be to allocate the income savings across all items. In that case, with food expenditure shares in India at 42%, the shifts noted would be reduced accordingly. If a fully behavioural model were available which included income distributional dimensions, different results could be estimated.

The impact on the government finances of the NFSA is considerable. The programme represents a substantive up-scaling of the previous programme, and while offer prices are set initially only for three years, if MSPs are inflation adjusted, the programme costs will also inflate over time. Adjusted for inflation, real programme costs (at 2013 prices), evaluated at projected MSP procurement prices less programme offer prices, are estimated to rise from around INR 1.1 trillion (USD 19 billion) in 2014, to around INR 1.3 trillion (USD 22 billion) by 2023. It is important to note that analyses of procurement and distribution, including its costs and impacts on both consumption and welfare, are conditional on programme operation. The procurement of 55 Mt of cereals and its distribution to an estimated 834 million people involves substantial infrastructure and coordination to prevent waste, product degradation and failure in reaching intended recipients.

Box 2.5. **India's National Food Security Act, 2013**

The National Food Security Act was adopted by the Indian Parliament on 10 September 2013 and extends to the whole of India. It foresees that every person belonging to a priority household is entitled to receive 5 kg of food grains per month at subsidised prices. Subsidised prices for rice, wheat and coarse cereals should not exceed INR 3, 2 and 1 per kg, respectively, for a period of three years. After that, prices may be adjusted by the Central Government. Addressing food security based on a rights based approach rather than a welfare approach is a major change in Indian food policy. The Ministry of Finance allocated INR 1.15 trillion in the 2014-15 budget to the implementation of the National Food Security Act, which is approximately 1% of India's GDP.

Eligible households will comprise up to 75% of the rural population and 50% of the urban population. This means that India's National Food Security Act could cover up to 834 million persons, or 67%, of the Indian population. The programme is, therefore, regarded as the largest food security programme in the world. Households covered under the "Antyoda Anna Yojana" scheme – a programme for the poorest of the poor – are entitled to 35 kg of food grains per household per month at the above-mentioned prices. Special entitlements shall also apply to pregnant and lactating women and children up to the age of 14. For example, every pregnant woman and lactating mother will be entitled to get food free of cost during pregnancy and six months after childbirth. Cash benefits of INR 1 000 per month would be provided for the first six months to meet increased food requirements of pregnant women. Children in the age group of six months to six years would be given food free of cost, and every child aged 6 to 14 years will be entitled to one free daily meal to be received at school. Special focus is also given to vulnerable groups in the remote areas of India. The state governments will be responsible for identifying priority households in rural and urban areas. The list of eligible households will be available publicly. The eldest woman (older than 18 years) in every eligible household will receive the ration cards for the household. In addition, reforms will be undertaken to make the public distribution system effective and transparent. These measures include the application of modern information and communication technologies and the use of biometric information for eligible households. Every state government will form a State Food Commission to monitor the implementation of the Food Security Act. The composition of the State Food Commission is regulated by the Food Security Act: it will consider experience, gender and caste. The act also makes provisions for vigilance committees and grievance redress mechanisms.

The Indian government will be responsible for procuring food grains to a central pool through the state agencies. The National Food Security Act specifies that 54.93 Mt of food grains will be distributed through the Public Distribution System (PDS) to all 35 Indian states per year. Additional allocations will have to be made by the government under other welfare schemes (8 Mt), buffer stocks (5 Mt) and the open market sale scheme (5 Mt). The total procurement will be approximately 70 Mt, which is 7 Mt higher than the amount procured during 2011-12 (Chand and Birthal, 2011). The central government will also be responsible for allocating food grains from the central pool to the different states, providing transportation and storage facilities. The state governments, on the other hand, will be implementing and monitoring the Food Security Act.

> ### Box 2.5. **India's National Food Security Act, 2013** *(cont.)*
>
> The National Food Security Act has been heavily debated within India. Some scholars argued that the act is more inclusive than current programmes, and eligible households will be more aware of their entitlements. This will make the PDS system more effective, because exclusion errors and leakages are better addressed (Drèze, 2013). Others stated that a further increase in procurement levels may aggravate the procurement challenges currently experienced, relating to infrastructure, stocking, transport, leakages and governance. These challenges would have to be addressed with substantial financial investments in market infrastructure. The central procurement of cereals may also crowd out private sector or state government initiatives that might be better tailored to local needs (Gulati et al., 2012).
>
> *Source:*
> Government of India (2013f), *The Gazette of India – National Food Security Act*, Government of India, New Delhi.
> Chand, R. and P.S. Birthal (2011), "Food Grain Stock Requirement during 12th Five-Year Plan", *NCAP Working Paper*, No. 9, National Centre for Agricultural Economics and Policy Research, New Delhi
> Drèze, J. (2013), "From the granary to the plate", *The Hindu*, 1 August 2013.
> Gulati, A., J. Gujral, and T. Nandakumar (2012), "National Food Security Bill – Challenges and Options", *Discussion Paper No. 2*, Commission for Agricultural Costs and Prices, Government of India: New Delhi.

The commodity outlook for India, 2014-23

Overview

The major question concerning the outlook for India, in the context of the policy environment and conditioning assumptions surrounding the outlook for its economy, is whether India will continue its recent increases in production, and if so will they serve higher domestic consumption, or larger exports. During the next decade, will India make gains toward reducing its number of food insecure people? The projections of this *Outlook* are affirmative. India's agriculture production growth will likely slow from the rapid pace of the previous decade, but it will still advance at more than double the rate of population increase, and consumption will advance at a similar pace. If international prices evolve as projected, all else being equal, India may export historical quantities at prices close to MSP levels. However, if the consumption of rice and wheat do not rise as projected, stock accumulation or trade would need to absorb production increases. In turn, higher exports particularly for rice, would depress international market prices and Indian exports could then not be achieved without subsidy, also reducing export revenue. The interaction of Indian agriculture's development and the government's policies have made India's agriculture an important influence on world markets.

A corollary to the question of how India's food security situation will evolve is the efficacy of government programmes. With rising price supports, how effective will input subsidies and food distribution programmes be in reducing food insecurity? These programmes may be key to increased production and consumption, but they absorb a large share of national finances. What are the opportunity costs of such programmes in terms of foregone alternative investments, for example? Assessing these questions is beyond the objective of this *Outlook* which is more to assess the implications on markets of sustaining existing policies. Summary indicators derived from the commodity projections included in the *Outlook* portray a cautiously optimistic scenario for the next decade. The measure of net agricultural production (commodity production less required inputs of seed and feed), evaluated at 2004-06 international reference prices, indicates growth in output 2.9% p.a.

over the next decade, which is in line with historical growth of India's agriculture sector (Table 2.1). It is, however, less than the very robust growth of 4.6% p.a. which was witnessed in the decade 2004-13.

The projection for aggregate consumption is also positive, as indicated in Figure 2.1. Based on food consumption projected in the *Outlook* by major commodity, average calorie and protein intake show a continuous rise to 2 830 kcal/day and 70 g/day by 2023, up from 2 450 kcal/day and 61 g/day, respectively, in the 2011-13 base period. These increases continue the trend that appears to have started around 2004-05, but they rise at a faster pace. It may appear counterintuitive that production is set to grow more slowly, but consumption more quickly. The reason for the result is that some of the increased production in the last decade went for both export and stock rebuilding, while in the *Outlook* the projection indicates more is used for increased consumption. Risks to this result are discussed in the final section of the chapter.

Figure 2.17. **India's calorie and protein consumption projected to increase**

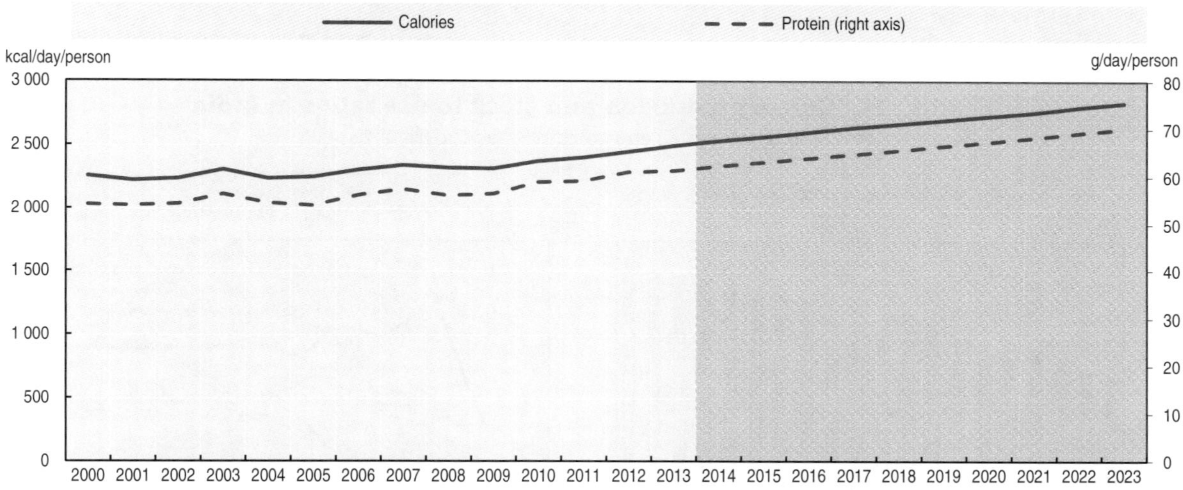

Source: OECD and FAO Secretariats.

StatLink ⎙ *http://dx.doi.org/10.1787/888933099333*

Cereals

Production growth strong, but slower than recent trend

Production of cereals may attain 282 Mt by 2023, as annual growth is anticipated to slow to 1.5%, with area remaining at near current levels. Yield growth remains robust, if slightly lower than the previous decade, at 1.7% p.a. Higher growth in cereals has been encouraged by the market support prices for rice and wheat which have been increased in recent years and are projected to be increased in line with increases in costs of production over the outlook period. However, higher production is the result of higher yields, as increases in the area harvested will be mainly allocated to other crops (Figure 2.19).

India is the second largest producer and consumer of rice in the world. Production is anticipated to reach 124 Mt by 2023, growing at a rate of 1.4% annually, led by yield growth of 1.9% p.a. Several programmes such as National Food Security Mission, Rashtriya Krishi Vikas Yojana and Bringing Green Revolution in Eastern India are being implemented by the

Figure 2.18. **Crop area increases in India but not for cereals**

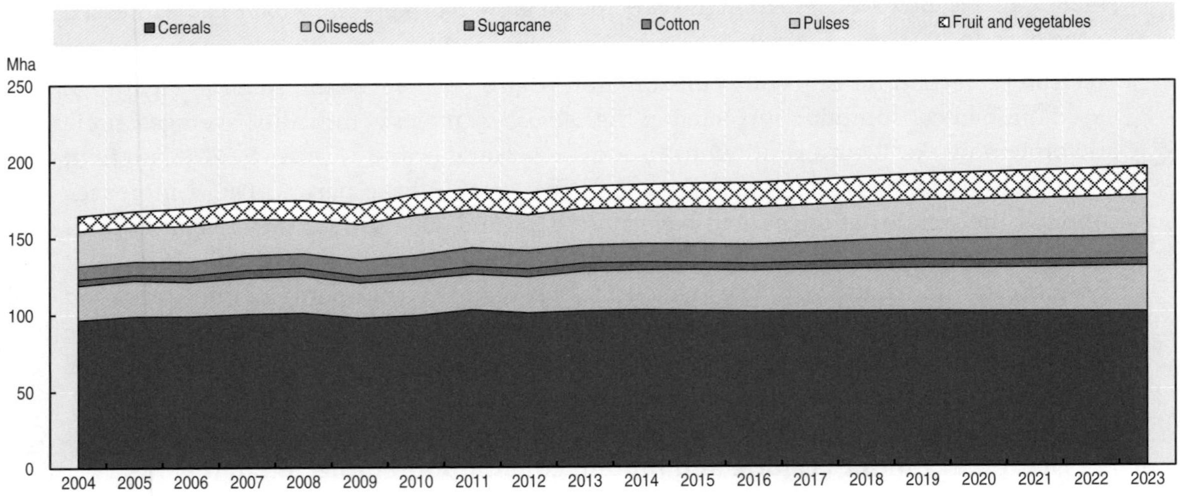

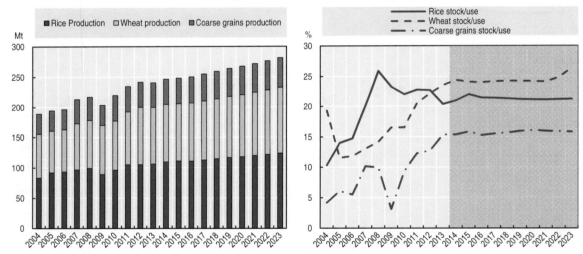

Source: OECD and FAO Secretariats.

StatLink http://dx.doi.org/10.1787/888933099352

Figure 2.19. **Cereal production and stock to use ratios in India**
Production (left panel) and stock-to-use ratio (right panel)

Source: OECD and FAO Secretariats.

StatLink http://dx.doi.org/10.1787/888933099371

government of India to increase the production and productivity of cereals and pulses in the country.

The production of wheat in the country has increased significantly from 75.1 Mt in 2006-07 to over 95 Mt in 2014. It is projected to attain 112 Mt by 2023, growing by 1.6% p.a. in the next decade, underpinned by yield growth at 1.7% p.a. Flat area growth compares to recent trends which have seen wheat area increase from 28 Mha in 2006-07 to almost 30 Mha in 2013-14.

Coarse grain production may reach 49 Mt by 2023, growing at 1.7% p.a. over the projection period, and as with wheat and rice, is mostly due to yield growth. In India, coarse grains are comprised of sorghum (*Jowar*), pearl millet (*Bajra*), maize, finger millet

(*Ragi*) and other small millets which are mainly grown in rain-fed conditions. These crops are grown in arid and semi-arid areas under low rainfall (200-600 mm), where fine cereals like wheat and rice cannot be grown profitably. Millets have more food, feed and fodder value, and they are more environmentally friendly and resilient to climate change. A majority of millet grains contain higher protein, fibre, calcium and minerals than fine cereals. Therefore, these are now being called "nutri-cereals" and are experiencing higher prices in recent years.

With such a strong orientation of the Indian diet toward cereals, and with policy on both the supply and demand sides oriented to increasing both production and consumption of cereals to enhance food security, a key question in the *Outlook* is how cereal food consumption will evolve over the next decade. The projections of this *Outlook* are optimistic, assuming that the income effect of the NFSA will lift rice and wheat consumption. Per capita cereal food consumption is projected to rise to 164 kg/person by 2023, compared to the base period quantity (2011-13) of 155 kg/person, or an increase of 5.8%. It is projected that per capita food consumption of rice, wheat and coarse grains will attain 78.8, 65.5 and 20.4 kg respectively. If this consumption level for cereals is attained, it would be a turnaround in the trend of diets of the Indian population experienced in the last decade. A key challenge will rest with the NFSA, and in particular the procurement and distribution systems that will provide about 55 Mt of cereals annually to an estimated 834 million people. Implications on markets if consumption does not increase as projected are assessed in the final section of this chapter.

Figure 2.20. **Per capita consumption of cereals to rise in India**

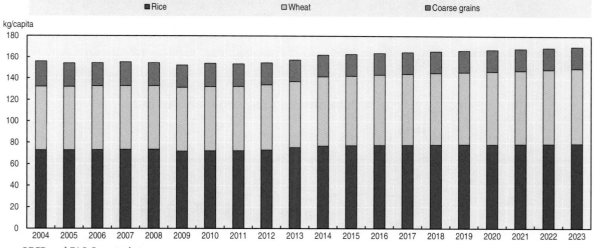

Source: OECD and FAO Secretariats.

StatLink ⫘ http://dx.doi.org/10.1787/888933099390

The important consequence of rising food consumption for rice and wheat is that increased production will largely be sold in the domestic market. A key concern, however, is the rapid build-up of stocks in recent years to near historical highs. The *Outlook* anticipates that stocks will remain high given the transaction requirements of the NFSA. Wheat, rice and coarse grain exports, which will be residual to supply and demand developments, are nevertheless projected to be higher in the next decade reaching over 17 Mt by 2023.

Figure 2.21. **Indian cereal exports may rise over the outlook period (2014-23)**

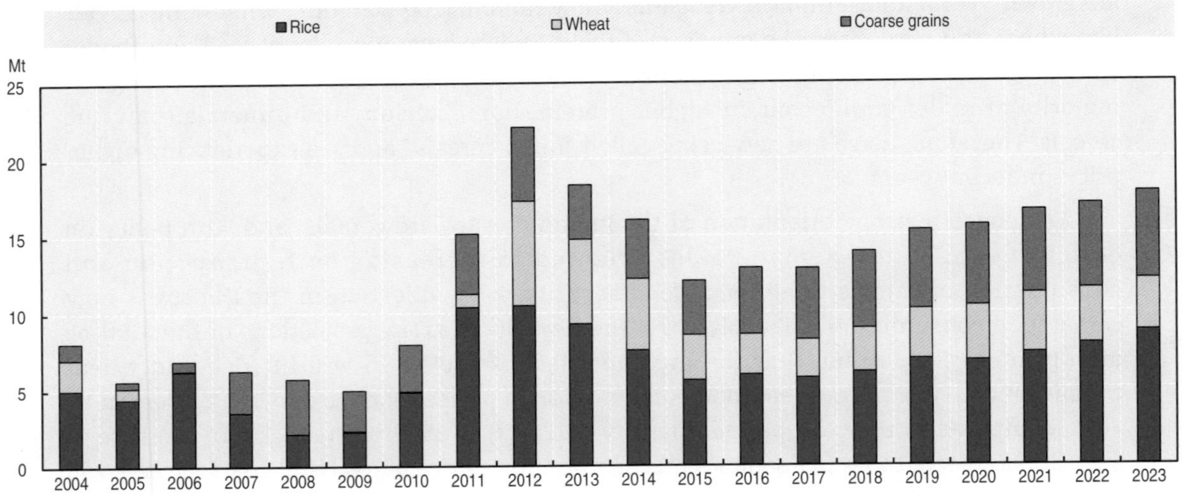

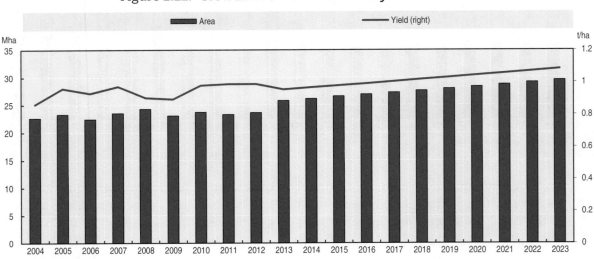

■ Rice   □ Wheat   ▨ Coarse grains

Source: OECD and FAO Secretariats.

StatLink ⬛⬛ *http://dx.doi.org/10.1787/888933099409*

Oilseeds and oilseed products

Oilseed production has grown more slowly than for most other crops. Area and yields have each increased about 0.8% p.a. in the last decade. Growth is anticipated to improve in the future with the encouragement of government programmes that aim to contain growth in vegetable oil imports. Oilseed output is projected to grow 2.6% p.a. India's trade in oilseeds will remain negligible, but higher demand for vegetable oil, at 3.7% p.a., will require imports growing to a level of 17 Mt by 2023, continuing India's position as the world's largest vegetable oil importer. Conversely, with a small feed market, and despite a growing livestock and aquaculture feed demand, oilseed meal exports are also anticipated to grow to 7.4 Mt.

Figure 2.22. **Growth in oilseed area and yields in India**

▬ Area   —— Yield (right)

Source: OECD and FAO Secretariats.

StatLink ⬛⬛ *http://dx.doi.org/10.1787/888933099428*

Figure 2.23. **Imports of vegetable oil continue to rise in India**

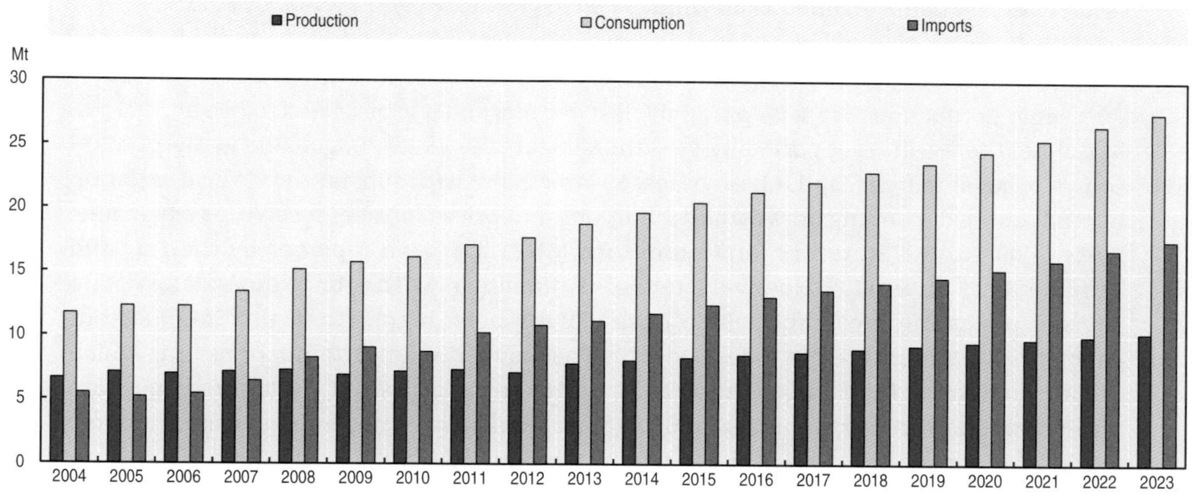

■ Production   □ Consumption   ■ Imports

Mt

Source: OECD and FAO Secretariats.

StatLink ⧉ *http://dx.doi.org/10.1787/888933099447*

Pulses

Being rich in protein, pulses form a vital part of the, largely vegetarian, Indian diet. India holds the first rank in pulse production and consumption, and the country grows the largest varieties of pulses in the world, accounting for about 32% of the area and 26% of world production. The important pulse crops are chickpea, pigeon pea, urd bean, mung bean, lentil and field pea. Yield of pulses has increased from 0.63 t/ha in 2007-08 to 0.79 t/ha in 2012-13. However, average productivity of pulses in India still remains below the world's average.

Pulse production has registered an increase from 15 Mt in 2007-08 to a record level of 18.4 Mt in 2012-13. Production is projected to attain 23 Mt by 2023, with annual growth in both area and yield at rates of 1% and 2% respectively. Food consumption, which grew at the rapid

Figure 2.24. **Growth in the pulse sector follows higher domestic demand in India**

—— Production   – – Food Use   — · — Other Use   – – – – Exports   — · · Imports

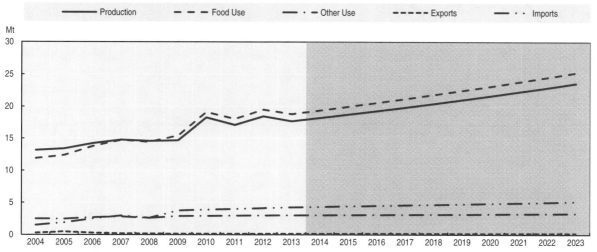

Mt

Source: OECD and FAO Secretariats

StatLink ⧉ *http://dx.doi.org/10.1787/888933099466*

pace of 5% p.a. in per capita terms, is projected to grow at 3% p.a. over the next decade. As a result of excess demand, imports are anticipated to grow to a level of 5.1 Mt by 2023.

Sugar

Sugar production rose 4.7% p.a. in the last decade, and it is projected to rise at 2.2% p.a. in the next ten years, supported by growth in sugarcane yields. Sugarcane is the primary source of sugar in India, and it has witnessed growth but with substantial cyclical variation in production, depending on weather conditions and prices farmers receive for sugarcane. Since 2009-10, the Statutory Minimum Price (SMP) has been replaced by the Fair and Remuneratory Price (FRP). However, state governments have announced mandatory state advised prices for sugarcane which have usually been higher than the SMP/FRP, but payments to farmers are often delayed. This has resulted in uncertainty of returns which caused production fluctuations. As a result, with low import tariffs, India's trade position may reflect shortages or surpluses, and, given its market size, may influence international markets. In view of past cyclical behaviour, a production cycle in the *Outlook* has been maintained.

The demand for sugar and by-products continues to grow, with per capita consumption projected to increase at 1% p.a. in the next decade, down from 1.6% p.a. in the last ten years. Consumption of molasses increased at almost 5% p.a. in the last ten years, largely due to higher demand for biofuel/ethanol production for which it is the major feedstock. In the next decade, molasses consumption is anticipated to be moderate as ethanol demand growth subsides.

Figure 2.25. **Indian sugar production grows but remains cyclical**

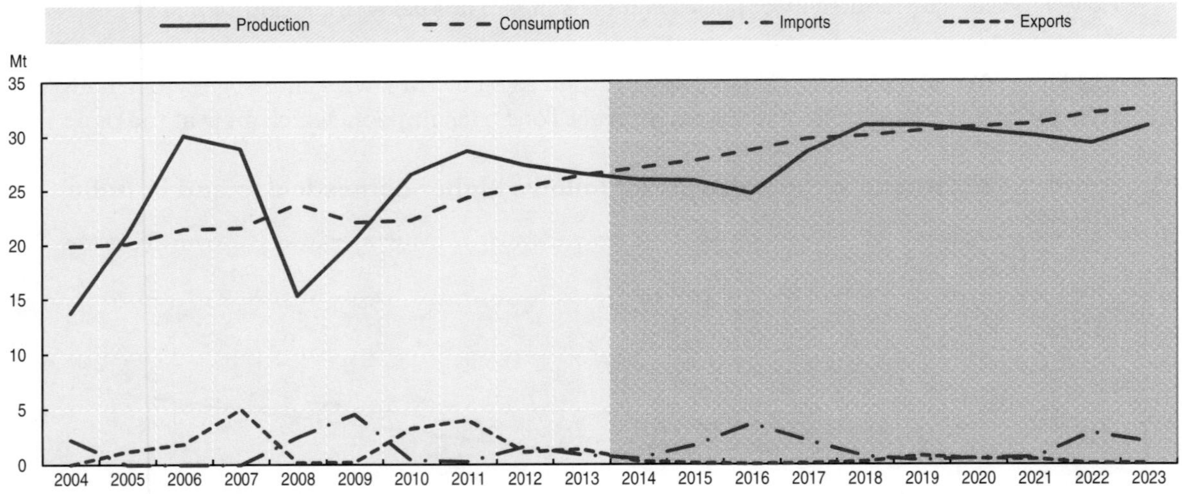

Source: OECD and FAO Secretariats.

StatLink ⟐ *http://dx.doi.org/10.1787/888933099485*

Vegetables and fruit

The *Outlook* does not cover fruits and vegetables in the wider international market. These sectors are, however, among the fastest growing and are now valuable sectors, particularly in agricultural zones favourable for production, such as in India. Indeed, the estimates of gross production value indicate that as a sector, the fruit and vegetable sector is one of India's most valuable sectors, exceeding that of cereals in 2012 (FAO, 2014). The highest valued items are mangoes, bananas, potatoes, tomatoes and onions. In the next decade, India's vegetable and fruit production is anticipated to grow 3.3% p.a. and 3.4% p.a., respectively, after having grown by 6.0% p.a. in the last decade (Figure 2.26), mainly as a result of expansion in area to almost 19 Mha. Growth in the vegetable and fruit sectors offers considerable opportunities for increased diversification of agricultural income and nutrition in the future.

Figure 2.26. **The vegetable and fruit sectors in India are growing at a fast pace**

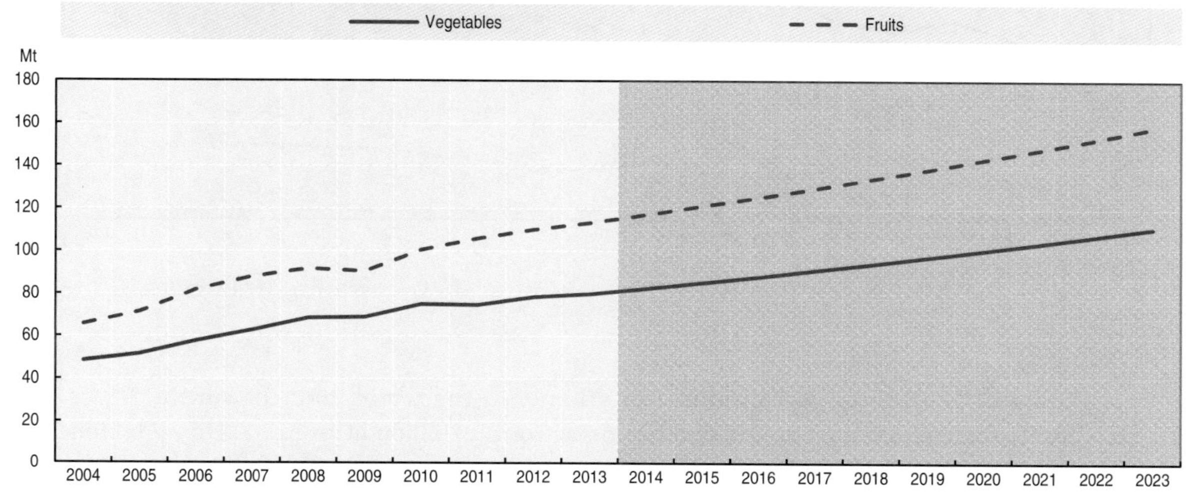

Source: OECD and FAO Secretariats.

StatLink http://dx.doi.org/10.1787/888933099504

Cotton

India now produces almost 25% of the world's cotton output and has a major influence on international cotton markets. In the past, India was also an important exporter of cotton textiles, but is less now because of the rise of other exporters, especially China. The adoption of *Bacillus thuringiensis* (Bt) genetically modified cotton, along with high yielding hybrids and increased irrigation, has underpinned further development of India's cotton sector. Cotton production increased rapidly from 2.3 Mt in 2000 to 6.3 Mt in 2013. With area projected to increase 4.2% p.a. and yield 1% p.a., India's cotton production may attain 9.2 Mt by 2023.

For cotton, the issue is how to continue the modernisation of production and bring yields closer to global norms. India's cotton yield in 2011-13 averaged 0.5 t/ha, compared to the global average of 0.8 t/ha. In terms of domestic demand for textile production, the question is whether India can capture higher international market shares, particularly from China where wage costs are rising. Based on demographics and industrial wage developments, India may capture more clothing trade from China in the future, but China's infrastructure and supply chain developments may help to maintain its advantage. Spinning cotton is much more capital-intensive than cutting and sewing apparel or garments, and China may continue spinning for even longer, as the United States did right up to 2000. In consideration of these issues, with higher production, India is projected to increase its cotton exports to more than 2 Mt by 2023, assuming no action is taken by government to limit exports.

Figure 2.27. **Indian cotton production and exports will rise**

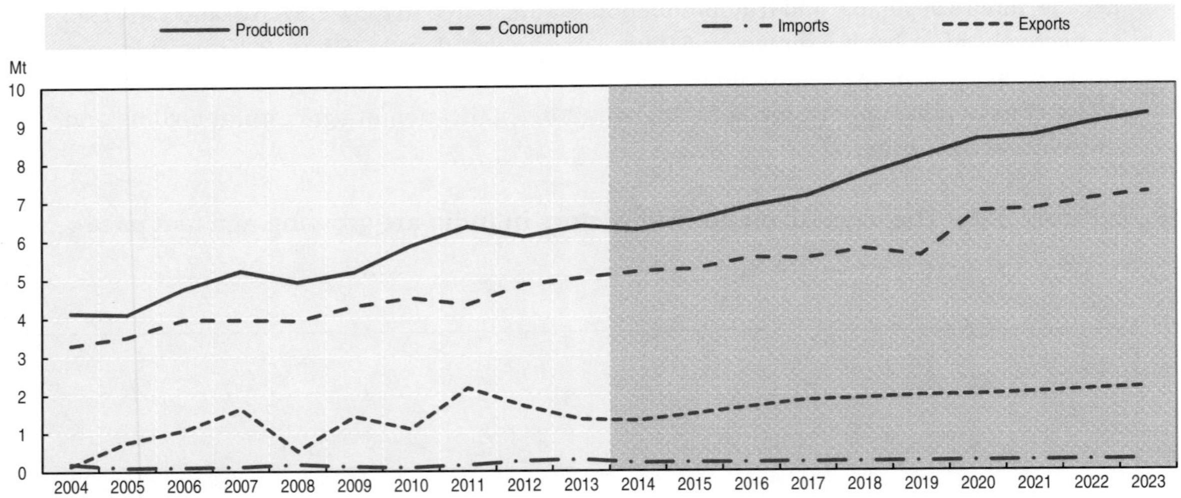

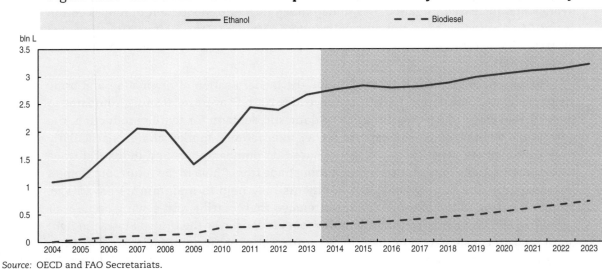

Source: OECD and FAO Secretariats.

StatLink ⬛ᵢₛ■ http://dx.doi.org/10.1787/888933099523

Biofuels

India is the fifth largest producer of ethanol in the world, and the ninth largest biodiesel producer. Ethanol production has risen from 1.5 billion litres in 2002 to 2.7 billion litres in 2013. Biodiesel production increased from non-existent to 300 million litres over the same period. India's National Biofuel Policy aims to replace 20% of its petroleum fuel consumption with biofuels by the end of its 12th Five-Year Plan (USDA, 2012). Ethanol production has been used primarily for non-fuel purposes, made from its large availability of molasses derived in the production of sugar. Based on 2013 estimates, the share of ethanol in petrol was still only 2.5%. Early projects to develop jatropha based biodiesel production have not been as promising as expected.

Figure 2.28. **Growth in India's biofuel production limited by feedstock availability**

Source: OECD and FAO Secretariats.

StatLink ⬛ᵢₛ■ http://dx.doi.org/10.1787/888933099542

Ethanol production is projected to rise to 3.2 billion litres by 2023, up 29% from the base period 2011-13. The production growth is limited by the availability of feedstock in the current projection, unless Indian sugar and molasses production increases more than projected in the outlook period. As a result, ethanol's share of petrol consumption over the outlook period will not rise above 3%. Biodiesel production is projected to remain low, rising by 150% to 730 million litres by 2023.

Meat

A crop-livestock mixed farming system prevails in most parts of India. Livestock is a significant source of income to rural households. With higher incomes, the consumption of products such as milk, meat, egg and fish has also risen, providing increased and more diversified incomes for farmers.

In the last decade, meat production increased by 3.9% p.a., led by a large 7.8% p.a. increase in poultry production. Meat production is projected to continue its fast growth at 3.1% p.a. to 2023, with poultry again dominating meat production. Strong demand for poultry meat reflects increasing diversification of diets and growth in income, but also cultural factors which are not favourable to bovine meat or pig meat in diets. Increased poultry consumption is among the fastest growing source of protein for the Indian population, although the traditional vegetarian diet will likely mean that per capita meat consumption will never reach anywhere near levels of other countries. In retail weight terms, India's per capita consumption may reach 4.3 kg/person by 2023, which compares to a world average of 36 kg/person and 94 kg/person in the United States.

An important development is the growth of bovine meat production from the buffalo herd, expressly for exports (Figure 2.30, and Box 7.2). Exports of bovine meat increased at a rate of 13.8% p.a. over the last decade. They are projected to rise to over 2 Mt by 2023, making India the largest bovine meat exporter in the world. The potential exists for even greater exports, given the number of buffalo animals in India.

Figure 2.29. **Poultry underpins meat consumption growth in India**

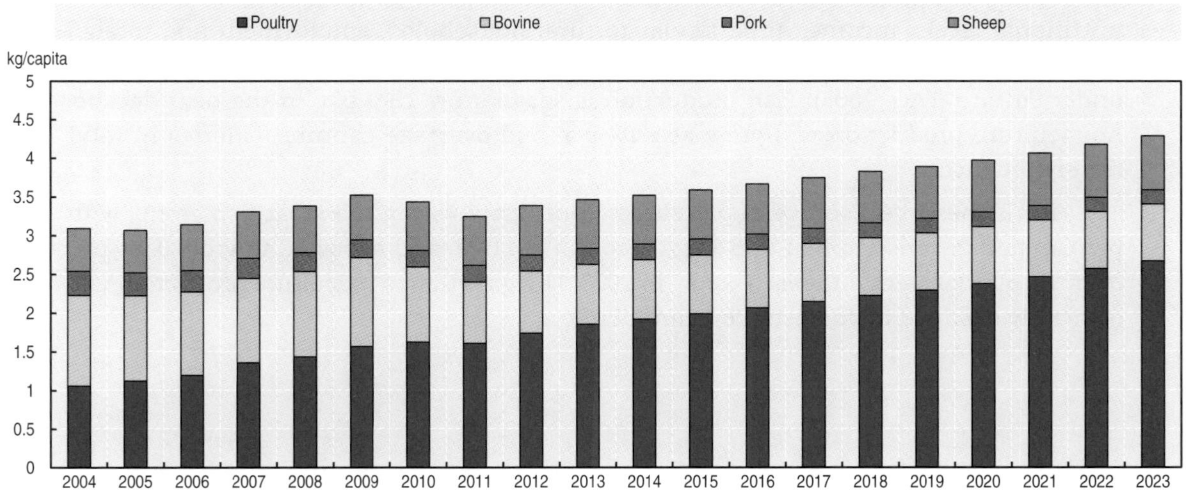

Source: OECD and FAO Secretariats.

StatLink ⟨⟩ http://dx.doi.org/10.1787/888933099561

Figure 2.30. **Bovine meat production and exports in India**

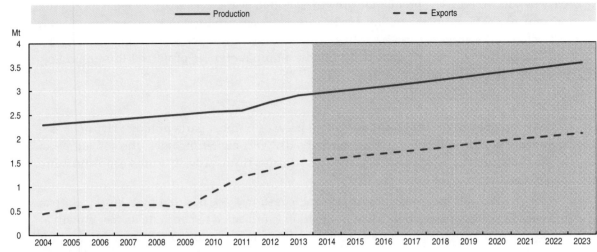

Source: OECD and FAO Secretariats.

StatLink ⟦⟧ http://dx.doi.org/10.1787/888933099958

Fish and seafood

India contributes around 6% to global fishery production, and it is the second largest producer of fish in the world. About 60% of the fish comes from inland waters, while the rest originates from marine waters. India's fishery production has grown 4.3% p.a. over the last decade, led by growth in aquaculture at 5.0% p.a. Aquaculture in India plays a major role in food security. At present, more than 90% of its production consists of freshwater finfish, in particular carps, which are almost fully consumed domestically. Shrimps and prawns from brackish water represent about 7% of the production and are mainly exported. In general, aquaculture is practised with the utilisation of low to moderate levels of inputs, especially organic-based fertilisers and feed. The impressive growth of aquaculture production has generated substantial socio-economic benefits, such as increased nutritional levels, income, in particular to rural households, employment and foreign exchange. It also brought vast un-utilised and under-utilised land and water resources under culture (FAO, 2005). Fish production is set to grow 1.3% p.a. in the next decade. Aquaculture production will grow at 2.1% p.a. and overtake capture fisheries in total fishery production.

Fish is the largest source of protein for consumers within the meat-fish group, with per capita fish consumption at 5.9 kg/person in 2011-13, and expected to grow 0.9% p.a. over the outlook period to reach 6.8 kg in 2023. The growth in aquaculture production will be mainly destined to domestic consumption.

Figure 2.31. **Aquaculture production dominates growth in fish production in India**

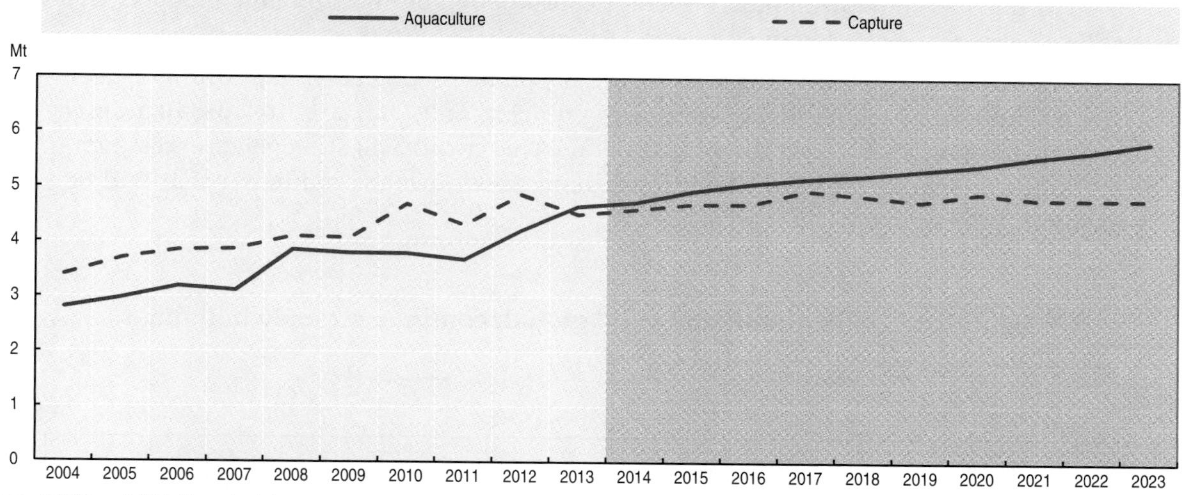

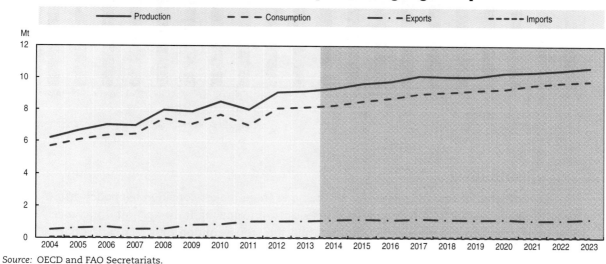

Source: OECD and FAO Secretariats.

StatLink 🔗 http://dx.doi.org/10.1787/888933099599

Figure 2.32. **More Indian fish production going for exports**

Source: OECD and FAO Secretariats.

StatLink 🔗 http://dx.doi.org/10.1787/888933099618

Dairy and dairy products

In the early 1970s, India started the "Operation Flood" programme, and since then has increased milk production six-fold (see also Box 2.1 above). Milk production is an important source of income for millions of farmers. With an estimated production of 140 Mt of milk in 2013, India is the largest producer of milk in the world.[14] Milk yields remain low by western standards, and the size of the cow herd is large, consisting in 2011 of some 45 million dairy cows, 38 million buffalo cows, 32 million goats, for a total of 115 million head. This number is projected to increase to 143 million by 2023. Milk production is projected to grow to 202 Mt by 2023, growing at a rate of 3.7% p.a. This is a considerable increase which, if attained, would make a major contribution to improved diets. However, even at this pace of growth, India's average consumption of milk and milk products will still be below those of Western Europe and Pakistan.

For the most part, India consumes fresh dairy products. One exception is butter (ghee), the production of which has been growing quickly at 3.7% p.a. Butter production is projected to grow 4% p.a. over the outlook period. This growth will also provide excess non-fat solids which will result in additional skim milk powder production that will be exported, primarily to Asian markets.

Figure 2.33. Milk output and yield growth continue strongly in India

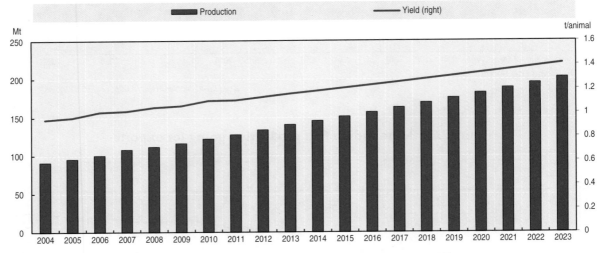

Source: OECD and FAO Secretariats.

StatLink ⬛⬛⬛ http://dx.doi.org/10.1787/888933099637

Risks and uncertainties

The outlook for India is relatively optimistic as India makes considerable policy effort to attain key objectives of reducing food insecurity, and raising farm and rural incomes. The projection shows higher agricultural output and consumption on a per capita basis and higher intake of calories, protein and other nutrients. The *Outlook* also suggests that India will continue to be a net exporter of food commodities. Exports of certain commodities such as rice, coarse grain, bovine meat, vegetable meal and cotton will likely be rising from current levels.

What are the key risks to this fairly optimistic future for India's agriculture? Aside from climate or yield shocks which may alter the base scenario, three alternative scenarios illustrate potential future issues. The first is associated with macroeconomic performance. If the economy does not resume higher economic growth, demand will not expand at the rates indicated in this *Outlook*. Second, an important risk is whether India's National Food Security Act will impact on food grain consumption as indicated in this *Outlook*. If the impact is less than estimated, excess production stemming from higher MSPs for wheat and rice will need to be stored or exported, with consequences for domestic and international markets. Third, if productivity growth does not continue at rates indicated by this *Outlook*, production will not increase as indicated. The consequences of lower supply would be lower exports, higher imports, or higher domestic prices and lower consumption. These risks are examined in three separate scenarios using the Aglink-Cosimo model which has been used to generate this *Outlook*.

i) *Lower growth scenario*

A scenario was assessed in which growth in India's GDP was decreased to 4% p.a. from the assumed average of 6.2% p.a. Lower growth may also impact other macroeconomic outcomes such as inflation and the exchange rate, but for purposes of this scenario, these have been assumed to remain unchanged. The result from this scenario is that per capita incomes would be 19% lower by 2023 than in the outlook. The implications are that consumption falls compared to the base projection, resulting in lower domestic prices, and hence lower production, lower imports, but higher exports. Demand effects vary according to the income elasticities of each product, and for example consumption of cereals falls 1.5%, milk 10%, vegetable oil 13% and poultry 10% (Figure 2.34). With calorie and protein intake reduced by 5% in this scenario, the gains in food security noted in the projection would be at risk. Economic growth is obviously critical to achieving food security objectives. The scenario also leads to lower imports of vegetable oil and higher exports of wheat, rice and coarse grain result in marginally lower international market prices. One scenario result illustrated in this case is that with weaker markets, domestic wheat prices fall to MSP levels, causing public stocks to build as additional wheat is procured to support prices.

Figure 2.34. **Lower GDP growth would reduce consumption gains in India**

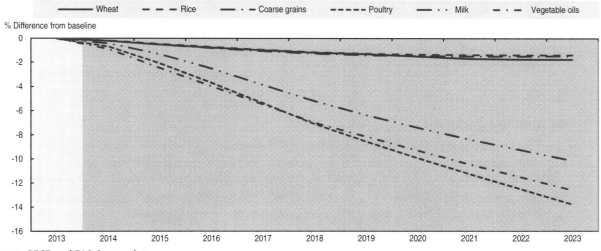

Source: OECD and FAO Secretariats.

StatLink ⬛ http://dx.doi.org/10.1787/888933099656

ii) *Income effect of NFSA*

A scenario was undertaken to assess the assumption made in the projection regarding the additional income effect of the NFSA. This scenario involves removing the shifts to the demand functions for each of the commodities as specified in the projection, and replacing them with a shift in income in those functions by the estimated size of the additional income provided by the subsidy and allowing the elasticities of demand to allocate the effect of the subsidy across all goods households consume. The size of the effective income subsidy provided by the programme is about 1% of per capita income in 2013, and this was used in the simulation. As Figure 2.35 shows, the effect is lower consumption across all commodities depending on the size of the income elasticities for each product. The implication is that if the cereal subsidy is diluted by spending on other commodities, the food consumption and food security impacts are less than projected.

Figure 2.35. **Comparison of assumptions on effects of NFSA on consumption in India**

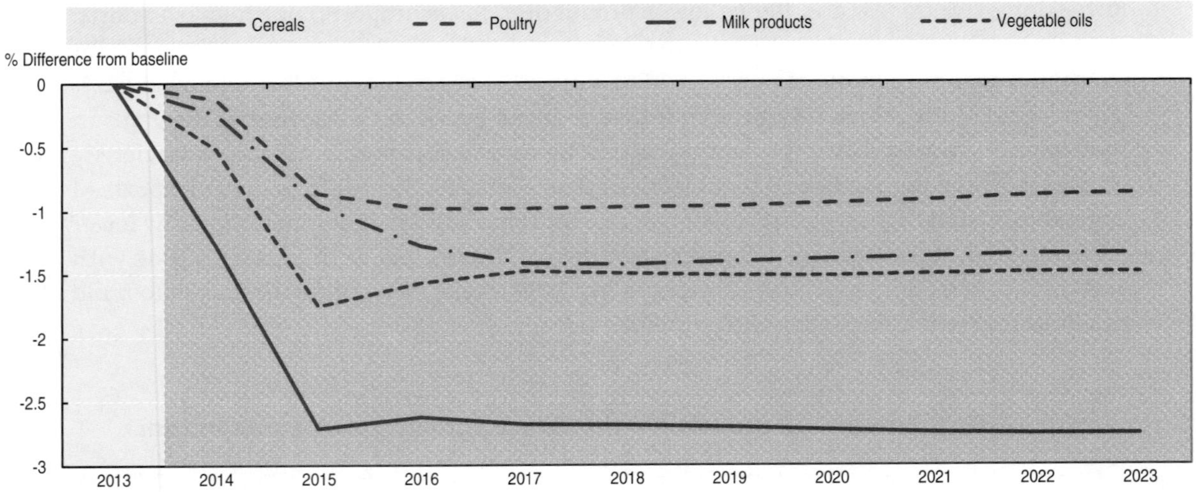

Note: The figure shows the percentage difference in consumption under the assumption that the National Food Security Act (NFSA) subsidy allocated according to the models income elasticities compared to the outlook projection which shifts consumption by the quantity that may be purchased by the subsidy allocated by survey expenditure shares.
Source: OECD and FAO Secretariats.

StatLink ᵐˢᵖ *http://dx.doi.org/10.1787/888933099675*

iii) *Lower yield scenario*

The projection is for yields to continue the strong performance achieved in the previous decade, given a very supportive policy framework including higher MSPs and input subsidies. One question is whether such yield growth is sustainable and what would be the consequences, if these are not attained in a context of domestic demand growth. Accordingly, a yield scenario was conducted in which the growth of yields for each crop was reduced by one-half percent per year from those projected. Lower output results in higher prices for cereals, as illustrated in Figure 2.36. Higher prices result in lower food consumption, lower exports but higher imports. The scenario underscores the importance that future growth in productivity will have in achieving India's food security objectives. Lower exports of rice, wheat and coarse grain result in higher world prices of about 6%, 1.5% and 1%, respectively.

Figure 2.36. **Impact of lower yield growth on domestic prices in India**

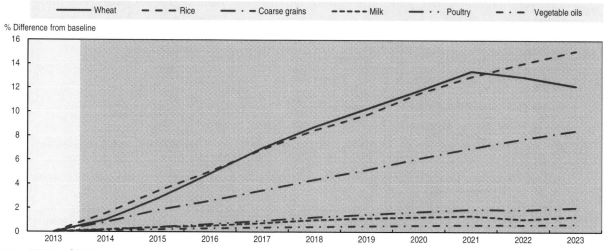

Source: OECD and FAO Secretariats.

StatLink 🖳🖧 *http://dx.doi.org/10.1787/888933099694*

Conclusions

The *Outlook* portrays a relatively optimistic scenario in which India will sustain recent production and consumption growth on a per capita basis over the next decade. The scenario is one for which India has considerable potential to reduce food insecurity.

While remaining largely vegetarian, Indian diets will diversify. Cereal consumption is anticipated to grow, but greater consumption of milk and milk products, pulses, fruits, vegetables and vegetable oil will contribute to the improved intake of food nutrients. Fish and meat consumption will grow strongly, although from a very low base, also providing an important source of protein.

India's policy effort will remain significant. Direct and indirect expenditures are estimated at USD 51 billion, or about 2.6% of India's current GDP. These may increase depending on settings of specific policy variables such as minimum support prices for commodities and maximum retail prices for fertilisers. The new National Food Security Act, which is the largest right to food programme of its kind ever attempted, may absorb as much as 40% of expenditures. The programme is expected to contribute to a marginal rise in cereal consumption, but it will also impact the consumption of other foods and goods.

Subsidies to encourage greater use of fertilisers, pesticides, seeds, water, electricity and credit, and market support prices, have played a role in the annual growth in agriculture and fish output of 4.6% in the last decade. Higher investment has also led to expansion of output. Growth is projected to slow to 3% p.a. over the next decade, still enough to raise per capita supplies considerably. Stocks of cereals are projected to stabilise or rise modestly over the next decade, largely as NFSA will require higher stocks for transaction purposes. Higher production will also cause India's trade surplus to widen modestly over the outlook period.

Key uncertainties in this scenario lie in India's macro performance, productivity/yield growth and the viability of government programmes. Sustained high income growth is the most critical ingredient to realisation of the outcomes of the *Outlook* scenario. But so is continued strong productivity growth, which, given the policy framework, will be key to preventing higher domestic prices that would reduce consumption. While the NFSA will transfer income to the poorest segment of the population, the procurement and distribution of 55 Mt of subsidised cereals to more than 800 million people, will present major challenges.

Notes

1. See FAO (2013) for estimates.

2. The measures are discussed in the section on Agricultural Policy.

3. Actual estimates by FAO are officially provided only up to 2009. These have been extended by extrapolation using consumption data used in this *Outlook* by the OECD and FAO Secretariats.

4. This reference is provided as a benchmark only for comparison purposes not an indication of what calorie or protein intake should be.

5. The biological potential reflects purely exogenous climate factors and varietal characteristics, but no other biotic or abiotic stresses (considered manageable), and hence represents a theoretical physical optimum. Attainable yield incorporates local soil factors and water control (area irrigated) to identify what is attainable given current level of water management but assuming that all other factors can be (at least theoretically) controlled.

6. Data refer only to Chapters 1-24 of the trade classification.

7. Mahatma Gandhi National Rural Employment Guarantee Act, which guarantees 100 days of work to every rural household.

8. MSPs are actually set on the basis of many factors, supply and demand. For this projection, MSPs have been indexed to production costs following cost of production index in the Aglink-Cosimo model, adjusted for 1% growth per year in productivity.

9. This is a simplified assessment, purely as an example to illustrate possible costs. The allocation of products by recipients does affect programme costs.

10. The estimates of per capita consumption provided by FAO using commodity balance sheets data indicate 158kg/person. Household consumer expenditure data for 2011 indicate 144 kg/person (NSSO, 2013).

11. This analysis abstracts from important issues of waste or programme inefficiencies which may mean that people do not receive the full benefits of the programme.

12. India has a Lorenz ratio of about 0.38 which implies a disproportionate number of people with incomes less than the average income used in the model. Expenditures on various food groups vary significantly over the income distribution, and by rural or urban location. For example, cereal expenditures as a share of total expenditures varied from 19% among the poorest in India to 3% in the highest class in urban areas.

13. The expenditure shares use the average of urban and rural, as found in NSSO (2013).

14. In these estimates, milk includes milk from all sources.

References

Chand, R. and P.S. Birthal (2011), "Food Grain Stock Requirement during 12th Five-Year Plan", NCAP *Working Paper 9*, National Centre for Agricultural Economics and Policy Research, New Delhi.

Chand, R. and S.K. Srivastava (2014), "Changes in the Rural Labour Market and Their Implications for Agriculture", *Economic and Political Weekly*, Vol XIIX, No. 10.

Conway, G.R. and E.B. Barbier (1988), "After the Green Revolution. Sustainable and equitable agricultural development", *Futures*, Vol. 20, pp. 651-670.

Cunningham, K. (2009), "Rural and urban linkages: Operation Flood's role in India's dairy development", *IFPRI Discussion Paper*, No. 00924, International Food Policy Research Institute, Washington, DC.

Divya J. and S.L. Belagali (2012), "Impact of Chemical Fertilisers in Selected Agricultural Areas of Mysore District, Karnatka, India", *Agris On-line Papers in Economics and Informatics*, Vol. 2 (3), pp. 1449-1458.

Drèze, J. (2013), "From the granary to the plate", in *The Hindu*, 1 August 2013.

FAO (2005), National Aquaculture Sector Overview Fact Sheets: India. *www.fao.org/fishery/countrysector/naso_india/en*.

FAO (2011). *The State of Food and Agriculture: Women in Agriculture*, Food and Agriculture Organization, Rome.

FAO (2013), *The State of Food Insecurity. The multiple dimensions of food security,* Food and Agriculture Organization, Rome.

FAO (2014), *FAOSTAT* (database), *http://faostat.fao.org/*.

Gautam M. and P.K. Aggarwal (2013), *Yield Gaps in Cereals: Progress and Potential*, Unpublished paper, World Bank, Washington D.C.

Global Trade Information Services (2014), *Global Trade Atlas* (database), *www.gtis.com/gta.*

Government of India, *India Labour Journal* (various issues), *http://labourbureau.nic.in/main2.html.*

Government of India (2010), *Agricultural Statistics at a Glance 2010*, Government of India, New Delhi.

Government of India (2012), *Agricultural Statistics at a Glance 2012*, Government of India, New Delhi.

Government of India (2013a), *Economic Survey 2012-13*, Government of India, New Delhi.

Government of India (2013b), *Agricultural Statistics at a Glance 2013*, Government of India, New Delhi.

Government of India (2013c), *Twelfth Five-Year Plan (2012-17)*, Government of India, New Delhi.

Government of India (2013d), *Toward Achieving the Millennium Development Goals – India 2013*, Government of India, New Delhi.

Government of India (2013e), *State of Indian Agriculture 2012-13*, Government of India, New Delhi

Government of India (2013f), *The Gazette of India – National Food Security Act*, Government of India, New Delhi.

Government of India (2014a), *Census 2010-2011*, Government of India, New Delhi.

Government of India (2014b), *Minimum Support Prices* (database), *http://cacp.dacnet.nic.inc.*

Government of India (2014c), *Seednet India Portal, http://seednet.gov.in/.*

Government of India (2014d), *Union Budget 2014-15, http://indiabudget.nic.in/.*

Gulati, A., J. Gujral, and T. Nandakumar (2012), "National Food Security Bill – Challenges and Options", Discussion Paper No. 2, *Commission for Agricultural Costs and Prices*, Government of India, New Delhi.

Gulati, A., J Surbhi and A Hoda (2013), "Farm trade: tapping the hidden potential", Discussion Paper No. 3, *Commission for Agricultural Costs and Prices*, Government of India, New Delhi.

ICAR (2010), *Degraded and Wastelands of India: status and spatial distribution*, Indian Council for Agricultural Research, New Delhi.

IMF (2014), *World Economic Outlook* (database), *www.imf.org/external/pubs/ft/weo/2013/02/weodata/index.aspx*

Kumar, P. (2013), *Demand and Supply of Commodities in India*, MacMillan Publishers, London.

Kumar, P., M. Gautam and P.K. Joshi (2013), "Total Factor Productivity: A State Level Analysis", Unpublished publication, World Bank, Washington, DC.

NCAER (2013a), *Agricultural Outlook and Situation Analysis Reports, First Semi-Annual Medium Term Agricultural Outlook Report, February 2013*, National Council of Applied Economic Research, New Delhi.

NCAER (2013b), *Agricultural Outlook and Situation Analysis Reports, Second Semi-Annual Medium Term Agricultural Outlook Report, September 2013*, National Council of Applied Economic Research, New Delhi.

NSSO (2012), *Nutritional Intake in India, NSS 66th Round*, National Sample Survey Organisation, New Delhi.

NSSO (2013), *Key Indicators of Household Consumer Expenditure in India, NSS 68th Round (July 2011-June 2012)*, National Sample Survey Organisation, New Delhi.

OECD (2013), *OECD Economic Outlook*, Vol. 2013/2, OECD Publishing. doi: *http://dx.doi.org/10.1787/eco_outlook-v2013-2-en*.

OECD (2014). SIGI Index (Database), *http://genderindex.org/*.

Papola, T.S. (2006), Employment Trends in India, *Institute for Studies in Industrial Development*, New Delhi, India.

Rabobank International (2001), *Indian Seed Industry – On the threshold of consolidation*, Rabobank International, Utrecht.

Rao, N. (2011), "Women's Access to Land: An Asian Perspective", Presentation at the UNWOMEN Expert Group Meeting on Enabling rural women's economic empowerment: institutions, opportunities and participation, Accra, 20-23 September 2011.

Sekhar, C.S.C. (2012), "Agricultural Market Integration in India", *Food Policy*, Vol. 37, pp. 309-322.

Shetty, P.K., S. Ayyappan and M.S. Swaminathan (eds.) (2013), *Climate Change and Sustainable Food Security*, National Institute of Advanced Studies, Bangalore.

Tara Satyavathi, C., Ch. Bharadwaj and P.S. Brahmanand (2010), "Role of Farm Women in Agriculture: Lessons Learned", *Gender, Technology and Development*, Vol. 14 (3), pp. 441-449.

Timmer, C.P. (1984), *A model of rice marketing margins in Indonesia*, Food Research Institute Studies, Vol. 13(2).

UNICEF (2014), *Statistics and Monitoring* (database), *www.unicef.org/statistics/*.

USDA (2012), "Global Agricultural Information Network – June 20, 2012", United States Department of Agriculture, Washington, DC. GAIN Report Number: IN2081.

World Bank (2014a), *World Development Indicators* (database), *http://data.worldbank.org/data-catalog/world-development-indicators*.

World Bank (2014b), *Commodity Price Data* (database), *http://data.worldbank.org/data-catalog/commodity-price-data*.

Chapter 3

Biofuels

This chapter describes the market situation and the latest set of quantitative medium-term projections for global and national biofuel markets for the ten-year period, 2014-23. It covers the developments expected in world and national ethanol and biodiesel prices, production, use, trade and stocks. The quantitative projections are developed with the aid of the partial equilibrium Aglink-Cosimo model of world agriculture. The chapter also includes three boxes that explain the uncertainties around the US Environmental Protection Agency (EPA) decision concerning the levels of biofuels mandates, the influence of petrol price controls on hydrous ethanol prices in Brazil, and, sub-national policies supporting biofuels. The chapter concludes with a discussion of some main issues and uncertainties that may have an impact on the medium-term outlook for biofuels. These include biofuel policies, and specific market developments influencing production, consumption and trade in biofuels.

Market situation

The year 2013 was marked by several policy decisions that have strongly influenced the market environment for biofuels. The European Union put in place trade measures against imports of biofuels from Argentina, Indonesia and the United States. There were also proposals towards lower first generation biofuels targets for 2020 in the European Renewable Energy Directive (RED). In Brazil, the ethanol blending requirement was raised to 25% for low blends.[1] At the same time, artificially lower domestic petrol prices in Brazil had some impacts on the use of high blends of ethanol. In Argentina and Indonesia, domestic biodiesel mandates were increased – partly in response to European anti-dumping measures. And for the first time, the EPA made proposals to reduce the total, advanced and cellulosic biofuel mandates for 2014.

The availability of cereals, oilseeds and palm oil in 2013 improved compared to 2012, and thus commodity prices edged lower. In 2013, world ethanol[2] and biodiesel[3] prices continued their declines from their historical high levels of 2011 in a context of ample supply for both ethanol and biodiesel.

Projection highlights

- Ethanol prices (Figure 3.1) are projected to increase in line with the inflation rates and crude oil prices over the next decade. Biodiesel prices are also expected to increase but their growth should be slower, mostly driven by the expected growth in vegetable oil prices and to a lesser extent by the growth in crude oil prices.

- Increasing domestic demand in key exporting countries is expected to raise biodiesel prices in 2016 and 2017. This trend is in line with the assumptions in this *Outlook* on the continuation of biofuel policies.

- Global ethanol and biodiesel production are both expected to expand to reach, respectively, 158 bln L and 40 bln L by 2023. Ethanol and biodiesel will continue to be mostly produced from feedstocks that can also be used for food. By 2023, 12%, 28% and 14% of world coarse grains, sugar cane, and vegetable oil production, respectively, are expected to be used to produce biofuels.

- Ethanol use in the United States will be limited by the ethanol blend wall[4] and should only grow marginally in the latter years of the projection period, leaving additional biodiesel use necessary to meet the advanced and total mandates. The policy driven imports of sugarcane based ethanol to fill the advanced gap[5] are also expected to flatten at the end of the next decade to reach 10 bln L by 2023. It is assumed that by 2023 only 12% of the US cellulosic mandate will be implemented.

- For the European Union, the *Outlook* assumes that the fulfilment percentage of the RED coming from biofuels should reach 8.5% in 2020.[6] Biodiesel use is expected to increase in the first part of the projection period and then to stay at a plateau of 19 bln L from 2020 onwards. The increase in production of second generation biofuel will remain very limited. Imports will be necessary to satisfy the RED target.

Figure 3.1. **Biofuel prices to remain almost constant in real terms**

Evolution of prices expressed in nominal terms (left) and in real terms (right)

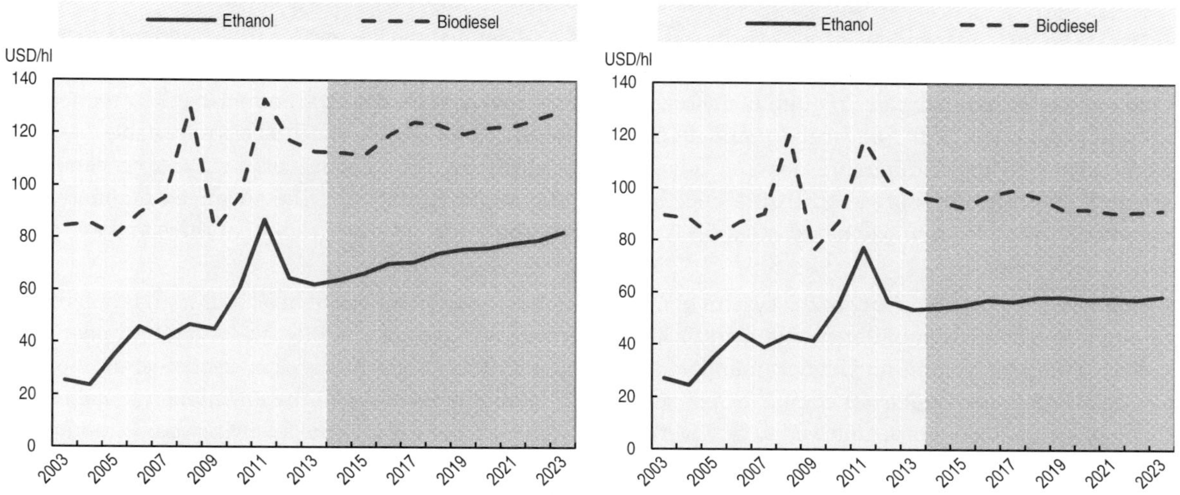

Notes: Ethanol: Brazil, Sao Paulo (anhydrous, ex-distillery), Biodiesel: Producer price, Germany, net of biodiesel tariff and energy tax.
Source: OECD and FAO Secretariats.

StatLink ⬛⬛⬛ http://dx.doi.org/10.1787/888933099713

Market trends and prospects

Main assumptions

Over the last seven years, a certain number of developed and developing countries have implemented ambitious biofuel targets or mandates as well as other support measures to the biofuel sector. Their motivation was based mainly on different, and in some cases complementary objectives, including achieving a high level of energy security, reducing greenhouse gas emission, and increasing domestic value added products for export as well as rural development.

In the United States, biofuel production and use are mainly driven by policies in place, namely the Renewable Fuel Standard (RFS2) set in 2007. It is important to note that this *Outlook* does not take into account the latest proposal[7] made by the EPA to reduce the total, the advanced and the cellulosic mandates for 2014. A final decision by the EPA is expected in June 2014 at the earliest. Uncertainties around this proposal are described in Box 3.1.

The *Outlook* assumes that it is unlikely that the strong increases for lingo-cellulosic biomass based biofuels, which are foreseen in the RFS2, can be met as the industry does not seem to be prepared for large scale production technologies in the upcoming years. It is assumed that by 2023 only 12% of the cellulosic mandate will be implemented and that the difference between the EISA cellulosic mandate and the assumed mandate will be entirely waived. This means that the *Outlook* assumes the United States advanced and the total mandates to be respectively 67% and 40% lower than what is specified in RFS2. The biodiesel mandate is assumed to remain constant. As a consequence, the advanced gap should reach 11.6 bln L by 2023. The biodiesel blender tax credit is not expected to be reinstated.

Box 3.1. **Uncertainties around the Environmental Protection Agency (EPA) decision concerning the levels of US biofuels mandates**

The US Energy Independence and Security Act (EISA) of 2007 defined the Renewable Fuel Standard programme known as RFS2.[1] Under this programme,[2] EISA established four quantitative annual mandates up to 2022. The total and advanced mandates require fuels to achieve respectively at least a 20% and a 50% GHG reduction. A minimum quantity of the advanced mandate must come from biodiesel and cellulosic renewable fuels. The biodiesel and cellulosic minimums leave an advanced gap which can be met with fuels such as sugarcane based ethanol. The conventional gap, the difference between the total mandate and the advanced mandate could potentially come from maize based ethanol. The mandates only restrict minimum quantities and are nested within each other.

Blenders, the obligated party in the system of mandates, must show compliance in all four mandate categories through the submission of Renewable Identification Numbers (RINs) to EPA. A RIN is a 38-digit number which indicates the year, volume and highest mandate classification the renewable fuel is capable of meeting. A blender can detach and use the RIN for compliance or sell the RIN to another blender on the RIN market to help satisfy their obligation. Blenders are allowed to "rollover" or run a "deficit" of RINs into the following year, although only up to 20% of a given mandate may be met with RINs produced in the previous or following year. RIN prices have experienced important variations over recent years as stakeholders may be concerned with issues such as the ethanol blend wall,[3] the availability of certain category of biofuels or the uncertainties concerning future mandate levels.

Since the establishment of EISA, the EPA has provided the minimum quantities for each of the four classes of biofuels required each year. Thus far, the production capacity for cellulosic ethanol has lagged well behind the mandated quantities. Until now the EPA has systematically chosen to reduce the applicable volume of cellulosic biofuels. In that situation, EPA would have been allowed to also reduce the applicable volume of advanced biofuel and total renewable fuel specified in RFS2. EPA has always kept the total and advanced mandate at their original levels given expected availability of biofuels (being biodiesel, imported sugarcane based ethanol or other advanced biofuels) to meet the advanced mandate.

The implementation decision of the EPA for 2014 is not yet known. In November 2013, EPA made a proposal to cut for the first time the total renewable fuel mandate, the total advanced biofuels mandate as well as the cellulosic mandate for 2014. This proposal is significantly below the final 2013 RFS and the initial numbers set by EISA for 2014 (Figure 3.2). The biodiesel mandate for 2014 is proposed to remain the same as in 2013.

Figure 3.2. **Structure of US biofuel mandates in 2013, in EISA 2014 and in the EPA proposal for 2014**

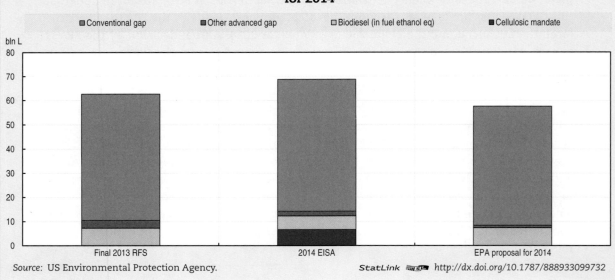

Source: US Environmental Protection Agency.

StatLink ⟐ http://dx.doi.org/10.1787/888933099732

Box 3.1. **Uncertainties around the Environmental Protection Agency (EPA)
decision concerning the levels of US biofuels mandates**

The main arguments behind this cut are:

● The limitations for the industry to produce cellulosic biofuels;

● The issue of ethanol blend wall. Quantitative biofuel mandates have been rising in the United States
since the establishment of EISA whereas motor fuel use has been decreasing. In 2012, the maximum
blend of ethanol for conventional petrol vehicles was set at 15% for vehicles produced in 2001 or later.
However, the dispensing of E15[4] and E85[5] is not widespread in the United States. For the EPA, the blend
wall problem represents a circumstance that warrants a reduction in the mandated volumes for 2014
under the "inadequate domestic supply" waiver provision in the RFS.

A period of comments on the proposal for all stakeholders ended at the end of January 2014. The final EPA
rule-making on 2014 mandates is expected in June 2014 and could be slightly different from the proposal.
EPA has announced that it will also propose a methodology to derive future mandates. This would prevent
periods of uncertainties on US biofuel markets and the RIN spot markets when the annual EPA decisions
are not known. This methodology is likely to take into account the fact that, unless retailers have strong
incentives to propose higher blends at the pump, ethanol use in the United States will be limited in the
future by the blend wall and will not be able to reach the level specified in EISA. Any reduction in total,
advanced and cellulosic mandates in the coming years will have an impact on US biofuel use and
production especially as the cellulosic mandates was set to expand massively. If the advanced gap is
reduced significantly it is likely that the two way ethanol trade between the United States and Brazil will be
reduced. The uncertainty around the EPA implementation decision comes at a period when the US
administration is seeking to develop its bioeconomy.[6]

1. www.epa.gov/OTAQ/fuels/renewablefuels/.
2. US biofuel policies were described in details in OECD – FAO (2012).
3. The blend wall term refers to short run technical constraints that act as an impediment to increased ethanol use.
4. E15 refers to gasohol with 15% volume of ethanol blended into gasoline. E10 is still the most commonly available gasohol in the
   United States.
5. E85 refers to gasohol with 85% volume of ethanol blended into gasoline. E85 is used by flex fuel vehicles.
6. The National bioeconomy blueprint was released in April 2012: www.whitehouse.gov/sites/default/files/microsites/ostp/
   national_bioeconomy_blueprint_april_2012.pdf.

In the United States the maximum amount of ethanol that can be mixed with petrol in
low blends is 15% for cars built after 2001. Since older cars will eventually leave the fleet,
the amount of ethanol being consumed in low blend mixes is assumed to increase over the
next decade to reach a maximum level of 14% by 2020. However, this assumption is subject
to uncertainty as at present the supply of E15 blends[8] to consumers is encountering some
difficulties. There are different reasons for this: retailers may not be willing to supply E15
due to the fact that earlier car warrantees may limit ethanol content to the previous 10%
limit; mis-fuelling of vehicles by consumers or simply problems of availability at the pump.
The quantity of ethanol to be used over the next decade in the United States will be limited
by the blend wall and by the expected decrease in petrol consumption.

In the European Union, the 2009 RED[9] states that renewable fuels (including non-
liquids) should increase to 10% of total transport fuel use by 2020 on an energy equivalent
basis. At the moment, the political environment for biofuels in the European Union is
marked by a certain degree of uncertainty. The European Parliament proposed a revision of
the RED in September 2013. Energy ministers did not reach a consensus on the reform in
December 2013.

In January 2014, the European Commission proposed a framework providing predictable and certain energy and climate objectives[10] applicable beyond 2020 and up to 2030. The framework underlined that first generation biofuels have a limited role in decarbonising the transport sector, and that a range of alternative renewable fuels and a mix of targeted policy measures are needed to address the challenges of the transport sector in a 2030 perspective, but it did not propose new targets for the transport sector after 2020.

Any reform in the coming years in the European Union will have some impact on global biodiesel and ethanol markets. This *Outlook* assumes a continuation of actual mandates and tax reductions by EU countries. When accounting for the fact that each unit of second generation biofuel (including those produced from used cooking oil) consumed counts double for the purpose of the Directive, the *Outlook* assumes that the fulfilment percentage coming from biofuels expressed in energy share should reach 8.5% in 2020.

In Brazil, the blending requirement (in volume share) in petrol is 25%. Flex-fuel vehicles can either run on E25 gasohol or on E100 (hydrous ethanol).[11] Box 3.2 describes the influence of petrol price controls on Brazilian hydrous ethanol prices. Contrary to what was done over the past few years to temper Brazilian price inflation, this *Outlook* assumes that Petrobras[12] will seek convergence between the international and the domestic retail prices of petrol over the next decade.[13]

Box 3.2. **The influence of petrol price controls on hydrous ethanol prices in Brazil**

Sugarcane based ethanol has been a key component of Brazil's energy policy for a long time. Just after the first oil crisis, the Brazilian government launched the PROALCOOL programme to improve the country's energy self-sufficiency and also the market for sugar cane. Since April 2011, the blend rate for anhydrous ethanol and petrol has to range between 18% and 25%. At present, gasohol sold at the pump is required to be E25. The Brazilian fleet of flex-fuel vehicles that can run either on gasohol or hydrous ethanol (E100) is about 20 million, the biggest in the world. Flex-fuel vehicles represented 87% of cars sold in Brazil in 2012.

With the discovery and development of huge pre-salt petroleum deposits offshore Brazil, the priority the government has given to ethanol as a domestic energy source has slackened. Along with this downgrading in importance, and ensuing credit problems, the sugarcane industry has undergone a downturn and found itself in a period of stagnation and reduced greenfield investment.

In addition to the sector's internal problems, the profitability of hydrous ethanol has also been negatively affected by:

● the relatively more attractive sugar prices in the international market

● price controls imposed on transport fuels sold by Petrobras.[1]

Since 2010, Brazil's rate of inflation has operated persistently between the centre of the target (4.5% p.a.) and its upper bound (6.5% p.a.). To avoid a rise in interest rates, the government resorted to various indirect policies to attenuate price inflation. One of these has been to regulate the prices of some of Petrobras' refined petroleum products. Those products that have a greater weight in the IPCA (Brazilian Consumer Price Index), such as diesel oil and especially petrol, have had their prices effectively controlled. Other products, such as naphtha and kerosene for aviation, which have a lower weight in the inflation index, have been subject to more frequent readjustments in prices.

Box 3.2. **The influence of petrol price controls on hydrous ethanol prices in Brazil** (cont.)

The Petrobras decision to not readjust petrol prices with world parity levels has hampered the sugarcane industry. Hydrous ethanol is a substitute for E20-E25 gasohol and remains competitive on an energy equivalent basis at a price up to 70%, on average, of the gasohol price. Since the price of petrol has remained fixed below international levels, with rising production costs, hydrous ethanol has become less a competitive with gasohol, cutting into the profit margins of ethanol producers.

The two simulations presented below estimate the impact of the Petrobras price policy on hydrous ethanol prices. However, while hydrous ethanol remains less profitable as long as petrol prices remain fixed, other government regulations requiring the blending of between 18 to 25% of anhydrous ethanol with petrol as gasohol has increased the demand for this alternative ethanol fuel.

Simulation 1: At what gasohol price is the production of hydrous ethanol economically viable, considering its energy equivalence to be 70% of gasohol?

Production costs compiled by PECEGE (Programme of Continuing Education in Economics and Management) from ESALQ/USP (Luiz de Queiroz College of Agriculture of the University of São Paulo), enabled a simulation of the sales price for gasohol at a gas station pump that would make the price of hydrous ethanol economically viable. Based on data from the 2012/13 harvest, this analysis was carried out in traditional ethanol producing states (São Paulo and Paraná) as well as in regions where the expansion of sugarcane for ethanol is taking place (Minas Gerais, Goiás, Mato Grosso do Sul and Mato Grosso) (Table 3.1).

Table 3.1. **Simulation of gasohol and hydrous ethanol prices based on the harvest data for 2012/13**

BRL/litre

Region	Operating cost	Economic cost[1]	Distribution cost	Econ. viable hydrous ethanol price	Econ. viable gasohol price	Hydrous ethanol price in 12/13 harvest[2]	Gasohol price in 12/13 harvest[2]
Traditional	1.10	1.30	0.67	1.97	2.81	1.83	2.67
Expansion	1.07	1.27	0.90	2.17	3.10	1.99	2.83

1. *Source:* PECEGE
2. *Source:* Brazilian National Agency of Petroleum, Natural Gas and Biofuels (ANP).

StatLink ᵐᵤₛₚ *http://dx.doi.org/10.1787/888933101157*

According to the simulation results, in order for it to be economically feasible to market hydrous ethanol, on average, a litre of gasohol would have to be sold for BRL 2.81 in São Paulo and in Paraná, and at BRL 3.10 in the other states. These values suggest that the price of hydrous ethanol was off by BRL 0.14 and by BRL 0.18 per litre in each region respectively.

Box 3.2. **The influence of petrol price controls on hydrous ethanol prices in Brazil** (cont.)

Simulation 2: What would be the price of hydrous ethanol if the price of petrol followed the price variation for crude oil in the international market and if Petrobras was not used to fight inflation?

Supposing Petrobras maintained since 2006 a direct relationship between i) the price of petrol in the domestic market and ii) variations of oil quotations in the international market, controlled by variations in the exchange rate, then on average a litre of gasohol would be sold in the Traditional Region at BRL 4.21 and in the Expansion Region at BRL 4.44[2]. Assuming that the ratio of 0.7 between hydrous ethanol and gasohol prices operates in these markets, a litre of hydrous ethanol would be sold, on average, at BRL 2.95 and BRL 3.11 in each region, respectively that is, at 61% and 56% higher than occurred (Table 3.2). These results clearly suggest, on the one hand, that the price controls on petrol have contributed to containing inflation but that on the other hand, they have severely reduced the profitability of the sugarcane industry. However, it is difficult to judge whether a total liberalisation of petrol prices in Brazil would result in a much greater use of hydrous ethanol because the supply of the latter is also a function of volatile sugar prices.

Table 3.2. **Price simulation presupposing that petrol had fully accompanied oil price variations and the Brazilian exchange rate**

BRL/litre

| Period | Traditional Area | | | | Expansion Area | | | |
| | Gasohol | | Hydrous Ethanol | | Gasohol | | Hydrous Ethanol | |
	Observed Price	Simulated Price	Observed Price	Simulated Price	Observed Price	Simulated Price	Observed Price	Simulated Price
Sep-06	2.44	2.26	1.32	1.58	2.58	2.38	1.71	1.67
Sep-07	2.40	2.44	1.11	1.71	2.45	2.57	1.41	1.80
Sep-08	2.41	2.65	1.29	1.86	2.51	2.79	1.59	1.95
Sep-09	2.39	2.22	1.32	1.55	2.47	2.34	1.53	1.64
Sep-10	2.46	2.22	1.44	1.56	2.53	2.34	1.62	1.64
Sep-11	2.67	3.23	1.89	2.26	2.84	3.40	2.00	2.38
Sep-12	2.63	3.82	1.77	2.68	2.80	4.03	1.93	2.82
Sep-13	2.72	4.21	1.75	2.95	2.89	4.44	1.95	3.11

Sources: Brazilian National Agency of Petroleum, Natural Gas and Biofuels (ANP), Central Bank and International Monetary Fund.

StatLink ᔑᘻᔑ *http://dx.doi.org/10.1787/888933101176*

Note: This box has been prepared by Antonio Carlos Kfouri Aidar, Director of Control, and Felipe Serigati, Project Coordinator at FGV Projetos. It is a summary of an article published in the Agroanalysis magazine entitled "The profitability of the sugar and ethanol sector depends on Petrobras".

1. Petrobras is a semi-public Brazilian multinational energy corporation. It is the largest company in the Southern Hemisphere (by market capitalisation) and the largest in Latin America (measured in 2011 revenues).
2. Obviously there are other factors influencing petrol prices in Brazil such as a transformation margin or taxes.

In response to anti-dumping duties on its biodiesel shipments, Argentina increased domestic biodiesel blending requirements to 10% in February 2014. A gradual increase to the 10% blending requirement is taken into account in this *Outlook*.

In developing countries, except for Brazil, the *Outlook* assumes that only 40% of biofuel targets can be reached. This assumption reduces the pressure on world biodiesel prices where developing countries account for a larger share of world trade compared to ethanol. In Indonesia, where a 25% biodiesel blending requirement is targeted for 2025, the *Outlook* assumes that only 20% of this target can be reached by 2023. A simulation, which assumed that Indonesia is going to reach its biodiesel target, revealed strong impacts and is described in Box 5.1 in the Oilseeds Chapter.

Prices

World ethanol prices are projected to increase by 9% in real terms over the projection period. Two elements are expected to strongly influence the level of ethanol prices. First, the *Outlook* expects an increase in market-driven demand of hydrous ethanol by owners of flex-fuel cars in Brazil, given the assumptions of strong crude oil prices and of Petrobas not freezing the retail price of petrol anymore. Second, policies in place such as the 25% blending requirement in Brazil and the level of the advanced gap in the United States should also reinforce ethanol prices. The domestic US corn-based ethanol price should not increase as much as the Brazilian world ethanol price, and the United States are expected to be exporting 8% of its domestic production by 2023.

In line with world vegetable oil prices, world biodiesel prices expressed in real terms are expected to decrease by 6% over the outlook period. They are not expected to be strongly influenced by the increasing crude oil prices as demand of biodiesel is mostly driven by policies in place and not by market forces. In the early years of the projections, increasing policy-dictated domestic demand in two key exporting countries, Argentina and Indonesia as well as anti-dumping measures in place in the European Union are expected to raise biodiesel prices above their medium-term trend.

Production and use of ethanol

After a significant decline in 2012, global ethanol production increased in 2013, surpassing the levels of 2011 due to lower prices for coarse grains and sugar. This increasing trend is assumed to prevail during the outlook period: world ethanol supply should reach some 158 bln L by 2023 (Figure 3.3). The three major ethanol producers are expected to remain the United States, Brazil and the European Union (Figure 3.4).

Ethanol production in developing countries is projected to increase from 45 bln L in 2013 to 71 bln L in 2023, with Brazil accounting for most of the supply increase. The growing use of ethanol in Brazil is linked to the mandatory 25% ethanol blending requirement in petrol, the development of the flex-fuel industry, and the import demand from the United States to fulfil the advanced biofuel mandate.

In the United States, the projected total biofuel production is driven by assumptions on how the EPA will deal with the total, the advanced, the biodiesel and the cellulosic mandates in the coming decade. The assumptions taken in this *Outlook* have been described at the beginning of this section. Ethanol production in the United States is projected to increase from 50 bln L in 2013 to 71 bln L by 2023. In 2015, the conventional gap[14] will reach its maximum level of almost 57 bln L. From 2016 onwards, the maize based

Figure 3.3. **Development of the world ethanol market**

■ World ethanol production   □ World ethanol trade

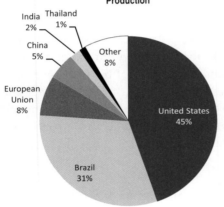

Source: OECD and FAO Secretariats.

StatLink ⭤ *http://dx.doi.org/10.1787/888933099751*

Figure 3.4. **Regional distributions of world ethanol production and use in 2023**

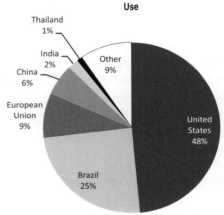

Source: OECD and FAO Secretariats.

StatLink ⭤ *http://dx.doi.org/10.1787/888933099770*

ethanol production in excess of the conventional gap is expected to be exported. The growth in US ethanol supply over the remaining part of the outlook period should mostly arise from ligno-cellulosic biomass based ethanol, where growth is assumed to accelerate after 2016 to reach 7.3 bln L by 2023.

The continuous increase in the total and advanced mandates is a major driver for the growth in US ethanol use over the projection period. However, this growth is limited by the blend wall and the declining petrol use prospects over the next decade. The blend wall is expected to reach its maximum level of 14% by 2020, leaving ethanol use to only grow marginally at the end of the projection period with the limited development of flex-fuel vehicles. Indeed, a flex-fuel car sector would develop in the United States only if the ethanol to petrol consumer price ratio would fall to the energy content of ethanol. This should not be the case in this outlook period. Although the advanced gap is expected to flatten from 2020 onwards, ethanol use is expected to remain above supply leaving the United States in a net import position throughout the projection period. Ethanol use is expected to reach almost 74 bln L in 2023.

In the European Union, fuel ethanol production mainly from wheat, coarse grains and sugar beet is projected to reach 12.1 bln L by 2023. Beginning in 2017, with the abolition of sugar quota, it is expected that the production of ethanol from sugar beets will be less profitable than the production of sugar for human consumption. Ethanol production based on sugar beets is thus projected to drop to 1.3 bln L. Ligno-cellulosic biomass based ethanol should grow towards the end of the projection period but should remain marginal. Ethanol fuel use is expected to amount to an average energy share of 6.6% in petrol types for transport fuels by 2023.

Ethanol markets in Brazil are driven by increasing domestic demand for hydrous and anhydrous ethanol due to the 25% blending requirement, and by the development of demand for hydrous ethanol by the flex-fuel vehicles fleet in the context of increasing crude oil prices as well as by import demand from the United States to fulfil the advanced mandate. Brazilian ethanol production is projected to almost double from 25 bln L in 2013 to 50 bln L in 2023, while net exports and use are expected to rise, respectively, from 2 to 11 bln L and 22.4 to 39 bln L.

Production and use of biodiesel

Global biodiesel production stagnated in 2013. In the major producing region, the European Union, biodiesel supply did not increase given the continuing debate on a possible reduction in support for first generation biodiesel linked to the sustainability criteria. Argentinean biodiesel production declined as the European Union introduced anti-dumping duties against their importation.

Global biodiesel production is, however, expected to reach 40 bln L in 2023 corresponding to a 54% increase from 2013 (Figure 3.5). The European Union is expected to be by far the major producer and user of biodiesel (Figure 3.6). Other significant players are Argentina, the United States and Brazil as well as Thailand and Indonesia. Policy will continue to influence consumption patterns in almost all countries.

In 2013, biodiesel production increased in Brazil, Indonesia, Thailand and Malaysia, offsetting the supply reduction in Argentina. Total biodiesel production in developing countries is projected to increase to 16 bln L in 2023. One factor limiting any increase in biodiesel production in developing countries is the availability of alternative feedstocks, such as jatropha, which are not yet suitable for biofuels production on a larger scale.

After a relatively strong decline in the European Union in 2013 (12 bln L versus 13.4 bln L in 2012), biodiesel use is projected to reach a plateau of 19 bln L from 2020 onwards given mandates and tax reductions by European member states. This should represent an average energy share of biodiesel in diesel type fuels of 7.4%. Domestic biodiesel production in the European Union is assumed to increase until 2020 to keep pace with demand. Second generation biodiesel production is not assumed to take off during the outlook period. About 3.2 bln L biodiesel imports will be necessary to satisfy the RED target.

In the United States, the mandate for biodiesel is assumed to stay constant over the projection period at 4.8 bln L. Given a decreasing biodiesel to diesel consumer price ratio, US biodiesel consumption is projected to increase and to be above the mandate in every

Figure 3.5. **Development of the world biodiesel market**

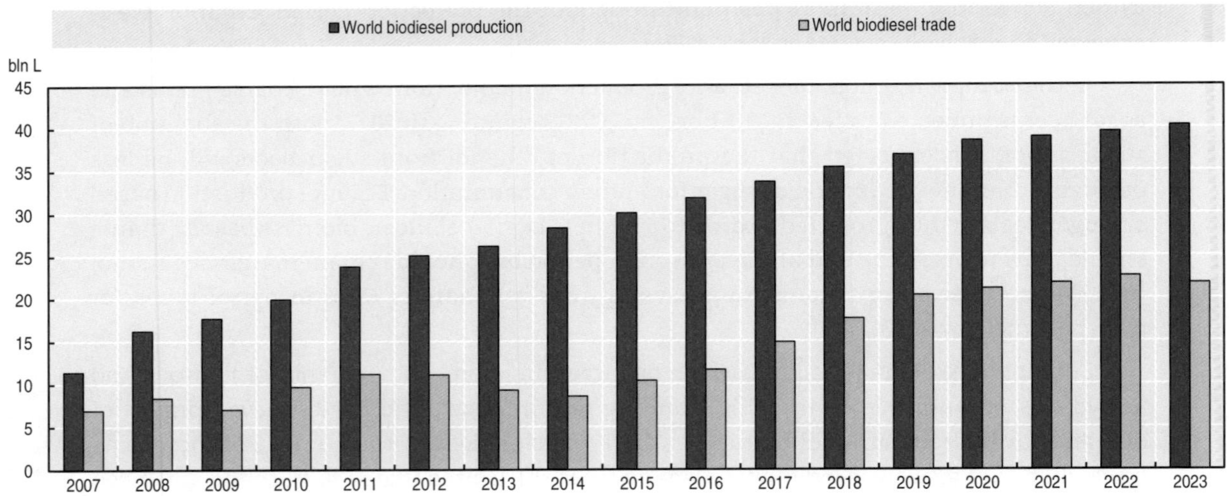

■ World biodiesel production   □ World biodiesel trade

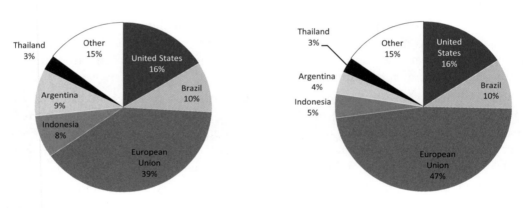

Source: OECD and FAO Secretariats.

StatLink ⏭ http://dx.doi.org/10.1787/888933099739

Figure 3.6. **Regional distributions of world biodiesel production and use in 2023**

Production

Thailand 3%
Other 15%
United States 16%
Brazil 10%
Argentina 9%
Indonesia 8%
European Union 39%

Use

Thailand 3%
Other 15%
United States 16%
Argentina 4%
Brazil 10%
Indonesia 5%
European Union 47%

Source: OECD and FAO Secretariats.

StatLink ⏭ http://dx.doi.org/10.1787/888933099808

year during the next decade. Biodiesel should therefore capture a share of the other advanced gap, lowering the need for imports of sugarcane based ethanol.

Due to the ethanol blend wall, biodiesel use should increase more strongly in the last years of the projection period to reach 6.5 bln L by 2023, helping the fulfilment of the advanced and total mandates.[15] If the EPA chooses lower total, advanced and cellulosic mandates than those that have been assumed in this *Outlook*, it is likely that biodiesel consumption would return very close to the mandate level. In a context of declining diesel consumption, biodiesel blending in diesel type fuels is expected to increase from 1.4% in 2013 to 2.7% in 2023. Biodiesel from tallow or other animal fat is expected to represent about 37% of total US production.

The *Outlook* assumes increasing biodiesel production in developing countries, mainly driven by the developments in Argentina and Indonesia. Argentinean biodiesel production is expected to be affected in 2014, as it was in 2013, by anti-dumping duties imposed by the European Union. It should reach 3.6 bln L by 2023 to satisfy both export and domestic demand. The *Outlook* assumes biodiesel use to rise in Argentina up to 1.7 bln L in 2023, given a stronger domestic biodiesel blending requirement at 10% and sustained demand for diesel. Competition between export and domestic demand is also expected to increase in Indonesia. Although the blending requirements will increase in the coming years, it is expected that Indonesia will satisfy both markets. Assuming that Indonesia can reach only 20% of their biodiesel targets, production increases from 1.8 bln L in 2013 to 3.3 bln L by 2023.

Trade in ethanol and biodiesel

Global ethanol trade is set to increase strongly. Most of this increase is due to the ethanol trade between Brazil and the United States. This trade[16] is expected to grow until 2020 when the ethanol blend wall should be reached, limiting additional ethanol use in the United States. The United States is expected to import about 10 bln L of sugarcane based ethanol from Brazil by 2023. At the same time, given strong world ethanol prices and relatively lower domestic corn based ethanol prices, the United States is expected to export 5 bln L of maize based ethanol by 2023. A large share of these exports will be destined to the Brazilian market to satisfy ethanol demand.

Canada and the European Union should also import US ethanol. The level of European imports would be strongly influenced by the conclusion of the actual trade dispute[17] between the United States and the European Union. Imports of ethanol into the European Union should be of about 1.6 bln L on average over the projection period, as domestic production is expected to grow at the same rate as demand. Developing countries are net exporters of ethanol. Brazil (11 bln L), India, Pakistan, South Africa and Thailand (1.2 bln L combined) are expected to dominate ethanol exports among developing countries.

Biodiesel trade is projected to increase only slightly over the next ten years, with Argentina remaining the major exporter followed by Indonesia. The export growth potential of both countries is expected to be limited due to domestic biodiesel targets and strong import restrictions in the European Union in 2014 and 2015. Net import demand in the European Union should stay at a plateau of 3.2 bln L during the last years of the projection period as the RED target is defined for 2020, and diesel use is expected to decrease slightly afterwards. The United States is expected to export a small surplus of biodiesel over the projection period. US exports are expected to decline in the last years of the projection period, when biodiesel use increases strongly to meet the total and advanced mandates.

Feedstocks used to produce biofuels

Coarse grains and sugarcane will remain the dominant ethanol feedstock (Figure 3.7), while vegetable oil continues to dominate biodiesel production (Figure 3.8). The share of coarse grain based ethanol production in global ethanol production is reduced by about 13% over the outlook period to 45% in 2023, which corresponds to 12% of global coarse grain production. The share of sugar crops share of world ethanol production increases from 25% in 2013 to 31% in 2023. 28% of global sugar cane production is expected to be used for ethanol production in 2023. Ligno-cellulosic biomass based ethanol is projected to account for 5% of world ethanol production by 2023. Cellulosic ethanol is expected to be mostly produced in the United States on the assumption that the cellulosic mandate would be filled at 12% in 2023.

Figure 3.7. **Share of feedstocks used for ethanol production**

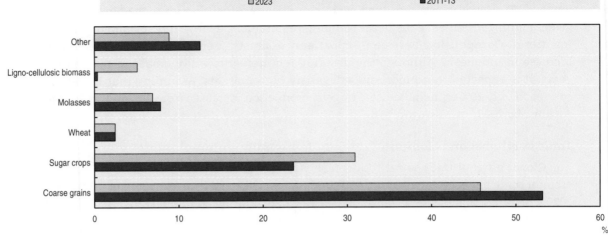

Note: Sugar crops include ethanol produced from sugar cane and from sugar beets.
Source: OECD and FAO Secretariats.

StatLink ꜟ http://dx.doi.org/10.1787/888933099827

Figure 3.8. **Share of feedstocks used for biodiesel production**

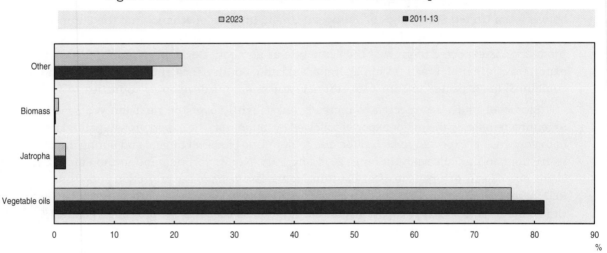

Source: OECD and FAO Secretariats.

StatLink ꜟ http://dx.doi.org/10.1787/888933099846

The share of biodiesel produced from vegetable oil in global biodiesel production decreases from 80% in 2013 to 76% in 2023, which corresponds to 14% of global vegetable oil production in 2023. The share of biodiesel produced from other sources, mostly used cooking oil and animal tallow, is expected to expand from 18% in 2013 to 21% in 2023 given the fact that each consumed unit of biodiesel produced from cooking oil in the European Union counts double for the RED targets.

Main issues and uncertainties

The outlook for biofuel markets is strongly influenced by policies in place. It is likely that the policy assumptions made in this *Outlook* are not going to reflect the reality of the coming decade. In the course of 2013, for the first time since the beginning of the biofuel era, it became clear that biofuel policies and implied targets or mandates may face explicit downward revisions in the future.

In November 2013, the EPA proposed to lower the total, the advanced, and the cellulosic mandates because of the blend wall issue and the limitations in large scale production of advanced biofuels such as second generation ones (Box 3.1). In December 2013, European ministers could not reach an agreement on the revision of the RED that was proposed by the European Parliament. This revision was seeking to limit at 6% the extent to which food-derived fuels can contribute to the 10% targets, and also to take indirect land use changes into account.

The question of energy security in a context of high crude oil prices was prioritised in the initial development of the biofuel sector. If major biofuel producing countries were to become less dependent on imported fossil fuels (like Brazil or the United States, for example), it is likely that the policy environment around biofuel production might become less favourable.

Box 3.3 describes sub-national policies supporting biofuels as these may play a bigger role in the coming years where national policies begin to be phased down. It is interesting to note that in the United States, even if mandates were to be reduced according to the EPA proposal of November 2013 and hence the policy driven two-way trade between the United States and Brazil was to almost disappear, the Low Carbon Fuel Standard[18] of the State of California would require some imports of sugarcane based ethanol.

Box 3.3. **Sub-national policies supporting biofuels**

Over the last decade, most OECD countries have adopted policies to support the production or use, or both, of liquid biofuels – mainly ethanol as a substitute for petrol and biodiesel and renewable diesel fuels as substitutes for petroleum diesel. National governments have traditionally played the most important supporting role, through providing capital grants for biofuel factories, bounties or tax benefits proportional to the volume produced or blended and exemptions from excise taxes on marketed biofuels.

In recent years, however, national support policies for first-generation biofuels – i.e. ethanol made from starch or sugar and renewable substitutes for diesel that are made from vegetable oils, tallow or used cooking oil – have been phased down, leaving mainly mandatory blending ratios or volumetric biofuel targets ("biofuel mandates", for short) as the main support mechanisms.

At the sub-national level, however, many other incentives remain in place. When assessing the effects of public policies on the supply and demand of biofuels, and of the feedstock agricultural commodities used for biofuels, it is important to take these additional policies into account. For example, in November 2013 the US Environmental Protection Agency (EPA) proposed to reduce the total annual quota for "advanced biofuels," which heretofore has been met mainly with biodiesel and imported sugarcane based ethanol. If this reduction is confirmed, then imports of ethanol from Brazil are likely to be affected. However, because the US State of California has a Low Carbon Fuel Standard that assigns a lower greenhouse gas value to cane ethanol, it is expected that some of that reduction would be offset by higher imports into California.

Box 3.3. **Sub-national policies supporting biofuels** (cont.)

In countries with strong federal systems, such as Australia, Canada, Mexico and the United States, some states and provinces have instituted biofuel mandates that exceed those of their federal governments. The Provinces of Saskatchewan and Manitoba require, respectively, 7.5% and 8.5% ethanol in their gasoline, in contrast with the federal Canadian requirement of 5%. Similarly, the Province of British Columbia specifies a minimum of 4% biodiesel in its diesel fuel, whereas the federal requirement is just 2%. In the United States, the effect of the Federal Renewable Fuel Standard has been to raise the average ethanol content of blended petrol fuel to almost 10%, which is currently the maximum allowed for most vehicles manufactured before 2001. Nonetheless, a law passed by the State of Minnesota calls for all gasoline blends sold in the state after 20 August 2015 to contain at least 20% ethanol by volume, or the maximum percent of ethanol by volume allowed by the EPA if that percentage is lower. A few US states have also set minimum blending shares for biodiesel.

In Australia, which has no national biofuel mandate, its most populous state, New South Wales, requires a 4% blend of ethanol in its petrol, and 2% biodiesel in its diesel fuel. Mexico likewise has no national mandate, but a 2% biodiesel mandate applies in the municipality of Guadalajara, and there are plans to expand the mandate to Mexico City and Monterrey.

Outside the OECD region, biofuel mandates have often first been introduced at the subnational level. China's current blending of 10% ethanol with petrol is applied only in nine provinces. Ethiopia has an ethanol mandate only for Addis Ababa, and Kenya only in the province of Kisumu. In India, the state government of Maharashtra has recently upped the blending percentage of ethanol with gasoline to 10%, which is twice the national mandate.

Several Canadian provinces (British Columbia, Saskatchewan, Manitoba and Quebec) and US states (Louisiana, Montana, Oregon and Washington) have linked implementation of their biofuel-content mandates with the development of in-state or in-province manufacturing capacity for the mandated fuel. For example, Washington State stipulated that, before for its mandate went into effect, a positive determination would have to be made by the State Department of Ecology that feedstock grown in Washington State could satisfy a 2% biodiesel blending requirement. The biodiesel requirement was increased to 5% once in-state feedstocks and oil-seed crushing capacity were determined to be able to meet the needs of a 3% average blend.

Whereas the federal governments of Canada and the United States formerly granted excise-tax reductions for biofuels, the United States no longer does, and Canada created a new system based on production-linked payments. Nonetheless, three Canadian provinces and thirteen US states offer some reductions in excise taxes or sales taxes for ethanol or biodiesel – sometimes on pure biofuels but in many cases for specific blends, such as E85. In addition, five Canadian provinces and 12 US states provide their own volumetric incentives to support in-state production of ethanol or biodiesel, many at rates equivalent to at least USD 0.05 per litre of pure biofuel.

Although the member states of the European Union are not "sub-national units" in the same sense as those outside the European Union, they are nonetheless subject to the EU-wide policy on biofuels. Seven of the EU's member states still offer exemptions or reductions on the excise tax normally applied to petrol or diesel transport fuels, in many cases only when the biofuel is used in a high-biofuel blend, such as E85.

Sometimes sub-national support policies require the use of locally harvested crops or locally produced biofuel. Ethanol-production plants operating in the US state of Louisiana and deriving their fuel from the distillation of maize must use maize harvested in Louisiana to meet at least 20% of the facility's total feedstock requirement. The US state of Montana's production tax incentive of USD 0.20 per gallon (USD 0.053 per litre) is available only for ethanol produced solely from agricultural products produced in Montana, unless Montana products are unavailable. Missouri's production incentive for ethanol, which pays up to USD 7.5 million cumulative per producer, is contingent on the use of Missouri agricultural products or qualified biomass. In the Canadian province of Nova Scotia, only biodiesel produced within the province is eligible for a CAD 0.154 fuel-tax exemption.

> ### Box 3.3. **Sub-national policies supporting biofuels** (cont.)
>
> The effects of these various sub-national measures on the markets for biofuels and their feedstocks depend on the situation in each country. Where a national biofuels mandate allows obligated parties to trade in biofuel credits, higher blending mandates in particular sub-national jurisdictions may only alter the internal pattern of production and consumption. Production or consumption incentives provided by sub-national governments may, however, increase overall domestic production or consumption if the blend limit for ethanol or biodiesel has not already been attained. If a production incentive is tied to the use of locally grown feedstock, the net effect of the policy will depend on the generosity of the incentive relative to the extra cost incurred by having to meet the local-content requirement.
>
> In countries with no national biofuels mandate, the effect of one or more sub-national jurisdiction applying a mandate or offering a financial incentive (as long as it is not contingent on the use of locally produced feedstock) will be to increase national consumption above what it would likely be in the absence of the sub-national measure.
>
> *Sources :*
> Bahar, H., J. Egeland and R. Steenblik (2013), "Domestic incentive measures for renewable energy with possible trade implications", OECD Trade and Environment Working Papers, 2013/01, OECD Publishing. *http://dx.doi.org/10.1787/5k44srlksr6f-en.*
> Lane, J. (2013), "Biofuels mandates around the world: 2014", Biofuels Digest, 31 December 2013. *www.biofuelsdigest.com/bdigest/2013/12/31/biofuels-mandates-around-the-world-2014/.*

This *Outlook* assumes that most of the biofuels to be produced in the next decade will be based on agricultural feedstocks. Biofuel production is thus likely to have direct and indirect effects on the environment and on land use in the medium-term. Any disturbance to agricultural production caused by climatic events, or in fossil fuel markets may have an impact on the availability of those biofuels.

A major uncertainty for biofuel markets is related to the availability of advanced biofuels produced from ligno-cellulosic biomass, waste or non-food feedstock. Their development depends strongly on current research and development spending to explore new technologies. The uncertainties regarding the future of biofuel policies in key countries might act as an impediment to new investment decisions.

Notes

1. Low blends refer gasohol sold at the pump for ordinary cars. By opposition, high blends refer to gasohol sold at the pump that only flex-fuel vehicles can accept.

2. Brazil, Sao Paolo (ex-distillery), anhydrous.

3. Producer price Germany net of biodiesel tariff and of energy tax.

4. The term blend wall refers to short run technical constraints that act as an impediment to increased ethanol use. It is assumed in this *Outlook* that US cars will not be able to consume gasohol with more than 14% of ethanol mixed with petrol. The blend wall should increase gradually from the current 10%, and it is assumed to be reached by 2020.

5. The advanced gap corresponds to the difference between the advanced mandate, and the biodiesel and cellulosic mandates. It corresponds to fuels being able to achieve a 50% greenhouse gas reduction. Sugarcane based ethanol qualifies as an advanced biofuel.

6. This assumption responds to likely market developments and is in line with the recently published Prospects for Agricultural Markets and Income in the EU 2013-23 (*www.eurocarne.com/pdf/informes/previsionesUE2013-2023.pdf*). The remainder of the target will be met from other renewable energy sources such as electric cars for example.

7. *www.epa.gov/OTAQ/fuels/renewablefuels/documents/420f13048.pdf.*

8. E15 refers to gasohol with 15% volume of ethanol blended into petrol. E10 is still the most commonly available gasohol in the United States.

9. *http://eur-lex.europa.eu/LexUriServ/LexUriServ.do?uri=OJ:L:2009:140:0016:0062:EN:PDF.*

10. *http://ec.europa.eu/energy/2030_en.htm.*

11. Hydrous ethanol – about 96% ethanol and 4% water – can be used as fuel for flex-fuel vehicles.

12. Petrobras is a semi-public Brazilian multinational energy corporation. It is the largest company in the Southern Hemisphere (by market capitalisation) and the largest in Latin America (measured in 2011 revenues).

13. This is a key assumption of the strategic plan for Petrobras issued in February 2014: *www.investidorpetrobras.com.br/en/business-management-plan/2030-strategic-plan-and-2014-2018-business-and-management-plan-presentation.htm.*

14. The conventional gap is the difference between the total and advanced mandates as defined by the Renewable Fuel Standard (RFS2). It is often seen as an implied maize based ethanol mandate.

15. Biodiesel like sugarcane based ethanol qualifies for the advanced mandate. It is important to note that a unit of biodiesel counts for 1.5 units of advanced mandate.

16. According to the RFS2, sugarcane based ethanol is classified to be an advanced biofuel, while maize based ethanol is not.

17. The European Union has launched an anti-dumping and anti-subsidy action against exports of American ethanol. A key element of the case is the credit from the US federal excise tax on petrol. That credit has not been renewed in 2012 and in 2013 and the same is assumed in all the years of the *Outlook*.

18. *www.energy.ca.gov/low_carbon_fuel_standard/.*

Chapter 4

Cereals

This chapter describes the market situation and the latest set of quantitative medium-term projections for world and national cereal markets for the ten-year period, 2014-23. It covers the developments expected in national and global wheat, coarse grains and rice prices, production, use (human consumption, industrial and feed use), trade (imports and exports) and stocks in the medium-term. The quantitative projections are developed with the aid of the partial equilibrium Aglink-Cosimo model of world agriculture. The chapter also includes four boxes that explain the importance of public stockholding for food security, the structural changes in world feed markets, the campaign to prevent bread waste in Turkey and the contribution of agricultural investments to stabilising international rice price volatility under climate change. The chapter concludes with a discussion of some main issues and uncertainties that may have an impact on the medium-term outlook for cereals. These include weather events, policies, and specific market events influencing cereal production, consumption and trade.

Market situation

While world cereal production in 2014 may not exceed its 2013 record,[1] large carryover stocks are expected to keep global supplies in the 2014 marketing year adequate relative to expected world demand. In Canada, reduced wheat plantings could result in a significant drop in production this year. By contrast, wheat production is anticipated to rise in 2014 in the United States and European Union, assuming good results from spring plantings. In Australia, wheat production could decline from last year's above average level, mostly on expected drier conditions. In the major producing states of the Commonwealth of Independent States (CIS), wheat yields are expected to fall from the relatively high levels in 2013, which may result in lower production in Kazakhstan, the Russian Federation and Ukraine. Regarding coarse grains, production prospects are mixed in the Southern hemisphere. The outlook is generally favourable in South Africa and Argentina. However, the first maize crop in Brazil could be adversely affected by unfavourable weather conditions. World rice production in 2014 could modestly rise, as growth is likely to be dampened by falling world prices and fears of a recurring El Niño event. Production is rising in Brazil, Indonesia and Madagascar, while drought problems are anticipated to depress output in Australia, Peru, Sri Lanka and Tanzania.

In 2014, food consumption of cereals is forecast to keep up with the rise in world population, resulting in a stable per capita consumption at the global level. The strongest growth in food consumption is expected in Asia, where wheat and rice are the main staples. Feed utilisation of cereals may decrease marginally in 2014, after a firm growth in 2013. In particular, feed use of wheat is likely to stagnate, and rice continues to be consumed primarily as food. Industrial use of coarse grains is projected to increase, but most of the rise is likely to reflect the continuing growth in the demand for other industrial uses, especially starch and starch derivatives in China, rather than any significant rise in biofuel use.

World cereal stocks in 2013 increased by 15%. As a result, the global cereal stocks-to-use ratio is expected to increase by 3 percentage points to almost 25% in 2014, its highest value since 2005. World cereal trade is also expected to increase in 2014, hitting a new record high for the second year in a row.

International prices of major cereals, namely wheat, rice and maize, are likely to remain mostly under downward pressure, resulting in average cereal prices falling slightly below their 2013 level in 2014.

Projection highlights

- After a good harvest in 2013, favourable supply prospects in 2014 are projected to keep downward pressure on prices. Grains prices will ease both in nominal and real terms over the outlook period.

- Ample world rice supplies are expected with developing countries accounting for most of the increase. The slowdown of rice production and consumption growth contrasts with a rapid expansion of trade.

- World cereal utilisation will increase, driven by larger non-food use in developed and emerging economies and food in least developed countries.

- A considerable rebuilding of grains stocks and increase of global trade are expected, with record carryover rice stocks in Asian countries.

Market trends and prospects

Prices

Cereal prices are projected to decrease compared to previous *Outlook* editions, mainly influenced by a slower economic growth and strong recovery of world grain supply after the 2012 droughts in the United States and CIS countries. Wheat prices are projected to approach USD 270/t in nominal terms by 2023, starting at USD 284/t in 2014, the lowest levels since 2010. In the first three years of the outlook period, wheat prices will further decrease due to ample production prospects in the United States, Canada and Brazil, reaching USD 267/t in 2016 (Figure 4.1).

Figure 4.1. **Cereal prices fall over the medium-term**

Evolution of prices expressed in nominal (left) and real terms (right)

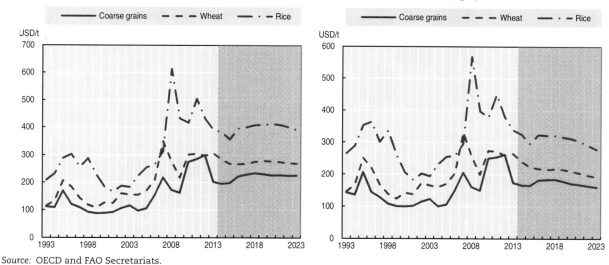

Source: OECD and FAO Secretariats.

StatLink ᎖ᎦᎵᏃ *http://dx.doi.org/10.1787/888933099865*

Coarse grain prices are also expected to considerably decrease in the first two years of the outlook period as a response to the ample production prospects in the United States, the Russian Federation and Argentina. Subject to average weather conditions, the representative maize Gulf price is projected to reach USD 195/t in 2014, 32% lower than the 2010-12 period of high prices and more in line with historical trends, and then to recover and stabilise over the second half of the projection period. At the end of the projection period, coarse grain prices are expected to be around USD 225/t in nominal terms (USD 160/t in real terms), significantly lower than in previous *Outlook* editions.

Rice prices over the projected period are anticipated follow the recent trend since 2011 and slide further down until reaching USD 391/t in 2023. This reflects the large supplies accumulated earlier in this decade. In particular exporting countries in Asia amassed large inventories, which will take long to offload on the market and will weigh on international prices at least until 2015. After this drop the nominal world rice price is projected to recover but to continue to fall in real terms.

Production

The potential for area expansion in the next decade is weak for cereals, and production growth will mostly be driven by yield increases. While the accumulated yield growth over the outlook versus the base period is projected at 10%, the increase in crop land devoted to wheat is less than 3% (Figure 4.2). World wheat production is expected to reach 778 Mt by 2023, about 12% higher than in the base period.[2] This represents an annual growth rate of around 1%, compared to 1.5% in the previous decade (Figure 4.3). The underlying factor for this sharp deceleration is the stabilisation of land use for wheat production over the outlook period.

Figure 4.2. **Limited potential to increase cereal production due to weak area expansion and moderate yield growth over the medium-term**

Evolution of global cereal harvested area and yields over the projection period

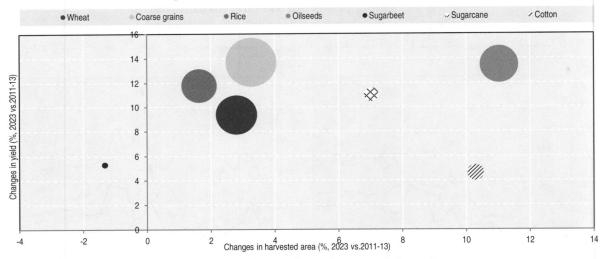

Note: The size of the bubbles indicates the proportion of harvested area of one crop relative to all crops.
Source: OECD and FAO Secretariats.

StatLink ⟋⟍⟋ *http://dx.doi.org/10.1787/888933099884*

Despite an unstable production trend, the Russian Federation is expected to further increase wheat production after last year's recovery from the severe drought in 2012. Production will outpace utilisation, contributing to a gradual rebuilding of stocks. Ukraine is projected to lead the developing world in both wheat and coarse grain production and net exports. Exports from Ukraine should be sustained by growing demand from East Asian countries, and China in particular.

World production of coarse grains is projected to reach 1 417 Mt by 2023, up 17% from the base period (Figure 4.4). As in the case of wheat, yields are projected to increase at a slower rate than in the past (0.8% p.a.), and crop land is only expected to moderately

Figure 4.3. **Recovery of wheat stocks led by production increases in the Russian Federation**

Evolution of supply, demand and stocks; World (left) and Russian Federation (right)

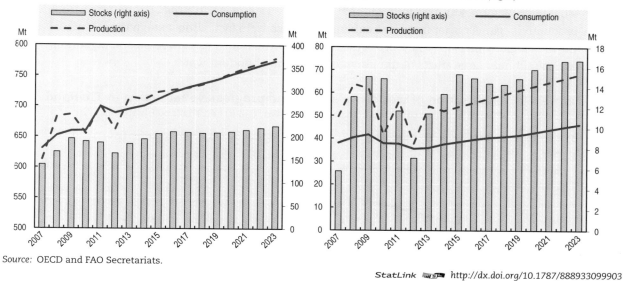

Source: OECD and FAO Secretariats.

StatLink ☞ *http://dx.doi.org/10.1787/888933099903*

expand, therefore, limiting the scope for a faster increase in production (Figure 4.2). Rebuilding of stocks in the United States is particularly strong in 2013 and 2014, while in 2015 and 2016 the country is expected to face a rebounding effect on production and stock, also driven by large export volumes.

The additional demand for biofuel production is behind the area expansion of coarse grains and oilseeds in developed countries. In developing countries the main driver is the feed demand for livestock production. Globally, coarse grains represent the largest share of the total harvested area (34%), followed by wheat (22%) and oilseeds (21%).

Figure 4.4. **A rapid recovery of coarse grains stocks is led by higher production of US corn**

Evolution of coarse grains supply, demand and stocks; World (left) and United States (right)

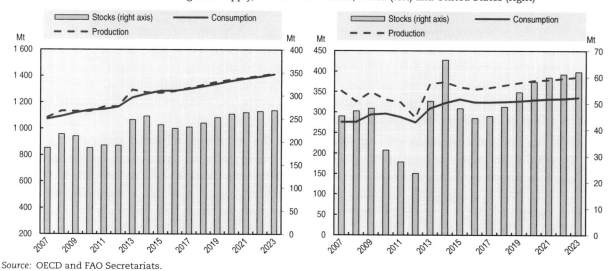

Source: OECD and FAO Secretariats.

StatLink ☞ *http://dx.doi.org/10.1787/888933099922*

World rice production is also projected to expand, but the projected 1.2% p.a. growth rate is about half of the 2.2% recorded in the previous ten years, implying a substantial slowdown (Figure 4.5). Virtually all of the expected increase in production stems from productivity gains rather than area expansion, which is, in fact, almost stagnating. Much of the area expansion is in Africa and some Asian countries, such as Cambodia and Myanmar, which still hold large tracts of uncultivated land and abundant water.

Figure 4.5. **Stabilisation of world rice stocks and progressive reduction in Thailand**
Evolution of rice supply, demand and stocks; World (left) and Thailand (right)

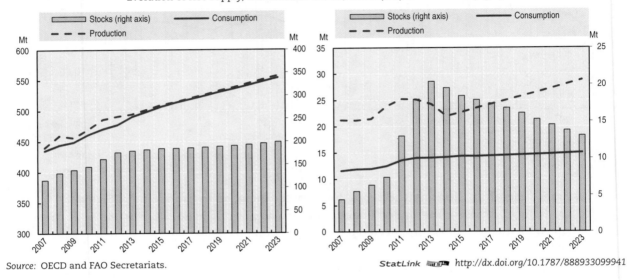

Source: OECD and FAO Secretariats.

StatLink http://dx.doi.org/10.1787/888933099941

Developing countries, which produce about 96% of world's rice crop, are foreseen to account for the bulk of the projected 67 Mt increase in output. Significant contributions are made by India, Cambodia, Myanmar and other Asian least developed countries, while more sluggish price projections result in a lower expansion of output in Africa than projected in the 2013 *Outlook*. Reversing earlier expectations and consistent with the policy line endorsed by the Chinese government early in 2014 to achieve self-sufficiency, China, the largest world rice producer, is expected to keep output rising, albeit modestly.

Thailand's government announced that official paddy procurements from farmers would be suspended, until further notice, by the end-February 2014, when the 2013 main crop buying scheme would be complete.[3] Such move could weigh on farmers' planting decisions and negatively affect production in the short run. In the medium-term, however, yields in Thailand have still much room for improvement, and productivity gains will contribute to a steady production growth.

The favourable outlook on supply allows for the rebuilding of world grain stocks, especially for coarse grains in the major exporting regions (i.e. Argentina, Australia, Canada, European Union, United States, Russian Federation, Ukraine and Kazakhstan). It is also important to recognise the importance of stockholding policies in some developing countries and the potential impacts on world markets, an issue largely debated at the 9th World Trade Organization Ministerial Conference in Bali (Box 1.9). For instance, China is projected to hold about 60%, 26% and 19% of world total stock of rice, coarse grains and wheat, respectively, in 2023. India is also expected to considerably increase grain stocks, especially in rice and wheat.

Use of cereals

Total wheat utilisation is projected to reach nearly 774 Mt by 2023, 295 Mt in developed countries and 479 Mt in developing countries (Figure 4.6). Wheat is expected to remain a commodity predominantly consumed for food, with direct human consumption reaching a stable 68% of its total use over the outlook period. At this level, per capita food consumption is projected to remain steady at around 66 kg p.a. World feed utilisation of wheat is expected to grow at a slower pace than in the historical period, but still represent around 20% of total consumption (38% in developed countries and 9% in developing countries). In developed countries wheat is also used for biofuel production, utilisation that is expected to moderately increase over the outlook period.

Figure 4.6. **Increasing food and feed demand for wheat in developing countries**

Evolution of wheat utilisation shares in developed and developing countries between the base year and 2023

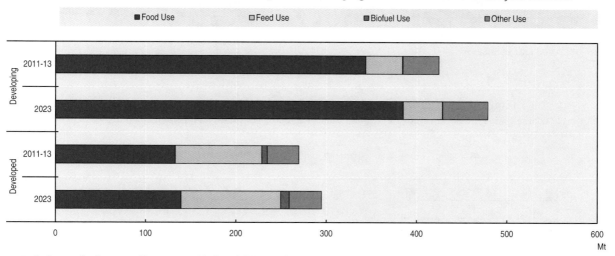

Note: In "other use" other non-disaggregated industrial demand sources (e.g. processing of straw) are included.
Source: OECD and FAO Secretariats.

StatLink ⟨⟩ *http://dx.doi.org/10.1787/888933099960*

Sustained by the demand for rice as food, the total utilisation of rice is to expand by about 1.1% p.a. to some 554 Mt in 2023 (Figure 4.7). In Asia, where much of the rice produced is consumed domestically, per capita rice consumption is expected to rise only marginally, as diets diversify. On the other hand, per capita rice consumption will keep growing in African countries, where rice is gaining relative importance as a major food staple. While demand continues to outpace production in Africa, rice imports are expected to increase, lifting Africa's share of world imports from 31% to 38%.

Despite a slower growth rate than in the previous decade, world utilisation of coarse grains is projected to increase by 20% by 2023 compared to the base period. This is driven largely by expansions in the demand for feed, which holds the largest share of total utilisation. Moderate increases in demand for industrial uses in developed countries and food in developing countries are also expected, the latter following larger population growth in these countries (Figure 4.8).

Figure 4.7. **African countries increase their share in world rice imports**

Evolution of rice imports in regional aggregates between 2004 and 2023

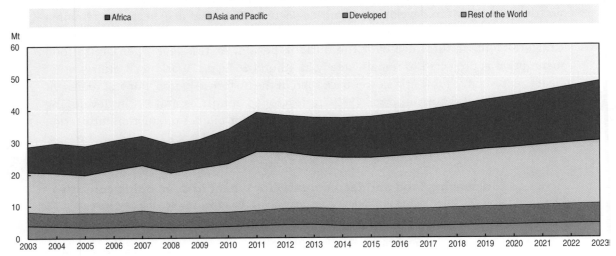

Source: OECD and FAO Secretariats.

StatLink ⟪s⟫ *http://dx.doi.org/10.1787/888933099979*

Figure 4.8. **Increasing biofuel and feed demand for coarse grains**

Evolution of coarse grains utilisation shares in China, other developing countries and developed countries between the base year and 2023

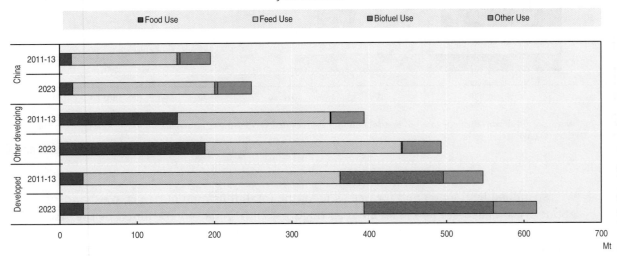

Note: In "other use" other non-disaggregated industrial demand sources (e.g. production of high fructose corn syrup or corn starch) are included.

Source: OECD and FAO Secretariats.

StatLink ⟪s⟫ *http://dx.doi.org/10.1787/888933099998*

The strong developments in feed use are mostly driven by strong growth in China, United States and Brazil. Among its industrial uses, maize-based ethanol production in the United States is projected to continue expanding after reaching the target of the Energy Independence and Security Act of 2007, with a considerable increase in ethanol exports. Within the United States, the share of maize used for ethanol production goes up to 44% of total domestic production. World use of coarse grains for production of biofuels is projected to reach 173 Mt, representing 12.2% of total world coarse grains utilisation.

With moderate increases in supply, the most important feature of the Chinese coarse grains markets in the coming ten years is the rapid increase in imports. The government's efforts to achieve self-sufficiency will likely concentrate on wheat and rice markets. While the *Outlook* projects considerable increases in meat imports (between 4% and 9% growth p.a.), this will not prevent coarse grains imports to follow a similar pattern with a 4% p.a. increase between 2014 and 2023, in order to satisfy demand. Feed demand is expected to increase the most, reaching 183 Mt in 2023 (Figure 4.8).

Starch and starch derivatives play a major role in Chinese food and non-food industries, and the demand of maize for processing into starch and other industrial uses increased rapidly between 2001 and 2007, when the government halted growth in the production of corn-based ethanol. Nevertheless, while restrictions on corn-based ethanol production are still in place, industrial processing of corn will continue growing, reaching a record high of 50 Mt in 2015. Over the outlook period, we expect the industrial use of maize to fall slightly to a 16% share of total coarse grains consumption.

In view of more efficient supply chains with high productivity to meet the growing demand, one of the challenges for agriculture is to reduce food loss and waste along the food chain. The problem of food loss and waste has drawn greater attention in many parts of the world. For example, 2014 is designated as the European year against Food Waste, and Turkey launched a campaign to reduce bread waste (Box 4.1). On the supply side, problems of food loss have been addressed through the recycling of waste into feed and fertilisers in an economic manner (Box 4.2). Entries of non-conventional feeds, such as distiller's dry grains (DDG), into feed markets have been significant in the last decade and are expected to continue during the projection period (Figure 4.9). If these measures are effective during the medium-term, they will further contribute to stable agricultural markets.

Figure 4.9. **Increasing use of non-conventional feeds led by dried distiller's grains**

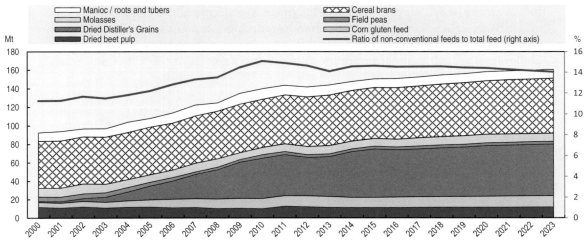

Source: OECD and FAO Secretariats.

StatLink ⧉ *http://dx.doi.org/10.1787/888933100017*

Box 4.1. **Campaign to prevent bread waste in Turkey**

Studies of the Food and Agriculture Organization (FAO) show that 1.3 Gt of food are wasted every year. This amount is equal to the total food production of Sub-Saharan Africa. Moreover, FAO estimates that one-third of the global food production is either wasted or lost.[1] If one-quarter of the food currently lost or wasted globally could be saved, it would be enough to feed the 840 million hungry people in the world.[2]

Against this background, the Turkish Government launched a campaign to decrease bread waste in the country, even though per capita household food waste is lower in Turkey compared to other OECD countries. The Turkish Grain Board, which is a subsidiary organisation of the Ministry of Food, Agriculture and Livestock, conducted research in 2008 and 2012 on the production, consumption, consumption habits and waste of bread in Turkey. The results of these studies were alarming, because they showed that the bread waste in Turkey reached serious amounts. As a consequence, a campaign was launched in January 2013 to inform and raise society's awareness of bread waste. The aims of the campaign are to create public awareness, prevent waste in bread production and consumption, ensure bread is bought as needed and preserved properly, inform society on different ways of using stale bread and contribute to the economy by preventing waste.

The bread waste campaign included a media campaign with estimated advertisement costs of USD 243 million,[3] spread on internet, TV commercials, newscasts, newspaper articles, a research book about bread waste, a stale bread recipe book and various brochures. Several conferences, exhibitions, press meetings, stale bread recipe competitions etc., have been organised with the co-operation of the universities, non-governmental organisations, the private sector and local administrators and reached all parts of the Turkish society.

At the end of 2013, the Turkish Grain Board carried out another study in order to evaluate the impact of the campaign on bread waste and consumption habits. The research results show that, between end of 2012 and 2013, daily bread waste in the country decreased by 18% from 5.95 million to 4.9 million loaves saving a total of 384 million loaves of bread. On a per capita basis, these improvements resulted in a 19% decrease in daily bread waste to 16.2 grams. Furthermore, the campaign resulted in a 10% decrease in the daily total bread production and consumption. Based on calculations by the Turkish Grain Board (Table 4.1), reducing bread waste saved USD 159 million and reducing unnecessary bread purchases saved USD 1.3 billion, for a total savings of USD 1.5 billion.[4]

1. Food losses refer to the decrease in edible food mass throughout the part of the supply chain that specifically leads to edible food for human consumption. Food losses occurring at the end of the food chain, which relates to retailers' and consumers' behaviour, are rather called "food waste". (*Source:* Global Food Losses and Food Waste (2011) – FAO).
2. Opening speech by Mustapha M. Sinaceur (FAO Representative in Turkey) on the campaign's results disclosure meeting, 17 January 2014. (Full speech can be accessed at: *www.ekmekisrafetme.com/ UploadResim/Kampanya/17012014EkmekFAO.pdf*).
3. 2013 average exchange rate 1.89 (USD/TRL) of Aglink-Cosimo Model is used.
4. "The Research on Bread Waste in Turkey" is the source of the figures in this paragraph. (The research can be accessed at *www.ekmekisrafetme.com/UploadResim/Kampanya/ArastirmaKitabi.pdf*.)

Box 4.1. **Campaign to prevent bread waste in Turkey** (cont.)

Table 4.1. **Bread waste statistics**

	Before the Campaign (End of 2012)	After the Campaign (End of 2013)
Annual expenditure on bread consumption (billion TRL)	26	23.5
Annual expenditure on bread consumption (billion USD)	13.8	12.4
Daily bread production (million loaves)	101	91
Daily bread consumption (million loaves)	95	86
Daily bread waste (million loaves)	5.95	4.9
Daily per capita bread consumption (g)	319	284
Daily per capita bread waste (g)	19.9	16.2

Sources: *The research on bread waste in Turkey*, The Turkish Grain Board, December 2013. (Accessible at: *www.ekmekisrafetme.com/UploadResim/Kampanya/ArastirmaKitabi.pdf*). The official internet site of the campaign (*www.ekmekisrafetme.com/*).

StatLink ᴍᴤ▀ *http://dx.doi.org/10.1787/888933101195*

Box 4.2. **Structural changes in the feed market**

Structural changes

The use of by-products in the feed market has expanded greatly with the massive arrival of distiller's dry grains (DDG). DDGs are a by-product of cereal based ethanol. The boom in the biofuel industry generated much larger supply of DDG and created a structural change in the feed market. The new regulation on the use of meat and bone meal (MBM) which was introduced in the European Union in the second half of the 1990s and in Japan in 2001 also created a structural change, albeit a smaller one. The decline in the share of coarse grains due to the increase in the relative price of maize is another important recent structural change. Additionally, the elimination of the European Union's cereal support price in 2001 combined with the higher world cereal prices experienced in recent years has reduced the competiveness of manioc and corn gluten feed substantially in the European market but strengthened it in Asia and the Americas.

But probably the most important structural change affecting the feed market in the last twenty years is the greater use of crop protein meals in the feed rations in many developing countries. This occurred as a result of the transition from backyard production to specialized, commercial livestock farms using concentrated feeds. In the 1990s this generated a sufficient improvement in the feed conversion ratio of non-ruminant production to offset the increasing use of concentrated feeds caused by the change in the farming structure. But a growing number of commercial farms in developing countries have reached the maximum amount of protein meal that can be used in the feed ration. In these countries improvement in the feed conversion ratio will be more limited in future and insufficient to offset increasing consumption of concentrated feeds. Going forward, this will become a key element of demand for cereals and other feeds.

Box 4.2. **Structural changes in the feed market** (cont.)

The use of by-products in the feed rations

DDG, MBM and corn gluten feed are all by-products of agricultural commodities. The same applies to cereal bran and dried beet pulp. An increasing share of fish meal production is also resulting from the use of fish residue. The feed market has provided a useful outlet for these by-products and they have become an important part of the system. The Aglink-Cosimo model was used to analyse these characteristics of the feed market. To capture their importance in the agricultural markets, a stylised counterfactual scenario was implemented, consisting of reducing the production of these by-products by 25% in every year of the outlook period. The reduction in supply increased prices and led to higher demand for the other concentrated feeds like cereals and crop protein meals. This stronger demand generated higher prices with average increases over the projection period of 9%, 6.3%, 18% and 6% for coarse grains, wheat, protein meal and oilseeds, respectively.

Under this scenario, by 2023, the total production of the six feeds derived from by-products is 75.9 Mt less. This represents almost 4.5% of the world concentrated feed use. A shock of this magnitude would generate major adjustments in the market. After ten years of these higher prices, production of cereals and oilseeds has increased respectively by 30 Mt and 10 Mt. This larger oilseed production generates almost 7.6 Mt of additional protein meal production. Therefore, on the production side, 37.6 Mt have become available to replace almost 50% of the imposed reduction in the scenario. The higher prices also reduce consumption; 25.4 Mt less concentrated feeds are used by livestock and fish farmers, 3.4 Mt less by the cereal food (including sweeteners) and other use sector and 4.2 Mt less by the biofuel sector for a total of 33 Mt or 43% of the imposed reduction in the scenario.[*] The remaining 5.3 Mt (75.9 minus 37.6, minus 33) have been replaced by fodder feeds (hay, pasture and cereal silage) in countries endowed with this type of resource.

These higher feed prices eventually reduce the supply of livestock and fish products and lead to lower world production levels for livestock (except beef) and fish and higher prices (Table 4.2). The resulting higher prices of beef substitutes have shifted beef demand upward sufficiently that it crosses the lower beef supply in the scenario at a higher production level, by 0.42% in 2023. Being less intensive in the use of these feeds, beef supply is not falling as much as the supply of non-ruminants. The substitution effect in demand is stronger than the supply effect resulting from higher feed prices.

Table 4.2. **Production and price changes of commodities requiring feeds in 2023 based on the counterfactual scenario**

%	Eggs	Poultry	Pork	Fish	Milk	Beef
Production	-3.8	-1.6	-0.74	-1.2[1]	-0.05	0.42
Price[2]	13.5	9.7	8.2	8	4	5.2

1. Aquaculture production.
2. Eggs is the price in the United States, pork and beef are the simple averages of the Atlantic and Pacific markets and milk is the cheese price.

StatLink ᴍᴤ☞ *http://dx.doi.org/10.1787/888933101214*

> ## Box 4.2. **Structural changes in the feed market** *(cont.)*
>
> The higher cereal prices affect also the ethanol and sweetener markets. By 2023, world ethanol and cereal sweetener production are both 1.2% lower and prices higher by 2.6% and 6% respectively. These higher prices contribute to higher sugar prices (2.6%) by shifting supply downward due to the higher price of ethanol and demand upward due to the higher price of high fructose corn syrup (HFCS).
>
> The hypothetical scenario illustrates the moderating effect the use of agricultural by-products in the feed markets has on cereal and animal product prices contributing to food security and mitigating to some extent the impact of the use of cereals for ethanol production.
>
> * This decline is due to the lower profitability caused by the higher price of maize and the lower receipts from the sale of DDG.

Trade of cereals

Continuing historical trends, the developed world continues to supply wheat and coarse grains to developing countries. Net trade flows from developed countries to developing countries will increase by 17%. For wheat and coarse grains combined, the United States and Canada are projected to be the major exporters in 2023, with 108 Mt, followed by the CIS countries (67 Mt between the Russian Federation, Ukraine and Kazakhstan). While the US wheat market balances remain fairly steady over time, Canada will considerably increase wheat production and gain share in world exports (Figure 4.10). Argentina is also expected to improve its share of international wheat markets.

Figure 4.10. **Wheat export shares for major countries**

2011-13

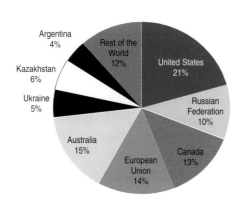

2023

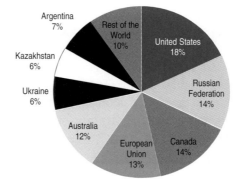

Source: OECD and FAO Secretariats.

StatLink ⟦msp⟧ *http://dx.doi.org/10.1787/888933100036*

Volatility of supply in wheat markets of the Russian Federation has been a historical issue and mainly due to severe periods of drought. Nevertheless, a positive trend has been observed in the last ten years, and further increase of wheat production and exports are expected. Similarly, Ukraine and Kazakhstan are expected to continue agricultural investments to achieve wheat exports in 2023 close to half of their domestic supply. Wheat imports by Egypt, the Middle East and Indonesia are projected to capture about 18% of the total volume in 2023, while coarse grain imports are more dispersed around the globe.

With 52 Mt, United States is projected to remain the main coarse grains exporter, followed by Argentina and Brazil, both adding another 56 Mt; making the Americas the principal port of origin for coarse grains (Figure 4.11). With yields growing steadily, area stabilises at 36 Mha during the second half of the outlook period, about 6% less than in the base year. This supply response is caused by lower coarse grains prices after the expected production surpluses in 2013 and 2014. Demand for feed will profit from lower prices and is expected to increase at 0.7% p.a.

Figure 4.11. **Rapid expansions of coarse grains exports**
The Americas will be the principal port of origin for coarse grains

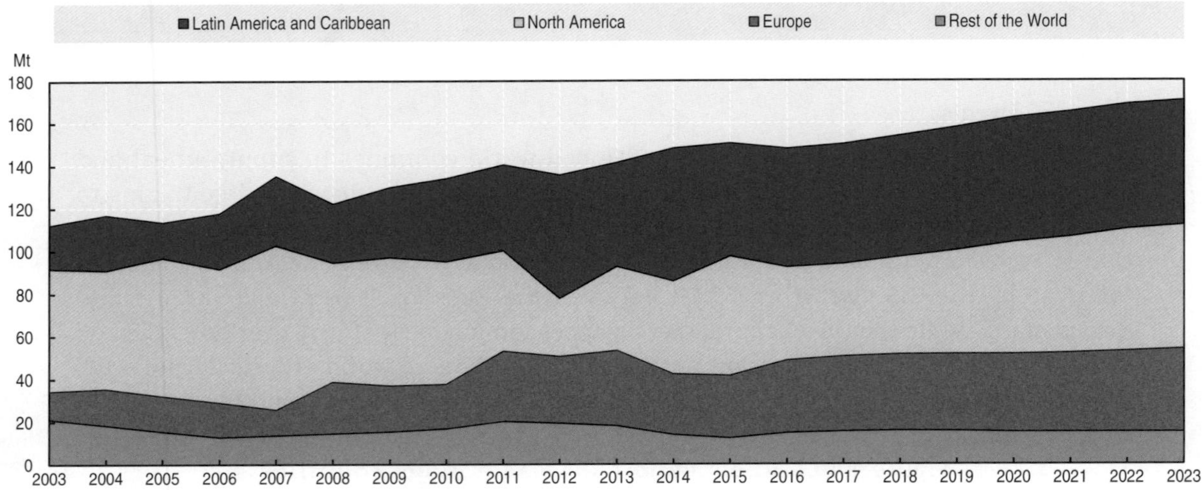

Source: OECD and FAO Secretariats.

StatLink http://dx.doi.org/10.1787/888933100055

Argentina's outlook on coarse grains is favourable, mainly due to the positive expected developments in barley markets and a clear orientation on exports. Out of 46 Mt of coarse grains production projected in 2023, 32 Mt will be exported and 10 Mt will be used for feed. Brazil's supply of coarse grains in 2023 is expected to be around 82 Mt, but only 24 Mt are for exports and 47 Mt for feed. Both countries expect expansions in harvested area over 1% p.a., which is more than double the world average growth. Among other countries, Ukraine is also expected to diversify its crop sector and increase plantings of coarse grains, mainly maize and barley for exports.

China has embarked on the transformation of its food security strategy at the end of 2013. The new strategy has clearly separated the positioning of staple food grains, namely rice and wheat, from oilseeds and feed grains, and the focus of food security has been placed on "absolute self-sufficiency" in the two staple food grains – wheat and rice. The projections of cereal net trades are in line with these ambitions (Figure 4.12). Yet, the policy allows international markets to compensate any production shortfall of non-staple food grains, while their domestic production is pursued to the extent possible. The transformation, which positioned imports as an important part of the food supply, is regarded as the historical turnaround from the strategy of "95% self-sufficiency in food production" launched in 1996.

Figure 4.12. **Cereal net trade in China**

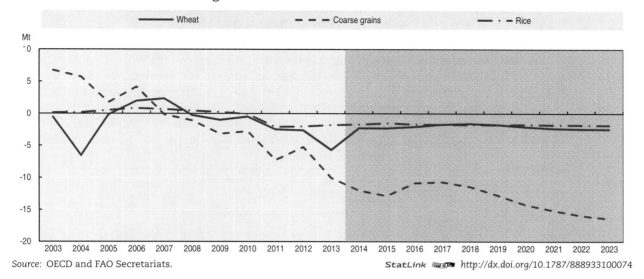

Source: OECD and FAO Secretariats.   StatLink ᠍᠍᠍ http://dx.doi.org/10.1787/888933100074

Despite being a thin market, compared with other agricultural commodities, international rice trade registered a particularly fast annual growth of 3.6% in the past ten years. A relatively fast pace of expansion of 3.1% p.a. is projected for the next ten years, which boosts the volume exchanged to 49 Mt by 2023. All of the traditional exporters, including India, Pakistan, Thailand, Viet Nam and the United States, are expected to increase their exports. Thailand, in particular, is foreseen to regain its leadership (Figure 4.13), following a relaxation of the high producer price policy applied in the past three years and on the back of the large inventories held in public warehouses, which will take several years for the market to absorb. Less attractive world prices, on the other hand, may prompt smaller exporters, such as Egypt, Brazil or the Russian Federation, to curtail international sales. However, one of the factors likely to dominate developments in the next decade is the probable rise of Cambodia and Myanmar (now included in the Asia Least Developed Country grouping) as major rice exporters which would further stoke competition among rice producers (Box 4.3).

Box 4.3. **Contribution of agricultural investments to stabilising international rice price volatility under climate change**

The role of agricultural investment growth in alleviating climate risks of rice production systems and rice markets was examined using a partial equilibrium model. The Rice Economy Climate Change (RECC) model covers rice markets in 15 countries and regions (Thailand, Viet Nam, Indonesia, Malaysia, the Philippines, Cambodia, Lao PDR, Myanmar, China, Japan, South Korea, India, the United States, EU27 and the rest of the world).[1] Rice yield in each economy is estimated from minimum and maximum temperatures, precipitation, and agricultural investments. Rice area harvested is estimated from rice and wheat producer prices and precipitation. All climate variables for the future period come from a climate change projection by BCM2 (Bergen Climate Model Version 2) Global Climate Model under A2 greenhouse gas emission scenario both in baseline and policy scenario projections.

Box 4.3. **Contribution of agricultural investments to stabilising international rice price volatility under climate change** (*cont.*)

It is assumed that the current growth rate of agricultural investments (land development[2] and machinery and equipment) from 2000-07 in each country will continue during the baseline projection period.[3] With this assumption, the coefficient of variation (CV) of the international rice price (milled 5% broken f.o.b. Ho Chi Minh price) in the baseline is 0.076 from 2010-12 to 2030[4] (Table 4.3).

Table 4.3. **Policy scenarios and simulation results for rice under climate change conditions**

	Countries	Growth rate of agricultural investment during the projection period (2010-30)		The coefficient of variation (CV) of international Rice Price (2010/12-2030)
		Land development	Machinery and Equipment	
Baseline	15 countries and regions	Same as 2000-2007 rate	Same as 2000-2007 rate	0.076
Policy scenario 1	ASEAN 8 countries	2.0% annum	1.0% annum	0.036
Policy scenario 2	The Philippines	2.0% annum	1.0% annum	0.072
Policy scenario 3	Thailand	2.0% annum	1.0% annum	0.055
Policy scenario 4	Viet Nam	2.0% annum	1.0% annum	0.059
Policy scenario 5	ASEAN 8 countries	0.0% annum (no growth)	0.0% annum (no growth)	0.125

StatLink ⬛📊 *http://dx.doi.org/10.1787/888933101233*

Projections were made under several scenarios of agricultural investments in selected countries for comparison against the baseline projection. These agricultural investments can be considered as climate change adaptation measures.

The simulation results suggest that the volatility in the rice price will increase compared to the baseline, if agricultural investment in ASEAN 8[5] countries do not grow during the projection period. However, a constant agricultural investment (2.0% p.a. increase for land development and 1.0% p.a increase for machinery and equipment) in ASEAN 8 countries will contribute to a decrease in the international rice price volatility. Particularly, investments in Thailand and Viet Nam are the most important in stabilising the international rice price under future climate change.

1. 14 countries and the EU account for 82% of total world rice production in 2010/12 (FAOSTAT). Other countries that produce rice are treated as "the rest of the world" in the model.
2. Land development includes land clearance, land contouring, creation of wells and watering holes, boundaries and irrigation channels built by farmers, and irrigation works, soil conservation works, flood control structures undertaken by government and other local bodies.
3. The growth rate of investments in land development in ASEAN 8 countries ranged from -0.1% to 1.9% and that in machinery and equipment in ASEAN 8 countries ranged from -0.1% to 1.0%.
4. The CV is the ratio of the standard deviation to the mean, measured by annual price from 2010/12 to 2030.
5. Thailand, Viet Nam, Indonesia, the Philippines, Malaysia, Cambodia, Lao PDR and Myanmar
Source: Koizumi, T. and H. Kanamaru (2014), *Contribution of Agricultural Investments to Stabilizing International Rice Price Volatility under Climate Change*, FAO website, *www.fao.org/climatechange/amicaf/85845/.*

Figure 4.13. **Rice export shares of major countries**

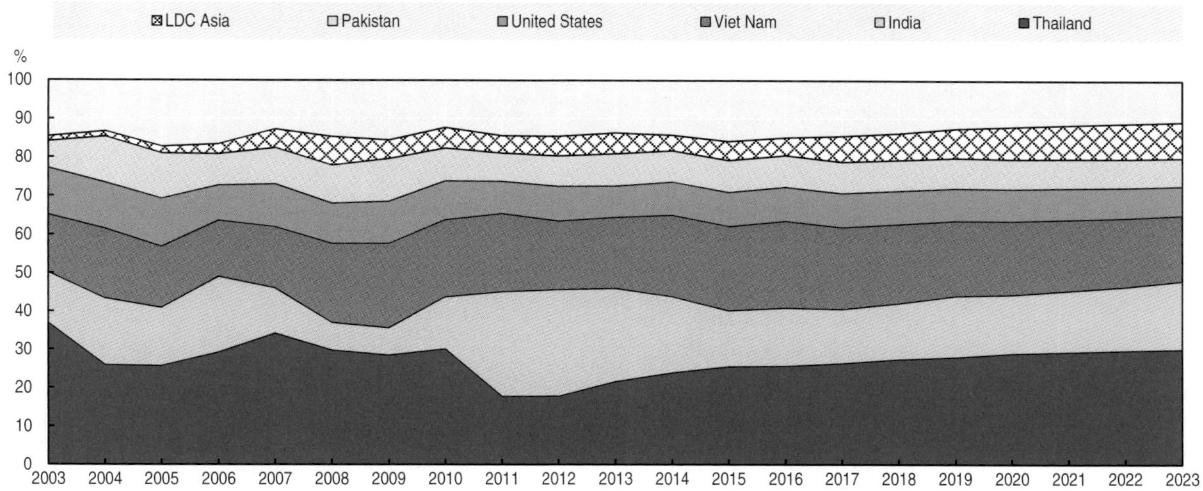

Source: OECD and FAO Secretariats.

StatLink ᵃᵐˢ᾿ http://dx.doi.org/10.1787/888933100093

Main issues and uncertainties

After a sharp recovery from the 2012 drought, current production prospects for the main producing regions (for instance United States, Russian Federation and Argentina) are rather optimistic. There is a high likelihood that adverse weather events such as *El Niño* will continue affecting cereal markets in these regions. In the *Outlook*, no weather cyclical patterns are projected, although adverse trends linked to extreme weather events in the past are part of the projections, with Australia as the typical example.

Cereal prices could be affected by a potential further slowdown of fast growing economies, such as China, and lower energy prices caused by new energy sources and new extraction technologies. Moreover, the reinforcement of food security and sustainability criteria in the reform and design of biofuel policies may also have the effect of lowering the demand of cereals. Additionally, unrests in exporting regions (i.e. Ukraine) or importing regions (i.e. Middle East), or changes to demographic policies such as the reform of China's one-child policy could provoke tensions on markets that are not reflected in the projections.

Notes

1. See the glossary for the definition of crop marketing years for wheat, coarse grains and rice in various countries.

2. The three-year average 2011, 2012 and 2013 is considered as the "base period".

3. IGC, (2014), *Grain Market Report*, 27 February.

References

Turkish Grain Board, (2013), The official internet site of the campaign to prevent bread waste, *www.ekmekisrafetme.com/*.

Koizumi, T., and H. Kanamaru (2014), *Contribution of Agricultural Investments to Stabilizing International Rice Price Volatility under Climate Change*, FAO website, *www.fao.org/climatechange/amicaf/85845*.

Chapter 5

Oilseeds and oilseed products

This chapter describes the market situation and the latest set of quantitative medium-term projections for global and national oilseed, protein meal and vegetable oil markets for the ten-year period, 2014-23. The discussion covers the developments expected in world and national prices, production, use (human consumption, industrial and feed use), trade (imports and exports) and stocks. The quantitative projections are developed with the aid of the partial equilibrium Aglink-Cosimo model of world agriculture. The chapter also includes a box that explains policy options for biofuel in Indonesia. It concludes with a discussion of main issues and uncertainties concerning the medium-term outlook for oilseeds. These include biodiesel policies, and specific market developments influencing production, consumption and trade of oilseeds and oilseed products.

Market situation

Recently the United States and Brazil[1] were affected by significant droughts which contributed to high prices of oilseeds and other crops. Farmers in many parts of the world responded to these higher prices, by strongly increasing oilseed production in 2013.[2] As a consequence, the global area under oilseeds cultivation and oilseed production reached new records. World coarse grain production also reached a new record. The large increase in crop production led to a significant decline in most crop prices, particularly in coarse grains, due to the large production increase in the United States. As a result, a shift in land to oilseeds is expected in the 2014 crop year which should lead to another record crop and further declines in the prices of the oilseed complex.

The lower oilseed prices will improve the crushing margin and lead to large expansion in crush and in oilseed meals and oils production. Global palm oil production is anticipated to continue to grow in the short term. Increases in income, population and biodiesel production are contributing to higher vegetable oil demand. This will avert large price declines for vegetable oil following the anticipated large increase in supply. Demand for protein meal will not be as strong due to a slowdown in world meat production in 2013 and 2014, resulting from the high feed prices since 2010.

The record crops of 2013 and 2014 will replenish oilseeds stock to levels that should buffer most unanticipated shortfalls in production in the short term.

Projection highlights

- World production of oilseeds has increased in marketing year 2013 and, in the absence of climate incidents, is expected to stay at this high level in 2014. These two large crops will significantly reduce international oilseeds and products prices. After this reduction, prices are expected to increase slowly, based on strong food and fuel demand for vegetable oil and a solid demand for protein meal once meat production grows stronger again.

- Relative profitability of coarse grains versus oilseeds is expected to favour the allocation of land toward oilseeds and lead to a 26%[3] increase in world production when combined with yield gains. With 91% of global exports in 2023, the Americas will continue to be the oilseeds basket of the world. China is expected to further solidify its position as the leading oilseeds importer, but its share of world oilseeds crush is expected to stabilise at 25% of world total.

- The share of palm oil production in total vegetable oil output is projected to continue to increase in the first seven years of the outlook period but to stabilise at almost 36% thereafter. World vegetable oil production will remain very concentrated in the coming decade as growth originates in the main producing regions of Indonesia and Malaysia. Demand of vegetable oils for food remains strong as global incomes and population grow, and the use of vegetable oils as fuel is supported by consumption mandates.

● Global protein meal output is projected to increase by 27% or 74 Mt. Almost two-thirds of this additional output comes from four countries: Argentina, Brazil, China and the United States. Compared to the past decade, consumption growth of protein meal slows down significantly, reflecting both slower absolute growth in global livestock production and slower growth in the share of protein meal in feed rations. This last phenomenon reflects the recent achievement of optimum use of protein meal in feed ration by commercial farms in some important developing countries.

Market trends and prospects

Prices

After the initial downward correction, all prices of the oilseed complex are expected to increase over the medium-term due to strong demands for vegetable oil and protein meal (Figure 5.1). The demand for protein meal is mainly driven by the growth in non-ruminant and milk production in developing countries and a greater incorporation rate of protein in feed rations in these countries. Vegetable oil demand is mainly driven by the food and biodiesel sectors. Despite the high crude oil price assumed in the projections, the bulk of global biodiesel demand will be driven by national mandates because generally biodiesel is not expected to be economically viable compared to diesel. Those mandates include the advanced biofuel mandate in the United States, which is expected to be filled partly by biodiesel in most years of the projection period.

Over the medium-term, the price of protein meal will stabilise around 5% above the average level of the period 2006-12; corresponding to the new higher price plateau. As of 2015, the price of vegetable oils is expected to increase again. Oilseed prices will increase from 2017 onwards, except in 2023 due to larger production generated by the lower coarse grains price in the two preceding years. In real terms, these prices are expected to fall but from very high levels (Figure 5.1). When compared to 2005 (i.e. before the new higher price plateau), the world price of vegetable oil, protein meal and oilseed in 2023 will be, respectively, 30%, 46% and 38% higher in real terms.

Figure 5.1. **Oilseed prices remain at a higher plateau**

Evolution of prices expressed in nominal (left) and in real terms (right)

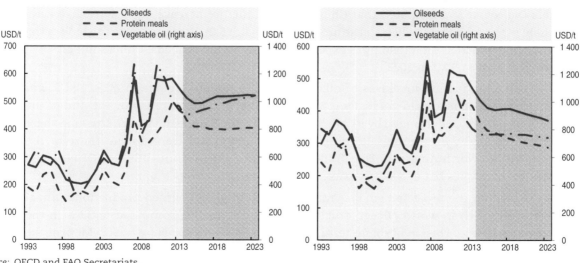

Source: OECD and FAO Secretariats.

StatLink http://dx.doi.org/10.1787/888933100112

The strong demand for vegetable oil drives the production of protein meals because both products are produced in fixed proportions. Despite solid meal demand from milk, pork, poultry and egg production in developing and certain developed countries, the protein meal price increases slowly because supply stays ahead of demand. Prices would be even lower if they were not supported by the high price of fishmeal, which is caused by high demand in the growing aquaculture sector and a somewhat stagnating fishmeal supply due to fishing quotas. Additionally, the prices for vegetable protein meal are strengthened by the prohibition and/or regulation in the use of meat and bone meal as farm animal feed in many countries.

Oilseed production and crush

Since maize production requires larger amounts of fertiliser and energy than oilseeds, the anticipated increase in the price of these inputs should give a cost advantage to soybean. As a result, the oilseeds' share of world area for the commodities covered in the *Outlook* is expected to grow slightly between the 2011-13 average and 2023 but at a slower pace than in the previous decade. Global area expansion of 11%, combined with yield improvements of 14%, generates a 26% increase in world oilseed production over the coming decade.

Founding countries of the *Mercado Común del Sur* (MERCOSUR, Argentina, Brazil, Paraguay and Uruguay) are expected to reach 36% of world production in 2023, compared to an average of 34% in 2011-13. In spite of a small decline, the United States remains the leading oilseeds producer, with a global share of 21% by 2023. The RUK countries (Russian Federation, Ukraine and Kazakhstan) and Canada are expected to maintain their 6.6% and 5% share, respectively, throughout the outlook period.

In the context of an increasing use of biodiesel to meet the Renewable Energy Directive, oilseeds production in the European Union will increase by 19% over the projection period and maintain more or less its 7% share of world total. This is mostly driven by yield increases.

Which regions of the world will crush these oilseeds depends on many factors, including transport cost, trade policies, acceptance of genetically modified crops, processing costs (e.g. labour and energy costs) and infrastructure (e.g. ports and roads). In this *Outlook*, it is anticipated that China will continue to increase oilseed crush, but its share of the world total will stabilise around 25% (Figure 5.2). However, since the bulk of the anticipated increase in crushing is expected from imported oilseeds, China's imports will reach almost 81.5 Mt in 2023.

Large production increases of oilseeds in more remote regions in MERCOSUR will enable these countries to gradually reach 25% of the world total crush by the end of the outlook period. Underpinned by its biodiesel policies, the European Union's crushing share only falls slightly over the outlook period. The downward trend in the share of the countries of North American Free Trade Agreement (NAFTA, United States, Canada and Mexico) continues but at a slower pace.

Based on the projected smaller rate of growth in global oilseed production, annual average growth in world oilseed crush is expected to be 2%, compared to 3.5% in the previous decade. This, in absolute terms, translates into an expansion of 96.5 Mt over the outlook period. The largest expansion in crush volume is projected to come from the MERCOSUR countries with 36.4 Mt, followed by China with 25 Mt.

Figure 5.2. **Share of global oilseed crush among leading regions**

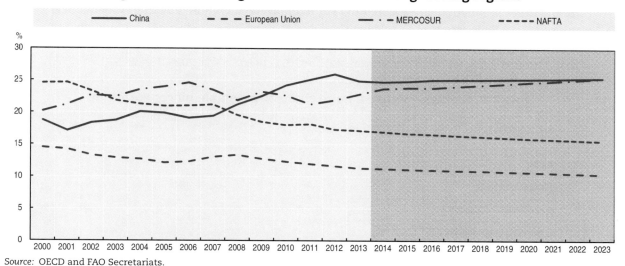

Source: OECD and FAO Secretariats.

StatLink ⊞⊑🖎 http://dx.doi.org/10.1787/888933100131

Since there are no new stock holding policies by any major producing or consuming country, the global stock-to-use ratio is expected to fall to 8% at the end of the outlook period. This limits the capacity to compensate potential production shortfalls in a major producing region and contributes to the continued risk of price volatility in the oilseed sector.

Vegetable oil production and consumption

World vegetable oil production is expected to increase by 28%, or 46 Mt, over the outlook period, relative to the 2011-13 average. It is likely to remain very concentrated with eight major producers (Indonesia, Malaysia, China, the European Union, the United States, Argentina, Brazil and India) accounting for almost 77% of total production throughout the projection period. Malaysia's and Indonesia's palm oil output is projected to grow on average at about 2.9% p.a., a slower rate than in the past as land restrictions, environmental restraints and labour costs become more constraining. The share of palm oil production in total vegetable oil output is projected to continue to increase in the first seven years of the outlook period but to be at almost 36% thereafter. Based on its use of imported seeds in domestic crush, China ranks second in vegetable oil production.

Rising per capita income is expected to lead to a 1.3% p.a. increase in per capita vegetable oil consumed as food in developing economies. Annual food vegetable oil use per capita is expected to average 20.3 kg across developing countries, but no more than 9.4 kg in Least Developed Countries (LDC) by 2023. As a group, developed countries are showing a stable consumption level of 24-25 kg, but individual countries differ based on tastes and dietary preferences.

Globally, the use of edible vegetable oil for biodiesel production is expected to expand by almost 10 Mt to 28.8 Mt over the outlook period. This constitutes a 50% increase over the base period and takes up almost one-quarter of the total production growth of vegetable oil. The European Union is expected to remain the largest producer of biodiesel, stabilising at about 40% of global output after 2017. Other important producing countries are Argentina, Brazil, Indonesia and the United States.

In developed countries, continuing sustained demand for non-food uses, in particular for biodiesel production, is expected to lead to an average annual growth of vegetable oil use of 1% p.a. This rate is much slower than during previous decade when biofuel policies were taking effect. The share of vegetable oil consumption used for world biodiesel production is expected to increase from 12% in 2011-13 to 14% in 2023 (Figure 5.3).

Figure 5.3. **Biodiesel to use a large share of vegetable oil consumption**

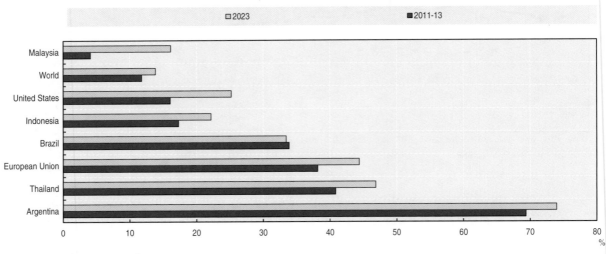

Source: OECD and FAO Secretariats.

StatLink http://dx.doi.org/10.1787/888933100150

Argentina is expected to maintain an export-oriented biodiesel industry: consumption of vegetable oil for biodiesel production is expected to reach 3 Mt by 2023, i.e. 74% of domestic vegetable oil use. In the European Union and Thailand, vegetable oil for biodiesel production is expected to account for 44% and 47%, respectively, of domestic vegetable oil consumption by 2023.

The use of maize oil for biodiesel production has emerged in the United States, and it is expected to amplify over the outlook period. Maize oil is extracted during the processing of maize into ethanol and sweeteners in wet milling plants. Since only about 10% of ethanol is produced in wet milling plants, the largest part of maize oil production is derived as a by-product of maize sweeteners.

Protein meal production and consumption

Global meal output is projected to increase by 27%, reaching almost 351 Mt by 2023. Production remains highly concentrated, with six producers (Argentina, Brazil, China, European Union, India and United States) accounting for almost 77% of global production. Almost two-thirds of the 74 Mt increase will come from only four countries: Argentina, Brazil, China and the United States. In China and the European Union, meal production will continue to rely on both domestically grown and imported seeds, while the others will barely import any seeds

Global meal consumption is expected to rise by 27%, with developing countries accounting for 84% of the increase and reaching 66% of global consumption by 2023. Compared to the past decade, annual consumption growth is expected to slow down markedly reflecting the lower growth of the livestock industry in developing countries and a slower growth in the inclusion of protein meal in feed rations.

In Least Developed Countries, protein meal use remains low, but its use is projected to grow faster in the coming ten years than over the previous decade because of a faster growth of livestock production and increasing feed intensity of protein meal. While this projected expansion represents a positive development for these countries, it is not a driving factor in the global protein meal market, since the increase in LDC consumption accounts for only 2.4% of the total growth. As for developed countries, growth in animal production is expected to follow the slow growth path of the past, and the penetration rate of protein meal in feed rations remains stable (Figure 5.4).

Figure 5.4. **Growth in protein meal consumption and animal production**
2011-13 vs. 2023

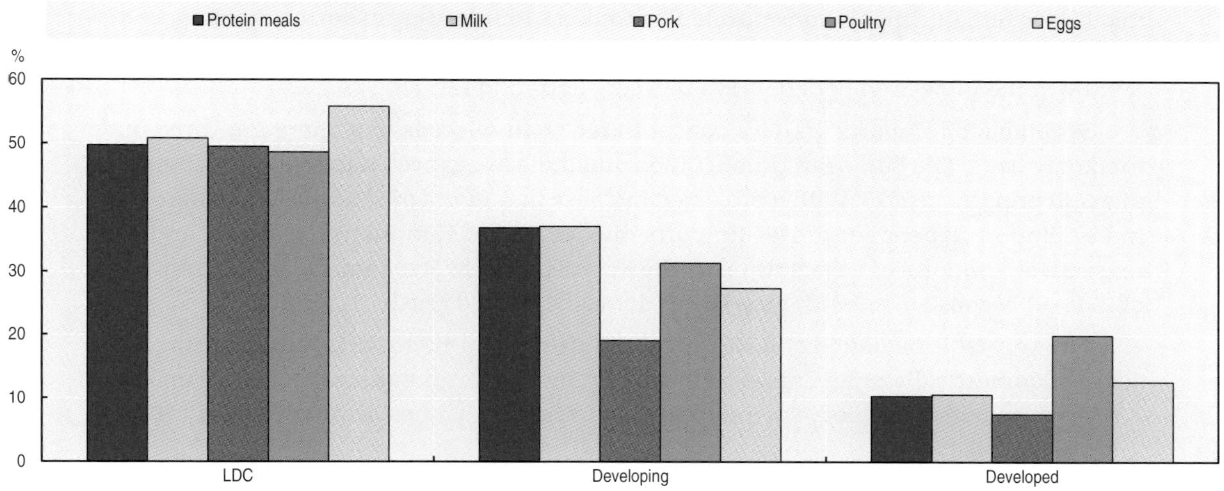

Source: OECD and FAO Secretariats.   StatLink ⬛ http://dx.doi.org/10.1787/888933100169

China and the European Union are expected to remain the leading protein meal consumers, followed by the United States, Brazil and India. The strong increase in demand for protein meal in China will not be entirely met by additional domestic production, which leads to 9 Mt of imports by 2023. In the United States, meal use is expected to expand, following a period of decline that was caused by rising availability of dried distillers grains (DDG). The massive increase in ethanol production in the United States led to a surge in the production of the by-product DDG which can replace, to some extent, protein meal in some feed rations. Approaching the Renewable Fuel Standard (RFS2) maximum amount of ethanol that can be produced from maize in 2015, DDG supply will eventually stabilise, contributing to rising demand for protein meal. The livestock industry in the Russian Federation is projected to increase the amount of protein meal used in the feed rations; yet, it will still remain much below the use rate of developed countries.

Trade in oilseeds and oilseed products

The average annual growth rate of world trade in oilseeds is expected to slow down considerably in the next decade, compared to the previous decade. This development is directly linked to the projected deceleration of the oilseed crush in China. The country is expected to expand its crush by only about 25 Mt in the coming decade compared to an increase of 46 Mt in the previous decade.

Imports by the second largest importer of oilseeds, the European Union, remain stable as increased crush demand is met primarily by rising domestic production. Many smaller importers are expected to expand their imports significantly relative to the base period, but in absolute volumes these additional shipments are small. Purchases by China and the European Union account for 71% of world oilseeds imports by 2023.

In terms of global oilseeds exports, growth over the next decade is expected to be slightly higher for developed than for developing countries. Exports from the United States should grow by 22% over the projection period. A similar growth is expected for Canada (21%) as a growing exportable surplus is generated through continued gains in canola cultivation in the Canadian prairies. Brazil's shipments of oilseeds will increase by 8%[4] over the next decade. Argentina's exports are expected to increase by 21%. Overall, world trade in oilseeds remains highly concentrated, with these four leading exporters holding an 82% market share in 2023. Additional exports by Paraguay and Uruguay, which are growing rapidly in the projection period, move this concentration ratio to 90%.

Vegetable oil imports are less concentrated than oilseeds, but there are three main market players. The European Union, China and India are expected to represent about 48% of world imports in 2023. With a projected increase in imports of 52% and 63%, China's and India's import dependency rates (imports divided by consumption) reach 36% and 64%, respectively. Imports of vegetable oil by the European Union will remain below the average of 2011-13 because of a 5.6 Mt increase in domestic oilseed crush.

The vegetable oil deficit of LDCs will continue to grow along with domestic usage. The share of domestically produced vegetable oil in this market is expected to fall from 35% to 32% over the outlook period. Their imports are expected to increase from 5.3 Mt in 2011-13 to 7.4 Mt by 2023.

Vegetable oil exports continue to be dominated by a few players (Figure 5.5). Indonesia and Malaysia will continue to account for almost two-thirds of total vegetable oil exports during the coming decade. Argentina is expected to be the third largest exporter with a share of 9%. A share of 65% of Argentina's domestic vegetable oil production is exported in 2023, as the differential export tax system continues to favour exports of oilseed products over oilseeds.

For meal, the projections indicate a slowdown in trade expansion from 48% in the previous decade to 28% in the next decade. The deceleration of imports will be much more pronounced in developed than in developing countries. Between the average of 2011-13 and 2023, global imports are projected to increase by 22 Mt, 90% of this anticipated expansion is projected to occur in the developing world.

The large increase in meal consumption in China is anticipated to change its trade balance from a small net exporter at the beginning of the century to a net importer of about 9 Mt in 2023. The European Union's trade deficit should remain mostly stable as the additional oilseeds produced to obtain the necessary oil for biodiesel production will also increase the domestic supply of protein meal.

Argentina will remain, by far, the largest meal exporter, because it is the only country among the large oilseed meal producers with a very small consumption base. This low level of consumption is directly tied to the composition of its livestock sector which requires small amounts of protein meal. The anticipated growth in crushing in Brazil will

Figure 5.5. **Share of vegetable oil exports in 2023**

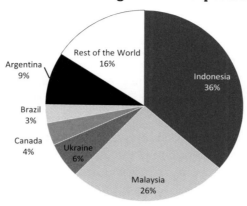

Source: OECD and FAO Secretariats.

StatLink ᠁᠁ *http://dx.doi.org/10.1787/888933100188*

generate a greater surplus of protein meal. Exports will therefore grow by 38%. The five significant American producers – Argentina, Paraguay, Brazil, the United States and Canada – account for a large share of protein meal trade, reaching 74% of world exports by 2023.

Main issues and uncertainties

In addition to the issues and uncertainties common to most commodities (e.g. macroeconomic environment, crude oil prices and weather conditions), each sector has its specific supply and demand sensitivities. The low stock level at the end of the outlook period is a source of uncertainty for the stability of prices, for example, if the sector is affected by adverse weather events.

Biofuel policies in the United States, European Union and Indonesia are a source of major uncertainties in the vegetable oil sector, because they have an impact on a large share of the demand in these countries. The proposal by the European Commission to limit the amount of first generation biofuels that can be counted towards the bloc's renewable energy targets from 10% to 5% remains an uncertainty. If, contrary to what is assumed in this *Outlook*, the new policy requiring Indonesia to replace 25% of its consumption of diesel oil with domestically produced biodiesel by 2025 is successful, the impact on the vegetable oil market would be significant according to the analysis presented in Box 5.1.

Since biodiesel is considered an advanced biofuel in the United States Renewable Fuel Standard mandates, all the uncertainties related to that policy are also relevant for the vegetable oil market.

The main uncertainties are the yearly decision by the United States Environment Protection Agency (EPA) regarding the cellulosic, advanced and total mandate. Until now, none of the reductions in the cellulosic mandate has translated into a reduction in the advanced and total mandates. As indicated in Box 3.1, the EPA's final implementation decision for 2014 is still outstanding. In November 2013, the EPA made a proposal to cut, for the first time, the total renewable fuel mandate, the total advanced biofuels mandate as well as the cellulosic mandate for 2014. This proposal is significantly below the final 2013 Renewable Fuel Standard and the initial numbers set by the Energy Independence and Security Act for 2014. The biodiesel mandate for 2014 is proposed to remain the same as in

2013. But since biodiesel is eligible to fulfil part of the other advanced gap, any decision affecting total and advanced mandates could have an impact on the biodiesel and vegetable oil sectors. An additional factor is the uncertain renewal of the biodiesel tax credit in the United States which can hugely affect the profitability of biodiesel production. The other factor affecting the incentives for blenders to use more biodiesel in the United States is the ethanol blend wall. In the *Outlook*, it is assumed that E15 blends (i.e. 15% ethanol and 85% fossil fuel) will be introduced in the market. However, this is far from being certain.

For protein meal, the European Commission announced in early 2013 that processed animal protein (PAP) from poultry and pigs would be allowed in fish farming as of 1 June 2013 (EU, 2013). There is also a possibility that the European Commission might reintroduce the use of PAP from pork and poultry to poultry and pig farming as of 2014. Both measures could affect the outlook for oilseed meal consumption in the European Union.

Box 5.1. **Policy options for biofuel in Indonesia: Implications for vegetable oil markets**

The Global Bioenergy Partnership (GBEP) is an initiative promoted by the G8 and G20 and launched in 2006 with the scope to support wider, cost effective bioenergy deployment, particularly in developing countries where biomass use is prevalent. Within this Partnership, 49 governments and 26 international organisations have agreed on a set of 24 indicators for bioenergy, designed to inform national policymaking about sustainability criteria of biofuel developments. The establishment of these indicators provides a framework that ensures the consideration of key factors related to sustainable policy decisions; however, they are not binding to pre-established thresholds, allowing individual countries to evaluate their envisioned policy goals independently.

Sustainable development is based on three pillars; economic development, social development and environmental protection. The indicators were designed to cover aspects related to all three pillars. Specifically related to the pillar of social development, one indicator assesses the impact of an emerging bioenergy sector on domestic food markets. Evaluation of this indicator involves three tiers. The first two tiers relate to qualitative assessments of the economic impacts that bioenergy could have on food prices, while the third tier is a model-based quantitative assessment of these impacts.

In Indonesia's case, the Aglink-Cosimo model was used to quantify the effects of proposed policy changes on different food product markets, with a special focus on vegetable oil. The study involved the simulation of four scenarios. The first scenario involved an ex-post simulation of a "no biodiesel" situation in Indonesia. It tested the effects of palm oil use for biofuel on domestic food prices from 2007 to 2012. Removing the biofuel use from the domestic vegetable oil demand increased vegetable oil exports proportionately leaving food demand and domestic prices unchanged.

The second scenario involved an increase in the blending requirements for biodiesel in diesel fuel from the currently achieved 1.5% to 10%, requiring approximately 1.5 billion litres of additional biodiesel by 2020, which was satisfied through a combination of significant production growth and almost complete elimination of biodiesel exports. The additional feedstock demand will be satisfied through slightly reduced exports of palm oil and a small production expansion of about 1% in 2020. No disturbance in the food sector was detected.

Scenario 3 involved an increase in domestic biodiesel production from 1.5 Mt to the currently installed annual processing capacity of 4.3 Mt, while maintaining the baseline blending ratio of 1.5%-3%. The effect on vegetable oil production was insignificant however as exports were reduced to supply the needed feedstock to biodiesel production.

Box 5.1. **Policy options for biofuel in Indonesia: Implications for vegetable oil markets** *(cont.)*

The policy options evaluated in the first three scenarios caused only marginal changes in vegetable oil prices. Changes to the domestic price of rice, wheat and coarse grains were also found to be minimal and vegetable oil consumption in Indonesia remained stable.[1] The impacts on the biofuel industry were mainly through minor changes in trade patterns but without significant shifts in the world market.

The fourth scenario assessed the effects of a new Indonesian policy requiring the use of 25% domestically produced biodiesel in domestically consumed diesel fuel by 2025.[2] The market impacts in this case are more significant. The domestic blending requirement implies additional production of approximately 10 bln of biodiesel and the elimination of biodiesel exports by 2020. The additional demand for biodiesel results in a 14% (approximately 3.5 Mt) reduction in vegetable oil exports. Domestic vegetable oil production increases 2.5% in response to the policy change, while domestic food consumption decreases approximately 1% by 2020. Due to Indonesia's importance within the global vegetable oil market, the projected decline in exports has global market implications. It results in an increase of 8% in the world vegetable oil price and 9% in the international biodiesel price by 2020 (Figure 5.6). As a result of the price increase, global vegetable oil food consumption decreased by 1.4% (approximately 2 Mt), while global vegetable oil production increased by 1.2% (approximately 2.3 Mt) in 2020.

Figure 5.6. **Potential influence of the National Indonesian Energy Policy (KEN) on global vegetable oil markets**

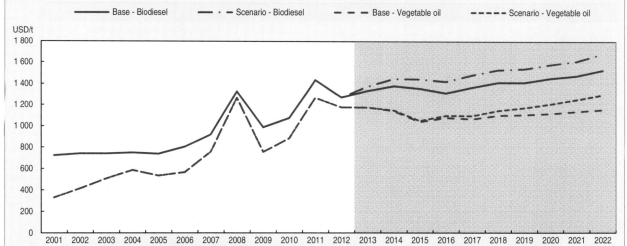

Source: FAO. 2014. Pilot Testing of GBEP Sustainability Indicators for Bioenergy in Indonesia – Indicator 10: Price and supply of a national food basket. Rome, Italy. Food and Agriculture Organization of the United Nations.

StatLink ⟐ *http://dx.doi.org/10.1787/888933100207*

This price increase stimulated global competitors to produce an additional 1.4 Mt of vegetable oil. Malaysia provided approximately one-third of this total, while the balance was shared equally among Canada, China, the European Union and Brazil. The greatest decline in vegetable oil consumption as food was observed in China, where consumption decreased by approximately 800 Kt in 2020.

Application of the GBEP indicators in Indonesia demonstrated their contribution to sustainable development through comprehensive policy guidance at the national level. Illustration of the extent to which domestic policy changes can influence global food markets further highlights the need to provide guidelines for sustainable development on a global scale.

1. Additional information available at *www.globalbioenergy.org/*
2. For all sectors including transport, industry and commerce, and electricity generation.

Notes

1. Brazilian oilseed sector data are reported on a calendar year basis.

2. See the glossary for the definition of crop marketing years for oilseeds and products in various countries.

3. Unless specified, these comparisons are between the average 2011-13 and 2023.

4. This low growth rate is partly due to fairly high levels in the base period and a rapid increase in crush in Brazil.

Reference

European Union (2013), *Official Journal of the European Union*, EU No 56/2013 Regulations, Brussels: European Union, Brussels.

Chapter 6

Sugar

This chapter describes the market situation and the latest set of quantitative medium-term projections for global and national sugar markets for the ten crop-year period, 2014-23. It covers the developments expected in world and national sugar prices, production, use, trade (imports and exports) and stocks (including stock-to-use). The quantitative projections are developed using the partial equilibrium Aglink-Cosimo model of world agriculture. The chapter also includes two boxes that explain market impacts of EU sweetener production quotas and the challenges that the US sugar programme faces in removing sugar surpluses. The chapter concludes with a discussion of some main issues and uncertainties that may have an impact on the medium-term outlook for sugar. These include sugar policies, and specific market developments influencing production, consumption and trade in sugar.

Market situation

After a fourth consecutive season of large global surplus (Figure 6.1), world sugar prices weakened in late 2013. Market fundamentals provide little support to prices during the remaining months of the current season (1 October 2013 to 30 September 2014). World sugar production is now expected to grow less rapidly at the beginning of the outlook period, signalling the end of the surplus phase in the world sugar cycle. But any world sugar price recovery is likely to be muted in the short term by the accumulation of large global stocks in a number of countries since the beginning of the surplus phase in 2011. Global stocks and the stocks-to-use ratio have reached a six year high at the start of the outlook period.

Figure 6.1. **World sugar balance moves into a fourth consecutive production surplus**

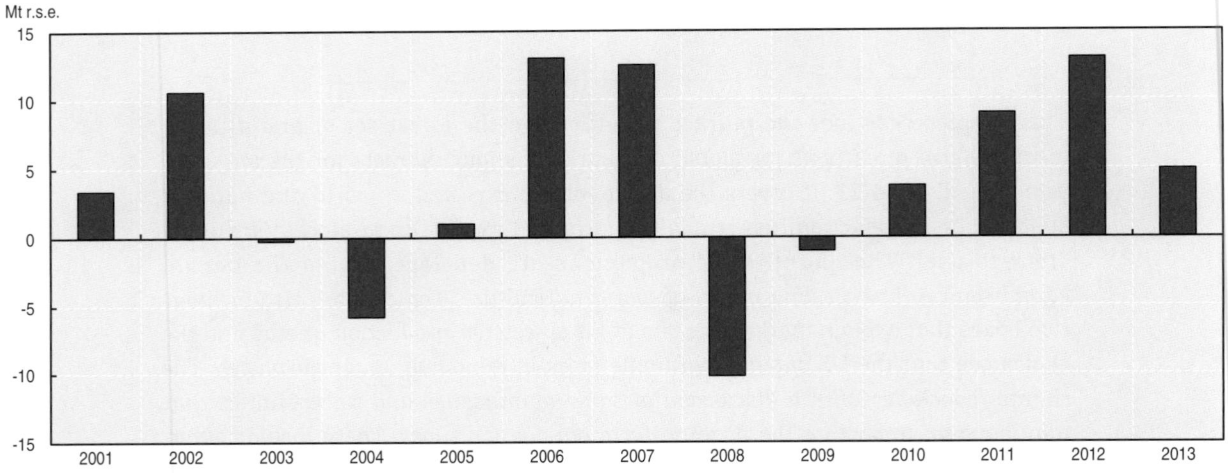

Mt r.s.e.

Source: International Sugar Organisation, world sugar balances.

StatLink ⬛ http://dx.doi.org/10.1787/888933100226

Projection highlights

- Global sugar production is projected to increase by 1.9% p.a. over the projection period and to reach nearly 216 Mt by 2023, an increase of around 36 Mt over the base period.* Most of the increase in production will originate from countries producing sugarcane rather than sugar beet, and is attributed to higher yields rather than area expansion, even though yields will continue to flatten in the short term. Global sugar consumption is projected to increase by 1.9% p.a., much slower than in the previous decade, and will reach 211 Mt in 2023. Growth in consumption of sugar will continue to be dominated by the sugar deficit regions of Asia and Africa.

- World sugar prices are expected to continue to be volatile over the course of the outlook period but will edge moderately upward on the back of rising costs of production

---

* See the glossary for the definition of the sugar crop year. The assumptions underlying the baseline projections can be found in the Overview, Box 1.1.

(Figure 6.2). Prices will remain attractive enough to enhance new investments in production capacity, notably in some exporting countries facing world market prices. The raw sugar price (Intercontinental Exchange No. 11 contract nearby futures) is projected to reach in nominal terms USD 431/t (USD 19.5 cts/lb) in 2023. The indicator world white sugar price (Euronext, Liffe futures Contract No.407, London) is projected to reach USD 519/t (USD 24 cts/lb) in nominal terms, in 2023. The white sugar premium is projected to narrow over the coming decade to reach USD 95/t. Brazil's cost of production and the allocation of its large sugarcane crop between sugar and ethanol production remains a key determinant of world sugar prices over the outlook period. World sugar prices are expected to remain on a raised plateau and to average higher over the projection period, but to continue to decline in real terms.

- Large stocks weighing on the market at the start of the outlook period are expected to slow price recovery. World sugar stocks are, on average, not foreseen to decline but stocks-to-use will, as countries respond to lower prices with increasing consumption (Figure 6.3).

- Production and consumption of high fructose corn syrup (HFCS), or isoglucose, is projected to grow by around 28 and 29%, respectively, to 2023 compared to the base period. The United States remains the leading producer, but the European Union will be responsible for a large share of the additional production in the coming decade, following the abolition of production quotas in 2017. Production will also grow in China and to a lesser extent in Mexico. These countries will also be the leading consumers. Imports and consumption of HFCS is expected to grow further in Mexico as well, as part of two way trade in sugar and HFCS with the United States in an integrated sweetener market under the North American Free Trade Agreement (NAFTA).

Figure 6.2. **World sugar prices to recover in the near term and to remain on a higher plateau**

Evolution of world sugar prices in nominal (left) and real terms (right) to 2023

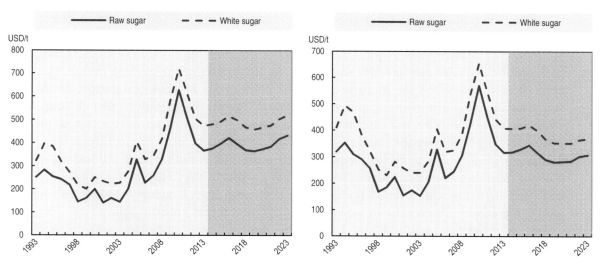

Note: Raw sugar world price, Intercontinental Exchange contract No. 11 nearby futures price; Refined sugar price, Euronext Liffe, Futures Contract No. 407, London. Real sugar prices are nominal world prices deflated by the US GDP deflator (2005 = 1)
Source: OECD and FAO Secretariats.

StatLink ⟨⟩ *http://dx.doi.org/10.1787/888933100245*

Figure 6.3. **The global sugar stock-to-use ratio to follow a downward trend**

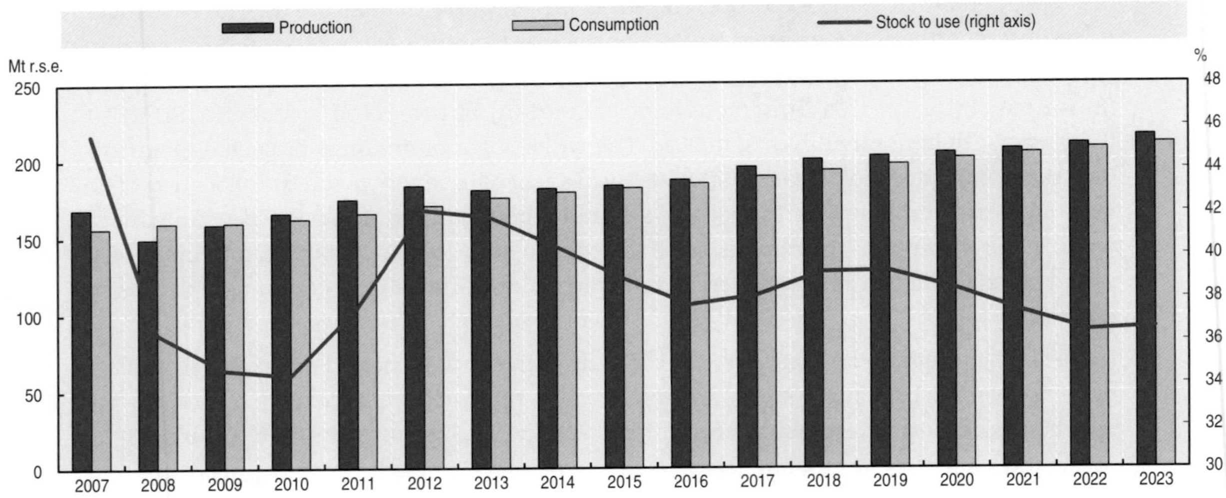

Source: OECD and FAO Secretariats.

StatLink ᴍᴐ http://dx.doi.org/10.1787/888933100264

Market trends and prospects

Prices

World sugar prices have weakened at the start of the outlook period in response to abundant supplies with the accumulation of large stocks after four years of global surpluses. Prices, nevertheless, are expected to recover in 2014, as the global sugar production growth will slow down for a second consecutive year. Four consecutive years of global surplus, with larger production in Brazil, Thailand and elsewhere, have led to abundant export availabilities and high stock-to-consumption cover of around 43% at the start of the outlook period.

Nominal prices are projected to strengthen more in the following two years, depending on production outcomes, before entering the downturn phase of the sugar production cycle once more. Beyond this period, prices are expected to follow an oscillating path around a moderately upward trend over the final years of the outlook period. This price pattern will reflect the longstanding production cycles in leading sugar producing countries of Asia, such as India, and its neighbours. These cycles result in periodic large switches in sugar imports and exports to the world market and cause adjustments in world prices. Sugar prices over the medium-term are expected to be underpinned by stronger demand with a return to broadly-based global economic growth, rising production of ethanol from sugarcane in Brazil and elsewhere, a stronger US Dollar, rising production costs and tighter stocks cover as stocks-to-use decline to 2023. Slowing yield growth and increasing constraints on the expansion of sugar production areas in many producing countries, other than perhaps Brazil, will help support higher sugar prices as demand continues to expand.

Both raw and white sugar prices are expected to follow a similar pattern over the projection period. The raw sugar price (Intercontinental Exchange No. 11 contract nearby futures) is projected in nominal terms at USD 431/t (USD 19.5 cts/lb) in 2023. The indicator world white sugar price (Euronext, Liffe Contract No.407, London) is projected to reach USD 519/t (USD 24 cts/lb), in nominal terms, in 2023. These price trends are predicated on growing demand for ethanol in Brazil as a fuel for the rapidly expanding domestic fleet of flex-fuel vehicles and other uses. Higher fuel demand arises from ethanol's use as a petrol substitute (100% hydrous ethanol) and as a petrol complement, anhydrous ethanol, which is a blend of 20-25% of ethanol and petrol to form gasohol. The production of ethanol for domestic fuel consumption and export is projected to utilise over 63% of Brazil's sugarcane harvest by 2023 and provide indirect support to world sugar prices. Should this additional sugarcane capacity be redirected to sugar production rather than ethanol, the results would be much lower world sugar prices. Sugar production costs in Brazil, as the main supplier to the world market, will provide an effective floor to world prices in the coming decade. However, the projected depreciation of the Brazilian Real against the US Dollar will imply a lower floor price, currently equivalent to a cost of production of around USD 19-20 cts/lb, when denominated in US Dollar terms.

The white sugar premium (difference between the white and raw sugar price), or refining margin, is anticipated to narrow to average around USD 95/t in the coming decade, compared to USD 106/t during the base period. This lower margin reflects the expected growth in refining capacity as additional destination and toll sugar refineries come on stream in various locations around the world such as in the Middle East, Africa and Asia. As these refineries process raw sugar, and increasingly high quality (VHP) raws, their higher demand will support raw sugar prices while the additional white sugar supplies they produce will put downward pressure on the refined product price and, thus, narrow the margin or premium between the two types of sugar over time.

Sugar remains one of the most volatile of all agricultural commodities. However, with abundant supplies, increased export availabilities and higher stock cover, sugar price volatility has abated to some extent in recent months. Despite this short-term development, world sugar prices are, nevertheless, expected to remain highly volatile in future years. This outcome reflects a combination of sugar market characteristics. These include reasonably steady, year-on-year consumption growth, but more variable production and its increasing concentration in regions of greater yield variation, continuing government interventions that impair market adjustment and growing links to more volatile energy markets. The concentration of production and trade in a handful of countries, including the dominant role of Brazil which is itself subject to periodic adverse weather events, is an important factor in this equation. Changes in crop prospects in Brazil are immediately reflected in world sugar prices and contribute to enhanced sugar price volatility.

Production and use of sugar

The sugar sector is capital intensive with a very high level of fixed costs. There has been a slowdown in the rate of expansion in primary processing capacity in recent years which continued in 2013. Despite some slowdown in production growth at the beginning of the outlook period, returns to sugar production are expected to remain sufficiently remunerative, on average, to encourage further investment and increased production over the coming decade. Although some expansion of sugar crop areas is expected in Brazil and a few other countries, additional production will come from higher yields. It is projected that sugarcane will account for virtually all of the additional sugar production and represent nearly 86% of sugar output in 2023, with only minimal additional contribution from sugar beets over the same period. Some expansion of sugar beet production is anticipated in the Russian Federation and the European Union following quota removal in 2017. In parallel, the share of sugarcane allocated to ethanol will continue to follow an upward trend and in 2023, 28% of sugarcane will be allocated to ethanol production (only 15% during the base period). The share of sugar beet allocated to ethanol (5%) will decrease slightly.

Figure 6.4. **Most of the additional ethanol and sugar increases will come from sugarcane production**

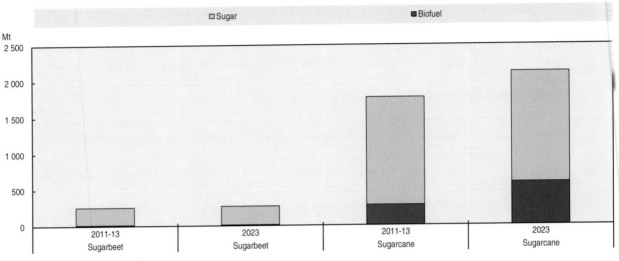

Source: OECD and FAO Secretariats

StatLink ᴍᴍᵖ *http://dx.doi.org/10.1787/888933100283*

World sugar production is projected to grow by 1.9% p.a. to reach 216 Mt by 2023, up nearly 36 Mt, or some 20%, above the average for the base period (2011-13). The developing countries share of global sugar production is projected at 79% in 2023 compared to just 21% in developed countries. In the developing world, the leading region is Latin America and Caribbean which accounts for 34% of global sugar production during the base period, where production is to increase by 22% by 2023. Sugar production in the Asia and Pacific region is expected to increase by 2.4% p.a. to 2023. This growth is driven mainly by higher output in China and Thailand. Finally, sugar output in Africa is projected to increase by 42% to the end of 2023 as a result of expansion in production in Sub-Saharan countries and Egypt. Higher internal demand for sugar will provide the incentive for an expansion of the sector in Africa. Trade opportunities offered under the Economic Partnership Agreements (EPAs) and the Everything But Arms (EBA) initiatives of the European Union are foreseen to reduce following the abolition of the EU quota in 2017. Regarding the developed countries, the European Union is the leading sugar producer with sugar output expected to increase by 1.3% p.a. to 2023, followed by North America where production grows by 0.8% p.a. and Oceania where production expands by 1.2% p.a. over the coming decade.

World sugar demand will be influenced by the recovery in global economic growth and the slightly slower growth in world population over the coming decade. Global consumption of sugar is projected to grow at around 1.9% p.a., slightly slower than in the previous decade, to reach 211 Mt in 2023. Developing countries as a group, with their dominant share of world sugar use, will continue to display the fastest growth in demand, driven by rising incomes, urbanisation and growing populations, although with considerable variation between countries (Figure 6.5). In contrast, sugar consumption is projected to show little or no growth in many of the developed countries consistent with their status as mature or saturated sugar markets. Slowly growing and ageing populations along with increased health consciousness and dietary changes are factors that are impeding sugar use in these countries. Compared to the base period, the sugar deficit regions of Asia and Pacific and Africa will account for most of the expansion in use to 2023 which is projected to increase faster than the world average (32% and 47% respectively). In the former region, it is expected that China and India will experienced the biggest increase in sugar consumption, but the growth in terms of per capita consumption is expected to be largest in China, Indonesia, Saudi Arabia and Thailand. Africa should see the highest growth in world consumption, but Sub-Saharan African countries will still face the lowest per capita consumption at the end of the projection period.

Figure 6.5. **Much higher growth in sugar demand is expected in developing countries**
Developed countries (left) and developing countries (right)

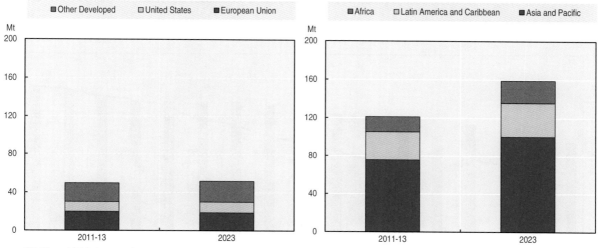

Source: OECD and FAO Secretariats.

StatLink ᴍ⊑🖳 *http://dx.doi.org/10.1787/888933100302*

Brazil is the world's leading sugar producer following the rapid expansion of the industry in the 1990s as a result of relatively low production costs and vast land resources suitable for increased sugar production. The last few years have witnessed a slowdown in the rate of expansion of the industry due to a combination of factors including adverse weather, the industry's limited access to credit and government fuel policy favouring petrol consumption. Adding to industry difficulties have been higher production costs in the short term associated with the mechanisation of harvesting, and rising labour and transport costs. These factors have lowered returns, reduced incentives for investment in the sector and contributed to slower growth in sugarcane output and mill capacity. However, with restored profitability anticipated in coming years, the area under sugar cane is expected to expand and to grow at an average of 1.3% p.a. to 2023. In addition to their considerable supply potential with favourable production advantages, Brazil's sugarcane producers have also benefited over many years from two competing outlets for their cane with strong demand from both sugar and ethanol productions, the latter as a domestic fuel. Ethanol's increasingly dominant share of the growing sugar cane harvest, expanding from around 52% in 2013 to over 63% by the close of the outlook period, will be a key factor influencing both global sugar production and price prospects to 2023.

In 2014, sugar production in Brazil is expected to be marginally lower than in the previous year with more of the reduced sugarcane crop going to ethanol production. However, increased sugarcane production is expected in the following years, leading to higher sugar (and ethanol) output aided in part by strengthening sugar prices in domestic currency terms, because the Brazilian Real is expected to weaken further against the US Dollar over the coming decade. This will boost the industry's competiveness and effectively lower the world's floor price for sugar. Brazil's sugar production is projected to grow at an average of around 1.7% p.a. in the coming decade to reach 49 Mt by 2023. The projected growth in sugar output will be faster in later years than in the near term but slower overall than in the last decade. Consumption of sugar is projected to continue to grow strongly, by around 1.8% p.a., to reach nearly 16.3 Mt in the same period (Figure 6.6).

Figure 6.6. **Sugar production and exports to increase in Brazil as ethanol output expands**

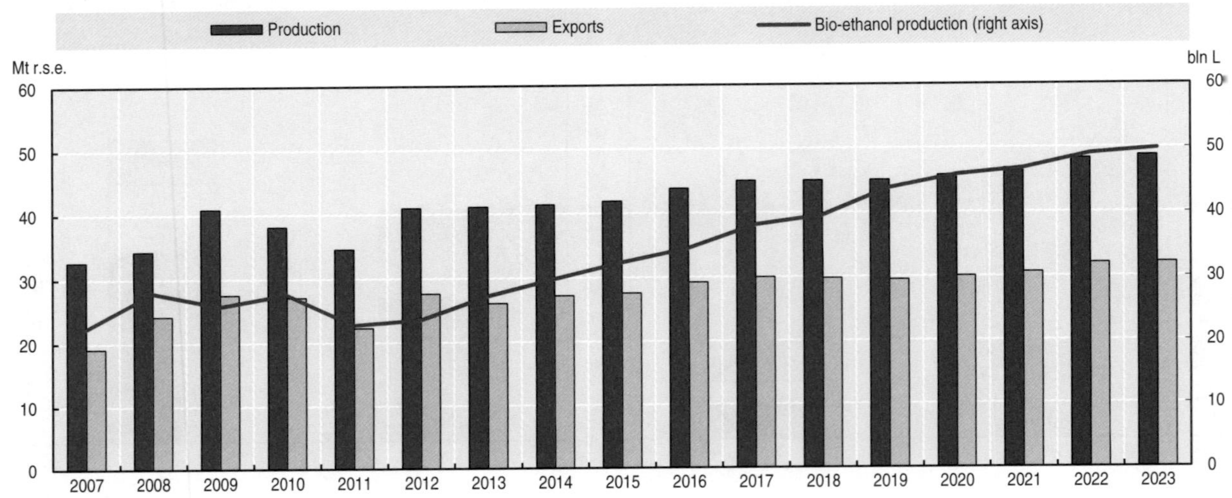

Source: OECD and FAO Secretariats.

StatLink http://dx.doi.org/10.1787/888933100321

India as the world's second largest sugar producer and the leading sugar consumer exerts an important influence on the world sugar market and global prices. Sugar production in the past has followed a cyclical pattern with periods of surplus followed by periods of deficit. This was the result of contrary movements between administered sugarcane and market determined sugar prices which could lead to payment arrears by mills. This production cycle is expected to continue over the projection period, if somewhat less pronounced, as initiatives to deregulate prices by the government have so far be limited to a two-year abolition of the levy sugar mechanism and system of quota release orders. High sugarcane prices at the beginning of the outlook period and limited competition from alternative crops have helped to maintain cane areas and slowing the fall in sugar production despite mounting payment arrears by mills. Lower sugar production is nevertheless anticipated in the near term period. India's production, although variable, is projected to grow at 2.2% p.a., on average, to reach about 31 Mt in 2023. Less variable and relatively strong growth in sugar demand is expected over the coming decade. Consumption is projected to rise to more than 32 Mt by 2023. Depending on the phase of the production cycle, these supply and demand trends are expected to result in India becoming a significant sugar importer in some years and a small, periodic exporter in other years of the coming decade.

Thailand as the world's second largest exporter has continued to produce large sugarcane crops following the surge in production in 2011. Sugar production at the start of the outlook period is projected to remain high but with the pace of production growth moderating in the first few years, as producers respond to weaker world prices. Faster production increases are expected in following years, and Thailand's sugar production will reach around 13.5 Mt by the close of the projection period which results in an average growth rate of 3.1% p.a. over the outlook period. This represents an additional 3.2 Mt over and above the average in the base period, with producers benefitting from higher prices in domestic currency terms as the Thai Baht weakens against the US Dollar. Sugar consumption with a continuation of the longstanding domestic pricing arrangements will grow by 2.9% p.a. to reach 4.1 Mt in 2023.

In China, the Far East Asia region's largest producer, it is expected that the outlook period will commence with only a slightly increase in production, because low sugar prices will discourage farmers to invest in their plantations. Going forward, with growth in cropping area and yields, sugar production from mainly sugarcane and a smaller crop of sugar beets is projected to increase at 2.6% p.a. but to struggle to keep up with demand growth. With sugar consumption significantly below the world's average, it is expected that China's sugar demand will continue to grow rapidly for both direct and indirect uses, but per capita consumption will stay low compared to other countries assuming that no radical changes in consumer food preferences take place over the coming decade. Stocks are foreseen to come down from their high level. As a result, the stock-to-use ratio will decrease slowly to reach 11.6% in 2023.

Figure 6.7. **China's sugar stock-to-use ratio to decline**

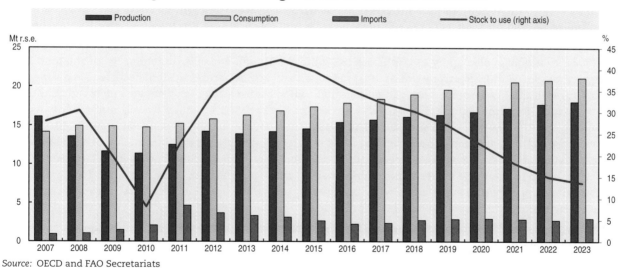

Source: OECD and FAO Secretariats

StatLink ⫘ http://dx.doi.org/10.1787/888933100340

In the developed countries, changes are expected to be less pronounced, and growth in production and consumption (1.4% and 0.5% p.a. respectively) is projected to be much lower than the growth from world levels over the forecast period. The growth in the OECD area will continue to shrink over the next decade and will account for about 20% of global production (down from 22% in the base period) and 22% of global consumption (down from 27% in the base period). Since its sugar reform in 2006, the European Union has turned from being a net exporter of sugar into a net importer. On 1 October 2017, the European Union will abolish production quotas for sugar beet and HFCS (Box 6.1). Based on the underlying assumptions of this *Outlook*, especially regarding the oil price and exchange rate, it is expected that after a rather steady production level in the short period, the removal of the quota will support EU sugar beet production. Both low cost and less efficient producers will expand their output at least at the beginning as the additional volumes will be used to produce sugar, a product more profitable than sugar beet used as feedstock for ethanol. On the other hand, the removal of HFCS quota will also create additional production and, even if there is a lot of uncertainty around this expansion, it will likely contribute to a large proportion of the internal sweetener demand as a lower priced product. According to the projections, sweetener consumption is expected to increase by about 0.5 Mt toward 2023 compared to the base period, with 11.2% attributed to HFCS, up from 3.5% before the removal of the quota. With this reform, domestic prices are projected to be significantly lower and closer to world price levels.

Box 6.1. **Some market impacts of EU sweetener production quotas**

A system of production quotas has operated in the EU sugar market for many years, dating back to the origins of the sugar regime in 1968, in order to limit excess production in response to high support prices. These quotas govern how much sugar domestic producers can sell in the internal market. As part of the fundamental sugar policy reforms initiated in November 2005, administered prices were significantly reduced (although market prices did not follow due to production shortfalls) and the production quota system was simplified and sugar producers were encouraged to renounce a quota of 6 Mt [white sugar value (wv)] by 2010. The quota is currently limited to a total production in the European Union of 14.5 Mt [raw sugar equivalent (rse)] which is allocated across member states. Out-of-quota production of sugar is what is produced in excess of the quota. The level of this production varies from year to year and depends mainly on growing conditions and the level of yields. The sugar made from out-of-quota production cannot (normally) be sold for food use in the European Union and must be sold for industrial uses (chemicals or biofuels) or else exported within annual limits.

Production quotas also apply to isoglucose (HFCS) in the Union, which is limited to 5% of the total EU sugar quota (0.665 Mt), effectively containing production and access to this sweetener. Isoglucose competes with sugar in mainly beverage and food preparations. EU subsidised sugar exports are subject to quantity (and value) limits of around 1.37 Mt (wv) under the GATT/WTO Uruguay Round agreement. As a consequence of the reform and with domestic sugar consumption reasonably stable at around 18 Mt p.a., the European Union has become a structural sugar deficit region requiring the importation of 3.5-4 Mt (wv) p.a. to satisfy its internal needs. As a result, the European Union has switched from being a large exporter of white sugar to the world's largest importer of mainly raw sugar. The bulk of imports enter the European Union under preferential agreements while others are subject to import duties. These large imports can have a significant impact on the world sugar market.

Under the latest Common Agricultural Policy (CAP) reforms of 2013, a new EU-wide sugar agreement will enter into force in 2017. This will lead the abolition of sugar and isoglucose quotas and minimum beet prices, but with existing high import barriers remaining in place. The termination of quotas after the 2016 season is reflected in the sugar baseline for the European Union. To assess the sugar market impacts of eliminating the production quotas, a counterfactual scenario is performed whereby the existing quotas for sugar and isoglucose (HFCS) are not abolished before the end of the projection period in 2023. The results of this scenario are compared with the EU sugar baseline in Table 6.1 below. This table shows, *inter alia*, the percentage differences of the continuing quota(s) scenario up to 2023 and with the no-quota(s) baseline projection.

Box 6.1. **Some market impacts of EU sweetener production quotas** (cont.)

The scenario results suggest that the continuation of quotas would, first and foremost, reduce EU domestic sugar production from 2017 onwards by nearly 11% by the end of the projection period, when compared to the baseline. This reduction would presumably be felt most by the more efficient producers and possibly with some additional production accruing to the less efficient and higher cost sugar producers within the European Union. Consumption of sugar appears to be slightly lower with production quotas, due to an increase in domestic sugar prices, as supplies of isoglucose, which are expected to expand strongly in a no-quota environment after 2017 and competing for a larger share of the sugar market, are restricted by quota. Domestic sugar prices will be higher than in the baseline and world levels with a continuation of quota and existing import barriers. This is because the significant shortfall between EU production and consumption under this scenario would need to be met by imports. Imports would increase by around 52% by the end of 2023, when compared with the baseline of no-quotas. This would potentially be beneficial to the EU's preferential suppliers who through the Everything But Arms (EBA) Initiative and the Economic Partnership Agreements (EPAs) of the Cotonou Agreement have first call in filling this larger import requirement. The EU refineries would see greater access to cane supplies which would be supportive of sugar production. While most imports would likely come from preferential suppliers duty free, some of these would likely be subject to import duties. These duties would have the effect of raising the average level of domestic prices above the world level. Furthermore, with the application of subsidised export limits in the production quota situation, EU exports would be lower, declining by over 36%, when compared to baseline value for 2023.

Table 6.1. **EU sugar market effects of continuing production quotas from 2013 to 2023**
(Comparison with baseline values)

		2013	2016	2023 Quota Scenario	2023 Baseline	2023 Difference from baseline (%)	2023 relative to 2013 Quota Scenario (%)	2023 relative to 2013 Baseline (%)
Sugar beet	Sugar beet area ('000 ha)	1 592	1 571	1 538	1 580	2.72	-3.37	-0.75
	Sugar beet yield (t/ha)	69	71	75	75	-0.45	8.95	8.46
	Sugar beet production ('000 t)	110 218	111 151	116 028	118 646	2.26	5.27	7.65
	Sugar beet for biofuel ('000 t)	14 181	16 942	21 033	13 137	-37.54	48.32	-7.36
	Sugar beet price (€/t)	31	31	30	26	-14.25	-2.70	-16.56
	Sugar beet out-of quota price (€/t)	17	18	21	26	23.13	24.51	53.31
	Sugar beet support price (€/t)	26	26	26	0	-100.00	0.00	-100.00
White sugar (r.s.e)	Sugar production ('000 t)	17 068	16 742	16 885	18 757	11.08	-1.07	9.90
	Sugar quota ('000 t)	14 496	14 496	14 496	0	-100.00	0.00	-100.00
	Sweetener total use* ('000 t)	20 401	19 687	20 441	21 086	3.16	0.20	3.36
	Sugar food and industry use ('000 t)	19 694	19 004	19 748	18 726	-5.17	0.27	-4.91
	Sugar exports ('000 t)	2 076	1 960	1 716	2 332	35.92	-17.35	12.34
	Sugar imports ('000 t)	4 413	3 760	4 767	2 313	-51.48	8.02	-47.59
	Sugar imports, EBA & EPA ('000 t)	2 080	2 128	3 388	1 390	-58.97	62.91	-33.16
	Share of white sugar in total imports (%)	32	36	38	38	0.03	18.75	18.78
	Sugar total stocks ('000 t)	2 884	1 596	1 856	1 504	-18.97	-35.63	-47.84
	White sugar producer price (€/t)	624	624	585	426	-27.13	-6.23	-31.67
	White sugar reference price (€/t)	404	404	404	0	-100.00	0.00	-100.00
	White sugar world price (€/t)	355	376	401	394	-1.93	13.19	11.01
Isoglucose	Isoglucose production ('000 t)	690	690	690	2 355	237.26	0.00	237.26
	Isoglucose use ('000 t)	650	627	638	2 171	240.42	-1.94	233.81
	Share of isoglucose in Sweetener use (%)	3.5	3.5	3.4	11.2	230.00	-2.13	222.96
	Isoglucose exports ('000 t)	60	80	91	155	84.60	54.95	186.04
	Isoglucose imports ('000 t)	20	16	39	16	-64.60	101.72	-28.59
	Isoglucose world price (€/t)	333	354	395	395	-1.28	20.77	19.23

Note: * Including white sugar and isoglucose.
Source: OECD and FAO Secretariats.

StatLink ᘳᗐ⬛ *http://dx.doi.org/10.1787/888933101252*

Box 6.1. Some market impacts of EU sweetener production quotas *(cont.)*

With the no-quota situation in the European Union, all sugar beet production is potentially available for higher value domestic sugar use or for export as a sweetener, such that secondary uses of sugar beets become less attractive including for ethanol production. With quotas remaining in place throughout the entire projection period, and continuing over-quota production, sugar beet use for ethanol production and other industrial purposes will be higher. Finally, the continuation of production quotas after 2017 would have the effect of raising world prices by 2% in 2023, when compared to baseline value as import demand in the European Union would increase significantly. In terms of isoglucose (HFCS), the prolongation of production quotas beyond 2017 to 2023 would lower production and consumption of this caloric sweetener by over 237% and 240%, respectively, by the end of 2023. In general, the reinstatement of production quotas would appear to constrain the potential of the EU sugar industry to expand globally (and nationally within member states with a comparative cost advantage), and to thus impair the efficiency and prospects of the sector.[1]

1. rse = raw sugar equivalent; wv = white sugar value, conversion factor raw to white of 0.92.

The sugar market of the United States is another market heavily influenced by the policy environment (Box 6.2). After a production record in 2012 and the need to trigger actions to maintain US prices above support levels, production is projected to be relatively stable at the start of the projections. It is expected that low prices will again result in some purchases by the Commodity Credit Corporation (CCC) of the United States Department for Agriculture (USDA) for resale to ethanol in 2013 in 2014 and 2018. Demand will stay firm over the outlook period. The low sugar prices will also affect Mexico, which forms with the United States a fully integrated market under NAFTA. Since 2009, the tendency was for food manufacturers in Mexico to substitute domestically produced sugar by lower cost imported HFCS from the United States, but recent lower prices have resulted in a reverse situation. The consumption of sugary drinks has placed Mexico on top of the global list of countries with the biggest weight problems, overtaking the United States. In order to address obesity concerns in Mexico, a tax of 8% per litre was imposed on soft drinks in 2014 but per capita consumption of sweeteners is expected to see only a little decline in the forecast period. It is forecasted that the share of HFCS in Mexico sweetener consumption will resume again at the start of the outlook period, to accelerate toward the end of the period and to reach a level of penetration of the sweetener market not far from the situation in the United States. Beginning 2019, production in both countries is forecasted to increase again, supported by higher prices.

Box 6.2. The US sugar programme under pressure to remove surpluses

The United States is one of the world's largest sugar producers, with production shared between sugarcane (42%) and sugar beets (58%), and is also a major global sugar importer. The US sugar market remains heavily influenced by government policies. In essence, the US sugar programme involves price support via the loan programme and supply control mechanisms, which include domestic marketing allotments, import restrictions and sales to bioenergy producers to manage the sugar market. One of the main selling points of the US sugar programme, particularly in the context of the recently completed 2014 Farm Bill negotiations, was that it operates at a zero costs to the US taxpayer to the extent practicable. However, with unrestricted sweetener trade with Mexico as sanctioned under the North American Free Trade Agreement (NAFTA), it has become increasingly difficult to control supply as demonstrated by the need in 2012 to reduce surplus sugar.

Box 6.2. **The US sugar programme under pressure to remove surpluses** (cont.)

The US government, through the US Department of Agriculture (USDA) and its Commodity Credit Corporation (CCC), implements a price support programme for sugar underpinned by a non-recourse loan rates scheme which allows the processor to repay the loan in full with sugar that was pledged as collateral for the loan when the price is low enough. The USDA operates the programme by seeking domestic prices high enough so that the likelihood of loan forfeitures to the CCC is minimized. Those prices have been above comparable world levels over the course of the sugar programme. Under World Trade Organization (WTO) obligations, the United States has a minimum import quota (TRQ) for raw and refined sugar of 1.14 Mt which is allocated between a wide-range of trading countries. The margin between the internal US price and the (usually lower) world price determines the attractiveness of shipping sugar from TRQ countries compared to shipping their sugar elsewhere. Under NAFTA, Mexico and the United States have formed a single integrated sugar market, with Mexico having gained unlimited, duty-free, access to the usually higher priced US market since 2008. The available amount of Mexican sugar export is influenced by domestic sugar production and the quantity of high fructose corn syrup (HFCS) consumed in Mexico which is mainly imported from the United States.

For many years prior to 2012, supplies of sugar to the US market have generally been tight, maintaining domestic prices well above support levels and making it unnecessary to implement various provisions of the US sugar programme designed to safeguard the domestic market from being over supplied. To help attain an adequate supply at reasonable prices, the USDA can increase TRQ access in addition to the United States' minimum WTO commitments, especially after 1 April, or six months into the October/September fiscal year. However, the situation changed fundamentally in the 2012 season with bumper harvests of sugar in both the United States and Mexico, resulting in record shipments from Mexico of 1.9 Mt and lifting the ending stocks to use ratio in the region to 26%. With US domestic prices in 2013, at or near loan levels, there was a high risk of sugar loan forfeitures. Under the legislation, the USDA is required to operate the sugar programme at the lowest possible cost and pre-empt forfeitures of sugar under loans by whatever means, including the purchase of surplus sugar for conversion to ethanol under the Feedstock Flexibility Program (FFP) provisions of the US Food, Conservation and Energy Act of 2008.

Despite a decline in TRQ imports in 2012, as the margin between the world and internal prices became unprofitable for many exporting countries, record Mexican sugar shipments pushed US sugar prices below loan rates for many sugar producing regions and required the USDA to take action. The CCC of USDA took ten separate measures in 2013 to manage the large sugar surplus in the domestic market. The first action by the CCC was to increase temporarily sugar refiner's limits for participation in the Refined Sugar Re-export Program (RSRP). To benefit from the RSRP scheme, refiners had to promise to surrender or forego RSRP imports of at least 2.5 times the amount of sugar awarded by USDA. This scheme implied that more exports would be sourced from domestic sugar, helping to clear some of the sugar surplus from the market, albeit with a delay and at a lower cost than the FFP facility. Under the FFP, USDA pays sugar producers the loan rate for their sugar production while selling it to ethanol factories at its ethanol value.

The CCC of USDA announced two invitations for the FFP measure in 2013. Under the first FFP action, results were modest with only 7 118 tonnes of forfeited sugar purchased and subsequently sold to an ethanol producer. According to USDA, the CCC paid USD 25.2 cts/lb for the beet sugar and received USD 6 cts/lb for its resale. The second FFP action was much larger with some 136 026 tonnes purchased at an average of USD 24.2 cts/lb but with a resale price for ethanol averaging only USD 4.6 cts/lb. In total, about 21.7% of CCC interventions were for FFP measures. Such interventions are expected to be repeated in some of the future years of the Outlook when forfeiture trigger levels are reached.

Trade

Over the coming decade, developments in some of the sugar producing countries known as deficit countries will provide a change in the pattern of global importing sugar markets. This is the case for the European Union, where sugar and isoglucose quotas will be abolished in 2017. From this date onward, more sugar beet will be devoted to sugar production for human consumption, which is more profitable than ethanol production, and this will affect the quantity of EU imports. The European Union is expected to lose its position as the world largest sugar importer with imports projected to regress by 1.9 Mt in 2023 compared with the base period. In the Russian Federation too, a decrease in sugar imports is anticipated over the forecast period as the growth in sugar production, combined with a decline in population, should help to slow the deficit.

Figure 6.8. **Contrasting trends among major sugar importers**

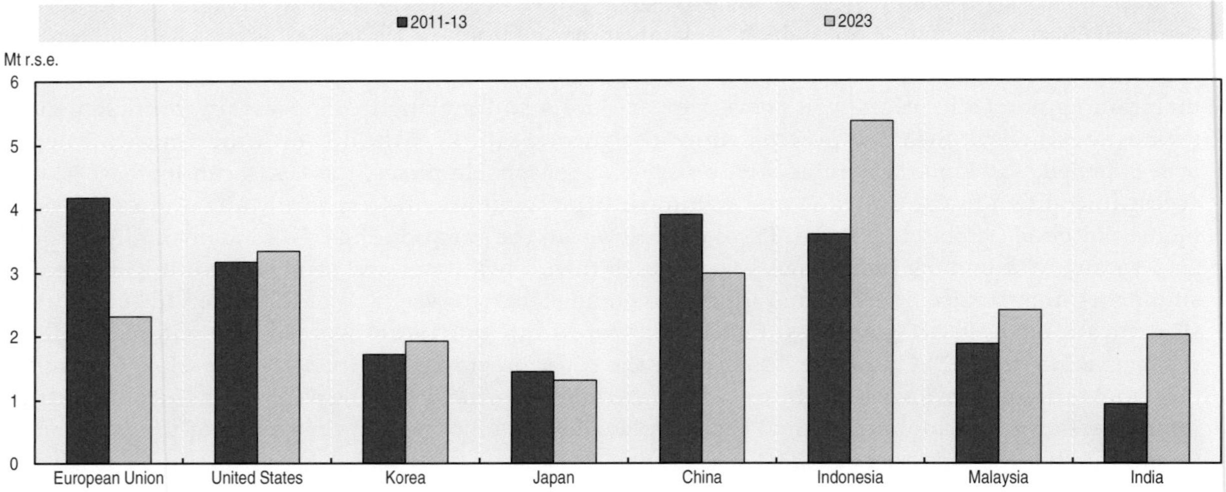

Source: OECD and FAO Secretariats.

StatLink http://dx.doi.org/10.1787/888933100359

Asia and Pacific and Africa will see the strongest growth in sugar demand, driving the growth in imports for those two regions. At the beginning of the outlook period, China and Indonesia are, after the European Union, the leading importers. However, over the forecast period, Indonesia is expected to turn into the leading sugar importer. The United States will recover from recent low world prices, but sugar supplies should stay relatively tight resulting in a continuation of TRQ imports from third countries as well as from Mexico as part of a fully integrated market under NAFTA. An average level of 3.2 Mt of imports is expected over the forecast period, which will make the United States the second largest importer worldwide in 2023. China, where a significant decrease in stocks will contribute to a decline of about 920 kt of imports, is anticipated to become the third largest sugar importer.

Sugar exports should remain highly concentrated. It is expected that Brazil will keep its position as the leading exporter. However, despite the fact that the sugar export volumes will continue to be related to the evolution of world sugar prices, they will become increasingly dependent on the development of the domestic and export markets for ethanol. After a slowdown at the beginning of the outlook period due to lower production growth, exports are anticipated to further expand, with Brazil accounting for about 48% of world trade in 2023, up from 45% during the base period. Good prospects are considered for the world's second largest exporter, Thailand, which will continue to invest in new irrigations schemes and technologies to improve sugarcane output, because the current price advantage over other crops such as cassava is anticipated to remain. This will result in an increase of export availabilities of 2.4 Mt over the outlook period. In Australia, public and private investments are expected to contribute to further developments in existing capacities as well as in new cane growing areas, improvements of cane varieties and the creation of new irrigation schemes. This should lead to a boost in the availability of sugar exports over the forecast period. Hence, Australian sugar exports are anticipated to increase by nearly 850 kt to reach 4 Mt in 2023.

Figure 6.9. **Sugar exports will stay concentrated and dominated by Brazil**

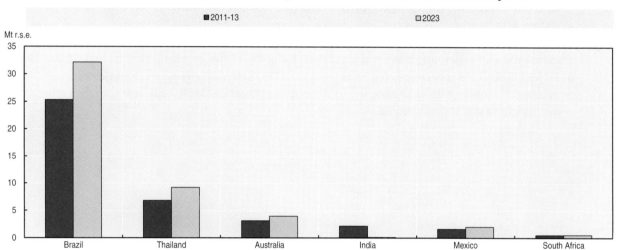

Source: OECD and FAO Secretariats.

StatLink ⟨ms⟩ *http://dx.doi.org/10.1787/888933100378*

Main issues and uncertainties

Sugar is a natural caloric sweetener produced from sugar cane or sugar beet. It competes with land for cereals, while sugar crops are also used to produce ethanol. Furthermore, other caloric sweeteners, such as HFCS, enter in direct competition with sugar for human consumption, and by-products of sugar cane and sugar beet can be used to produce ethanol or complete feed rations. Moreover, the sugar sector is a capital intensive sector with a high level of fixed costs. As a result of these features, changes occurring in other agricultural markets and in macroeconomic factors can have a significant impact on the sugar outlook.

The projections in this *Outlook* are based on the assumption that sugar prices, after a slowdown at the start of the projection period, will be sufficiently attractive to encourage new investments in producing countries, both at the farm and processing level. Any shocks, such as structural changes in sugar policies, originating from the major producing countries, could impact the results of this *Outlook*, with consequences for producers and consumers.

Sweetener demand is expected to stay steady in the medium-term, particularly in developing countries driven by population growth, rising per capita income and urbanisation. Health concerns, often associated with high sugar consumption, could impact the demand in some of these countries over the medium-term of this *Outlook*, and hence lower the projected consumption growth. In addition, expansion in the demand for alternative sweeteners, such as starch sweeteners (e.g high fructose syrup) and intense sweeteners (e.g, sucralose and stevia), could alter the projected consumption levels.

The share of the sugarcane crop allocated to ethanol production at the expense of sugar used as food in Brazil adds another dimension of uncertainty for the *Outlook*. That share remains tightly linked to Brazil's energy policy. Any changes to this share driven by energy/biofuel policies, such as higher blending rates in Brazil and/or new biofuel mandates in the United States, could affect sugar availabilities in Brazil.

The world sugar market and prices are largely influenced by government policies; the sugar market remains one of the most protected markets. It is dominated by border measures, including high import tariffs and price supports. Indirect support, through assistance to the biofuel sector, also provides some price support. Reforms have taken place in some producing countries, but more efforts are required to create a more transparent and efficient global sugar market. Reforms of the sugar market in India have been less ambitious than expected, while the new US Farm Act leaves much of the existing provisions in place. All these policies influence the sugar outlook, and any changes will result in a new set of projections.

Chapter 7

Meat

This chapter describes the market situation and the latest set of quantitative medium-term projections for global and national meat markets for the ten-year period, 2014-23. It covers the developments expected in world and national meat production, use, trade and stocks. The quantitative projections are developed with the aid of the partial equilibrium Aglink-Cosimo model of world agriculture. The chapter also includes three boxes that describe the income-meat demand relationship across countries, the driving factors of India's rise as the top bovine meat exporter and the importance of closing efficiency gaps in meat production. The chapter concludes with a discussion of some main issues and uncertainties that may have an impact on the medium-term outlook for meat. These include the uncertainties surrounding herd rebuilding in North America, animal disease outbreaks and the increasing trend in China to import meat.

Market situation

FAOs Meat Price Index, a measure of global meat prices, has remained at historically high levels since 2011. It currently stands some 90% higher than ten years earlier, reflecting the impact of higher feed costs, which more than doubled over the decade. Though a rapid fall of feed costs in 2013 has set the stage for renewed profitability in the meat sector, supply growth is hampered by tighter sanitary and environmental regulations, and sustained costs of energy, water and labour. The structure of world meat trade is evolving due to shifts in the size and location of demand. Market growth is underpinned by higher demand from emerging regions, particularly from rising incomes, population growth and urbanisation, while the location of demand is reshaped by falling or stagnant demand in many OECD countries.

Global meat production rose just over 1% in 2013, led by growth in pig and sheep meat, but slower growth in bovine meat and poultry. Growth in poultry meat production, at 0.5% was the slowest in at least the last twenty years. It reflects not only the impact of high feed prices which persisted in the first half of the year, but also falling production in China, following consumer reaction to its H7N9 avian influenza outbreak. The United States and Canada have been coping with an outbreak of the Porcine Epidemic Diarrhoea virus (PEDv), which has also reduced pigmeat supplies.

Meat trade has stagnated in the past three years at around 30 Mt. This outcome stems from higher prices that limit demand growth in emerging countries, many of which are net importers of various meat products. In 2013, higher imports of bovine and sheep meats were somewhat offset by lower pig and poultry meat imports – particularly from the Russian Federation, as higher domestic production lowered import demand from this typically large meat importer.

A number of current issues, enumerated below, may impact the medium-term market outlook. The first of these is the situation in the North American, and particularly the bovine, meat market. A confluence of factors, such as higher productivity, higher feed costs, disease related issues and the occurrences of droughts, resulted in the North American beef cow herd declining since 2005. Estimates of the United States cow herd in January 2014 indicate the smallest inventory in decades. The recent decline in feed costs, combined with short supplies, has pushed US fed beef prices to record levels, and a herd rebuilding process appears to have started. Conditions in the United States have a significant impact on global bovine markets, and particularly on the Pacific market where it trades. A second issue is linked to the impact disease outbreaks in major meat markets, in particular PEDv in North America and avian influenza in Asia will have in the next years. The third issue relates to the duration of the sharp increase in net meat imports from China. Though most of increased trade can be attributed to the avian influenza H7N9 outbreak in the case of poultry meat, imports of bovine meat, pig meat and sheep meat have all increased in recent years, pointing to a trend increase that would have important implications for global meat markets.

Projection highlights

- Nominal meat prices are expected to remain high throughout the outlook period. Feed costs remain above historic norms and rising costs related to other inputs such as energy, labour, water and land will also support higher prices. The price of bovine meat in the Pacific Market, which is currently at historic record levels, will rise to around USD 4 800/t by 2016 before falling under increased supplies. Pigmeat prices will oscillate up to the USD 2 000/t level over the projection period, while poultry prices follow feed costs closely over the outlook period, reaching USD 1 550/t by 2023. Sheepmeat prices which fell sharply from high levels in 2013, should resume rising over the medium-term in line with the prices of other competing meats (Figure 7.1a). In real terms, however, meat prices have already, or will soon, peak, and will decline moderately by 2023 (Figure 7.1b).

- Global meat production is projected to rise by 1.6% p.a. over the *Outlook* period, down from 2.3% p.a. in the last ten years. Driven largely by demand preferences, poultry meat will become the largest meat sector by 2020. Over the projection period poultry meat production will capture almost half of the increase in global meat production by 2023, compared to the base period. The sheep meat sector will also exhibit strong growth, recovering from slow growth during the past decade.

- Global meat consumption per capita is expected to reach 36.3 kg in retail weight by 2023, an increase of 2.4 kg compared to the base period. This additional consumption will mostly (72%) consist of poultry, followed by pig, sheep and bovine meat. Consumption growth in developed countries will be slower than that of the developing countries, but in absolute terms, at 69 kg per capita, will remain more than double that in developing countries by the end of the projection period.

- Meat trade is projected to grow slower than in the past decade and in global terms just over 10.6% of meat output will be traded. The most significant import demand growth originates from Asia, which represents the greatest share of additional imports for all meat types.

Figure 7.1a. **World prices in nominal terms**

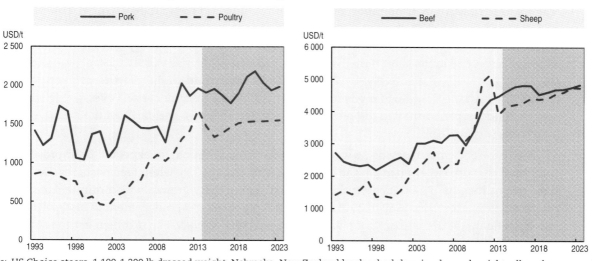

Note: US Choice steers, 1 100-1 300 lb dressed weight, Nebraska. New Zealand lamb schedule price dressed weight, all grade average. US Barrows and gilts, No. 1-3, 230-250 lb dressed weight, Iowa/South Minnesota. Brazil average chicken producer price ready to cook.
Source: OECD and FAO Secretariats.

StatLink http://dx.doi.org/10.1787/888933100397

Figure 7.1b. **World prices in real terms**

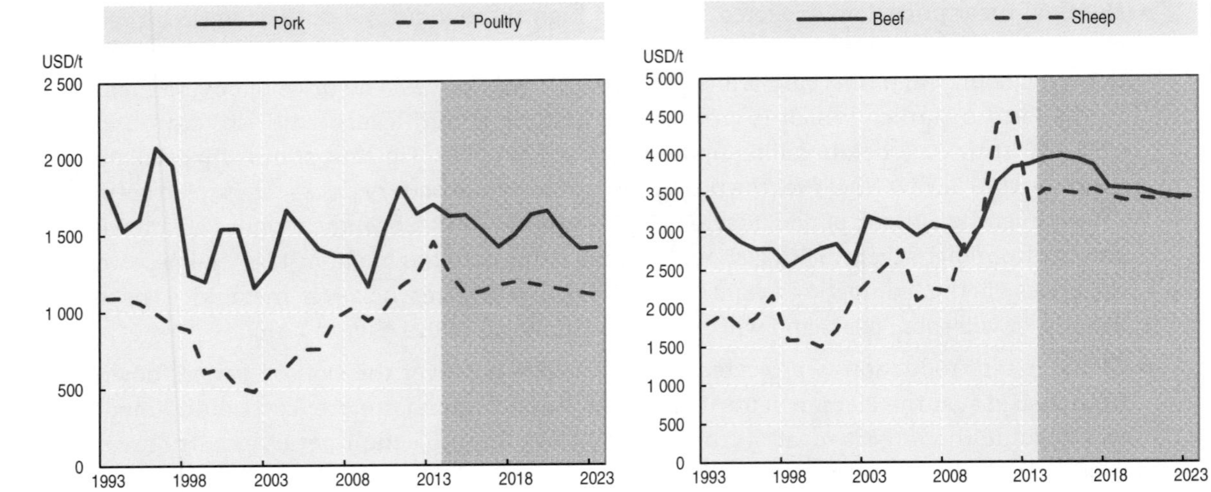

Note: US Choice steers, 1 100-1 300 lb dressed weight, Nebraska. New Zealand lamb schedule price dressed weight, all grade average. US Barrows and gilts, No. 1-3, 230-250 lb dressed weight, Iowa/South Minnesota. Brazil average chicken producer price ready to cook.
Source: OECD and FAO Secretariats.

StatLink ⫘ *http://dx.doi.org/10.1787/888933100416*

Market trends and prospects

Prices

Nominal beef prices in the Pacific market are expected to remain firm in the short term, as herd rebuilding constrains the supply response from the United States, the biggest beef producer in the world. The expected rise in Pacific prices will open up a higher margin with Atlantic prices as the latter pasture based market has sustained larger supplies in recent years. Sheep meat prices reached record levels in 2012 as competition with dairy for pasture in Australia and New Zealand in recent years reduced exports. A strong supply response from those countries brought prices down sharply in 2013. They are projected to rise again over the medium-term to a level of around USD 4 750/t carcass weight equivalent (c.w.e.), underpinned by firm import demand from China and the European Union. Poultry and pig production relies on more intensive use of feed grains, with the result that prices demonstrate a closer correlation to feed prices. The prices of both poultry and pigmeat are expected to decline in the short term in line with feed costs, then rise to USD 1 550/t c.w.e. and USD 1 980/t c.w.e., respectively, by 2023 as feed costs trend higher in the projection (Figure 7.1a). After accounting for general price inflation, real meat prices will average higher over the outlook period than in the previous decade, but they will decline from their current high levels (Figure 7.1b).

Meat-to-feed price margins as well as feed conversion ratios are expected to improve compared to those experienced in the last three years (Figure 7.2), when feed costs reached their recent heights. The *Outlook* anticipates that productivity growth will continue. Long run trend estimates from 1980 to 2013 suggest that pig meat and poultry meat to feed price ratios are falling at the rate of 1.5% p.a. and 0.8% p.a., respectively. The bovine meat to feed price ratio over this period does not reveal a significant downward trend. Over the medium-term, farm price to feed price ratios will remain at or above trend levels as a result of higher non-feed costs, due in particular to factors related to energy, services and environmental regulations.

Figure 7.2. **Meat to feed price ratios should return to historical trend**

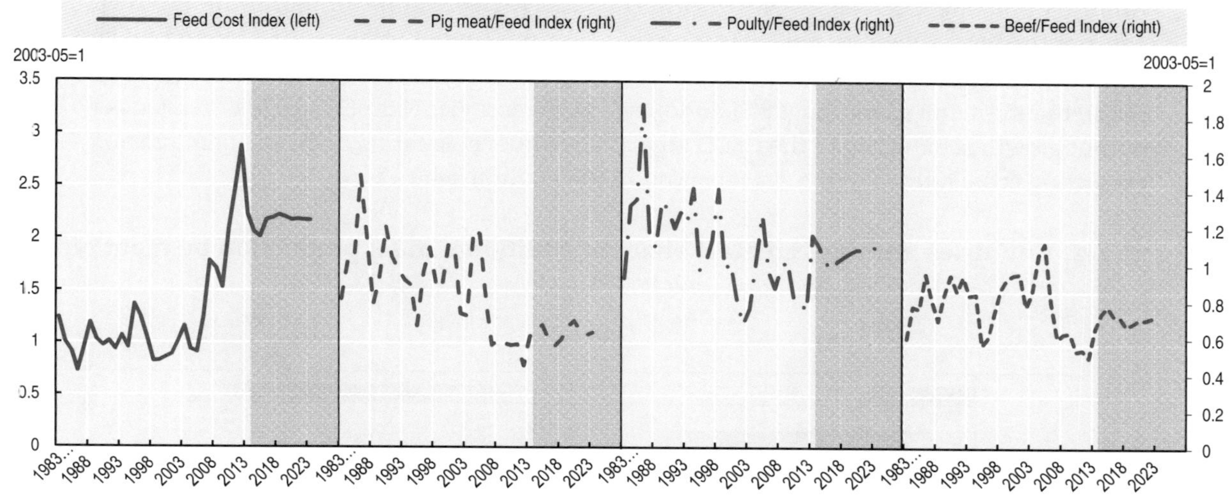

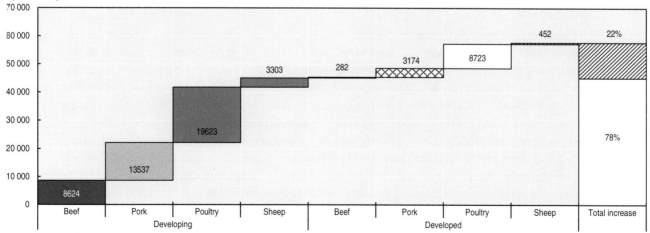

Source: OECD and FAO Secretariats

StatLink ⧉ *http://dx.doi.org/10.1787/888933100435*

Production

While the recent decline in feed costs from their peak in 2012 imply improved profitability for the meat sector, feed costs are nevertheless projected to remain relatively high through the next decade. With other input costs rising – including those associated with meeting more stringent regulations and requirements for the environment, animal welfare and health, as well as water and labour – production growth will be restrained. Global meat production will increase by 19% in 2023 compared to the base period, and of the additional 57.7 Mt, developing countries as a group are projected to account for 45.1 Mt, or 78%, of the total (Figure 7.3).

Figure 7.3. **Growth of meat production by region and meat type**
2023 vs. 2011-13

Note: c.w.e. is carcass weight equivalent, r.t.c is ready to cook equivalent.
Source: OECD and FAO Secretariats.

StatLink ⧉ *http://dx.doi.org/10.1787/888933100454*

Contributing to the increased production, in order of importance, are Asia, Latin America and the Caribbean, North America and Africa. China remains the greatest contributor, with an additional 15.3 Mt, followed by the United States with 6 Mt and Brazil with 4.5 Mt (Figure 7.4). Of the major meat producers, the fastest growers are Argentina (30%), the Russian Federation (28%), Indonesia (47%) and Viet Nam (39%). However, slower output growth is expected in the OECD area as a result of stagnating domestic demand and escalating costs related to the preservation of the environment.

Figure 7.4. **Countries with the greatest share of additional meat production by meat type**

2023 vs. 2011-13

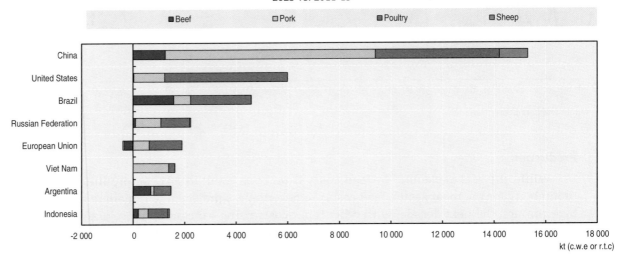

Note: c.w.e. is carcass weight equivalent, r.t.c. is ready to cook equivalent.
Source: OECD and FAO Secretariats.

StatLink http://dx.doi.org/10.1787/888933100475

Of the projected 57.7 Mt of additional meat production in 2023, 28.3 Mt is poultry meat, 16.7 Mt is pigmeat, 9 Mt is bovine meat, and 3.8 Mt is sheep meat. By the end of this decade poultry production will overtake pigmeat production. While both poultry and pig meat production growth will be slower through the outlook period than in the past decade, production of both bovine and sheep meat are expected to increase more rapidly than they did in the last decade.

In terms of output growth, poultry has some clear advantages over other meats. Production does not require a large land base, and it is often situated close to highly populated, growing and richer urban markets. Its short production cycle enables a quicker response from producers in adapting to profitability conditions, and a high feed conversion ratio (meat/feed) results in the lowest production costs of all meats. These attributes are favourable in stimulating growth, especially in developing regions with competitive feed grain prices. Recently, however, poultry has faced problems with high density production, which can be problematic for the spread of diseases. Asia will remain the world's fastest growing market for poultry meat, and it will be critical to resolve disease issues. In India, meat production is dominated by poultry, and output is anticipated to advance around 5% p.a., albeit from still a small base. China's production will recover as consumers regain confidence in the safety of poultry meat.

Global pigmeat production is projected to increase at 1.1% p.a. In developed countries, production will be just 8% higher by 2023 compared to the 2011-13 base period, due mainly to slow growth in the United States and Europe. Considerable uncertainty exists in the United States due to the recent outbreak of the Porcine Epidemic Diarrhoea virus (PEDv), which will reduce production and, given the importance of US trade, will raise pigmeat prices across the Pacific markets until the disease is arrested. The *Outlook*'s assessment is a 2% reduction in US production in 2014 with growth resuming thereafter as the problem is solved. Elsewhere, Asia will account for two-thirds of the growth in pigmeat supplies. This is largely due to China, which represents almost half of additional global pigmeat production. As domestic pigmeat demand becomes more satiated, with the world highest per capita pigmeat consumption, China's, domestic production growth will slow to 0.9% p.a. in the projection period. Brazil and Argentina continue to grow comparatively strongly at 1.9% p.a. and 3% p.a. respectively, bolstered by domestic demand.

In bovine markets, an important event is the herd rebuilding phase which is currently underway in North America, and in particular in the United States, a country which accounts for about one sixth of global supplies. Liquidation in the United States, which started in 2006 and has continued for eight years, was encouraged mainly by high feed and other input prices and weak domestic demand. The drought of 2012 also induced high cow slaughter. Figure 7.5 indicates the depth of cow herd liquidation and the projected expansion over the outlook period, which is anticipated to have a major impact on Pacific meat markets. After weak growth in the last decade, US beef supplies are expected to advance 1.2% p.a. in the *Outlook* period.

Figure 7.5. **Cattle cycle: Inventory of beef cows in the United States**

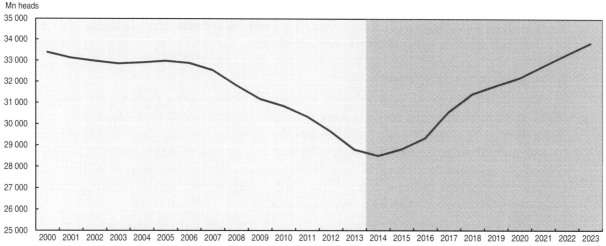

Source: OECD and FAO Secretariats.

StatLink ⟦⟧ *http://dx.doi.org/10.1787/888933100492*

A noticeable turnaround is also expected in the Russian Federation and Argentina, following a decade of diminishing output. Significant production growth will also occur in the least developed countries in Africa, traditionally a pastoral production system. India will account for almost 10% of additional bovine meat produced by 2023 as programmes to encourage commercial slaughter for export are implemented by the government (Box 7.1).

Global sheep meat production, based largely on pastoral systems, is projected to advance rapidly, due to stronger growth in Africa and Asia, encouraged by the higher prices of recent years. These two regions together account for 71% of global supplies, and their share should continue to increase in the medium-term. Australia and New Zealand, whose combined shipments account for 75% of global sheep meat trade, witnessed declining production in the last decade, as high grain and dairy product prices increased the cost of pasture. Reduction in output from these countries was the reason for the large upswing in sheep meat prices during the last ten years. Production of sheep meat is expected to resume at a stronger pace in Australia, but to remain flat in New Zealand, given the high milk prices which are anticipated over the outlook period.

The livestock supply response in some countries is being conditioned by environmental and food safety regulations that stem from concerns for the environment and sustainability; especially, but not exclusively, in developed markets. In many areas of the developing world, a considerable productivity gap remains, with potential for meat output expansion, if higher productivity can be realised.

Consumption

While production costs are the key determinant of prices, it is mostly consumer preferences, together with income and population growth, that lead and drive the meat sector over time. These drivers clearly support higher growth in poultry demand compared to other meats – it is the cheapest and most accessible meat, it is also free of the cultural barriers that affect pigmeat. Aggregate meat consumption remains strongest in developing countries, but recent trends suggest that they have weakened in developed/higher income countries, where per capita levels of meat consumption are already high. However, poultry consumption growth is more robust everywhere. Basic demand analysis suggests that poultry meat is most sensitive to income changes in developing countries (Box 7.1).

Developing countries will account for 83% of extra meat consumed in 2023, relative to the base period, with Asian markets consuming more than half of it. In Asia, total meat consumption is expected to increase by 26%, driven by both strong income growth and a growing and increasingly urban population.

Consumption growth in developed economies remains slow through the *Outlook* period relative to emerging markets. Consumption growth in the United States, and to a lesser extent in Europe, is projected to be positive again following a decline through the past decade. Within the BRICS region, consumption growth is expected to decline, as consumption levels on a per capita basis rise to those of high income markets. While meat consumption growth in India is rapid, the world's largest vegetarian country will still consume on average less than 5 kg per capita by 2023.

In Africa, and despite rapid growth through the past decade, the level of meat consumption per capita remains low, at only 34% of the global average. Population growth, however, is expected to cause a significant increase in total meat consumption. Poultry meat is projected to overtake bovine meat as the most consumed meat product. Poultry and bovine meat together account for 70% of total meat consumption, with sheep meat accounting for a further 20% of the total.

Poultry meat will continue to dominate growth in meat consumption through the outlook period, increasing by 27% in 2023, relative to the base period. It is noteworthy that the United States is projected to increase per capita consumption of poultry from 51 kg to 57 kg by 2023, encouraged by its lower price relative to other meats. Consequently poultry's share of meat consumption expands after slipping in the previous decade. Some of the

Box 7.1. **Income and meat consumption**

Drivers of meat consumption differ significantly across regions, with different cultures and traditions and economic circumstances. However, as meat is a relatively expensive food, consumer incomes play an important role in driving consumption. Economic growth in the past decade has supported higher meat consumption per capita in most countries although in some it has already reached saturation levels.

Figure 7.6 shows per capita consumption of different meats in relation to income on a purchasing power parity basis. Higher income elasticities are expected for more expensive meats like beef and sheep meat; however the data suggests that on a country by country basis this is not the case. Poultry shows the most elastic response to changes in income, despite the fact that it is the cheapest meat. Lower income consumers tend to enter the meat market through poultry and, to a lesser extent, pork, leading to higher consumption as incomes increase, even at low levels of income. Nevertheless, for all meats, as income per capita increases and food becomes a smaller share of total expenditure, the income elasticity decreases significantly.

Figure 7.6. **Yearly meat consumption per capita increases as income levels rise**

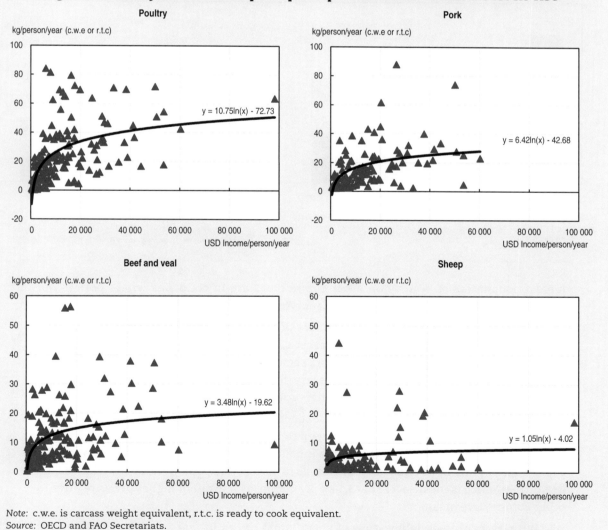

Note: c.w.e. is carcass weight equivalent, r.t.c. is ready to cook equivalent.
Source: OECD and FAO Secretariats.

StatLink ⬛⬛ *http://dx.doi.org/10.1787/888933100511*

Box 7.1. **Income and meat consumption** (*cont.*)

Apart from providing the lowest cost option, poultry is perceived as low in fat, a factor that influences higher income consumers. It is consumed widely across regions (Figure 7.7). Pork provides the most direct competition in terms of price; however regions like the Middle East and Africa consume hardly any pork.

Beef and veal is consumed widely in the Americas as well as in Oceania, while also providing a significant share of meat consumption in Africa, where it is often produced on small scale at household level. On a per capita basis, sheep meat is consumed mainly in the Oceania region and to a lesser extent in the Middle East, providing an alternative to beef and poultry in the absence of pork consumption. The differences in consumption patterns across regions points to the fact that while income remains important, there are many additional factors that influences meat consumption levels.

Figure 7.7. **Regional composition of meat consumption**
base period 2010-13

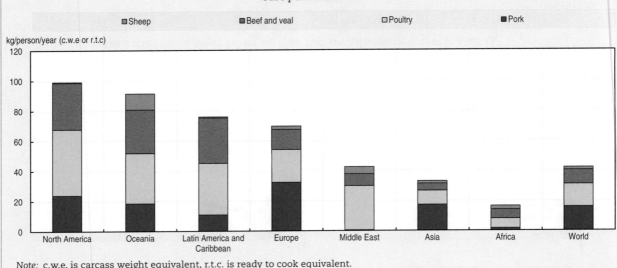

Note: c.w.e. is carcass weight equivalent, r.t.c. is ready to cook equivalent.
Source: OECD and FAO Secretariats.

StatLink http://dx.doi.org/10.1787/888933100530

largest consumers of poultry on a per capita basis are in countries where pork is not consumed, such as Malaysia, Israel and Saudi Arabia.

While pork represents the greatest share of meat consumption in the historical base period, slower growth will see it lose market share to the benefit of poultry in the next decade. In China, which has the largest pork sector in the world, consumption growth rates will decline indicating that consumers are reaching near saturation levels and are diversifying to alternative sources of animal proteins.

Global bovine meat consumption is expected to advance again in the next decade, although it will rise only by 0.1 kg on a per capita basis by 2023, compared to the base period average, having fallen by the same amount in the last ten years. Consumption per capita falls slightly in developed countries, as it rises in developing countries. The decline in North America is most severe at -3.1 kg per capita, as a result of higher prices relative to other competitive meats.

With an expected stabilisation of sheep meat prices in real terms, consumption is projected to grow in the projection period. However, sheep meat will still represent only a

Figure 7.8. **Per capita meat consumed in the world**
2023 vs. base period 2011-13

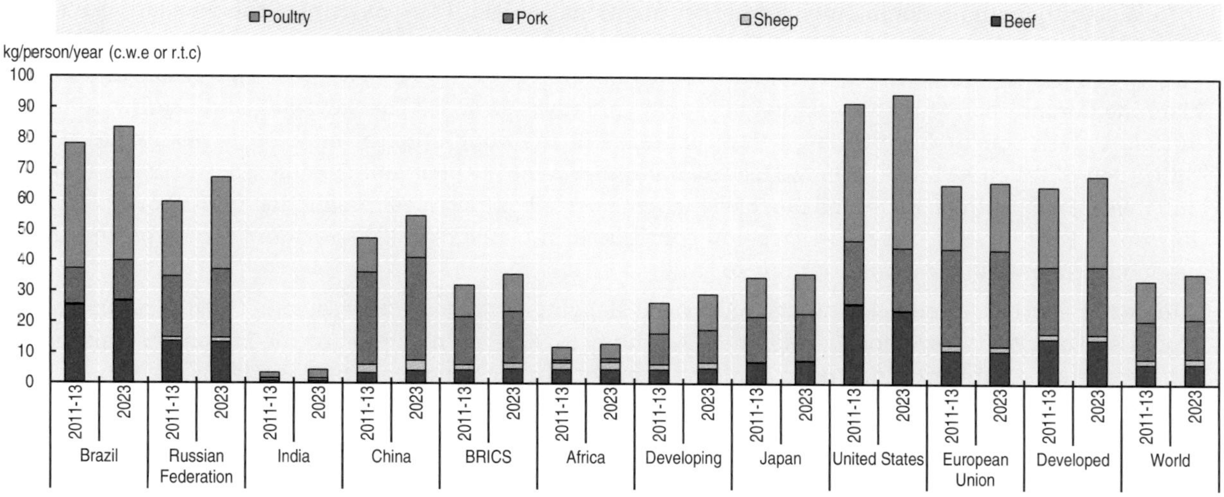

Note: c.w.e. is carcass weight equivalent, r.t.c. is ready to cook equivalent.
Source: OECD and FAO Secretariats.

StatLink ⟨⟨⟨ *http://dx.doi.org/10.1787/888933100549*

small share of global meat consumed. The most significant growth in sheep meat consumption will be in Africa, China, and other economies in the Middle East and Asia.

Trade

Meat trade expansion is anticipated to increase at a slower pace in the next decade when compared to the previous one, but nevertheless will outpace production growth. Higher domestic production in traditionally importing developing and least developed countries is the reason for the slower trade growth. Total meat trade will remain around 10% of production, with bovine meat having the highest trade share at 15.8%.

Developed countries are expected to account for 54% of global meat exports by 2023, down from 56% in the base period. Traditional exporting countries are expected to maintain a high share of the global trade, notably North America (31%) and South America (28%) which also account for 60% of the additional shipments. In these regions, production growth is declining and yet outpaces consumption growth, resulting in an expansion of export supplies. In contrast, the position of the European Union as world meat exporter, while still significant, will continue to weaken through the next decade. Its decline is driven by the combined effect of a strong Euro and higher production costs, following the implementation of stringent animal welfare requirements, notably in the pig meat sector.

Some developing exporting countries, notably Argentina, Brazil, India and Thailand, are expected to benefit from higher global prices and strengthen their strategic position within the structure of international meat trade. A significant development is the consolidation of India as a giant exporter of beef to developing regions, notably with low priced buffalo meat (Box 7.2).

Figure 7.10 illustrates the absolute change in imports and exports for specific meat types across regions from the base period to 2023. Most of the additional meat traded is poultry meat accounting for just over half of additional trade through the outlook period, followed by beef and pork. Sheep trade represents a very small share of the additional trade.

Box 7.2. **Exports of buffalo meat from India**

For a country with predominantly vegetarian traditions, and with the majority of the population averse to consuming beef, it is remarkable that India is currently counted as a major beef exporter. Beef from India largely comprises buffalo meat, also known as carabeef. Under the 11th Five Year Plan (2007-12) of the Planning Commission of the Government of India, initiatives such as "The Salvaging and Rearing of Male Buffalo Calves Scheme" contributed to an increase in the population of male buffaloes, while "The Utilization of Fallen Animals" scheme led to an improvement in carcass utilisation. These two key policy initiatives, along with an increased rate of slaughter, boosted buffalo meat production from about 2.5 Mt in 2009 to 3.75 Mt in 2013. These policies will continue in the 12th Plan (2012-17) and it is expected that production of buffalo meat will continue to grow.

India has also enhanced investments in the meat slaughter and food safety sectors. The Agricultural and Processed Food Products Export Development Authority (APEDA) of India has provided financial assistance for setting up a number of integrated abattoirs, slaughterhouses and meat processing plants. It has also supported the modernisation of a large number of abattoirs across the country. These have contributed to improving the quality of the meat and also meeting safety requirements for exports.

For a number of reasons, India is considered to have a comparative advantage in producing and exporting carabeef as against traditional beef producers and exporters like Brazil and Australia. First, commercial beef-ranching is not practised in India and the male and unproductive female buffaloes are allowed to be slaughtered. Since these animals do not produce milk, they are rarely fed expensive nutritious feeds and therefore the cost of producing meat is much lower than other beef exporting countries. Second, as the production is going up while the domestic market is limited, India will have a substantial surplus to export which, at present, stands at around 30% of its total production. Third, the beef produced in India is *halal* meat, which is preferred in a number of South Asian, African and the Middle Eastern markets. The potential for India to increase its exports competitively is therefore enormous.

The bulk of the buffalo meat that is exported comes from Uttar Pradesh, a large State in India's north and the Southern Indian State of Andhra Pradesh. Most of India's buffalo meat is shipped to South East Asian countries, followed by Middle-Eastern and African countries. Viet Nam with a 30% share, is the largest market. Sanitary standards have limited India's access to new markets, especially to OECD countries to which exports are minuscule.

Figure 7.9. **Buffalo meat exports from India, 2012-13**

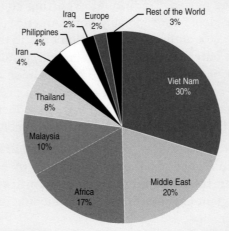

Source: Agricultural and Processed Food Products Export Development Authority (APEDA), Ministry of Commercie and Industry, Government of India (*www.apeda.gov.in*).

StatLink ᵃˢᵖ *http://dx.doi.org/10.1787/888933100568*

The most significant growth in import demand originates from Asia, which represents the greatest share of additional imports for all meat types. Africa also accounts for a significant share of additional meat imports, as consumption growth exceeds growth in domestic production. Japan and China are the largest net importer of meat products, followed by Viet Nam, Saudi Arabia and the Russian Federation. The Russian Federation's net import position is expected to fall significantly, relative to the base period, as efforts to lower import dependency through government programmes are expected to yield some results in stimulating production. The origin of additional exports differs across meat types. South America seizes a significant share of additional exports for all meat types except sheep, which originates mainly from Oceania.

Figure 7.10. **Changes in the net trade of meat by type and region**

2023 vs. base period

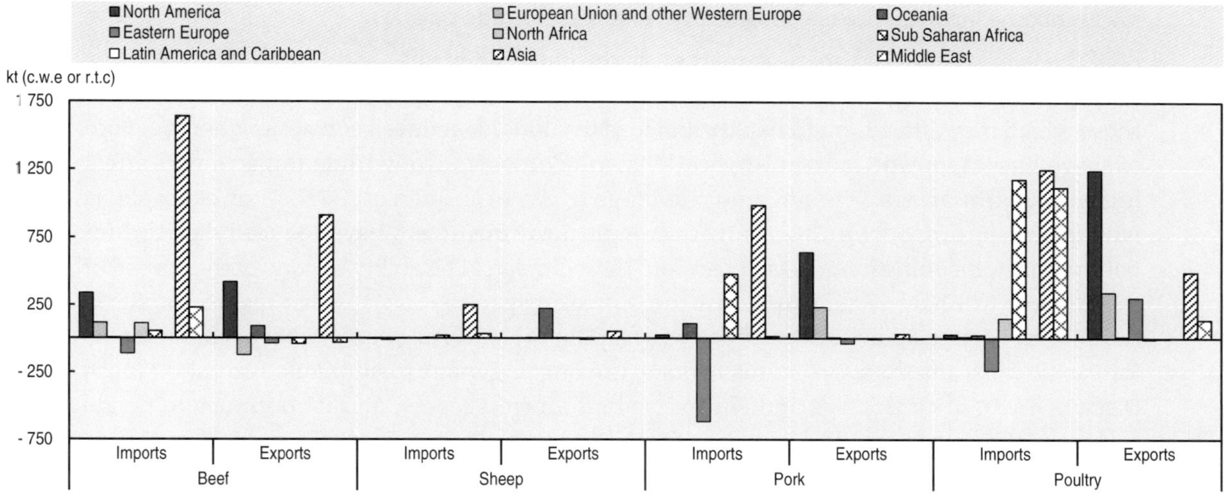

Note: c.w.e. is carcass weight equivalent, r.t.c. is ready to cook equivalent.
Source: OECD and FAO Secretariats.

StatLink ⬛⬛ http://dx.doi.org/10.1787/888933100587

Considering specific meat types, additional poultry exports originate mainly from North and South America, but Ukraine is also showing a substantial expansion of its poultry sector, leading to substantial export growth and contributing to a positive trade balance for poultry products in Europe. Continued unrest in the area, however, could reduce this expected export growth. The most significant importers after Asia are North Africa and the Middle East.

The majority of additional pork exports are expected to originate from North America, where exports are projected to grow through the ten-year period, while the only other significant net exporting region is the European Union. The greatest demand for additional imports is from Asia, followed by Sub-Saharan Africa and South America.

The demand for additional beef imports is centred in Asia, followed by the Middle East and North Africa, while the bulk of additional exports are expected to originate from South America, thanks to export growth of 2.4% p.a. through the outlook period. Exports from North America and Europe are anticipated to decline through the outlook period.

Australia and New Zealand continue to be the world's largest sheep meat exporters, growing 1.9% p.a. over the projection period. Sheep meat exports from Australia are expected to grow faster than those from New Zealand. This growth will be driven by increasing demand from the expanding middle class in the Middle East and Asia, particularly China, which has now surpassed the United Kingdom as New Zealand's number one market in terms of volume.

Main issues and uncertainties

The rate of growth in the meat sector differs by country and meat type, but at aggregate level the meat sector of developing countries is among the fastest growing of all major agricultural sectors. In developed countries, meat production is growing, but consumption per person, as well as the population growth rate is relatively stagnant, implying growing exports. Trade agreements have fostered increased trade by reducing tariff and non-tariff barriers, while global agreements have also improved the capacity to cope with animal disease outbreaks, which have often disturbed national and international markets unexpectedly as interdependence has increased with time. This stylistic portrayal of a globally growing sector also points to the standard risks and uncertainties in the *Outlook*, whether they are higher or lower income growth, disease outbreaks or changes in trade policies.

The ever present risk to meat markets is the outbreak of animal diseases, which may be of two types. Those which may affect herd capital, forcing liquidation of existing animals, and those which may affect human health, and lead to suddenly reduced consumer demand. Both of these have domestic market implications, in addition to likely trade impacts that affect international markets. The ongoing challenge of Avian Influenza (H7N9), for example, is having a major impact on China's meat complex, as consumers have reduced demand for poultry meat, resulting in increased demand for red meats. The ability to control the spread of this disease will have ramifications for the outlook, especially in the Asian region. Similarly, the current Porcine Epidemic Diarrhoea virus (PEDv) in North America will have repercussions for Pacific meat markets. In various regions, the ongoing effort to eliminate Foot and Mouth Disease (FMD) in cattle, pigs and sheep has had mixed success, and it continues to divide commercial markets and opportunities for the industry. African Swine Fever (ASF), which is endemic in parts of Africa and has spread at various times to other countries, could also potentially disrupt markets in the future.

The prospect of various trade agreements over the outlook period could increase meat trade substantially. In October 2013, the European Union signed a free trade agreement with Canada, which is likely to increase agricultural trade between the two and provide increased access to the pig and bovine meat sectors. The United States is currently discussing with the European Union the creation of the Transatlantic Trade and Investment Partnership (TTIP), which would reduce tariffs and trade restrictions and likely enhance trade between the two partners. Few analyses have tried to quantify the effect on the meat market of such trade agreement. Nevertheless, the TTIP would likely improve US exports of high quality beef to the European Union (Agri-Benchmark, 2013). The European Union is also negotiating with countries of the Mercado Común del Sur (MERCOSUR; Brazil, Argentina, Uruguay, Paraguay and Venezuela), and depending on the outcomes, an agreement could have a substantive impact on meat trade between these regions (Burrell et al., 2011). An outcome of the discussions for a Trans Pacific Partnership (TPP) Free Trade Agreement could also affect meat trade during the outlook period.

Environmental regulations and concerns continue to affect meat production. These imply higher costs of compliance, either by affecting the location of production, or in the form of specific requirements related to animal housing, waste disposal etc. Estimates of global animal numbers used in this *Outlook* indicate that in 2013 the inventory of cattle, pigs, sheep and poultry birds stood at 1.6 billion, 1.0 billion, 2.1 billion, and 22.6 billion respectively. From 1995 to 2013, the trend growth of cattle inventory was negligible, while for pigs, sheep and poultry it grew by 0.7%, 1.1%, and 2.8% p.a, respectively. For the outlook period, the rate of growth in herds for cattle (1.1%), pigs (0.6%), sheep (2.6%) and poultry (2.2%) are significant, and it indicates that further growth in farm animal herds will be required in order to meet the growing demand for meat, eggs and dairy products. Growing herd numbers further implies potentially higher environmental pressures and other externalities. These trends have caused policy makers to draw attention to the importance of improved animal efficiency/productivity in supplying market requirements (Box 7.3).

There are certain specific risks associated with the outlook. One is cattle herd rebuilding, which is projected to continue into the early years of the outlook period in North America, impacting significantly on Pacific meat markets. The current projection portrays Pacific bovine meat prices as peaking in 2015, and declining thereafter as supplies come on stream. However, the projection also includes a large margin between Pacific and Atlantic bovine meat markets which may not sustain if Atlantic market suppliers, particularly Brazil and Argentina, gain better access to the Pacific market. If this occurs, it would bring Pacific bovine meat prices down, limiting the resulting growth in both supply and exports from North America.

The potential for increased meat imports by China is an important risk which could underpin higher prices in meat markets. As noted in the 2013 *Outlook*, whether China increases domestic meat production by growing or importing more feed grain, or alternatively imports more meat directly (or both), has implications for global markets of these commodities. In fact, the recent meat trade situation in China points to much higher meat imports than previously expected. If these were to rise more than projected, they could considerably impact markets. On a reverse perspective, India's potential to increase bovine meat exports is substantial, given the low rate of commercial slaughter relative to the size of its buffalo cattle inventory. The projection indicates that bovine meat exports from India will exceed 2 Mt by 2023, while its slaughter remains only some 1% of inventory. Simulations using the Aglink-Cosimo model indicate that if that ratio increased to 1.5% by 2023, exports would increase to 3.5 Mt and depress Atlantic market prices by up to 8%.

Box 7.3. **Global agenda for sustainable livestock**

The livestock sector is vital to global nutrition and food security, provides livelihoods to an estimated one billion people, and delivers important products and services such as asset savings, traction, manure for fuel and fertilisers, and fibre. However, the sector is facing unprecedented challenges. By 2050, the demand for livestock products will grow by 70% driven by rising world population, increasing affluence, and urbanisation. This growth in demand is happening at a time when concerns about resource scarcity, climate change and the need for more equitable development are assuming ever greater importance.

Realizing that the complexity of the challenges facing the sector can be addressed only through concerted and collective action, stakeholders have formed a partnership to build a **Global Agenda for Sustainable Livestock (*www.livestockdialogue.org*)**. The Agenda is a multi-stakeholder partnership committed to sustainable livestock sector development, whose purpose is to catalyse and guide the continuous improvement of livestock sector practices towards more efficient, safe, and responsible use of natural resources. Through a more efficient use of natural resources, the sector can enhance its environmental performance and generate significant economic and social benefits, contributing to food security, income generation and poverty reduction.

Box 7.3. **Global agenda for sustainable livestock** (cont.)

The partnership develops harmonised metrics and methodologies, conducts independent sector analyses and produces voluntary guidance and strategic recommendations to catalyse the continuous improvement of livestock sector resource use. Land, water, nutrients and greenhouse gas emissions are the initial focus, particularly on areas where large environmental, social and economic gains can be made:

a) Focus area: *Closing the efficiency gap* aims to stimulate the application of existing, but not widely used technologies, by the bulk of the world's producers whose use of natural resources is often greatly inefficient.

b) Focus area: *Restoring value to grasslands* pursues better management of grazing land which contributes to carbon sequestration, protection of water resources and biodiversity, whilst enhancing productivity and livelihoods.

c) Focus area: *Waste to worth* aims to recover and recycle nutrients and energy contained in animal manure from intensive and confined livestock production operations.

The adoption of more efficient technologies and practices is the key to increased productivity and to mitigating emissions from livestock, and increasing the sector's contribution to economic growth and poverty reduction. Possible interventions to improve productivity are generally those that improve efficiency at animal and herd levels. Feeding practices and feed additives, manure handling (treatment, storage, application, housing), and general animal husbandry practices (genetic selection, animal health, reduced mortality, reproductive management) all offer avenues for significant social, economic and environmental benefits.

Some examples of where productivity gains can be made and also result in simultaneous improvements of environmental performance include: (Gerber et al., 2013[1]):

- Herd management and feed quality improvement in South Asia to produce same or even greater amounts of milk out of a reduced cattle and buffalo population;

- In South America, feasible improvements in grazing management and forage quality, and animal health and husbandry in beef production, could lead to a 19% to 30% reduction of CO_2-equivalent emissions;

- In the West African small ruminant sector, emissions reductions and greater supply of beef and milk could potentially be achieved by improving forage digestibility, grazing management, and animal health, husbandry, and breeding;

- Dairy systems in OECD countries could reduce their emissions by 14% to 17% through the adoption of improved pasture management, feed supplementation and energy saving equipment;

- Industrial pig production systems in East and Southeast Asia could, by improving manure management and adopting energy saving technologies (and using low carbon energy), reduce emissions by 16% to 25% and achieve further environmental benefits related to reduced nutrient losses into the environment.

1. FAO (2013), *Tackling Climate Change Through Livestock*, Food and Agriculture Organization of the United Nations, Rome *www.fao.org/docrep/018/i3437e/i3437e.pdf*.

References

Agri-Benchmark (2013), *Cost of production and competiveness of beef production in Canada, the US and EU*, Working Paper, 2013/5. *www.agribenchmark.org*/beefandsheep/publications.

Burrell, A., E. Ferrari, A. González Mellado, M. Himics, J. Michalek, S. Shrestha and B. Van Doorslaer (2011), *Potential EU-Mercosur Free Trade Agreement Impact Assessment*, Joint Research Centre, European Commission, Seville.

FAO (2013), *Tackling Climate Change Through Livestock*, Food and Agriculture Organization of the United Nations, Rome

Gerber, P.J., H. Steinfeld, B. Henderson, A. Mottet, C. Opio, J. Dijkman, A. Falcucci and G.Tempio (2013). *Tackling climate change through livestock – A global assessment of emissions and mitigation opportunities*. Food and Agriculture Organization of the United Nations, Rome.

Chapter 8

Fish and seafood

This chapter illustrates the market situation and the latest set of quantitative medium-term projections for the fish sector for 2014-23. The analysis of the market prospects for fish covers the developments expected in its prices, production, use (human consumption, fishmeal and fish oil) and trade (imports and exports). The quantitative projections are developed with the aid of the dynamic policy specific partial equilibrium fish model. At present, it is a stand-alone model using the same macroeconomic assumptions and the same feed and food prices employed or generated by the agricultural market model Aglink-Cosimo. The chapter also includes a box that discusses the recycling of fish residue in the fishmeal and oil market. The chapter concludes with a discussion of some main issues and uncertainties which might affect the medium-term outlook for fish. Major emphasis is given to fisheries policies, and specific constraints influencing capture and aquaculture production.

Market situation

The fish and seafood[1] sector has been recently characterised by rather high and volatile prices. With the 2002-04 average price set to 100, the aggregate FAO Fish Price Index climbed steeply to a record high of 164 in December 2013. This growth reflects an inadequate supply that pushes prices upward for selected farmed species, e.g. salmon and shrimps/prawns that are two of the world's major traded species, but also increases in prices for some wild species such as cod and certain pelagic species. In contrast, fishmeal prices, after having reached historic highs in January 2013, experienced a downward trend (minus 20% during January 2013-January 2014), but still remain on a high plateau.

After a period of instability, that started in the mid-end of 2012 and early 2013, fishery trade bounced back during the rest of 2013 and early 2014. In 2013 the overall exports of fish and fishery products peaked at over USD 136 billion, representing a more than 5% increase compared with the previous year. This strengthening was in part a reflection of higher prices, but it was also stimulated by a recovery in high-income economies, which are the main importers of seafood. Overall exports from developing countries increased partly because of this revitalised import demand but also because of flourishing demand for high value species such as salmon, tuna, bivalves and shrimp, by emerging economies.

Led by continued growth in aquaculture output, global fishery production (aquaculture plus capture) reached a new record in 2013, at more than 160 Mt. Per capita apparent[2] fish consumption grew by more than 2%, compared to previous year, reflecting the increased availability of farmed products, which are in the process of overtaking capture fisheries as the main source of fish food supply, but also the growing volumes of wild species going to direct human consumption instead of being reduced into fishmeal/fish oil.

Projection highlights

- Despite the instability experienced in 2012 and part of 2013, the medium-term trend for the fish sector remains positive. Developing countries will drive major changes and expansion in fisheries and aquaculture production, trade and consumption.

- The outlook for fish in the next decade reflects the response to sustained high costs in a context of firm demand, in particular in developing countries. By 2023, fish prices in nominal terms are projected to be well above their historical average. In real terms, fish prices are expected to slightly decline, yet remaining above levels in previous decades.

- World fishery production is expected to be 17% higher by 2023. The growth will be primarily driven by gains in aquaculture output, which is projected to reach 49% of total fishery production in 2023. However, growth in aquaculture production is anticipated to slow down to 2.5% p.a., dampened by higher costs during the outlook period, which compares to 5.6% p.a. for the previous decade.

● Fish and fishery products will continue to be highly traded, but overall trade is projected to increase at a slightly slower pace than in the past due to higher transportation cost, slower output growth and weaker demand in selected importing countries.

● World per capita apparent fish food consumption is projected to reach 20.9 kg per capita in 2023, up from 19.2 kg per capita in 2011-13. Relative to the previous decade, fish consumption growth in the outlook period will decelerate due to high fish prices and slower population growth.

Market trends and prospects

Prices

Fishery prices are currently at very high levels, and little moderation is expected as long as production costs, in particular for feed and energy, remain high. The main drivers affecting world fish prices for capture, aquaculture and traded products will be income and population growth, limited growth of capture fisheries production, sustained demand for fish, increasing meat prices, and high costs for feed, energy and crude oil. All these factors will contribute to fish prices continuing to rally over the medium-term (Figure 8.1) in nominal terms relative to the previous decade. In real terms, however, fish prices are assumed to slightly decline, but they will remain on an elevated plateau over the next decade. This decline can be explained by further productivity gains in aquaculture production and by a decline in real terms of some input prices.

Figure 8.1. **World fish prices in real terms expected to remain high**

Nominal (left) *vs* real (right) fish prices

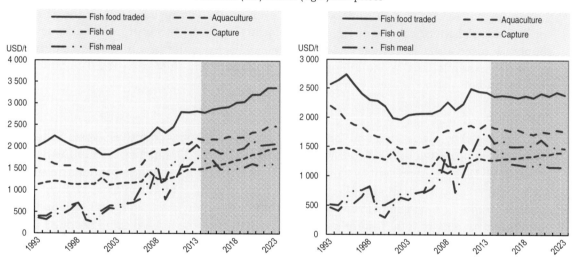

Note: Fish food traded: world unit value of trade (sum of exports and imports). Aquaculture: FAO world unit value of aquaculture fisheries production (live weight basis). Capture: FAO estimated value of world ex-vessel value of capture fisheries production excluding for reduction. Fishmeal: 64-65% protein, Hamburg, Germany. Fish oil: any origin, N.W. Europe.
Source: OECD and FAO Secretariats.

StatLink ⟨⟨⟩⟩ http://dx.doi.org/10.1787/888933100606

Capture fisheries are expected to remain under restrictive capture quotas, with its average price (excluding fish for reduction) projected to grow more than the one for aquaculture fish (31% compared to 15%) during 2014-23. However, the overall price of fish caught in the wild will remain lower than that for farmed fish. This is partially explained by the increasing share of lower value fish in overall catches. Both coarse grains and fishmeal will continue to be to be used as ingredients for raising fed aquaculture species. As in the case of meats, the price ratio between aquaculture fish and coarse grains is expected to remain stable over next decade, at a higher level than during the 2006-12 period but at a much lower level than in the 1990s. The ratio of the price of fish raised in aquaculture to the fishmeal price will gradually stabilise over the projected period.

Starting from a high plateau, the average fishmeal price is projected to remain stable over the projection period. Since the demand for fishmeal from aquaculture is growing faster than supply, an increase in the price ratio between fishmeal and oilseed meal is expected due to the strong preference for fishmeal in certain stages of animal rearing (e.g. in the weaning stage for pigs and initial stages of salmon rearing). This will be more relevant in years of the El Niño phenomenon, affecting catches in South America, in particular anchoveta species in Peru and Chile, which are mainly used for reduction into fishmeal and fish oil. However, since fishmeal and protein meal prices are starting from very high levels, a small decline is expected in nominal terms over 2014-23.

Due to slower growth in supply than in demand, fish oil prices will increase in nominal terms by 14% between the 2011-13 base period and 2023. The popularity of the Omega-3 fatty acids in human diets and the growth of aquaculture production have both contributed to an increase in the fish to oilseed oil price ratio. The popularity of Omega-3, in particular, is the source of a structural change in the ratio of these two prices since 2012. The resulting ratio is assumed to be maintained over the medium-term except in the years where the El Niño phenomenon occurs.

The price of traded fish products in nominal terms will increase by 20% over the outlook period, though in real terms it is projected to stabilise at a slightly lower level than the recent peak reached in 2011, but below the levels reached at the beginning of the 1990s. For individual fishery commodities, price volatility could be more pronounced due to supply swings caused by changes in catch quotas, disease outbreaks in the aquaculture sector (for example, as the one affecting shrimps production in Mexico and Thailand at present) as well as fluctuations in feed costs.

Production

Stimulated by higher demand for fish and led by developing countries, world fishery production is projected to reach 186 Mt in 2023. This is about 17% higher than in the base period 2011-13, but it represents a slower annual growth compared to the previous decade (1.2% versus 2.1%). Notwithstanding the diminishing growth rate, the total amount of fisheries production will remain higher than that of the individual beef, pork or poultry outputs. About 89% of total fishery production, or 166 Mt, is estimated to be destined for direct human consumption. Developing countries are expected to account for about 96% of the projected production growth, and their share in total production will increase from 82% in the base period to 84% in 2023. A more marked expansion is expected in Asia, with its share in the total production going up from 68% to 71% (Figure 8.2).

Capture production is projected to slightly increase by 2% over the projection period, from 92.6 Mt to about 95 Mt in 2023. This improvement is due to a combination of factors, including the recovery of certain catches resulting from progress in rebuilding fish stocks and establishing robust management regimes by some countries; some growth of catches in those few countries not subject to strict production quotas; and enhanced use of fishery production through reduced discards, waste and losses as required by changes in

Figure 8.2. **Asian countries dominate fisheries production**

Fishery production in live weight equivalent for aquaculture (left) and capture (right)

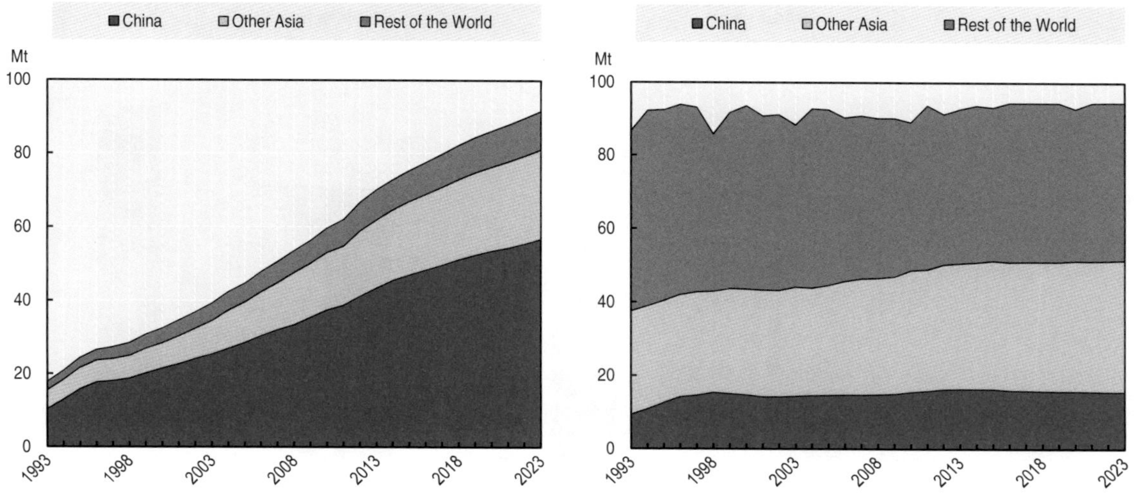

Source: OECD and FAO Secretariats.

StatLink http://dx.doi.org/10.1787/888933100625

legislation or stimulated by higher fish prices (including for fishmeal and fish oil). Capture production is not expected to increase very much at the beginning of the outlook period due to announced restraining production quotas in Chile in 2014. The El Niño effect on catches by Peru and Chile could cause a 2% decline in world capture fisheries in years in which it occurs. As a periodical phenomenon and based on past trends, the model was adjusted to reflect this occurrence in 2015 and 2020 although actual occurrence may vary.

Expanding aquaculture production will drive overall growth. Aquaculture production is projected to reach about 92 Mt in 2023, an increase of 38% over next decade. This amounts to an annual growth rate of 2.5%, which is significantly lower than the growth rate of 5.6% p.a. experienced in the previous decade (2004-13). This slowdown in expansion will mainly be due to restrictions caused by environmental impacts of production and competition from other users of water and coastal spaces. For example, aquaculture farming along coasts, lakes or rivers can conflict with urban development or tourism. This can create problems related to water quality and scarcity and push aquaculture expansion into less optimal production locations. Furthermore, the high costs of fishmeal, fish oil and other related feeds will serve as a drag on growth as an essential component of production for many species, in particular carnivorous ones. Despite the slower growth rate, aquaculture will still remain one of the fastest growing sectors when compared to other food-producing systems. The share of aquaculture in total fishery production should grow from an average of 42% in the base year (2011-13) to 49% in 2023. Excluding non-food uses, aquaculture fish production is expected to surpass capture fisheries in 2014 as the main source of fish for human consumption, and this share should reach 53% by 2023 (Figure 8.3).

Aquaculture will expand in all continents, with different growth levels, ranging from 39% for Africa to 30% for Oceania. The bulk of aquaculture production will continue to originate from Asian countries, which account for about 88% of world production. China will remain the main producer with a share of 62% of total production. China, India and Indonesia are expected to represent the majority of growth in quantity terms. In percentage terms, a

Figure 8.3. **Aquaculture surpassing capture fisheries for human consumption**
Fishery production in live weight equivalent

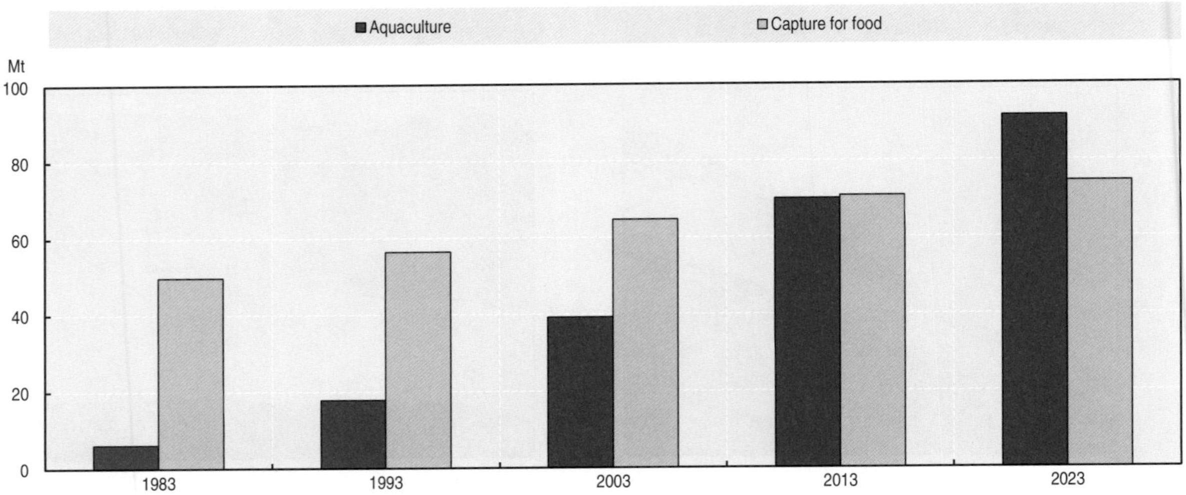

Source: OECD and FAO Secretariats.

StatLink ⟨⟩ *http://dx.doi.org/10.1787/888933100644*

significant expansion is projected for Mexico (84%), Norway (77%), Iran (77%), Turkey (74%), Russian Federation (72%), Indonesia (64%) and Brazil (62%).

In 2023, fishmeal production will reach 5.5 Mt (product weight) and fish oil 1.2 Mt (product weight), which is equivalent to an increase of 6% and 7%, respectively, compared to the averages of 2011-13. Fishmeal and fish oil can be produced from whole fish, fish cut-offs or other fish by-products, such as heads, tails, bones and other offal resulting from processing (Box 8.1). Fishmeal and fish oil originating from whole fish are entirely produced from species caught in the wild. It is expected that the proportion of capture fisheries used to produce fishmeal will gradually decline to around 16% by 2023 from an average of about 19% in the period 2004-13. The decrease will be caused by a reduced availability of raw material due to limits set by government agencies based on stock assessments. It will also be caused by increased use of fish species for human consumption that were previously used for reduction

---

Box 8.1. **Recycling fish residue in the fishmeal and oil market**

The market for fishmeal and fish oil went through a revolution in the 1980s with the advent of aquaculture. Until aquaculture became a major outlet for fishmeal and fish oil, these products were predominantly parts of the larger protein meal and vegetable oil markets. They were both used in pigs and chicken feed ration. Fishmeal and fish oil are preferred feed inputs for aquaculture because of their unique ability to meet the nutritional needs of some fish species. Fishmeal is widely used in aquaculture while fish oil is primarily being used for carnivore finfish such as salmon, sea bass and sea bream.

From around 2000, there has been increasing pressure on fishmeal and fish oil prices due to strong demand from aquaculture and lower landings from the most significant reduction fisheries. The introduction of more stringent fisheries management practices first in Scandinavia and the United States, and then in Chile and Peru has led to lower landings. Moreover, a larger share of landings is being used for direct human consumption. In fact, captured fish used directly for reduction to fishmeal and fish oil dropped by 43% between 1992 and 2012.

Box 8.1. **Recycling fish residue in the fishmeal and oil market** (*cont.*)

More recently the increased awareness of the health benefits associated with Omega-3 consumption has led to a surge in the demand for fish oil for direct human consumption. According to IFFO, the Marine Ingredients Organisation, the share of fish oil in the Omega-3 market has increased from 5% in 1990 to 22% in 2012. While still 74% of the fish oil is going to aquaculture, fish farmers find themselves competing with a buyer that is able to pay substantially higher prices. Looking forward, aquaculture's share of fish oil consumption is therefore likely to decline.

Higher prices for marine materials have produced new sources of supply. The fillet yield for most fish species varies between 30% and 65% of the mass of the fish. Trimmings and cut-offs that once were discarded are now being processed into fishmeal and fish oil. This development has been supported by the growth of more large scale processing facilities that provide enough waste to justify the investment in a fishmeal plant at the end of the processing line.

In most cases, official data do not directly break down fishmeal and fish oil production originating from reduction fisheries versus that obtained from fish residues. However, total production of these commodities and the quantity of fish reduced into fishmeal and fish oil are known. Combining this with an estimate of the fishmeal and oil yield from reduction fisheries, the quantity of fishmeal and oil produced from residues can be inferred. Data from Peru, where fishmeal and oil production is dominated by the reduction fishery, were used to estimate these yields.

In fact, yields will be smaller or higher in different countries because of differences in species used, but Peru seems to be a good representative of the global average. This is confirmed by the World Bank study "Fish to 2030: Prospects for Fisheries and Aquaculture", based on the International Food Policy Research Institute (IFPRI)'s International Model for Policy Analysis of Agricultural Commodities and Trade (IMPACT model) which shows different yields by species and hence by countries, but arrives at a world average equal to the yields generated with the Peruvian data. Based on this approach, the share of world fish oil production originating from fish residue was estimated to have increased from 25% to 34% between 1995 and 2012. For fishmeal the same share has grown from 14% to 29% over the same period. Given the expected high prices over the next decade these shares should reach 40% and 35% respectively by 2023 according to the OECD-FAO Outlook.

A hypothetical scenario was studied with the FAO fish model, investigating the impact of a 25% reduction in the use of fish residues for oil and meal production in each country.

By 2023 that generates a 498 Kt and 120 Kt decline in fishmeal and fish oil production from fish residue respectively. This decline in supply leads to higher prices, by 16% and 18% respectively. Because of the fishing quotas, the resulting larger crushing margin only generates a small increase in fish reduction (0.9%). As a result, additional fishmeal and fish oil production from whole fish can only replace 50 Kt and 9 Kt of the assumed loss in production or 10% and 8% respectively. The decline in total fishmeal and fish oil production reaches 8% and 9.5% respectively in 2023. The resulting higher fishmeal and fish oil price reduces world aquaculture production by 0.66% in 2023 and capture, again because of the fishing quotas, can only replace 8% of the losses. The overall reduction in supply of fish leads to a 2% higher world price of fish in 2023.

This rather small impact is partly due to the fact that even though many aquaculture species use fishmeal only a limited number of species use large quantities in the compound feed ration. However, the impact is much stronger if the results of the agricultural scenario presented in the Box 4.2 "Structural changes in the feed market" are combined to the reduction in fishery recycling activities.

This is because many aquaculture species are fed with agricultural products or by-products. In the broader scenario, by 2023 the weighted average price of all feeds in China, the United States and the European Union increases by 15-17%. This leads to higher meat prices generating stronger fish demand. Consequently demand for fish and fishmeal is stronger and feed cost of producing aquaculture is larger. The world prices of fish and fishmeal in 2023 are therefore much stronger at 9.6% and 34% respectively compared to the baseline.

as is already the case for some pelagic species in Norway and Iceland. The share of capture fisheries used for fishmeal will be slightly smaller in years of El Niño, owing to reduced anchoveta catches.

Sustained demand and high prices are expected to lead to more fishmeal and fish oil to be produced from fish waste and by-products obtained from the processing of fish into fillets, portions and similar forms. In 2023, fishmeal obtained from by-products is expected reach 36% of total production in 2023, up from 28% in 2011-13. For fish oil, this share could reach 41% of total production, compared with 33% in 2011-13. The use of fish by-products can affect the composition and quality of the resulting fishmeal/fish oil, because they contain, in general, less protein, more ash (minerals) and increased levels of small amino acids (such as glycine, proline, hydroxyproline) compared to fishmeal and fish oil obtained from whole fish. This difference in the composition may affect its potential for use aquaculture and livestock farming. However, this is not taken into consideration in the fish model and in the Outlook.

Consumption

Fish is expected to remain predominantly consumed as food. It is a valuable and nutritious contribution to diversified and healthy diets, because it is a concentrated source of protein and of many other essential fatty acids and micronutrients. Fish that is not consumed as food is reduced into fishmeal and fish oil and serves other non-food uses, such as for ornamental fish, culturing, fingerlings and fry, bait, pharmaceutical inputs, and as direct feed for aquaculture, livestock and other animals. World per capita apparent fish consumption is projected to reach 20.9 kg in 2023, up from an average of 19.2 kg in 2011-13. The driving force behind this increase will be a combination of rising incomes and urbanisation, interlinked with the expansion of fish production, and improved distribution channels. However, the pace of this increase will slow in particular in the second half of the outlook period, when fish starts to become more expensive in comparison with meat. Overall, per capita apparent fish food consumption will increase by 0.5% p.a. during 2014-23, compared to 1.7% p.a. in 2004-13.

Despite the overall increase in the availability of fish to most consumers (Figure 8.4), growth patterns of apparent per capita fish consumption will be very uneven. For example, the most substantial rises will occur in Brazil (+45%, from 10.5 kg in the base period to 15.3 kg in 2023, mostly because of the significant expansion in domestic aquaculture production and of national initiatives to increase seafood consumption), Saudi Arabia (+37%, from 11.7 kg to 16 kg), other Eastern European countries (+29%, from 9.2 kg to 11.9 kg) and China (+ 23%, from 35 kg to 43 kg). Apparent fish consumption will remain static or decreasing in Japan (-5%, from 52.8 kg to 49.9 kg), in Canada (-7%), in selected Latin American countries and in Africa (-5%), in particular in Sub-Saharan Africa. Per capita apparent fish consumption in Africa is projected to decline during 2014-23, from 10.0 kg in 2011-13 to 9.5 kg in 2023. This decrease will be mainly caused by population growing more than supply. Between 2011-13 and 2023, the population in Africa is estimated to increase at 2.3% p.a., while the supply of fish for food consumption will increase by only 1.7% p.a. Projected production increases will be limited (+0.6% p.a.). In order to satisfy the growing demand, Africa is expected to become further dependent on fish imports (overall increase to 25%, at 2.5% p.a.), representing 38% of total fish consumed in Africa. The decline in per capita fish consumption in Africa can impact food security by reducing the intake of fish proteins and micronutrients. At present Africa has a higher proportion of fish to total animal protein intake compared to the world average.

Figure 8.4. **Increase in fish consumption by region between the base period and 2023**

Consumption growth of 30 Mt is projected by 2023; predominantly in Asia

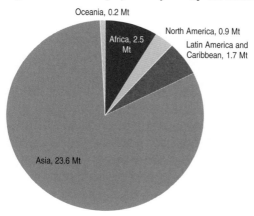

Source: OECD and FAO Secretariats.

StatLink *http://dx.doi.org/10.1787/888933100663*

Disparities in fish consumption will continue to remain between developed and developing countries, with the latter having lower levels of consumption, though the gap is narrowing. In developing countries annual per capita fish consumption will rise from 18.4 kg in the base period to 20.4 kg in 2023. In the same period, per capita fish consumption in developed countries is estimated to increase from 22.6 kg to 23.2 kg. A sizeable and growing share of fish consumed in developed countries will be met by imports.

Population growth in the period 2014-23 is projected to be concentrated in urban areas, in particular in developing countries. In 2023, more than 57% of the world population will live in urban areas. The rural population is expected to decline in every continent except in Africa. Urbanisation will be one of the major driving forces that influence food consumption patterns including the demand for fishery products. City dwellers spend a higher proportion of their income on food purchases and change the composition of their food baskets towards more processed, convenience and higher value-added products that – like fish – contain high levels of proteins. However, marked differences exist, and will continue to remain, between and within countries and regions in terms of quantity and variety consumed per head and the subsequent nutritional contribution. These dissimilarities in consumption depend on the availability and cost of fish and other alternative foods, disposable incomes, and the interaction of several socio-economic and cultural factors. These factors include food traditions, tastes, demand, income levels, seasons, prices, health infrastructure and communication facilities.

Fishmeal and fish oil production will be constrained by risks of demand being higher than supply. Demand for fishmeal for high protein feed comes from both the aquaculture and livestock industries. Due to high prices and major innovation efforts, it is expected that the percentage of fishmeal and fish oil in compound feeds in aquaculture will continue its downward trend (Figure 8.5), and fishmeal and fish oil will be more frequently used as strategic ingredients to enhance growth at specific stages of fish production, e.g. in fry. Fish oil is still expected to be used in the aquaculture industry, but will also be increasingly processed for direct human consumption. The reason for this is that fish oil – being rich in Omega-3 fatty acids – is considered to be beneficial for a wide range of human biological functions.

Figure 8.5. **Reduction in the inclusion rate of fishmeal in animal feed rations**

Ratio of fishmeal consumption to aquaculture production

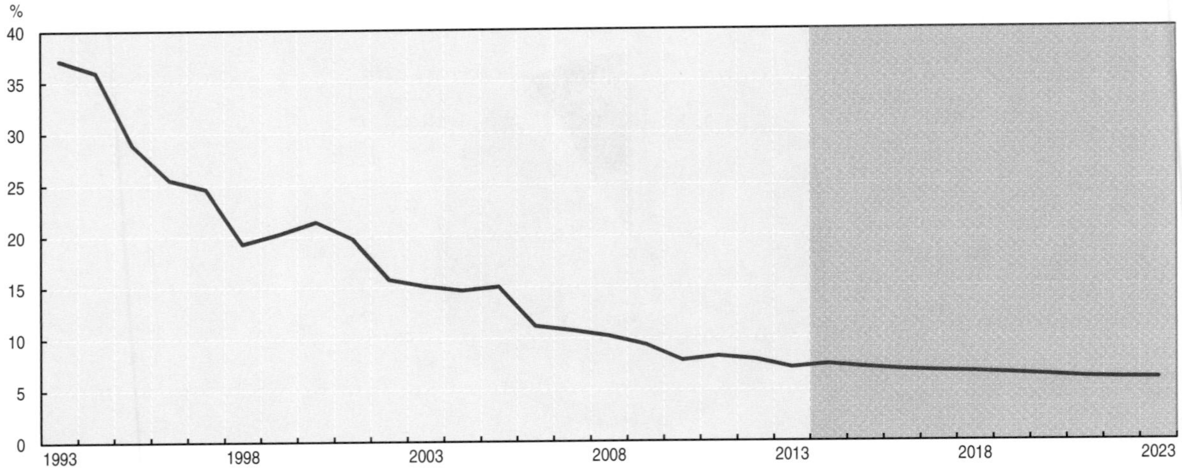

Source: OECD and FAO Secretariats.

StatLink http://dx.doi.org/10.1787/888933100682

Trade

Fish and fishery products will continue to be highly traded, fuelled by increasing consumption of fishery commodities, trade liberalisation policies, globalisation of food systems, and technological innovations in processing, preservation, packaging and transportation. About 37% of total fishery production is expected to be imported (32% excluding intra-EU trade)[3] in the form of products for human consumption or for non-edible purposes by 2023. A share of this trade might consist of repeated trading of products in different processing stages among countries and regions. This practice of outsourcing processing activities at regional and world levels is expected to increase in the next decade, with raw material usually sent from European and North American markets to Asia (China in particular, but also in other countries such as India, Indonesia and Viet Nam) and Central and Eastern Europe for filleting and packaging, and then re-imported. This makes the fishery value chains complex and the sector highly globalised.

World trade of fish for human consumption is expected to reach 45 Mt in live weight equivalent in 2023, up 20% from the base period, but with the annual growth rate slowing from 2.7% in 2004-13 to 1.7% in 2014-23. This decline will be caused by increasing transportation costs, slower growth of fishery production and sustained domestic demand in some of the major exporting countries. Aquaculture will contribute to a growing share of the international trade in fishery commodities for human consumption with high-value species, such as salmon, sea bass, sea bream, shrimp and prawns, bivalves and other molluscs, but also relatively low-value species, such as tilapia, catfish (including *Pangasius*) and carps.

The next decade will be characterised by an increasing role played by developing countries in fishery trade (Figure 8.6) and the corresponding decline in the share of developed economies. Trade in fish is a significant source of foreign currency earnings, employment, income generation and food security for some developing countries. During next decade, developing countries will continue to lead fishery exports of fish for human consumption, slightly increasing their share in world trade from 67% to 68%. Due to their primary role in fishery production, 53% of world fish exports for human consumption will originate from Asia in 2023, with Asian countries being responsible for 62% of the overall growth of world exports. China will remain the major global exporter, accounting for over 22% of world trade and over 29% of all additional fishery exports by the close of the projection period. It is expected that Chinese exports will continue to be composed by goods produced from domestic and imported raw material. Among the non-Asian countries, Brazil and Mexico are projected to substantially increase their exports with growth rates of 66% and 44%, respectively.

Figure 8.6. **Trade of fish for human consumption**

Exports (left) and imports (right) of fish for human consumption in live weight equivalent

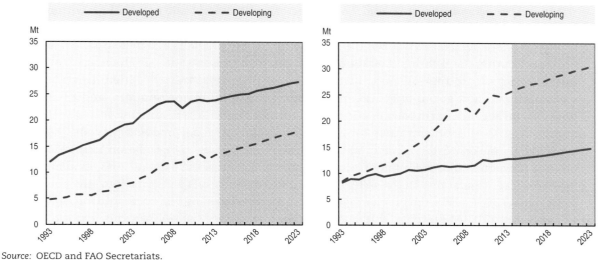

Source: OECD and FAO Secretariats.

StatLink ⬛⬛ http://dx.doi.org/10.1787/888933100701

Economic recovery in Europe and United States will revitalise demand for seafood while demand and consumption in Japan is projected to decline. Since production in Japan is not expected to fall, the decline in consumption will reduce imports of fish for human consumption by 16%. Limited growth prospects for domestic fishery production will mean that developed countries will remain highly dependent on external supplies to satisfy their domestic demand. Their imports are expected to increase by 13% over the outlook period. However, overall market growth will erode the developed countries' share in global imports from 55% in 2011-13 to 51% in 2023. Developing countries will increase imports for domestic consumption but also for raw material for processing and re-export, in particular for species not produced locally. Increasing imports are expected to be recorded by several Asian countries (including China, India, Indonesia and the Philippines), Brazil, selected countries in the Middle East and in Africa

Exports of fishmeal are projected to remain steady with 2.8 Mt product weight exported in 2014, increasing by only 2% in 2023. Developing countries led by Asia will remain the main exporters and importers of fishmeal, with a share of 76% and 72% of world trade, respectively. China alone should have a 35% share of world fishmeal imports in 2023, slightly declining from 38% in 2011-13. High international prices of fishmeal will push China's domestic production of fishmeal to satisfy its aquaculture and livestock (in particular pigs) industries. Peru and Chile will continue to be leading exporters of fishmeal, but their combined share in total exports will decrease from 52% in 2011-13 to 46% in 2023. Fish oil exports are expected to increase by 6% over next decade, with developing countries exporting 65% of the total. Due to salmon farming and growing demand for fish to be consumed as food, European countries will represent the main importers with a 48% share of global fish oil imports, and with Norway alone accounting for 24% of the world imports in 2023.

Main issues and uncertainties

The fish projections reported in this chapter are based on specific assumptions. The future prospects of the fishery and aquaculture sector will depend on its capacity to deal with different challenges, both globally and locally. These include the allocation of fishing rights and the economic sustainability of the sector; multilateral trade negotiations within the World Trade Organization (WTO), including the focus on fishery subsidies; and economic crises, which can weaken the demand for fishery products and increase the risk of import barriers and tariffs. Market changes can also present a major challenge. The outsourcing of production and introduction of private standards, including for environmental and social purposes, their endorsement by major retailers, and their possible effect on market access for developing countries will challenge current approaches. More stringent rules for quality and safety of food products may also be expected. In this context, it is important to mention that the new EU Regulation 1169/2011 on the provision of food information to consumers will change the existing legislation on food labelling. Regulations on the sell-by/expiry dates of foodstuffs will come into effect on 13 December 2014, while the articles regarding nutritional labelling will come into force on 13 December 2016. At present, there is no obligation to specify the sell-by/expiry dates of imported fishery products in fresh form into the European Union, but from December 2014 onwards countries exporting fresh fishery products to the European Union will have to bring their products into conformity with the new regulations. Exporters to the European Union will need to label the goods properly to avoid any alerts, rejections or blocks regarding the quality of their products. This might imply the need to conduct internationally certified and valid laboratory tests for knowing the shelf life of the various categories of their fishery products.

Model projections call for stable capture fisheries production over the next decade, with a slight increase by 2023. This reflects stable production trends since the 1990s, with production fluctuating around 90 Mt, but also the way the fish model is constructed.[4] The effective prospects of capture fisheries are rather difficult to determine, because they depend on the natural productivity of fish stocks and ecosystems and are subject to many variables and uncertainties. According to FAO estimates,[5] the percentage of stock groups monitored by FAO which are underexploited is diminishing, with 30% at a biologically unsustainable level and therefore overfished. A share of current catches has also been obtained by fleets moving their operations from depleted areas to new areas, a practice which can cause a long term decline in global catches as overexploitation spreads. At the same time, owing to better resource management practices, some fisheries and stocks are showing signs of recovery, which could help to maintain and stabilise overall catches.

There is a risk that the effects of reduced ecosystem productivity and changing ecosystem structures can worsen, in particular in areas beyond national jurisdiction (ABNJs). The marine ABNJ are those areas of oceans for which no one nation has the specific or sole management responsibility. They comprise about 64% of the surface of the oceans and almost 95% of their volume but a minority of the total catch. They include complex ecosystems that are subject to impacts from a variety of sectors, including shipping, pollution and deep-sea mining. ABNJs are sometimes characterised by lack of institutional frameworks that regulate access. Sustainable management of fisheries resources and biodiversity conservation in those areas are difficult and challenging. Issues related to the conservation and sustainable management of biodiversity in ABNJ are currently being discussed by a dedicated UN Ad Hoc Open-ended Informal Working Group. In accordance with the RIO+20 declaration "The future we want", a decision on whether to launch negotiations on a United Nations Convention on the Law of the Sea (UNCLOS) implementing agreement will be taken before the end of the United Nations General Assembly 69th session in 2015. Furthermore, the overcapacity of fishing fleets globally and illegal unreported and unregulated (IUU) fishing are other important threats affecting the sustainability of fisheries resources. They can be found in all types and dimensions of fisheries, including inland waters. They concern all aspects and stages of the harvest and utilisation of fish, and in some instances IUU fishing is associated with organised crime. These situations are also linked with, and exacerbated by, the poor governance characterising several fisheries activities. The fishery sector can also be affected by competition from other sectors over the use of natural resources and ecosystems, and by effects of climate change, pollution, and ocean acidification with resulting damage to habitats, ecological functions and biodiversity.

The projections indicate that majority of future growth in fish production will come from aquaculture. However, the prospects for this sector can be limited by concerns over the environmental, spatial or legal impacts and as competition for land, water, financial and other productive resources increase. In particular the growth will depend on several factors, including the availability and accessibility to technology, financial resources, and areas and water of good quality; availability, sustainability and cost of fishmeal and fish oil and of other alternative sources of feeding for fed species, in particular carnivorous ones; and the availability of fish seeds.[6] The future of aquaculture also depends on environmental externalities including climate change, pollution and problems that can originate from not guided and monitored aquaculture practices such as degradation of land and marine habitats and pollution (as, for example, from discharges of organic wastes, nitrogen and phosphorous), endangered biodiversity through escapees and transfer of non-native and native diseases and parasites to surrounding production areas; inadequate biosecurity measures and disease outbreaks. In order to grow further, the aquaculture sector needs to address these environmental externalities it can cause. It also requires an accommodating governance framework that supports innovation in production and environmental prevention and mitigation. For example, the current limited aquaculture production of several OECD countries is not simply a question of competitiveness, but it is also caused by the regulatory framework. Governments can spur new growth in the sector by addressing the limitations of current approaches to unleash the potential of the sector. National development plans, institutional innovation, certification, aquaculture licencing systems, co-operation among the various stakeholders and spatial planning (including addressing user conflicts) have all been identified as ways to improve the prospects of aquaculture. Future growth of aquaculture will also depend on how the sector will invest to enhance productivity in a sustainable manner through technological development and better management practices. Improvements in genetics, breeding and nutrition are particularly important as well as progress in developing substitutes for fishmeal and fish oil in feeds used to farm aquaculture species.

To meet some of the challenges faced by the fisheries and aquaculture sectors and identified in the outcome document of the United Nations Conference on Sustainable Development (United Nations, 2012) and the post-2015 development agenda (United Nations, 2014), FAO has formulated the "Blue Growth" initiative as a coherent approach for the sustainable, integrated and socio-economically sensitive management of oceans and wetlands focusing on four components: capture fisheries, aquaculture, ecosystem services, and trade and social protection of coastal communities. The initiative is grounded on the principles of the 1995 FAO Code of Conduct for Responsible Fisheries and its associated guidelines (FAO, 1995). The Blue Growth framework promotes responsible and sustainable fisheries and aquaculture by way of an integrated approach involving all stakeholders. Through capacity development, it will strengthen the policy environment, institutional arrangements and the collaborative processes that empower fishing communities, civil society organisations and public entities. To achieve its integrated approach to Blue Growth, FAO is collaborating with a wide array of other UN agencies, intergovernmental organisations and other initiatives or processes where synergies exist with the work of FAO.

The OECD Green Growth Strategy, based on the idea that it is both possible and necessary to achieve sustained economic growth while reducing the human impact on the environment, is also particularly relevant for fisheries and aquaculture that depend more than most economic sectors on environmental resources. Some potential avenues for growth have been investigated already by the OECD Committee for Fisheries in its work on Green Growth, including energy use, waste and governance, and there remain many other areas to be tackled in the future.

Fishery projections presented in this *Outlook* for the European Union do not take into consideration the effects that can be generated by the implementation of the new Common Fisheries Policy (CFP) which could increase EU capture fisheries and aquaculture production during the next decade. The CFP has been agreed by Council and Parliament and is effective from 1 January 2014.[7] The main goals of the new CFP are to bring fish stocks back to sustainable levels (by setting fishing levels at maximum sustainable yield levels by 2015 where possible, and at the latest by 2020 for all fish stocks), put an end to wasteful fishing practices, and create new opportunities for jobs and growth in coastal areas. To achieve this CFP focuses on banning discards, empowering the sector and decentralising decision making, emphasising aquaculture, supporting small scale fisheries, improving the scientific knowledge on the state of stocks and taking responsibility in foreign waters through the EU's international agreements. The European Maritime and Fisheries Fund (EMFF) is the funding instrument that will support the implementation of the reformed CFP and should come into force during 2014. Through the new CFP, overall EU production from both capture fisheries as well as aquaculture could increase in the next decade.

Among the policies introduced by the CFP, it is important to mention a landing obligation, with the scope to reduce the current high levels of unwanted catches and to gradually eliminate discards. An obligation to land all catches ("the landing obligation") of species which are subject to catch limits and, in the Mediterranean Sea, also catches of species which are subject to minimum sizes, has been established and will be gradually implemented. The landing obligation will be gradually introduced between 2015 and 2019 for different regions and different fisheries, starting with all pelagic fisheries and fisheries in the Baltic Sea. The Basic Regulation stipulates a clear timetable and a framework for implementing the landing obligation. However, this framework needs to be specified and operationalised on a regional level. Specific measures and rules of implementation avoiding unwanted catches could be for example more selective gear, restricting access to juvenile aggregation areas, exemption from the discard ban due to high survival, real time closures and rules on documentation.

Notes

1. The terms "fish and seafood" or simply "fish" indicate fish, crustaceans, molluscs and other aquatic invertebrates but excludes aquatic mammals and aquatic plants.

2. The term *apparent* refers to the average food available for consumption, which is not equal to average food intake or average food consumption for a number of reasons, e.g. food waste at household level.

3. Including fishmeal converted into a live weight equivalent basis.

4. In the fish model, production of capture fisheries is kept exogenous for most countries as being tightly managed, while it is endogenous responding to prices for other countries not subject to quotas and it is endogenous with no price elasticity for the South American countries affected by El Niño.

5. See sections on the Status of the Fisheries Resources, in part 1 of State of World Fisheries and Aquaculture (SOFIA) 2012 and 2014 available at *www.fao.org/fishery/sofia/en*.

6. Fish seeds indicate eggs, spawn, offspring, progeny or brood of the aquatic organism (including aquatic plants) being cultured. At this infantile stage, seed may also be referred to or known as fry, larvae, postlarvae, spat and fingerlings. They may originate from two principal sources: captive breeding programmes or caught from the wild.

7. More information is available at *http://ec.europa.eu/fisheries/reform/index_en.htm*.

References

United Nations (2012), "The future we want", *www.uncsd2012.org*.

United Nations (2014). "Millennium Development Goals and post-2015 Development Agenda", *www.un.org/en/ecosoc/about/mdg.shtml*.

FAO (1995), *Code of Conduct for Responsible Fisheries*, Food and Agriculture Organization, Rome.

Chapter 9

Dairy

This chapter describes the market situation and the latest set of quantitative medium-term projections for global and national dairy markets for the ten-year period, 2014-23. The discussion of the medium-term market prospects for dairy covers the developments expected in national milk production, and world and national dairy product prices, production, food consumption and trade (imports and exports). The quantitative projections are developed with the aid of the partial equilibrium Aglink-Cosimo model of world agriculture. Included in the chapter are two boxes on i) challenges and opportunities facing China's dairy sector and ii) milk and dairy products in human nutrition. The chapter concludes with a discussion of some main issues and uncertainties affecting the medium-term outlook for dairy. These include dairy policies, and specific market development influencing production, consumption and trade in dairy.

Market situation

In early 2012, high returns and excellent pasture conditions in Oceania, and parts of South America, generated a supply response triggering a fall in milk and dairy prices. With demand continuing to expand, especially from China, prices bottomed out in mid-2012 at levels much higher than during the previous downturn in 2009. The decline in Chinese milk production by 5.7% in 2013 led to strong import demand for dairy products and to higher world dairy prices. Additionally, during the first half of 2013, major players on the world dairy market – the United States, the European Union, New Zealand and Australia – produced less milk than a year ago. The main reasons were high feed cost and adverse weather conditions in Oceania and parts of Europe. Prices for skim milk powder (SMP) and whole milk powder (WMP) reached a new peak in April 2013, above the level of the 2007/08 commodity boom. Production in the major dairy exporting countries started to increase in mid-2013, as feed prices declined and milk margins improved. Nevertheless, due to continued strong demand on the world market, prices of dairy products remain high into the year 2014.

Projection highlights

- World milk production is projected to increase by 180 Mt by 2023 when compared to the base years (2011-13), the majority of which (78%) is anticipated to come from developing countries. The average growth rate for the projection period is estimated at 1.9% which is below the 2.2% witnessed in the last decade. The slowdown in growth reflects growing shortages of water and suitable land in developing countries combined with a slow introduction of modern dairy production systems.

- Several dairy product prices reached new highs during 2013, and a correction is expected in the near future, followed by firming nominal prices over the medium-term. Real prices are projected to decline slightly in the next decade, albeit remaining considerably above the pre-2007 levels.

- Per capita consumption of dairy products in developing countries is expected to increase by 1.2% to 1.9% p.a. The expansion in demand reflects robust income growth and further globalisation of diets. By contrast, per capita consumption in the developed world is projected to increase between 0.2% and 0.9% p.a.

- A general expansion of trade in dairy products is expected over the coming decade. Strong growth is expected for whey, cheese and SMP, at more than 2% p.a. Lower growth is expected for WMP, at 1.7% p.a., and especially butter at 0.7% p.a. The bulk of this growth will be satisfied by expanded exports from the United States, the European Union, New Zealand, Australia and Argentina.

Market trends and prospects

Prices

Milk and dairy product prices increased in 2013 due to a large production shortfall in China and increasing feed costs. Additionally, during the first half of 2013, major players on the world dairy market – the United States, the European Union, New Zealand and Australia – produced less milk than a year ago. Production in the major dairy exporting countries started to react to the price signals during 2013. In addition, starting mid-2013, prices for feed grains became considerably lower, compared to last year. Combined with an expected recovery of the domestic milk production in China, this will likely lead to declining dairy and milk prices in the near future (Figure 9.1).

Figure 9.1. **World dairy prices in nominal terms**

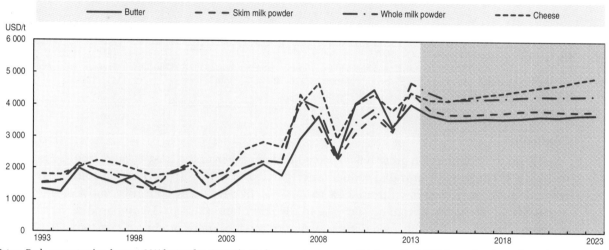

Notes: F.o.b. export price, butter, 82% butterfat, Oceania; F.o.b. export price, non-fat dry milk, 1.25% butterfat, Oceania; F.o.b. export price, WMP 26% butterfat, Oceania; F.o.b. export price, cheddar cheese, 39% moisture, Oceania.
Source: OECD and FAO Secretariats.

StatLink ᵃᵐˢᴾ *http://dx.doi.org/10.1787/888933100720*

Over the medium-term, increasing incomes and globalisation of diets are expected to raise the demand for milk and dairy products in developing countries. Most of the growth in demand will be satisfied domestically by increasing dairy herds and rising yields. The increasing import demand will support prices of dairy products during the next decade. Cheese prices are expected to develop the strongest over the outlook period. On the other hand, butter prices are expected to remain below SMP prices in the next decade.

Over the next ten years, it is expected that real dairy product prices will decline slightly. This is partly due to the current higher price levels but also to the expected continued productivity growth in the dairy sector (Figure 9.2). Nevertheless, real prices will be substantially higher than in the period before 2007.

The *Outlook* price projections reflect the usual assumptions of stability in weather and in economic and policy conditions. Under these "normal" conditions, prices are not expected to reach the peak levels of 2007/08, 2011 or 2013. However, actual price outcomes are likely to exhibit significant variations around the projection trend.

Figure 9.2. **World dairy prices in real terms**
2005 USD

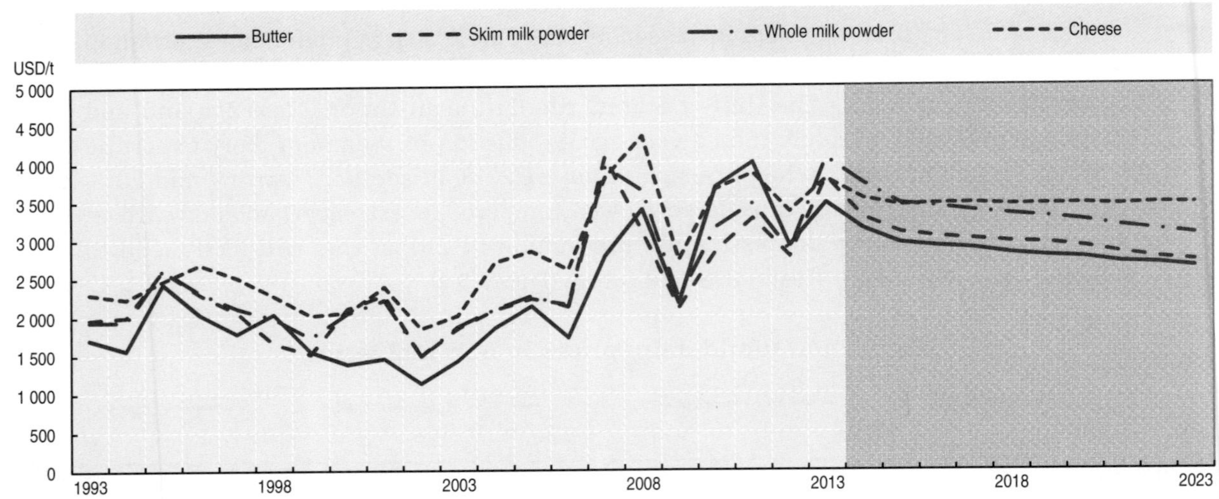

Notes: F.o.b. export price, butter, 82% butterfat, Oceania; F.o.b. export price, non-fat dry milk, 1.25% butterfat, Oceania; F.o.b. export price, WMP 26% butterfat, Oceania; F.o.b. export price, cheddar cheese, 39% moisture, Oceania.
Source: OECD and FAO Secretariats.

StatLink http://dx.doi.org/10.1787/888933100739

Production

World milk production growth is expected to decrease over the next decade, from 2.2% to 1.9% p.a. The growth in milk production originates to 78% from developing countries, where growth rates slowdown from 3.6% to 2.8% p.a. In developing countries, most of the production growth stems from an increase in the dairy herd (1.6% p.a.), compared to yield growth (1.2% p.a.), reflecting a slow introduction of modern dairy production systems; but especially the herd growth is limited due to constraints in water and land availability. In Asia, for example, the milk yield growth will contribute more to production increases in the coming decade as the environmental constraints are more binding than in Africa and Latin America.

India is expected to outpace the European Union and will become the largest milk producer in the world. Almost the entire Indian production, with a very high share of buffalo milk, is consumed fresh, and only very small amounts are further processed (Figure 9.3).

China, although a much smaller producer and consumer of milk and dairy products than India, is more important for international dairy markets. China's self-sufficiency in milk and dairy products has declined substantially in recent years, which was partly fuelled by slow growth in domestic milk production in the last five years, following food safety problems related to milk adulterated with melamine in 2008, and a substantial decline in 2013. It is expected that the Chinese dairy sector can overcome its challenges in the coming decade and a further deterioration in self-sufficiency is limited (Box 9.1).

In developed countries milk yield growth (0.84% p.a.) is projected at a higher rate than total production growth (0.80% p.a.), which implies a slightly declining dairy herd. This observation is a continuation of the trend in the last decade. Nevertheless, there are considerable differences between major milk producing countries and regions.

The rate of production expansion in New Zealand, the largest milk exporter, is expected to fall, compared to the previous decade, from 4.5% to 1.9% p.a., because of an

Figure 9.3. **Outlook for milk production**

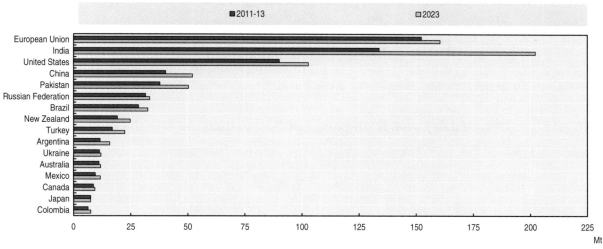

Source: OECD and FAO Secretariats.

StatLink ⫘ http://dx.doi.org/10.1787/888933100758

Box 9.1. Challenges and opportunities facing China's dairy sector

China's dairy sector is characterised by scattered small-scale production and low milk yields. Small-scale farmers accounted for 40% of the dairy cows at the end of 2013. As a result of this small-scale structure, prospects for improving total milk production are limited.

China's raw milk price leaped from USD 0.46/kg in the early part of 2008 to USD 0.68/kg in the early part of 2014. In 2013, average milk prices in China were about 30% higher than the average world price. Main drivers behind this increase were increasing feed costs (37.7% for maize and 13.9% for soybean meal since 2008), and rapid growth in labour and land costs. This led to a situation where, despite the surge in milk prices, milk production margins have declined.

The majority of China's dairy processing enterprises have been operating at a loss, and a large number of farmers have abandoned milk production. Consequently, China's inventory of dairy cows fell by about 10% in 2013, which caused China's total milk production to decline by 5.7%. The resulting cow milk production of 35.3 Mt was 2.1 Mt below the 2012 level representing China's biggest annual fall since 1949. This was far more significant than the fall in milk production caused by the food safety problems related to milk adulterated with melamine in 2008.

Considering that China's per capita consumption of dairy products is less than one-third of the world average, the Chinese dairy market has significant growth potential. This is mainly driven by urbanisation and rapidly increasing household incomes. By 2023, the consumption of dairy products in China is expected to increase by around 35% from the 2011-13 base period, with fresh dairy products, butter, cheese, skim milk powder (SMP) and whole milk powder (WMP) gaining 2.2%, 1.5%, 4.3%, 3.5% and 3.0% p.a., respectively. China's total milk production is expected to reach almost 52.1 Mt by 2023, with an estimated average growth rate of 2.7% p.a., which is below the 3.5% p.a. witnessed in the last decade and the expected 2.8% p.a. growth in consumption. To meet the growing demand, China's imports of dairy products will continue to increase over the outlook period. China's imports of butter, cheese, SMP and WMP are expected to reach 57, 128, 315, and 616 Kt, respectively, in 2023. This marks an increase of 23.9% for butter, 228.2% for cheese, 86.4% for SMP and 43.9% for WMP compared to the base period (Figure 9.4). Imports of SMP and WMP will account for 83.4% of total dairy product imports in 2023.

Box 9.1. **Challenges and opportunities facing China's dairy sector** *(cont.)*

China's dairy industry is at a crossroad facing a number of challenges and opportunities. A growing share of imported dairy products in Chinese dairy consumption will increase the pressure on the Chinese dairy sector, especially on small-scale farmers and dairy processing enterprises. However, increasing competition from imports, may also spur China's dairy sector to transform and upgrade, providing a platform for large-scale development, which could lead to significant increases in milk yields.

Figure 9.4. **China's dairy product imports continue to increase over the outlook period**

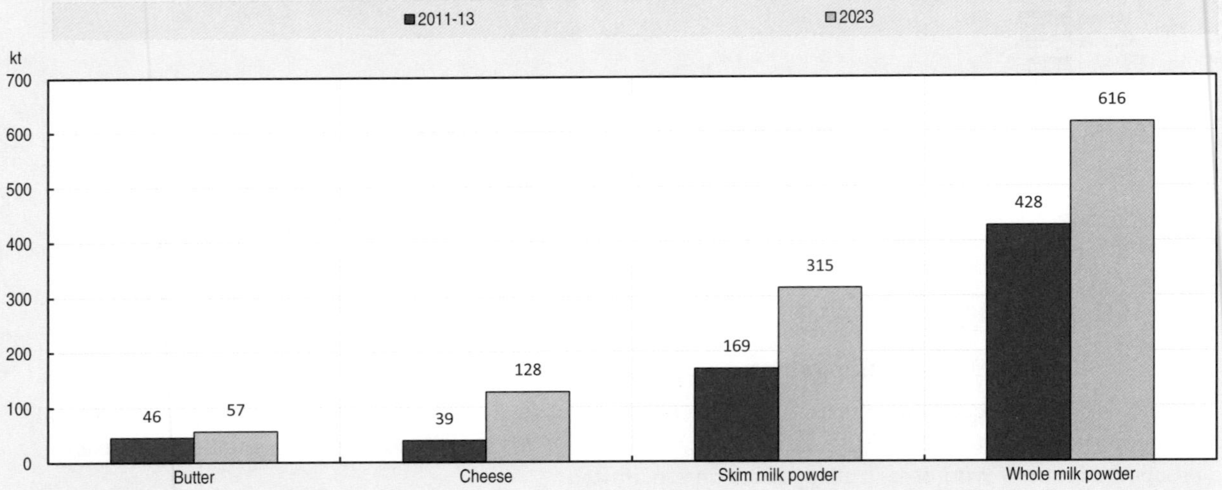

Source: OECD and FAO Secretariats.

StatLink ⇗ http://dx.doi.org/10.1787/888933100777

---

appreciating exchange rate, increasing production costs and environmental factors that constrain milk output growth. Most of the growth will come from a further increase in the dairy herd, assuming that the mainly pasture-based, extensive milk production, implying a low yield per dairy cow, will be maintained.

Following declining dairy herds in Australia during the last decade (-2.3% p.a.), a turnaround is projected (+0.6% p.a.). Consequently, milk production will grow by 2.0% p.a. which will satisfy additional import demand during the next decade.

An increase of the US milk production by 0.9% p.a. is expected during the next decade, implying a slightly declining dairy herd (-0.1% p.a.). So far no effects of the policy changes due to the 2014 Farm Act are incorporated in the baseline.

Sluggish growth in EU milk production is projected over the coming decade (0.5% p.a.) in response to slow growth in domestic demand and relatively high costs. The latter constrains the European Union's ability to participate in the faster growing export markets. The end of the EU milk quota in 2015 is likely to have a small impact on overall milk production in the European Union, but it may lead to a further concentration of milk production in some regions. In addition, the environmental constraints in these regions might limit further growth. Overall, due to the shifts, a faster increase in average yields is expected during the outlook period (2.3% p.a.) than in the decade before (1.3% p.a.).

The processing of milk into the four main dairy products – butter, cheese, SMP and WMP – is increasing at world level at similar pace as milk production. In the outlook period it is expected that butter (2.1% p.a.), SMP (1.9% p.a.) and WMP (2.2% p.a.) increase slightly faster than world milk production (1.9% p.a.), whereas cheese (1.6% p.a.) grows slower. The growth rates also reflect that in the case of butter and WMP the majority of the production occurs in developing countries with a faster growth in milk production, whereas in the case of cheese and SMP it is in the developed ones.

Consumption

The largest share of milk and dairy product consumption is in the form of fresh dairy products, taking up about 70% of total milk production. This share continues to increase due to raising milk production in developing countries where this share is considerably higher. A publication by the FAO (2013) looks into milk and dairy products in human nutrition and assesses especially the situation in developing countries (Box 9.2).

Per capita consumption of dairy products in developing countries is expected to increase on average by 1.9% p.a. for cheese and butter and by 1.2% p.a. for SMP and WMP. The expansion in demand reflects robust income growth, expanding populations and a further globalisation of diets.

By 2023, per capita consumption of fresh dairy products in India is expected to increase to around 171 kg per capita, compared to per capita consumption of 104 kg in Australia, 93 kg in the European Union, 86 kg in New Zealand, 75 kg in Canada, 72 kg in the United States and 26 kg in China. Nevertheless, total consumption of dairy products in milk equivalent is considerably higher in developed countries than in developing ones (Figure 9.5). The difference stems mostly from the per capita consumption of cheese which is more than tenfold in developed countries compared to developing ones.

Figure 9.5. **Major dairy product consumption**
in milk equivalent

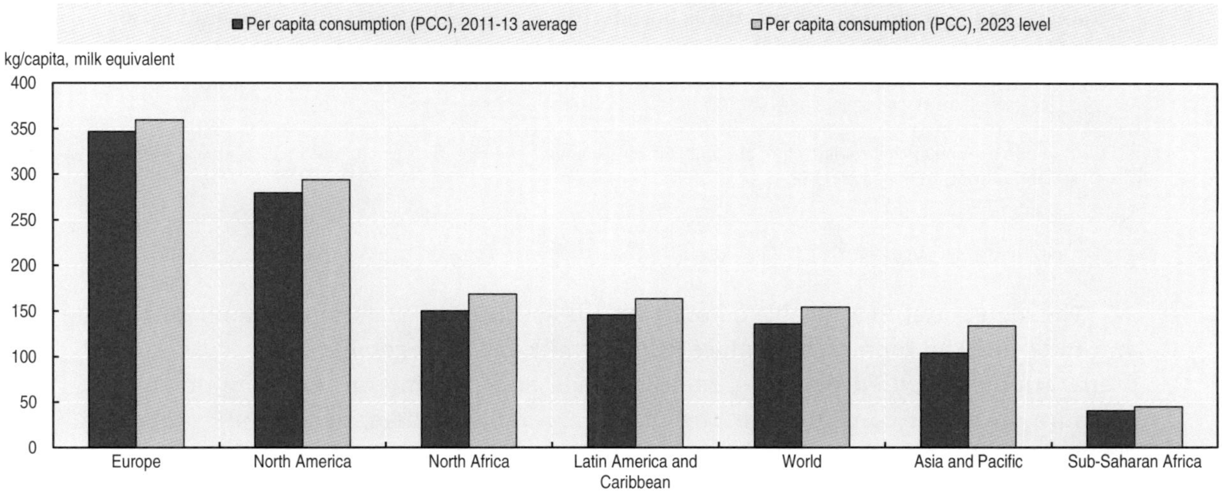

Note: The coefficients used to calculate the consumption in milk equivalent are: Fresh dairy products 1, butter 18.2, cheese 9.247, skim milk powder 11.944, and whole milk powder 8.37.
Source: OECD and FAO Secretariats.

StatLink ᵃˢᵖ *http://dx.doi.org/10.1787/888933100796*

Box 9.2. **Milk and dairy products in human nutrition**

Billions of people consume milk and dairy products every day. Not only are milk and dairy products a vital source of nutrition, they also present livelihood opportunities for farmers, processors, shopkeepers and others in the dairy value chain. The FAO has just published a book entitled *Milk and Dairy Products in Human Nutrition*,[1] which draws together information on nutrition, dairy farming and dairy-industry development from a wide range of sources and explores the linkages between them. An important focus is the development of dairy value chains, a key strategy for improving diets and raising income levels amongst the poorest segments of the world's population.

With rising incomes and increased production, milk and dairy products have become an important part of the diet in some parts of the world where little milk was consumed in the 1970s – particularly in Asia. The interconnectivity between dairying, human nutrition and health are highlighted. While, growing consumption of dairy and livestock products brings important nutritional benefits to large segments of the population in developing countries, there are still many millions who cannot afford better-quality diets owing to the higher cost.

The report highlights the role of dairy-industry development programmes in promoting food and nutrition security and reducing poverty. Increasing demand and relatively high prices for milk and dairy products provide an opportunity for millions of smallholder dairy farmers to improve their livelihood. In many parts of the world, milk and dairy products are highly valued and have an important role in both household food security and income generation. Experience has shown that dairy-industry development projects often have a positive effect on household health and nutrition, in addition to providing employment and income, and can make a substantial and sustainable contribution to poverty reduction. In examining sustainable approaches, the report concludes that support to national or regional groupings, such as co-operatives or associations, assisted by the integrated supply of inputs and support services, can benefit tens of millions of farm families.

Dairying is important in agriculture in that it can provide not only daily food at the household level but also a regular income. Moreover, dairy animals may be used for traction and provide manure for use as both fertiliser and fuel. Strategic investment in, and promotion of, dairy farming can raise farm income, contribute to improved nutrition and create employment in the wider community via processing and distribution and related activities.

1. The book represents a revisiting of the subject by FAO, with the title first published in 1959 and a revised second edition released in 1972.

The high butter to vegetable oil price ratio is assumed to constrain demand for butter and milk fat. The increasing replacement of milk fat by vegetable oils occurs in food preparations, fat-filled powders, table spreads and cooking oil, exerting downward pressure on butter consumption and prices. Overall, the demand for milk protein is growing faster than the demand for milk fat over the next decade, which implies that the butter price will remain below the SMP price on the world market.

Trade

A general expansion in dairy trade is expected over the coming decade. The growth rates differ between dairy products at 0.7% annually for butter, cheese (2.4% p.a.), SMP (2.5% p.a.) and WMP (1.7% p.a.). The vast bulk of this growth will be met by increased exports from the United States, European Union, New Zealand and Australia. These four countries account jointly for 74% of world cheese, 74% of world WMP, 81% of world butter and 86% of world SMP exports in 2023 (Figure 9.6).

Figure 9.6. **Dairy product exporters**

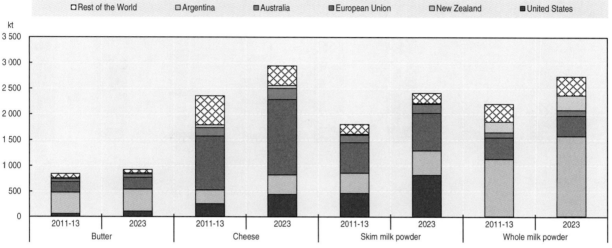

Source: OECD and FAO Secretariats.

StatLink http://dx.doi.org/10.1787/888933100815

The European Union will remain the main cheese exporter (accounting for 39% of world exports in 2023), but its growth rate is below that of the other major cheese exporters, i.e. New Zealand, the United States and Australia. Several other countries like Saudi Arabia, Belarus, Ukraine, Egypt, Turkey and Argentina export considerable amounts of cheese predominantly to neighbouring markets. New Zealand remains the primary source for butter on the international market, at 47% market share, although losing some share to the other major exporters. In case of WMP, it is expected that New Zealand can increase its share in world trade over the next decade to 57% in 2023. Other important exporters are the European Union, Argentina and Australia. The United States is the largest source of SMP exports, at 34% in 2023, and is expected to expand more rapidly than the other major suppliers like the European Union, New Zealand and Australia. Considerable increases are expected for Indian SMP exports, to about 90 Kt by 2023. Country coverage of the whey powder market is limited, but trade is projected to increase considerably in the coming decade. Exports of the European Union, the United States and New Zealand are all expected to grow by more than 3% p.a. and will reach a combined 1.2 Mt of exports in 2023.

In recent years, considerable growth has occurred in fresh dairy trade, which is not incorporated in this *Outlook*. This comprises not only products like yogurts and cream but also liquid milk. One important trade flow is liquid milk exported from the European Union to China (100 Kt in 2013, up from 56 Kt in 2012). Nevertheless, this remains small in relation to the trade in the dairy products covered and might only be a temporary phenomenon.

In contrast to dairy exports, imports are much wider spread and generally the dominant destinations for dairy products are developing countries, especially in Asia and Africa. Only for cheese considerable imports occur in developed countries (Figure 9.7).

Figure 9.7. **Major dairy product importers**

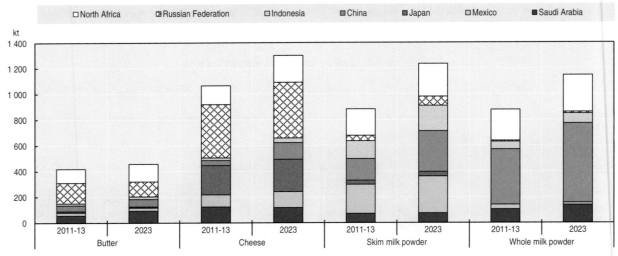

Source: OECD and FAO Secretariats.

StatLink 🔗 http://dx.doi.org/10.1787/888933100834

Cheese imports in developed countries are currently higher than in developing countries, but it is expected that cheese imports in developing countries will grow at a much faster rate (4.4% p.a.) than in developed countries (0.7% p.a.). The Russian Federation remains the primary importer followed by Japan. China is expected to overtake Mexico, the United States, Saudi Arabia and Korea, which are all projected to import more than 80 Kt (3% of world imports) by 2023. Butter imports by developed countries continue to decline (-2.3% p.a.). The Russian Federation remains the main destination of butter, but domestic production increases faster than consumption. Increases in butter imports are expected in developing countries. The two main destinations are Egypt and Saudi Arabia which are closing the gap on the Russian Federation. WMP imports skyrocketed in recent years in China, and a further continuation in growth is expected but at a much slower rate (0.6% p.a.). Other important destinations remain Algeria, Nigeria and Saudi Arabia. In the case of SMP, China will become the world's major importer. Mexico, Indonesia, Algeria, Malaysia and Egypt are other important importers; all with continued growth but at a considerably slower pace than in the preceding decade.

Main issues and uncertainties

The development of Chinese self-sufficiency in milk and dairy products is a main determinant of the future price development on world dairy markets. It is currently expected that the Chinese milk production will start to grow again from this year onwards. Any delay would result in higher dairy prices worldwide.

In 2015, the EU system of milk quotas is scheduled to end. The *Outlook* projects a smooth transition, because actual output remained well below EU quota levels in historic years for most EU member states. Other observers expect a strong supply reaction in the European Union to the end of quota which would increase exports and result in lower world market prices for dairy products. This may also cause higher volatility of milk production and dairy product supply from the European Union.

The 2014 US Farm Act redesigned the support to dairy in the United States. The new Margin Protection Program (MPP) makes payments to dairy producers when the difference between milk prices and feed costs falls below a minimum level. The differences will be calculated nationally on a rolling two-month's average, and producers can opt to secure differences in the range from USD 4 to USD 8 per hundredweight (cwt) for 25% to 90% of their historic production. The baseline makes no assumption about the effect of the policy change. Nevertheless, it could result in increasing US output and exports.

As we have seen in recent years, unusual weather events can have a major impact on dairy markets through their impact on feed grains or pasture conditions. The *Outlook* assumes normal weather conditions from 2013 onwards. However, as climate change models increasingly predict an increase in the incidence and severity of extreme weather events, the probability of abnormal conditions may be increasing. The largest supplier of dairy exports, New Zealand, is weather dependent due to the predominantly pasture-based production.

Environmental legislation can have strong impacts on the future development of dairy production. The greenhouse-gas emissions from dairy activities make up a considerable share of the total emissions in some countries, and any changes in related policies could affect dairy production. Water access and manure management are additional areas where policy changes could have an impact on the dairy industry.

Dairy demand and export opportunities could also be affected by the outcome of various Free Trade Agreements (FTA) and Regional Trade Agreements (RTA) agreements currently under discussion. These agreements could increase international dairy trade through specific market access changes and also by simplifying bilateral sanitary requirements. Another important point for international trade are applied tariffs among developing countries which are often set below their bound WTO levels and thus can be varied at short notice.

Underlying the outlook for international dairy prices is the assumption of continued strong growth in incomes among developing countries, especially in the Middle East, North Africa, South East Asia and China. Any slowdown in economic activity in any of these regions could trigger a significant downturn in dairy prices. It is also assumed that no major outbreaks of animal diseases occur during the outlook period, which could alter the setting rapidly.

Reference

FAO (2013), *Milk and Dairy Products in Human Nutrition*, FAO publications, Rome, *http://www.fao.org/ docrep/018/i3396e/i3396e.pdf*

Chapter 10

Cotton

This chapter summarises the current situation and medium-term projections for world cotton markets during 2014-23. Expected developments in national and global cotton prices, production, use, trade (imports and exports) and stocks, and the background to these developments, are discussed. The underlying quantitative projections are developed with the aid of the partial equilibrium Aglink-Cosimo model of world agriculture. A separate section examines China's cotton policies, which are a significant source of variation and uncertainty during the outlook period. Other sources of uncertainty addressed include shifts in consumer demand and trends in both agricultural and industrial technology.

Market situation

World cotton prices in 2013 were influenced by competing forces, with world demand again rising after a prolonged decline that began in 2007 and elevated stock levels creating uncertainty about future prospects. Falling prices for grains and oilseeds helped reduce cotton prices, but tight supplies of high quality cotton in the United States offset some of this impact. World cotton stocks rose for the fourth consecutive year, but again most of the increase was accounted for by official reserve building in China. Consumption continued to decline in China – the world's largest industrial consumer by a large margin – but increased in a number of other countries as China's yarn imports rose sharply. Steady to higher world production is widely foreseen in the coming year, with early reports indicating an intention of US farmers to plant 4.5 Mha, a 7% increase. China's area is expected to decline, as the support for farmers in China's eastern provinces is reduced.

Projection highlights

World cotton use is expected to grow at 2.4% p.a., a rate slightly above the long term average of 1.9% over the coming decade. In 2007, world consumption reached a peak of 26.7 Mt, and following significant declines during 2008-11 – and with a relatively slow recovery – this peak is not likely to be surpassed again until 2016.

- World production is expected to grow more slowly than consumption during the first years of the outlook period, reflecting the large global stocks that accumulated between 2010 and 2014. World cotton area grows throughout the projection period, finally surpassing in 2020 the recent peaks seen in 2004 and 2011. Yields rise around the world, but global average yield grows very slowly as global output switches from relatively high-yielding countries, like China, to relatively low-yielding ones in South Asia and Sub-Saharan Africa.

- World trade rises at a rate above its long-term average in the *Outlook*, with exports in 2023 12% above those in the base period. The United States retains its position as the world's largest exporter accounting for 24% of world trade. India retains its position as the world's second largest source of cotton while increasing its global share from 18% in the base period to 20% of exports by 2023.

- China retains its position as the world's largest import market for cotton throughout the outlook period. But, by 2023 China's share of world trade is foreseen 16 percentage points below its base period 47% share. Bangladesh's share rises more than any other importer, up from 8% to 12%. Viet Nam, Turkey, Pakistan and Indonesia are also expected to realise larger shares.

Market trends and prospects

Prices

The benchmark A Index measure of cotton prices delivered to Asian ports is expected to average below its 2012 level (USD 1 938/t) during 2013, despite a mid-season recovery (Figure 10.1). World cotton markets in 2013 continue to be indirectly influenced by the 2010 price spike, as the stock-building efforts begun by China in the wake of the price spike continue to support prices. After rising 78% in 2010, the A Index fell 28% in 2011 and is estimated down an additional 15% from that point in 2013. Variable prices are expected over the outlook period, generally falling through 2016, but rising afterwards. While rising, prices remain below USD 2 200/t in every year of the projection period.

Figure 10.1. **Cotton prices rise between 2000-09 and 2014-23**

Evolution of world cotton prices in nominal (left) and real terms (right) to 2023[a]

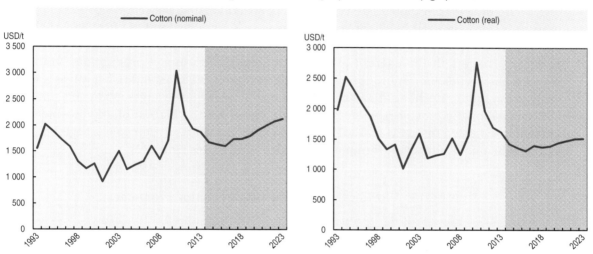

Note: Cotlook Ltd A Index: *a)* Real cotton prices are nominal world prices deflated by the US GDP deflator (2005 = 1).
Sources: Cotlook Ltd and OECD and FAO Secretariats.

StatLink ⬛⬛ http://dx.doi.org/10.1787/888933100853

China's efforts to ensure its producers receive about USD 3 200/t resulted in a significant accumulation of stocks starting in 2011. In addition to a significant share of the domestic crop, the reserve authorities have purchased cotton from outside of China. The withdrawal of millions of tons of cotton from world markets has supported world prices, particularly after December 2012, as the world economy strengthened. China has signalled its intention to reform its cotton support programme, and to move to reduce its stocks. The shift from building stocks to reducing them in China is one of the major factors behind a decline foreseen in world cotton prices during the early years of the outlook period.

The outlook period's highest level for world cotton prices is 6% above the base period average. Cotton prices in 2014-23 are expected to be significantly higher than in previous decades. They are expected to average USD 1 835/t, 38% more than in 2000-09. However, this is a smaller long term gain compared with wheat and corn, which are forecast to average 40% and 68% higher than in 2000-09. Cotton prices shifted downward relative to a variety of other commodities during 2000-09, including crops that compete with cotton for planted area, like wheat, corn, and soybeans. Cotton prices are not expected to rise enough in the projection period to return to their earlier relative price levels.

Production of cotton

World cotton production is projected to grow 2.2% annually in the *Outlook*, reaching 31.0 Mt in 2023. This total is expected to be 15% higher than production in the base period. Following the 2008 global financial crisis and subsequent cotton price volatility, world cotton production starts from a relatively low level in 2013, and rises as world consumption rebounds. Cotton yields are expected to rise in most countries, but the simple global average yield is expected to rise only 4.6% over the projection period as global production becomes increasingly concentrated in countries with relatively low yields. In particular, the roles of India and China will switch, with India replacing China as the world's largest producer starting in the first year of the outlook period.

Output is expected to fall in China, the world's largest producer since 1982 (Figure 10.2). While achieving high per hectare yields, China's cotton producers – particularly in its eastern provinces – utilise relatively labour-intensive technology. With a high share of labour in production costs, China's steadily rising wages have constrained profits for cotton growers, while rising subsidies for grain production have further eroded the relative attractiveness of producing cotton. Fragmented land holdings limit the ability of cotton growers in the eastern provinces to adopt mechanised production, while demographic trends indicate continued declines in rural population and rising wages are likely in the future. Mechanisation has been more applicable for the larger producing units in China's Xinjiang province, where per hectare yields are the highest of any province. China has indicated that 2014 will begin a period of reform for its cotton policy, beginning with a reduction of support to farmers in the eastern provinces (Box 10.1).

Figure 10.2. **World cotton production by major producer**

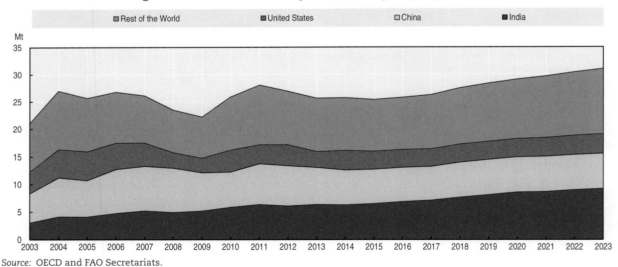

Source: OECD and FAO Secretariats.

StatLink 📊 *http://dx.doi.org/10.1787/888933100872*

India is expected to replace China as the world's largest cotton producer in 2014, and is expected to account for 30% of world output in 2023. As Indian farmers continue to apply new and existing technology to capture currently unrealised yield potential, rising relative cotton prices on world markets will add additional incentives for Indian farmers to

Box 10.1. **China's cotton policies drive large changes in world ending stocks**

Between 2010 and 2013, China's ending stocks of cotton rose by almost 350%. China's share of world cotton stocks rose from 19% to 54% during this time, with government-owned reserves accounting for the entire increase. The size of global cotton ending stocks in 2013 and the share of these stocks held by a single country are unprecedented in at least the last 50 years. The rise of China's official reserve stocks has noticeably affected world cotton supply and demand in recent years, and changes in China's cotton policies are expected to continue influencing cotton markets in the forecast period.

The government significantly altered its cotton policy in 2011, announcing a fixed price below which it would purchase cotton for its reserve through the annual harvest. This price was set below peak levels that occurred in 2010, but significantly above the levels that have prevailed on world markets since then. China is expected to begin altering its policy in the 2014 marketing year (September-August), reducing the amount of support offered to farmers and the gap introduced between cotton prices in China and the rest of the world since 2011. The large size of official reserve stocks makes the evolution of China's cotton policy in 2014 and beyond important to world cotton markets.

While China's share of world cotton stocks rose, its share of world cotton consumption fell. The rise in the domestic price of cotton in China relative to the world market price significantly constrained the profitability of spinning cotton fibre in yarn. China's trade deficit in cotton yarn rose significantly, and the textile industries of countries like India, Pakistan and others increased their consumption of cotton to meet this demand. One of the aims of China's cotton policy reform will be to limit the distortionary impact of support for cotton farmers. If China's domestic cotton prices can be returned to a level closer to world prices, the textile industry will probably be able to recover much of the share of world spinning lost during 2011-13. The appreciation of the Chinese Yuan Renminbi during this time, and steadily rising wages, will limit China's ability to return to the peak share of 42% realised before 2011, but could be significantly higher than the 33% realised in 2013.

China indicated that support for cotton producers will shift to a more targeted, less distortionary policy in 2014. Cotton producers in Xinjiang province will be the only producers to receive new, target price based direct subsidies. Producers in other provinces can expect to receive lower returns, and lower cotton production in 2014 is expected as a result. Lower production, combined with higher consumption, will begin the process of lowering China's reserve stocks. Other policy changes, likely in 2014 or in later years, include changes in trade policy and efforts to sell reserve stocks at lower prices. Production policy in 2014 is described as a pilot program, and the evolution of policies regarding cotton production, trade and management of official reserves will have potentially significant impacts on world markets for several years.

Figure 10.3. **Cotton ending stocks rise sharply**
Stock to use ratio

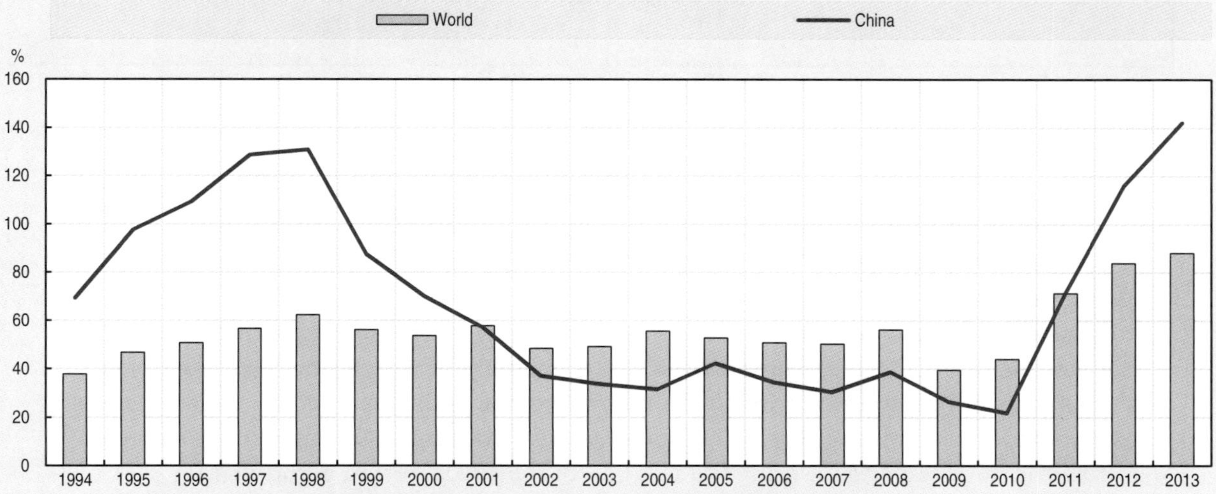

Source: International Cotton Advisory Committee, Cotton: World Statistics, September 2013.

StatLink http://dx.doi.org/10.1787/888933100891

increase planted area and output. While there is a scientific debate around the use of genetically modified (GM) crops, the adoption of GM cotton in India has been part of shift in practices and technology that led India's cotton production to more than double between 2000 and the base period. While GM adoption there is nearly complete, yields are expected to continue to grow, albeit at far below the 7.7% annual rate realised during 2000-09. With cotton area in India also rising slightly faster than harvested area for all grains and oilseeds, India accounts for the largest share of the expected gain in world production through 2023 (Figure 10.4).

Pakistan accounts for the second largest share of increased global production, and like India is expected to realise slightly faster growth in cotton area than in total grains and oilseeds area. However, this growth over 2014-23 will begin at a relatively lower base than in India. Cotton accounts for a larger share of Pakistan's planted area than in India, but this share fell after 2005 (Figure 10.4). Pakistan has lagged behind India considerably in the adoption of GM cotton, and cotton's share of planted area in the base period is down 9% from the last half of the 1990s.

Figure 10.4. **Cotton area relative to area for total grains and oilseeds in major producing countries**

Index: 1995-99 average cotton share of cropland = 1.0 (actual shares projected in 2023, %, right axis)

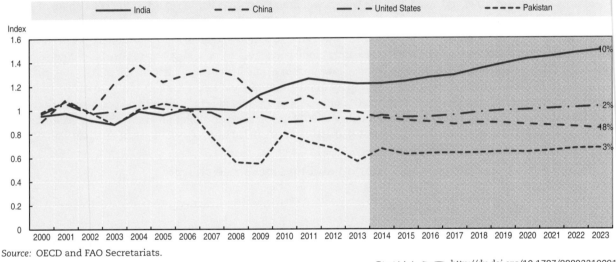

Source: OECD and FAO Secretariats.

StatLink ⟶ *http://dx.doi.org/10.1787/888933100910*

Globally, the area planted to cotton is equivalent to 3-4% of the area planted to grains, oilseeds, and sugar crops. Total global area planted to these crops is expected to grow slowly during 2014-23 (0.4% p.a.), well below the rate of cotton area's expansion. However, cotton's share of this area total is still foreseen to be only marginally higher in 2023 than in the base period, 3.7% compared with 3.5%. The volatility of cotton prices in recent years and China's efforts to reduce its stocks mean that the early years of the projection are expected to be an unusually low point for cotton area, magnifying the growth rate expected during the outlook period. During the last half of the 1990s, cotton accounted for 3.8% of this global area total, but with substantial increases in productivity, a smaller share of crop area is now needed to sustain growing cotton production.

Consumption of cotton

Total demand for cotton is expected to reach 30.8 Mt in 2023, surpassing its previous record-high by 4.3 Mt. While cotton consumption is expected to grow slightly more rapidly than it has over the very long-term, it is expected to grow significantly more slowly than the 3% rate realised during 2000-09. While consumption grows faster than the world's population in the *Outlook*, consumption on a per capita basis in 2023 is nonetheless expected to remain below the peaks seen in the last half of the 1980s and again during 2004-07 (Figure 10.5).

Figure 10.5. **World per capita consumption of cotton remains below peak**

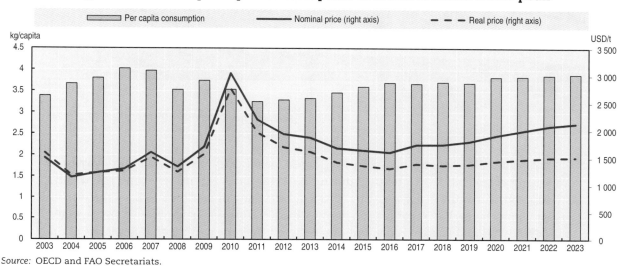

Source: OECD and FAO Secretariats.

StatLink ꜱ᎑ *http://dx.doi.org/10.1787/888933100929*

In recent years, cotton consumption has been disrupted by global economic volatility, an unprecedented price shock, and policy changes in China (Box 10.1). From a peak of 26.5 Mt in 2006 and 2007, world cotton consumption is estimated to have fallen 14% to 22.7 Mt in 2011. The outlook for world economic growth in the coming decade is more promising than during the base period and cotton prices have stabilised at more favourable levels relative to competing fibres. However, cotton prices are expected to remain high by historical standards and the global shift of textile production away from China's highly developed infrastructure may raise the average cost of supplying textiles to importing countries.

China is expected to remain the largest consumer of cotton fibre, its position since the 1960s. But China's share of world consumption is expected to decline, continuing a shift underway since 2007 (Figure 10.6). The age structure of China's population points to a decline in new labour-force entrants in coming years. With wages already rising steadily, China's comparative advantage is shifting away from labour-intensive industries like clothing. Government policies in minimum wages, pollution control, and investment will likely support this trend. Compounding this, the price of cotton in China has risen substantially relative to the world price since 2010 due to support policies for cotton farmers. While the reform of China's cotton programme is expected to boost China's share and level of cotton consumption early in the outlook period, China's share of world cotton consumption in 2023 is projected at 32%, down from 36% in the base period.

Figure 10.6. **World cotton consumption rebounds, but relatively slowly**

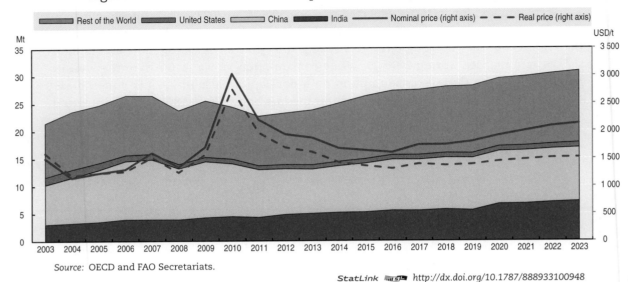

Source: OECD and FAO Secretariats.

StatLink ᵃˢˡ http://dx.doi.org/10.1787/888933100948

India's textile industry has been the largest beneficiary of China's shift away from processing cotton fibre into textiles during 2011-13. India recently became the world's largest exporter of cotton yarn, and by 2023 will be closing in on China to have the world's largest domestic market in population terms. China's reforms starting in 2014 are expected to moderate India's increased consumption between the base and the first few years of the outlook period. At 7.2 Mt expected in 2023, India's cotton consumption continues on its trend of a growing world share, which rises from 20% to 23%.

The fastest growth among major consumers is expected in Bangladesh and Viet Nam. Consumption is expected to grow at a 4-5% rate in each country, as their textile industries continue the rapid expansion each has enjoyed since 2000. While Bangladesh had been widely expected to see a reduction in its textile exports after the phase-out of the Multi-fibre Arrangement (MFA) in 2005, its garment exports and cotton spinning have instead flourished. Cotton consumption in Bangladesh grew at a 6.6% rate during 2004-13, and at a 14.0% rate in Viet Nam.

Cotton trade

Cotton trade is expected to grow relatively strongly during the outlook period. Trade will be boosted by China's return to world markets in the latter part of the projection period and by the continued expansion of textile output in countries which are large net cotton importers. Traditionally, cotton has been a relatively highly trade-dependent crop, with a ratio of world trade to world consumption of 30-45%, compared with ratios below 20% for grains and below 30% for soybeans. In the *Outlook*, exports are expected to grow at above the rate of world consumption, reaching 10.6 Mt by 2023. The ratio of trade to consumption is expected to fall from a relatively high 41% in the base period, reaching 34% in 2023.

The leading exporter throughout the *Outlook* will be the United States, while India's exports are expected to remain the world's second largest (Figure 10.7). In the decades before its post-2000 surge in productivity and production, India was a minor factor on world markets. India frequently imposed export quotas to maintain low cotton prices for its textile industry, and it was a net importer for seven consecutive years between 1998 and 2004. But more recently, India has at times accounted for as much as 24% of the world's cotton exports. By 2023, its share is forecast to be larger than in the base period, but only by a small margin as consumption gains begin to approach growth in output.

Figure 10.7. **World cotton trade shares by exporter**
2011-13 and 2023

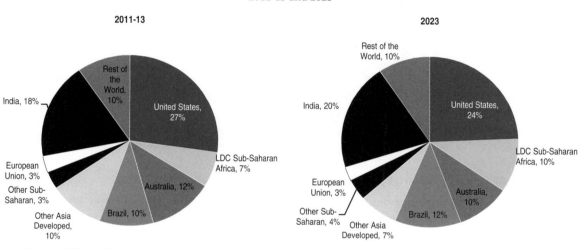

Source: OECD and FAO Secretariats.

StatLink ᵃˢᵖ *http://dx.doi.org/10.1787/888933100967*

Least Developed (LDC) Sub-Saharan Africa is expected to see a recovery of its share of world trade by 2023, growing from 7% to 10%. However, the region's share of world trade has been relatively variable in the last few decades, typically ranging between 7% and 13%. Cotton consumption is limited throughout Sub-Saharan Africa, and many countries export virtually all of their production. From a high of 926 000 t in 2004, LDC Sub-Saharan Africa's production fell below 400 000 t by 2009 as relative cotton prices reached new lows. With the recovery of world cotton prices, and expected yield gains in the region, production, exports and share of world trade are expected to rise through 2023.

Like exports, shifts in the composition of importers represent the continuation of recent trends in the world cotton economy. China is expected to retain the role as world largest importer that it has held since shortly after its World Trade Organization (WTO) accession drove its consumption up sharply, but at a reduced level (Figure 10.8). As China's share of world imports falls from 47% in the base period to 31% in 2023, Bangladesh's 2023 share of world trade is expected to be nearly 60% larger than in the base period, and gains are also expected for Viet Nam, Turkey and Pakistan. As China's role in world textile production diminishes, cotton consumption is expected to grow more rapidly in a variety of countries, most of which are significant net importers.

Figure 10.8. **World cotton trade shares by importer**
2011-13 and 2023

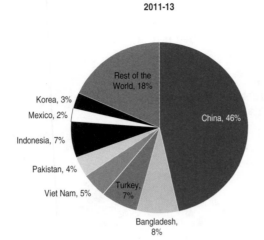

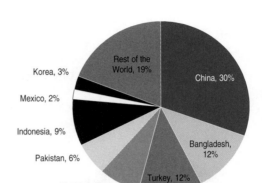

Source: OECD and FAO Secretariats.

StatLink 🔗 *http://dx.doi.org/10.1787/888933100986*

Main issues and uncertainties

The level of consumer demand and its relationship to industrial demand for cotton fibre is an important source of uncertainty in the *Outlook*. The consumption of cotton projected is ultimately a derived demand: textile mills consume cotton to produce yarn used in clothing and other consumer goods. Due to textile trade, the geographic distribution of the consumption of these consumer products can differ significantly from the distribution of cotton fibre consumption. Due to significant value-added in the production of consumer products, and substantial opportunities to substitute other fibres for cotton, the relationship between consumer spending on clothing and the volume of cotton consumed can vary significantly. World cotton consumption over the long run has grown at a 1.9% p.a. and is expected to grow 2.4% in the *Outlook*. World consumption typically does not grow smoothly at the long run rate, but has periods of relatively high or low growth. If the *Outlook's* assumptions of relatively strong economic growth and no significant technical change prove incorrect, then cotton consumption might grow at a different rate.

China's cotton policies are another important source of uncertainty in the *Outlook*. As the world's largest producer, consumer and importer in the base period, China's developments are important to understand under any circumstances, and its recent policy changes have heightened this importance. During 2011-13, China provided substantially more support to its cotton farmers than earlier, and did so primarily through maintenance of high domestic cotton prices. The *Outlook* assumes that the steps China has indicated to reform its cotton policies in 2014 will be expanded in the following years. While the changes that have been most clearly outlined to date have focused on support for farmers, there are also indications that policy-makers regard the unusually large stocks that China has accumulated since 2010 as unsustainable (Figure 10.9). The result could be higher consumption by China's textile industry, but possible changes in trade policy could also be used by China to accelerate a reduction in stocks. These changes would have implications for the outlook in other countries as well.

Figure 10.9. **World cotton stocks shift out of China**

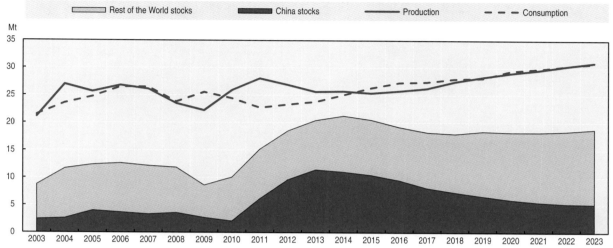

Source: OECD and FAO Secretariats.

StatLink *http://dx.doi.org/10.1787/888933101005*

Prospects for productivity gains around the world are another uncertainty, particularly in India. The adoption of GM crops has been associated with an increase in total factor productivity in cotton in China, and significantly higher yields, area and output in India. In the United States, GM adoption and boll weevil eradication have reduced the cost of growing cotton, and in Australia the adoption of GM varieties specific to Australia has also raised productivity. It is likely that these factors account for some of the downward shift of cotton prices relative to other commodity prices since 2000. Many countries have been more cautious in their approach to GM adoption, motivated in part by trade restrictions some countries maintain on imports of food and feed products based on GM crops. Similar restrictions are not applied to cotton fibre, yarn, or other textile products, but GM adoption has been slow in many countries nonetheless.

Future productivity gains are also possible through the adoption of other technologies and farming practices. Thus, the completion of GM adoption by India's farmers in recent years does not necessarily mean that further significant yield gains are not possible. For example, newer GM traits have progressed to near-final approval stages. If the yield increases foreseen in this *Outlook* are not realised, cotton prices and cotton area in other countries would likely be higher.

Glossary of terms

A-H1N1

This is an influenza virus that had never been identified as a cause of infections in people before the current H1N1 pandemic. Genetic analyses of this virus have shown that it originated from animal influenza viruses and is unrelated to the human seasonal H1N1 viruses that have been in general circulation among people since 1977.

Average Crop Revenue Election (ACRE) program

A new programme introduced with the 2008 US FCE Act allowing farmers to choose revenue-based protection against yield and market fluctuations.

APEC

Asia-Pacific Economic Co-operation – a forum for 21 Pacific-rim member economies that seeks to promote open trade and practical economic co-operation throughout the Asia-Pacific region. Co-operation is based on three pillars: trade and investment liberalization, business facilitation, and economic and technical co-operation. The primary goal is to support sustainable economic growth and prosperity in the region. Established in 1989, membership comprises Australia; Brunei Darussalam; Canada; Chile; People's Republic of China; Hong Kong, China; Indonesia; Japan; Republic of Korea; Malaysia; Mexico; New Zealand; Papua New Guinea; Peru; Philippines; Russian Federation; Singapore; Chinese Taipei; Thailand; United States; and Viet Nam.

Aquaculture

The farming of aquatic organisms including fish, molluscs, crustaceans and aquatic plants, etc. Farming implies some form of intervention in the rearing process to enhance production, such as regular stocking, feeding and protection from predators. Farming also implies individual or corporate ownership of the stock being cultivated. For statistical purposes, aquatic organisms that are harvested by an individual or corporate body that has owned them throughout their rearing period contribute to aquaculture, while aquatic organisms that are exploitable by the public as a common property resource, with or without appropriate licenses, are the harvest of capture fisheries.

Australia-US Free Trade Agreement (AUSFTA)

A Bilateral Agreement negotiated between the United States and Australia that came into force on 1 January 2005. AUSFTA covers goods, services, investment, financial services, government procurement, standards and technical regulations, telecommunications, competition-related matters, electronic commerce, intellectual property rights, labour and the environment.

Avian influenza

Avian influenza is an infectious disease of birds caused by type A strains of the influenza virus. The disease, which was first identified in Italy more than 100 years ago, occurs worldwide. The quarantining of infected farms, destruction of infected or potentially exposed flocks, and recently inoculation are standard control measures.

Atlantic beef/pigmeat market

The Atlantic market consists of countries producing and trading livestock, bovine and porcine, that are Foot and Mouth Disease (FMD) free with vaccination or contain FMD free zones. Most countries parts of this market are located around the Atlantic rim and typically trade grass fed bovine and grain fed porcine. The main countries that are part of that market are; South America, European Union, Russian Federation, North Africa, Iran, Israel, Kazakhstan, Malaysia, Peru, Philippines, Saudi Arabia, Turkey, Ukraine, Uruguay, Viet Nam, South Africa.

Baseline

The set of market projections used for the outlook analysis in this report and as a benchmark for the analysis of the impact of different economic and policy scenarios. A detailed description of the generation of the baseline is provided in the chapter on Methodology in this report.

Biofuels

In the wider sense defined as all solid, fluid or gaseous fuels produced from biomass. More narrowly, the term biofuels comprises those that replace petroleum-based road-transport fuels, i.e. bioethanol produced from sugar crops, cereals and other starchy crops that can be used as an additive to, in a blend with or as a replacement of gasoline, and biodiesel produced mostly from vegetable oils, but also from waste oils and animal fats, that can be used in blends with or as a replacement of petroleum-based diesel.

Biomass

Biomass is defined as any plant matter used directly as fuel or converted into other forms before combustion. Included are wood, vegetal waste (including wood waste and crops used for energy production), animal materials/wastes and industrial and urban wastes, used as feedstocks for producing bio-based products. In the context of the *Outlook* it does not include agricultural commodities used in the production of biofuels (e.g. vegetable oils, sugar or grains).

Bovine Spongiform Encephalopathy (BSE)

A fatal disease of the central nervous system of cattle, first identified in the United Kingdom in 1986. On 20 March 1996 the UK Spongiform Encephalopathy Advisory Committee (SEAC) announced the discovery of a new variant of Creutzfeldt-Jacob Disease (vCJD), a fatal disease of the central nervous system in humans, which might be linked to consumption of beef affected by exposure to BSE.

BRICS

Refers to the emerging economies of Brazil, the Russian Federation, India, China and South Africa.

Capture fisheries

Capture fisheries refer to the hunting, collecting and gathering activities directed at removing or collecting live wild aquatic organisms (predominantly fish, molluscs and crustaceans) including plants from the oceanic, coastal or inland waters for human consumption and other purposes by hand or more usually by various types of fishing gear such as nets, lines and stationary traps. The production of capture fisheries is measured by nominal catches (in live weight basis) of fish, crustaceans, molluscs and other aquatic animals and plants, killed, caught, trapped or collected for all commercial, industrial, recreational and subsistence purposes.

Cereals

Defined as wheat, coarse grains and rice.

Common Agricultural Policy (CAP)

The European Union's agricultural policy, first defined in Article 39 of the Treaty of Rome signed in 1957.

Coarse grains

Defined as barley, maize, oats, sorghum and other coarse grains in all countries except Australia, where it includes triticale and in the European Union where it includes rye and other mixed grains.

Conservation Reserve Program (CRP)

A major provision of the United States' Food Security Act of 1985 and extended under the Food and Agriculture Conservation and Trade Act of 1990, the Food and Agriculture Improvement and Reform Act of 1996, and the Farm Security and Rural Investment Act of 2002 is designed to reduce erosion on 40 to 45 million acres (16 to 18 million hectares) of farm land. Under the programme, producers who sign contracts agree to convert erodible crop land to approved conservation uses for ten years. Participating producers receive annual rental payments and cash or payment in kind to share up to 50% of the cost of establishing permanent vegetative cover. The CRP is part of the *Environmental Conservation Acreage Reserve Program*. The 1996 FAIR Act authorised a 36.4 million acre (14.7 million hectares) maximum under CRP, its 1995 level. The maximum area enrolled in the CRP was increased to 39.2 million acres in the 2002 FSRI Act.

Consumer price index for food (CPIF)

FAO's Global and Regional Food Consumer Price Indices (CPI) measure food inflation at sub-regional (e.g. South America), regional (e.g. Americas) and global (world, all countries). The Global Food CPI covers approximately 150 countries worldwide, representing more than 90% of the world population.

The aggregation procedure is based on the use of population weights. Population weights may better reflect regional food inflation and its impacts on households, while using the Gross Domestic Product (GDP) or any other measure of national income may better reflect the impact on the economy as a whole. Using GDP would also mean giving a higher weight to countries less exposed to food insecurity, because households in countries with higher GDP tend to be richer, spend a lower proportion of their income on food and benefit from an economic environment characterised by lower and less volatile consumer price inflation.

Common Market Organisation (CMO) for sugar

The common organisation of the sugar market (CMO) in the European Union was established in 1968 to ensure a fair income to community sugar producers and self-supply of the Community market. At present the CMO is governed by Council Regulation (EC) No. 318/2006 (the basic regulation) which establishes a restructuring fund financed by sugar producers to assist the restructuring process needed to render the industry more competitive.

Crop year, coarse grains

Refers to the crop marketing year beginning 1 April for Japan, 1 July for the European Union and New Zealand, 1 August for Canada and 1 October for Australia. The US crop year begins 1 June for barley and oats and 1 September for maize and sorghum.

Crop year, cotton

Refers to the crop marketing year beginning 1 August for all countries.

Crop year, oilseeds

Refers to the crop marketing year beginning 1 April for Japan, 1 July for the European Union and New Zealand, 1 August for Canada and 1 October for Australia. The US crop year begins 1 June for rapeseed, 1 September for soyabeans and for sunflower seed.

Crop year, rice

Refers to the crop marketing year beginning 1 April for Japan, Australia, 1 August for the United States, 1 September for the European Union, 1 November for Korea and 1 January for other countries.

Crop year, sugar

A common crop marketing year beginning 1 October and extending to 31 September, used by ISO (International Sugar Organization).

Crop year, wheat

Refers to the crop marketing year beginning 1 April for Japan, 1 June for the United States, 1 July for the European Union and New Zealand, 1 August for Canada and 1 October for Australia.

Decoupled payments

Budgetary payments paid to eligible recipients who are not linked to current production of specific commodities or livestock numbers or the use of specific factors of production.

Developed countries

See summary table at the end of the Glossary.

Developing countries

See summary table at the end of the Glossary.

Direct payments

Payments made directly by governments to producers.

Doha Development Agenda

The current round of multilateral trade negotiations in the World Trade Organisation that were initiated in November 2001, in Doha, Qatar.

Domestic support

Refers to the annual level of support, expressed in monetary terms, provided to agricultural production. It is one of the three pillars of the Uruguay Round Agreement on Agriculture targeted for reduction.

Economic Partnership Agreements (EPAs)

Free trade agreements currently being negotiated between the EU and the African, Caribbean Pacific (ACP) group of developing countries to replace the Cotonou Agreement which expired in 2007.

El Niño

In this publication, El Niño is used to indicate a broader term of quasi-periodic ocean climate conditions including La Niña, Southern Oscillation, or ENSO, which are characterised by anomalies in the temperature of the surface of eastern coast of Latin America (centred on Peru) -warming or cooling known as *El Niño* and *La Niña* respectively- and air surface pressure in the tropical western Pacific (the Southern Oscillation), often around Christmas time. The abnormal warm ocean climate conditions are accompanied by dramatic changes in species abundance and distribution, higher local rainfall and flooding, massive deaths of fish and their predators (including birds).

Energy Independence and Security Act (EISA) 2007

US legislation passed in December 2007 that is designed to increase US energy security by lessening dependence on imported oil, to improve energy conservation and efficiency, expand the production of renewable fuels, and to make America's air cleaner for future generations.

Ethanol

A biofuel that can be used as a fuel substitute (hydrous ethanol) or a fuel extender (anhydrous ethanol) in mixes with petroleum, and which is produced from agricultural feed-stocks such as sugar cane and maize.

Everything-But-Arms (EBA)

The Everything-But-Arms (EBA) Initiative eliminates EU import tariffs for numerous goods, including agricultural products, from the least developed countries. The tariff elimination is scheduled in four steps from 2006/07 to 2009/10.

Export credits (with official support)

Government financial support, direct financing, guarantees, insurance or interest rate support provided to foreign buyers to assist in the financing of the purchase of goods from national exporters.

Export restitutions (refunds)

EU export subsidies provided to cover the difference between internal prices and world market prices for particular commodities.

Export subsidies

Subsidies given to traders to cover the difference between internal market prices and world market prices, such as for example the EU *export restitutions*. Export subsidies are now subject to value and volume restrictions under the *Uruguay Round Agreement on Agriculture*.

FCE Act, 2008

Officially known as the Food, Conservation and Energy Act of 2008. This US farm legislation replaces the FSRI Act of 2002 and covers the period 2008-13.

Gur, jaggery, khandasari

Semi-processed sugars (plantation whites) extracted from sugarcane in India.

Health Check Reform of the Common Agricultural Policy

On 20 November 2008 the EU agriculture ministers reached a political agreement on the Health Check of the Common Agricultural Policy. Among a range of measures, the agreement abolishes arable set-aside, increases milk quotas gradually leading up to their abolition in 2015, and converts market intervention into a genuine safety net. Ministers also agreed to increase modulation, whereby direct payments to farmers are reduced and the money transferred to the Rural Development Fund.

High Fructose Corn Syrup (HFCS)

Isoglucose sweetener extracted from maize.

Industrial oilseeds

A category of oilseed production in the European Union for industrial use (i.e. biofuels).

Intervention purchases

Purchases by the EC Commission of certain commodities to support internal market prices.

Intervention purchase price

Price at which the European Commission will purchase produce to support internal market prices. It usually is below 100% of the intervention price, which is an annually decided policy price.

Intervention stocks

Stocks held by national intervention agencies in the European Union as a result of *intervention* buying of commodities subject to market price support. Intervention stocks may be released onto the internal markets if internal prices exceed intervention prices; otherwise, they may be sold on the world market with the aid of *export restitutions*.

Inulin

Inulin syrups are extracted from chicory through a process commercially developed in the 1980s. They usually contain 83% fructose. Inulin syrup production in the European Union is covered by the sugar regime and subject to a production quota.

Isoglucose

Isoglucose is a starch-based fructose sweetener, produced by the action of glucose isomerase enzyme on dextrose. This isomerisation process can be used to produce glucose/fructose blends containing up to 42% fructose. Application of a further process can raise the fructose content to 55%. Where the fructose content is 42%, isoglucose is equivalent in sweetness to sugar. Isoglucose production in the European Union is covered by the sugar regime and subject to a production quota.

Least squares growth rate

The **least-squares growth rate**, r, is estimated by fitting a linear regression trend line to the logarithmic annual values of the variable in the relevant period, as follows: $Ln(xt) = a + r * t$ and is calculated as $[exp (r) - 1]$.

Live weight

The weight of meat, finfish and shellfish at the time of their capture or harvest. Calculated on the basis of conversion factors from landed to nominal weight and on rates prevailing among national industries for each type of processing.

Loan rate

The commodity price at which the *Commodity Credit Corporation* (CCC) offers *non-recourse loans* to participating farmers. The crops covered by the programme are used as collateral for these loans. The loan rate serves as a floor price, with the effective level lying somewhat above the announced rate, for participating farmers in the sense that they can default on their loan and forfeit their crop to the CCC rather than sell it in the open market at a lower price.

Market access

Governed by provisions of the *Uruguay Round Agreement* on *Agriculture* which refer to concessions contained in the country schedules with respect to bindings and reductions of tariffs and to other minimum import commitments.

Marketing allotments (US sugar program)

Marketing allotments designate how much sugar can be sold by sugar millers and processors on the US internal market and were established by the 2002 FSRI Act as a way to guarantee the US sugar loan program operates at no cost to the Federal Government.

Marketing year, protein meals

Refers to the marketing year beginning 1 October.

Marketing year, vegetable oils

Refers to the marketing year beginning 1 October.

Market Price Support (MPS) Payment

Indicator of the annual monetary value of gross transfers from consumers and taxpayers to agricultural producers arising from policy measures creating a gap between domestic market prices and *border prices* of a specific agricultural commodity, measured at the farm gate level. Conditional on the production of a specific commodity, MPS includes the transfer to producers associated with both production for domestic use and exports, and is measured by the price gap applied to current production. The MPS is net of financial contributions from individual producers through producer levies on sales of the specific commodity or penalties for not respecting regulations such as production quotas (*Price levies*), and in the case of livestock production is net of the market price support on domestically produced coarse grains and oilseeds used as animal feed (*Excess feed cost*).

Methyl Tertiary Butyl Ether (MTBE)

A chemical gasoline additive that can be used to boost the octane number and oxygen content of the fuel, but can render contaminated water undrinkable.

Milk quota scheme

A supply control measure to limit the volume of milk produced or supplied. Quantities up to a specified quota amount benefit from full *market price support*. Over-quota volumes may be penalised by a levy (as in the European Union, where the "super levy" is 115% of the target price) or may receive a lower price. Allocations are usually fixed at individual producer level. Other features, including arrangements for quota reallocation, differ according to scheme.

Non-Recourse loan programme

Programme to be implemented under the US FAIR Act of 1996 for butter, non-fat dry milk and cheese after 1999 in which loans must be repaid with interest to processors to assist them in the management of dairy product inventories.

North American Free Trade Agreement (NAFTA)

A trilateral agreement on trade, including agricultural trade, between Canada, Mexico and the United States, phasing out tariffs and revising other trade rules between the three countries over a 15-year period. The agreement was signed in December 1992 and came into effect on 1 January 1994.

Oilseed meals

Defined as rapeseed meal (canola), soyabean meal, and sunflower meal in all countries, except in Japan where it excludes sunflower meal.

Oilseeds

Defined as rapeseed (canola), soyabeans, sunflower seed, peanuts and cotton seeds in all countries, except in Japan where it excludes sunflower seed.

Pacific beef/pigmeat market

The Pacific meat market consists of countries or zones within countries that produce and trade livestock free from/of, Foot and Mouth Disease (FMD) without vaccination. FMD status is given by the OIE according to strict guidelines (*www.oie.int/en/animal-health-in-the-world/official-disease-status/fmd/*) and include, inter alia, Australia, New Zealand, Japan, Korea, North America and the vast majority of Western Europe. The name "Pacific" refers to the fact that most of them are located around the Pacific rim.

Payment-In-Kind (PIK)

A programme used in the US to help dispose of public stocks of commodities. Under PIK, government payments in the form of Commodity Credit Corporation (CCC)-owned commodities are given to farmers in return for additional reductions in harvested acreage.

PROCAMPO

A programme of direct support to farmers in Mexico. It provides for direct payments per hectare on a historical basis.

Producer Support Estimate (PSE)

Indicator of the annual monetary value of gross transfers from consumers and taxpayers to agricultural producers, measured at farm gate level, arising from policy measure, regardless of their nature, objectives or impacts on farm production or income. The PSE measure support arising from policies targeted to agriculture relative to a situation without such policies, i.e. when producers are subject only to general policies (including economic, social, environmental and tax policies) of the country. The PSE is a gross notion implying that any costs associated with those policies and incurred by individual producers are not deducted. It is also a nominal assistance notion meaning that increased costs associated with import duties on inputs are not deducted. But it is an indicator net of producer contributions to help finance the policy measure (*e.g.* producer levies) providing a given transfer to producers. The PSE includes implicit and explicit payments. The percentage PSE is the ration of the PSE to the value of total gross farm receipts, measured by the value of total production (at farm gate prices), plus budgetary support. The nomenclature and definitions of this indicator replaced the former Producer Subsidy Equivalent in 1999.

Protein meals

Defined as oilseed meals, coconut meal, cotton meal and palm kernel meal.

Purchasing Power Parity (PPP)

Purchasing power parities (PPPs) are the rates of currency conversion that eliminate the differences in price levels between countries. The PPPs are given in national currency units per US Dollar.

Renewable Energy Directive (RED)

EU directive legislating binding mandates of 20% for the share of renewable energy in all member states' energy mix by the year 2020, with a specific mandate of 10% for the renewable energy share in transport fuels.

Renewable Fuel Standard (RFS and RFS2)

A standard in the United States for the use of renewable fuel use in the transport sector in the Energy Act (EISA). RFS2 is a revision of the RFS program for 2010 and beyond.

Saccharin

A low calorie, artificial sweetener used as a substitute for sugar mainly in beverage preparations.

Scenario

A model-generated set of market projections based on alternative assumptions than those used in the baseline. Used to provide quantitative information on the impact of changes in assumptions on the outlook.

Single Farm Payment

With the 2003 CAP reform, the EU introduced a farm-based payment largely independent of current production decisions and market developments, but based on the level of former payments received by farmers. To facilitate land transfers, entitlements are calculated by dividing the reference amount of payment by the number of eligible hectares (incl. forage area) in the reference year. Farmers receiving the new SFP are obliged to keep their land in good agricultural and environmental condition and have the flexibility to produce any commodity on their land except fruits, vegetables and table potatoes.

SPS Agreement

WTO Agreement on Sanitary and Phyto-sanitary measures, including standards used to protect human, animal or plant life and health.

Stock-to-use ratio

The stock-to-use ratio for cereals is defined as the ratio of cereal stocks to its domestic utilisation.

Stock-to-disappearance ratio

The stock-to-disappearance ratio is defined as the ratio of stocks held by the main exporters to their disappearance (i.e. domestic utilisation plus exports). For wheat the eight major exporters are considered, namely the United States, Argentina, the European Union, Canada, Australia, Russian Federation, Ukraine and Kazakhstan. In the case of coarse grains, United States, Argentina, the European Union, Canada, Australia, Russian

Federation, Ukraine and Brazil are considered. For rice Viet Nam, Thailand, India, Pakistan and the United States enter this ratio calculation.

Support price

Prices fixed by government policy makers in order to determine, directly or indirectly, domestic market or producer prices. All administered price schemes set a minimum guaranteed support price or a target price for the commodity, which is maintained by associated policy measures, such as quantitative restrictions on production and imports; taxes, levies and tariffs on imports; export subsidies; and public stockholding.

Tariff-rate quota (TRQ)

Resulted from the Uruguay Round Agreement on Agriculture. Certain countries agreed to provide minimum import opportunities for products previously protected by non-tariff barriers. This import system established a quota and a two-tier tariff regime for affected commodities. Imports within the quota enter at a lower (in-quota) tariff rate while a higher (out-of-quota) tariff rate is used for imports above the concessionary access level.

Uruguay Round Agreement on Agriculture (URAA)

The terms of the URAA are contained in the section entitled the "Agreement on Agriculture" of the Final Act Embodying the Results of the Uruguay Round of Multilateral Trade Negotiations. This text contains commitments in the areas of *market access*, domestic support, and *export subsidies*, and general provisions concerning monitoring and continuation. In addition, each country's schedule is an integral part of its contractual commitment under the URAA. There is a separate agreement entitled the Agreement on the Application of Sanitary and Phyto-sanitary Measures. This agreement seeks establishing a multilateral framework of rules and disciplines to guide the adoption, development and the enforcement of sanitary and phyto-sanitary measures in order to minimise their negative effects on trade. See also *Phyto-sanitary regulations* and *Sanitary regulations*.

Vegetable oils

Defined as rapeseed oil (canola), soyabean oil, sunflower seed oil, coconut oil, cotton oil, palm kernel oil, peanuts oil and palm oil, except in Japan where it excludes sunflower seed oil.

Voluntary Quota Restructuring Scheme

Established as part of the reform of the European Union's Common Market Organisation (CMO) for sugar in February 2006 to apply for four years from 1 July 2006. Under the scheme, sugar producers receive a degressive payment for permanently surrendering sugar production quota, in part or in entirety, over the period 2006-07 to 2009-10.

WTO

World Trade Organisation created by the Uruguay Round agreement.

Summary table for developed and developing countries

DEVELOPED	North America		Canada, United States
	Europe		Albania, Andorra, Belarus, Bosnia and Herzegovina, European Union, Faeroe Islands, Gibraltar, Holy See, Iceland, Monaco, Montenegro, Republic of Moldova, Russian Federation, San Marino, Serbia, The former Yugoslav Republic of Macedonia, Ukraine, Switzerland
	Oceania developed		Australia, New Zealand
	Other developed		Armenia, Georgia, Israël, Japan, Kasakhtan, Kyrgyzstan, Republic of Azerbaijan, South Africa, Tajikistan, Turkmenistan, Uzbekistan
DEVELOPING	Africa	North Africa	Algeria, Egypt, Libyan Arab Jamahiriya, Morocco, Tunisia
		Sub-Saharan Africa	Angola, Benin, Botswana, Burkina Faso, Burundi, Cameroon, CapeVerde, Central African Republic, Chad, Comoros, Congo, Côte d'Ivoire, Democratic Republic of the Congo, Djibouti, Equatorial Guinea, Eritrea, Ethiopia, Gabon, Gambia, Ghana, Guinea, Guinea-Bissau, Kenya, Lesotho, Liberia, Madagascar, Malawi, Mali, Mauritania, Mauritius, Mayotte, Mozambique, Namibia, Niger, Nigeria, Republic of the Congo, Reunion, Rwanda, Saint Helena, SaoTome and Principe, Senegal, Seychelles, Sierra Leone, Somalia, Soudan, Swaziland, Tanzania, Togo, Uganda, Western Sahara, Zambia, Zimbabwe
	Latin America and Caribbean		Anguilla, Antigua and Barbuda, Argentina, Aruba, Bahamas, Barbados, Belize, Bolivia, Brazil, British Virgin Islands, Cayman Islands, Chile, Colombia, Costa Rica, Cuba, Dominica, Dominican Republic, Ecuador, El Salvador, Falkland Islands (Malvinas), French Guiana, Grenada, Guadeloupe, Guatemala, Guyana, Haiti, Honduras, Jamaica, Martinique, Mexico, Montserrat, Netherlands Antilles, Nicaragua, Panama, Paraguay, Peru, Puerto Rico, Saint Kitts and Nevis, Saint Lucia, Saint Vincent and the Grenadines, South Georgia/Sandwich Islands, Suriname, Trinidad and Tobago, Turks and Caicos Islands, United States Virgin Islands, Uruguay, Venezuela
	Asia and Pacific		Afghanistan, American Samoa, Bahrain, Bangladesh, Bhutan, Brunei Darussalam, Cambodia, China, Chinese Taipei, Christmas Island, Cocos (Keeling) Islands, CookIslands, Democratic People's Republic of Korea, Fiji Islands, French Polynesia, GAZA, Gaza Strip (Palestine), Guam, Hong Kong (China), India, Indonesia, Iran, Iraq, Johnston Islands, Jordan, Kiribati, Korea, Kuwait, Lao People's Democratic Republic, Lebanon, Macau, Malaysia, Maldives, Marshall Islands, Micronesia (Federated States of), Mongolia, Myanmar, Nauru, Nepal, Neutral Zone, New Caledonia, Niue, Norfolk Island, Northern Mariana Islands, Oman, Pacific Islands, Pakistan, Philippines, Palau, Palestine Occupied Tr, Papua New Guinea, Pitcairn Islands, Qatar, Samoa, Saudia Arabia, Singapore, Solomon Islands, Sri Lanka, Syrian Arab Republic, Thailand, Timor-Leste, Tokelau, Tonga, Turkey, Tuvalu, United Arab Emirates, US Minor Outlying Islands, Vanuatu, Viet Nam, Wallis and Futuna Islands, West Bank, Yemen
	LDC		Afghanistan, Angola, Bangladesh, Benin, Bhutan, Burkina Faso, Burundi, Cambodia, Central African Republic, Chad, Comoros, Democratic Republic of the Congo, Djibouti, Equatorial Guinea, Eritrea, Ethiopia, Gambia, Guinea, Guinea-Bissau, Haiti, Kiribati, Lao People's Democratic Republic, Lesotho, Liberia, Madagascar, Malawi, Mali, Mauritania, Mozambique, Myanmar, Nepal, Niger, Rwanda, Samoa, Sao Tome and Principe, Senegal, Sierra Leone, Solomon Islands, Somalia, Soudan, Tanzania, Timor-Leste, Togo, Tuvalu, Uganda, Vanuatu, Yemen, Zambia
BRICS			Brazil, Russian Federation, India, China, South Africa

Methodology

This section provides information on the methodological aspects of the generation of the present *Agricultural Outlook*. It discusses the main aspects in the following order: First, a general description of the agricultural baseline projections and the *Outlook* report is given. Second, the compilation of a consistent set of the assumptions on macroeconomic projections is discussed in more detail. A third part presents how production costs are taken into account in the model's supply equations. The fourth part presents the new feed demand system that has been incorporated in the 2014 version of the model. Then the fifth part presents the methodology developed for the stochastic analysis conducted with the Aglink-Cosimo model.

The generation of the OECD-FAO Agricultural Outlook

The projections presented and analysed in this document are the result of a process that brings together information from a large number of sources. The use of a model jointly developed by the OECD and FAO Secretariats, based on the OECD's Aglink model and extended by FAO's Cosimo model, facilitates consistency in this process. A large amount of expert judgement, however, is applied at various stages of the Outlook process. The *Agricultural Outlook* presents a single, unified assessment, judged by the OECD and FAO Secretariats to be plausible given the underlying assumptions, the procedure of information exchange outlined below and the information to which they had access.

The starting point of the outlook process is the reply by OECD countries (and some non-member countries) to an annual questionnaire circulated in the autumn. Through these questionnaires, the OECD Secretariat obtains information from these countries on future commodity market developments and on the evolution of their agricultural policies. The starting projections for the country modules handled by the FAO Secretariat are developed through model based projections and consultations with FAO commodity specialists. External sources, such as the IMF, the World Bank and the UN, are also used to complete the view of the main economic forces determining market developments. This part of the process is aimed at creating a first insight into possible market developments and at establishing the key assumptions which condition the outlook. The main economic and policy assumptions are summarised in the Overview chapter and in specific commodity tables of the present report. The sources and assumptions for those assumptions are discussed in more detail further below.

As a next step, the modelling framework jointly developed by the OECD and FAO Secretariats is used to facilitate a consistent integration of this information and to derive an initial set of global market projections (baseline). In addition to quantities produced, consumed and traded, the baseline also includes projections for nominal prices (in local currency units) for the commodities concerned. Unless otherwise stated, prices referred to in the text are also in nominal terms. The data series for the projections are drawn from OECD and FAO databases. For the most part, information in these databases has been taken from national statistical sources. For further details on particular series, enquiries should be directed to the OECD and FAO Secretariats.

The model provides a comprehensive dynamic economic and policy specific representation of the main temperate-zone commodities as well as rice, cotton and vegetable oils. The Aglink and Cosimo country and regional modules are all developed by the OECD and FAO Secretariats in conjunction with country experts and, in some cases, with assistance from other national administrations. The initial baseline results for the countries under the OECD Secretariat's responsibility are compared with those obtained from the questionnaire replies and issues arising are discussed in bilateral exchanges with country experts. The initial projections for individual country and regional modules developed by the FAO Secretariat are reviewed by a wider circle of in-house and international experts. In this stage, the global projection picture emerges and refinements are made according to a consensus view of both Secretariats and external advisors. On the basis of these discussions and of updated information, a second baseline is produced. The information generated is used to prepare market assessments for biofuels, cereals, oilseeds, sugar, meats, fish and seafood, dairy products and cotton over the course of the outlook period, which is discussed at the annual meetings of the Group on Commodity Markets of the OECD *Committee for Agriculture*. Following the receipt of comments and final data revisions, a last revision is made to the baseline projections. The revised projections form the basis of a draft of the present *Agricultural Outlook* publication, which is discussed by the *Senior Management Committee* of FAO's Department of Economic and Social Development and the OECD's *Working Party on Agricultural Policies and Markets of the Committee for Agriculture*, in May 2014, prior to publication. In addition, the Outlook will be used as a basis for analysis presented to the FAO's *Committee on Commodity Problems* and its various *Intergovernmental Commodity Groups*.

The Outlook process implies that the baseline projections presented in this report are a combination of projections developed by collaborators for countries under the OECD Secretariat's responsibility and original projections for the 42 countries and regions under the FAO Secretariat's responsibility. The use of a formal modelling framework reconciles inconsistencies between individual country projections and forms a global equilibrium for all commodity markets. The review process ensures that judgement of country experts is brought to bear on the projections and related analyses. However, the final responsibility for the projections and their interpretation rests with the OECD and FAO Secretariats.

Sources and assumptions for the macroeconomic projections

Population estimates from the 2012 Revision of the United Nations Population Prospects database provide the population data used for all countries and regional aggregates in the *Outlook*. For the projection period, the medium variant set of estimates was selected for use from the four alternative projection variants (low, medium, high and constant fertility). The UN Population Prospects database was chosen because it represents a comprehensive source of reliable estimates which includes data for non-OECD developing countries. For consistency reasons, the same source is used for both the historical population estimates and the projection data.

The other macroeconomic series used in the Aglink-Cosimo model are real GDP, the GDP deflator, the private consumption expenditure (PCE) deflator, the Brent crude oil price (in US Dollars per barrel) and exchange rates expressed as the local currency value of 1 USD. Historical data for these series in OECD countries as well as Brazil, Argentina, China and Russian Federation are consistent with those published in the *OECD Economic Outlook No. 94*, November 2013 and *No. 93*, June 2013. For other economies, historical macroeconomic data were obtained from the IMF, World Economic Outlook, October 2013. Assumptions for 2014-23 are based on the recent medium-term macroeconomic projections of the OECD Economics Department, projections of the *OECD Economic Outlook No. 93* and projections of the IMF.

The model uses indices for real GDP, consumer prices (PCE deflator) and producer prices (GDP deflator) which are constructed with the base year 2005 value being equal to 1. The assumption of constant real exchange rates implies that a country with higher (lower) inflation relative to the United States (as measured by the US GDP deflator) will have a depreciating (appreciating) currency and therefore an increasing (decreasing) exchange rate over the projection period, since the exchange rate is measured as the local currency value of 1 USD. The calculation of the nominal exchange rate uses the percentage growth of the ratio "country-GDP deflator/US GDP deflator".

The oil price used to generate the *Outlook* is based on information from the *OECD Economic Outlook No. 94* until 2015 (short term update) and the growth rate of the International Energy Agency, World Energy Outlook, November 2013, for future paths.

The representation of production costs in Aglink-Cosimo

Changes in production costs are an important variable for farmers' decisions on crop and livestock production quantities, in addition to output returns and, if applicable, policy measures.

While supply in Aglink-Cosimo is largely determined by gross returns, production costs are represented in the model in the form of a cost index used to deflate gross production revenues. In other words, supply equations in the model in most cases depend on gross returns per unit of activity (such as returns per hectare or the meat price) relative to the overall production cost level as expressed by the index. Consequently, equations for harvested areas in crop production and for livestock production quantities take the following general forms:

$$AH = f\left(\frac{RH}{CPCI}\right); \quad QP = f\left(\frac{PP}{CPCI}\right);$$

respectively with:

AH   area harvested (crop production)

RH   returns per hectare (crop production)

CPCI Commodity production cost index

QP   production quantity (livestock production)

PP   producer price (livestock production)

Among others, energy prices, increased by rising crude oil prices, have fostered attention to agricultural production costs in agricultural commodity models. Energy prices can significantly impact on international markets for agricultural products as production costs for both crops and livestock products are highly dependent on energy costs. Fuels for tractors and other machinery, as well as heating and other forms of energy are directly used in the production process. In addition, other inputs such as fertilisers and pesticides have high energy content, and costs for these inputs are driven to a significant extent by energy prices. It is therefore important to explicitly consider energy prices in the representation of production costs.

The production cost indices employed in Aglink-Cosimo for livestock products is constructed from three sub-indices representing non-tradable inputs, energy inputs, and other tradable inputs, respectively. While the non-tradable sub-index is approximated by the domestic GDP deflator, the energy sub-index is affected by changes in the world crude oil price and the country's exchange rate. Finally, the tradable sub-index is linked to global inflation (approximated by the US GDP deflator) and the country's exchange rate. This relationship is shown in the following equation:

$$CPCI_{r,t} = CPCS_{r,t}^{NT} * GDPD_{r,t} \big/ GDPD_{r,bas}$$
$$+ CPCS_{r,t}^{EN} * \left(XP_t^{OIL} * XR_{r,t} \right) \big/ \left(XP_{bas}^{OIL} * XR_{r,bas} \right)$$
$$+ \left(1 - CPCS_{r,t}^{NT,I} - CPCS_{r,t}^{EN,I} \right) * \left(XR_{r,t} * GDPD_{USA,t} \right) \big/ \left(XR_{r,bas} * GDPD_{USA,bas} \right)$$

with:

CPCI   commodity production cost index for livestock

$CPCS^{NT}$ share of non-tradable input in total base commodity production costs

$CPCS^{EN}$ share of energy in total base commodity production costs

GDPD   deflator for the gross domestic product

XP^{OIL} world crude oil price

XR   nominal exchange rate with respect to the US Dollar

r,t   region and time index, respectively

bas   base year (2000 or 2005 or 2008) value

The production cost index is different for each *crop product* and is constructed from five sub-indices representing seeds inputs, fertiliser inputs, energy inputs, other tradable inputs and non-tradable inputs, respectively.

$$CPCI_{r,t}^c = CPCS_{r,t}^{NT} * GDPD_{r,t} \big/ GDPD_{r,bas}$$
$$+ CPCS_{r,t}^{EN} * \left(XP_t^{OIL} * XR_{r,t} \right) \big/ \left(XP_{bas}^{OIL} * XR_{r,bas} \right)$$
$$+ CPCS_{r,t}^{FT} * \left(XP_t^{FT} * XR_{r,t} \right) \big/ \left(XP_{bas}^{FT} * XR_{r,bas} \right)$$
$$+ CPCS_{r,t}^{TR} * \left(XR_{r,t} * GDPD_{USA,t} \right) \big/ \left(XR_{r,bas} * GDPD_{USA,bas} \right)$$
$$+ CPCS_{r,t}^{SD} * PP_{r,t}^c(-1) \big/ PP_{r,bas}^c$$

with:

$CPCI^C$ commodity production cost index for crop product c

$CPCS^{NT}$ share of non-tradable input in total base commodity production costs

$CPCS^{EN}$ share of energy in total base commodity production costs

$CPCS^{FT}$ share of fertiliser in total base commodity production costs

$CPCS^{TR}$ share of other tradable input in total base commodity production costs

$CPCS^{SD}$ share of seeds input in total base commodity production costs

GDPD   deflator for the gross domestic product

XP^{OIL} world crude oil price

XP^{FT} world fertiliser price

PP^c producer price for crop product c

XR   nominal exchange rate with respect to the US Dollar

c   Crop product

r,t   region and time index, respectively

bas   base year (2000 or 2005 or 2008) value

The shares of the various cost categories are country specific. They were estimated based on historic cost structures in individual countries. Shares vary depending on the development stages of the countries and regions. Developed countries tend to have higher shares of energy, fertiliser and tradable inputs than developing nations.

The fertiliser price is an index produced by the World Bank (Pink Sheets). It is formed as an index as follows:

$$XP^{FT} = 0.2 * DAP + 0.16 * MOP + 0.02 * TSP + 0.62 * Urea$$

With:

DAP   US Diammonium Phosphate

MOP   Canada Potassium Chloride

TSP   Triple superphosphate

Urea (Black Sea)

And is represented by an equation in the Aglink-Cosimo model:

$$
\begin{aligned}
XP_t^{FT} = CON &+ elas_{FT}^{lag1} * (XP_{t-1}^{FT} - XP_{t-2}^{FT}) \\
&+ elas_{FT}^{lag2} * (XP_{t-2}^{FT} - XP_{t-3}^{FT}) \\
&+ elas_{FT}^{OIL1} * (XP_{t-1}^{OIL} - XP_{t-2}^{OIL}) \\
&+ elas_{FT}^{OIL2} * (XP_{t-2}^{OIL} - XP_{t-3}^{OIL}) \\
&+ elas_{FT}^{crop1} * (XP_{t-1}^{crop} - XP_{t-2}^{crop}) \\
&+ elas_{FT}^{crop2} * (XP_{t-2}^{crop} - XP_{t-3}^{crop})
\end{aligned}
$$

With:

$$XP_t^{crop} = 0.5 * XP_t^{CG} + 0.2 * XP_t^{WT} + 0.2 * XP_t^{OS} + 0.1 * XP_t^{PRI}$$

With:

XP^{OIL} world crude oil price

XP^{FT} world fertiliser price

XP^{CG} world coarse grain price

XP^{WT} world wheat price

XP^{OS} world oilseed price

XP^{RI} world rice price

The new feed demand system

A new feed demand system, the final element of the Aglink/Cosimo review, has been fully incorporated in the 2014 version of the model. That improvement insures a greater consistency between animal requirement and amount of feed consumed. To achieve this many new feeds had to be included in the model such as distiller's dry grain, corn gluten feed, dried beet pulp, cereal bran, meat, bone and feather meals, field peas, manioc, fishmeal, whey powder and molasses. Complete balance sheets[*] and world market clearing price were introduced for all of these products except field peas. Fodder feeds (pasture, hay and cereal silage) are implicitly taken into account in the feed demand functions of countries endowed with these resources. The cross price demand elasticities of these products with coarse grains or protein meals are high insuring a consistent evolution of their price with their main competitor in the model.

The methodology of stochastic simulations with Aglink-Cosimo

The stochastic analysis methodology can be summarised in four steps: i) for the drivers that are treated stochastically, historical deviations around their trends or their expected values are estimated using past data; ii) from these deviations, the stochastic behaviour of the drivers is formalised: iii) 600 sets of future alternative values for these drivers, based on their stochastic behaviour, are generated; and iv) the Aglink-Cosimo model is run for each alternative set of values of the drivers. These steps are further explained below.

Step i): Estimating variability based on historical data

For the macroeconomic variables, deviations from expected values are computed as the ratio of the one-year-ahead forecast to the observed outcome. The forecasts come from past OECD Economic Outlooks and from the International Monetary Fund, and are available from 2003 onwards. This generates a time series of forecast errors from 2004 to 2012. The coefficient of variation (CV) of the errors is given in Table 3.

Table 1. **Macroeconomic variables treated as uncertain and the calculated CV of the one-year-ahead forecast errors (in %)**

	AUS	BRA	CAN	CHN	EUN	IND	JPN	NZL	RUS	USA	WLD	Total
Consumer Price Index (CPI)	2.2	7.2	1.6	6.6	1.8	9.7	1.3	2.6	7.2	1.1		**10.0**
Gross Domestic Product Deflator (GDP)	2.6	4.6	2.2	9.1	1.1	6.9	2.1	1.7	10.0	1.9		**10.0**
Gross Domestic Product (GDP)	1.3	3.5	2.4	4.3	2.8	3.8	4.2	3.0	8.1	2.2		**10.0**
Exchange rate (national currency/USD)	13.0	21.0	8.0	4.4	11.5	10.3	9.3	14.8	13.5			**9.0**
Crude oil price										26.1		**1.0**
Total	**4.0**	**4.0**	**4.0**	**4.0**	**4.0**	**4.0**	**4.0**	**4.0**	**4.0**	**3.0**	**1.0**	**40.0**

Note: the countries are denoted as follows, (AUS) Australia, (BRA) Brazil, (CAN) Canada, (EUN) European Union, (IND) India, (JPN) Japan, (NZL) New Zealand, (USA) United States, and (WLD) World
Source: Institute for Prospective Technological Studies (European Commission) calculations.

StatLink ᴪᴸᴸ *http://dx.doi.org/10.1787/888933101271*

The deviations around expected yield are measured as the ratio of the estimated yield to the observed outcome, where the estimated yield is obtained by an OLS regression over the period 1996-2012 using the same yield equations as in Aglink-Cosimo.

---

[*] Fishmeal is included in the satellite fish model.

Table 2. **Commodity yields treated as uncertain and the calculated CV (in %)**

	EU		Eurasia			South America				North America			South East Asia				Others				Total
	E15	NMS	KAZ	UKR	RUS	ARG	BRA	PRY	URY	CAN	MEX	USA	IND	MYS	THA	VNM	AUS	CHN	IND	NZL	
Wheat																					
Soft	4.3	10	26.5	26.8	12	14.6	14.7	21.8	25.8	11.2	5.4	6.2					33.9	3.1	4.1		15
Durum	9.6	16.5																			2
Coarse grains																					
C. Grains				13.5				14.3	10.9												3
Barley	4.3	8				16.7				11							30				5
Maize	5.8	23.6				10.7	7.6			7.7	4.4	7.2						3.2			8
Oats	4.6	9.5								8											3
Rye	10.3	10.6																			2
Other cereals	5.3	9.1																			2
Oilseeds																					
Oilseed			33	12.4				18.3													3
Rape	6.3	11.6								11							29				4
Soybean	9.8					15.7	7.5			17.4		5.6									5
Sunflower	6.6	14.1			15.5	10.6															4
Others																					
Rice	3.5											3.5			2.9	1.7		1.5	4.7		6
Palm oil													6.3	6.1							2
Sugarbeet	4.7	5.3			19.2							6.3						8.3			5
Sugarcane						7.7	3					5.7			11.4		8.7	7.4	5.4		7

Notes: The following abbreviations are used:

Countries: (EU) European Union, (E15) EU member states that joined before 2004, (NMS) EU member states that joined after 2004, (KAZ) Kazakhstan, (UKR) Ukraine, (RUS) Russia, (ARG) Argentina, (BRA) Brazil, (PRY) Paraguay, (URY) Uruguay, (CAN) Canada, (MEX) Mexico, (USA) United States, (IDN) Indonesia, (MYS) Malaysia, (THA) Thailand, (VNM) Viet Nam, (AUS) Australia, (CHN) China, (IND) India, and (NZL) New Zealand.

Commodities: (WTS/WT) soft wheat, (WTD) durum wheat, (CG) coarse grains, (BA) barley, (MA) maize, (OT) oats, (RY) rye, (OC) other cereals, (OS) Oilseeds, (RP) rapeseed, (SB) soybeans, (SF) sunflower seeds, (RI) rice, (PL) palm oil, (SBE) sugar beet, (SCA) sugar cane, (MK) milk.

Source: Institute for Prospective Technological Studies (European Commission) calculations.

StatLink ᴍᴵˢ▣ http://dx.doi.org/10.1787/888933101290

Steps (ii and iii): deriving the stochastic behaviour of the drivers and generating 600 sets of alternative values of the stochastic terms that mimic this stochastic behaviour

These steps are performed by the software SIMETAR. Step ii) uses the deviations and errors estimated in step i), and in step iii) the 600 alternative values are generated for each year of the projection period 2014-23. The assumptions underlying these steps are: a) deviations and errors are normally distributed and b) the covariance between exogenous drivers is relevant information. Estimated covariances are used only for the macroeconomic drivers and for yields within each regional block (e.g. the EU), but not between regional blocks. Thus, covariances between yield uncertainties in different regional blocks are assumed to be zero. For the macroeconomic variables, the stochastic deviation is assumed to increase over time; for the simulation of the crude oil and exchange rate stochastic terms a correction factor of 0.8 was used. By contrast, yield uncertainty is assumed not to cumulate over time.

Then, SIMETAR is run with these underlying assumptions and its output provides the final stochastic terms. A comparison of the two panels of Figure 1 illustrates the consequences of these two approaches to simulating the stochastic terms of macroeconomic and yield variables.

Figure 1. **Box plots of the multiplicative stochastic terms (2014-23)**

Australian wheat (left figure) and Russian GDP (right figure)

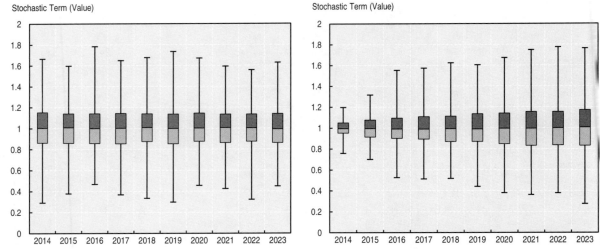

Source: Institute for Prospective Technological Studies (European Commission) calculations.

StatLink ᴹᵊ🔗 *http://dx.doi.org/10.1787/888933101024*

Step iv): running the Aglink-Cosimo model for each of the 600 alternative uncertainty scenarios

The stochastic terms are incorporated as multiplicative factors into the equations in which one of the stochastic drivers appears. This has the effect of shifting the relevant function above or below its "central" position in the deterministic baseline run. The model is run for each of the 600 alternative sets of stochastic drivers, providing 600 sets of different possible sets of the model's output variables.

For most of the scenarios presented in the Overview chapter, not all the 600 sets yield to a solution. The following table summarises the percentage of solved runs ("rate of success") for each of the five scenarios.

Table 3. **Rate of success in the solutions for the five scenarios**

Scenario	Rate of Success (%)
Milk yield uncertainty	100
Crop yield uncertainty	73
Crop + milk yield uncertainty	73
Macroeconomic uncertainty	80
Macroeconomic + yield (crop & milk) uncertainty	74

Source: Institute for Prospective Technological Studies (European Commission) calculations.

StatLink ᴹᵊ🔗 *http://dx.doi.org/10.1787/888933101309*

Statistical Annex

Part I. ANNEX A

Table A.1. Economic assumptions

Calendar year

		Average 2011-13est	2014	2015	2016	2017	2018	2019	2020	2021	2022	2023
REAL GDP[1]												
Australia	%	2.9	2.6	3.1	3.8	3.7	3.6	3.5	3.4	3.3	3.2	3.1
Canada	%	2.0	2.3	2.6	2.2	2.2	2.3	2.3	2.3	2.3	2.3	2.2
Chile	%	5.2	4.5	4.9	4.8	4.6	4.3	4.1	4.0	3.8	3.6	3.4
European Union	%	0.3	1.3	1.9	1.7	1.8	1.7	1.7	1.7	1.8	1.7	1.7
Japan	%	1.0	1.0	0.9	0.9	0.9	0.9	0.9	1.8	0.9	0.9	1.1
Korea	%	2.8	3.8	4.0	5.5	5.0	4.7	4.4	4.2	4.0	3.8	3.6
Mexico	%	2.9	3.8	4.2	3.2	3.4	3.5	3.5	3.6	3.6	3.6	3.6
New Zealand	%	2.5	2.6	3.4	2.5	2.4	3.1	2.3	2.2	2.9	2.1	2.6
Norway	%	1.8	2.8	3.1	3.6	3.4	3.3	3.1	3.0	2.8	2.7	2.5
Switzerland	%	1.6	2.2	2.7	2.7	2.6	2.5	2.4	2.4	2.3	2.3	2.2
Turkey	%	4.9	3.7	4.3	6.2	5.8	5.5	5.2	4.9	4.7	4.5	4.5
United States	%	2.1	2.9	3.4	2.7	2.5	2.4	2.3	2.2	2.2	2.1	2.1
Algeria	%	3.0	3.7	3.7	3.6	3.8	3.8	3.7	3.7	3.7	3.7	3.7
Argentina	%	5.7	3.0	1.8	2.5	2.7	2.9	2.9	3.0	3.0	3.0	3.0
Bangladesh	%	6.1	6.0	6.5	6.8	7.0	7.0	6.7	6.7	6.7	6.7	6.7
Brazil	%	2.0	2.2	2.5	4.2	4.0	3.9	3.8	3.7	3.7	3.6	3.6
China	%	8.2	8.2	7.5	8.2	7.8	7.5	7.1	6.8	6.4	6.0	5.7
Egypt	%	1.9	2.8	4.0	4.2	4.1	4.0	3.8	3.8	3.8	3.8	3.8
India	%	4.5	5.1	6.3	6.5	6.7	6.7	6.3	6.3	6.3	6.3	6.3
Indonesia	%	6.0	5.5	6.0	6.0	6.0	6.0	5.9	5.9	5.9	5.9	5.9
Iran	%	-0.1	1.3	2.0	2.2	2.2	2.4	2.0	2.0	2.0	2.0	2.0
Malaysia	%	5.2	4.9	5.2	5.2	5.2	5.2	5.1	5.1	5.1	5.1	5.1
Pakistan	%	3.9	2.5	3.5	3.7	4.5	5.0	3.8	3.8	3.8	3.8	3.8
Russian Federation	%	3.1	2.3	2.9	3.8	3.5	3.3	3.1	3.0	2.9	2.8	2.8
Saudi Arabia	%	5.8	4.4	4.3	4.3	4.3	4.3	4.3	4.3	4.3	4.3	4.3
South Africa	%	2.7	2.9	3.3	3.4	3.5	3.5	3.3	3.3	3.3	3.3	3.3
Ukraine	%	1.9	1.5	1.5	1.6	1.8	2.0	1.7	1.7	1.7	1.7	1.7
Uruguay	%	4.7	3.3	3.1	3.3	3.7	3.9	3.5	3.5	3.5	3.5	3.5
OECD[2,3]	%	1.5	2.2	2.6	2.4	2.3	2.2	2.2	2.3	2.1	2.1	2.1
PCE DEFLATOR[1]												
Australia	%	2.2	2.1	1.9	2.7	2.7	2.8	2.8	2.8	2.7	2.7	2.7
Canada	%	1.5	1.1	1.4	2.3	2.3	2.3	2.3	2.3	2.2	2.2	2.2
Chile	%	3.5	3.0	3.6	2.8	2.7	3.3	3.2	2.5	3.0	3.6	2.7
European Union	%	2.4	1.6	1.5	1.9	2.0	1.9	1.9	1.9	2.0	1.9	1.9
Japan	%	-0.6	2.0	1.8	2.1	2.1	2.1	2.1	2.1	2.1	2.0	2.0
Korea	%	2.3	1.9	2.7	2.5	2.7	2.8	2.9	3.0	3.0	3.0	3.0
Mexico	%	3.8	3.5	4.1	3.9	3.1	3.7	3.5	4.0	3.3	3.2	3.1
New Zealand	%	1.4	1.4	1.7	2.1	2.1	2.1	2.1	2.1	2.1	2.1	2.1
Norway	%	1.4	2.3	2.2	3.3	3.2	3.2	3.2	3.2	2.9	2.9	2.9
Switzerland	%	-0.5	0.1	0.3	1.8	1.9	2.0	2.0	2.0	2.0	2.0	2.0
Turkey	%	8.3	6.3	5.6	4.4	4.6	4.8	4.9	4.9	5.0	5.0	5.0
United States	%	1.8	1.6	1.8	1.8	1.9	2.0	2.0	2.0	2.0	2.0	2.0
Algeria	%	6.1	4.5	4.0	4.0	4.0	4.0	4.1	4.1	4.1	4.1	4.1
Argentina	%	19.3	26.1	9.1	5.3	4.2	4.3	4.1	4.0	4.3	3.9	4.1
Bangladesh	%	9.0	6.5	6.0	5.6	5.5	5.5	5.9	5.9	5.9	5.9	5.9
Brazil	%	6.8	6.0	6.0	4.4	4.5	4.5	4.5	4.6	4.6	4.6	4.6
China	%	3.5	2.4	2.4	3.9	4.0	4.0	4.0	4.0	4.0	4.0	4.0
Egypt	%	8.9	10.3	10.7	11.1	11.8	12.3	11.3	11.3	11.3	11.3	11.3
India	%	9.9	8.9	7.5	7.0	6.8	6.7	7.4	7.4	7.4	7.4	7.4
Indonesia	%	5.6	7.5	5.8	5.2	4.7	4.5	5.5	5.5	5.5	5.5	5.5
Iran	%	2.2	1.5	1.8	1.9	2.1	2.2	1.9	1.9	1.9	1.9	1.9
Malaysia	%	2.3	2.6	2.6	2.4	2.2	2.2	2.4	2.4	2.4	2.4	2.4
Pakistan	%	10.7	7.9	9.0	7.0	6.0	6.0	7.2	7.2	7.2	7.2	7.2
Russian Federation	%	6.7	5.7	4.5	3.7	3.8	3.9	3.9	4.0	4.0	4.0	4.0
Saudi Arabia	%	3.5	3.6	3.5	3.5	3.5	3.5	3.5	3.5	3.5	3.5	3.5
South Africa	%	5.5	5.5	5.1	5.0	5.0	5.0	5.1	5.1	5.1	5.1	5.1
Ukraine	%	2.8	1.9	3.3	3.9	4.0	4.0	3.4	3.4	3.4	3.4	3.4
Uruguay	%	8.2	8.6	8.1	7.8	7.4	7.0	7.8	7.8	7.8	7.8	7.8
OECD[2,3]	%	2.1	1.9	2.0	2.1	2.2	2.2	2.2	2.3	2.2	2.2	2.2

Table A.1. Economic assumptions (cont.)

Calendar year

		Average 2011-13est	2014	2015	2016	2017	2018	2019	2020	2021	2022	2023
GDP DEFLATOR[1]												
Australia	%	1.4	1.5	2.4	2.7	2.7	2.8	2.8	2.8	2.7	2.7	2.7
Canada	%	1.8	1.7	1.7	2.5	2.4	2.4	2.3	2.3	2.2	2.2	2.2
Chile	%	2.2	2.6	3.0	3.0	3.0	3.0	3.0	3.0	3.0	3.0	3.0
European Union	%	1.5	1.4	1.5	1.8	1.9	1.8	1.8	1.9	1.8	1.8	1.8
Japan	%	-1.1	1.2	1.3	2.1	2.1	2.1	2.1	2.1	2.1	2.0	2.0
Korea	%	1.5	0.9	1.7	2.5	2.4	3.2	3.1	3.0	2.9	2.8	2.9
Mexico	%	3.5	3.8	3.8	3.7	3.6	3.6	3.6	3.6	3.3	3.2	3.2
New Zealand	%	1.4	2.2	1.7	2.1	2.1	2.1	2.1	2.1	2.1	2.1	2.1
Norway	%	3.8	2.5	2.6	3.3	3.2	3.2	3.2	3.2	2.9	2.9	2.9
Switzerland	%	0.2	0.6	0.8	1.8	1.9	2.0	2.0	2.0	2.0	2.0	2.0
Turkey	%	7.1	6.0	5.5	4.4	4.6	4.8	5.0	5.0	4.8	4.9	5.0
United States	%	1.7	1.8	2.0	1.8	1.9	2.0	2.0	2.0	2.0	2.0	2.0
Algeria	%	9.8	3.4	2.5	2.4	3.3	1.7	2.7	2.7	2.7	2.7	2.7
Argentina	%	17.7	22.8	17.8	5.3	4.4	4.2	4.1	4.1	4.1	4.1	4.0
Bangladesh	%	7.5	6.9	6.3	5.8	5.6	5.6	6.0	6.0	6.0	6.0	6.0
Brazil	%	6.0	5.8	5.8	4.4	4.5	4.5	4.5	4.6	4.6	4.6	4.6
China	%	3.5	1.2	1.8	3.9	4.0	4.0	4.0	4.0	4.0	4.0	4.0
Egypt	%	9.9	10.8	11.0	11.2	11.7	12.3	11.4	11.4	11.4	11.4	11.4
India	%	8.1	7.3	6.4	6.4	5.6	5.4	6.2	6.2	6.2	6.2	6.2
Indonesia	%	5.8	5.6	5.7	5.2	4.7	5.0	5.3	5.3	5.3	5.3	5.3
Iran	%	1.7	1.8	2.0	1.8	1.9	2.0	2.0	2.0	2.0	2.0	2.0
Malaysia	%	2.3	2.5	3.1	2.8	2.6	2.6	2.7	2.7	2.7	2.7	2.7
Pakistan	%	11.3	7.9	9.0	7.0	6.0	6.0	7.2	7.2	7.2	7.2	7.2
Russian Federation	%	10.1	5.4	4.7	3.7	3.8	3.9	3.9	4.0	4.0	4.0	4.0
Saudi Arabia	%	5.2	-0.4	-1.0	-0.6	0.0	0.3	-0.4	-0.4	-0.4	-0.4	-0.4
South Africa	%	6.1	6.1	6.4	6.4	6.4	6.4	6.3	6.3	6.3	6.3	6.3
Ukraine	%	7.8	2.5	4.8	5.3	5.5	5.5	4.7	4.7	4.7	4.7	4.7
Uruguay	%	8.6	8.2	8.4	7.8	7.7	7.4	7.9	7.9	7.9	7.9	7.9
OECD[3]	%	1.6	1.8	2.0	2.1	2.1	2.2	2.2	2.2	2.2	2.2	2.2
WORLD INPUT PRICES												
Brent crude oil[4]	USD/barrel	110.6	113.1	118.1	121.4	124.7	128.1	131.6	135.2	139.0	143.0	147.1
Fertiliser[5]	USD/t	424.3	325.1	326.5	327.7	353.8	358.8	361.7	362.4	359.7	362.1	361.8
EXCHANGE RATES												
Australia	AUD/USD	0.99	1.04	1.07	1.10	1.14	1.17	1.20	1.23	1.26	1.28	1.31
Canada	CAD/USD	1.01	1.05	1.06	1.08	1.10	1.11	1.13	1.14	1.15	1.16	1.18
Chile	CLP/USD	487.18	505.95	509.78	513.14	516.07	518.74	521.24	523.67	526.06	528.44	530.85
European Union	EUR/USD	0.75	0.72	0.73	0.73	0.74	0.74	0.74	0.75	0.75	0.76	0.76
Japan	JPY/USD	85.44	97.02	97.97	98.98	99.88	100.68	101.41	102.08	102.71	103.32	103.89
Korea	'000 KRW/USD	1.11	1.06	1.06	1.06	1.06	1.06	1.06	1.06	1.06	1.06	1.06
Mexico	MXN/USD	12.78	12.88	13.07	13.24	13.39	13.53	13.67	13.81	13.91	14.00	14.09
New Zealand	NZD/USD	1.24	1.21	1.23	1.26	1.28	1.30	1.32	1.34	1.36	1.38	1.39
Algeria	DZD/USD	76.95	84.86	89.70	93.28	97.69	97.70	101.58	105.61	109.80	114.15	118.68
Argentina	ARS/USD	4.70	5.88	6.35	6.62	6.84	7.04	7.23	7.42	7.62	7.81	8.00
Bangladesh	BDT/USD	77.85	79.03	81.49	83.82	86.15	88.56	90.64	92.78	94.96	97.19	99.47
Brazil	BRL/USD	1.92	2.18	2.30	2.41	2.52	2.63	2.74	2.85	2.97	3.09	3.21
China	CNY/USD	6.31	6.08	6.23	6.38	6.53	6.67	6.81	6.95	7.08	7.21	7.34
Egypt	EGP/USD	6.10	7.02	7.24	7.52	8.06	8.57	9.06	9.58	10.13	10.71	11.33
India	INR/USD	55.38	72.32	75.08	77.83	80.08	82.77	87.19	91.85	96.75	101.92	107.36
Indonesia	'000 IDR/USD	9.55	11.74	12.06	12.30	12.62	12.92	13.47	14.04	14.63	15.26	15.90
Malaysia	MYR/USD	3.11	3.29	3.29	3.29	3.29	3.29	3.31	3.34	3.36	3.38	3.41
Pakistan	PKR/USD	90.49	110.26	120.97	126.92	131.58	134.92	144.17	154.05	164.60	175.88	187.94
Russian Federation	RUB/USD	30.70	31.80	32.10	32.40	32.60	32.90	33.20	33.50	33.80	34.20	34.53
Saudi Arabia	SAR/USD	3.75	3.75	3.75	3.75	3.75	3.75	3.75	3.75	3.75	3.75	3.75
South Africa	ZAR/USD	8.39	10.10	10.51	10.93	11.38	11.84	12.32	12.82	13.34	13.88	14.45
Ukraine	UAH/USD	8.03	8.15	8.15	8.15	8.15	8.15	8.15	8.16	8.16	8.16	8.17
Uruguay	UYU/USD	19.89	21.37	22.66	23.94	25.17	26.34	27.82	29.39	31.04	32.79	34.63

Table A.1. Economic assumptions (cont.)

Calendar year

		Average 2011-13est	2014	2015	2016	2017	2018	2019	2020	2021	2022	2023
POPULATION[1]												
Australia	%	1.3	1.2	1.2	1.3	1.3	1.2	1.2	1.2	1.2	1.2	1.1
Canada	%	1.0	1.0	1.0	1.0	1.0	1.0	0.9	0.9	0.9	0.8	0.8
Chile	%	0.9	0.9	0.9	0.8	0.8	0.8	0.8	0.7	0.7	0.7	0.7
European Union	%	0.2	0.2	0.2	0.2	0.2	0.2	0.1	0.1	0.1	0.1	0.1
Japan	%	-0.1	-0.1	-0.1	-0.2	-0.2	-0.2	-0.3	-0.3	-0.3	-0.3	-0.3
Korea	%	0.5	0.5	0.5	0.5	0.4	0.4	0.4	0.4	0.4	0.3	0.3
Mexico	%	1.2	1.2	1.2	1.1	1.1	1.0	1.0	1.0	1.0	1.0	0.9
New Zealand	%	1.0	1.0	1.0	1.0	0.9	0.9	0.9	0.9	0.9	0.9	0.8
Norway	%	1.0	1.0	1.0	1.0	1.0	1.0	1.0	0.9	0.9	0.8	0.8
Switzerland	%	1.0	1.0	1.0	1.0	1.0	1.0	1.0	1.0	1.0	1.0	1.0
Turkey	%	1.2	1.1	1.1	1.1	1.0	1.0	1.0	0.9	0.9	0.9	0.9
United States	%	0.8	0.8	0.8	0.8	0.8	0.8	0.8	0.8	0.8	0.7	0.7
Algeria	%	1.9	1.8	1.8	1.7	1.6	1.5	1.4	1.4	1.3	1.2	1.2
Argentina	%	0.9	0.9	0.8	0.8	0.8	0.8	0.8	0.8	0.7	0.7	0.7
Bangladesh	%	1.2	1.2	1.2	1.2	1.1	1.1	1.1	1.1	1.0	1.0	1.0
Brazil	%	0.9	0.8	0.8	0.8	0.7	0.7	0.7	0.7	0.6	0.6	0.6
China	%	0.6	0.6	0.6	0.5	0.5	0.4	0.4	0.4	0.3	0.3	0.2
Egypt	%	1.7	1.6	1.6	1.5	1.5	1.5	1.4	1.4	1.3	1.3	1.3
India	%	1.2	1.2	1.2	1.1	1.1	1.1	1.1	1.0	1.0	1.0	1.0
Indonesia	%	1.2	1.2	1.1	1.1	1.1	1.0	1.0	1.0	1.0	0.9	0.9
Iran	%	1.3	1.3	1.3	1.2	1.2	1.2	1.1	1.1	1.0	1.0	0.9
Malaysia	%	1.6	1.6	1.5	1.5	1.4	1.4	1.4	1.3	1.3	1.3	1.3
Pakistan	%	1.7	1.6	1.6	1.6	1.6	1.6	1.5	1.5	1.5	1.4	1.4
Russian Federation	%	-0.2	-0.3	-0.3	-0.3	-0.3	-0.3	-0.3	-0.3	-0.4	-0.4	-0.4
Saudi Arabia	%	1.9	1.9	1.8	1.7	1.7	1.6	1.5	1.4	1.3	1.2	1.1
South Africa	%	0.7	0.7	0.7	0.6	0.6	0.6	0.6	0.6	0.6	0.6	0.6
Ukraine	%	-0.6	-0.7	-0.7	-0.7	-0.7	-0.7	-0.7	-0.7	-0.7	-0.7	-0.8
Uruguay	%	0.3	0.3	0.3	0.3	0.3	0.3	0.3	0.3	0.3	0.3	0.3
OECD[3]	%	0.6	0.5	0.5	0.5	0.5	0.5	0.5	0.5	0.4	0.4	0.4
World	%	1.2	1.1	1.1	1.1	1.1	1.0	1.0	1.0	1.0	1.0	0.9

Note: For OECD member countries, as well as Brazil, China and Russia, historical data for real GDP, private consumption expenditure deflator and GDP deflator were obtained from the OECD Economic Outlook No. 94, November 2013. For other economies, historical macroeconomic data were obtained from the IMF, World Economic Outlook, October 2013. Assumptions for the projection period draw on the recent short term update of the OECD Economics Department, projections of the OECD Economic Outlook No. 93, projections of the IMF, and for population, projections from the United Nations World Population Prospects Database, 2012 Revision (medium variant). Data for the European Union are euro area aggregates except for population.

Average 2011-13est and 2013est: Data for 2013 are estimated.

1. Annual per cent change. The price index used is the private consumption expenditure deflator.
2. Annual weighted average real GDP and CPI growth rates in OECD countries are based on weights using purchasing power parities (PPPs).
3. Excludes Iceland.
4. Short term update for crude oil price from the OECD Economic Outlook No.94, November 2013 and projections from IEA World Energy Outlook 2013.
5. World Bank. Data for 2013 are estimated, projections by OECD and FAO Secretariats.

Source: OECD and FAO Secretariats.

StatLink ᐧᐧᐧ *http://dx.doi.org/10.1787/888933101328*

Table A.2. World prices

Nominal price

		Average 2011-13est	2014	2015	2016	2017	2018	2019	2020	2021	2022	2023
CEREALS												
Wheat[1]	USD/t	302.9	283.8	268.4	266.8	267.7	276.0	278.7	277.8	274.9	271.0	269.4
Coarse Grains[2]	USD/t	262.0	195.0	197.9	222.2	228.6	234.0	230.6	226.0	226.2	224.9	225.2
Rice[3]	USD/t	442.5	381.9	356.6	395.2	400.1	407.8	409.7	412.3	409.1	401.0	390.8
Distiller's dry grains[4]	USD/t	231.0	201.4	198.2	211.6	212.8	215.0	213.3	211.8	213.0	213.7	213.2
OILSEEDS												
Oilseeds[5]	USD/t	567.3	511.7	493.4	494.2	507.1	518.3	518.6	519.4	521.2	523.4	522.0
Protein meals[6]	USD/t	466.3	430.3	408.4	408.8	400.1	400.2	398.5	399.8	402.9	404.3	403.8
Vegetable oils[7]	USD/t	1 036.0	900.1	918.8	937.2	953.8	981.5	991.2	1 010.3	1 018.1	1 030.1	1 042.0
SWEETENERS												
Raw sugar[8]	USD/t rse	422.7	374.1	395.3	420.3	393.2	368.3	363.2	372.6	382.9	416.1	430.7
Refined sugar[9]	USD/t rse	529.1	479.2	490.2	514.0	497.1	466.1	456.5	465.4	474.3	501.5	5 8.6
HFCS[10]	USD/t	565.7	440.9	449.3	476.1	484.0	493.9	501.9	508.4	517.2	526.4	522.9
Molasses[11]	USD/t	171.2	177.9	181.7	189.7	180.5	171.2	167.5	165.9	166.0	170.3	168.8
MEAT												
Beef and veal												
Price, EU[12]	USD/t dw	4 961.6	5 411.7	5 606.1	5 562.5	5 593.2	5 168.0	5 296.7	5 339.2	5 325.4	5 283.6	5 23 .1
Price, United States[13]	USD/t dw	4 308.3	4 644.2	4 776.4	4 817.7	4 809.2	4 534.5	4 602.7	4 685.8	4 693.2	4 753.7	4 83 .5
Price, Brazil[14]	USD/t pw	3 243.7	2 849.3	2 975.1	3 105.5	3 173.1	2 895.7	2 900.7	2 926.1	2 952.6	2 933.9	2 90 .7
Pigmeat												
Price, EU[15]	USD/t dw	2 221.3	2 500.2	2 428.0	2 435.1	2 599.6	2 509.9	2 650.6	2 747.3	2 791.7	2 736.1	2 665 9
Price, United States[16]	USD/t dw	1 949.9	1 906.3	1 953.8	1 869.3	1 768.6	1 904.2	2 108.8	2 183.9	2 032.4	1 935.4	1 981 3
Price, Brazil[17]	USD/t dw	1 566.9	1 669.5	1 516.4	1 600.2	1 617.7	1 613.7	1 705.6	1 757.7	1 675.7	1 757.7	1 732
Poultry meat												
Price, EU[18]	USD/t rtc	2 609.0	2 489.3	2 348.0	2 398.5	2 470.1	2 508.2	2 517.5	2 510.9	2 505.1	2 483.0	2 461.
Price, United States[19]	USD/t rtc	1 203.2	1 237.7	1 114.2	1 150.9	1 213.9	1 257.3	1 269.5	1 270.3	1 266.7	1 267.2	1 270.
Price, Brazil[20]	USD/t rtc	1 465.3	1 474.1	1 332.8	1 383.4	1 458.7	1 511.4	1 528.2	1 533.9	1 535.3	1 542.0	1 550.2
Sheep meat												
Price, New Zealand[21]	USD/t dw	4 663.7	4 166.8	4 215.5	4 264.8	4 415.6	4 385.6	4 404.8	4 545.6	4 604.2	4 754.6	4 740.8
FISH AND SEAFOOD												
Product traded[22]	USD/t	2 810.2	2 791.7	2 867.8	2 903.3	2 925.7	3 025.9	3 044.7	3 208.6	3 212.3	3 367.0	3 368.1
Aquaculture[23]	USD/t	2 118.6	2 149.9	2 177.7	2 171.4	2 239.2	2 217.9	2 222.9	2 335.5	2 356.6	2 468.0	2 484.1
Capture[24]	USD/t	1 455.3	1 498.5	1 552.8	1 593.9	1 632.5	1 695.2	1 733.6	1 817.9	1 850.8	1 932.6	1 967.3
Meal[25]	USD/t	1 614.1	1 674.3	1 691.1	1 481.8	1 489.1	1 495.2	1 524.6	1 610.1	1 560.8	1 591.1	1 616.1
Oil[26]	USD/t	1 821.2	1 843.2	1 947.4	1 844.1	1 879.5	1 925.2	1 974.4	2 153.9	2 034.1	2 051.7	2 072.4
DAIRY PRODUCTS												
Butter[27]	USD/t	3 939.1	3 686.1	3 538.1	3 551.0	3 581.1	3 569.2	3 593.3	3 644.0	3 629.5	3 680.7	3 695.0
Cheese[28]	USD/t	4 174.5	4 151.6	4 130.8	4 222.9	4 314.4	4 377.3	4 466.8	4 566.1	4 633.4	4 755.7	4 851.4
Skim milk powder[29]	USD/t	3 740.4	3 864.6	3 706.0	3 701.8	3 731.7	3 758.3	3 815.7	3 828.8	3 799.5	3 787.6	3 806.3
Whole milk powder[30]	USD/t	3 936.6	4 389.9	4 158.9	4 178.3	4 188.8	4 214.1	4 253.8	4 274.5	4 267.9	4 279.7	4 292.7
Whey powder[31]	USD/t	1 240.9	1 236.0	1 209.3	1 240.5	1 257.4	1 248.9	1 243.5	1 233.6	1 188.8	1 196.4	1 204.4
Casein[32]	USD/t	8 735.0	8 882.8	8 829.2	8 808.0	8 899.2	8 923.1	9 043.6	9 120.5	9 088.7	9 127.0	9 216.0
BIOFUEL												
Ethanol[33]	USD/hl	70.9	63.6	66.1	69.9	70.5	73.9	75.5	76.0	77.9	78.9	82.1
Biodiesel[34]	USD/hl	120.7	112.2	111.3	119.0	123.8	122.9	119.4	121.8	122.5	125.3	128.7
COTTON												
Cotton[35]	USD/t	2 005.4	1 681.9	1 641.3	1 607.1	1 744.9	1 747.0	1 803.1	1 913.7	2 000.6	2 084.1	2 131.2

Table A.2. World prices (cont.)

Real price

		Average 2011-13est	2014	2015	2016	2017	2018	2019	2020	2021	2022	2023
CEREALS												
Wheat[1]	USD/t	265.6	240.7	223.1	217.9	214.5	216.9	214.7	209.7	203.4	196.5	191.4
Coarse Grains[2]	USD/t	230.1	165.5	164.5	181.4	183.1	183.8	177.6	170.6	167.3	163.1	160.0
Rice[3]	USD/t	388.6	324.0	296.5	322.6	320.6	320.4	315.6	311.2	302.7	290.8	277.7
Distiller's dry grains[4]	USD/t	202.6	170.8	164.8	172.8	170.5	168.9	164.3	159.9	157.6	154.9	151.5
OILSEEDS												
Oilseeds[5]	USD/t	497.6	434.0	410.1	403.5	406.3	407.2	399.4	392.1	385.6	379.5	370.9
Protein meals[6]	USD/t	408.6	365.0	339.5	333.8	320.5	314.4	306.9	301.8	298.1	293.2	287.0
Vegetable oils[7]	USD/t	909.6	763.5	763.8	765.2	764.2	771.2	763.4	762.6	753.2	746.9	740.5
SWEETENERS												
Raw sugar[8]	USD/t rse	371.3	317.3	328.6	343.2	315.0	289.4	279.7	281.2	283.3	301.7	306.1
Refined sugar[9]	USD/t rse	464.6	406.5	407.5	419.7	398.3	366.2	351.6	351.3	350.9	363.6	368.5
HFCS[10]	USD/t	496.7	374.0	373.5	388.7	387.8	388.0	386.6	383.8	382.6	381.7	371.6
Molasses[11]	USD/t	150.1	150.9	151.0	154.9	144.6	134.5	129.0	125.2	122.8	123.5	120.0
MEAT												
Beef and veal												
Price, EU[12]	USD/t dw	4 350.0	4 590.6	4 660.3	4 541.8	4 481.3	4 060.5	4 079.6	4 030.4	3 939.9	3 831.1	3 720.9
Price, United States[13]	USD/t dw	3 776.0	3 939.4	3 970.6	3 933.6	3 853.2	3 562.8	3 545.0	3 537.1	3 472.3	3 446.9	3 437.0
Price, Brazil[14]	USD/t pw	2 848.1	2 417.0	2 473.2	2 535.7	2 542.3	2 275.1	2 234.1	2 208.8	2 184.4	2 127.3	2 061.3
Pigmeat												
Price, EU[15]	USD/t dw	1 946.8	2 120.8	2 018.4	1 988.2	2 082.8	1 972.0	2 041.5	2 073.8	2 065.4	1 984.0	1 894.4
Price, United States[16]	USD/t dw	1 710.1	1 617.0	1 624.1	1 526.3	1 417.0	1 496.2	1 624.2	1 648.5	1 503.7	1 403.4	1 408.4
Price, Brazil[17]	USD/t dw	1 372.2	1 416.2	1 260.5	1 306.6	1 296.1	1 267.8	1 313.6	1 326.8	1 239.8	1 274.5	1 231.2
Poultry meat												
Price, EU[18]	USD/t rtc	2 287.8	2 111.5	1 951.9	1 958.4	1 979.0	1 970.7	1 939.0	1 895.3	1 853.3	1 800.4	1 749.2
Price, United States[19]	USD/t rtc	1 053.9	1 049.9	926.2	939.7	972.6	987.8	977.8	958.9	937.2	918.8	902.9
Price, Brazil[20]	USD/t rtc	1 283.2	1 250.4	1 107.9	1 129.5	1 168.7	1 187.5	1 177.0	1 157.9	1 135.9	1 118.1	1 101.6
Sheep meat												
Price, New Zealand[21]	USD/t dw	4 094.1	3 534.5	3 504.3	3 482.2	3 537.8	3 445.8	3 392.6	3 431.3	3 406.4	3 447.5	3 368.9
FISH AND SEAFOOD												
Product traded[22]	USD/t	2 810.2	2 368.0	2 384.0	2 370.6	2 344.1	2 377.5	2 345.1	2 422.0	2 376.5	2 441.4	2 393.4
Aquaculture[23]	USD/t	2 118.6	1 823.7	1 810.3	1 773.0	1 794.1	1 742.6	1 712.1	1 763.0	1 743.5	1 789.5	1 765.3
Capture[24]	USD/t	1 455.3	1 271.1	1 290.8	1 301.4	1 308.0	1 331.9	1 335.2	1 372.3	1 369.3	1 401.3	1 398.1
Meal[25]	USD/t	1 614.1	1 420.3	1 405.8	1 209.9	1 193.1	1 174.8	1 174.3	1 215.4	1 154.7	1 153.7	1 148.4
Oil[26]	USD/t	1 821.2	1 563.5	1 618.9	1 505.7	1 505.9	1 512.6	1 520.7	1 625.9	1 504.9	1 487.7	1 472.7
DAIRY PRODUCTS												
Butter[27]	USD/t	3 456.6	3 126.8	2 941.2	2 899.4	2 869.2	2 804.3	2 767.6	2 750.7	2 685.3	2 668.9	2 625.8
Cheese[28]	USD/t	3 660.4	3 521.6	3 433.9	3 448.0	3 456.7	3 439.3	3 440.3	3 446.7	3 428.0	3 448.4	3 447.6
Skim milk powder[29]	USD/t	3 276.6	3 278.1	3 080.8	3 022.5	2 989.9	2 952.9	2 938.9	2 890.2	2 811.0	2 746.4	2 704.8
Whole milk powder[30]	USD/t	3 448.4	3 723.8	3 457.2	3 411.6	3 356.1	3 311.0	3 276.3	3 226.6	3 157.6	3 103.2	3 050.5
Whey powder[31]	USD/t	1 087.0	1 048.4	1 005.3	1 012.9	1 007.4	981.2	957.7	931.2	879.5	867.5	855.9
Casein[32]	USD/t	7 661.7	7 534.9	7 339.7	7 191.7	7 130.1	7 010.9	6 965.4	6 884.7	6 724.2	6 618.0	6 549.2
BIOFUEL												
Ethanol[33]	USD/hl	62.3	54.0	54.9	57.1	56.5	58.0	58.2	57.4	57.6	57.2	58.4
Biodiesel[34]	USD/hl	105.9	95.2	92.5	97.1	99.2	96.6	92.0	91.9	90.7	90.9	91.5
COTTON												
Cotton[35]	USD/t	1 760.1	1 426.7	1 364.4	1 312.2	1 398.0	1 372.7	1 388.7	1 444.5	1 480.1	1 511.2	1 514.5

Note: This table is a compilation of price information presented in the detailed commodity tables further in this annex. Prices for crops are on marketing year basis and those for meat and dairy products on calendar year basis. See Glossary of Terms for definitions.
Average 2011-13est: Data for 2013 are estimated.

1. No.2 hard red winter wheat, ordinary protein, United States f.o.b. Gulf Ports (June/May), less EEP payments where applicable.
2. No.2 yellow corn, United States f.o.b. Gulf Ports (September/August).
3. Milled 5% broken, f.o.b. Ho Chi Minh (January/December).
4. Wholesale price, Central Illinois.
5. Weighted average oilseed price, European port.
6. Weighted average meal price, European port.
7. Weighted average price of oilseed oils and palm oil, European port.
8. Raw sugar world price, ICE contract No11 nearby, October/September.
9. Refined sugar price,Euronext,Liffe,Contract No. 407 London,Europe,October/September.
10. United States wholesale list price HFCS-55, October/September.
11. Unit import price, Europe (October/September).
12. EU average beef producer price.
13. Choice steers, 1100-1300 lb lw, Nebraska - lw to dw conversion factor 0.63.
14. Brazil average beef producer price.
15. EU average pigmeat producer price.
16. Barrows and gilts, No. 1-3, 230-250 lb lw, Iowa/South Minnesota - lw to dw conversion factor 0.74.
17. Brazil average pigmeat producer price.
18. EU average producer price.
19. Wholesale weighted average broiler price 12 cities.
20. Brazil average chicken for slaughter producer price.
21. Lamb schedule price, all grade average.
22. World unit value of trade (sum of exports and imports).
23. World unit value of aquaculture fisheries production (live weight basis).
24. FAO estimated value of world ex-vessel value of capture fisheries production excluding for reduction.
25. Fishmeal, 64-65% protein, Hamburg, Germany.
26. Fish oil any origin, N.W. Europe.
27. F.o.b. export price, butter, 82% butterfat, Oceania.
28. F.o.b. export price, cheddar cheese, 39% moisture, Oceania.
29. F.o.b. export price, non-fat dry milk, 1.25% butterfat,Oceania.
30. F.o.b. export price, WMP 26% butterfat, Oceania.
31. Dry whey, Wholesale price, West region, United States.
32. Export price, New Zealand.
33. Brazil, Sao Paulo (ex-distillery).
34. Producer price Germany net of biodiesel tariff.
35. Cotlook A index, Middling 1 3/32", c.f.r. far Eastern ports (August/July).

Source: OECD and FAO Secretariats.

StatLink ⌨ *http://dx.doi.org/10.1787/888933101347*

Table A.3.1. World trade projections, imports

		Average 2011-13est	2014	2015	2016	2017	2018	2019	2020	2021	2022	2023
Wheat												
World Trade	kt	139 997	135 881	138 754	141 109	143 033	144 410	146 762	148 986	151 339	153 612	155 540
OECD[1]	kt	32 373	28 300	28 606	29 377	29 758	29 720	29 532	29 577	29 875	30 166	30 479
Developing countries	kt	111 885	110 528	112 873	114 753	116 236	117 332	119 521	121 380	123 306	125 010	126 374
Least Developed Countries	kt	14 905	16 778	17 448	17 955	18 360	18 747	19 126	19 425	19 710	20 017	20 268
Coarse grains												
World Trade	kt	132 766	144 745	147 016	144 592	146 839	150 732	154 593	159 049	161 833	165 281	167 156
OECD[1]	kt	56 962	53 575	53 806	53 348	52 980	55 094	55 888	57 186	57 839	58 781	58 868
Developing countries	kt	95 651	113 488	116 110	113 664	115 842	117 586	121 049	125 093	128 116	131 371	133 532
Least Developed Countries	kt	2 125	3 703	4 293	4 199	4 196	4 110	4 293	4 485	4 669	4 772	4 935
Rice												
World Trade	kt	38 293	37 378	37 715	38 688	39 797	41 112	42 769	44 026	45 502	47 036	48 613
OECD[1]	kt	4 815	4 943	5 060	5 175	5 294	5 417	5 548	5 669	5 804	5 960	6 080
Developing countries	kt	33 381	32 169	32 466	33 378	34 410	35 632	37 191	38 394	39 774	41 175	42 664
Least Developed Countries	kt	6 898	6 865	6 789	6 910	6 838	7 087	7 400	7 661	7 920	8 146	8 423
Oilseeds												
World Trade	kt	115 128	122 682	123 857	125 865	126 669	128 179	129 601	131 431	133 115	134 855	136 874
OECD[1]	kt	32 882	33 466	33 701	33 974	33 917	33 711	33 632	33 710	33 629	33 573	33 534
Developing countries	kt	90 006	97 208	98 472	100 434	101 345	103 048	104 548	106 340	108 201	110 061	112 190
Least Developed Countries	kt	397	313	317	303	298	295	299	309	318	331	342
Protein Meals												
World Trade	kt	77 167	81 563	83 521	84 412	86 280	88 672	90 522	92 760	94 761	96 720	98 952
OECD[1]	kt	43 424	45 279	45 308	45 353	45 594	45 994	46 521	46 730	47 177	47 547	47 840
Developing countries	kt	38 758	42 134	44 326	45 400	47 193	49 301	50 851	53 087	54 887	56 645	58 674
Least Developed Countries	kt	594	722	840	921	976	1 031	1 097	1 184	1 268	1 340	1 407
Vegetable Oils												
World Trade	kt	67 639	70 542	72 546	74 374	75 999	77 717	79 383	81 239	82 960	84 641	86 233
OECD[1]	kt	17 929	17 954	18 206	18 179	18 444	18 584	18 804	19 249	19 300	19 111	19 014
Developing countries	kt	50 467	53 430	55 151	56 991	58 337	59 922	61 372	62 805	64 512	66 412	68 168
Least Developed Countries	kt	5 257	5 516	5 749	5 942	6 117	6 307	6 503	6 706	6 916	7 136	7 350
Sugar												
World Trade	kt	53 659	53 623	54 945	56 679	55 875	56 179	57 540	59 010	60 310	62 916	64 222
OECD[1]	kt	13 813	13 738	13 946	13 640	12 304	12 481	12 703	12 844	12 765	12 682	12 813
Developing countries	kt	37 977	38 206	39 284	41 561	42 303	42 374	43 638	44 999	46 340	48 935	49 958
Least Developed Countries	kt	6 685	7 268	7 206	7 288	7 790	8 141	8 643	9 083	9 557	9 692	10 172
Beef[2]												
World Trade	kt	7 592	8 189	8 434	8 567	8 775	8 986	9 311	9 566	9 803	9 990	10 215
OECD[1]	kt	3 199	3 316	3 416	3 482	3 529	3 573	3 673	3 710	3 760	3 793	3 835
Developing countries	kt	4 120	4 682	4 817	4 952	5 157	5 329	5 506	5 649	5 819	5 953	6 119
Least Developed Countries	kt	182	178	191	209	243	232	241	241	239	218	205
Pigmeat[2]												
World Trade	kt	6 633	6 753	6 877	7 064	7 245	7 408	7 554	7 640	7 787	7 903	8 024
OECD[1]	kt	3 282	3 226	3 221	3 260	3 326	3 388	3 457	3 387	3 354	3 354	3 356
Developing countries	kt	3 298	3 589	3 753	3 886	4 051	4 211	4 314	4 467	4 665	4 840	5 042
Least Developed Countries	kt	188	244	274	292	307	354	379	422	461	499	546
Poultry												
World Trade	kt	12 101	12 249	12 881	13 207	13 486	13 840	14 190	14 573	15 011	15 461	15 859
OECD[1]	kt	2 979	2 731	2 678	2 659	2 629	2 600	2 567	2 526	2 480	2 441	2 405
Developing countries	kt	9 048	9 220	9 754	10 057	10 319	10 599	10 938	11 279	11 680	12 079	12 444
Least Developed Countries	kt	967	1 051	1 152	1 153	1 167	1 205	1 253	1 276	1 321	1 361	1 405
Fish												
World Trade	kt	37 058	38 167	39 035	39 772	40 309	41 359	42 274	43 005	43 922	44 632	45 432
OECD	kt	20 109	20 266	20 615	21 014	21 319	21 521	21 781	21 984	22 257	22 420	22 677
Developing countries	kt	16 654	17 673	18 307	18 694	18 873	19 687	20 294	20 797	21 411	21 908	22 428
Least Developed Countries	kt	811	789	768	779	780	779	789	783	813	836	873
Fishmeal												
World Trade	kt	3 021	3 029	2 765	3 002	2 952	2 956	2 942	2 717	2 854	2 772	2 813
OECD	kt	1 169	1 143	1 102	1 104	1 069	1 066	1 069	942	1 012	977	998
Developing countries	kt	1 945	1 991	1 795	2 022	2 027	2 043	2 038	1 948	2 017	1 983	2 012
Least Developed Countries	kt	26	29	29	29	29	29	29	29	29	29	29
Fish oil												
World Trade	kt	818	822	812	845	846	870	870	849	853	876	887
OECD	kt	657	668	662	674	676	691	690	679	657	688	692
Developing countries	kt	276	297	291	312	313	324	324	314	338	338	347
Least Developed Countries	kt	1	1	1	1	1	1	1	1	1	1	1
Butter												
World Trade	kt	823	865	853	860	867	873	884	890	900	900	905
OECD[1]	kt	131	145	141	140	138	136	134	131	129	126	124
Developing countries	kt	534	579	585	596	609	622	637	648	662	669	680
Least Developed Countries	kt	15	25	17	16	16	16	18	19	20	19	18

Table A.3.1. **World trade projections, imports** (cont.)

		Average 2011-13est	2014	2015	2016	2017	2018	2019	2020	2021	2022	2023
Cheese													
World Trade	kt	2 145	2 183	2 216	2 273	2 342	2 404	2 462	2 531	2 611	2 683	2 732
OECD[1]	kt	822	849	833	841	852	869	877	885	889	900	911
Developing countries	kt	1 042	1 057	1 103	1 165	1 218	1 256	1 297	1 365	1 446	1 515	1 558
Least Developed Countries	kt	34	45	56	61	65	75	87	103	113	119	120
Whole milk powder													
World Trade	kt	2 210	2 383	2 432	2 451	2 487	2 536	2 583	2 624	2 673	2 715	2 762
OECD[1]	kt	80	70	74	76	78	75	74	72	70	68	67
Developing countries	kt	2 157	2 327	2 375	2 393	2 428	2 473	2 517	2 557	2 605	2 646	2 692
Least Developed Countries	kt	185	198	204	209	213	219	224	228	233	239	244
Skim milk powder													
World Trade	kt	1 808	1 926	1 982	2 028	2 076	2 137	2 189	2 241	2 297	2 351	2 401
OECD[1]	kt	314	312	323	334	340	348	355	365	375	383	392
Developing countries	kt	1 670	1 748	1 801	1 844	1 888	1 946	1 994	2 042	2 095	2 146	2 195
Least Developed Countries	kt	88	93	98	101	103	107	110	113	117	121	124
Cotton													
World Trade	kt	9 271	7 692	8 011	8 395	8 790	8 888	9 169	9 477	9 900	10 366	10 800
OECD[1]	kt	1 416	1 743	1 828	1 761	1 936	1 878	1 894	1 924	1 948	1 981	2 007
Developing countries	kt	8 894	7 313	7 606	7 943	8 335	8 435	8 717	9 033	9 458	9 923	10 343
Least Developed Countries	kt	709	946	926	988	1 184	1 085	1 153	1 196	1 242	1 286	1 330

Note: The values do not add up to world trade due to double counting of certains countries and statistical differences (i.e. LDC are already included in the Developing countries aggregate).

Average 2011-13est: Data for 2013 are estimated.

1. Excludes Iceland but includes all EU28 member countries.
2. Excludes trade of live animals.

Source: OECD and FAO Secretariats.

StatLink ᴍˢᴾ *http://dx.doi.org/10.1787/888933101366*

Table A.3.2. World trade projections, exports

		Average 2011-13est	2014	2015	2016	2017	2018	2019	2020	2021	2022	2023
Wheat												
OECD[1]	kt	91 920	92 994	95 148	92 954	92 535	91 408	91 894	92 368	92 347	92 836	92 792
Developing countries	kt	20 437	20 476	19 597	20 002	20 320	21 191	22 131	23 027	23 827	24 066	24 350
Least Developed Countries	kt	54	61	56	53	51	49	47	43	40	37	34
Coarse grains												
OECD[1]	kt	52 922	55 865	67 563	57 430	57 527	59 769	62 444	66 048	67 919	70 859	72 098
Developing countries	kt	60 559	70 330	60 112	64 510	65 938	67 097	67 815	68 277	68 578	68 402	68 478
Least Developed Countries	kt	5 289	2 002	1 704	2 386	2 791	3 009	2 839	2 565	2 408	2 296	2 280
Rice												
OECD[1]	kt	3 941	3 982	4 125	4 245	4 343	4 398	4 423	4 472	4 514	4 565	4 526
Developing countries	kt	33 745	33 758	33 937	34 776	35 776	37 040	38 682	39 936	41 372	42 870	44 502
Least Developed Countries	kt	1 992	1 606	1 939	1 843	2 726	2 928	3 346	3 786	4 093	4 437	4 674
Oilseeds												
OECD[1]	kt	52 995	58 110	57 315	58 491	59 603	60 383	60 731	61 225	62 022	62 779	63 725
Developing countries	kt	57 276	61 127	63 418	63 867	63 444	63 878	64 737	65 879	66 444	67 210	67 995
Least Developed Countries	kt	100	87	77	75	80	86	101	117	133	146	163
Protein Meals												
OECD[1]	kt	14 725	14 384	14 176	14 121	14 371	14 315	14 290	14 516	14 750	14 959	15 382
Developing countries	kt	57 077	62 229	64 284	64 949	66 379	68 671	70 308	72 023	73 574	75 100	76 721
Least Developed Countries	kt	176	204	132	122	126	130	129	117	113	102	93
Vegetable Oils												
OECD[1]	kt	6 175	5 848	6 047	6 339	6 378	6 435	6 501	6 560	6 675	6 841	6 972
Developing countries	kt	56 355	60 386	62 197	63 526	64 974	66 434	67 780	69 309	70 650	71 966	73 202
Least Developed Countries	kt	225	223	221	218	216	214	211	209	207	204	202
Sugar												
OECD[1]	kt	7 577	7 954	8 563	8 192	7 241	7 142	7 287	7 587	7 948	8 489	8 934
Developing countries	kt	49 612	50 145	51 209	52 762	52 728	52 943	54 091	55 271	56 266	58 253	59 268
Least Developed Countries	kt	1 514	1 540	1 794	1 967	1 562	1 765	1 947	2 128	2 317	2 437	2 729
Beef[2]												
OECD[1]	kt	3 885	3 628	3 694	3 741	3 804	3 861	3 966	4 023	4 082	4 129	4 179
Developing countries	kt	4 269	4 838	4 990	5 064	5 202	5 356	5 571	5 739	5 883	6 017	6 183
Least Developed Countries	kt	6	3	3	2	2	2	2	2	3	3	3
Pigmeat[2]												
OECD[1]	kt	6 007	5 902	5 990	6 121	6 307	6 430	6 548	6 634	6 765	6 859	6 963
Developing countries	kt	1 127	1 092	1 072	1 128	1 137	1 179	1 262	1 315	1 320	1 377	1 380
Least Developed Countries	kt	0	0	0	0	0	0	0	0	0	0	0
Poultry												
OECD[1]	kt	5 653	5 878	6 078	6 351	6 403	6 500	6 589	6 745	6 955	7 166	7 338
Developing countries	kt	6 817	6 747	7 179	7 225	7 442	7 680	7 912	8 105	8 305	8 508	8 695
Least Developed Countries	kt	1	1	1	0	0	0	0	0	0	0	0
Fish												
OECD	kt	12 792	13 230	13 413	13 644	13 893	14 126	14 341	14 491	14 784	15 005	15 142
Developing countries	kt	25 329	26 364	26 923	27 399	27 657	28 349	28 950	29 297	29 897	30 258	30 745
Least Developed Countries	kt	1 425	1 453	1 513	1 478	1 461	1 450	1 429	1 458	1 445	1 463	1 454
Fishmeal												
OECD	kt	954	885	1 016	933	1 014	1 021	1 021	1 014	990	1 035	1 036
Developing countries	kt	2 133	2 137	1 868	2 160	2 120	2 138	2 129	1 887	2 061	1 985	2 034
Least Developed Countries	kt	76	74	74	74	74	74	74	74	74	74	74
Fish oil												
OECD	kt	411	399	434	436	447	455	455	460	445	467	468
Developing countries	kt	520	517	489	529	524	551	551	524	539	558	575
Least Developed Countries	kt	9	11	11	11	11	11	11	11	11	11	11
Butter												
OECD[1]	kt	670	714	703	710	717	725	736	741	752	753	760
Developing countries	kt	101	84	83	84	84	82	82	84	84	85	84
Least Developed Countries	kt	5	4	5	8	9	9	9	12	14	16	15
Cheese												
OECD[1]	kt	1 571	1 719	1 769	1 849	1 923	1 980	2 049	2 127	2 219	2 294	2 339
Developing countries	kt	604	505	493	470	456	456	449	441	429	422	422
Least Developed Countries	kt	0	0	0	0	0	0	0	0	0	0	0
Whole milk powder												
OECD[1]	kt	1 640	1 742	1 800	1 813	1 848	1 885	1 924	1 957	1 998	2 030	2 070
Developing countries	kt	551	607	597	601	603	614	622	630	638	648	656
Least Developed Countries	kt	10	6	6	6	6	6	6	6	6	6	5
Skim milk powder												
OECD[1]	kt	1 517	1 631	1 704	1 761	1 820	1 876	1 930	1 977	2 033	2 076	2 121
Developing countries	kt	187	211	196	188	177	179	176	181	184	195	199
Least Developed Countries	kt	5	2	2	2	2	2	2	2	2	2	2
Biofuel[3]												
Ethanol World Trade	Mn L	3 430	3 937	5 868	6 548	8 295	10 118	11 901	12 405	11 716	11 726	10 812
Biodiesel World Trade	Mn L	1 859	1 556	1 904	1 977	1 884	1 843	2 157	2 238	2 298	2 241	2 174

Table A.3.2. World trade projections, exports *(cont.)*

		Average 2011-13est	2014	2015	2016	2017	2018	2019	2020	2021	2022	2023
Cotton												
OECD[1]	kt	4 092	3 176	3 384	3 305	3 440	3 343	3 381	3 517	3 695	3 873	3 988
Developing countries	kt	4 426	3 575	3 641	3 876	4 299	4 465	4 717	4 898	5 141	5 423	5 726
Least Developed Countries	kt	796	843	857	843	897	991	1 063	1 098	1 143	1 187	1 241

Note: Average 2011-13est: Data for 2013 are estimated.

1. Excludes Iceland but includes all EU28 member countries.
2. Excludes trade of live animals.
3. Sum of all positive net trade positions.

Source: OECD and FAO Secretariats.

StatLink ⬛📊 *http://dx.doi.org/10.1787/888933101385*

Table A.4.1. Biofuel projections: Ethanol

	PRODUCTION (Mn L)		Growth (%)[1]	DOMESTIC USE (Mn L)		Growth (%)[1]	FUEL USE (Mn L)		Growth (%)[1]	SHARE IN GASOLINE TYPE FUEL USE (%)				NET TRADE (Mn L)[2]	
										Energy share		Volume share			
	Average 2011-13est	2023	2014-23	Average 2011-13est	2023	2014-23	Average 2011-13est	2023	2014-23	Average 2011-13est	2023	Average 2011-13est	2023	Average 2011-13est	2023
NORTH AMERICA															
Canada	1 788	1 935	0.34	2 060	2 472	2.21	2 060	2 472	2.21	3.4	3.9	5.0	5.7	-272	-537
United States	48 468	70 717	2.26	47 197	76 617	2.96	44 840	74 124	3.05	5.9	9.9	8.6	14.0	1 264	-5 887
of which second generation	1	7 300	..	..	..	..	..	..	..	..	..	..	..	..	..
EUROPE															
European Union	6 674	12 072	6.00	8 113	13 562	5.87	5 636	11 348	7.35	3.2	6.6	4.7	9.5	-1 282	-1 490
of which second generation	60	426	..	..	..	..	..	..	..	..	..	..	..	..	..
OCEANIA DEVELOPED															
Australia	340	315	-0.33	376	397	-0.27	376	397	-0.27	1.4	1.4	2.0	2.1	-37	-83
OTHER DEVELOPED															
Japan	317	333	0.05	1 173	1 773	3.88	350	954	8.94	0.0	..	0.0	..	-855	-1 439
of which second generation	293	309	..	..	..	..	..	..	..	..	..	..	..	..	..
South Africa	259	285	0.27	111	98	0.11	5	6	1.16	..	..	..	..	148	187
SUB-SAHARAN AFRICA															
Mozambique	32	44	1.79	33	39	1.12	8	16	2.65	..	..	..	..	-2	5
Tanzania	32	48	2.71	38	48	2.70	11	28	4.94	..	..	..	..	-6	0
LATIN AMERICA AND CARRIBBEAN															
Argentina	502	1 127	7.59	604	1 282	7.13	383	1 076	9.23	3.4	6.6	5.0	9.5	-102	-155
Brazil	24 479	49 757	6.05	22 396	38 945	4.72	20 679	37 009	4.96	45.3	59.0	55.2	68.3	2 083	10 812
Colombia	400	609	3.17	466	623	2.13	372	530	2.54	..	..	..	..	-66	-14
Mexico	218	220	-0.86	355	352	-0.86	0	0	..	0.0	..	0.0	..	-137	-132
Peru	226	327	2.90	173	226	1.97	109	179	2.51	..	..	..	..	53	101
ASIA AND PACIFIC															
China	8 170	7 702	1.18	8 135	9 199	3.10	2 212	4 383	7.79	1.3	1.3	1.9	1.9	35	-1 497
India	2 497	3 210	1.76	2 338	3 093	2.57	397	1 227	7.93	..	..	..	..	159	117
Indonesia	195	218	1.04	141	178	1.28	36	59	1.98	..	..	..	..	54	40
Malaysia	73	75	0.70	113	127	0.41	0	0	-0.04	..	..	..	..	-40	-52
Philippines	158	286	0.88	450	660	1.91	319	533	2.39	..	..	..	..	-292	-375
Thailand	1 042	1 909	3.13	866	1 540	2.44	663	1 334	2.86	..	..	..	..	176	369
Turkey	94	147	3.45	132	159	1.80	50	60	1.76	..	..	..	..	-38	-11
Viet Nam	406	500	3.33	343	532	2.21	166	335	3.70	..	..	..	..	63	-32
TOTAL	100 546	158 044	3.58	100 050	157 913	3.58	79 494	136 887	4.04	6.2	..	8.9	..	3 430	10 812

.. Not available

Note: Average 2011-13est: Data for 2013 are estimated.

1. Least-squares growth rate (see glossary).
2. For total net trade exports are shown.

Source: OECD and FAO Secretariats.

StatLink ⬛⬛ http://dx.doi.org/10.1787/888933101404

Table A.4.2. Biofuel projections: Biodiesel

	PRODUCTION (Mn L)		Growth (%)[1]	DOMESTIC USE (Mn L)		Growth (%)[1]	SHARE IN DIESEL TYPE FUEL USE (%)				NET TRADE (Mn L)[2]	
							Energy share		Volume share			
	Average 2011-13est	2023	2014-23	Average 2011-13est	2023	2014-23	Average 2011-13est	2023	Average 2011-13est	2023	Average 2011-13est	2023
NORTH AMERICA												
Canada	305	603	-0.01	530	834	2.36	1.5	2.3	1.9	2.9	-226	-232
United States	4 104	6 549	2.30	3 706	6 339	2.15	1.5	2.7	1.9	3.4	261	209
EUROPE												
European Union	10 250	15 868	5.09	12 967	19 069	4.66	5.1	7.4	6.2	9.1	-2 717	-3 201
of which second generation	45	210	..	..	..	..	..	..	..	..	..	..
OCEANIA DEVELOPED												
Australia	657	742	1.10	657	742	1.10	2.8	2.5	3.4	3.1	0	0
OTHER DEVELOPED												
South Africa	75	108	3.36	75	108	3.36	..	..	..	..	0	0
SUB-SAHARAN AFRICA												
Mozambique	70	96	2.92	19	47	5.09	..	..	..	..	51	49
Tanzania	62	130	7.29	0	57	64.21	..	..	..	..	62	72
LATIN AMERICA AND CARIBBEAN												
Argentina	2 607	3 650	3.29	1 009	1 743	3.82	6.4	9.2	7.8	11.3	1 598	1 907
Brazil	2 744	3 894	1.90	2 748	3 836	1.75	4.6	4.6	5.7	5.7	-4	58
Colombia	604	946	3.41	604	945	3.41	..	..	..	..	1	1
Peru	93	175	6.34	272	338	2.34	..	..	..	..	-179	-163
ASIA AND PACIFIC												
India	290	730	10.04	400	886	7.51	..	..	..	..	-110	-155
Indonesia	1 785	3 255	4.37	568	1 832	6.98	..	..	..	..	1 217	1 423
Malaysia	159	837	11.50	89	648	14.91	..	..	..	..	69	188
Philippines	156	419	8.09	156	419	8.09	..	..	..	..	0	0
Thailand	823	1 161	1.96	823	1 161	1.96	..	..	..	..	0	0
Turkey	12	27	8.30	12	28	8.49	..	..	..	..	0	0
Viet Nam	24	98	10.42	24	97	10.37	..	..	..	..	0	1
TOTAL	**25 037**	**40 260**	**4.03**	**24 878**	**40 106**	**4.05**	**3.0**	**4.3**	**3.7**	**5.3**	**1 859**	**2 174**

.. Not available

Note: Average 2011-13est: Data for 2013 are estimated.

1.   Least-squares growth rate (see glossary).

2.   For total net trade exports are shown.

Source: OECD and FAO Secretariats.

StatLink ⫶⫶⫶ *http://dx.doi.org/10.1787/888933101423*

Table A.5. Main policy assumptions for biofuel markets

		2013est	2014	2015	2016	2017	2018	2019	2020	2021	2022	2023
ARGENTINA												
Biodiesel												
Export tax	%	20.7	21.6	22.4	23.8	24.0	24.0	24.0	24.0	24.0	24.0	24.0
BRAZIL												
Ethanol												
Import tariffs	%	0.0	0.0	0.0	0.0	0.0	0.0	0.0	0.0	0.0	0.0	0.0
Incorporation mandate[1]	%	17.5	18.3	18.3	18.3	18.3	18.3	18.3	18.3	18.3	18.3	18.3
Biodiesel												
Tax concessions[2]	BRL/hl	6.7	6.7	6.7	6.7	6.7	6.7	6.7	6.7	6.7	6.7	6.7
Import tariffs	%	4.6	4.6	4.6	4.6	4.6	4.6	4.6	4.6	4.6	4.6	4.6
CANADA												
Ethanol												
Tax concessions[2]	CAD/hl	6.4	6.4	6.4	6.4	6.4	6.4	6.4	6.4	6.4	6.4	6.4
Import tariffs	CAD/hl	5.0	5.0	5.0	5.0	5.0	5.0	5.0	5.0	5.0	5.0	5.0
Incorporation mandate[1]	%	3.4	3.4	3.4	3.4	3.4	3.4	3.4	3.4	3.4	3.4	3.4
Direct support												
Federal	CAD/hl	6.0	5.0	4.0	3.0	0.0	0.0	0.0	0.0	0.0	0.0	0.0
Provincial	CAD/hl	4.3	4.3	4.3	4.3	0.0	0.0	0.0	0.0	0.0	0.0	0.0
Biodiesel												
Tax concessions[2]	CAD/hl	7.7	7.7	7.7	7.7	7.7	7.7	7.7	7.7	7.7	7.7	7.7
Incorporation mandate[1]	%	1.8	1.8	1.8	1.8	1.8	1.8	1.8	1.8	1.8	1.8	1.8
Direct support												
Federal	CAD/hl	12.0	10.0	8.0	6.0	0.0	0.0	0.0	0.0	0.0	0.0	0.0
Provincial	CAD/hl	0.0	0.0	0.0	0.0	0.0	0.0	0.0	0.0	0.0	0.0	0.0
COLOMBIA												
Ethanol												
Import tariffs	%	9.7	9.7	9.7	9.7	9.7	9.7	9.7	9.7	9.7	9.7	9.7
Blending target[3,4]	%	10.0	10.0	10.0	10.0	10.0	10.0	10.0	10.0	10.0	10.0	10.0
Biodiesel												
Blending target[4]	%	5.0	5.0	5.0	5.0	5.0	5.0	5.0	5.0	5.0	5.0	5.0
EUROPEAN UNION												
Biofuel												
Energy share in fuel consumption[5]	%	4.7	5.4	5.9	6.3	6.8	7.4	7.9	8.5	8.5	8.5	8.5
Ethanol												
Tax concessions[2]	EUR/hl	18.3	18.3	18.3	18.3	18.3	18.3	18.3	18.3	18.3	18.3	18.3
Import tariffs	EUR/hl	19.2	19.2	19.2	19.2	19.2	19.2	19.2	19.2	19.2	19.2	19.2
Biodiesel												
Tax concessions[2]	EUR/hl	19.4	19.4	19.4	19.4	19.4	19.4	19.4	19.4	19.4	19.4	19.4
Import tariffs	%	6.5	6.5	6.5	6.5	6.5	6.5	6.5	6.5	6.5	6.5	6.5
INDIA												
Ethanol												
Import tariffs	%	8.0	8.0	8.0	8.0	8.0	8.0	8.0	8.0	8.0	8.0	8.0
Share of biofuel mandates in total fuel consumption	%	5.0	5.0	5.0	5.0	5.0	5.0	5.0	5.0	5.0	5.0	5.0
Biodiesel												
Import tariffs	%	7.8	7.8	7.8	7.8	7.8	7.8	7.8	7.8	7.8	7.8	7.8
Share of biofuel mandates in total fuel consumption	%	2.8	3.7	4.6	5.5	6.4	7.3	8.2	8.2	8.2	8.2	8.2
INDONESIA												
Ethanol												
Import tariffs	%	26.3	26.3	26.3	26.3	26.3	26.3	26.3	26.3	26.3	26.3	26.3
Blending target[4]	%	0.0	0.0	0.0	0.0	0.0	0.0	0.0	0.0	0.0	0.0	0.0
Biodiesel												
Blending target[4]	%	3.0	3.0	7.0	7.0	7.0	7.0	7.0	7.0	7.0	7.0	7.0
MALAYSIA												
Ethanol												
Import tariffs	%	0.0	0.0	0.0	0.0	0.0	0.0	0.0	0.0	0.0	0.0	0.0
Blending target[4]	%	0.0	0.0	0.0	0.0	0.0	0.0	0.0	0.0	0.0	0.0	0.0
Biodiesel												
Blending target[4]	%	5.0	5.0	5.0	5.0	5.0	5.0	5.0	5.0	5.0	5.0	5.0
PERU												
Ethanol												
Import tariffs	%	0.0	0.0	0.0	0.0	0.0	0.0	0.0	0.0	0.0	0.0	0.0
Blending target[4]	%	7.8	7.8	7.8	7.8	7.8	7.8	7.8	7.8	7.8	7.8	7.8
Biodiesel												
Import tariffs	%	0.0	0.0	0.0	0.0	0.0	0.0	0.0	0.0	0.0	0.0	0.0
Blending target[4]	%	5.0	5.0	5.0	5.0	5.0	5.0	5.0	5.0	5.0	5.0	5.0

Table A.5. **Main policy assumptions for biofuel markets** *(cont.)*

		2013est	2014	2015	2016	2017	2018	2019	2020	2021	2022	2023
THAILAND												
Ethanol												
Import tariffs	%	0.0	0.0	0.0	0.0	0.0	0.0	0.0	0.0	0.0	0.0	0.0
Blending target[4]	%	5.2	5.2	5.2	5.2	5.2	5.2	5.2	5.2	5.2	5.2	5.2
Biodiesel												
Blending target[4]	%	5.0	5.0	5.0	5.0	5.0	5.0	5.0	5.0	5.0	5.0	5.0
UNITED STATES												
Renewable Fuel Standard[6]												
Total	Mn L	62 648	63 492	68 069	70 007	72 399	75 479	78 654	80 013	81 715	83 008	83 008
advanced mandate	Mn L	10 410	8 982	11 288	13 226	15 618	18 698	21 873	23 232	24 934	26 227	26 227
cellulosic ethanol	Mn L	23	108	400	800	1 600	2 600	3 700	4 800	6 100	7 300	7 300
biodiesel	Mn L	4 845	4 845	4 845	4 845	4 845	4 845	4 845	4 845	4 845	4 845	4 845
Ethanol												
Import surcharge	USD/hl	0.00	0.00	0.00	0.00	0.00	0.00	0.00	0.00	0.00	0.00	0.00
Import tariffs (undenatured)	%	2.40	2.40	2.40	2.40	2.40	2.40	2.40	2.40	2.40	2.40	2.40
Import tariffs (denatured)	%	1.90	1.90	1.90	1.90	1.90	1.90	1.90	1.90	1.90	1.90	1.90
Blenders tax credit	USD/hl	0.00	0.00	0.00	0.00	0.00	0.00	0.00	0.00	0.00	0.00	0.00
Biodiesel												
Import tariffs	%	4.60	4.60	4.60	4.60	4.60	4.60	4.60	4.60	4.60	4.60	4.60
Blenders tax credit	USD/hl	26.42	0.00	0.00	0.00	0.00	0.00	0.00	0.00	0.00	0.00	0.00

Note: 2013est: Data for 2013 are estimated.

For many countries, shares for ethanol and biodiesel are not individually specified in the legislation.

Figures are based on a combination of the EU mandate in the context of the Renewable Energy Directive and the National Renewable Energy Action Plans (NREAP) in the EU member states.

1. Share in respective fuel type, energy equivalent.
2. Difference between tax rates applying to fossil and biogen fuels.
3. Applies to cities with more than 500 000 inhabitants.
4. Expressed in volume share.
5. According to the current Renewable energy Directive 2009/28/EC, the energy content of biofuel other than first-generation biofuels counts twice towards meeting the target. It is assumed that a certain share of the 10% transport energy target is filled by other sources than biofuel.
6. The total, advanced and cellulosic mandates are not at the levels defined in EISA. As those mandates are subject to uncertainties regarding EPA implementation, the following assumptions were taken to construct the baseline: The total and advanced mandates have been reduced by a portion of the shortfall in cellulosic production. That portion starts at 80% in 2014 and reaches 100% in 2023.

Source: OECD and FAO Secretariats.

StatLink ⇒ *http://dx.doi.org/10.1787/888933101442*

Table A.6. World cereal projections

Crop year

		Average 2011-13est	2014	2015	2016	2017	2018	2019	2020	2021	2022	2023
WHEAT												
World												
Production	Mt	692.1	710.5	722.6	726.5	729.4	735.0	743.6	753.6	762.6	771.0	778.1
Area	Mha	221.7	227.1	229.8	228.6	226.8	226.0	226.4	227.5	227.9	228.1	227.9
Yield	t/ha	3.12	3.13	3.14	3.18	3.22	3.25	3.28	3.31	3.35	3.38	3.41
Consumption	Mt	694.2	700.2	711.2	722.3	730.4	736.8	743.0	751.4	758.8	766.5	773.6
Feed use	Mt	136.2	130.0	133.8	138.4	140.7	141.5	142.4	145.0	147.5	150.5	153.8
Food use	Mt	476.4	488.4	493.5	498.3	502.4	506.2	509.7	513.5	517.5	521.4	524.3
Biofuel use	Mt	6.6	6.8	7.4	7.8	8.5	9.4	10.2	10.8	10.5	10.2	9.8
Other use	Mt	75.0	75.0	76.6	77.7	78.8	79.8	80.8	82.1	83.3	84.4	85.6
Exports	Mt	139.6	135.9	138.8	141.1	143.0	144.4	146.8	149.0	151.3	153.6	155.5
Closing stocks	Mt	178.2	194.6	206.1	210.3	209.2	207.4	208.0	210.2	214.0	218.4	223.0
Price[1]	USD/t	302.9	283.8	268.4	266.8	267.7	276.0	278.7	277.8	274.9	271.0	269.4
Developed countries												
Production	Mt	359.0	364.4	373.6	374.4	375.2	377.8	382.3	387.3	391.5	395.2	398.1
Consumption	Mt	269.6	269.6	273.4	277.9	280.7	282.5	284.1	287.5	289.8	292.4	294.6
Closing stocks	Mt	71.8	77.7	84.5	86.3	84.9	84.1	84.9	86.4	88.6	90.5	92.0
Developing countries												
Production	Mt	333.1	346.1	349.1	352.1	354.1	357.2	361.2	366.3	371.1	375.7	380.0
Consumption	Mt	424.6	430.6	437.8	444.4	449.7	454.4	458.9	463.9	469.0	474.1	478.9
Closing stocks	Mt	106.3	117.0	121.5	124.0	124.3	123.3	123.0	123.8	125.4	127.9	131.0
OECD[2]												
Production	Mt	280.5	285.4	292.0	290.4	288.4	288.4	290.3	292.7	294.3	295.6	295.9
Consumption	Mt	222.7	219.1	221.4	224.7	226.4	227.3	227.8	229.7	230.5	231.6	232.3
Closing stocks	Mt	49.1	52.0	56.1	58.2	57.5	56.9	57.0	57.2	58.5	59.8	61.0
COARSE GRAINS												
World												
Production	Mt	1 207.6	1 273.3	1 269.1	1 281.8	1 307.0	1 331.0	1 354.2	1 372.3	1 385.7	1 401.2	1 417.6
Area	Mha	332.1	329.8	327.6	329.6	333.0	336.0	338.4	339.7	340.6	341.7	342.9
Yield	t/ha	3.64	3.86	3.87	3.89	3.92	3.96	4.00	4.04	4.07	4.10	4.13
Consumption	Mt	1 180.7	1 262.0	1 284.6	1 286.2	1 300.3	1 318.7	1 339.1	1 361.1	1 378.9	1 395.0	1 412.2
Feed use	Mt	665.6	699.5	709.0	711.1	719.7	731.6	746.4	761.8	775.0	788.5	799.6
Food use	Mt	197.9	204.8	208.0	211.0	214.1	217.6	221.4	225.2	228.7	232.3	235.7
Biofuel use	Mt	138.8	161.2	169.8	166.3	168.1	170.6	171.5	173.3	173.3	171.3	172.7
Other use	Mt	133.9	149.7	150.3	149.7	149.2	148.8	148.8	148.7	148.8	148.8	149.4
Exports	Mt	139.3	148.2	150.5	148.1	150.3	154.2	158.1	162.5	165.3	168.8	170.6
Closing stocks	Mt	210.9	255.7	236.7	228.9	232.1	240.9	252.5	260.3	263.6	266.3	268.3
Price[3]	USD/t	262.0	195.0	197.9	222.2	228.6	234.0	230.6	226.0	226.2	224.9	225.2
Developed countries												
Production	Mt	619.4	671.3	662.1	662.4	670.7	680.6	690.3	697.8	701.9	707.2	713.0
Consumption	Mt	570.7	610.8	620.7	613.4	615.7	621.2	626.8	633.5	637.6	639.7	644.0
Closing stocks	Mt	89.8	124.2	106.2	102.5	104.0	109.5	116.3	120.3	121.6	122.6	123.1
Developing countries												
Production	Mt	588.2	602.0	607.0	619.4	636.3	650.3	663.9	674.5	683.8	694.1	704.6
Consumption	Mt	610.0	651.2	663.9	672.7	684.6	697.5	712.3	727.6	741.4	755.3	768.2
Closing stocks	Mt	121.1	131.4	130.6	126.4	128.1	131.4	136.2	139.9	142.0	143.7	145.2
OECD[2]												
Production	Mt	563.0	616.7	605.7	603.2	610.5	619.5	628.4	635.2	638.5	643.2	648.6
Consumption	Mt	560.2	601.0	610.0	602.5	604.5	609.5	615.2	622.5	627.2	630.2	634.9
Closing stocks	Mt	85.3	120.0	101.9	98.5	100.0	105.3	111.9	115.8	117.0	117.9	118.4

Table A.6. **World cereal projections** (*cont.*)

Crop year

		Average 2011-13est	2014	2015	2016	2017	2018	2019	2020	2021	2022	2023
RICE												
World												
Production	Mt	490.8	502.0	510.0	514.6	521.1	526.6	533.1	538.4	545.0	551.3	557.6
Area	Mha	162.0	163.1	163.9	163.6	163.9	164.1	164.3	164.2	164.4	164.6	164.7
Yield	t/ha	3.03	3.08	3.11	3.15	3.18	3.21	3.24	3.28	3.31	3.35	3.39
Consumption	Mt	479.7	498.9	507.0	513.7	519.4	524.9	530.9	536.3	542.1	548.1	554.1
Feed use	Mt	16.9	17.7	18.3	18.9	19.4	19.9	20.3	20.8	21.3	21.9	22.4
Food use	Mt	404.1	417.1	423.1	428.3	433.3	438.2	443.5	448.2	453.1	458.2	463.1
Exports	Mt	37.9	37.9	38.3	39.2	40.3	41.7	43.3	44.6	46.1	47.6	49.2
Closing stocks	Mt	172.7	182.5	184.8	185.1	186.3	187.5	189.2	190.8	193.2	195.8	198.8
Price[4]	USD/t	442.5	381.9	356.6	395.2	400.1	407.8	409.7	412.3	409.1	401.0	390.8
Developed countries												
Production	Mt	17.7	18.4	18.5	18.8	18.9	18.9	19.0	19.0	19.1	19.1	19.1
Consumption	Mt	18.5	19.4	19.4	19.6	19.8	19.9	20.1	20.2	20.3	20.5	20.6
Closing stocks	Mt	5.0	5.0	5.0	5.0	5.0	4.8	4.7	4.5	4.3	4.1	4.0
Developing countries												
Production	Mt	473.1	483.7	491.4	495.8	502.2	507.7	514.2	519.4	525.9	532.2	538.5
Consumption	Mt	461.2	479.5	487.6	494.1	499.6	505.0	510.8	516.1	521.8	527.7	533.4
Closing stocks	Mt	167.7	177.4	179.8	180.1	181.4	182.6	184.5	186.3	188.8	191.7	194.9
OECD[2]												
Production	Mt	21.3	22.1	22.2	22.3	22.4	22.4	22.4	22.4	22.5	22.5	22.5
Consumption	Mt	22.2	23.0	23.1	23.3	23.4	23.6	23.7	23.8	23.9	24.1	24.2
Closing stocks	Mt	6.8	6.8	6.8	6.7	6.7	6.5	6.3	6.1	5.9	5.7	5.5

Note: Crop year: See Glossary of Terms for definitions.

Average 2011-13est: Data for 2013 are estimated.

1. No.2 hard red winter wheat, ordinary protein, United States f.o.b. Gulf Ports (June/May), less EEP payments where applicable.
2. Excludes Iceland but includes all EU28 member countries.
3. No.2 yellow corn, United States f.o.b. Gulf Ports (September/August).
4. Milled, 5% broken, f.o.b. Ho Chi Minh (January/December).

Source: OECD and FAO Secretariats.

StatLink http://dx.doi.org/10.1787/888933101461

Table A.7.1. Wheat projections: Production and trade

Crop year

	PRODUCTION (kt)		Growth (%)[4]		IMPORTS (kt)		Growth (%)[4]		EXPORTS (kt)		Growth (%)[4]	
	Average 2011-13est	2023	2004-13	2014-23	Average 2011-13est	2023	2004-13	2014-23	Average 2011-13est	2023	2004-13	2014-23
WORLD	**692 113**	**778 096**	**1.51**	**0.99**	**139 997**	**155 540**	**3.45**	**1.48**	**139 635**	**155 540**	**3.25**	**1.48**
DEVELOPED COUNTRIES	**359 022**	**398 127**	**0.95**	**0.93**	**28 112**	**29 167**	**2.08**	**1.44**	**119 198**	**131 191**	**3.71**	**1.27**
NORTH AMERICA	86 570	92 362	1.07	0.17	3 658	4 087	5.94	1.61	47 070	50 293	1.10	-0.11
Canada	28 555	32 971	2.08	0.82	74	70	21.38	0.00	18 194	22 290	1.86	0.51
United States	58 015	59 391	0.59	-0.17	3 583	4 017	5.73	1.64	28 876	28 003	0.69	-0.57
EUROPE	215 095	245 498	0.44	1.29	8 334	7 291	-2.53	0.87	41 902	53 079	5.25	3.57
European Union	139 204	145 824	0.21	0.42	6 120	5 566	-1.63	1.51	19 746	20 231	5.69	0.91
Russian Federation	49 353	68 191	0.31	3.04	206	60	-27.40	8.56	14 319	22 059	1.76	5.94
Ukraine	19 867	23 932	2.06	2.61	10	5	-32.72	0.35	7 207	9 740	7.98	5.36
OCEANIA DEVELOPED	26 651	26 061	4.97	-0.50	365	342	0.28	0.40	21 038	18 671	7.38	-1.08
Australia	26 193	25 622	4.99	-0.51	15	0	20.60	..	21 038	18 671	7.38	-1.08
New Zealand	458	439	4.91	-0.13	350	342	-0.15	0.40	0	0	..	..
OTHER DEVELOPED[1]	30 706	34 206	1.48	1.65	15 755	17 447	4.47	1.68	9 188	9 148	7.94	3.09
Japan	803	929	-1.78	1.43	6 242	5 770	1.73	0.15	0	0	..	..
South Africa	1 884	1 857	-0.51	0.51	1 572	1 809	5.53	0.53	264	177	6.32	-0.53
DEVELOPING COUNTRIES	**333 091**	**379 969**	**2.15**	**1.05**	**111 885**	**126 374**	**3.80**	**1.48**	**20 437**	**24 350**	**0.80**	**2.63**
AFRICA	23 996	30 552	2.68	1.39	37 349	45 474	2.86	2.18	858	487	-2.62	-2.85
NORTH AFRICA	19 043	24 693	2.27	1.35	22 721	24 191	3.43	1.51	233	38	-5.95	-3.91
Algeria	3 117	4 300	3.96	2.00	6 300	6 559	2.47	0.97	0	0	0.00	-0.07
Egypt	8 655	11 313	1.47	1.30	10 033	10 952	3.99	1.49	0	0	0.00	-0.11
SUB-SAHARAN AFRICA	4 953	5 860	4.41	1.53	14 628	21 284	2.04	2.99	624	449	-1.23	-2.75
LATIN AMERICA and CARIBBEAN	23 269	32 021	-1.09	2.45	21 602	23 146	2.11	0.92	9 862	16 072	-2.05	4.84
Argentina	9 900	16 208	-5.12	4.32	0	0	..	..	6 041	10 729	-8.07	6.82
Brazil	5 305	6 268	2.95	0.86	6 454	7 756	2.71	1.16	1 045	2 471	..	3.34
Chile	1 421	1 621	-2.32	0.83	902	1 059	13.91	1.73	0	0	0.00	-0.12
Mexico	3 442	4 221	2.79	0.65	4 314	3 025	2.28	-0.90	745	823	7.06	0.04
Uruguay	1 642	1 834	16.67	1.20	30	31	-0.88	-1.02	1 067	1 133	59.36	1.16
ASIA and PACIFIC	285 827	317 395	2.42	0.89	52 934	57 753	5.33	1.19	9 717	7 790	4.08	-0.32
Bangladesh	1 177	1 108	2.64	0.48	2 143	3 146	3.02	1.13	0	0	0.00	-0.08
China[2]	119 825	120 924	2.81	-0.09	3 967	2 769	17.44	1.38	375	326	-15.55	0.72
India	91 753	108 584	3.67	1.61	23	65	-28.62	0.40	4 391	3 356	43.32	0.94
Indonesia	0	0	0.00	1.35	6 788	8 218	5.15	1.50	60	60	11.70	-1.48
Iran, Islamic Republic of	13 767	15 285	-0.60	0.58	3 462	3 256	24.62	2.80	200	210	129.44	-0.68
Korea	39	37	24.63	0.00	5 078	4 828	5.34	0.99	50	53	-8.37	0.50
Malaysia	0	0	0.00	1.23	1 392	1 573	1.99	1.16	134	125	4.35	-1.14
Pakistan	24 306	28 938	2.16	1.63	450	1 113	-11.41	3.85	138	0	-68.48	-1.39
Saudi Arabia	827	797	-16.31	1.42	2 600	3 220	73.66	1.35	0	0	-63.47	-0.10
Turkey	21 317	23 832	0.57	1.17	3 067	2 968	28.16	-0.24	3 267	2 670	6.78	-1.21
LEAST DEVELOPED COUNTRIES (LDC)	**12 029**	**15 424**	**4.25**	**2.14**	**14 905**	**20 268**	**2.82**	**2.03**	**54**	**34**	**-14.91**	**-5.97**
OECD[3]	**280 474**	**295 868**	**0.86**	**0.32**	**32 373**	**30 479**	**3.34**	**0.67**	**91 920**	**92 792**	**3.37**	**-0.14**
BRICS	**268 121**	**305 823**	**2.59**	**1.16**	**12 222**	**12 459**	**0.25**	**1.11**	**20 395**	**28 389**	**5.17**	**4.68**

.. Not available

Note: Crop year: See Glossary of Terms for definitions.

Average 2011-13est: Data for 2013 are estimated.

1. Includes Israel and also transition economies: Kazakhstan, Kyrgyzstan, Tajikistan, Turkmenistan, Uzbekistan, Armenia, Azerbaijan and Georgia.
2. Refers to mainland only. The economies of Chinese Taipei, Hong Kong (China) and Macau (China) are included in the Other Asia Pacific aggregate.
3. Excludes Iceland but includes all EU28 member countries.
4. Least-squares growth rate (see glossary).

Source: OECD and FAO Secretariats.

StatLink ᕫ᠍᠍ᕬᒲᔐ *http://dx.doi.org/10.1787/888933101480*

Table A.7.2. Wheat projections: Consumption, food use, per capita

Crop year

	CONSUMPTION (kt)		Growth (%)[4]		FOOD USE (kt)		Growth (%)[4]		PER CAPITA (kg)		Growth (%)[4]	
	Average 2011-13est	2023	2004-13	2014-23	Average 2011-13est	2023	2004-13	2014-23	Average 2011-13est	2023	2004-13	2014-23
WORLD	**694 222**	**773 569**	**1.55**	**1.07**	**476 426**	**524 299**	**1.10**	**0.78**	**67.4**	**66.2**	**-0.09**	**-0.24**
DEVELOPED COUNTRIES	**269 638**	**294 644**	**0.35**	**0.95**	**132 821**	**139 183**	**0.22**	**0.38**	**95.6**	**96.8**	**-0.26**	**0.09**
NORTH AMERICA	45 097	44 940	1.71	0.85	28 473	30 810	0.22	0.79	80.8	80.2	-0.69	0.00
Canada	10 088	10 745	2.53	1.35	2 745	2 802	-1.00	0.15	78.8	72.6	-2.08	-0.77
United States	35 009	34 195	1.47	0.70	25 728	28 009	0.36	0.85	81.0	81.0	-0.53	0.08
EUROPE	181 628	199 705	-0.10	0.87	80 692	82 208	-0.08	0.12	108.6	110.6	-0.25	0.13
European Union	124 799	131 209	-0.22	0.43	56 183	58 888	0.20	0.39	110.5	113.9	-0.13	0.25
Russian Federation	36 387	46 155	-0.20	2.24	14 133	13 530	-0.92	-0.49	98.7	97.9	-0.84	-0.16
Ukraine	12 560	14 184	0.82	1.27	5 351	4 893	-0.80	-0.81	117.5	115.9	-0.29	-0.13
OCEANIA DEVELOPED	7 134	7 733	-0.56	1.14	2 272	2 703	-0.05	1.09	82.5	86.4	-1.59	-0.07
Australia	6 312	6 952	-0.94	1.24	1 897	2 319	-0.22	1.24	82.2	88.0	-1.85	0.03
New Zealand	821	781	2.83	0.30	375	384	0.76	0.24	84.1	77.7	-0.33	-0.67
OTHER DEVELOPED[1]	35 780	42 266	1.26	1.39	21 384	23 462	1.42	0.73	80.0	84.0	0.77	0.35
Japan	6 696	6 694	0.89	0.13	5 348	5 421	0.28	0.08	42.0	43.7	0.25	0.33
South Africa	3 218	3 487	1.76	0.64	3 052	3 328	1.49	0.62	58.3	59.4	0.31	0.03
DEVELOPING COUNTRIES	**424 584**	**478 925**	**2.38**	**1.15**	**343 606**	**385 116**	**1.46**	**0.93**	**60.5**	**59.4**	**0.08**	**-0.26**
AFRICA	60 244	75 238	3.18	1.93	51 562	63 942	2.48	1.92	50.5	48.0	-0.07	-0.51
NORTH AFRICA	40 944	48 657	3.06	1.47	33 785	39 344	2.06	1.36	200.2	200.5	0.50	0.03
Algeria	9 000	10 796	2.64	1.45	7 750	9 183	1.86	1.49	201.4	201.9	0.06	0.03
Egypt	18 638	22 196	3.29	1.45	15 872	18 673	2.09	1.44	196.6	197.2	0.39	0.02
SUB-SAHARAN AFRICA	19 300	26 581	3.43	2.83	17 777	24 598	3.33	2.88	20.9	21.6	0.55	0.23
LATIN AMERICA and CARIBBEAN	36 344	39 030	1.45	0.76	33 312	35 130	1.76	0.66	54.6	51.7	0.59	-0.30
Argentina	5 093	5 494	0.68	0.68	4 850	5 141	0.96	0.48	118.0	114.7	0.08	-0.29
Brazil	10 880	11 512	1.60	0.57	10 433	11 037	1.58	0.58	52.5	51.3	0.64	-0.12
Chile	2 260	2 678	0.46	1.20	2 073	2 296	1.35	0.82	118.7	120.6	0.38	0.05
Mexico	7 011	6 423	2.10	-0.03	5 850	4 937	3.59	-0.30	48.4	36.4	2.31	-1.32
Uruguay	641	724	4.28	1.10	394	413	1.15	0.37	116.2	117.5	0.85	0.07
ASIA and PACIFIC	327 996	364 657	2.34	1.04	258 731	286 043	1.23	0.75	63.9	63.9	0.10	-0.13
Bangladesh	3 524	4 236	1.72	1.24	3 206	3 678	1.12	1.14	20.7	21.1	0.00	0.06
China[2]	125 817	123 015	2.58	0.14	89 502	84 838	0.06	-0.70	65.0	58.7	-0.56	-1.09
India	84 600	103 335	1.91	1.57	75 255	91 317	1.71	1.46	60.8	65.5	0.36	0.40
Indonesia	6 445	8 100	4.48	1.66	4 660	5 287	2.21	0.96	18.9	19.1	0.84	-0.06
Iran, Islamic Republic of	15 800	18 267	0.57	1.09	12 711	14 525	1.23	1.12	166.3	167.7	0.00	0.02
Korea	5 101	4 812	5.50	0.91	2 340	2 344	0.37	-0.10	47.8	45.7	-0.22	-0.49
Malaysia	1 236	1 441	1.00	1.45	875	1 034	-1.05	1.41	29.9	30.3	-2.78	0.04
Pakistan	25 001	30 051	2.19	1.70	23 751	28 794	3.00	1.72	132.6	135.6	1.17	0.18
Saudi Arabia	3 510	3 983	4.18	1.55	2 770	3 294	3.32	1.56	97.9	98.2	1.29	0.07
Turkey	20 950	24 095	1.05	1.33	15 465	17 467	1.35	1.15	205.8	208.2	0.01	0.18
LEAST DEVELOPED COUNTRIES (LDC)	**27 520**	**35 530**	**3.79**	**2.15**	**24 423**	**31 287**	**3.20**	**2.23**	**28.2**	**28.4**	**0.89**	**0.03**
OECD[3]	**222 699**	**232 345**	**0.51**	**0.62**	**120 096**	**127 128**	**0.53**	**0.56**	**92.5**	**92.8**	**-0.13**	**0.09**
BRICS	**260 903**	**287 504**	**1.89**	**0.98**	**192 376**	**204 051**	**0.70**	**0.32**	**64.0**	**62.8**	**-0.20**	**-0.35**

Note: Crop year: See Glossary of Terms for definitions.

Average 2011-13est: Data for 2013 are estimated.

1. Includes Israel and also transition economies: Kazakhstan, Kyrgyzstan, Tajikistan, Turkmenistan, Uzbekistan, Armenia, Azerbaijan and Georgia.
2. Refers to mainland only. The economies of Chinese Taipei, Hong Kong (China) and Macau (China) are included in the Other Asia Pacific aggregate.
3. Excludes Iceland but includes all EU28 member countries.
4. Least-squares growth rate (see glossary).

Source: OECD and FAO Secretariats.

StatLink ⟐ *http://dx.doi.org/10.1787/888933101499*

Table A.8.1. Coarse grain projections: Production and trade

Crop year

	PRODUCTION (kt)		Growth (%)[4]		IMPORTS (kt)		Growth (%)[4]		EXPORTS (kt)		Growth (%)[4]	
	Average 2011-13est	2023	2004-13	2014-23	Average 2011-13est	2023	2004-13	2014-23	Average 2011-13est	2023	2004-13	2014-23
WORLD	**1 207 589**	**1 417 614**	**2.49**	**1.35**	**132 766**	**167 156**	**2.78**	**1.80**	**139 325**	**170 638**	**2.38**	**1.76**
DEVELOPED COUNTRIES	**619 394**	**713 019**	**0.83**	**0.87**	**37 115**	**33 624**	**1.17**	**1.23**	**78 766**	**102 160**	**-1.00**	**2.62**
NORTH AMERICA	350 678	412 774	0.88	0.74	4 513	4 307	-0.60	1.76	37 890	57 882	-6.68	2.72
Canada	24 460	27 099	-0.50	1.03	686	1 388	-16.20	11.99	4 520	5 612	-0.64	2.12
United States	326 218	385 675	0.98	0.72	3 827	2 919	7.95	-0.88	33 370	52 270	-7.44	2.83
EUROPE	236 457	266 905	0.61	1.10	11 304	8 404	9.07	4.84	33 021	38 806	10.12	3.17
European Union	153 167	169 338	-0.39	0.61	9 855	7 369	12.63	6.11	9 155	9 616	1.65	2.09
Russian Federation	32 609	39 170	0.44	1.84	415	241	-5.85	-1.64	4 603	5 420	13.31	2.02
Ukraine	33 554	38 351	6.87	2.42	35	50	-3.93	0.01	17 323	20 652	15.82	3.87
OCEANIA DEVELOPED	13 827	13 159	1.09	0.32	18	13	7.87	-2.00	5 133	4 167	3.26	0.08
Australia	13 188	12 524	1.08	0.34	0	0	..	..	5 127	4 162	3.26	0.08
New Zealand	639	635	2.08	-0.10	18	13	11.09	-2.00	6	6	20.44	0.00
OTHER DEVELOPED[1]	18 432	20 180	3.31	0.98	21 279	20 899	-1.00	-0.09	2 722	1 305	9.25	-2.72
Japan	218	201	-0.44	-1.26	18 844	17 924	-1.07	-0.35	0	0	..	..
South Africa	12 546	14 178	4.02	0.79	276	216	-16.05	2.20	2 242	1 255	12.56	-2.47
DEVELOPING COUNTRIES	**588 195**	**704 595**	**4.50**	**1.86**	**95 651**	**133 532**	**3.49**	**1.95**	**60 559**	**68 478**	**8.76**	**0.66**
AFRICA	103 816	131 163	4.08	2.56	17 255	25 161	2.03	1.82	5 278	2 311	12.40	-0.59
NORTH AFRICA	12 284	13 378	0.60	1.60	13 729	18 049	3.33	1.69	50	35	-4.19	-3.12
Algeria	1 654	2 238	5.26	3.24	3 331	3 883	5.23	1.70	0	0	0.00	-0.12
Egypt	7 626	8 543	-0.47	1.47	5 973	6 288	3.42	-0.21	0	0	0.00	-0.80
SUB-SAHARAN AFRICA	91 531	117 785	4.64	2.68	3 525	7 112	-1.99	2.16	5 228	2 276	12.73	-0.55
LATIN AMERICA and CARIBBEAN	156 120	183 438	5.11	1.90	27 375	36 505	2.76	2.02	48 983	58 300	11.01	0.30
Argentina	35 792	45 917	6.61	2.13	0	0	..	..	23 267	31 816	8.82	2.34
Brazil	71 876	81 849	7.33	1.73	996	1 288	3.13	1.20	22 753	23 805	13.10	-1.64
Chile	2 063	2 221	0.85	2.12	1 504	2 895	1.14	5.11	127	65	2.38	-4.95
Mexico	28 448	32 984	0.31	1.92	10 994	14 378	0.83	2.06	297	175	37.01	6.43
Uruguay	1 041	990	5.90	1.96	52	62	-4.50	0.53	100	66	4.12	-6.86
ASIA and PACIFIC	328 259	389 994	4.36	1.62	51 021	71 865	4.50	1.96	6 298	7 866	-2.73	4.43
Bangladesh	2 197	2 489	22.38	1.43	33	425	-16.80	12.17	0	0	0.00	-12.84
China[2]	212 799	255 972	5.02	1.47	7 882	16 904	22.10	4.20	358	443	-31.69	1.21
India	41 736	48 692	2.70	1.74	8	2	-16.35	-2.62	4 080	5 650	24.70	4.99
Indonesia	18 514	20 496	6.70	1.91	2 515	4 875	19.78	3.53	25	22	-6.87	-0.64
Iran, Islamic Republic of	4 477	5 278	-0.87	2.23	5 266	5 675	7.50	0.52	0	0	0.00	-0.40
Korea	188	184	-7.41	-0.64	8 338	8 835	-0.58	-0.34	0	0	10.61	1.77
Malaysia	56	88	-0.16	1.98	3 233	4 111	3.39	2.37	8	8	0.05	2.26
Pakistan	5 117	6 172	5.25	1.97	21	75	-0.27	1.95	167	79	175.41	2.74
Saudi Arabia	376	390	-0.66	2.67	11 076	12 751	4.64	0.84	0	0	0.00	-1.18
Turkey	13 138	16 422	0.01	2.08	418	605	-2.32	-0.78	321	193	4.37	-2.09
LEAST DEVELOPED COUNTRIES (LDC)	**73 666**	**92 313**	**5.98**	**2.77**	**2 125**	**4 935**	**-2.57**	**2.52**	**5 289**	**2 280**	**14.90**	**1.83**
OECD[3]	**562 986**	**648 602**	**0.45**	**0.79**	**56 962**	**58 868**	**0.99**	**1.29**	**52 922**	**72 098**	**-4.69**	**2.41**
BRICS	**371 566**	**439 860**	**4.67**	**1.56**	**9 578**	**18 651**	**12.27**	**3.84**	**34 038**	**36 573**	**8.54**	**-0.40**

.. Not available

Note: Crop year: See Glossary of Terms for definitions.

Average 2011-13est: Data for 2013 are estimated.

1. Includes Israel and also transition economies: Kazakhstan, Kyrgyzstan, Tajikistan, Turkmenistan, Uzbekistan, Armenia, Azerbaijan and Georgia.
2. Refers to mainland only. The economies of Chinese Taipei, Hong Kong (China) and Macau (China) are included in the Other Asia Pacific aggregate.
3. Excludes Iceland but includes all EU28 member countries.
4. Least-squares growth rate (see glossary).

Source: OECD and FAO Secretariats.

StatLink ᴹᴵˢᴸ *http://dx.doi.org/10.1787/888933101518*

Table A.8.2. Coarse grain projections: Consumption, feed use, per capita

Crop year

	CONSUMPTION (kt)		Growth (%)[4]		FEED USE (kt)		Growth (%)[4]		PER CAPITA (kg)		Growth (%)[4]	
	Average 2011-13est	2023	2004-13	2014-23	Average 2011-13est	2023	2004-13	2014-23	Average 2011-13est	2023	2004-13	2014-23
WORLD	**1 180 715**	**1 412 186**	**2.42**	**1.27**	**665 570**	**799 576**	**1.03**	**1.57**	**28.0**	**29.7**	**0.65**	**0.57**
DEVELOPED COUNTRIES	**570 741**	**643 987**	**1.22**	**0.59**	**331 900**	**362 619**	**-1.36**	**0.61**	**21.7**	**21.3**	**-0.02**	**-0.18**
NORTH AMERICA	310 533	358 147	2.30	0.38	138 473	158 963	-3.45	0.73	24.7	23.6	0.08	-0.62
Canada	20 057	22 732	-1.52	0.84	13 399	15 282	-4.21	1.02	72.2	71.6	-0.06	-0.56
United States	290 477	335 415	2.61	0.35	125 073	143 681	-3.36	0.70	19.4	18.2	0.08	-0.69
EUROPE	214 095	236 858	-0.03	0.96	162 485	170 674	0.47	0.53	20.7	20.3	0.02	-0.02
European Union	154 007	167 551	0.05	0.83	115 100	116 833	0.15	0.08	19.0	19.4	0.29	0.12
Russian Federation	28 261	33 914	-1.05	1.73	24 119	27 168	1.85	2.09	17.2	15.0	-1.46	-0.15
Ukraine	15 656	17 737	1.38	0.78	10 255	12 364	2.01	1.12	44.7	44.1	0.99	-0.13
OCEANIA DEVELOPED	8 762	9 005	-0.27	0.22	6 223	6 583	-1.96	0.47	20.1	16.9	-0.86	-1.87
Australia	8 111	8 363	-0.44	0.25	5 699	6 079	-2.27	0.52	18.4	14.8	-1.39	-2.06
New Zealand	651	642	2.26	-0.13	524	503	2.40	-0.09	28.5	28.1	1.62	-1.20
OTHER DEVELOPED[1]	37 350	39 977	0.46	0.45	24 719	26 400	0.62	0.40	21.0	21.1	-0.32	0.12
Japan	18 818	18 363	-0.96	-0.47	14 014	13 348	-0.97	-0.77	2.5	2.5	-0.91	0.01
South Africa	11 437	13 133	2.56	1.16	5 085	6 270	3.77	1.94	93.2	91.7	-0.58	-0.10
DEVELOPING COUNTRIES	**609 975**	**768 200**	**3.66**	**1.88**	**333 670**	**436 956**	**3.98**	**2.44**	**29.5**	**31.6**	**0.74**	**0.64**
AFRICA	116 588	153 643	3.57	2.43	26 203	34 460	4.36	2.35	72.9	75.4	0.42	0.27
NORTH AFRICA	26 080	31 333	2.21	1.57	18 469	22 901	2.72	1.76	39.6	38.7	-0.11	-0.13
Algeria	4 968	6 104	5.68	2.05	4 118	5 135	6.94	2.18	18.6	18.2	-0.59	0.04
Egypt	13 622	14 826	1.20	0.71	9 171	9 926	1.34	0.57	49.9	48.7	-0.17	-0.16
SUB-SAHARAN AFRICA	90 507	122 310	3.99	2.67	7 734	11 559	9.51	3.62	79.5	81.7	0.38	0.20
LATIN AMERICA and CARIBBEAN	129 279	161 194	2.31	2.13	84 828	108 840	2.97	2.47	52.1	53.7	0.22	0.34
Argentina	12 424	13 940	3.76	1.50	8 951	10 157	4.53	1.80	48.6	47.3	5.27	0.01
Brazil	45 539	59 194	3.24	2.45	35 472	47 060	3.67	2.70	25.5	25.0	1.34	-0.35
Chile	3 381	5 036	0.79	3.78	2 704	4 218	1.08	4.36	18.7	18.3	0.46	-0.07
Mexico	39 295	47 161	0.30	1.87	20 522	24 738	-0.07	2.01	132.2	139.8	-0.11	0.69
Uruguay	843	987	2.75	1.70	280	333	2.63	2.70	22.4	20.1	-1.39	-0.08
ASIA and PACIFIC	364 108	453 363	4.20	1.62	222 640	293 657	4.34	2.44	15.2	15.2	0.38	0.05
Bangladesh	2 147	2 908	18.71	2.33	1 250	1 884	24.20	3.09	4.5	4.5	11.30	-0.12
China[2]	213 904	272 161	5.34	1.65	136 283	183 436	4.90	2.72	11.3	11.9	1.89	0.56
India	36 871	42 970	1.18	1.42	5 840	8 613	5.19	3.72	21.1	20.4	-1.09	-0.32
Indonesia	20 520	25 254	7.23	2.02	9 413	13 066	13.81	3.09	29.2	28.6	0.57	-0.13
Iran, Islamic Republic of	9 426	10 949	2.91	1.14	8 944	10 390	3.10	1.15	1.3	1.3	-1.25	-0.08
Korea	8 642	9 026	-0.59	-0.35	6 391	6 789	-0.82	-0.44	4.4	4.4	-0.24	-0.23
Malaysia	3 318	4 188	3.55	2.33	3 124	3 990	3.74	2.45	1.6	1.6	-1.33	-0.01
Pakistan	4 855	6 138	5.71	1.92	1 995	2 702	6.58	2.60	9.7	10.0	1.48	0.25
Saudi Arabia	10 752	13 116	3.74	0.79	10 505	12 823	3.82	0.78	3.4	3.3	-1.97	-0.08
Turkey	13 102	16 790	-0.62	1.89	10 603	14 118	-0.56	2.17	17.1	17.6	-0.38	0.41
LEAST DEVELOPED COUNTRIES (LDC)	**70 969**	**94 686**	**5.19**	**2.69**	**8 712**	**12 547**	**10.98**	**3.34**	**58.3**	**62.6**	**1.60**	**0.69**
OECD[3]	560 241	634 938	1.20	0.62	317 376	349 090	-1.67	0.59	28.7	30.1	0.26	0.44
BRICS	336 013	421 373	3.82	1.72	206 798	272 547	4.31	2.66	18.0	17.9	0.07	0.03

Note: Crop year: See Glossary of Terms for definitions.

Average 2011-13est: Data for 2013 are estimated.

1. Includes Israel and also transition economies: Kazakhstan, Kyrgyzstan, Tajikistan, Turkmenistan, Uzbekistan, Armenia, Azerbaijan and Georgia.
2. Refers to mainland only. The economies of Chinese Taipei, Hong Kong (China) and Macau (China) are included in the Other Asia Pacific aggregate.
3. Excludes Iceland but includes all EU28 member countries.
4. Least-squares growth rate (see glossary).

Source: OECD and FAO Secretariats.

StatLink 🖩🖳 *http://dx.doi.org/10.1787/888933101537*

Table A.9.1. Rice projections: Production and trade

Crop year

	PRODUCTION (kt)		Growth (%)[5]		IMPORTS (kt)		Growth (%)[5]		EXPORTS (kt)		Growth (%)[5]	
	Average 2011-13est	2023	2004-13	2014-23	Average 2011-13est	2023	2004-13	2014-23	Average 2011-13est	2023	2004-13	2014-23
WORLD	**490 800**	**557 584**	**2.22**	**1.15**	**38 293**	**48 613**	**3.41**	**3.12**	**37 917**	**49 165**	**3.59**	**3.08**
DEVELOPED COUNTRIES	**17 735**	**19 122**	**0.17**	**0.42**	**4 911**	**5 949**	**2.01**	**1.53**	**4 172**	**4 662**	**1.73**	**1.15**
NORTH AMERICA	6 044	7 521	-1.31	0.99	1 031	1 363	2.50	2.93	3 231	3 782	-0.28	1.60
Canada	0	0	..	..	384	463	2.18	1.79	0	0	..	..
United States	6 044	7 521	-1.31	0.99	647	900	2.79	3.56	3 231	3 782	-0.28	1.60
EUROPE	2 633	2 630	3.08	0.64	1 361	1 622	-0.74	1.22	396	254	16.11	-2.19
European Union	1 815	1 830	1.06	0.26	915	1 155	1.77	1.99	140	95	1.60	-0.76
Russian Federation	691	675	9.33	1.89	170	179	-8.38	-2.54	243	149	53.38	-3.12
Ukraine	109	104	8.96	-0.44	57	53	-9.37	-0.93	9	8	20.89	0.93
OCEANIA DEVELOPED	713	730	20.58	0.94	186	165	3.68	0.50	383	464	53.41	0.22
Australia	713	730	20.58	0.94	144	124	4.25	0.68	383	464	53.41	0.22
New Zealand	0	0	..	..	42	41	1.75	0.00	0	0	..	..
OTHER DEVELOPED[1]	8 345	8 241	-0.12	-0.19	2 333	2 799	3.57	1.13	162	162	-1.44	-0.06
Japan	7 828	7 577	-0.28	-0.35	813	768	0.88	0.00	131	120	-2.14	0.00
South Africa	2	12	0.00	16.44	1 176	1 650	5.98	1.78	0	0	0.00	-1.75
DEVELOPING COUNTRIES	**473 066**	**538 462**	**2.30**	**1.18**	**33 381**	**42 664**	**3.64**	**3.36**	**33 745**	**44 502**	**3.86**	**3.30**
AFRICA	17 403	23 072	4.21	2.44	11 831	18 430	3.56	4.65	521	378	-11.21	-4.28
NORTH AFRICA	4 110	4 816	-1.81	1.03	757	1 098	13.54	4.76	407	293	-13.78	-5.71
Algeria	1	1	0.00	0.64	109	133	6.01	1.90	0	0	0.00	-1.86
Egypt	4 068	4 769	-1.89	1.04	333	461	72.03	6.04	407	293	-13.78	-5.71
SUB-SAHARAN AFRICA	13 294	18 255	6.66	2.85	11 075	17 332	3.07	4.64	115	85	6.61	3.60
LATIN AMERICA and CARIBBEAN	18 836	22 179	0.86	1.52	4 004	4 453	1.81	2.63	3 390	3 261	10.52	-1.18
Argentina	999	1 185	4.86	1.61	0	0	..	..	586	733	5.78	0.79
Brazil	8 294	9 881	-0.77	1.64	750	834	1.43	5.57	1 049	842	32.13	-6.57
Chile	92	75	0.66	-0.87	117	154	2.89	1.74	1	1	59.56	-0.20
Mexico	123	189	-5.91	3.13	882	1 308	2.53	4.36	2	35	-5.18	22.68
Uruguay	1 033	1 009	1.80	1.22	2	1	158.01	-0.30	938	922	4.11	1.25
ASIA and PACIFIC	436 826	493 211	2.30	1.11	17 546	19 781	4.16	2.45	29 834	40 863	3.77	3.87
Bangladesh	34 017	38 563	3.73	1.16	84	348	-25.31	11.32	2	0	-58.09	-9.69
China[2]	139 235	143 771	1.67	0.26	2 346	2 424	21.46	1.15	386	603	-11.89	0.77
India	105 577	124 240	2.23	1.40	100	63	8.46	0.27	10 069	8 775	9.59	3.41
Indonesia	43 193	50 483	3.45	1.04	1 837	645	8.92	2.36	3	5	216.10	0.38
Iran, Islamic Republic of	1 520	1 721	-1.20	0.67	1 644	1 956	4.76	1.55	0	0	0.00	-0.11
Korea	4 157	4 010	-1.97	-0.56	390	448	9.13	0.89	3	3	-31.04	0.00
Pakistan	5 897	7 029	1.07	1.75	60	57	84.48	-0.60	3 001	3 601	-0.52	1.70
Philippines	11 598	12 025	2.21	0.13	1 150	2 937	-6.62	10.66	7	9	186.60	-0.76
Thailand	24 873	28 858	3.35	3.05	540	251	55.81	-4.28	7 205	14 803	-0.83	5.69
Turkey	536	535	6.43	0.24	220	433	1.52	3.95	51	26	73.63	-3.80
Viet Nam	28 948	32 844	2.67	0.92	583	501	24.81	-0.05	7 147	8 346	5.70	0.10
LDC Asia[3]	29 635	40 439	2.28	2.93	1 284	1 284	4.79	-11.74	1 889	4 599	18.75	13.47
LEAST DEVELOPED COUNTRIES (LDC)	**73 392**	**92 691**	**3.52**	**2.19**	**6 898**	**8 423**	**0.80**	**2.57**	**1 992**	**4 674**	**17.37**	**13.24**
OECD[4]	**21 307**	**22 468**	**-0.49**	**0.17**	**4 815**	**6 080**	**2.55**	**2.34**	**3 941**	**4 526**	**0.40**	**1.38**
BRICS	**253 798**	**278 578**	**1.82**	**0.80**	**4 542**	**5 151**	**8.74**	**1.79**	**11 747**	**10 369**	**8.59**	**1.78**

.. Not available

Note: Crop year: See Glossary of Terms for definitions.

Average 2011-13est: Data for 2013 are estimated.

1. Includes Israel and also transition economies: Kazakhstan, Kyrgyzstan, Tajikistan, Turkmenistan, Uzbekistan, Armenia, Azerbaijan and Georgia.
2. Refers to mainland only. The economies of Chinese Taipei, Hong Kong (China) and Macau (China) are included in the Other Asia Pacific aggregate.
3. LDC Asia includes Afghanistan, Bhutan, Myanmar, Cambodia, Lao Peoples' Democratic Republic, Nepal, Yemen, Timor Meste, Maldives.
4. Excludes Iceland but includes all EU28 member countries.
5. Least-squares growth rate (see glossary).

Source: OECD and FAO Secretariats.

StatLink ᴬᴵˢᴾ *http://dx.doi.org/10.1787/888933101556*

Table A.9.2. Rice projections: Consumption, per capita

Crop year

	CONSUMPTION (kt)		Growth (%)[1]		PER CAPITA (kg)		Growth (%)[1]	
	Average 2011-13est	2023	2004-13	2014-23	Average 2011-13est	2023	2004-13	2014-23
WORLD	**479 709**	**554 051**	**1.92**	**1.14**	**57.2**	**58.4**	**0.25**	**0.13**
DEVELOPED COUNTRIES	**18 490**	**20 607**	**0.15**	**0.70**	**12.4**	**13.2**	**-0.51**	**0.24**
NORTH AMERICA	4 056	5 098	-0.29	1.18	11.5	13.3	-1.20	0.40
Canada	384	463	2.18	1.79	11.0	12.0	1.06	0.86
United States	3 673	4 636	-0.52	1.13	11.6	13.4	-1.41	0.35
EUROPE	3 611	3 996	0.11	1.09	4.9	5.4	-0.08	1.10
European Union	2 590	2 888	0.57	0.95	5.1	5.6	0.24	0.81
Russian Federation	630	705	-2.16	2.06	4.4	5.1	-2.07	2.39
Ukraine	156	149	-1.16	-0.70	3.3	3.4	-1.00	-0.08
OCEANIA DEVELOPED	382	485	0.52	2.06	13.9	15.5	-1.03	0.88
Australia	340	444	0.41	2.27	14.8	16.9	-1.23	1.04
New Zealand	42	41	1.75	0.00	9.5	8.3	0.65	-0.91
OTHER DEVELOPED[2]	10 440	11 028	0.32	0.30	34.4	33.8	-0.64	-0.44
Japan	8 454	8 379	-0.47	-0.10	57.3	55.6	-1.00	-0.41
South Africa	1 158	1 660	5.54	1.83	21.0	28.4	4.72	1.27
DEVELOPING COUNTRIES	**461 219**	**533 444**	**2.00**	**1.15**	**68.1**	**68.5**	**0.14**	**-0.01**
AFRICA	28 955	40 998	4.64	3.42	25.0	27.8	1.87	1.17
NORTH AFRICA	4 441	5 600	1.95	2.15	23.7	25.8	0.88	0.88
Algeria	111	134	6.07	1.89	2.9	2.9	4.20	0.42
Egypt	3 978	4 918	1.53	1.97	43.7	46.2	0.33	0.60
SUB-SAHARAN AFRICA	24 514	35 398	5.19	3.64	25.3	28.1	2.07	1.21
LATIN AMERICA and CARIBBEAN	19 719	23 266	0.45	2.21	30.6	32.5	-0.67	1.29
Argentina	414	451	2.35	3.21	10.1	10.1	1.46	2.42
Brazil	8 248	9 798	-0.95	3.20	41.5	45.6	-1.87	2.48
Chile	207	227	1.69	0.77	11.6	11.7	0.82	-0.01
Mexico	1 004	1 452	1.06	3.97	8.3	10.7	-0.20	2.91
Uruguay	98	88	-2.15	0.93	7.4	7.5	-4.66	0.50
ASIA and PACIFIC	412 545	469 180	1.91	0.93	84.6	86.0	0.25	0.04
Bangladesh	34 333	38 716	3.24	1.18	166.9	167.7	0.89	-0.07
China[3]	133 062	143 114	1.00	0.22	76.6	76.2	-0.21	-0.03
India	95 341	115 009	1.80	1.32	73.4	78.0	0.11	0.17
Indonesia	44 693	51 015	3.30	1.06	161.7	162.7	1.00	-0.02
Iran, Islamic Republic of	3 081	3 668	1.27	1.07	35.8	38.2	0.38	-0.01
Korea	4 530	4 490	-1.08	-0.42	68.7	51.3	-2.09	-2.80
Pakistan	2 939	3 476	4.01	1.70	13.6	13.9	4.08	0.27
Philippines	13 048	14 888	1.49	1.48	120.9	117.0	0.81	-0.14
Thailand	13 875	15 021	2.99	0.61	141.9	146.3	1.55	0.06
Turkey	712	940	3.07	1.93	8.9	10.6	1.52	0.98
Viet Nam	21 717	24 894	1.64	1.12	189.4	192.7	0.50	0.12
LDC Asia[4]	30 238	36 015	2.81	1.79	124.4	126.5	0.19	0.35
LEAST DEVELOPED COUNTRIES (LDC)	**79 934**	**96 018**	**3.45**	**1.83**	**67.7**	**64.9**	**0.25**	**-0.33**
OECD[5]	**22 196**	**24 245**	**-0.21**	**0.57**	**15.3**	**15.2**	**-1.07**	**-0.27**
BRICS	**238 439**	**270 286**	**1.25**	**0.79**	**68.5**	**71.1**	**-0.09**	**0.22**

Note: Crop year: See Glossary of Terms for definitions.

Average 2011-13est: Data for 2013 are estimated.

1. Least-squares growth rate (see glossary).
2. Includes Israel and also transition economies: Kazakhstan, Kyrgyzstan, Tajikistan, Turkmenistan, Uzbekistan, Armenia, Azerbaijan and Georgia.
3. Refers to mainland only. The economies of Chinese Taipei, Hong Kong (China) and Macau (China) are included in the Other Asia Pacific aggregate.
4. LDC Asia includes Afghanistan, Bhutan, Myanmar, Cambodia, Lao Peoples' Democratic Republic, Nepal, Yemen, Timor Meste, Maldives.
5. Excludes Iceland but includes all EU28 member countries.

Source: OECD and FAO Secretariats.

StatLink ⟩⟩ http://dx.doi.org/10.1787/888933101575

Table A.10. Main policy assumptions for cereal markets

Crop year

		Average 2011-13est	2014	2015	2016	2017	2018	2019	2020	2021	2022	2023
ARGENTINA												
Crops export tax	%	21.0	21.0	21.0	21.0	21.0	21.0	21.0	21.0	21.0	21.0	21.0
Rice export tax	%	5.0	5.0	5.0	5.0	5.0	5.0	5.0	5.0	5.0	5.0	5.0
CANADA												
Tariff-quotas[2]												
Wheat	kt	350.0	350.0	350.0	350.0	350.0	350.0	350.0	350.0	350.0	350.0	350.0
In-quota tariff	%	1.1	1.1	1.1	1.1	1.1	1.1	1.1	1.1	1.1	1.1	1.1
Out-of-quota tariff	%	61.7	61.7	61.7	61.7	61.7	61.7	61.7	61.7	61.7	61.7	61.7
Barley	kt	399.0	399.0	399.0	399.0	399.0	399.0	399.0	399.0	399.0	399.0	399.0
In-quota tariff	%	0.7	0.7	0.7	0.7	0.7	0.7	0.7	0.7	0.7	0.7	0.7
Out-of-quota tariff	%	58.0	58.0	58.0	58.0	58.0	58.0	58.0	58.0	58.0	58.0	58.0
EUROPEAN UNION[3]												
Cereal reference price[4]	EUR/t	101.3	101.3	101.3	101.3	101.3	101.3	101.3	101.3	101.3	101.3	101.3
Direct aids ceilings[5]	bln EUR	42.6	42.6	42.6	42.8	42.8	42.9	42.9	42.9	43.0	43.0	43.0
Rice reference price[6]	EUR/t	150.0	150.0	150.0	150.0	150.0	150.0	150.0	150.0	150.0	150.0	150.0
Direct payment for rice	EUR/ha	112.0	0.0	0.0	0.0	0.0	0.0	0.0	0.0	0.0	0.0	0.0
Wheat tariff-quota[2]	kt	3 346.0	3 346.0	3 346.0	3 346.0	3 346.0	3 346.0	3 346.0	3 346.0	3 346.0	3 346.0	3 346.0
Coarse grain tariff-quota[2]	kt	3 518.3	3 518.3	3 518.3	3 518.3	3 518.3	3 518.3	3 518.3	3 518.3	3 518.3	3 518.3	3 518.3
Subsidised export limits (WTO)[2]												
Wheat	Mt	15.4	15.4	15.4	15.4	15.4	15.4	15.4	15.4	15.4	15.4	15.4
Coarse grains[7]	Mt	10.5	10.5	10.5	10.5	10.5	10.5	10.5	10.5	10.5	10.5	10.5
JAPAN												
Wheat tariff-quota	kt	5 740.0	5 740.0	5 740.0	5 740.0	5 740.0	5 740.0	5 740.0	5 740.0	5 740.0	5 740.0	5 740.0
In-quota tariff	'000 JPY/t	0.0	0.0	0.0	0.0	0.0	0.0	0.0	0.0	0.0	0.0	0.0
Out-of-quota tariff	'000 JPY/t	55.0	55.0	55.0	55.0	55.0	55.0	55.0	55.0	55.0	55.0	55.0
Barley tariff-quota	kt	1 369.0	1 369.0	1 369.0	1 369.0	1 369.0	1 369.0	1 369.0	1 369.0	1 369.0	1 369.0	1 369.0
In-quota tariff	'000 JPY/t	0.0	0.0	0.0	0.0	0.0	0.0	0.0	0.0	0.0	0.0	0.0
Out-of-quota tariff	'000 JPY/t	39.0	39.0	39.0	39.0	39.0	39.0	39.0	39.0	39.0	39.0	39.0
Rice tariff-quota	kt	682.2	682.2	682.2	682.2	682.2	682.2	682.2	682.2	682.2	682.2	682.2
In-quota tariff	'000 JPY/t	0.0	0.0	0.0	0.0	0.0	0.0	0.0	0.0	0.0	0.0	0.0
Out-of-quota tariff	'000 JPY/t	341.0	341.0	341.0	341.0	341.0	341.0	341.0	341.0	341.0	341.0	341.0
KOREA												
Wheat tariff	%	5.4	5.4	5.4	5.4	5.4	5.4	5.4	5.4	5.4	5.4	5.4
Maize tariff-quota	kt	6 102.0	6 102.0	6 102.0	6 102.0	6 102.0	6 102.0	6 102.0	6 102.0	6 102.0	6 102.0	6 102.0
In-quota tariff	%	1.7	1.7	1.7	1.7	1.7	1.7	1.7	1.7	1.7	1.7	1.7
Out-of-quota tariff	%	403.5	403.5	403.5	403.5	403.5	403.5	403.5	403.5	403.5	403.5	403.5
Barley tariff-quota	kt	53.6	53.6	53.6	53.6	53.6	53.6	53.6	53.6	53.6	53.6	53.6
In-quota tariff	%	22.5	22.5	22.5	22.5	22.5	22.5	22.5	22.5	22.5	22.5	22.5
Out-of-quota tariff	%	359.3	359.3	359.3	359.3	359.3	359.3	359.3	359.3	359.3	359.3	359.3
Rice quota[8]	kt	205.2	205.2	205.2	205.2	205.2	205.2	205.2	205.2	205.2	205.2	205.2
In-quota tariff	%	5.0	5.0	5.0	5.0	5.0	5.0	5.0	5.0	5.0	5.0	5.0
MERCOSUR												
Wheat tariff	%	10.0	10.0	10.0	10.0	10.0	10.0	10.0	10.0	10.0	10.0	10.0
Coarse grain tariff	%	8.0	8.0	8.0	8.0	8.0	8.0	8.0	8.0	8.0	8.0	8.0
Rice tariff	%	10.0	10.0	10.0	10.0	10.0	10.0	10.0	10.0	10.0	10.0	10.0
MEXICO												
Barley import tariff	%	110.1	60.0	45.0	15.0	0.0	0.0	0.0	0.0	0.0	0.0	0.0
UNITED STATES												
ACRE participation rate												
Wheat	%	10.0	10.0	10.0	10.0	10.0	10.0	10.0	10.0	10.0	10.0	10.0
Coarse grains	%	10.0	10.0	10.0	10.0	10.0	10.0	10.0	10.0	10.0	10.0	10.0
Rice	%	0.1	0.1	0.1	0.1	0.1	0.1	0.1	0.1	0.1	0.1	0.1
Wheat loan rate	USD/t	108.0	108.0	108.0	108.0	108.0	108.0	108.0	108.0	108.0	108.0	108.0
Maize loan rate	USD/t	76.8	76.8	76.8	76.8	76.8	76.8	76.8	76.8	76.8	76.8	76.8
Prod. flex. contract payment												
Wheat	USD/t	16.9	16.9	16.9	16.9	16.9	16.9	16.9	16.9	16.9	16.9	16.9
Maize	USD/t	10.3	10.3	10.3	10.3	10.3	10.3	10.3	10.3	10.3	10.3	10.3
CRP areas[9]												
Wheat	Mha	3.1	3.2	3.3	3.3	3.3	3.3	3.3	3.3	3.3	3.3	3.3
Coarse grains	Mha	2.8	2.9	3.0	3.0	3.0	3.0	3.0	3.0	2.6	2.6	2.6
Subsidised export limits (WTO)[2]												
Wheat	Mt	14.5	14.5	14.5	14.5	14.5	14.5	14.5	14.5	14.5	14.5	14.5
Coarse grains	Mt	1.6	1.6	1.6	1.6	1.6	1.6	1.6	1.6	1.6	1.6	1.6

Table A.10. Main policy assumptions for cereal markets (cont.)

Crop year

		Average 2011-13est	2014	2015	2016	2017	2018	2019	2020	2021	2022	2023
CHINA												
Wheat tariff-quota	kt	9 636	9 636	9 636	9 636	9 636	9 636	9 636	9 636	9 636	9 636	9 636
In-quota tariff	%	2.3	2.3	2.3	2.3	2.3	2.3	2.3	2.3	2.3	2.3	2.3
Out-of-quota tariff	%	65.0	65.0	65.0	65.0	65.0	65.0	65.0	65.0	65.0	65.0	65.0
Coarse grains tariff	%	2.0	2.0	2.0	2.0	2.0	2.0	2.0	2.0	2.0	2.0	2.0
Maize tariff-quota	kt	7 200	7 200	7 200	7 200	7 200	7 200	7 200	7 200	7 200	7 200	7 200
In-quota tariff	%	3.7	3.7	3.7	3.7	3.7	3.7	3.7	3.7	3.7	3.7	3.7
Out-of-quota tariff	%	41.7	41.7	41.7	41.7	41.7	41.7	41.7	41.7	41.7	41.7	41.7
Rice tariff-quota	kt	5 320	5 320	5 320	5 320	5 320	5 320	5 320	5 320	5 320	5 320	5 320
In-quota tariff	%	2.3	2.3	2.3	2.3	2.3	2.3	2.3	2.3	2.3	2.3	2.3
Out-of-quota tariff	%	51.7	51.7	51.7	51.7	51.7	51.7	51.7	51.7	51.7	51.7	51.7
INDIA												
Minimum support price												
Rice	INR/t	12 250	14 400	15 158	15 832	16 632	17 349	18 212	19 113	20 080	21 063	22 076
Wheat	INR/t	13 371	15 477	16 252	17 063	17 800	18 579	19 619	20 713	21 860	23 073	24 397
Wheat tariff	%	51.0	51.0	51.0	51.0	51.0	51.0	51.0	51.0	51.0	51.0	51.0
Maize tariff	%	18.9	51.5	51.5	51.5	51.5	51.5	51.5	51.5	51.5	51.5	51.5
Rice tariff	%	80.0	80.0	80.0	80.0	80.0	80.0	80.0	80.0	80.0	80.0	80.0
RUSSIAN FEDERATION												
Wheat ad valorem import tax	%	3.3	0.0	0.0	0.0	0.0	0.0	0.0	0.0	0.0	0.0	0.0
Rice tariff equivalent of import barriers	%	9.4	11.7	10.0	0.0	0.0	0.0	0.0	0.0	0.0	0.0	0.0
Coarse grains tariff equivalent of import barriers	%	2.7	2.7	2.7	0.0	0.0	0.0	0.0	0.0	0.0	0.0	0.0
Coarse grain specific tariff	RUB/t	3.2	4.5	4.5	0.0	0.0	0.0	0.0	0.0	0.0	0.0	0.0
Coarse grain ad valorem import tax	%	2.7	2.7	2.7	0.0	0.0	0.0	0.0	0.0	0.0	0.0	0.0

Note: Crop year: See Glossary of Terms for definitions.

Average 2011-13est: Data for 2013 are estimated.

The sources for tariffs and Tariff Rate Quotas are the national questionnaire reply, UNCTAD and WTO.

1. Indian input subsidies consist of those for electricty, fertiliser and irrigation.
2. Year beginning 1 July.
3. Till 2014, EU farmers can be granted the Single payment scheme (SPS) or the Single area payment scheme (SAPS), which provides flat-rate payments independent from current production decisions and market developments. From 2015, it becomes the Basic payment scheme (BPS) and it shall account for 68% maximum of the national direct payment envelopes. On top of this, from 2015 onwards, new compulsory policy instruments are introduced: the Green Payment (30%) and young farmer scheme (2%).
4. Buying-in at the fixed reference price is operable automatically only for common wheat up to a maximum quantity of 3 million tons per marketing year. Above that ceiling and for durum wheat, maize and barley intervention can take place only via tender.
5. Estimated net amounts for all direct payments based on EU Regulation No 1307/2013. Possible reductions of the payments due to the degressivity as well as potential transfers between direct aids and rural development envelopes are not accounted for.
6. Intervention is set at zero tonnes per marketing year. However, the Commission may initiate intervention if market requires.
7. The export volume excludes 0.4 Mt of exported potato starch. The original limit on subsidised exports is 10.8 Mt.
8. Husked rice basis.
9. Includes wheat, barley, maize, oats and sorghum.

Source: OECD and FAO Secretariats.

StatLink ᎒᎒ᏚᏞ http://dx.doi.org/10.1787/888933101594

Table A.11. World oilseed projections

		Average 2011-13est	2014	2015	2016	2017	2018	2019	2020	2021	2022	2023
OILSEED (crop year)[1]												
World												
Production	Mt	402.6	433.9	432.8	442.1	450.2	459.7	468.3	477.5	486.8	496.5	507.1
Area	Mha	190.1	197.3	196.0	198.8	199.6	201.4	202.9	204.9	207.1	209.0	211.1
Yield	t/ha	2.12	2.20	2.21	2.22	2.26	2.28	2.31	2.33	2.35	2.38	2.40
Consumption	Mt	402.6	426.1	434.2	443.9	451.8	459.9	468.1	477.5	487.4	496.9	506.9
Crush	Mt	350.6	372.1	379.3	388.2	395.6	403.1	410.6	419.5	428.7	437.6	447.1
Exports	Mt	114.5	123.1	124.3	126.3	127.1	128.6	130.0	131.8	133.5	135.2	137.3
Closing stocks	Mt	39.3	51.5	49.7	47.5	45.5	45.0	44.8	44.3	43.3	42.6	42.4
Price[2]	USD/t	567.3	511.7	493.4	494.2	507.1	518.3	518.6	519.4	521.2	523.4	522.0
Developed countries												
Production	Mt	173.0	180.1	181.4	185.0	187.8	191.4	193.9	197.0	200.8	203.9	207.6
Consumption	Mt	140.8	144.0	145.2	148.2	150.0	151.9	153.6	155.9	158.5	160.5	162.7
Crush	Mt	128.1	130.2	131.6	134.1	135.8	137.7	139.3	141.5	143.9	146.0	148.1
Closing stocks	Mt	14.4	16.4	16.8	16.7	16.3	16.2	16.3	16.6	16.7	16.9	17.1
Developing countries												
Production	Mt	229.5	253.7	251.5	257.1	262.4	268.3	274.4	280.5	286.0	292.6	299.6
Consumption	Mt	261.8	282.1	288.8	295.7	301.9	308.0	314.5	321.6	328.9	336.3	344.2
Crush	Mt	222.5	241.9	247.7	254.1	259.8	265.4	271.3	278.0	284.7	291.7	299.0
Closing stocks	Mt	25.0	35.1	32.9	30.8	29.3	28.7	28.5	27.8	26.6	25.8	25.3
OECD[3]												
Production	Mt	144.9	153.4	153.5	155.9	157.9	160.4	162.1	164.1	166.6	168.8	171.3
Consumption	Mt	124.8	128.7	129.6	131.5	132.6	133.8	134.9	136.4	138.0	139.5	140.9
Crush	Mt	113.4	116.5	117.2	119.0	120.0	121.2	122.1	123.5	125.0	126.4	127.8
Closing stocks	Mt	13.0	15.4	15.8	15.6	15.2	15.2	15.2	15.5	15.6	15.7	15.9
PROTEIN MEALS (marketing year)												
World												
Production	Mt	276.8	294.4	299.0	305.2	310.6	316.8	322.8	329.5	336.6	343.5	350.8
Consumption	Mt	277.0	292.9	298.7	304.9	310.1	316.9	322.6	329.4	336.5	343.4	350.6
Closing stocks	Mt	17.0	19.1	19.5	20.0	20.6	20.7	21.0	21.2	21.5	21.8	22.1
Price[4]	USD/t	466.3	430.3	408.4	408.8	400.1	400.2	398.5	399.8	402.9	404.3	403.8
Developed countries												
Production	Mt	90.0	91.3	91.5	93.0	93.8	95.0	95.8	97.2	98.8	100.1	101.4
Consumption	Mt	108.3	111.4	111.6	112.7	113.2	114.5	115.4	116.3	117.6	118.7	119.6
Closing stocks	Mt	1.5	1.6	1.7	1.7	1.7	1.7	1.7	1.7	1.7	1.7	1.8
Developing countries												
Production	Mt	187.5	203.1	207.5	212.3	216.8	221.8	226.9	232.3	237.8	243.4	249.4
Consumption	Mt	168.7	181.5	187.1	192.3	196.9	202.4	207.2	213.2	218.9	224.7	231.0
Closing stocks	Mt	15.6	17.4	17.8	18.3	19.0	19.0	19.3	19.5	19.8	20.0	20.4
OECD[3]												
Production	Mt	84.3	86.1	86.0	87.1	87.7	88.4	89.0	90.0	91.1	92.1	93.1
Consumption	Mt	113.0	116.9	117.1	118.4	118.9	120.1	121.2	122.2	123.5	124.7	125.5
Closing stocks	Mt	1.6	1.7	1.7	1.7	1.8	1.8	1.8	1.8	1.8	1.8	1.8
VEGETABLE OILS (marketing year)												
World												
Production	Mt	162.5	172.7	176.7	181.2	185.0	189.0	192.8	196.9	200.9	204.8	208.7
Of which palm oil	Mt	55.6	60.1	62.0	63.8	65.6	67.3	68.9	70.5	72.0	73.4	74.8
Consumption	Mt	161.5	172.2	176.2	180.6	184.6	188.8	192.6	196.8	200.3	204.0	207.9
Food	Mt	132.6	140.9	143.8	146.8	149.3	152.1	154.7	157.6	160.7	164.1	167.4
Biofuel	Mt	19.0	20.6	21.6	22.9	24.3	25.6	26.6	27.8	28.0	28.3	28.8
Exports	Mt	67.3	70.8	72.8	74.6	76.2	78.0	79.6	81.5	83.2	84.9	86.5
Closing stocks	Mt	22.9	23.7	24.0	24.4	24.5	24.5	24.4	24.3	24.7	25.2	25.7
Price[5]	USD/t	1 036.0	900.1	918.8	937.2	953.8	981.5	991.2	1 010.3	1 018.1	1 030.1	1 042.0
Developed countries												
Production	Mt	41.2	41.5	41.9	42.8	43.3	44.0	44.6	45.3	46.1	46.8	47.5
Consumption	Mt	47.3	47.7	48.2	49.0	49.9	50.6	51.1	52.0	52.0	51.9	52.1
Closing stocks	Mt	3.7	4.6	5.1	5.2	5.0	4.8	4.4	3.9	4.0	4.1	4.3
Developing countries												
Production	Mt	121.5	131.2	134.8	138.4	141.7	145.0	148.3	151.6	154.8	158.0	161.2
Consumption	Mt	114.2	124.5	128.0	131.6	134.7	138.2	141.5	144.8	148.3	152.1	155.8
Closing stocks	Mt	19.2	19.1	18.9	19.1	19.4	19.7	20.1	20.4	20.7	21.1	21.4
OECD[3]												
Production	Mt	34.7	35.3	35.4	36.0	36.3	36.7	36.9	37.4	37.8	38.3	38.7
Consumption	Mt	46.2	46.7	47.1	47.8	48.5	49.1	49.6	50.5	50.5	50.4	50.5
Closing stocks	Mt	3.3	4.4	4.9	5.0	4.8	4.5	4.1	3.6	3.6	3.8	3.9

Note: Average 2011-13est: Data for 2013 are estimated.
1. Crop year : See Glossary of Terms for definitions.
   Cotton seeds have been extracted from the oilseed total. Based on the cotton outlook, cotton seed production and crush would reach about 50 Mt in 2022.
2. Weighted average oilseed price, European port.
3. Excludes Iceland but includes all EU28 member countries.
4. Weighted average protein meal, European port.
5. Weighted average price of oilseed oils and palm oil, European port.
Source: OECD and FAO Secretariats.

StatLink ▤▤ *http://dx.doi.org/10.1787/888933101613*

Table A.12.1. Oilseed projections: Production and trade

Crop year

	PRODUCTION (kt)		Growth (%)[4]		IMPORTS (kt)		Growth (%)[4]		EXPORTS (kt)		Growth (%)[4]	
	Average 2011-13est	2023	2004-13	2014-23	Average 2011-13est	2023	2004-13	2014-23	Average 2011-13est	2023	2004-13	2014-23
WORLD	**402 593**	**507 126**	**3.12**	**1.86**	**115 128**	**136 874**	**6.13**	**1.21**	**114 480**	**137 268**	**6.01**	**1.21**
DEVELOPED COUNTRIES	**173 049**	**207 551**	**3.25**	**1.62**	**25 121**	**24 684**	**-0.30**	**-0.35**	**57 204**	**69 273**	**6.12**	**1.38**
NORTH AMERICA	109 961	129 848	1.72	1.15	1 865	1 787	3.09	0.26	49 481	60 110	5.07	1.07
Canada	20 389	24 347	8.05	2.06	511	515	-3.46	0.18	11 256	13 576	9.19	1.88
United States	89 572	105 501	0.65	0.95	1 353	1 272	7.24	0.29	38 225	46 534	4.16	0.85
EUROPE	56 604	69 808	6.12	2.45	17 140	17 491	0.37	0.06	4 709	6 021	14.63	4.55
European Union	28 604	33 938	2.87	1.71	15 920	16 383	-0.23	0.08	671	549	-2.49	0.38
Russian Federation	11 969	12 884	7.58	2.81	724	472	63.48	-1.28	370	230	5.83	-0.18
Ukraine	13 873	19 942	15.30	3.43	31	35	7.21	-0.05	3 238	4 232	30.78	4.69
OCEANIA DEVELOPED	3 767	4 252	15.66	2.50	39	31	-1.61	-0.01	2 750	2 952	22.79	2.48
Australia	3 757	4 242	15.68	2.51	32	27	-1.37	0.00	2 750	2 952	22.80	2.48
New Zealand	10	10	12.37	0.00	7	5	-1.56	-0.08	0	0	-0.13	-1.48
OTHER DEVELOPED[1]	2 717	3 642	6.95	2.63	6 077	5 374	-2.72	-1.76	263	189	13.90	1.42
Japan	256	255	1.78	0.00	5 228	4 379	-3.28	-2.08	0	0	-14.88	0.00
South Africa	1 486	2 096	7.00	1.44	49	3	-3.71	-19.08	103	0	21.50	-99.97
DEVELOPING COUNTRIES	**229 544**	**299 575**	**3.03**	**2.03**	**90 006**	**112 190**	**8.68**	**1.59**	**57 276**	**67 995**	**5.93**	**1.03**
AFRICA	9 925	11 578	0.88	1.55	3 029	3 942	9.51	1.88	280	448	8.13	12.90
NORTH AFRICA	556	659	0.23	1.66	2 920	3 757	10.05	1.77	39	24	4.46	-2.04
Algeria	119	138	1.48	2.00	218	241	11.58	0.53	0	0	0.00	-0.04
Egypt	268	314	-0.36	1.42	1 863	2 359	13.95	1.98	33	21	12.54	-1.94
SUB-SAHARAN AFRICA	9 369	10 920	0.92	1.54	110	185	0.08	4.66	241	425	9.06	14.77
LATIN AMERICA and CARIBBEAN	141 477	188 987	4.46	1.94	7 490	7 367	-0.46	-0.40	54 901	65 115	6.13	0.87
Argentina	52 031	73 002	2.32	2.23	294	1	-55.17	0.00	11 914	14 427	1.61	-0.36
Brazil	74 718	92 554	5.30	1.28	213	66	-2.17	-7.18	34 851	37 725	7.25	0.38
Chile	86	106	1.50	1.98	196	363	-1.47	1.57	4	4	-7.37	-1.29
Mexico	331	331	5.90	-0.54	5 398	5 578	1.97	-0.09	11	12	7.67	0.00
Uruguay	3 160	5 382	22.10	5.03	4	3	-7.53	-1.11	2 881	4 846	23.88	4.99
ASIA and PACIFIC	78 142	99 010	1.03	2.27	79 488	100 881	9.94	1.74	2 095	2 432	1.13	4.66
Bangladesh	370	434	3.32	1.51	256	265	-1.84	2.14	0	0	0.00	-0.16
China[2]	45 495	55 805	0.18	2.12	63 826	81 457	12.08	1.87	1 034	943	-4.57	0.54
India	23 633	31 936	1.78	2.62	175	173	45.89	5.67	628	982	10.60	13.54
Indonesia	2 099	2 641	1.56	3.20	2 083	2 513	6.32	1.31	2	2	-5.58	-0.11
Iran, Islamic Republic of	505	643	2.28	2.13	698	971	-1.23	0.03	3	3	0.00	0.00
Korea	147	153	0.44	0.00	1 202	1 453	-1.16	1.55	0	0	-1.54	0.00
Malaysia	7	8	5.02	1.75	582	796	0.09	1.46	29	29	0.64	-1.44
Pakistan	1 066	1 120	9.08	1.62	1 193	1 574	5.39	0.95	53	44	147.17	-0.96
Saudi Arabia	4	4	0.00	0.00	5	6	0.00	1.42	0	0	0.00	-1.40
Turkey	1 545	2 265	8.60	1.54	1 957	2 154	2.58	1.41	58	78	45.51	2.22
LEAST DEVELOPED COUNTRIES (LDC)	**6 932**	**8 258**	**1.69**	**1.54**	**397**	**342**	**-1.04**	**0.90**	**100**	**163**	**3.53**	**9.12**
OECD[3]	**144 859**	**171 308**	**2.22**	**1.29**	**32 882**	**33 534**	**-0.15**	**-0.05**	**52 995**	**63 725**	**5.41**	**1.13**
BRICS	**157 302**	**195 276**	**3.20**	**1.82**	**64 987**	**82 171**	**12.15**	**1.82**	**36 985**	**39 880**	**6.80**	**0.53**

Note: Crop year: See Glossary of Terms for definitions.

Average 2011-13est: Data for 2013 are estimated.

1. Includes Israel and also transition economies: Kazakhstan, Kyrgyzstan, Tajikistan, Turkmenistan, Uzbekistan, Armenia, Azerbaijan and Georgia.
2. Refers to mainland only. The economies of Chinese Taipei, Hong Kong (China) and Macau (China) are included in the Other Asia Pacific aggregate.
3. Excludes Iceland but includes all EU28 member countries.
4. Least-squares growth rate (see glossary).

Source: OECD and FAO Secretariats.

StatLink ᴍᴤ⌐ *http://dx.doi.org/10.1787/888933101632*

Table A.12.2. Oilseed projections: Consumption, domestic crush

Crop year

	CONSUMPTION (kt)		Growth (%)[1]		DOMESTIC CRUSH (kt)		Growth (%)[1]	
	Average 2011-13est	2023	2004-13	2014-23	Average 2011-13est	2023	2004-13	2014-23
WORLD	**402 644**	**506 926**	**3.24**	**1.93**	**350 586**	**447 109**	**3.50**	**2.05**
DEVELOPED COUNTRIES	**140 812**	**162 728**	**1.94**	**1.37**	**128 106**	**148 098**	**2.35**	**1.45**
NORTH AMERICA	62 179	71 336	0.10	1.17	56 088	64 007	0.46	1.23
Canada	9 416	11 169	6.79	1.75	8 433	10 181	8.01	1.55
United States	52 763	60 167	-0.79	1.07	47 654	53 826	-0.51	1.17
EUROPE	68 998	81 255	4.28	1.72	63 673	75 316	4.76	1.80
European Union	43 986	49 767	2.03	1.14	40 651	46 258	2.41	1.18
Russian Federation	12 361	13 123	8.93	2.66	11 704	12 330	9.35	2.72
Ukraine	10 470	15 734	12.83	2.95	9 515	14 502	14.36	3.19
OCEANIA DEVELOPED	957	1 331	3.70	2.47	931	1 307	3.94	2.53
Australia	941	1 317	3.67	2.50	920	1 295	3.89	2.55
New Zealand	17	14	5.51	0.02	12	12	8.37	0.02
OTHER DEVELOPED[2]	8 677	8 804	-0.60	-0.15	7 414	7 469	-0.81	-0.18
Japan	5 562	4 632	-3.01	-1.89	4 711	3 742	-3.27	-2.36
South Africa	1 520	2 083	5.97	2.20	1 356	2 000	5.93	3.09
DEVELOPING COUNTRIES	**261 831**	**344 198**	**3.99**	**2.21**	**222 480**	**299 012**	**4.20**	**2.36**
AFRICA	12 720	15 066	2.40	1.42	7 911	9 376	3.47	1.32
NORTH AFRICA	3 460	4 387	8.19	1.77	3 242	4 145	8.73	1.81
Algeria	341	378	7.29	1.04	320	353	7.44	0.95
Egypt	2 104	2 648	11.21	1.94	1 967	2 500	12.36	2.02
SUB-SAHARAN AFRICA	9 260	10 679	0.79	1.28	4 669	5 231	0.82	0.95
LATIN AMERICA and CARIBBEAN	93 013	131 680	2.75	2.56	86 459	124 551	2.50	2.68
Argentina	39 671	58 564	1.60	2.94	38 621	57 442	1.57	2.98
Brazil	39 944	55 382	3.49	2.45	35 409	50 586	2.78	2.67
Chile	281	465	-0.30	1.69	271	452	-0.38	1.69
Mexico	5 717	5 897	2.14	-0.11	5 375	5 542	3.21	-0.13
Uruguay	265	534	11.26	5.41	239	500	11.95	5.72
ASIA and PACIFIC	156 098	197 452	4.95	2.04	128 110	165 085	5.54	2.18
Bangladesh	623	699	1.71	1.74	538	578	1.12	1.43
China[3]	108 768	136 380	6.12	2.08	88 775	113 646	7.26	2.32
India	23 184	31 077	1.52	2.46	19 491	26 050	0.93	2.28
Indonesia	4 162	5 150	3.62	2.09	2 239	3 499	5.92	3.44
Iran, Islamic Republic of	1 183	1 610	0.18	0.83	1 126	1 541	0.09	0.80
Korea	1 401	1 605	-0.29	1.39	996	1 078	-0.22	1.06
Malaysia	543	774	-0.25	1.26	537	767	-0.27	1.26
Pakistan	2 198	2 646	6.86	1.26	1 966	2 364	6.96	1.13
Saudi Arabia	9	10	0.00	0.85	6	7	0.00	1.03
Turkey	3 501	4 339	4.84	1.48	3 202	3 912	4.44	1.35
LEAST DEVELOPED COUNTRIES (LDC)	**7 248**	**8 437**	**1.58**	**1.42**	**4 601**	**5 263**	**0.97**	**1.23**
OECD[4]	**124 797**	**140 917**	**0.81**	**1.01**	**113 414**	**127 825**	**1.19**	**1.04**
BRICS	**185 777**	**238 045**	**5.02**	**2.24**	**156 734**	**204 612**	**5.33**	**2.43**

Note: Crop year: See Glossary of Terms for definitions.

Average 2011-13est: Data for 2013 are estimated.

1. Least-squares growth rate (see glossary).
2. Includes Israel and also transition economies: Kazakhstan, Kyrgyzstan, Tajikistan, Turkmenistan, Uzbekistan, Armenia, Azerbaijan and Georgia.
3. Refers to mainland only. The economies of Chinese Taipei, Hong Kong (China) and Macau (China) are included in the Other Asia Pacific aggregate.
4. Excludes Iceland but includes all EU28 member countries.

Source: OECD and FAO Secretariats.

StatLink 🔗 *http://dx.doi.org/10.1787/888933101651*

Table A.13.1. Protein meal projections: Production and trade

Marketing year

	PRODUCTION (kt)		Growth (%)[4]		IMPORTS (kt)		Growth (%)[4]		EXPORTS (kt)		Growth (%)[4]	
	Average 2011-13est	2023	2004-13	2014-23	Average 2011-13est	2023	2004-13	2014-23	Average 2011-13est	2023	2004-13	2014-23
WORLD	**276 764**	**350 778**	**3.17**	**1.98**	**77 167**	**98 952**	**3.43**	**2.19**	**77 125**	**98 794**	**2.87**	**2.20**
DEVELOPED COUNTRIES	**89 997**	**101 422**	**1.44**	**1.22**	**38 408**	**40 278**	**1.03**	**0.31**	**20 048**	**22 073**	**7.32**	**1.62**
NORTH AMERICA	46 624	51 944	0.07	1.06	4 225	5 097	5.15	2.11	13 276	14 060	5.64	0.83
Canada	5 191	6 214	6.76	1.50	967	920	-4.14	3.32	3 537	3 823	12.02	1.09
United States	41 433	45 731	-0.57	1.00	3 257	4 177	10.00	1.88	9 739	10 237	3.90	0.73
EUROPE	36 332	42 145	3.91	1.62	27 660	27 250	-0.80	-0.29	6 434	7 663	11.71	3.25
European Union	25 634	28 835	1.68	1.08	25 357	25 063	-1.12	-0.42	1 055	1 101	4.31	0.27
Russian Federation	5 453	5 945	10.18	2.66	517	696	-5.17	3.86	1 719	1 104	11.13	5.23
Ukraine	4 469	6 806	16.45	3.19	56	32	-5.48	-3.35	3 352	5 274	16.63	3.76
OCEANIA DEVELOPED	978	1 194	5.53	1.55	2 261	2 754	17.23	1.51	64	85	20.74	0.00
Australia	970	1 187	5.53	1.56	659	832	3.82	1.94	64	85	20.75	0.00
New Zealand	8	8	7.09	0.00	1 602	1 922	31.87	1.32	0	0	..	..
OTHER DEVELOPED[1]	6 063	6 139	-1.14	-0.12	4 263	5 177	6.58	1.35	274	265	6.45	1.47
Japan	3 237	2 607	-3.65	-2.40	2 403	2 659	6.98	0.54	2	0	-31.08	0.00
South Africa	862	1 254	5.78	3.01	1 310	1 759	5.62	1.68	52	48	35.65	-1.60
DEVELOPING COUNTRIES	**187 516**	**249 356**	**4.05**	**2.31**	**38 758**	**58 674**	**6.31**	**3.72**	**57 077**	**76 721**	**1.63**	**2.37**
AFRICA	7 026	8 812	2.42	1.90	3 354	4 983	6.53	3.62	423	522	-0.37	-6.77
NORTH AFRICA	2 514	3 189	7.64	1.76	3 018	4 579	6.61	3.54	6	5	5.28	-0.57
Algeria	209	236	9.19	0.95	989	1 473	7.70	3.66	0	0	0.00	-0.26
Egypt	1 596	1 984	9.23	1.91	897	1 369	6.32	3.75	2	2	0.00	-0.29
SUB-SAHARAN AFRICA	4 512	5 623	0.23	1.99	335	405	5.92	4.68	417	516	-0.44	-6.82
LATIN AMERICA and CARIBBEAN	67 464	97 681	2.52	2.69	8 151	10 679	2.33	2.47	42 821	60 394	1.01	2.68
Argentina	29 424	43 432	1.76	2.91	0	0	0.00	0.00	26 269	37 984	1.13	2.50
Brazil	28 377	40 984	2.73	2.77	12	35	-34.50	9.43	13 278	18 356	-0.56	3.33
Chile	197	331	-0.36	1.69	1 059	1 710	4.46	3.89	4	1	35.79	-1.79
Mexico	3 917	4 243	2.48	0.00	1 657	2 275	-0.28	2.46	29	33	13.17	0.00
Uruguay	134	295	11.50	5.68	271	316	16.35	0.91	20	18	20.33	-0.90
ASIA and PACIFIC	113 026	142 863	5.19	2.08	27 254	43 011	7.75	4.07	13 833	15 805	3.95	1.73
Bangladesh	371	421	0.68	1.68	403	747	11.38	4.48	0	0	0.00	-0.48
China[2]	69 102	84 441	6.98	1.92	1 147	9 332	12.57	17.98	1 027	277	-0.65	-3.35
India	18 870	26 118	2.46	2.93	79	71	1.92	-0.56	4 817	7 437	2.89	4.86
Indonesia	5 666	8 089	7.19	2.80	3 657	4 023	7.85	0.36	3 646	3 712	7.75	-0.35
Iran, Islamic Republic of	1 001	1 322	0.71	0.85	2 310	2 620	22.61	0.75	167	238	31.25	-0.74
Korea	831	894	-0.18	0.99	3 487	4 160	2.49	1.34	0	0	..	..
Malaysia	3 052	3 941	1.80	1.78	1 278	1 256	5.75	-0.61	2 445	2 780	2.07	0.61
Pakistan	3 609	4 672	0.94	2.36	630	885	15.02	3.96	130	94	15.59	-2.82
Saudi Arabia	38	3	3.71	0.96	721	988	0.98	1.52	0	0	-3.96	-0.26
Turkey	2 541	2 980	2.50	1.09	1 846	3 205	10.74	3.63	190	97	13.15	-3.48
LEAST DEVELOPED COUNTRIES (LDC)	**3 140**	**4 006**	**0.54**	**2.21**	**594**	**1 407**	**9.07**	**7.23**	**176**	**93**	**-2.16**	**-5.60**
OECD[3]	**84 333**	**93 089**	**0.58**	**0.91**	**43 424**	**47 840**	**1.28**	**0.68**	**14 725**	**15 382**	**5.57**	**0.75**
BRICS	**122 664**	**158 741**	**5.23**	**2.33**	**3 066**	**11 893**	**3.70**	**12.32**	**20 893**	**27 222**	**0.86**	**3.69**

.. Not available

Note: Average 2011-13est: Data for 2013 are estimated.

1. Includes Israel and also transition economies: Kazakhstan, Kyrgyzstan, Tajikistan, Turkmenistan, Uzbekistan, Armenia, Azerbaijan and Georgia.
2. Refers to mainland only. The economies of Chinese Taipei, Hong Kong (China) and Macau (China) are included in the Other Asia Pacific aggregate.
3. Excludes Iceland but includes all EU28 member countries.
4. Least-squares growth rate (see glossary).

Source: OECD and FAO Secretariats.

StatLink ᴴᵗᵗᵖ *http://dx.doi.org/10.1787/888933101670*

Table A.13.2. Protein meal projections: Consumption
Marketing year

	CONSUMPTION (kt)		Growth (%)[1]	
	Average 2011-13est	2023	2004-13	2014-23
WORLD	**277 044**	**350 576**	**3.36**	**2.01**
DEVELOPED COUNTRIES	**108 297**	**119 603**	**0.47**	**0.83**
NORTH AMERICA	37 605	42 979	-1.00	1.25
Canada	2 630	3 311	-1.79	2.51
United States	34 975	39 669	-0.94	1.16
EUROPE	57 516	61 719	0.93	0.57
European Union	49 937	52 797	0.15	0.36
Russian Federation	4 247	5 530	6.81	2.34
Ukraine	1 135	1 561	14.11	1.42
OCEANIA DEVELOPED	3 170	3 863	12.23	1.56
Australia	1 560	1 933	4.16	1.80
New Zealand	1 610	1 930	31.98	1.32
OTHER DEVELOPED[2]	10 006	11 042	1.29	0.50
Japan	5 645	5 265	-0.19	-1.09
South Africa	2 064	2 956	4.86	2.40
DEVELOPING COUNTRIES	**168 748**	**230 973**	**5.62**	**2.68**
AFRICA	9 183	13 258	4.46	3.15
NORTH AFRICA	5 494	7 750	6.93	2.80
Algeria	1 154	1 700	7.32	3.36
Egypt	2 512	3 350	7.60	2.64
SUB-SAHARAN AFRICA	3 689	5 508	1.48	3.65
LATIN AMERICA and CARIBBEAN	33 171	47 925	4.84	2.87
Argentina	3 295	5 367	7.49	4.46
Brazil	15 233	22 725	6.55	3.11
Chile	1 244	2 035	3.61	3.58
Mexico	5 544	6 484	1.56	0.80
Uruguay	385	592	14.34	3.12
ASIA and PACIFIC	126 394	169 789	5.93	2.59
Bangladesh	768	1 168	5.14	3.42
China[3]	69 767	93 335	7.35	2.80
India	14 072	18 714	2.64	2.29
Indonesia	5 534	8 378	7.07	3.14
Iran, Islamic Republic of	3 111	3 700	10.81	0.94
Korea	4 316	5 054	2.01	1.28
Malaysia	1 885	2 414	3.83	1.83
Pakistan	4 083	5 458	1.91	2.74
Saudi Arabia	742	990	1.05	1.57
Turkey	4 152	6 078	4.96	2.53
LEAST DEVELOPED COUNTRIES (LDC)	**3 552**	**5 317**	**1.79**	**3.59**
OECD[4]	**113 009**	**125 529**	**0.32**	**0.84**
BRICS	**105 383**	**143 261**	**6.42**	**2.75**

Note: Average 2011-13est: Data for 2013 are estimated.
1. Least-squares growth rate (see glossary).
2. Includes Israel and also transition economies: Kazakhstan, Kyrgyzstan, Tajikistan, Turkmenistan, Uzbekistan, Armenia, Azerbaijan and Georgia.
3. Refers to mainland only. The economies of Chinese Taipei, Hong Kong (China) and Macau (China) are included in the Other Asia Pacific aggregate.
4. Excludes Iceland but includes all EU28 member countries.
Source: OECD and FAO Secretariats.

StatLink ⟦⟧ *http://dx.doi.org/10.1787/888933101689*

Table A.14.1. Vegetable oil projections: Production and trade

Marketing year

	PRODUCTION (kt)		Growth (%)[4]		IMPORTS (kt)		Growth (%)[4]		EXPORTS (kt)		Growth (%)[4]	
	Average 2011-13est	2023	2004-13	2014-23	Average 2011-13est	2023	2004-13	2014-23	Average 2011-13est	2023	2004-13	2014-23
WOLRD	**162 470**	**208 690**	**4.32**	**2.12**	**67 639**	**86 233**	**5.15**	**2.24**	**67 268**	**86 470**	**4.83**	**2.23**
DEVELOPED COUNTRIES	**41 224**	**47 492**	**3.45**	**1.53**	**17 172**	**18 065**	**3.33**	**0.76**	**10 913**	**13 268**	**12.10**	**2.75**
NORTH AMERICA	15 016	16 547	0.95	1.07	3 997	4 953	8.38	-0.58	3 905	5 188	9.30	2.93
Canada	3 353	4 058	9.83	1.63	347	369	3.53	0.00	2 686	3 240	13.31	2.00
United States	11 663	12 489	-0.77	0.90	3 649	4 584	8.98	-0.63	1 219	1 948	3.43	4.67
EUROPE	23 078	27 703	5.88	1.97	10 623	10 185	1.74	1.32	6 759	7 818	14.30	2.69
European Union	14 350	16 513	3.76	1.34	8 784	8 292	1.87	1.51	1 465	954	9.06	-2.35
Russian Federation	4 261	4 486	8.20	2.81	820	954	-1.51	2.19	1 574	1 366	17.56	6.94
Ukraine	4 071	6 214	14.02	3.19	375	295	2.49	-2.91	3 487	5 249	17.22	3.00
OCEANIA DEVELOPED	494	651	3.66	1.94	512	574	6.26	0.90	145	188	17.23	1.99
Australia	489	646	3.63	1.96	406	467	9.01	1.08	145	188	17.31	1.99
New Zealand	5	5	7.77	0.00	107	108	-0.70	0.14	0	0	-0.69	-0.19
OTHER DEVELOPED[1]	2 636	2 591	0.18	-0.03	2 040	2 353	3.22	1.30	104	74	1.67	-0.55
Japan	1 481	1 133	-1.46	-2.30	750	953	1.63	2.50	1	0	16.35	0.00
South Africa	401	561	4.26	2.90	847	869	4.04	0.21	66	46	-0.27	-0.21
DEVELOPING COUNTRIES	**121 486**	**161 198**	**4.60**	**2.29**	**50 467**	**68 168**	**5.84**	**2.68**	**56 355**	**73 202**	**3.81**	**2.14**
AFRICA	5 781	7 378	2.58	2.24	7 362	9 910	5.02	3.04	1 200	1 135	10.90	-1.07
NORTH AFRICA	770	936	5.98	1.54	3 027	3 789	2.57	1.94	424	340	14.48	-1.91
Algeria	92	99	4.74	0.96	577	731	-1.09	2.25	33	31	-12.64	-2.20
Egypt	419	519	7.85	1.88	1 724	2 204	4.93	1.93	339	289	34.63	-1.90
SUB-SAHARAN AFRICA	5 011	6 442	2.13	2.34	4 335	6 121	7.04	3.79	776	795	9.86	-0.69
LATIN AMERICA and CARIBBEAN	21 647	30 669	2.90	2.57	4 290	4 881	4.74	1.38	8 305	13 243	-2.83	3.17
Argentina	7 840	11 811	1.22	3.13	13	17	4.09	-0.09	4 646	7 680	-3.94	3.43
Brazil	7 581	10 592	2.82	2.42	423	626	15.27	3.34	1 470	2 690	-8.65	4.26
Chile	69	106	-0.16	1.69	351	376	2.27	0.76	2	1	-9.38	-0.31
Mexico	1 670	1 793	3.00	0.25	886	960	4.28	1.47	26	4	-11.89	-3.33
Uruguay	68	133	12.04	5.69	83	113	11.79	3.90	2	2	0.00	-2.48
ASIA and PACIFIC	94 058	123 151	5.17	2.23	38 816	53 377	6.13	2.74	46 850	58 824	5.34	2.00
Bangladesh	228	256	2.35	1.78	1 616	2 215	4.69	2.63	0	0	0.00	-0.19
China[2]	22 525	27 771	5.92	1.91	10 049	15 306	4.00	3.17	266	464	8.52	3.09
India	7 424	10 278	1.01	2.75	10 754	17 510	9.94	4.36	199	181	1.59	-2.52
Indonesia	32 611	45 715	8.32	2.66	52	61	0.52	-0.30	22 695	31 314	7.30	2.70
Iran, Islamic Republic of	303	385	0.65	0.86	1 839	2 329	6.20	1.28	236	228	8.81	-1.26
Korea	239	257	0.00	0.93	851	908	5.28	0.39	10	5	6.72	0.00
Malaysia	21 407	26 496	2.82	1.88	1 882	1 428	8.03	-1.47	19 390	22 491	3.62	1.49
Pakistan	1 311	1 652	2.64	2.02	2 407	3 036	3.94	1.98	119	102	-3.62	-1.94
Saudi Arabia	14	3	3.19	0.90	482	591	1.93	1.62	1	1	-22.06	-1.63
Turkey	1 270	1 548	4.00	1.19	1 368	1 548	4.31	0.35	543	555	26.92	-0.35
LEAST DEVELOPED COUNTRIES (LDC)	**2 742**	**3 400**	**1.70**	**1.92**	**5 257**	**7 350**	**4.68**	**3.18**	**225**	**202**	**3.46**	**-1.09**
OECD[3]	**34 702**	**38 690**	**2.15**	**1.05**	**17 929**	**19 014**	**3.79**	**0.79**	**6 175**	**6 972**	**9.99**	**1.71**
BRICS	**42 192**	**53 687**	**4.51**	**2.25**	**22 892**	**35 265**	**6.30**	**3.63**	**3 576**	**4 747**	**-0.67**	**4.37**

Note: Average 2011-13est: Data for 2013 are estimated.
1. Includes Israel and also transition economies: Kazakhstan, Kyrgyzstan, Tajikistan, Turkmenistan, Uzbekistan, Armenia, Azerbaijan and Georgia.
2. Refers to mainland only. The economies of Chinese Taipei, Hong Kong (China) and Macau (China) are included in the Other Asia Pacific aggregate.
3. Excludes Iceland but includes all EU28 member countries.
4. Least-squares growth rate (see glossary).
Source: OECD and FAO Secretariats.

StatLink ᴍᴵˢ▤ http://dx.doi.org/10.1787/888933101708

Table A.14.2. Vegetable oil projections: Consumption, per capita food use

Marketing year

	CONSUMPTION (kt)		Growth (%)[1]		PER CAPITA FOOD USE (kg)		Growth (%)[1]	
	Average 2011-13est	2023	2004-13	2014-23	Average 2011-13est	2023	2004-13	2014-23
WORLD	**161 549**	**207 920**	**4.43**	**2.11**	**18.8**	**21.1**	**1.61**	**0.87**
DEVELOPED COUNTRIES	**47 310**	**52 091**	**2.16**	**1.07**	**25.0**	**24.6**	**-0.71**	**-0.32**
NORTH AMERICA	15 214	16 291	1.23	0.12	36.4	31.6	-1.58	-1.48
Canada	995	1 187	1.23	-0.06	25.3	21.9	-1.69	-0.94
United States	14 218	15 104	1.23	0.13	37.6	32.7	-1.57	-1.51
EUROPE	26 710	29 895	2.84	1.68	22.6	23.7	-0.08	0.24
European Union	21 462	23 693	2.64	1.76	22.8	22.8	-1.52	-0.23
Russian Federation	3 496	4 057	3.41	1.27	24.4	29.3	3.49	1.61
Ukraine	929	1 259	4.26	2.12	19.3	20.9	4.08	0.38
OCEANIA DEVELOPED	858	1 037	3.70	1.34	27.7	29.5	1.42	0.16
Australia	747	925	4.42	1.50	28.2	30.8	1.87	0.29
New Zealand	111	112	-0.31	0.13	24.9	22.7	-1.39	-0.78
OTHER DEVELOPED[2]	4 529	4 867	1.26	0.61	16.6	17.0	0.40	0.17
Japan	2 193	2 085	-0.71	-0.36	17.2	16.8	-0.74	-0.11
South Africa	1 183	1 383	4.11	1.22	21.0	22.5	2.11	0.46
DEVELOPING COUNTRIES	**114 239**	**155 829**	**5.50**	**2.49**	**17.2**	**20.3**	**2.71**	**1.28**
AFRICA	11 638	16 133	3.48	2.99	11.2	11.9	0.82	0.53
NORTH AFRICA	3 326	4 375	2.33	2.17	19.5	22.1	0.77	0.83
Algeria	624	798	0.89	2.26	16.1	17.4	-0.89	0.81
Egypt	1 765	2 427	3.81	2.42	21.6	25.4	2.09	1.00
SUB-SAHARAN AFRICA	8 312	11 758	3.98	3.32	9.6	10.1	1.05	0.64
LATIN AMERICA and CARIBBEAN	17 484	22 278	7.44	1.86	19.7	21.7	1.02	0.65
Argentina	3 151	4 138	18.37	2.63	23.5	24.0	-0.62	0.20
Brazil	6 482	8 518	8.20	1.71	21.6	26.4	1.09	1.43
Chile	412	481	1.80	0.94	23.4	25.0	0.84	0.17
Mexico	2 493	2 749	3.54	0.67	20.6	20.2	2.26	-0.36
Uruguay	149	244	12.12	4.88	16.2	18.0	2.14	0.86
ASIA and PACIFIC	85 117	117 418	5.42	2.55	18.4	22.7	3.42	1.64
Bangladesh	1 832	2 468	4.36	2.52	11.7	14.0	3.20	1.43
China[3]	31 530	42 528	4.78	2.34	22.5	29.0	3.99	1.95
India	17 864	27 562	5.64	3.76	14.2	19.4	4.16	2.65
Indonesia	9 980	14 392	11.34	2.52	19.3	23.2	2.23	1.65
Iran, Islamic Republic of	1 851	2 482	4.53	1.40	23.9	28.4	3.26	0.31
Korea	1 080	1 160	3.70	0.51	22.0	22.6	3.10	0.12
Malaysia	4 059	5 382	2.56	2.31	24.3	25.2	2.95	0.12
Pakistan	3 584	4 581	3.95	2.07	19.4	20.0	1.79	0.18
Saudi Arabia	485	592	2.06	1.58	17.0	17.5	0.05	0.09
Turkey	2 054	2 537	1.43	1.01	26.9	29.6	0.17	-0.02
LEAST DEVELOPED COUNTRIES (LDC)	**7 751**	**10 541**	**3.54**	**2.84**	**8.8**	**9.4**	**1.10**	**0.64**
OECD[4]	**46 235**	**50 549**	**2.03**	**0.97**	**26.0**	**25.0**	**-1.02**	**-0.58**
BRICS	**60 555**	**84 048**	**5.26**	**2.64**	**19.1**	**24.6**	**3.65**	**2.02**

Note: Average 2011-13est: Data for 2013 are estimated.

1. Least-squares growth rate (see glossary).
2. Includes Israel and also transition economies: Kazakhstan, Kyrgyzstan, Tajikistan, Turkmenistan, Uzbekistan, Armenia, Azerbaijan and Georgia.
3. Refers to mainland only. The economies of Chinese Taipei, Hong Kong (China) and Macau (China) are included in the Other Asia Pacific aggregate.
4. Excludes Iceland but includes all EU28 member countries.

Source: OECD and FAO Secretariats.

StatLink 🔗 http://dx.doi.org/10.1787/888933101727

Table A.15. Main policy assumptions for oilseed markets

Crop year

		Average 2011-13est	2014	2015	2016	2017	2018	2019	2020	2021	2022	2023
ARGENTINA												
Oilseed export tax	%	33.5	33.5	33.5	33.5	33.5	33.5	33.5	33.5	33.5	33.5	33.5
Protein meal export tax	%	31.0	31.0	31.0	31.0	31.0	31.0	31.0	31.0	31.0	31.0	31.0
Oilseed oil export tax	%	31.0	31.0	31.0	31.0	31.0	31.0	31.0	31.0	31.0	31.0	31.0
AUSTRALIA												
Tariffs												
Soybean oil	%	8.0	8.0	8.0	8.0	8.0	8.0	8.0	8.0	8.0	8.0	8.0
Rapeseed oil	%	8.0	8.0	8.0	8.0	8.0	8.0	8.0	8.0	8.0	8.0	8.0
CANADA												
Tariffs												
Rapeseed oil	%	6.4	6.4	6.4	6.4	6.4	6.4	6.4	6.4	6.4	6.4	6.4
EUROPEAN UNION[2]												
Tariffs												
Soybean oil	%	6.00	6.00	6.00	6.00	6.00	6.00	6.00	6.00	6.00	6.00	6.00
Rapeseed oil	%	6.00	6.00	6.00	6.00	6.00	6.00	6.00	6.00	6.00	6.00	6.00
JAPAN												
New output payments												
Soybeans	JPY/kg	188.5	188.5	188.5	188.5	188.5	188.5	188.5	188.5	188.5	188.5	188.5
Tariffs												
Soybean oil	JPY/kg	10.9	10.9	10.9	10.9	10.9	10.9	10.9	10.9	10.9	10.9	10.9
Rapeseed oil	JPY/kg	10.9	10.9	10.9	10.9	10.9	10.9	10.9	10.9	10.9	10.9	10.9
KOREA												
Soybean tariff-quota	kt	1 032	1 032	1 032	1 032	1 032	1 032	1 032	1 032	1 032	1 032	1 032
In-quota tariff	%	5	5	5	5	5	5	5	5	5	5	5
Out-of-quota tariff	%	487	487	487	487	487	487	487	487	487	487	487
Soybean (for food) mark up	'000 KRW/t	150	141	138	134	130	127	123	119	115	112	108
MEXICO												
Tariffs												
Soybeans	%	33	33	33	33	33	33	33	33	33	33	33
Soybeans meal	%	23.8	23.8	23.8	23.8	23.8	23.8	23.8	23.8	23.8	23.8	23.8
Soybeans oil	%	45	45	45	45	45	45	45	45	45	45	45
UNITED STATES												
ACRE participation rate												
Soybeans	%	10.0	10.0	10.0	10.0	10.0	10.0	10.0	10.0	10.0	10.0	10.0
Soybeans loan rate	USD/t	183.7	183.7	183.7	183.7	183.7	183.7	183.7	183.7	183.7	183.7	183.7
CRP area												
Soybeans	Mha	1.8	1.8	1.9	1.9	1.9	1.9	1.9	1.9	1.9	1.9	1.9
Tariffs												
Rapeseed	%	3	3	3	3	3	3	3	3	3	3	3
Soybean meal	%	2.2	2.2	2.2	2.2	2.2	2.2	2.2	2.2	2.2	2.2	2.2
Rapeseed meal	%	1.2	1.2	1.2	1.2	1.2	1.2	1.2	1.2	1.2	1.2	1.2
Soybean oil	%	12.7	12.7	12.7	12.7	12.7	12.7	12.7	12.7	12.7	12.7	12.7
Rapeseed oil	%	3.2	3.2	3.2	3.2	3.2	3.2	3.2	3.2	3.2	3.2	3.2
Subsidised export limits (WTO)												
Oilseed oils	kt	141	141	141	141	141	141	141	141	142	142	142
CHINA												
Tariffs												
Soybeans	%	2.4	2.4	2.4	2.4	2.4	2.4	2.4	2.4	2.4	2.4	2.4
Soybean meal	%	6.3	6.3	6.3	6.3	6.3	6.3	6.3	6.3	6.3	6.3	6.3
Soybean oil in-quota tariff	%	9.0	9.0	9.0	9.0	9.0	9.0	9.0	9.0	9.0	9.0	9.0
Vegetable oil tariff-quota	kt	7 998.1	7 998.1	7 998.1	7 998.1	7 998.1	7 998.1	7 998.1	7 998.1	7 998.1	7 998.1	7 998.1
INDIA												
Input subsidy rate, oilseeds[3]	INR/t	4 888.3	4 888.3	4 888.3	4 888.3	4 888.3	4 888.3	4 888.3	4 888.3	4 888.3	4 888.3	4 888.3
Soybean tariff	%	30.0	30.0	30.0	30.0	30.0	30.0	30.0	30.0	30.0	30.0	30.0
Rapeseed tariff	%	30.0	30.0	30.0	30.0	30.0	30.0	30.0	30.0	30.0	30.0	30.0
Sunflower tariff	%	30.0	30.0	30.0	30.0	30.0	30.0	30.0	30.0	30.0	30.0	30.0
Oilseed tariff	%	30.0	30.0	30.0	30.0	30.0	30.0	30.0	30.0	30.0	30.0	30.0
Soybean meal tariff	%	100.0	100.0	100.0	100.0	100.0	100.0	100.0	100.0	100.0	100.0	100.0
Rapeseed meal tariff	%	100.0	100.0	100.0	100.0	100.0	100.0	100.0	100.0	100.0	100.0	100.0
Sunflower meal tariff	%	100.0	100.0	100.0	100.0	100.0	100.0	100.0	100.0	100.0	100.0	100.0
Soybean oil tariff	%	0.0	0.0	0.0	0.0	0.0	0.0	0.0	0.0	0.0	0.0	0.0
Rapeseed oil tariff	%	7.5	7.5	7.5	7.5	7.5	7.5	7.5	7.5	7.5	7.5	7.5
Sunflower oil tariff	%	0.0	0.0	0.0	0.0	0.0	0.0	0.0	0.0	0.0	0.0	0.0
Palm oil tariff	%	0.0	0.0	0.0	0.0	0.0	0.0	0.0	0.0	0.0	0.0	0.0

Note: Crop year: See Glossary of Terms for definitions.

Average 2011-13est: Data for 2013 are estimated.

The sources for tariffs and Tariff Rate Quotas are the national questionnaire reply, UNCTAD and WTO.

1. Estimated net amounts for all direct payments. Possible reductions of the payments due to the degressivity as well as potential transfers between direct aids and rural development envelopes are not accounted for.

2. Till 2014, EU farmers can be granted the Single payment scheme (SPS) or the Single area payment scheme (SAPS), which provides flat-rate payments independent from current production decisions and market developments. From 2015, it becomes the Basic payment scheme (BPS) and it shall account for 68% maximum of the national direct payment envelopes. On top of this, from 2015 onwards, new compulsory policy instruments are introduced: the Green Payment (30%) and young farmer scheme (2%).

3. Indian input subsidies consist of those for electricty, fertiliser and irrigation.

Source: OECD and FAO Secretariats.

StatLink 🔍 *http://dx.doi.org/10.1787/888933101746*

Table A.16. World sugar projections

Crop year

		Average 2011-13est	2014	2015	2016	2017	2018	2019	2020	2021	2022	2023
WORLD												
SUGARBEET												
Production	Mt	265.8	254.1	256.5	260.8	265.0	267.1	269.1	270.0	271.7	273.1	276.3
Area	Mha	4.8	4.7	4.7	4.7	4.8	4.8	4.8	4.8	4.8	4.7	4.7
Yield	t/ha	55.32	54.55	54.76	55.09	55.59	56.07	56.31	56.71	57.10	57.62	58.24
Biofuel use	Mt	14.1	15.5	16.2	16.9	13.4	13.4	13.3	13.3	13.2	13.2	13.1
SUGARCANE												
Production	Mt	1 827.5	1 873.7	1 903.1	1 911.9	1 975.6	2 030.2	2 067.6	2 087.3	2 111.6	2 123.6	2 172.2
Area	Mha	26.2	26.7	26.7	26.5	27.0	27.6	27.8	27.9	27.9	27.8	28.0
Yield	t/ha	69.88	70.28	71.20	72.12	73.04	73.65	74.25	74.92	75.71	76.47	77.60
Biofuel use	Mt	282.8	350.6	383.2	409.8	455.0	475.2	528.4	553.1	564.7	592.2	601.5
SUGAR												
Production	Mt rse	179.9	182.0	183.8	187.2	195.4	200.2	202.4	204.6	207.2	210.6	215.7
Consumption	Mt rse	170.9	179.6	182.1	185.0	189.5	193.2	197.3	201.3	204.7	207.9	210.9
Closing stocks	Mt rse	69.2	72.5	70.8	69.6	72.1	75.7	77.4	77.3	76.4	75.8	77.2
Price, raw sugar[1]	USD/t	422.7	374.1	395.3	420.3	393.2	368.3	363.2	372.6	382.9	416.1	430.7
Price, white sugar[2]	USD/t	529.1	479.2	490.2	514.0	497.1	466.1	456.5	465.4	474.3	501.5	518.6
Price, HFCS[3]	USD/t	565.7	440.9	449.3	476.1	484.0	493.9	501.9	508.4	517.2	526.4	522.9
DEVELOPED COUNTRIES												
SUGARBEET												
Production	Mt	212.5	199.1	200.6	203.9	206.8	208.4	210.2	210.9	212.3	213.0	215.3
SUGARCANE												
Production	Mt	75.9	79.8	79.9	80.6	81.7	83.0	83.7	84.2	84.8	85.4	85.9
SUGAR												
Production	Mt rse	42.2	40.8	41.2	41.9	43.5	44.0	44.4	44.7	45.1	45.5	46.1
Consumption	Mt rse	49.7	50.0	50.2	50.0	50.3	50.7	51.1	51.5	51.7	51.7	51.8
Closing stocks	Mt rse	15.2	14.5	14.0	13.7	14.0	14.4	14.9	14.9	14.9	14.6	14.9
HFCS												
Production	Mt	9.8	10.0	10.2	10.3	10.7	10.9	11.1	11.5	11.9	12.3	12.7
Consumption	Mt	8.1	8.1	8.2	8.2	8.6	8.8	9.0	9.3	9.6	10.0	10.3
DEVELOPING COUNTRIES												
SUGARBEET												
Production	Mt	53.3	55.0	55.9	57.0	58.1	58.6	58.8	59.1	59.5	60.1	61.0
SUGARCANE												
Production	Mt	1 751.6	1 793.9	1 823.3	1 831.3	1 893.9	1 947.1	1 983.9	2 003.1	2 026.8	2 038.2	2 086.3
SUGAR												
Production	Mt rse	137.7	141.1	142.6	145.4	151.9	156.2	158.0	159.9	162.1	165.1	169.6
Consumption	Mt rse	121.2	129.5	131.9	135.0	139.2	142.5	146.2	149.8	153.0	156.2	159.1
Closing stocks	Mt rse	54.0	57.9	56.8	55.9	58.1	61.2	62.5	62.4	61.6	61.2	62.3
HFCS												
Production	Mt	3.0	3.2	3.3	3.3	3.4	3.4	3.4	3.5	3.6	3.6	3.7
Consumption	Mt	4.0	4.3	4.5	4.6	4.7	4.7	4.8	4.8	5.0	5.2	5.4
OECD[4]												
SUGARBEET												
Production	Mt	170.0	160.5	161.2	163.3	166.4	167.8	168.1	168.4	169.2	170.4	172.7
SUGARCANE												
Production	Mt	111.1	116.6	116.2	116.3	116.8	117.0	116.5	116.4	116.7	117.2	118.9
SUGAR												
Production	Mt rse	40.4	40.1	40.0	39.9	40.9	41.2	41.4	41.6	42.0	42.5	43.4
Consumption	Mt rse	45.6	45.9	45.9	45.6	45.8	46.2	46.5	46.9	47.0	46.9	47.0
Closing stocks	Mt rse	12.2	12.4	11.8	11.5	11.7	11.9	12.1	12.1	11.9	11.7	12.0
HFCS												
Production	Mt	11.1	11.3	11.6	11.7	12.1	12.3	12.6	12.9	13.4	13.9	14.3
Consumption	Mt	10.4	10.6	10.9	11.0	11.4	11.6	11.9	12.2	12.7	13.2	13.6

Note: Crop year: See Glossary of Terms for definitions.

Average 2011-13est: Data for 2013 are estimated.

rse : raw sugar equivalent.

HFCS: High fructose corn syrup.

1. Raw sugar world price, ICE contract No11 nearby, October/September.
2. Refined sugar price, White Sugar Futures Contract No. 407, Euronext market, Liffe, London, Europe, October/September.
3. United States wholesale list price HFCS-55 , October/September.
4. Excludes Iceland but includes all EU28 member countries.

Source: OECD and FAO Secretariats.

StatLink http://dx.doi.org/10.1787/888933101765

Table A.17.1. Sugar projections: Production and trade

Crop year

	PRODUCTION (kt)		Growth (%)[4]		IMPORTS (kt)		Growth (%)[4]		EXPORTS (kt)		Growth (%)[4]	
	Average 2011-13est	2023	2004-13	2014-23	Average 2011-13est	2023	2004-13	2014-23	Average 2011-13est	2023	2004-13	2014-23
WORLD	**179 882**	**215 705**	**2.34**	**1.92**	**53 659**	**64 222**	**2.70**	**1.88**	**56 688**	**67 590**	**2.30**	**1.77**
DEVELOPED COUNTRIES	**42 191**	**46 098**	**-0.65**	**1.37**	**15 682**	**14 264**	**-0.06**	**-1.08**	**7 076**	**8 322**	**-7.37**	**1.83**
NORTH AMERICA	8 047	8 615	1.33	0.76	4 471	4 786	4.29	0.33	283	275	-0.57	0.00
Canada	125	101	0.75	1.11	1 298	1 444	0.38	0.28	67	95	3.54	0.00
United States	7 922	8 513	1.34	0.76	3 173	3 342	6.30	0.36	216	180	-1.63	0.00
EUROPE	26 817	28 211	-0.79	1.47	6 343	4 026	-2.38	-4.86	2 934	3 434	-9.00	2.84
European Union	18 141	18 757	-2.27	1.30	4 185	2 313	4.68	-5.97	2 035	2 332	-10.33	1.88
Russian Federation	4 914	5 508	6.63	1.87	1 069	862	-13.51	-5.37	66	20	-21.55	0.00
Ukraine	2 157	2 122	-0.94	2.06	10	4	-24.25	-5.37	135	185	16.84	59.17
OCEANIA DEVELOPED	4 099	5 140	-2.70	1.25	343	353	5.29	0.80	3 154	3 988	-4.18	1.36
Australia	4 099	5 140	-2.70	1.25	112	100	43.90	0.00	3 139	3 983	-4.18	1.36
New Zealand	0	0	..	..	231	253	-0.04	1.14	16	5	-7.36	0.00
OTHER DEVELOPED[1]	3 229	4 133	-1.30	2.19	4 525	5 099	-0.30	1.43	704	624	-11.41	1.02
Japan	733	859	-3.26	1.70	1 448	1 314	0.34	-1.41	2	5	-3.59	0.00
South Africa	2 410	3 182	-0.54	2.39	354	710	0.73	9.60	520	564	-10.62	1.30
DEVELOPING COUNTRIES	**137 690**	**169 607**	**3.43**	**2.08**	**37 977**	**49 958**	**4.07**	**2.90**	**49 612**	**59 268**	**4.64**	**1.77**
AFRICA	8 486	12 047	2.38	3.07	10 677	15 273	3.50	4.00	2 837	3 589	1.98	2.70
NORTH AFRICA	2 433	3 260	1.83	2.59	4 755	6 082	2.84	2.89	405	270	28.77	-3.31
Algeria	0	0	..	..	1 670	2 182	2.32	2.79	254	240	117.95	-0.31
Egypt	2 100	2 805	3.55	2.80	1 513	1 936	4.05	4.03	152	30	7.82	15.34
SUB-SAHARAN AFRICA	6 053	8 787	2.61	3.26	5 922	9 191	4.14	4.81	2 431	3 318	0.27	3.38
LATIN AMERICA and CARIBBEAN	60 974	74 096	2.94	1.56	2 527	2 784	2.64	1.58	33 079	41 122	4.24	1.52
Argentina	2 167	2 490	-0.65	1.29	4	5	10.84	0.00	302	375	-8.52	-0.50
Brazil	38 905	48 752	3.86	1.73	0	0	..	..	25 341	32 178	4.53	1.71
Chile	337	358	-0.80	1.81	486	608	6.96	2.04	0	0	0.00	0.17
Mexico	6 407	6 467	1.43	-0.94	217	148	11.98	0.19	1 655	2 043	21.89	1.06
Uruguay	33	58	27.61	4.40	111	116	-1.28	0.68	3	10	-20.51	-0.67
ASIA and PACIFIC	68 230	83 464	4.11	2.42	24 773	31 900	4.49	2.52	13 696	14 558	6.34	2.29
Bangladesh	135	162	-1.35	0.13	1 671	2 800	9.89	4.14	220	541	189.73	7.48
China[2]	13 540	18 025	2.67	2.63	3 904	2 987	16.31	0.98	117	81	-8.38	-2.42
India	27 478	30 860	4.66	2.20	938	2 023	147.25	1.00	2 187	107	32.26	.89
Indonesia	2 717	3 223	1.11	1.95	3 598	5 370	9.73	3.17	0	0	-19.30	-1.29
Iran, Islamic Republic of	1 342	1 450	0.22	1.35	1 353	1 826	2.79	3.40	43	0	-35.72	20.58
Korea	0	0	..	..	1 719	1 929	1.24	1.91	366	238	1.70	-3.30
Malaysia	28	30	-11.00	0.08	1 876	2 405	3.16	3.01	219	79	-6.86	-2.93
Pakistan	5 425	7 092	6.00	2.56	39	39	-25.45	-0.58	378	609	37.90	2.96
Saudi Arabia	0	0	..	..	1 395	2 058	3.51	3.79	261	312	4.84	0.14
Thaïland	10 293	13 450	8.30	3.06	7	15	9.12	-0.25	6 831	9 223	10.35	2.39
Turkey	2 377	2 944	2.32	2.06	125	453	28.60	2.73	76	48	15.71	-7.33
LEAST DEVELOPED COUNTRIES (LDC)	**4 182**	**6 954**	**4.24**	**4.17**	**6 685**	**10 172**	**6.51**	**4.32**	**1 514**	**2 729**	**6.54**	**5.70**
OECD[3]	**40 421**	**43 388**	**-0.86**	**0.88**	**13 813**	**12 813**	**3.13**	**-0.89**	**7 577**	**8 934**	**-4.01**	**0.10**
BRICS	**87 246**	**106 327**	**3.81**	**2.04**	**6 266**	**6 582**	**1.57**	**0.15**	**28 232**	**32 950**	**4.05**	**1.71**

.. Not available

Note: Crop year: See Glossary of Terms for definitions.
Average 2011-13est: Data for 2013 are estimated.
Sugar data are expressed in raw sugar equivalent.

1. Includes Israel and also transition economies: Kazakhstan, Kyrgyzstan, Tajikistan, Turkmenistan, Uzbekistan, Armenia, Azerbaijan and Georgia.
2. Refers to mainland only. The economies of Chinese Taipei, Hong Kong (China) and Macau (China) are included in the Other Asia Pacific aggregate.
3. Excludes Iceland but includes all EU28 member countries.
4. Least-squares growth rate (see glossary).

Source: OECD and FAO Secretariats.

StatLink http://dx.doi.org/10.1787/888933101784

Table A.17.2. Sugar projections: Consumption, per capita
Crop year

	CONSUMPTION (kt)		Growth (%)[1]		PER CAPITA (kg)		Growth (%)[1]	
	Average 2011-13est	2023	2004-13	2014-23	Average 2011-13est	2023	2004-13	2014-23
WORLD	**170 898**	**210 930**	**1.83**	**1.89**	**24.2**	**26.6**	**0.62**	**0.86**
DEVELOPED COUNTRIES	**49 672**	**51 805**	**0.19**	**0.46**	**35.7**	**36.0**	**-0.29**	**0.16**
NORTH AMERICA	11 890	12 959	1.65	0.68	33.6	33.7	0.67	-0.11
Canada	1 388	1 451	0.68	0.35	39.9	37.6	-0.42	-0.56
United States	10 501	11 509	1.78	0.72	32.9	33.3	0.82	-0.05
EUROPE	29 505	28 835	-0.58	-0.03	39.7	38.8	-0.75	-0.02
European Union	19 771	18 726	-0.11	-0.33	38.9	36.2	-0.43	-0.47
Russian Federation	5 786	6 355	-1.64	0.71	40.4	46.0	-1.56	1.04
Ukraine	2 024	1 980	-2.13	0.60	44.5	46.9	-1.63	1.29
OCEANIA DEVELOPED	1 271	1 434	0.13	1.00	46.2	45.8	-1.41	-0.16
Australia	1 055	1 186	0.30	0.98	45.8	45.0	-1.33	-0.23
New Zealand	216	248	-0.65	1.11	48.5	50.1	-1.73	0.19
OTHER DEVELOPED[2]	7 006	8 577	1.30	1.83	26.2	30.7	0.65	1.45
Japan	2 200	2 165	-0.90	-0.12	17.3	17.4	-0.93	0.13
South Africa	2 180	3 308	4.11	3.86	41.6	59.0	2.90	3.25
DEVELOPING COUNTRIES	**121 226**	**159 125**	**2.57**	**2.40**	**21.3**	**24.5**	**1.17**	**1.19**
AFRICA	15 904	23 422	3.07	3.58	15.6	17.6	0.50	1.11
NORTH AFRICA	6 487	8 946	1.93	2.81	38.4	45.6	0.38	1.46
Algeria	1 370	1 915	1.87	3.11	35.6	42.1	0.08	1.63
Egypt	3 253	4 661	2.79	3.33	40.3	49.2	1.09	1.89
SUB-SAHARAN AFRICA	9 417	14 476	3.92	4.08	11.1	12.7	1.13	1.40
LATIN AMERICA and CARIBBEAN	29 501	35 366	0.92	1.67	48.4	52.1	-0.24	0.70
Argentina	1 813	2 132	0.35	1.52	44.1	47.6	-0.53	0.74
Brazil	13 282	16 373	1.24	1.76	66.9	76.1	0.30	1.05
Chile	837	940	2.84	1.01	47.9	49.4	1.86	0.23
Mexico	4 833	4 616	-0.69	-0.21	40.0	34.0	-1.93	-1.22
Uruguay	133	164	1.80	1.71	39.2	46.6	1.50	1.40
ASIA and PACIFIC	75 821	100 337	3.17	2.40	18.7	22.4	2.02	1.51
Bangladesh	1 627	2 406	8.08	3.29	10.5	13.8	6.88	2.18
China[3]	15 768	21 128	3.57	2.67	11.4	14.6	2.92	2.26
India	25 319	32 443	2.94	1.96	20.5	23.3	1.58	0.90
Indonesia	5 965	8 612	4.86	2.58	24.1	31.1	3.45	1.54
Iran, Islamic Republic of	2 595	3 285	2.74	2.04	33.9	37.9	1.49	0.93
Korea	1 255	1 683	0.26	2.89	25.6	32.8	-0.32	2.49
Malaysia	1 628	2 329	3.98	2.82	55.6	68.2	2.16	1.43
Pakistan	5 010	6 481	2.97	2.36	28.0	30.5	1.14	0.81
Saudi Arabia	1 077	1 706	4.24	4.26	38.0	50.9	2.19	2.73
Thaïland	2 986	4 141	3.08	2.85	44.7	61.0	2.79	2.73
Turkey	2 559	3 321	3.43	2.56	34.1	39.6	2.06	1.58
LEAST DEVELOPED COUNTRIES (LDC)	**9 282**	**14 248**	**5.61**	**4.05**	**10.7**	**12.9**	**3.25**	**1.81**
OECD[4]	**45 644**	**46 995**	**0.42**	**0.35**	**35.1**	**34.3**	**-0.25**	**-0.12**
BRICS	**62 335**	**79 607**	**2.24**	**2.07**	**20.7**	**24.5**	**1.32**	**1.39**

Note: Crop year: See Glossary of Terms for definitions.
Average 2011-13est: Data for 2013 are estimated.
Sugar data are expressed in raw sugar equivalent.
1. Least-squares growth rate (see glossary).
2. Includes Israel and also transition economies: Kazakhstan, Kyrgyzstan, Tajikistan, Turkmenistan, Uzbekistan, Armenia, Azerbaijan and Georgia.
3. Refers to mainland only. The economies of Chinese Taipei, Hong Kong (China) and Macau (China) are included in the Other Asia Pacific aggregate.
4. Excludes Iceland but includes all EU28 member countries.
Source: OECD and FAO Secretariats.

StatLink http://dx.doi.org/10.1787/888933101803

Table A.18. Main policy assumptions for sugar markets

Crop year

		Average 2011-13est	2014	2015	2016	2017	2018	2019	2020	2021	2022	2023
ARGENTINA												
Tariff, sugar	ARS/t	35.0	35.0	35.0	35.0	35.0	35.0	35.0	35.0	35.0	35.0	35.0
BANGLADESH												
Tariff, white sugar	%	32.5	32.5	32.5	32.5	32.5	32.5	32.5	32.5	32.5	32.5	32.5
BRAZIL												
Tariff, raw sugar	%	16.0	16.0	16.0	16.0	16.0	16.0	16.0	16.0	16.0	16.0	16.0
Tariff, white sugar	%	16.0	16.0	16.0	16.0	16.0	16.0	16.0	16.0	16.0	16.0	16.0
CANADA												
Tariff, raw sugar	CAD/t	24.7	24.7	24.7	24.7	24.7	24.7	24.7	24.7	24.7	24.7	24.7
Tariff, white sugar	CAD/t	30.9	30.9	30.9	30.9	30.9	30.9	30.9	30.9	30.9	30.9	30.9
CHINA[1]												
TRQ sugar	kt	1 954.0	1 954.0	1 954.0	1 954.0	1 954.0	1 954.0	1 954.0	1 954.0	1 954.0	1 954.0	1 954.0
In-quota tariff, raw sugar	%	15.0	15.0	15.0	15.0	15.0	15.0	15.0	15.0	15.0	15.0	15.0
In-quota tariff, white sugar	%	20.0	20.0	20.0	20.0	20.0	20.0	20.0	20.0	20.0	20.0	20.0
Tariff, over-quota	%	50.0	50.0	50.0	50.0	50.0	50.0	50.0	50.0	50.0	50.0	50.0
EUROPEAN UNION												
Reference price, white sugar	EUR/t	404.4	404.4	404.4	404.4	404.4	404.4	404.4	404.4	404.4	404.4	404.4
Production quota[2]	Mt wse	13.3	13.3	13.3	13.3	0.0	0.0	0.0	0.0	0.0	0.0	0.0
WTO export limit[3]	kt wse	1 375.0	1 375.0	1 375.0	1 375.0	1 375.0	1 375.0	1 375.0	1 375.0	1 375.0	1 375.0	1 375.0
Tariff, raw sugar	EUR/t	339.0	339.0	339.0	339.0	339.0	339.0	339.0	339.0	339.0	339.0	339.0
Tariff, white sugar	EUR/t	419.0	419.0	419.0	419.0	419.0	419.0	419.0	419.0	419.0	419.0	419.0
INDIA												
Intervention price, sugarcane	INR/t	1 750.0	2 100.0	2 100.0	2 100.0	2 100.0	2 100.0	2 100.0	2 100.0	2 100.0	2 100.0	2 100.0
Applied tariff, raw sugar	%	60.0	60.0	60.0	60.0	60.0	60.0	60.0	60.0	60.0	60.0	60.0
INDONESIA												
Tariff, white sugar	%	25.0	25.0	25.0	25.0	25.0	25.0	25.0	25.0	25.0	25.0	25.0
JAPAN												
Minimum stabilisation price, raw sugar	JPY/kg	153.2	153.2	153.2	153.2	153.2	153.2	153.2	153.2	153.2	153.2	153.2
Tariff, raw sugar	JPY/kg	71.8	71.8	71.8	71.8	71.8	71.8	71.8	71.8	71.8	71.8	71.8
Tariff, white sugar	JPY/kg	103.1	103.1	103.1	103.1	103.1	103.1	103.1	103.1	103.1	103.1	103.1
KOREA												
Tariff, raw sugar	%	18.0	18.0	18.0	18.0	18.0	18.0	18.0	18.0	18.0	18.0	18.0
MEXICO												
Mexico common external tariff, raw sugar	MXN/t	4 326.1	4 361.2	4 425.6	4 482.1	4 533.5	4 581.8	4 628.7	4 675.1	4 708.9	4 740.4	4 771.6
Mexico common external tariff, white sugar	MXN/t	4 565.5	4 602.6	4 670.5	4 730.2	4 784.4	4 835.4	4 884.9	4 933.8	4 969.5	5 002.7	5 035.7
RUSSIAN FEDERATION												
Minimum tariff, raw sugar	USD/t	148.0	140.0	140.0	140.0	140.0	140.0	140.0	140.0	140.0	140.0	140.0
Minimum tariff, white sugar	USD/t	340.0	340.0	340.0	340.0	340.0	340.0	340.0	340.0	340.0	340.0	340.0
UNITED STATES												
Loan rate, raw sugar	USD/t	413.4	413.4	413.4	413.4	413.4	413.4	413.4	413.4	413.4	413.4	413.4
Loan rate, white sugar	USD/t	531.1	531.1	531.1	531.1	531.1	531.1	531.1	531.1	531.1	531.1	531.1
TRQ, raw sugar	kt rse	1 518	1 416	1 419	1 424	1 427	1 431	1 434	1 435	1 436	1 437	1 439
TRQ, refined sugar	kt rse	49.0	49.0	49.0	49.0	49.0	49.0	49.0	49.0	49.0	49.0	49.0
Raw sugar 2nd tier WTO tariff	USD/t	338.6	338.6	338.6	338.6	338.6	338.6	338.6	338.6	338.6	338.6	338.6
White sugar 2nd tier WTO tariff	USD/t	357.4	357.4	357.4	357.4	357.4	357.4	357.4	357.4	357.4	357.4	357.4
SOUTH AFRICA												
Tariff, raw sugar	%	105.0	105.0	105.0	105.0	105.0	105.0	105.0	105.0	105.0	105.0	105.0
TANZANIA												
Applied tariff, white sugar	%	25.0	25.0	25.0	25.0	25.0	25.0	25.0	25.0	25.0	25.0	25.0
VIET NAM												
Applied tariff, white sugar	%	40.0	40.0	40.0	40.0	40.0	40.0	40.0	40.0	40.0	40.0	40.0

Note: Crop year: See Glossary of Terms for definitions.

Average 2011-13est: Data for 2013 are estimated.

The sources for tariffs and Tariff Rate Quotas are the national questionnaire reply, UNCTAD and WTO.

1. Refers to mainland only.
2. Production that receives official support, Croatia not included.
3. It is assumed that no export subsidies will be granted for sugar after the abolition of the quota.

Source: OECD and FAO Secretariats.

StatLink *http://dx.doi.org/10.1787/888933101822*

Table A.19. World meat projections

Calendar year

		Average 2011-13est	2014	2015	2016	2017	2018	2019	2020	2021	2022	2023
WORLD												
BEEF AND VEAL												
Production	kt cwe	66 764	67 439	68 173	68 670	69 784	70 994	72 127	72 920	73 876	74 796	75 623
Consumption	kt cwe	66 172	67 086	67 841	68 340	69 441	70 630	71 752	72 531	73 476	74 392	75 208
PIGMEAT												
Production	kt cwe	112 716	116 894	118 764	120 328	121 435	122 744	123 838	125 241	126 740	128 084	129 427
Consumption	kt cwe	112 231	116 714	118 596	120 136	121 237	122 574	123 679	125 063	126 539	127 887	129 248
POULTRY MEAT												
Production	kt rtc	106 164	109 970	112 586	115 297	117 816	120 480	123 340	126 302	129 027	131 809	134 511
Consumption	kt rtc	106 045	109 794	112 406	115 125	117 650	120 308	123 165	126 124	128 853	131 637	134 341
SHEEP MEAT												
Production	kt cwe	13 496	14 040	14 408	14 770	15 143	15 488	15 807	16 158	16 518	16 890	17 251
Consumption	kt cwe	13 427	13 977	14 353	14 715	15 089	15 436	15 756	16 108	16 469	16 841	17 203
TOTAL MEAT												
Per capita consumption[1]	kg rwt	33.8	34.1	34.4	34.6	34.8	35.0	35.3	35.5	35.7	36.0	36.2
DEVELOPED COUNTRIES												
BEEF AND VEAL												
Production	kt cwe	29 349	28 481	28 312	28 126	28 471	28 815	29 123	29 277	29 456	29 562	29 631
Consumption	kt cwe	29 254	28 483	28 367	28 141	28 421	28 726	29 070	29 245	29 395	29 505	29 576
PIGMEAT												
Production	kt cwe	41 818	42 180	42 920	43 396	43 484	43 851	43 900	44 146	44 463	44 735	44 992
Consumption	kt cwe	39 200	39 464	40 055	40 454	40 380	40 656	40 646	40 749	40 875	41 008	41 098
POULTRY MEAT												
Production	kt rtc	43 700	45 183	45 984	47 061	47 817	48 558	49 388	50 282	51 001	51 735	52 423
Consumption	kt rtc	41 350	42 541	43 237	44 062	44 778	45 471	46 191	46 935	47 456	47 996	48 508
SHEEP MEAT												
Production	kt cwe	3 266	3 329	3 368	3 435	3 478	3 543	3 574	3 615	3 651	3 683	3 718
Consumption	kt cwe	2 720	2 698	2 730	2 777	2 809	2 847	2 857	2 879	2 895	2 917	2 942
TOTAL MEAT												
Per capita consumption[1]	kg rwt	64.6	64.7	65.2	65.6	66.0	66.5	66.9	67.3	67.6	67.9	68.2
DEVELOPING COUNTRIES												
BEEF AND VEAL												
Production	kt cwe	37 369	38 959	39 861	40 544	41 313	42 179	43 004	43 642	44 420	45 234	45 993
Consumption	kt cwe	36 917	38 603	39 474	40 200	41 020	41 904	42 682	43 286	44 081	44 886	45 632
PIGMEAT												
Production	kt cwe	70 898	74 714	75 844	76 932	77 951	78 893	79 938	81 096	82 277	83 349	84 435
Consumption	kt cwe	73 031	77 249	78 542	79 682	80 857	81 917	83 033	84 314	85 664	86 879	88 149
POULTRY MEAT												
Production	kt rtc	62 464	64 787	66 602	68 236	69 999	71 922	73 952	76 019	78 026	80 074	82 088
Consumption	kt rtc	64 694	67 253	69 169	71 063	72 872	74 837	76 974	79 189	81 397	83 642	85 833
SHEEP MEAT												
Production	kt cwe	10 230	10 711	11 040	11 336	11 665	11 945	12 233	12 543	12 867	13 207	13 533
Consumption	kt cwe	10 706	11 279	11 624	11 938	12 281	12 588	12 900	13 229	13 574	13 924	14 261
TOTAL MEAT												
Per capita consumption[1]	kg rwt	26.3	26.8	27.1	27.3	27.5	27.8	28.0	28.3	28.6	28.8	29.1
OECD[2]												
BEEF AND VEAL												
Production	kt cwe	27 234	26 455	26 309	26 133	26 472	26 830	27 165	27 363	27 581	27 729	27 836
Consumption	kt cwe	26 393	26 040	25 927	25 774	26 085	26 407	26 727	26 891	27 090	27 219	27 307
PIGMEAT												
Production	kt cwe	40 002	40 269	40 882	41 380	41 393	41 722	41 812	42 099	42 434	42 721	42 883
Consumption	kt cwe	37 002	37 359	37 888	38 270	38 157	38 452	38 504	38 615	38 765	38 960	39 039
POULTRY MEAT												
Production	kt rtc	42 723	44 132	45 035	46 125	46 887	47 650	48 459	49 334	50 067	50 797	51 469
Consumption	kt rtc	40 075	40 983	41 631	42 433	43 119	43 751	44 435	45 110	45 589	46 071	46 536
SHEEP MEAT												
Production	kt cwe	2 584	2 625	2 648	2 672	2 719	2 741	2 774	2 787	2 800	2 805	2 816
Consumption	kt cwe	2 050	2 013	2 027	2 034	2 066	2 061	2 068	2 063	2 054	2 050	2 050
TOTAL MEAT												
Per capita consumption[1]	kg rwt	65.0	64.9	65.3	65.6	65.8	66.3	66.6	66.9	67.1	67.3	67.4

Note: Calendar Year: Year ending 30 September for New Zealand.

Average 2011-13est: Data for 2013 are estimated.

1. Per capita consumption expressed in retail weight. Carcass weight to retail weight conversion factors of 0.7 for beef and veal, 0.78 for pigmeat and 0.88 for both sheep meat and poultry meat.
2. Excludes Iceland but includes all EU28 member countries.

Source: OECD and FAO Secretariats.

StatLink ⟶ http://dx.doi.org/10.1787/888933101841

Table A.20.1. Beef and veal projections: Production and trade

Calendar year

	PRODUCTION (kt cwe)[4]		Growth (%)[5]		IMPORTS (kt cwe)[6]		Growth (%)[5]		EXPORTS (kt cwe)[6]		Growth (%)[5]	
	Average 2011-13est	2023	2004-13	2014-23	Average 2011-13est	2023	2004-13	2014-23	Average 2011-13est	2023	2004-13	2014-23
WORLD	**66 764**	**75 623**	**0.79**	**1.34**	**7 592**	**10 215**	**2.67**	**2.54**	**8 152**	**10 386**	**1.14**	**2.33**
DEVELOPED COUNTRIES	**29 349**	**29 631**	**-0.12**	**0.60**	**3 444**	**4 095**	**-1.34**	**1.79**	**3 882**	**4 203**	**2.59**	**1.64**
NORTH AMERICA	12 609	12 755	-0.05	1.19	1 246	1 579	-4.23	1.96	1 533	1 904	7.79	3.67
Canada	1 334	1 448	-2.24	0.97	258	275	9.66	0.64	358	369	-5.72	2.49
United States	11 276	11 307	0.24	1.22	987	1 304	-6.15	2.26	1 175	1 535	19.94	3.98
EUROPE	10 664	10 350	-1.02	-0.22	1 259	1 405	0.14	1.62	365	216	-0.57	-1.94
European Union	7 991	7 654	-0.65	-0.28	288	395	-7.75	2.54	228	114	0.68	0.09
Russian Federation	1 631	1 725	-1.56	0.09	874	854	5.01	0.65	0	0	..	..
Ukraine	371	290	-6.29	-1.46	7	47	-16.87	23.78	11	1	-18.92	-21.62
OCEANIA DEVELOPED	3 034	3 232	0.40	0.83	14	14	1.93	0.00	1 971	2 077	0.25	0.49
Australia	2 407	2 644	0.85	1.16	6	5	-0.17	0.00	1 447	1 644	0.80	1.49
New Zealand	627	587	-1.20	-0.53	8	9	4.45	0.00	524	433	-1.12	-2.62
OTHER DEVELOPED[1]	3 042	3 294	2.67	0.82	925	1 097	1.62	1.83	14	6	0.41	-5.19
Japan	509	506	0.15	0.14	744	794	2.34	0.59	1	1	36.92	0.00
South Africa	832	958	2.22	1.76	9	32	-14.48	18.55	8	1	-3.25	-5.56
DEVELOPING COUNTRIES	**37 369**	**45 993**	**1.52**	**1.85**	**4 120**	**6 119**	**7.28**	**3.08**	**4 269**	**6 183**	**-0.02**	**2.83**
AFRICA	5 823	7 636	3.08	2.49	723	909	5.00	1.27	62	40	2.93	-5.21
NORTH AFRICA	1 135	1 296	2.96	0.63	464	580	5.30	0.90	1	2	7.34	1.43
Algeria	117	152	3.34	1.75	81	132	-1.34	4.14	0	0	-25.52	-2.26
Egypt	795	805	3.61	-0.67	351	447	8.54	0.99	1	2	4.99	0.51
SUB-SAHARAN AFRICA	4 688	6 340	3.11	2.91	259	329	4.47	1.91	61	38	2.83	-5.46
LATIN AMERICA and CARIBBEAN	16 917	20 319	0.22	1.58	775	798	0.77	-0.50	2 494	3 569	-4.66	2.52
Argentina	2 582	3 271	-2.40	1.91	6	7	-0.16	0.00	211	612	-14.49	6.16
Brazil	8 731	10 305	0.14	1.37	44	38	2.70	-0.62	1 399	1 895	-6.05	2.24
Chile	198	253	-1.43	2.12	176	189	2.09	-0.04	8	0	-11.41	-29.58
Mexico	1 776	1 989	1.96	1.07	245	276	-4.39	1.45	120	71	17.46	-3.41
Uruguay	502	621	-1.34	1.84	0	0	-31.20	-0.17	306	381	-2.25	2.12
ASIA and PACIFIC	14 629	18 038	2.58	1.88	2 622	4 412	10.93	4.34	1 712	2 574	13.23	3.46
Bangladesh	200	259	0.88	2.49	0	0	9.14	6.91	0	0	-5.09	-14.94
China[2]	6 529	7 774	1.97	1.71	155	840	65.17	9.38	78	127	-3.86	7.06
India	2 748	3 568	2.34	2.14	1	1	22.35	-0.25	1 360	2 098	13.87	3.34
Indonesia	447	650	2.67	2.43	59	83	12.39	8.14	1	1	2.65	-1.87
Iran, Islamic Republic of	220	256	-6.97	1.14	167	207	15.90	3.54	2	3	49.64	-0.54
Korea	309	385	6.80	1.37	339	383	5.24	1.64	5	9	14.96	0.00
Malaysia	14	14	-1.65	-0.17	168	218	0.81	1.66	10	8	17.67	-1.63
Pakistan	1 517	1 819	4.90	1.85	3	3	11.30	-1.83	27	44	38.38	8.35
Saudi Arabia	42	54	12.77	2.95	160	216	7.87	2.46	25	21	31.82	-2.40
Turkey	543	789	5.32	2.67	6	14	121.27	5.54	17	0	46.59	-26.60
LEAST DEVELOPED COUNTRIES (LDC)	**4 602**	**6 218**	**3.17**	**2.84**	**182**	**205**	**5.50**	**1.77**	**6**	**3**	**13.42**	**1.96**
OECD[3]	27 234	27 836	0.07	0.73	3 199	3 835	-2.03	1.59	3 885	4 179	3.12	1.64
BRICS	20 470	24 330	0.90	1.50	1 083	1 765	6.71	4.11	2 846	4 121	0.00	2.90

.. Not available

Note: Calendar year: Year ending 30 September for New Zealand.
Average 2011-13est: Data for 2013 are estimated.

1. Includes Israel and also transition economies: Kazakhstan, Kyrgyzstan, Tajikistan, Turkmenistan, Uzbekistan, Armenia, Azerbaijan and Georgia.
2. Refers to mainland only. The economies of Chinese Taipei, Hong Kong (China) and Macau (China) are included in the Other Asia Pacific aggregate.
3. Excludes Iceland but includes all EU28 member countries.
4. Gross indigenous production.
5. Least-squares growth rate (see glossary).
6. Excludes trade of live animals.

Source: OECD and FAO Secretariats.

StatLink ⊞⊒⊒ *http://dx.doi.org/10.1787/888933101860*

Table A.20.2. Beef and veal projections: Consumption, per capita

Calendar year

	CONSUMPTION (kt cwe)		Growth (%)[1]		PER CAPITA (kg rwt)[5]		Growth (%)[1]	
	Average 2011-13est	2023	2004-13	2014-23	Average 2011-13est	2023	2004-13	2014-23
WORLD	**66 172**	**75 208**	**0.89**	**1.33**	**6.6**	**6.6**	**-0.30**	**0.31**
DEVELOPED COUNTRIES	**29 254**	**29 576**	**-0.53**	**0.57**	**14.7**	**14.4**	**-1.00**	**0.27**
NORTH AMERICA	12 664	12 715	-1.13	0.96	25.2	23.2	-2.03	0.17
Canada	992	1 062	-0.35	0.40	19.9	19.3	-1.44	-0.51
United States	11 672	11 653	-1.20	1.01	25.7	23.6	-2.08	0.24
EUROPE	11 697	11 459	-0.81	-0.05	11.0	10.8	-0.98	-0.04
European Union	7 910	7 803	-1.15	-0.18	10.9	10.6	-1.47	-0.32
Russian Federation	2 781	2 626	1.20	-0.02	13.6	13.3	1.28	0.30
Ukraine	367	336	-5.79	0.19	5.6	5.6	-5.32	0.89
OCEANIA DEVELOPED	906	960	0.33	0.77	23.1	21.5	-1.22	-0.39
Australia	793	855	0.30	0.76	24.1	22.7	-1.34	-0.45
New Zealand	113	105	0.55	0.84	17.8	14.9	-0.54	-0.07
OTHER DEVELOPED[2]	3 987	4 441	2.42	1.07	10.4	11.1	1.76	0.69
Japan	1 241	1 298	1.20	0.42	6.8	7.3	1.17	0.68
South Africa	824	986	1.79	2.08	11.0	12.3	0.60	1.48
DEVELOPING COUNTRIES	**36 917**	**45 632**	**2.14**	**1.86**	**4.5**	**4.9**	**0.75**	**0.66**
AFRICA	6 526	8 513	3.32	2.40	4.5	4.5	0.75	-0.04
NORTH AFRICA	1 627	1 903	3.52	0.70	6.7	6.8	1.94	-0.62
Algeria	207	296	-0.34	2.66	3.8	4.6	-2.10	1.18
Egypt	1 157	1 258	4.90	-0.11	10.0	9.3	3.15	-1.50
SUB-SAHARAN AFRICA	4 899	6 609	3.25	2.94	4.0	4.1	0.48	0.29
LATIN AMERICA and CARIBBEAN	14 669	16 978	1.12	1.28	16.8	17.5	-0.04	0.32
Argentina	2 378	2 666	-0.31	1.10	40.5	41.7	-1.18	0.32
Brazil	7 146	8 150	1.42	1.15	25.2	26.5	0.48	0.45
Chile	366	442	0.42	1.31	14.7	16.2	-0.54	0.54
Mexico	1 590	1 925	0.07	1.22	9.2	9.9	-1.17	0.19
Uruguay	187	231	-0.05	1.47	38.6	46.1	-0.34	1.16
ASIA and PACIFIC	15 722	20 142	2.68	2.15	2.7	3.2	1.54	1.26
Bangladesh	200	259	0.88	2.50	0.9	1.0	-0.24	1.40
China[3]	6 558	8 501	2.31	2.19	3.3	4.1	1.67	1.78
India	1 391	1 474	-3.37	0.63	0.8	0.7	-4.64	-0.42
Indonesia	594	819	3.73	2.61	1.7	2.1	2.33	1.57
Iran, Islamic Republic of	391	468	-0.91	2.12	3.6	3.8	-2.11	1.00
Korea	615	759	4.57	1.52	8.8	10.4	3.96	1.13
Malaysia	188	239	0.46	1.56	4.5	4.9	-1.29	0.18
Pakistan	1 487	1 772	4.60	1.76	5.8	5.8	2.74	0.22
Saudi Arabia	178	250	6.77	3.10	4.4	5.2	4.67	1.59
Turkey	633	872	7.13	2.74	5.9	7.3	5.71	1.76
LEAST DEVELOPED COUNTRIES (LDC)	**4 768**	**6 395**	**3.45**	**2.82**	**3.8**	**4.1**	**1.14**	**0.61**
OECD[4]	**26 393**	**27 307**	**-0.60**	**0.68**	**14.2**	**14.0**	**-1.25**	**0.21**
BRICS	**18 701**	**21 737**	**1.26**	**1.39**	**4.4**	**4.7**	**0.35**	**0.72**

Note: Calendar year: Year ending 30 September New Zealand.

Average 2011-13est: Data for 2013 are estimated.

1. Least-squares growth rate (see glossary).
2. Includes Israel and also transition economies: Kazakhstan, Kyrgyzstan, Tajikistan, Turkmenistan, Uzbekistan, Armenia, Azerbaijan and Georgia.
3. Refers to mainland only. The economies of Chinese Taipei, Hong Kong (China) and Macau (China) are included in the Other Asia Pacific aggregate.
4. Excludes Iceland but includes all EU28 member countries.
5. Per capita consumption expressed in retail weight. Carcass weight to retail weight conversion factors of 0.7 for beef and veal, 0.78 for pigmeat and 0.88 for both sheep meat and poultry meat.

Source: OECD and FAO Secretariats.

StatLink ⟐⟐ *http://dx.doi.org/10.1787/888933101879*

Table A.21.1. Pigmeat projections: Production and trade

Calendar year

	PRODUCTION (kt cwe)[4]		Growth (%)[5]		IMPORTS (kt cwe)[6]		Growth (%)[5]		EXPORTS (kt cwe)[6]		Growth (%)[5]	
	Average 2011-13est	2023	2004-13	2014-23	Average 2011-13est	2023	2004-13	2014-23	Average 2011-13est	2023	2004-13	2014-23
WORLD	**112 716**	**129 427**	**1.96**	**1.10**	**6 633**	**8 024**	**5.54**	**1.95**	**7 066**	**8 141**	**4.50**	**1.97**
DEVELOPED COUNTRIES	**41 818**	**44 992**	**0.93**	**0.63**	**3 335**	**2 982**	**2.19**	**-0.46**	**5 938**	**6 761**	**6.66**	**1.74**
NORTH AMERICA	12 451	13 749	1.26	0.76	588	573	-0.39	0.70	3 579	4 179	6.80	1.97
Canada	2 148	2 256	-0.98	0.67	223	273	8.37	2.58	1 229	1 315	2.24	1.00
United States	10 303	11 493	1.77	0.77	365	301	-3.67	-0.67	2 351	2 864	10.11	2.45
EUROPE	27 050	28 768	0.77	0.58	1 206	705	6.07	-3.56	2 305	2 521	6.93	1.37
European Union	22 630	23 258	0.26	0.40	19	19	-15.62	-0.87	2 140	2 394	6.77	1.57
Russian Federation	2 618	3 600	6.64	1.82	797	241	5.22	-9.17	0	0	..	..
Ukraine	614	572	1.66	-0.44	193	257	17.21	2.98	19	3	5.09	-10.96
OCEANIA DEVELOPED	405	446	-1.32	1.06	332	418	8.99	1.32	48	55	-4.83	2.00
Australia	356	392	-1.39	1.01	289	370	9.67	1.43	48	55	-4.85	2.00
New Zealand	49	55	-0.81	1.48	43	48	5.08	0.54	0	0	2.68	0.00
OTHER DEVELOPED[1]	1 912	2 029	1.69	0.41	1 209	1 287	-0.72	0.59	6	7	4.38	-2.80
Japan	1 292	1 287	0.51	-0.25	1 112	1 148	-0.98	0.26	1	0	..	..
South Africa	322	406	11.22	2.14	41	54	3.49	2.96	4	6	5.86	-1.30
DEVELOPING COUNTRIES	**70 898**	**84 435**	**2.60**	**1.36**	**3 298**	**5 042**	**10.17**	**3.75**	**1 127**	**1 380**	**-3.18**	**3.17**
AFRICA	983	1 389	3.39	3.19	244	714	16.22	8.44	5	1	-6.45	-10.84
NORTH AFRICA	2	2	-8.23	0.47	1	1	3.37	5.20	0	0	29.80	-4.38
Algeria	0	0	-1.38	0.00	0	0	-17.83	0.00	0	0	-1.38	0.00
Egypt	0	0	-18.63	-0.51	0	1	8.65	5.52	0	0	38.24	-5.23
SUB-SAHARAN AFRICA	981	1 387	3.42	3.19	244	713	16.28	8.45	5	1	-7.02	-11.09
LATIN AMERICA and CARIBBEAN	7 116	8 902	3.32	2.14	1 014	1 311	10.74	2.00	793	939	1.14	2.71
Argentina	309	429	5.13	3.04	35	33	1.71	0.02	10	35	27.56	10.74
Brazil	3 462	4 113	3.31	1.88	12	11	28.68	-0.84	529	555	-0.67	1.91
Chile	577	872	4.73	3.42	30	28	44.91	-4.90	157	262	3.88	5.28
Mexico	1 237	1 459	2.25	1.30	643	781	10.42	1.74	73	66	10.11	-0.84
Uruguay	22	31	2.24	1.41	28	34	14.79	1.15	0	0	-53.52	-0.08
ASIA and PACIFIC	62 799	74 144	2.51	1.24	2 040	3 017	9.29	3.68	329	440	-10.22	4.26
Bangladesh	0	0	-19.59	0.00	0	0	33.25	0.00	0	0	-1.38	0.00
China[2]	52 706	60 856	2.50	0.94	524	1 403	36.69	7.08	100	351	-25.63	7.77
India	329	322	-3.59	-0.30	1	0	27.42	-5.13	0	0	-7.33	2.41
Indonesia	752	1 132	4.58	4.19	1	2	-14.48	0.00	0	0	-21.34	-21.25
Iran, Islamic Republic of	0	0	-21.89	0.00	1	2	39.58	0.00	1	2	84.54	0.00
Korea	1 023	1 396	1.37	2.00	543	373	7.10	-1.46	2	3	-29.02	0.00
Malaysia	230	300	1.79	2.85	15	21	17.71	3.57	6	1	24.02	-13.44
Pakistan	0	0	-29.45	0.00	0	0	-35.41	0.00	0	0	-20.51	0.00
Saudi Arabia	0	0	-29.45	0.00	10	12	15.63	0.00	0	0	-31.78	0.00
Turkey	1	1	-0.96	0.00	0	1	-12.90	0.00	0	1	-6.41	0.00
LEAST DEVELOPED COUNTRIES (LDC)	**1 411**	**2 109**	**4.88**	**3.74**	**188**	**546**	**16.48**	**9.36**	**0**	**0**	**15.50**	**-3.08**
OECD[3]	40 002	42 883	0.71	0.64	3 282	3 356	2.60	0.52	6 007	6 963	6.50	1.90
BRICS	59 438	69 297	2.69	1.04	1 374	1 710	10.87	2.10	635	912	-7.77	3.83

.. Not available

Note: Calendar year: Year ending 30 September New Zealand.

Average 2011-13est: Data for 2013 are estimated.

1. Includes Israel and also transition economies: Kazakhstan, Kyrgyzstan, Tajikistan, Turkmenistan, Uzbekistan, Armenia, Azerbaijan and Georgia.
2. Refers to mainland only. The economies of Chinese Taipei, Hong Kong (China) and Macau (China) are included in the Other Asia Pacific aggregate.
3. Excludes Iceland but includes all EU28 member countries.
4. Gross indigenous production.
5. Least-squares growth rate (see glossary).
6. Excludes trade of live animals.

Source: OECD and FAO Secretariats.

StatLink ⬛ᵐˢᴸ *http://dx.doi.org/10.1787/888933101898*

Table A.21.2. Pigmeat projections: Consumption, per capita

Calendar year

	CONSUMPTION (kt cwe)		Growth (%)[1]		PER CAPITA (kg rwe)[5]		Growth (%)[1]	
	Average 2011-13est	2023	2004-13	2014-23	Average 2011-13est	2023	2004-13	2014-23
WORLD	112 231	129 248	2.00	1.10	12.4	12.7	0.80	0.08
DEVELOPED COUNTRIES	39 200	41 098	0.39	0.37	22.0	22.3	-0.09	0.07
NORTH AMERICA	9 227	9 928	-0.43	0.28	20.4	20.2	-1.33	-0.50
Canada	766	796	-0.65	0.29	17.1	16.1	-1.74	-0.63
United States	8 461	9 132	-0.40	0.28	20.8	20.6	-1.29	-0.49
EUROPE	26 160	27 053	0.57	0.36	27.5	28.4	0.40	0.37
European Union	20 468	20 858	-0.30	0.28	31.4	31.5	-0.62	0.14
Russian Federation	3 642	3 940	6.25	0.45	19.8	22.2	6.34	0.78
Ukraine	806	847	4.36	0.59	13.8	15.7	4.89	1.29
OCEANIA DEVELOPED	688	809	3.05	1.13	19.5	20.2	1.46	-0.03
Australia	597	707	3.28	1.15	20.2	20.9	1.60	-0.07
New Zealand	91	102	1.60	1.03	15.9	16.1	0.50	0.11
OTHER DEVELOPED[2]	3 124	3 309	0.83	0.53	9.1	9.2	0.19	0.15
Japan	2 413	2 434	-0.06	0.03	14.8	15.3	-0.10	0.28
South Africa	358	453	10.53	2.31	5.3	6.3	9.24	1.71
DEVELOPING COUNTRIES	73 031	88 149	2.96	1.46	10.0	10.6	1.56	0.27
AFRICA	1 220	2 103	5.18	4.72	0.9	1.2	2.56	2.22
NORTH AFRICA	2	2	-7.54	1.95	0.0	0.0	-8.95	0.61
Algeria	0	0	-6.15	0.00	0.0	0.0	-7.81	-1.44
Egypt	1	1	-14.29	2.98	0.0	0.0	-15.71	1.54
SUB-SAHARAN AFRICA	1 218	2 101	5.22	4.72	1.1	1.4	2.39	2.03
LATIN AMERICA and CARIBBEAN	7 340	9 278	4.31	2.06	9.4	10.7	3.11	1.09
Argentina	335	427	4.36	2.33	6.4	7.4	3.45	1.55
Brazil	2 944	3 570	4.24	1.87	11.6	12.9	3.27	1.16
Chile	450	637	5.98	2.23	20.1	26.1	4.98	1.45
Mexico	1 810	2 178	3.96	1.53	11.7	12.5	2.67	0.50
Uruguay	50	65	7.92	1.27	11.5	14.5	7.61	0.96
ASIA and PACIFIC	64 471	76 769	2.78	1.32	12.4	13.4	1.63	0.43
Bangladesh	0	0	20.72	0.00	0.0	0.0	19.37	-1.07
China[3]	53 077	61 870	2.79	1.03	30.1	33.4	2.16	0.63
India	330	323	-3.55	-0.31	0.2	0.2	-4.82	-1.35
Indonesia	730	1 109	4.46	4.30	2.3	3.1	3.06	3.24
Iran, Islamic Republic of	0	0	-7.83	0.00	0.0	0.0	-8.95	-1.09
Korea	1 548	1 766	3.04	1.14	24.6	26.9	2.45	0.75
Malaysia	239	320	2.07	3.03	6.4	7.3	0.28	1.64
Pakistan	0	0	-34.33	0.00	0.0	0.0	-35.49	-1.51
Saudi Arabia	10	12	15.67	0.00	0.3	0.3	13.39	-1.47
Turkey	0	0	-24.76	0.00	0.0	0.0	-25.76	-0.96
LEAST DEVELOPED COUNTRIES (LDC)	1 614	2 665	5.89	4.66	1.5	1.9	3.52	2.40
OECD[4]	37 002	39 039	0.11	0.42	22.2	22.2	-0.54	-0.05
BRICS	60 350	70 155	3.03	1.04	15.6	16.9	2.10	0.37

Note: Calendar year: Year ending 30 September for New Zealand.
   Average 2011-13est: Data for 2013 are estimated.
1. Least-squares growth rate (see glossary).
2. Includes Israel and also transition economies: Kazakhstan, Kyrgyzstan, Tajikistan, Turkmenistan, Uzbekistan, Armenia, Azerbaijan and Georgia.
3. Refers to mainland only. The economies of Chinese Taipei, Hong Kong (China) and Macau (China) are included in the Other Asia Pacific aggregate.
4. Excludes Iceland but includes all EU28 member countries.
5. Per capita consumption expressed in retail weight. Carcass weight to retail weight conversion factors of 0.7 for beef and veal, 0.78 for pigmeat and 0.88 for both sheep meat and poultry meat.
Source: OECD and FAO Secretariats.

StatLink ⧉ *http://dx.doi.org/10.1787/888933101917*

Table A.22.1. Poultry meat projections: Production and trade

Calendar year

	PRODUCTION (kt rtc)		Growth (%)[4]		IMPORTS (kt rtc)		Growth (%)[4]		EXPORTS (kt rtc)		Growth (%)[4]	
	Average 2011-13est	2023	2004-13	2014-23	Average 2011-13est	2023	2004-13	2014-23	Average 2011-13est	2023	2004-13	2014-23
WORLD	**106 164**	**134 511**	**3.80**	**2.27**	**12 101**	**15 859**	**7.46**	**2.77**	**12 244**	**16 026**	**6.27**	**2.73**
DEVELOPED COUNTRIES	**43 700**	**52 423**	**2.54**	**1.67**	**3 053**	**3 415**	**-1.57**	**1.24**	**5 427**	**7 331**	**5.44**	**2.73**
NORTH AMERICA	20 905	25 861	0.93	1.97	303	333	4.19	0.61	3 797	5 043	4.73	2.37
Canada	1 210	1 392	0.78	1.38	246	274	2.43	0.69	179	209	4.37	1.14
United States	19 695	24 469	0.94	2.00	57	59	16.86	0.25	3 618	4 834	4.75	2.42
EUROPE	17 839	20 821	4.34	1.38	1 574	1 329	-5.64	-1.42	1 554	2 206	7.37	3.60
European Union	12 608	13 873	1.99	0.90	841	850	2.35	0.11	1 320	1 667	5.39	3.00
Russian Federation	3 544	4 657	14.16	2.17	466	255	-13.40	-4.35	35	178	90.24	12.74
Ukraine	1 040	1 437	11.79	3.06	87	26	-10.79	-14.11	90	226	35.12	5.05
OCEANIA DEVELOPED	1 209	1 567	3.36	2.44	0	0	..	..	45	57	6.95	3.56
Australia	1 041	1 357	3.79	2.51	0	0	..	..	45	57	6.95	3.56
New Zealand	168	210	0.96	1.97	0	0	..	..	0	0	..	..
OTHER DEVELOPED[1]	3 748	4 175	3.89	1.08	1 176	1 753	5.42	4.00	31	25	7.25	1.23
Japan	1 418	1 436	1.47	0.38	435	408	1.77	-1.52	7	10	26.43	0.00
South Africa	1 517	1 717	6.85	1.02	382	855	7.57	8.74	12	14	13.31	2.67
DEVELOPING COUNTRIES	**62 464**	**82 088**	**4.77**	**2.68**	**9 048**	**12 444**	**12.74**	**3.23**	**6 817**	**8 695**	**6.98**	**2.74**
AFRICA	3 437	4 723	4.20	3.13	1 337	2 196	16.27	4.12	14	4	21.05	-9.80
NORTH AFRICA	2 122	2 850	4.57	2.94	207	360	59.09	3.02	11	3	49.88	-9.51
Algeria	285	389	0.93	2.91	3	4	11.66	1.26	0	0	108.35	-0.59
Egypt	877	1 056	3.44	1.83	130	214	76.27	3.16	3	2	35.38	-4.35
SUB-SAHARAN AFRICA	1 316	1 873	3.63	3.42	1 130	1 836	13.72	4.35	3	1	3.31	-10.96
LATIN AMERICA and CARIBBEAN	23 975	29 895	4.78	2.09	1 673	1 893	8.52	1.17	4 328	5 570	5.24	2.68
Argentina	1 883	2 543	9.37	2.32	16	12	-0.16	0.00	268	618	19.86	5.86
Brazil	13 097	15 445	4.78	1.68	3	3	28.78	0.00	3 869	4 801	4.42	2.50
Chile	690	841	3.00	1.32	80	20	27.59	-13.22	120	67	6.84	-5.85
Mexico	2 809	3 731	2.16	2.74	639	543	6.24	-1.47	15	21	101.29	7.46
Uruguay	94	122	9.29	2.10	3	4	25.79	-3.37	14	16	104.26	4.99
ASIA and PACIFIC	35 052	47 470	4.82	3.03	6 038	8 355	13.44	3.52	2 476	3 121	10.70	2.90
Bangladesh	189	278	2.71	4.40	0	2	6.39	24.39	0	0	-1.45	-26.63
China[2]	17 573	22 385	4.10	2.76	512	933	5.92	3.71	481	723	-1.56	7.81
India	2 447	4 231	7.81	4.79	0	0	24.11	1.95	7	4	22.33	-2.52
Indonesia	1 665	2 432	4.52	3.85	1	1	-20.02	1.98	0	0	-39.20	-1.88
Iran, Islamic Republic of	1 737	2 336	4.68	2.84	42	65	24.81	8.79	31	49	9.95	6.55
Korea	715	950	5.22	2.59	143	103	13.85	-3.35	30	33	37.64	0.00
Malaysia	1 435	1 886	5.84	2.71	45	75	12.45	3.97	30	32	20.26	0.05
Pakistan	845	1 453	10.28	4.05	1	1	2.98	1.65	18	15	136.33	1.66
Saudi Arabia	589	689	1.80	0.99	807	1 292	9.54	4.97	30	29	-5.06	-1.44
Turkey	1 679	2 402	8.68	2.69	489	97	40.70	-8.28	307	439	34.03	1.14
LEAST DEVELOPED COUNTRIES (LDC)	**2 270**	**3 374**	**5.77**	**4.11**	**967**	**1 405**	**12.13**	**2.93**	**1**	**0**	**24.14**	**-32.62**
OECD[3]	**42 723**	**51 469**	**1.75**	**1.72**	**2 979**	**2 405**	**6.35**	**-1.37**	**5 653**	**7 338**	**5.72**	**2.31**
BRICS	**38 179**	**48 435**	**5.35**	**2.44**	**1 362**	**2 046**	**-4.20**	**3.84**	**4 405**	**5 720**	**4.04**	**3.17**

.. Not available

Note: Calendar year: Year ending 30 September for New Zealand.

Average 2011-13est: Data for 2013 are estimated.

1. Includes Israel and also transition economies: Kazakhstan, Kyrgyzstan, Tajikistan, Turkmenistan, Uzbekistan, Armenia, Azerbaijan and Georgia.
2. Refers to mainland only. The economies of Chinese Taipei, Hong Kong (China) and Macau (China) are included in the Other Asia Pacific aggregate.
3. Excludes Iceland but includes all EU28 member countries.
4. Least-squares growth rate (see glossary).

Source: OECD and FAO Secretariats.

StatLink ▆▅▆ *http://dx.doi.org/10.1787/888933101936*

Table A.22.2. Poultry meat projections: Consumption, per capita
Calendar year

	CONSUMPTION (kt rtc)		Growth (%)[1]		PER CAPITA (kg rwt)[5]		Growth (%)[1]	
	Average 2011-13est	2023	2004-13	2014-23	Average 2011-13est	2023	2004-13	2014-23
WORLD	**106 045**	**134 341**	**3.91**	**2.28**	**13.2**	**14.9**	**2.69**	**1.24**
DEVELOPED COUNTRIES	**41 350**	**48 508**	**1.87**	**1.49**	**26.2**	**29.7**	**1.39**	**1.19**
NORTH AMERICA	17 435	21 151	0.31	1.85	43.6	48.4	-0.60	1.06
Canada	1 277	1 456	0.69	1.28	32.2	33.2	-0.41	0.35
United States	16 158	19 695	0.28	1.90	44.8	50.1	-0.61	1.12
EUROPE	17 858	19 944	2.84	0.95	21.2	23.6	2.66	0.95
European Union	12 128	13 055	1.69	0.61	21.0	22.2	1.36	0.47
Russian Federation	3 973	4 734	5.91	1.44	24.4	30.1	6.00	1.78
Ukraine	1 037	1 236	6.14	1.83	20.0	25.8	6.68	2.53
OCEANIA DEVELOPED	1 163	1 509	3.24	2.40	37.2	42.5	1.65	1.22
Australia	996	1 300	3.67	2.47	38.0	43.4	1.98	1.24
New Zealand	168	210	0.96	1.97	33.0	37.3	-0.13	1.04
OTHER DEVELOPED[2]	4 894	5 903	4.28	1.86	16.1	18.6	3.61	1.49
Japan	1 848	1 835	1.64	-0.07	12.8	13.0	1.61	0.18
South Africa	1 887	2 558	6.94	3.03	31.7	40.1	5.69	2.42
DEVELOPING COUNTRIES	**64 694**	**85 833**	**5.41**	**2.75**	**10.0**	**11.6**	**3.98**	**1.54**
AFRICA	4 760	6 914	6.61	3.45	4.1	4.6	3.95	0.99
NORTH AFRICA	2 318	3 206	5.88	2.98	12.1	14.4	4.27	1.63
Algeria	287	393	0.98	2.90	6.6	7.6	-0.80	1.42
Egypt	1 004	1 267	5.53	2.06	10.9	11.8	3.78	0.63
SUB-SAHARAN AFRICA	2 442	3 708	7.34	3.88	2.5	2.9	4.45	1.20
LATIN AMERICA and CARIBBEAN	21 319	26 215	4.95	1.90	30.8	34.0	3.74	0.93
Argentina	1 631	1 937	8.10	1.38	34.9	38.0	7.16	0.61
Brazil	9 231	10 647	4.95	1.34	40.9	43.6	3.97	0.63
Chile	650	794	3.79	1.31	32.8	36.7	2.80	0.54
Mexico	3 433	4 253	2.76	2.07	25.0	27.6	1.49	1.04
Uruguay	83	110	7.37	1.52	21.4	27.5	7.06	1.21
ASIA and PACIFIC	38 615	52 704	5.52	3.11	8.4	10.4	4.35	2.21
Bangladesh	189	280	2.71	4.48	1.1	1.4	1.57	3.35
China[3]	17 604	22 595	4.22	2.69	11.2	13.8	3.57	2.28
India	2 439	4 227	7.79	4.80	1.7	2.7	6.37	3.71
Indonesia	1 666	2 433	4.49	3.85	5.9	7.7	3.08	2.80
Iran, Islamic Republic of	1 748	2 352	4.75	2.90	20.1	23.9	3.47	1.78
Korea	828	1 020	5.81	1.89	14.9	17.5	5.20	1.50
Malaysia	1 450	1 928	5.82	2.81	43.7	49.7	3.97	1.42
Pakistan	828	1 439	9.92	4.07	4.1	6.0	7.97	2.50
Saudi Arabia	1 366	1 953	5.89	3.51	42.5	51.2	3.80	1.99
Turkey	1 861	2 060	9.85	2.11	21.8	21.6	8.40	1.13
LEAST DEVELOPED COUNTRIES (LDC)	**3 235**	**4 778**	**7.34**	**3.75**	**3.3**	**3.8**	**4.94**	**1.52**
OECD[4]	**40 075**	**46 536**	**1.58**	**1.44**	**27.2**	**29.9**	**0.91**	**0.96**
BRICS	**35 135**	**44 761**	**4.96**	**2.41**	**10.3**	**12.1**	**4.01**	**1.73**

Note: Calendar year: Year ending 30 September for New Zealand.
   Average 2011-13est: Data for 2013 are estimated.
1. Least-squares growth rate (see glossary).
2. Includes Israel and also transition economies: Kazakhstan, Kyrgyzstan, Tajikistan, Turkmenistan, Uzbekistan, Armenia, Azerbaijan and Georgia.
3. Refers to mainland only. The economies of Chinese Taipei, Hong Kong (China) and Macau (China) are included in the Other Asia Pacific aggregate.
4. Excludes Iceland but includes all EU28 member countries.
5. Per capita consumption expressed in retail weight. Carcass weight to retail weight conversion factors of 0.7 for beef and veal, 0.78 for pigmeat and 0.88 for both sheep meat and poultry meat.
Source: OECD and FAO Secretariats.

StatLink ⬛᠍᠍᠍᠍ http://dx.doi.org/10.1787/888933101955

Table A.23.1. Sheep meat projections: Production and trade

Calendar year

	PRODUCTION (kt cwe)[4]		Growth (%)[5]		IMPORTS (kt cwe)[6]		Growth (%)[5]		EXPORTS (kt cwe)[6]		Growth (%)[5]	
	Average 2011-13est	2023	2004-13	2014-23	Average 2011-13est	2023	2004-13	2014-23	Average 2011-13est	2023	2004-13	2014-23
WORLD	**13 496**	**17 251**	**1.27**	**2.29**	**864**	**1 173**	**0.75**	**1.89**	**911**	**1 183**	**0.32**	**1.78**
DEVELOPED COUNTRIES	**3 266**	**3 718**	**-0.25**	**1.25**	**367**	**350**	**-3.10**	**-0.37**	**805**	**1 025**	**0.03**	**1.80**
NORTH AMERICA	91	87	-2.51	-0.25	93	88	-1.36	-0.37	8	11	6.79	0.11
Canada	15	14	-2.25	0.10	19	17	-0.56	-1.14	0	0	-12.40	3.00
United States	76	73	-2.57	-0.32	73	71	-1.57	-0.17	8	11	7.52	0.08
EUROPE	1 275	1 254	-1.48	-0.20	234	217	-2.44	-0.67	30	22	17.93	-2.83
European Union	963	899	-2.50	-0.57	207	194	-3.31	-0.82	23	20	27.18	-1.94
Russian Federation	195	234	3.62	0.92	11	12	6.79	-0.26	0	0	..	..
Ukraine	19	20	2.95	0.42	0	0	28.25	10.55	0	0	-34.59	-9.55
OCEANIA DEVELOPED	1 123	1 302	-1.29	1.43	3	4	-2.70	0.00	766	991	-0.41	1.96
Australia	660	815	-0.74	2.29	0	0	..	..	362	528	0.93	3.64
New Zealand	463	487	-2.05	0.12	3	4	-2.70	0.00	404	463	-1.54	0.30
OTHER DEVELOPED[1]	777	1 075	4.55	3.14	37	40	-9.24	1.47	0	0	11.06	-9.64
Japan	0	0	..	..	30	30	-6.97	0.22	0	0	..	..
South Africa	163	191	1.82	1.72	6	4	-19.12	0.94	0	0	-2.46	-4.02
DEVELOPING COUNTRIES	**10 230**	**13 533**	**1.80**	**2.60**	**497**	**823**	**4.50**	**3.03**	**106**	**158**	**2.68**	**1.61**
AFRICA	2 674	3 831	2.56	3.81	23	55	-2.73	5.92	32	27	7.08	-0.89
NORTH AFRICA	699	903	4.62	2.31	7	12	-13.31	2.17	0	0	0.60	22.19
Algeria	297	399	6.28	2.37	2	5	-37.23	5.25	0	0	-9.08	-15.95
Egypt	127	155	6.85	2.27	2	2	11.50	1.77	0	0	3.07	-31.63
SUB-SAHARAN AFRICA	1 974	2 928	1.91	4.32	16	43	6.70	7.32	32	27	7.09	-0.88
LATIN AMERICA and CARIBBEAN	380	436	0.57	1.41	24	22	-12.08	-0.35	25	32	0.54	2.07
Argentina	58	62	-0.62	0.38	0	0	-8.50	0.00	4	4	-8.18	0.40
Brazil	83	86	1.14	0.60	5	6	..	..	0	0	-14.31	8.43
Chile	18	18	2.43	-0.02	0	0	-36.29	0.53	6	3	1.32	-5.80
Mexico	57	64	3.22	0.86	9	2	-20.54	-11.35	0	0	..	..
Uruguay	34	46	-1.43	2.69	0	0	41.50	-0.32	14	25	4.24	1.03
ASIA and PACIFIC	7 177	9 265	1.60	2.19	449	746	7.20	2.97	49	98	1.51	1.32
Bangladesh	211	341	3.48	4.76	0	1	-12.45	9.74	0	0	-8.61	-31.03
China[2]	4 033	5 132	2.12	1.91	155	372	20.70	3.74	6	16	-21.05	0.15
India	909	1 159	3.16	2.26	0	0	14.07	-6.25	14	50	10.25	6.67
Indonesia	118	178	-0.84	4.17	1	1	8.30	2.54	0	0	-2.16	-23.47
Iran, Islamic Republic of	268	290	-6.85	1.03	9	15	175.52	5.13	0	0	-15.09	-15.92
Korea	1	1	-9.92	0.00	5	5	7.76	0.00	0	0	0.21	0.36
Malaysia	1	1	11.63	-1.57	21	36	5.48	3.56	0	0	41.80	-3.44
Pakistan	450	547	-0.95	1.78	0	0	-41.43	-1.36	18	27	18.61	1.37
Saudi Arabia	11	12	-0.10	0.80	28	32	-10.38	4.72	5	3	4.10	-4.51
Turkey	291	403	-1.32	2.68	1	4	45.59	17.54	0	0	-13.16	-14.52
LEAST DEVELOPED COUNTRIES (LDC)	**1 845**	**2 705**	**2.54**	**3.97**	**5**	**11**	**-3.52**	**7.84**	**20**	**16**	**11.55**	**-1.57**
OECD[3]	**2 584**	**2 816**	**-1.70**	**0.82**	**357**	**340**	**-3.91**	**-0.53**	**803**	**1 026**	**-0.01**	**1.81**
BRICS	**5 383**	**6 802**	**2.32**	**1.91**	**177**	**394**	**12.36**	**3.46**	**20**	**66**	**-7.02**	**4.41**

.. Not available

Note: Calendar year: Year ending 30 September for New Zealand.

Average 2011-13est: Data for 2013 are estimated.

1. Includes Israel and also transition economies: Kazakhstan, Kyrgyzstan, Tajikistan, Turkmenistan, Uzbekistan, Armenia, Azerbaijan and Georgia.
2. Refers to mainland only. The economies of Chinese Taipei, Hong Kong (China) and Macau (China) are included in the Other Asia Pacific aggregate.
3. Excludes Iceland but includes all EU28 member countries.
4. Gross indigenous production.
5. Least-squares growth rate (see glossary).
6. Excludes trade of live animals.

Source: OECD and FAO Secretariats.

StatLink *http://dx.doi.org/10.1787/888933101974*

Table A.23.2. Sheep meat projections: Consumption, per capita

Calendar year

	CONSUMPTION (kt cwe)		Growth (%)[4]		PER CAPITA (kg rwt)[5]		Growth (%)[4]	
	Average 2011-13est	2023	2004-13	2014-23	Average 2011-13est	2023	2004-13	2014-23
WORLD	**13 427**	**17 203**	**1.26**	**2.31**	**1.7**	**1.9**	**0.07**	**1.27**
DEVELOPED COUNTRIES	**2 720**	**2 942**	**-0.86**	**0.93**	**1.7**	**1.8**	**-1.33**	**0.63**
NORTH AMERICA	170	158	-2.13	-0.35	0.4	0.4	-3.03	-1.13
Canada	35	31	-0.86	-0.61	0.9	0.7	-1.94	-1.52
United States	135	127	-2.44	-0.28	0.4	0.3	-3.31	-1.05
EUROPE	1 444	1 394	-2.07	-0.23	1.7	1.7	-2.24	-0.23
European Union	1 118	1 033	-3.19	-0.61	1.9	1.8	-3.50	-0.74
Russian Federation	201	231	4.27	0.90	1.2	1.5	4.36	1.23
Ukraine	19	20	3.01	0.43	0.4	0.4	3.53	1.12
OCEANIA DEVELOPED	294	275	-3.45	0.19	9.4	7.7	-4.94	-0.97
Australia	255	242	-1.57	0.01	9.7	8.1	-3.18	-1.19
New Zealand	39	33	-12.34	1.72	7.7	5.9	-13.29	0.80
OTHER DEVELOPED[1]	812	1 114	3.27	3.08	2.7	3.5	2.61	2.70
Japan	30	30	-6.97	0.22	0.2	0.2	-7.00	0.47
South Africa	168	195	-0.47	1.71	2.8	3.1	-1.63	1.11
DEVELOPING COUNTRIES	**10 706**	**14 261**	**1.86**	**2.62**	**1.7**	**1.9**	**0.48**	**1.41**
AFRICA	2 588	3 779	2.36	3.98	2.2	2.5	-0.18	1.50
NORTH AFRICA	706	914	4.24	2.31	3.7	4.1	2.65	0.96
Algeria	299	404	5.49	2.40	6.8	7.8	3.63	0.93
Egypt	129	157	6.87	2.27	1.4	1.5	5.09	0.84
SUB-SAHARAN AFRICA	1 882	2 864	1.72	4.57	1.9	2.2	-1.01	1.88
LATIN AMERICA and CARIBBEAN	384	427	-0.48	1.15	0.6	0.6	-1.62	0.19
Argentina	54	58	0.08	0.38	1.2	1.1	-0.80	-0.39
Brazil	90	93	1.49	0.58	0.4	0.4	0.55	-0.11
Chile	12	15	2.89	1.68	0.6	0.7	1.91	0.90
Mexico	69	66	-4.02	-0.58	0.5	0.4	-5.21	-1.59
Uruguay	19	20	0.61	1.35	4.8	5.0	0.31	1.04
ASIA and PACIFIC	7 734	10 055	1.83	2.21	1.7	2.0	0.69	1.32
Bangladesh	211	342	3.39	4.76	1.2	1.7	2.24	3.64
China[2]	4 183	5 488	2.63	2.03	2.7	3.3	1.99	1.63
India	893	1 108	3.06	2.12	0.6	0.7	1.70	1.06
Indonesia	119	179	-0.70	4.16	0.4	0.6	-2.03	3.10
Iran, Islamic Republic of	249	274	-7.29	1.33	2.9	2.8	-8.41	0.22
Korea	7	7	1.26	0.00	0.1	0.1	0.67	-0.39
Malaysia	23	38	5.47	3.31	0.7	1.0	3.63	1.92
Pakistan	431	519	-1.38	1.80	2.1	2.2	-3.13	0.26
Saudi Arabia	120	130	-3.26	1.22	3.7	3.4	-5.16	-0.27
Turkey	302	411	-0.85	2.72	3.5	4.3	-2.16	1.74
LEAST DEVELOPED COUNTRIES (LDC)	**1 757**	**2 627**	**2.17**	**4.16**	**1.8**	**2.1**	**-0.11**	**1.92**
OECD[3]	**2 050**	**2 050**	**-2.79**	**0.18**	**1.4**	**1.3**	**-3.43**	**-0.29**
BRICS	**5 535**	**7 114**	**2.62**	**1.98**	**1.6**	**1.9**	**1.70**	**1.30**

Note: Calendar year: Year ending 30 September for New Zealand.

Average 2011-13est: Data for 2013 are estimated.

1. Includes Israel and also transition economies: Kazakhstan, Kyrgyzstan, Tajikistan, Turkmenistan, Uzbekistan, Armenia, Azerbaijan and Georgia.
2. Refers to mainland only. The economies of Chinese Taipei, Hong Kong (China) and Macau (China) are included in the Other Asia Pacific aggregate.
3. Excludes Iceland but includes all EU28 member countries.
4. Least-squares growth rate (see glossary).
5. Per capita consumption expressed in retail weight. Carcass weight to retail weight conversion factors of 0.7 for beef and veal, 0.78 for pigmeat and 0.88 for both sheep meat and poultry meat.

Source: OECD and FAO Secretariats.

StatLink ⬛ *http://dx.doi.org/10.1787/888933101993*

Table A.24. **Main policy assumptions for meat markets**

		Average 2011-13est	2014	2015	2016	2017	2018	2019	2020	2021	2022	2023
ARGENTINA												
Beef export tax	%	15.0	15.0	15.0	15.0	15.0	15.0	15.0	15.0	15.0	15.0	15.0
CANADA												
Beef tariff-quota	kt pw	76.4	76.4	76.4	76.4	76.4	76.4	76.4	76.4	76.4	76.4	76.4
In-quota tariff	%	0.0	0.0	0.0	0.0	0.0	0.0	0.0	0.0	0.0	0.0	0.0
Out-of-quota tariff	%	26.5	26.5	26.5	26.5	26.5	26.5	26.5	26.5	26.5	26.5	26.5
Poultry meat tariff-quota	kt pw	45.4	45.4	45.4	45.4	45.4	45.4	45.4	45.4	45.4	45.4	45.4
In-quota tariff	%	2.5	2.5	2.5	2.5	2.5	2.5	2.5	2.5	2.5	2.5	2.5
Out-of-quota tariff	%	196.6	196.6	196.6	196.6	196.6	196.6	196.6	196.6	196.6	196.6	196.6
EUROPEAN UNION[1]												
Beef budget ceiling[2]	'000 EUR	1 606 431	1 661 058	..	..	..	..	..	..	..	..	..
Beef basic price[3]	EUR/kg dw	2.2	2.2	2.2	2.2	2.2	2.2	2.2	2.2	2.2	2.2	2.2
Beef buy-in price[3,4]	EUR/kg dw	1.6	1.9	1.9	1.9	1.9	1.9	1.9	1.9	1.9	1.9	1.9
Pigmeat basic price	EUR/kg dw	1.5	1.5	1.5	1.5	1.5	1.5	1.5	1.5	1.5	1.5	1.5
Sheep basic rate[5]	EUR/head	10.5	10.5	..	..	..	..	..	..	..	..	..
Beef tariff-quota	kt cwe	288.9	313.4	313.4	313.4	313.4	313.4	313.4	313.4	313.4	313.4	313.4
Pig tariff-quota	kt cwe	114.6	116.2	116.2	116.2	116.2	116.2	116.2	116.2	116.2	116.2	116.2
Poultry tariff-quota	kt rtc	890.7	959.4	959.4	959.4	959.4	959.4	959.4	959.4	959.4	959.4	959.4
Sheep meat tariff-quota	kt cwe	285.2	285.2	285.2	285.2	285.2	285.2	285.2	285.2	285.2	285.2	285.2
Subsidised export limits (WTO)												
Beef[6]	kt cwe	989.6	989.6	989.6	989.6	989.6	989.6	989.6	989.6	989.6	989.6	989.6
Pigmeat[6]	kt cwe	588.4	588.4	588.4	588.4	588.4	588.4	588.4	588.4	588.4	588.4	588.4
Poultry meat	kt cwe	430.8	430.8	430.8	430.8	430.8	430.8	430.8	430.8	430.8	430.8	430.8
JAPAN[7]												
Beef stabilisation prices												
Upper price	JPY/kg dw	1 063.3	1 070.0	1 070.0	1 070.0	1 070.0	1 070.0	1 070.0	1 070.0	1 070.0	1 070.0	1 070.0
Lower price	JPY/kg dw	818.3	825.0	825.0	825.0	825.0	825.0	825.0	825.0	825.0	825.0	825.0
Beef tariff	%	38.5	38.5	38.5	38.5	38.5	38.5	38.5	38.5	38.5	38.5	38.5
Pigmeat stabilisation prices												
Upper price	JPY/kg dw	546.7	550.0	550.0	550.0	550.0	550.0	550.0	550.0	550.0	550.0	550.0
Lower price	JPY/kg dw	401.7	405.0	405.0	405.0	405.0	405.0	405.0	405.0	405.0	405.0	405.0
Pigmeat import system[8]												
Tariff	%	4.3	4.3	4.3	4.3	4.3	4.3	4.3	4.3	4.3	4.3	4.3
Standard import price	JPY/kg dw	409.9	409.9	409.9	409.9	409.9	409.9	409.9	409.9	409.9	409.9	409.9
Poultry meat tariff	%	7.4	7.4	7.4	7.4	7.4	7.4	7.4	7.4	7.4	7.4	7.4
KOREA												
Beef tariff	%	37.3	32.0	29.3	26.7	18.0	16.0	14.0	12.0	10.0	8.0	6.0
Beef mark-up		0.0	0.0	0.0	0.0	0.0	0.0	0.0	0.0	0.0	0.0	0.0
Pigmeat tariff	%	22.5	22.5	22.5	22.5	15.8	14.6	13.5	12.4	11.3	11.3	11.3
Poultry meat tariff	%	21.0	21.0	21.0	21.0	21.0	21.0	21.0	21.0	21.0	21.0	21.0
MEXICO												
Pigmeat tariff	%	45.0	45.0	45.0	45.0	45.0	45.0	45.0	45.0	45.0	45.0	45.0
Pigmeat NAFTA tariff	%	0.0	0.0	0.0	0.0	0.0	0.0	0.0	0.0	0.0	0.0	0.0
Poultry meat tariff-quota	kt pw	127.0	300.0	300.0	300.0	300.0	300.0	300.0	300.0	300.0	300.0	300.0
In-quota tariff	%	33.3	0.0	0.0	0.0	0.0	0.0	0.0	0.0	0.0	0.0	0.0
Out-of-quota tariff	%	214.3	150.0	125.0	100.0	75.0	75.0	75.0	75.0	75.0	75.0	75.0
RUSSIAN FEDERATION												
Beef tariff-quota	kt pw	566.7	570.0	570.0	570.0	570.0	570.0	570.0	0.0	0.0	0.0	0.0
In-quota tariff	%	15.0	15.0	15.0	15.0	15.0	15.0	15.0	0.0	0.0	0.0	0.0
Out-of-quota tariff	%	50.0	55.0	55.0	55.0	55.0	55.0	55.0	27.5	27.5	9.2	0.0
Pigmeat tariff-quota	kt pw	453.3	430.0	430.0	430.0	430.0	430.0	430.0	0.0	0.0	0.0	0.0
In-quota tariff	%	5.0	0.0	0.0	0.0	0.0	0.0	0.0	0.0	0.0	0.0	0.0
Out-of-quota tariff	%	68.3	65.0	65.0	65.0	65.0	65.0	65.0	25.0	25.0	25.0	25.0
Poultry tariff-quota	kt pw	368.7	378.0	378.0	378.0	378.0	378.0	378.0	0.0	0.0	0.0	0.0
In-quota tariff	%	25.0	25.0	25.0	25.0	25.0	25.0	25.0	0.0	0.0	0.0	0.0
Out-of-quota tariff	%	80.0	80.0	80.0	80.0	80.0	80.0	80.0	37.5	37.5	37.5	38.0
UNITED STATES												
Beef tariff-quota	kt pw	696.6	696.6	696.6	696.6	696.6	696.6	696.6	696.6	696.6	696.6	696.6
In-quota tariff	%	4.8	4.8	4.8	4.8	4.8	4.8	4.8	4.8	4.8	4.8	4.8
Out-of-quota tariff	%	26.4	26.4	26.4	26.4	26.4	26.4	26.4	26.4	26.4	26.4	26.4

Table A.24. **Main policy assumptions for meat markets** (*cont.*)

		Average 2011-13est	2014	2015	2016	2017	2018	2019	2020	2021	2022	2023
CHINA												
Beef tariff	%	15.5	15.5	15.5	15.5	15.5	15.5	15.5	15.5	16.5	16.5	16.5
Pigmeat tariff	%	16.0	16.0	16.0	16.0	16.0	16.0	16.0	16.0	16.0	16.0	16.0
Sheep meat tariff	%	15.0	15.0	15.0	15.0	15.0	15.0	15.0	15.0	15.0	15.0	15.0
Poultry meat tariff	%	19.1	19.1	19.1	19.1	19.1	19.1	19.1	19.1	19.1	19.1	19.1
INDIA												
Beef tariff	%	100.0	100.0	100.0	100.0	100.0	100.0	100.0	100.0	100.0	100.0	100.0
Pigmeat tariff	%	100.0	100.0	100.0	100.0	100.0	100.0	100.0	100.0	100.0	100.0	100.0
Sheep meat tariff	%	91.9	91.9	91.9	91.9	91.9	91.9	91.9	91.9	91.9	91.9	91.9
Poultry meat tariff	%	87.0	87.0	87.0	87.0	87.0	87.0	87.0	87.0	87.0	87.0	87.0
Eggs tariff	%	150.0	150.0	150.0	150.0	150.0	150.0	150.0	150.0	150.0	150.0	150.0
SOUTH AFRICA												
Sheep meat tariff-quota	kt pw	6.0	6.0	6.0	6.0	6.0	6.0	6.0	6.0	6.0	6.0	6.0
In-quota tariff	%	20.0	20.0	20.0	20.0	20.0	20.0	20.0	20.0	20.0	20.0	20.0
Out-of-quota tariff	%	96.0	96.0	96.0	96.0	96.0	96.0	96.0	96.0	96.0	96.0	96.0

.. Not available

Note: Average 2011-13est: Data for 2013 are estimated.

1. Till 2014, EU farmers can be granted the Single payment scheme (SPS) or the Single area payment scheme (SAPS), which provides flat-rate payments independent from current production decisions and market developments. From 2015, it becomes the Basic payment scheme (BPS) and it shall account for 68% maximum of the national direct payment envelopes. On top of this, from 2015 onwards, new compulsory policy instruments are introduced: the Green Payment (30%) and young farmer scheme (2%).
2. EU budget ceiling for coupled suckler cow premium, applicable to Belgium, Spain, France, Austria and Portugal. The situation after 2014 is not yet known as member states shall inform the Commission on their decision to grant coupled payments on the 1st of august 2014.
3. Price for R3 grade male cattle.
4. Safety-net trigger.
5. 80% of this basic rate is granted to milk ewes and goats; an additional premium of EUR 3.5/head is granted in Less Favoured Areas. This payment scheme applies only in Portugal and Finland. The situation after 2014 is not yet known as member states shall inform the Commission on their decision to grant coupled payments on the 1st of august 2014.
6. Includes live trade.
7. Year beginning 1 April.
8. Pig carcass imports. Emergency import procedures triggered from November 1995 to March 1996, from July 1996 to June 1997, from August 2001 to March 2002, from August 2002 to March 2003, from August 2003 to March 2004 and from August 2004 to March 2005.

Source: OECD and FAO Secretariats.

StatLink ⌐⌐⌐ *http://dx.doi.org/10.1787/888933102012*

Table A.25. World fish and seafood projections

Calendar year

		Average 2011-13est	2014	2015	2016	2017	2018	2019	2020	2021	2022	2023
FISH												
World												
Production	kt	158 828	166 515	168 448	171 963	174 218	176 618	178 758	178 903	182 263	184 130	18 095
of which aquaculture	kt	66 254	72 830	75 304	77 508	79 774	82 187	84 330	86 083	87 796	89 625	9 562
Consumption	kt	158 082	165 506	167 539	171 104	173 559	176 009	178 324	178 419	181 929	183 946	18 986
of which for food	kt	135 794	143 762	147 002	149 591	152 253	154 924	157 504	159 097	161 389	163 681	16 890
of which for reduction	kt	16 082	15 697	14 688	15 762	15 654	15 532	15 365	13 944	15 133	14 930	1 833
Price												
Aquaculture[1]	USD/t	2 118.6	2 149.9	2 177.7	2 171.4	2 239.2	2 217.9	2 222.9	2 335.5	2 356.6	2 468.0	2 4 4.1
Capture[2]	USD/t	1 455.3	1 498.5	1 552.8	1 593.9	1 632.5	1 695.2	1 733.6	1 817.9	1 850.8	1 932.6	1 9 7.3
Product traded[3]	USD/t	2 810.2	2 791.7	2 867.8	2 903.3	2 925.7	3 025.9	3 044.7	3 208.6	3 212.2	3 367.0	3 3 8.1
Developed countries												
Production	kt	28 650	29 518	29 572	29 325	29 261	29 336	29 474	29 570	29 613	29 660	29 32
of which aquaculture	kt	4 263	4 524	4 551	4 663	4 817	5 006	5 189	5 343	5 490	5 616	5 37
Consumption	kt	36 576	37 210	37 289	37 231	37 345	37 398	37 630	37 669	37 800	37 811	37 49
of which for food	kt	31 467	32 014	32 160	32 285	32 489	32 615	32 890	32 976	33 169	33 225	33 99
of which for reduction	kt	4 035	4 193	4 133	3 957	3 874	3 807	3 769	3 728	3 666	3 621	3 55
Developing countries												
Production	kt	130 178	136 996	138 876	142 638	144 958	147 282	149 284	149 334	152 650	154 470	156 34
of which aquaculture	kt	61 991	68 306	70 753	72 846	74 957	77 181	79 141	80 740	82 306	84 009	85 85
Consumption	kt	121 506	128 296	130 251	133 874	136 214	138 611	140 695	140 751	144 130	146 135	148 03
of which for food	kt	104 327	111 749	114 842	117 307	119 764	122 309	124 613	126 121	128 221	130 456	132 49
of which for reduction	kt	12 046	11 505	10 555	11 805	11 780	11 724	11 595	10 216	11 467	11 309	11 24
OECD												
Production	kt	31 472	31 915	32 144	32 429	32 558	32 767	32 919	32 536	33 142	33 155	33 21
of which aquaculture	kt	5 921	6 273	6 348	6 520	6 755	7 028	7 296	7 543	7 776	7 940	8 12
Consumption	kt	38 815	38 951	39 347	39 749	40 034	40 162	40 359	40 029	40 590	40 595	40 747
of which for food	kt	31 543	32 131	32 341	32 568	32 856	33 024	33 314	33 420	33 634	33 762	33 948
of which for reduction	kt	6 092	5 717	5 909	6 092	6 096	6 063	5 975	5 544	5 891	5 767	5 734
FISHMEAL												
World												
Production	kt	5 181.9	5 336.2	5 178.0	5 460.3	5 466.6	5 476.6	5 469.6	5 161.5	5 487.2	5 477.6	5 491.5
from whole fish	kt	3 753.1	3 673.8	3 443.3	3 700.5	3 682.9	3 661.2	3 629.4	3 304.1	3 587.6	3 546.7	3 530.0
Consumption	kt	5 121.7	5 398.7	5 359.3	5 324.1	5 380.8	5 452.1	5 479.8	5 428.5	5 371.9	5 397.6	5 481.4
Variation in stocks	kt	60.2	-62.5	-181.3	136.1	85.7	24.5	-10.2	-266.9	115.3	80.0	10.1
Price[4]	USD/t	1 614.1	1 674.3	1 691.1	1 481.8	1 489.1	1 495.2	1 524.6	1 610.1	1 560.8	1 591.1	1 616.1
Developed countries												
Production	kt	1 345.0	1 402.2	1 404.7	1 372.3	1 363.4	1 360.3	1 365.3	1 367.8	1 365.8	1 366.9	1 370.0
from whole fish	kt	948.7	992.2	983.5	943.4	925.6	911.6	904.5	896.6	883.6	874.6	867.9
Consumption	kt	1 787.6	1 732.0	1 688.2	1 605.5	1 575.7	1 555.3	1 536.8	1 413.2	1 406.1	1 389.0	1 392.3
Variation in stocks	kt	-4.3	-3.0	-50.3	45.1	0.7	-0.5	-0.2	-45.9	44.3	0.0	0.1
Developing countries												
Production	kt	3 836.9	3 934.0	3 773.3	4 087.9	4 103.2	4 116.3	4 104.3	3 793.7	4 121.5	4 110.7	4 121.4
from whole fish	kt	2 804.4	2 681.6	2 459.8	2 757.1	2 757.3	2 749.6	2 724.9	2 407.6	2 704.0	2 672.1	2 662.1
Consumption	kt	3 334.1	3 666.7	3 671.1	3 718.6	3 805.1	3 896.8	3 943.0	4 015.3	3 965.8	4 008.6	4 089.0
Variation in stocks	kt	64.4	-59.5	-131.0	91.0	85.0	25.0	-10.0	-221.0	71.0	80.0	10.0
OECD												
Production	kt	1 771.5	1 706.0	1 763.0	1 810.3	1 819.0	1 821.0	1 811.8	1 723.2	1 810.5	1 790.9	1 791.5
from whole fish	kt	1 389.7	1 311.7	1 358.4	1 398.8	1 399.4	1 391.4	1 370.9	1 272.7	1 349.9	1 321.1	1 312.7
Consumption	kt	1 972.3	1 967.4	1 943.8	1 891.3	1 873.5	1 866.9	1 860.2	1 742.0	1 743.0	1 733.0	1 754.3
Variation in stocks	kt	15.1	-3.0	-95.3	90.1	0.7	-0.5	-0.2	-90.9	89.3	0.0	0.1

Table A.25. **World fish and seafood projections** (cont.)

Calendar year

		Average 2011-13est	2014	2015	2016	2017	2018	2019	2020	2021	2022	2023
FISH OIL													
World													
Production	kt	1 084.3	1 073.1	1 035.4	1 108.4	1 118.0	1 123.8	1 127.0	1 065.3	1 139.6	1 152.1	1 162.8
from whole fish	kt	716.0	707.1	656.5	717.7	715.3	711.6	705.1	633.4	697.8	689.6	686.7
Consumption	kt	1 073.3	1 081.3	1 077.9	1 078.4	1 099.5	1 124.2	1 127.4	1 121.5	1 095.6	1 141.5	1 162.1
Variation in stocks	kt	11.0	-8.2	-42.5	30.0	18.6	-0.3	-0.4	-56.3	43.9	10.6	0.7
Price[5]	USD/t	1 821.2	1 843.2	1 947.4	1 844.1	1 879.5	1 925.2	1 974.4	2 153.9	2 034.1	2 051.7	2 072.4
Developed countries													
Production	kt	389.5	376.0	379.1	377.4	380.2	382.0	385.0	387.4	388.9	391.1	393.7
from whole fish	kt	177.3	187.1	183.9	176.4	172.9	169.9	167.9	165.7	162.6	160.3	158.4
Consumption	kt	616.7	581.0	576.6	578.4	588.9	602.3	607.4	605.6	580.1	611.0	620.8
Variation in stocks	kt	5.0	-0.2	-12.5	5.0	-6.4	-0.3	-0.4	-11.3	8.9	0.6	0.7
Developing countries													
Production	kt	694.8	697.1	656.3	731.0	737.8	741.9	742.0	677.9	750.7	761.0	769.1
from whole fish	kt	538.7	520.1	472.6	541.3	542.4	541.8	537.2	467.7	535.3	529.3	528.3
Consumption	kt	456.7	500.2	501.3	500.0	510.6	521.9	519.9	515.9	515.5	530.4	541.4
Variation in stocks	kt	6.0	-8.0	-30.0	25.0	25.0	0.0	0.0	-45.0	35.0	10.0	0.0
OECD													
Production	kt	597.2	560.4	578.5	595.8	604.2	609.1	611.4	595.4	619.9	630.8	639.5
from whole fish	kt	309.5	293.9	303.9	313.5	313.8	312.1	307.5	285.1	303.1	296.7	295.0
Consumption	kt	839.6	829.5	818.8	818.9	829.8	845.0	846.9	840.0	808.5	851.3	863.2
Variation in stocks	kt	3.3	-0.2	-12.5	15.0	3.6	-0.3	-0.4	-26.3	23.9	0.6	0.7

Note: The term "fish" indicates fish, crustaceans, molluscs and other aquatic animals, but excludes aquatic mammals, crocodiles, caimans, alligators and aquatic plants.

Average 2011-13est: Data for 2013 are estimated.

1. World unit value of aquaculture fisheries production (live weight basis).
2. FAO estimated value of world ex vessel value of capture fisheries production excluding for reduction.
3. World unit value of trade (sum of exports and imports).
4. Fishmeal, 64-65% protein, Hamburg, Germany.
5. Fish oil, any origin, N.W. Europe.

Source: OECD and FAO Secretariats.

StatLink ⟨⟨⟨ http://dx.doi.org/10.1787/888933102031

Table A.26.1. Fish and seafood projections: Production and trade

Calendar year

	PRODUCTION (kt)		Growth (%)[3]		IMPORTS (kt)		Growth (%)[3]		EXPORTS (kt)		Growth (%)[3]	
	Average 2011-13est	2023	2004-13	2014-23	Average 2011-13est	2023	2004-13	2014-23	Average 2011-13est	2023	2004-13	2014-23
WORLD	**158 828**	**186 095**	**2.11**	**1.22**	**37 058**	**45 432**	**2.18**	**1.97**	**37 838**	**45 532**	**2.73**	**1.70**
DEVELOPED COUNTRIES	**28 650**	**29 732**	**-0.42**	**0.10**	**20 405**	**23 004**	**0.55**	**1.30**	**12 509**	**14 787**	**1.72**	**1.96**
NORTH AMERICA	6 550	6 497	-0.53	-0.08	5 470	6 637	1.19	1.77	2 942	3 231	0.42	1.27
Canada	1 013	1 118	-3.08	0.99	654	812	1.41	2.46	796	1 031	-2.82	3.01
United States	5 537	5 379	0.01	-0.29	4 817	5 824	1.16	1.67	2 146	2 200	1.90	2.75
EUROPE	16 173	17 243	0.26	0.30	10 234	12 040	1.16	1.90	8 353	10 219	2.63	-0.10
European Union	6 198	6 075	-1.80	-0.73	7 754	9 218	1.31	1.94	2 233	2 713	-0.06	-4.90
Norway	3 559	4 601	2.27	2.24	262	212	2.21	-2.51	2 985	4 083	5.73	0.30
Russian Federation	4 408	4 640	4.46	0.32	1 171	1 465	0.67	3.20	1 749	2 253	2.63	0.39
OCEANIA DEVELOPED	776	838	-2.01	0.77	517	633	2.44	1.78	450	413	-2.58	-0.07
Australia	239	287	-1.48	1.26	463	583	2.23	1.95	56	30	-4.30	2.01
New Zealand	537	551	-2.24	0.53	54	50	4.57	0.00	394	383	-2.32	1.73
OTHER DEVELOPED[1]	5 151	5 154	-1.97	-0.42	4 183	3 694	-1.68	-1.16	764	925	0.28	1.60
Japan	4 395	4 364	-1.92	-0.41	3 699	3 118	-2.46	-1.67	556	688	0.60	3.11
South Africa	637	664	-2.90	-0.71	163	247	10.36	4.36	162	204	0.12	-2.24
DEVELOPING COUNTRIES	**130 178**	**156 364**	**2.75**	**1.45**	**16 654**	**22 428**	**4.53**	**2.70**	**25 329**	**30 745**	**3.28**	**1.11**
AFRICA	8 890	10 244	2.94	0.74	3 896	4 832	4.12	2.48	1 712	1 509	0.06	-1.47
NORTH AFRICA	2 767	3 208	4.02	0.43	628	1 000	6.02	5.81	462	418	3.58	-1.95
Egypt	1 439	1 784	6.85	0.86	343	610	2.67	6.58	18	8	14.79	1.71
SUB-SAHARAN AFRICA	6 123	7 036	2.47	0.89	3 268	3 832	3.76	1.73	1 250	1 091	-1.05	-1.99
Ghana	380	415	-0.26	0.56	306	337	-0.58	0.88	31	42	-7.78	2.26
Nigeria	908	1 145	7.00	1.92	1 398	1 662	2.61	1.91	8	5	-0.22	1.25
LATIN AMERICA and CARIBBEAN	16 483	17 353	-3.16	1.12	1 988	3 131	6.97	3.41	4 127	5 147	0.60	5.92
Argentina	814	903	-2.81	0.51	60	60	4.49	0.00	650	771	-2.04	2.31
Brazil	1 554	2 088	6.00	2.50	638	1 318	11.72	6.00	41	68	-12.52	3.07
Chile	3 632	4 366	-5.44	2.38	63	60	4.49	0.00	1 361	1 834	-0.82	3.17
Mexico	1 694	1 715	2.21	0.30	317	459	6.12	2.41	178	256	2.87	1.17
Peru	6 387	5 968	-5.71	0.60	98	70	10.45	-5.11	659	855	6.10	0.10
ASIA and PACIFIC	104 805	128 767	3.92	1.56	10 770	14 465	4.27	2.63	19 490	24 090	4.26	0.60
China[2]	57 098	72 113	4.12	1.72	3 502	4 470	5.38	1.58	8 082	10 335	4.37	2.20
India	8 735	10 639	4.27	1.30	20	305	7.28	38.51	1 035	1 155	8.52	-0.27
Indonesia	8 799	11 277	5.82	2.12	226	441	22.54	5.65	1 320	2 016	4.79	2.85
Korea	2 193	2 192	0.37	0.44	1 590	1 848	-0.39	1.40	720	720	6.73	-0.21
Philippines	3 143	3 456	1.55	0.42	276	549	12.07	14.22	359	92	9.55	-12.05
Thailand	2 992	3 307	-4.27	1.37	1 671	2 001	2.71	1.45	2 278	3 190	0.50	4.10
Viet Nam	5 671	6 811	7.45	1.21	260	375	19.48	3.09	2 370	2 825	11.73	1.37
LEAST DEVELOPED COUNTRIES (LDC)	**12 651**	**15 150**	**5.62**	**1.30**	**811**	**873**	**11.01**	**1.07**	**1 425**	**1 454**	**2.12**	**-0.22**
OECD	**31 472**	**33 212**	**-1.36**	**0.42**	**20 109**	**22 677**	**0.47**	**1.21**	**12 792**	**15 142**	**1.61**	**1.55**
BRICS	**72 432**	**90 144**	**4.11**	**1.59**	**5 493**	**7 805**	**4.90**	**3.13**	**11 069**	**14 015**	**4.19**	**2.12**

Note: Fish: The term "fish" indicates fish, crustaceans, molluscs and other aquatic animals, but excludes aquatic mammals, crocodiles, caimans, alligators and aquatic plants. Imports and exports refer to trade of food fish i.e. for human consumption.

Average 2011-13est: Data for 2013 are estimated.

1. Includes Israel and also transition economies: Kazakhstan, Kyrgyzstan, Tajikistan, Turkmenistan, Uzbekistan, Armenia, Azerbaijan and Georgia.
2. Refers to mainland only. The economies of Chinese Taipei, Hong Kong (China) and Macau (China) are included in the Other Asia Pacific aggregate.
3. Least-squares growth rate (see glossary).

Source: OECD and FAO Secretariats.

StatLink ᴍᴀᴘ *http://dx.doi.org/10.1787/888933102050*

Table A.26.2. Fish and seafood projections: Reduction, food use, per capita

Calendar year

	REDUCTION (kt)		Growth (%)[3]		FOOD USE (kt)		Growth (%)[3]		PER CAPITA (kg)		Growth (%)[3]	
	Average 2011-13est	2023	2004-13	2014-23	Average 2011-13est	2023	2004-13	2014-23	Average 2011-13est	2023	2004-13	2014-23
WORLD	**16 082**	**14 833**	**-3.79**	**-0.58**	**135 794**	**165 890**	**2.95**	**1.57**	**19.2**	**20.9**	**1.73**	**0.54**
DEVELOPED COUNTRIES	**4 035**	**3 585**	**-4.08**	**-1.71**	**31 467**	**33 399**	**-0.22**	**0.48**	**22.6**	**23.2**	**-0.69**	**0.19**
NORTH AMERICA	802	723	0.93	-0.68	7 954	8 864	-0.21	0.79	22.6	23.1	-1.12	0.01
Canada	42	57	-7.95	0.98	796	817	0.69	0.10	22.9	21.2	-0.41	-0.82
United States	760	666	1.73	-0.82	7 158	8 047	-0.31	0.87	22.5	23.3	-1.19	0.10
EUROPE	2 057	1 862	-6.61	-1.99	15 372	16 652	0.50	0.77	20.7	22.4	0.33	0.77
European Union	762	534	-3.55	-3.88	10 607	11 696	-0.29	0.99	20.9	22.6	-0.61	0.85
Norway	390	300	-10.71	-3.51	287	330	2.61	1.39	57.5	59.6	1.50	0.42
Russian Federation	353	329	3.93	-0.83	3 361	3 424	3.67	-0.04	23.5	24.8	3.75	0.29
OCEANIA DEVELOPED	121	117	-2.73	-0.25	722	941	1.69	2.03	26.3	30.1	0.12	0.85
Australia	39	36	-2.85	-1.02	607	804	1.87	2.22	26.3	30.5	0.21	0.99
New Zealand	81	81	-2.60	0.12	116	137	0.76	0.96	25.9	27.7	-0.33	0.04
OTHER DEVELOPED[1]	1 056	881	-1.35	-2.08	7 418	6 942	-1.73	-0.69	27.7	24.9	-2.36	-1.06
Japan	739	496	-1.90	-4.05	6 716	6 198	-1.90	-0.77	52.8	49.9	-1.93	-0.53
South Africa	317	386	0.24	1.26	317	321	-4.03	-1.23	6.0	5.7	-5.15	-1.81
DEVELOPING COUNTRIES	**12 046**	**11 248**	**-3.66**	**-0.18**	**104 327**	**132 492**	**4.08**	**1.86**	**18.4**	**20.4**	**2.67**	**0.66**
AFRICA	495	506	-1.37	-0.60	10 381	12 886	4.13	1.77	10.2	9.7	1.54	-0.66
NORTH AFRICA	296	304	1.35	-0.97	2 602	3 461	4.84	2.30	15.4	17.6	3.24	0.95
Egypt	0	0	..	..	1 764	2 387	5.87	2.24	21.8	25.2	4.11	0.81
SUB-SAHARAN AFRICA	198	202	-4.65	0.00	7 779	9 425	3.90	1.58	9.1	8.3	1.11	-1.04
Ghana	0	0	..	..	647	710	0.09	0.59	25.5	22.6	-2.32	-1.31
Nigeria	0	0	..	..	2 298	2 802	4.23	1.92	13.6	12.3	1.43	-0.79
LATIN AMERICA and CARIBBEAN	7 949	7 361	-4.63	0.39	5 960	7 657	2.70	2.04	9.8	11.3	1.52	1.07
Argentina	0	0	..	..	231	192	-2.90	-2.14	5.6	4.3	-3.75	-2.89
Brazil	57	45	1.99	-2.48	2 093	3 293	8.69	3.78	10.5	15.3	7.68	3.06
Chile	1 990	2 209	-6.18	2.35	254	282	-0.53	0.94	14.6	14.8	-1.47	0.17
Mexico	566	485	7.67	0.03	1 268	1 432	0.87	0.58	10.5	10.5	-0.38	-0.45
Peru	5 078	4 354	-5.36	-0.31	685	809	3.01	2.46	22.8	23.7	1.85	1.27
ASIA and PACIFIC	3 603	3 381	-1.58	-1.24	87 986	111 949	4.17	1.86	21.7	25.0	3.01	0.97
China[2]	1 194	1 129	-5.82	-1.85	48 224	62 120	4.26	1.81	35.0	43.0	3.61	1.41
India	264	242	-0.81	-0.79	7 272	9 447	3.77	1.95	5.9	6.8	2.41	0.89
Indonesia	30	30	0.06	0.00	7 417	9 622	5.84	2.38	30.0	34.7	4.42	1.34
Korea	54	38	-11.47	-0.91	2 846	3 183	0.92	1.17	58.1	62.0	0.33	0.77
Philippines	0	0	..	..	3 060	3 913	1.47	2.21	31.7	33.8	-0.25	0.58
Thailand	716	616	-3.58	-1.79	1 652	1 502	-3.84	-1.65	24.7	22.1	-4.11	-1.76
Viet Nam	414	334	11.41	-3.01	3 155	4 026	5.31	1.70	34.7	40.7	4.32	0.97
LEAST DEVELOPED COUNTRIES (LDC)	**374**	**434**	**9.61**	**1.22**	**10 834**	**13 765**	**6.24**	**1.95**	**12.5**	**12.5**	**3.86**	**-0.25**
OECD	**6 092**	**5 734**	**-4.66**	**-0.37**	**31 543**	**33 948**	**-0.39**	**0.62**	**24.3**	**24.8**	**-1.05**	**0.14**
BRICS	**2 187**	**2 130**	**-3.07**	**-1.10**	**61 266**	**78 605**	**4.23**	**1.80**	**20.4**	**24.2**	**3.30**	**1.13**

.. Not available

Note: Fish: The term "fish" indicates fish, crustaceans, molluscs and other aquatic animals, but excludes aquatic mammals, crocodiles, caimans, alligators and aquatic plants. Imports and exports refer to trade of food fish i.e. for human consumption.
Average 2011-13est: Data for 2013 are estimated.

1. Includes Israel and also transition economies: Kazakhstan, Kyrgyzstan, Tajikistan, Turkmenistan, Uzbekistan, Armenia, Azerbaijan and Georgia.
2. Refers to mainland only. The economies of Chinese Taipei, Hong Kong (China) and Macau (China) are included in the Other Asia Pacific aggregate.
3. Least-squares growth rate (see glossary).

Source: OECD and FAO Secretariats.

StatLink ⓘ⫘ *http://dx.doi.org/10.1787/888933102069*

Table A.27.1. World dairy projections: Butter and cheese

Calendar year

		Average 2011-13est	2014	2015	2016	2017	2018	2019	2020	2021	2022	2023
BUTTER												
World												
Production	kt pw	9 885	10 460	10 651	10 887	11 125	11 364	11 596	11 842	12 102	12 358	12 620
Consumption	kt pw	9 880	10 422	10 627	10 861	11 101	11 340	11 578	11 825	12 085	12 337	12 598
Stock changes	kt pw	-8	20	6	7	5	5	-1	-2	-1	2	3
Price[1]	USD/t	3 939	3 686	3 538	3 551	3 581	3 569	3 593	3 644	3 630	3 681	3 695
Developed countries												
Production	kt pw	4 473	4 640	4 647	4 681	4 712	4 749	4 769	4 795	4 834	4 868	4 906
Consumption	kt pw	3 997	4 107	4 121	4 142	4 163	4 185	4 196	4 214	4 239	4 264	4 289
Developing countries												
Production	kt pw	5 412	5 820	6 004	6 206	6 413	6 615	6 827	7 047	7 268	7 490	7 714
Consumption	kt pw	5 882	6 315	6 506	6 719	6 938	7 155	7 382	7 611	7 846	8 074	8 308
OECD[2]												
Production	kt pw	4 149	4 311	4 305	4 338	4 365	4 395	4 411	4 432	4 467	4 495	4 526
Consumption	kt pw	3 579	3 721	3 737	3 761	3 780	3 801	3 809	3 824	3 845	3 866	3 887
Stock changes	kt pw	31	20	6	7	6	5	0	-2	-1	2	2
CHEESE												
World												
Production	kt pw	21 210	21 791	22 231	22 645	23 028	23 412	23 786	24 173	24 524	24 879	25 251
Consumption	kt pw	21 042	21 609	22 010	22 427	22 811	23 198	23 573	23 960	24 308	24 667	25 039
Stock changes	kt pw	-42	-33	7	3	3	1	0	-1	1	-2	-1
Price[3]	USD/t	4 175	4 152	4 131	4 223	4 314	4 377	4 467	4 566	4 633	4 756	4 851
Developed countries												
Production	kt pw	17 030	17 493	17 844	18 185	18 469	18 713	18 963	19 270	19 527	19 796	20 025
Consumption	kt pw	16 414	16 760	17 013	17 272	17 491	17 699	17 901	18 134	18 294	18 490	18 676
Developing countries												
Production	kt pw	4 180	4 298	4 387	4 460	4 558	4 699	4 823	4 903	4 996	5 083	5 226
Consumption	kt pw	4 628	4 849	4 997	5 155	5 320	5 499	5 671	5 826	6 014	6 177	6 362
OECD[2]												
Production	kt pw	16 408	16 800	17 145	17 460	17 731	17 968	18 216	18 507	18 744	18 992	19 200
Consumption	kt pw	15 655	15 963	16 201	16 449	16 658	16 856	17 045	17 266	17 413	17 600	17 774
Stock changes	kt pw	3	-33	7	3	3	1	0	-1	1	-2	-1

Note: Calendar year: Year ending 30 June for Australia and 31 May for New Zealand in OECD aggregate.

　　Average 2011-13est: Data for 2013 are estimated.

1. F.o.b. export price, butter, 82% butterfat, Oceania.
2. Excludes Iceland but includes all EU28 member countries.
3. F.o.b. export price, cheddar cheese, 39% moisture, Oceania.

Source: OECD and FAO Secretariats

StatLink ᵃᵐˢᵖ *http://dx.doi.org/10.1787/888933102088*

Table A.27.2. World dairy projections: Powders and casein

Calendar year

		Average 2011-13est	2014	2015	2016	2017	2018	2019	2020	2021	2022	2023
SKIM MILK POWDER												
World												
Production	kt pw	3 759	3 907	4 001	4 085	4 175	4 256	4 329	4 400	4 486	4 560	4 633
Consumption	kt pw	3 800	3 932	4 017	4 093	4 159	4 238	4 298	4 370	4 451	4 543	4 616
Stock changes	kt pw	-17	-43	-34	-25	-3	0	12	11	17	-1	-1
Price[1]	USD/t	3 740	3 865	3 706	3 702	3 732	3 758	3 816	3 829	3 799	3 788	3 806
Developed countries												
Production	kt pw	3 279	3 443	3 531	3 608	3 685	3 761	3 819	3 881	3 962	4 029	4 093
Consumption	kt pw	1 880	1 872	1 912	1 940	1 959	1 976	1 981	2 000	2 026	2 062	2 080
Developing countries												
Production	kt pw	480	464	470	477	489	495	509	519	524	531	540
Consumption	kt pw	1 920	2 060	2 104	2 153	2 200	2 261	2 317	2 370	2 425	2 482	2 536
OECD[2]												
Production	kt pw	3 091	3 235	3 322	3 396	3 472	3 541	3 597	3 656	3 735	3 799	3 856
Consumption	kt pw	1 953	1 900	1 943	1 973	1 994	2 012	2 019	2 041	2 069	2 106	2 127
Stock changes	kt pw	-67	14	-4	-5	-3	0	2	1	7	-1	-1
WHOLE MILK POWDER												
World												
Production	kt pw	4 705	4 928	5 055	5 183	5 279	5 412	5 530	5 662	5 772	5 899	6 022
Consumption	kt pw	4 717	4 947	5 074	5 202	5 298	5 431	5 549	5 681	5 790	5 918	6 040
Stock changes	kt pw	31	0	0	0	0	0	0	0	0	0	0
Price[3]	USD/t	3 937	4 390	4 159	4 178	4 189	4 214	4 254	4 274	4 268	4 280	4 293
Developed countries												
Production	kt pw	2 129	2 214	2 280	2 299	2 336	2 376	2 417	2 454	2 500	2 536	2 579
Consumption	kt pw	527	513	521	525	531	536	541	546	551	557	562
Developing countries												
Production	kt pw	2 576	2 714	2 775	2 884	2 943	3 037	3 113	3 208	3 272	3 363	3 442
Consumption	kt pw	4 189	4 434	4 553	4 677	4 767	4 895	5 008	5 135	5 239	5 361	5 479
OECD[2]												
Production	kt pw	2 357	2 458	2 522	2 539	2 580	2 626	2 673	2 713	2 762	2 804	2 852
Consumption	kt pw	796	787	797	803	810	816	822	828	834	842	849
Stock changes	kt pw	0	0	0	0	0	0	0	0	0	0	0
WHEY POWDER												
Wholesale price, United States[4]	USD/t	1 241	1 236	1 209	1 241	1 257	1 249	1 243	1 234	1 189	1 196	1 204
CASEIN												
Price[5]	USD/t	8 735	8 883	8 829	8 808	8 899	8 923	9 044	9 121	9 089	9 127	9 216

Note: Calendar year: Year ending 30 June for Australia and 31 May for New Zealand in OECD aggregate.

    Average 2011-13est: Data for 2013 are estimated.

1. F.o.b. export price, non-fat dry milk, 1.25% butterfat, Oceania.
2. Excludes Iceland but includes all EU28 member countries.
3. F.o.b. export price, WMP 26% butterfat, Oceania.
4. Dry whey, West Region, United States.
5. Export price, New Zealand.

Source: OECD and FAO Secretariats.

StatLink ⟐⟐ *http://dx.doi.org/10.1787/888933102107*

Table A.28.1. Butter projections: Production and trade

Calendar year

	PRODUCTION (kt)		Growth (%)[4]		IMPORTS (kt)		Growth (%)[4]		EXPORTS (kt)		Growth (%)[4]	
	Average 2011-13est	2023	2004-13	2014-23	Average 2011-13est	2023	2004-13	2014-23	Average 2011-13est	2023	2004-13	2014-23
WORLD	**9 885**	**12 620**	**1.79**	**2.12**	**823**	**905**	**-1.72**	**0.68**	**844**	**924**	**-1.05**	**0.66**
DEVELOPED COUNTRIES	**4 473**	**4 906**	**0.53**	**0.64**	**288**	**225**	**-6.96**	**-2.34**	**743**	**840**	**-1.64**	**0.72**
NORTH AMERICA	929	1 106	4.02	1.67	20	13	-9.00	-4.38	60	111	25.46	5.49
Canada	91	84	1.35	-1.11	7	6	-8.20	0.00	0	0	-3.81	0.00
United States	838	1 021	4.35	1.93	13	8	-9.36	-6.56	60	111	27.08	5.50
EUROPE	2 790	2 984	-0.41	0.30	204	147	-8.54	-2.61	208	227	-8.45	-0.10
European Union	2 237	2 330	-0.23	0.09	29	23	-14.33	-1.56	124	138	-11.89	0.73
Russian Federation	272	358	-2.66	2.20	159	116	-8.07	-2.82	3	3	-4.23	0.00
Ukraine	84	84	-4.10	-0.12	8	2	141.77	-8.42	2	5	-32.59	3.11
OCEANIA DEVELOPED	621	666	0.74	0.44	22	25	11.46	0.51	474	500	1.57	0.31
Australia	121	139	-2.52	1.60	21	24	10.93	0.52	52	67	-5.39	3.07
New Zealand	501	527	1.68	0.15	1	1	..	0.00	423	433	2.77	-0.05
OTHER DEVELOPED[1]	133	150	-0.92	1.16	44	41	-1.73	-2.09	2	1	-1.90	-1.70
Japan	67	67	-2.28	-0.06	9	8	-15.61	-4.75	0	0	..	..
South Africa	13	12	0.75	-0.06	4	7	7.26	3.51	1	1	4.17	-3.55
DEVELOPING COUNTRIES	**5 412**	**7 714**	**2.93**	**3.19**	**534**	**680**	**2.40**	**1.91**	**101**	**84**	**4.85**	**0.11**
AFRICA	301	410	2.97	2.87	126	164	2.59	2.53	4	3	28.39	-0.63
NORTH AFRICA	172	207	2.28	1.72	108	136	3.35	2.90	3	2	58.58	-1.26
Algeria	3	4	2.09	2.38	16	23	2.71	3.54	0	0	0.00	-3.42
Egypt	128	147	1.24	1.43	72	99	10.73	3.93	3	2	77.10	-1.33
SUB-SAHARAN AFRICA	129	202	3.95	4.19	18	28	-0.60	1.11	1	1	12.63	0.67
LATIN AMERICA and CARIBBEAN	243	275	1.58	1.00	51	61	-3.71	0.52	58	39	10.44	-1.83
Argentina	54	64	3.39	1.83	0	0	..	..	23	20	22.80	0.18
Brazil	81	90	0.62	0.94	3	3	28.54	1.38	1	1	-5.93	5.83
Chile	23	30	6.72	1.78	3	5	6.89	1.74	4	5	18.86	-1.71
Mexico	14	14	-2.79	0.24	24	25	-8.66	-3.12	3	1	20.22	-21.86
Uruguay	17	16	-0.80	-0.68	0	0	0.00	0.88	17	12	3.71	-0.87
ASIA and PACIFIC	4 868	7 029	2.99	3.31	358	454	3.45	1.90	39	41	-0.83	2.40
Bangladesh	27	39	4.04	3.32	4	9	2.33	9.27	0	0	10.50	-0.65
China[2]	109	137	1.12	1.69	46	57	19.79	1.13	2	0	47.66	0.00
India	3 543	5 321	3.35	3.72	3	2	2.00	1.05	9	8	7.95	-1.21
Indonesia	0	0	0.00	-53.38	16	21	2.41	2.79	1	0	29.34	-2.72
Iran, Islamic Republic of	187	207	-1.25	1.16	46	66	4.50	1.00	1	0	-10.10	-0.12
Korea	5	7	-1.14	2.53	8	8	25.83	1.25	0	0	..	..
Malaysia	0	0	0.00	-2.45	14	16	2.86	0.94	4	4	17.23	-0.93
Pakistan	689	912	2.68	2.53	0	0	-8.18	2.32	1	1	82.07	-2.62
Saudi Arabia	6	3	1.35	-8.26	57	93	4.94	5.03	3	2	-18.24	-4.79
Turkey	182	236	4.96	1.13	14	13	15.25	-0.96	1	0	25.87	-4.26
LEAST DEVELOPED COUNTRIES (LDC)	**216**	**330**	**2.92**	**3.91**	**15**	**18**	**1.29**	**-0.21**	**5**	**15**	**15.47**	**14.30**
OECD[3]	**4 149**	**4 526**	**0.96**	**0.57**	**131**	**124**	**-5.80**	**-1.63**	**670**	**760**	**-1.66**	**0.88**
BRICS	**4 018**	**5 919**	**2.72**	**3.51**	**215**	**184**	**-4.78**	**-1.46**	**16**	**13**	**3.40**	**-0.73**

.. Not available

Note: Calendar year: Year ending 30 June for Australia and 31 May for New Zealand.

Average 2011-13est: Data for 2013 are estimated.

1. Includes Israel and also transition economies: Kazakhstan, Kyrgyzstan, Tajikistan, Turkmenistan, Uzbekistan, Armenia, Azerbaijan and Georgia.
2. Refers to mainland only. The economies of Chinese Taipei, Hong Kong (China) and Macau (China) are included in the Other Asia Pacific aggregate.
3. Excludes Iceland but includes all EU28 member countries.
4. Least-squares growth rate (see glossary).

Source: OECD and FAO Secretariats.

StatLink http://dx.doi.org/10.1787/888933102126

Table A.28.2. Butter projections: Consumption, per capita
Calendar year

	CONSUMPTION (kt)		Growth (%)[1]		PER CAPITA (kg)		Growth (%)[1]	
	Average 2011-13est	2023	2004-13	2014-23	Average 2011-13est	2023	2004-13	2014-23
WORLD	**9 880**	**12 598**	**1.93**	**2.14**	**1.4**	**1.6**	**0.73**	**1.11**
DEVELOPED COUNTRIES	**3 997**	**4 289**	**0.30**	**0.48**	**2.9**	**3.0**	**-0.18**	**0.18**
NORTH AMERICA	877	1 006	2.78	1.27	2.5	2.6	1.84	0.48
Canada	96	88	0.55	-0.54	2.7	2.3	-0.55	-1.46
United States	781	918	3.08	1.47	2.5	2.7	2.16	0.69
EUROPE	2 781	2 903	-0.62	0.20	3.7	3.9	-0.79	0.21
European Union	2 135	2 215	0.40	0.09	4.2	4.3	0.07	-0.05
Russian Federation	434	472	-4.86	0.73	3.0	3.4	-4.77	1.06
Ukraine	87	81	-1.59	-0.63	1.9	1.9	-1.10	0.06
OCEANIA DEVELOPED	162	191	6.27	0.78	5.9	6.1	4.64	-0.39
Australia	83	96	1.17	0.43	3.6	3.7	-0.48	-0.77
New Zealand	79	94	14.74	1.14	17.7	19.1	13.50	0.22
OTHER DEVELOPED[2]	178	190	-0.36	0.37	0.7	0.7	-0.99	0.00
Japan	77	76	-2.26	-0.70	0.6	0.6	-2.29	-0.45
South Africa	15	18	2.20	1.27	0.3	0.3	1.01	0.67
DEVELOPING COUNTRIES	**5 882**	**8 308**	**3.17**	**3.12**	**1.0**	**1.3**	**1.77**	**1.90**
AFRICA	418	571	2.78	2.79	0.4	0.4	0.23	0.34
NORTH AFRICA	269	342	2.24	2.20	1.6	1.7	0.68	0.86
Algeria	18	26	4.37	3.37	0.5	0.6	2.53	1.89
Egypt	188	245	2.66	2.41	2.3	2.6	0.96	0.98
SUB-SAHARAN AFRICA	149	229	3.83	3.74	0.2	0.2	1.04	1.07
LATIN AMERICA and CARIBBEAN	244	296	-0.45	1.30	0.4	0.4	-1.59	0.34
Argentina	32	45	0.49	2.51	0.8	1.0	-0.38	1.73
Brazil	83	91	1.10	0.86	0.4	0.4	0.16	0.16
Chile	22	30	5.54	2.45	1.3	1.6	4.54	1.67
Mexico	35	38	-7.74	-0.71	0.3	0.3	-8.89	-1.72
Uruguay	1	4	-43.37	-0.08	0.2	1.1	-43.53	-0.39
ASIA and PACIFIC	5 220	7 442	3.40	3.22	1.3	1.7	2.25	2.32
Bangladesh	30	48	3.88	4.18	0.2	0.3	2.73	3.06
China[3]	152	194	4.39	1.52	0.1	0.1	3.75	1.12
India	3 570	5 315	3.70	3.72	2.9	3.8	2.34	2.64
Indonesia	15	21	3.09	2.83	0.1	0.1	1.71	1.78
Iran, Islamic Republic of	243	273	1.68	1.13	3.2	3.1	0.44	0.02
Korea	13	16	8.32	1.83	0.3	0.3	7.69	1.44
Malaysia	10	12	0.61	1.73	0.3	0.4	-1.15	0.36
Pakistan	685	912	2.63	2.53	3.8	4.3	0.80	0.98
Saudi Arabia	56	94	7.64	4.55	2.0	2.8	5.52	3.02
Turkey	190	249	4.92	1.01	2.5	3.0	3.53	0.04
LEAST DEVELOPED COUNTRIES (LDC)	**229**	**333**	**3.09**	**3.29**	**0.3**	**0.3**	**0.78**	**1.07**
OECD[4]	**3 579**	**3 887**	**1.26**	**0.47**	**2.8**	**2.8**	**0.60**	**0.00**
BRICS	**4 254**	**6 090**	**2.48**	**3.33**	**1.4**	**1.9**	**1.56**	**2.64**

Note: Calendar year: Year ending 30 June for Australia and 31 May for New Zealand.

Average 2011-13est: Data for 2013 are estimated.

1. Least-squares growth rate (see glossary).
2. Includes Israel and also transition economies: Kazakhstan, Kyrgyzstan, Tajikistan, Turkmenistan, Uzbekistan, Armenia, Azerbaijan and Georgia.
3. Refers to mainland only. The economies of Chinese Taipei, Hong Kong (China) and Macau (China) are included in the Other Asia Pacific aggregate.
4. Excludes Iceland but includes all EU28 member countries.

Source: OECD and FAO Secretariats.

StatLink ᵐⁱˢᴾ *http://dx.doi.org/10.1787/888933102145*

Table A.29.1. Cheese projections: Production and trade

Calendar year

	PRODUCTION (kt)		Growth (%)[4]		IMPORTS (kt)		Growth (%)[4]		EXPORTS (kt)		Growth (%)[4]	
	Average 2011-13est	2023	2004-13	2014-23	Average 2011-13est	2023	2004-13	2014-23	Average 2011-13est	2023	2004-13	2014-23
WORLD	**21 210**	**25 251**	**1.78**	**1.63**	**2 145**	**2 732**	**4.03**	**2.65**	**2 359**	**2 946**	**5.03**	**2.43**
DEVELOPED COUNTRIES	**17 030**	**20 025**	**1.49**	**1.49**	**1 103**	**1 174**	**1.65**	**0.66**	**1 755**	**2 524**	**3.36**	**3.38**
NORTH AMERICA	5 309	6 652	2.35	2.08	160	135	-5.44	1.14	270	453	19.81	5.12
Canada	384	439	1.27	1.18	23	22	1.07	0.00	10	10	-1.23	-0.15
United States	4 925	6 213	2.44	2.15	137	113	-6.28	1.38	260	443	21.91	5.27
EUROPE	10 699	12 082	1.20	1.11	591	586	3.51	-0.28	1 044	1 465	3.78	3.15
European Union	9 547	10 690	1.19	1.03	76	66	-4.08	-1.36	744	1 143	3.96	3.59
Russian Federation	459	596	2.28	2.23	414	433	4.98	-0.04	17	13	7.35	-0.08
Ukraine	186	237	-4.49	1.76	16	6	16.22	-9.08	70	102	-2.98	4.91
OCEANIA DEVELOPED	667	862	-0.42	2.46	79	83	5.80	0.47	434	601	-1.91	2.84
Australia	341	414	-1.55	2.10	74	78	4.74	0.50	166	221	-3.74	2.80
New Zealand	326	448	0.88	2.81	5	5	..	0.00	268	380	-0.64	2.86
OTHER DEVELOPED[1]	355	428	1.84	1.74	273	371	2.30	2.24	7	6	-2.94	-1.81
Japan	47	60	3.44	3.08	227	252	0.80	0.28	0	0	..	..
South Africa	45	55	1.43	1.65	10	20	11.58	7.56	3	3	6.26	-2.68
DEVELOPING COUNTRIES	**4 180**	**5 226**	**3.03**	**2.21**	**1 042**	**1 558**	**7.21**	**4.44**	**604**	**422**	**12.00**	**-1.97**
AFRICA	955	1 125	1.08	1.13	173	293	11.30	7.32	147	74	18.47	-5.29
NORTH AFRICA	697	781	0.98	0.75	146	209	12.99	6.44	147	74	18.59	-5.29
Algeria	2	2	0.00	0.33	25	31	0.67	3.31	0	0	-25.67	-3.21
Egypt	645	698	0.71	0.36	64	77	29.98	5.56	133	74	34.02	-5.27
SUB-SAHARAN AFRICA	257	344	1.35	2.07	27	84	4.64	9.84	0	0	-5.61	-4.66
LATIN AMERICA and CARIBBEAN	1 989	2 549	4.55	2.42	295	375	8.31	2.86	144	91	2.33	-4.64
Argentina	559	759	4.25	2.78	3	0	..	..	54	58	2.07	-1.74
Brazil	700	860	4.90	2.08	32	13	33.82	-6.10	3	3	-14.17	1.87
Chile	77	82	1.49	1.35	35	72	23.44	6.20	9	5	-6.75	-5.83
Mexico	175	196	3.13	1.09	94	123	3.36	1.73	3	0	21.25	-24.64
Uruguay	96	118	9.48	2.20	2	2	24.01	2.75	32	4	2.32	-19.30
ASIA and PACIFIC	1 237	1 552	2.37	2.70	574	890	5.72	4.33	313	256	17.69	0.53
Bangladesh	1	1	0.00	0.52	0	1	13.23	8.25	0	0	-8.93	-7.63
China[2]	263	342	-0.30	3.23	39	128	24.77	7.88	0	0	-8.88	1.40
India	2	2	24.36	3.36	1	1	13.57	-1.30	3	3	25.56	1.31
Indonesia	0	0	0.00	-4.51	20	36	9.28	5.71	1	0	12.13	-5.40
Iran, Islamic Republic of	252	268	-1.47	1.01	0	0	13.38	-0.24	40	11	51.98	-7.59
Korea	25	31	-0.61	1.73	80	99	8.83	1.46	0	0	..	..
Malaysia	0	0	0.00	3.74	14	27	10.16	6.08	0	0	29.65	-5.73
Pakistan	0	0	0.00	-0.26	1	3	7.50	5.47	0	0	-4.65	-5.18
Saudi Arabia	221	285	23.52	3.58	125	119	3.00	0.14	188	154	17.60	-0.14
Turkey	172	229	2.62	4.42	6	12	2.62	1.38	35	63	14.68	10.96
LEAST DEVELOPED COUNTRIES (LDC)	**371**	**497**	**2.74**	**2.10**	**34**	**120**	**5.62**	**12.07**	**0**	**0**	**-1.61**	**-5.24**
OECD[3]	**16 408**	**19 200**	**1.50**	**1.47**	**822**	**911**	**0.77**	**0.96**	**1 571**	**2 339**	**3.37**	**3.60**
BRICS	**1 469**	**1 855**	**2.80**	**2.32**	**496**	**595**	**6.81**	**1.23**	**25**	**23**	**1.95**	**-0.03**

.. Not available

Note: Calendar year: Year ending 30 June for Australia and 31 May for New Zealand.

Average 2011-13est: Data for 2013 are estimated.

1. Includes Israel and also transition economies: Kazakhstan, Kyrgyzstan, Tajikistan, Turkmenistan, Uzbekistan, Armenia, Azerbaijan and Georgia.
2. Refers to mainland only. The economies of Chinese Taipei, Hong Kong (China) and Macau (China) are included in the Other Asia Pacific aggregate.
3. Excludes Iceland but includes all EU28 member countries.
4. Least-squares growth rate (see glossary).

Source: OECD and FAO Secretariats.

StatLink ᓄᗏ *http://dx.doi.org/10.1787/888933102164*

Table A.29.2. Cheese projections: Consumption, per capita
Calendar year

	CONSUMPTION (kt)		Growth (%)[1]		PER CAPITA (kg)		Growth (%)[1]	
	Average 2011-13est	2023	2004-13	2014-23	Average 2011-13est	2023	2004-13	2014-23
WORLD	**21 042**	**25 039**	**1.75**	**1.64**	**3.0**	**3.2**	**0.55**	**0.61**
DEVELOPED COUNTRIES	**16 414**	**18 676**	**1.35**	**1.20**	**11.8**	**13.0**	**0.88**	**0.90**
NORTH AMERICA	5 202	6 336	1.57	1.85	14.8	16.5	0.65	1.06
Canada	401	451	1.56	1.21	11.5	11.7	0.45	0.29
United States	4 801	5 885	1.57	1.90	15.1	17.0	0.67	1.12
EUROPE	10 273	11 203	1.14	0.79	13.8	15.1	0.97	0.79
European Union	8 880	9 613	0.93	0.74	17.5	18.6	0.60	0.60
Russian Federation	858	1 016	3.53	1.22	6.0	7.3	3.62	1.55
Ukraine	155	140	0.16	-0.64	3.4	3.3	0.66	0.04
OCEANIA DEVELOPED	313	344	2.73	1.36	11.4	11.0	1.14	0.19
Australia	250	270	1.11	1.10	10.9	10.3	-0.54	-0.11
New Zealand	63	74	12.02	2.34	14.1	14.9	10.81	1.42
OTHER DEVELOPED[2]	625	793	2.47	2.00	2.3	2.8	1.81	1.63
Japan	274	312	1.29	0.76	2.2	2.5	1.25	1.01
South Africa	52	72	2.73	3.27	1.0	1.3	1.53	2.66
DEVELOPING COUNTRIES	**4 628**	**6 362**	**3.24**	**3.08**	**0.8**	**1.0**	**1.84**	**1.87**
AFRICA	995	1 344	1.40	2.77	1.0	1.0	-1.12	0.32
NORTH AFRICA	709	916	1.31	2.56	4.2	4.7	-0.24	1.21
Algeria	26	34	1.55	2.75	0.7	0.7	-0.24	1.27
Egypt	597	701	0.34	1.68	7.4	7.4	-1.33	0.26
SUB-SAHARAN AFRICA	285	428	1.63	3.24	0.3	0.4	-1.10	0.58
LATIN AMERICA and CARIBBEAN	2 130	2 833	4.92	2.81	3.5	4.2	3.71	1.83
Argentina	508	701	4.66	3.24	12.4	15.6	3.75	2.45
Brazil	729	869	5.61	1.92	3.7	4.0	4.63	1.21
Chile	94	149	6.14	3.84	5.4	7.8	5.14	3.05
Mexico	266	319	3.09	1.49	2.2	2.4	1.81	0.46
Uruguay	62	117	11.71	5.59	18.4	33.2	11.39	5.27
ASIA and PACIFIC	1 504	2 185	2.35	3.64	0.4	0.5	1.21	2.74
Bangladesh	1	2	1.72	2.95	0.0	0.0	0.59	1.84
China[3]	302	470	1.28	4.30	0.2	0.3	0.65	3.89
India	1	0	-29.27	5.22	0.0	0.0	-30.20	4.12
Indonesia	19	36	9.28	5.94	0.1	0.1	7.80	4.87
Iran, Islamic Republic of	224	257	-1.35	1.69	2.9	3.0	-2.55	0.59
Korea	105	130	5.79	1.52	2.1	2.5	5.18	1.13
Malaysia	13	27	9.13	6.29	0.5	0.8	7.23	4.85
Pakistan	1	3	8.01	5.47	0.0	0.0	6.09	3.87
Saudi Arabia	151	250	7.31	4.43	5.3	7.4	5.20	2.89
Turkey	142	178	1.24	2.58	1.9	2.1	-0.10	1.59
LEAST DEVELOPED COUNTRIES (LDC)	**408**	**618**	**2.99**	**3.55**	**0.5**	**0.6**	**0.68**	**1.32**
OECD[4]	15 655	17 774	1.28	1.19	12.1	13.0	0.62	0.71
BRICS	1 942	2 427	3.81	2.06	0.6	0.7	2.87	1.39

Note: Calendar year: Year ending 30 June for Australia and 31 May for New Zealand.
　　　Average 2011-13est: Data for 2013 are estimated.
1. Least-squares growth rate (see glossary).
2. Includes Israel and also transition economies: Kazakhstan, Kyrgyzstan, Tajikistan, Turkmenistan, Uzbekistan, Armenia, Azerbaijan and Georgia.
3. Refers to mainland only. The economies of Chinese Taipei, Hong Kong (China) and Macau (China) are included in the Other Asia Pacific aggregate.
4. Excludes Iceland but includes all EU28 member countries.
Source: OECD and FAO Secretariats.

StatLink ᕳᕱᔒ *http://dx.doi.org/10.1787/888933102183*

Table A.30.1. Skim milk powder projections: Production and trade

Calendar year

	PRODUCTION (kt)		Growth (%)[4]		IMPORTS (kt)		Growth (%)[4]		EXPORTS (kt)		Growth (%)[4]	
	Average 2011-13est	2023	2004-13	2014-23	Average 2011-13est	2023	2004-13	2014-23	Average 2011-13est	2023	2004-13	2014-23
WORLD	**3 759**	**4 633**	**2.29**	**1.89**	**1 808**	**2 401**	**5.54**	**2.49**	**1 804**	**2 418**	**6.24**	**2.47**
DEVELOPED COUNTRIES	**3 279**	**4 093**	**2.35**	**1.91**	**138**	**206**	**0.84**	**1.74**	**1 617**	**2 219**	**6.28**	**2.76**
NORTH AMERICA	1 023	1 511	4.37	3.28	3	3	-4.37	0.00	477	829	8.99	4.24
Canada	82	81	0.49	-0.78	3	3	-0.72	0.00	11	9	-0.83	-3.52
United States	941	1 430	4.78	3.57	0	0	..	..	465	821	9.39	4.36
EUROPE	1 353	1 545	1.22	1.00	53	91	-2.33	1.31	591	732	8.86	2.32
European Union	1 097	1 243	2.09	0.95	2	3	-28.03	-1.28	481	624	14.23	2.80
Russian Federation	50	64	-8.97	3.69	43	71	0.54	1.19	1	1	-13.07	0.00
Ukraine	118	128	0.10	0.71	3	2	83.80	1.76	22	13	-15.98	-4.10
OCEANIA DEVELOPED	735	875	3.49	1.69	8	8	13.65	0.17	542	649	2.64	1.65
Australia	226	256	2.38	1.47	4	4	3.18	0.35	148	177	-0.37	1.95
New Zealand	509	619	4.02	1.78	4	4	..	0.00	394	473	3.96	1.53
OTHER DEVELOPED[1]	167	161	-2.95	0.41	74	104	3.07	2.32	8	9	-0.76	-1.22
Japan	138	132	-3.68	0.43	30	35	-1.88	-0.71	0	0	..	..
South Africa	15	13	0.73	-0.56	7	13	7.15	3.27	6	7	21.52	-1.51
DEVELOPING COUNTRIES	**480**	**540**	**1.90**	**1.77**	**1 670**	**2 195**	**6.03**	**2.56**	**187**	**199**	**5.68**	**-0.35**
AFRICA	4	4	0.38	0.00	283	390	5.63	3.24	6	2	12.47	-3.01
NORTH AFRICA	0	0	0.00	-17.02	205	255	6.34	2.50	1	1	11.26	-2.91
Algeria	0	0	0.00	-15.18	122	149	5.20	2.40	0	0	-3.70	-2.34
Egypt	0	0	0.00	-20.49	68	88	19.94	3.00	1	1	17.58	-2.92
SUB-SAHARAN AFRICA	4	4	0.38	0.13	79	135	4.46	4.82	4	1	12.78	-3.06
LATIN AMERICA and CARIBBEAN	258	297	3.06	1.16	328	404	5.91	2.48	47	37	4.57	-1.42
Argentina	36	36	2.11	-0.11	0	0	..	..	17	16	0.93	-0.19
Brazil	140	174	2.90	1.77	24	25	42.76	-1.12	0	1	-54.35	-3.11
Chile	14	18	4.68	2.50	16	22	17.18	4.50	3	1	34.61	-4.31
Mexico	33	35	0.55	0.47	227	287	5.53	2.83	1	0	16.67	-13.86
Uruguay	24	19	7.72	-1.90	0	1	79.46	2.12	23	17	9.45	-2.08
ASIA and PACIFIC	218	240	0.73	2.62	1 059	1 402	6.22	2.40	135	161	5.86	-0.04
Bangladesh	0	0	0.00	-10.33	27	42	1.76	4.15	0	0	-18.11	-3.98
China[2]	57	53	82.49	2.07	169	315	18.36	3.80	0	1	-23.55	0.00
India	142	176	-0.78	3.00	16	3	72.53	-1.12	51	90	-2.38	1.13
Indonesia	0	0	0.00	31.64	138	197	6.89	3.00	1	1	-10.03	-2.91
Iran, Islamic Republic of	0	0	0.00	-10.98	17	24	8.54	2.70	6	6	78.60	-2.62
Korea	13	6	-13.20	2.40	23	24	20.42	2.75	0	0	1.09	0.00
Malaysia	0	0	0.00	-3.82	101	127	7.51	1.39	16	18	7.76	-1.37
Pakistan	0	0	0.00	-3.87	32	42	30.67	3.42	0	0	-8.51	-3.31
Saudi Arabia	0	0	0.00	7.86	72	75	2.60	0.79	25	25	27.59	-0.78
Turkey	0	0	0.00	0.50	1	2	-40.10	0.39	3	1	50.68	-0.39
LEAST DEVELOPED COUNTRIES (LDC)	**0**	**0**	**0.00**	**-8.51**	**88**	**124**	**5.19**	**3.16**	**5**	**2**	**25.29**	**-2.77**
OECD[3]	3 091	3 856	2.68	1.94	314	392	3.79	2.49	1 517	2 121	7.18	2.91
BRICS	404	480	-0.17	2.41	259	428	14.24	2.90	58	99	-1.20	0.85

.. Not available

Note: Calendar year: Year ending 30 June for Australia and 31 May for New Zealand.

Average 2011-13est: Data for 2013 are estimated.

1. Includes Israel and also transition economies: Kazakhstan, Kyrgyzstan, Tajikistan, Turkmenistan, Uzbekistan, Armenia, Azerbaijan and Georgia.
2. Refers to mainland only. The economies of Chinese Taipei, Hong Kong (China) and Macau (China) are included in the Other Asia Pacific aggregate.
3. Excludes Iceland but includes all EU28 member countries.
4. Least-squares growth rate (see glossary).

Source: OECD and FAO Secretariats.

StatLink 🔗 http://dx.doi.org/10.1787/888933102202

Table A.30.2. Skim milk powder projections: Consumption, per capita
Calendar year

	CONSUMPTION (kt)		Growth (%)[1]		PER CAPITA (kg)		Growth (%)[1]	
	Average 2011-13est	2023	2004-13	2014-23	Average 2011-13est	2023	2004-13	2014-23
WORLD	**3 800**	**4 616**	**1.52**	**1.77**	**0.5**	**0.6**	**1.43**	**0.85**
DEVELOPED COUNTRIES	**1 880**	**2 080**	**-0.81**	**1.07**	**1.2**	**1.3**	**0.48**	**0.95**
NORTH AMERICA	550	687	0.10	2.17	1.5	1.7	-0.46	1.58
Canada	74	76	1.72	-0.30	1.1	0.9	-2.36	-0.82
United States	476	611	0.24	2.53	1.5	1.8	0.01	1.74
EUROPE	905	905	-2.48	0.12	1.0	1.1	0.54	0.26
European Union	688	622	-3.00	-0.57	1.0	1.0	1.05	-0.65
Russian Federation	92	134	-5.01	2.31	0.6	1.0	-4.93	2.64
Ukraine	97	117	4.83	1.46	2.1	2.8	5.36	2.16
OCEANIA DEVELOPED	192	232	15.35	1.77	7.0	7.4	13.57	0.59
Australia	73	83	11.24	0.47	3.2	3.2	9.43	-0.74
New Zealand	119	149	18.75	2.56	26.8	30.1	17.46	1.63
OTHER DEVELOPED[2]	232	256	-2.08	1.24	0.8	0.8	-2.64	0.98
Japan	172	167	-3.87	0.21	1.2	1.1	-4.11	0.44
South Africa	16	20	-1.36	2.32	0.3	0.4	-2.51	1.72
DEVELOPING COUNTRIES	**1 920**	**2 536**	**4.40**	**2.37**	**0.3**	**0.4**	**3.01**	**1.18**
AFRICA	271	391	4.63	3.25	0.3	0.3	2.03	0.79
NORTH AFRICA	189	254	4.98	2.52	1.1	1.3	3.38	1.17
Algeria	115	149	3.44	2.39	3.0	3.3	1.61	0.92
Egypt	57	88	14.32	3.08	0.7	0.9	12.42	1.63
SUB-SAHARAN AFRICA	82	137	3.86	4.77	0.1	0.1	1.07	2.07
LATIN AMERICA and CARIBBEAN	533	664	4.14	2.05	0.8	0.9	3.04	1.11
Argentina	19	20	2.74	-1.67	0.5	0.4	1.84	-2.42
Brazil	164	198	5.15	1.36	0.6	0.6	4.98	0.54
Chile	24	38	5.72	3.95	1.4	2.0	4.72	3.15
Mexico	258	322	4.76	2.54	2.1	2.4	3.47	1.50
Uruguay	3	2	-2.04	0.48	0.8	0.7	-2.33	0.18
ASIA and PACIFIC	1 116	1 481	4.47	2.30	0.3	0.3	3.31	1.40
Bangladesh	27	42	3.49	4.15	0.2	0.2	2.34	3.03
China[3]	226	368	15.47	3.54	0.2	0.3	14.75	3.13
India	109	90	-2.73	-1.54	0.1	0.1	-4.01	-2.57
Indonesia	133	196	6.93	3.03	0.5	0.7	5.49	1.99
Iran, Islamic Republic of	10	19	7.92	5.07	0.1	0.2	6.61	3.93
Korea	37	30	0.99	2.68	0.8	0.6	0.41	2.28
Malaysia	84	109	5.12	1.92	2.9	3.2	3.28	0.54
Pakistan	26	42	26.59	3.43	0.1	0.2	24.34	1.87
Saudi Arabia	40	50	1.68	1.65	1.4	1.5	-0.32	0.15
Turkey	2	1	-18.72	1.36	0.0	0.0	-19.80	0.38
LEAST DEVELOPED COUNTRIES (LDC)	**84**	**123**	**3.24**	**3.25**	**0.1**	**0.1**	**0.93**	**1.03**
OECD[4]	**1 953**	**2 127**	**-0.25**	**1.15**	**1.3**	**1.4**	**0.96**	**0.86**
BRICS	**606**	**810**	**3.28**	**2.08**	**0.2**	**0.2**	**2.36**	**1.43**

Note: Calendar year: Year ending 30 June for Australia and 31 May for New Zealand.
Average 2011-13est: Data for 2013 are estimated.
1. Least-squares growth rate (see glossary).
2. Includes Israel and also transition economies: Kazakhstan, Kyrgyzstan, Tajikistan, Turkmenistan, Uzbekistan, Armenia, Azerbaijan and Georgia.
3. Refers to mainland only. The economies of Chinese Taipei, Hong Kong (China) and Macau (China) are included in the Other Asia Pacific aggregate.
4. Excludes Iceland but includes all EU28 member countries.
Source: OECD and FAO Secretariats.

StatLink ⬛⬛ *http://dx.doi.org/10.1787/888933102221*

Table A.31.1. Whole milk powder projections: Production and trade

Calendar year

	PRODUCTION (kt)		Growth (%)[4]		IMPORTS (kt)		Growth (%)[4]		EXPORTS (kt)		Growth (%)[4]	
	Average 2011-13est	2023	2004-13	2014-23	Average 2011-13est	2023	2004-13	2014-23	Average 2011-13est	2023	2004-13	2014-23
WORLD	4 705	6 022	2.88	2.24	2 210	2 762	4.02	1.66	2 204	2 743	3.16	1.67
DEVELOPED COUNTRIES	2 129	2 579	2.42	1.65	53	69	-7.28	2.78	1 653	2 087	4.05	1.88
NORTH AMERICA	38	40	2.19	0.85	11	12	-15.37	0.00	11	16	0.42	2.47
Canada	11	10	-6.33	-0.60	4	4	-23.50	0.00	1	1	6.17	0.00
United States	27	31	8.16	1.36	7	8	-2.03	0.00	10	15	0.64	2.58
EUROPE	793	796	-2.28	0.44	15	19	-11.03	1.19	420	398	-2.87	0.12
European Union	667	638	-1.99	0.05	3	3	-1.82	-1.28	381	348	-2.77	0.01
Russian Federation	55	80	-6.04	4.29	8	11	-15.95	1.12	1	0	..	..
Ukraine	11	12	-8.82	0.92	1	1	97.57	2.21	1	1	-31.37	-2.14
OCEANIA DEVELOPED	1 255	1 702	6.85	2.37	10	15	3.85	4.65	1 219	1 671	7.89	2.35
Australia	134	138	-4.36	2.25	10	14	2.58	5.02	99	110	-1.61	1.99
New Zealand	1 122	1 564	9.11	2.38	1	1	..	0.00	1 120	1 561	9.17	2.38
OTHER DEVELOPED[1]	43	41	-0.45	-0.78	17	23	2.74	4.85	3	2	1.50	3.96
Japan	12	12	-2.51	1.56	0	0	..	..	0	0	..	..
South Africa	15	14	-0.52	-0.23	2	5	-1.75	4.13	3	2	2.09	-1.96
DEVELOPING COUNTRIES	2 576	3 442	3.30	2.70	2 157	2 692	4.49	1.63	551	656	0.85	1.04
AFRICA	8	7	1.34	-1.24	483	628	1.52	2.48	17	10	8.37	-2.64
NORTH AFRICA	0	0	0.00	-5.82	240	285	3.11	1.76	2	2	40.61	-3.46
Algeria	0	0	0.00	-6.12	181	202	0.62	1.19	0	0	-0.79	-1.17
Egypt	0	0	0.00	-12.07	44	61	23.16	3.59	2	2	78.37	-3.16
SUB-SAHARAN AFRICA	8	7	1.34	-1.23	243	343	0.14	3.13	15	8	6.93	-2.65
LATIN AMERICA and CARIBBEAN	1 339	1 624	3.15	1.37	404	421	1.61	1.04	296	374	1.34	1.03
Argentina	283	339	1.52	0.81	2	0	-8.49	..	206	293	2.10	1.73
Brazil	532	651	2.39	1.60	67	55	13.23	0.13	1	1	-43.43	4.15
Chile	84	101	3.49	1.16	12	14	14.33	-0.95	15	22	10.56	0.98
Mexico	277	337	6.91	1.63	36	18	-10.57	-4.99	11	11	34.48	-0.25
Uruguay	59	56	7.80	-0.82	0	0	-16.58	0.42	37	25	1.75	-4.20
ASIA and PACIFIC	1 229	1 811	3.50	4.08	1 270	1 644	6.87	1.48	238	272	0.06	1.23
Bangladesh	0	0	0.00	-7.87	34	52	7.53	4.02	0	0	-14.69	-3.86
China[2]	1 155	1 677	2.98	4.04	428	616	30.04	0.56	7	4	-15.16	3.11
India	0	30	-59.00	21.95	2	0	26.78	-20.16	1	28	-32.48	25.25
Indonesia	70	99	203.64	2.40	59	77	-3.53	3.35	8	5	-12.35	-3.25
Iran, Islamic Republic of	1	0	-1.08	-3.09	5	7	0.72	1.67	2	1	79.99	-1.65
Korea	3	5	-3.73	2.02	3	2	4.05	2.56	0	0	-14.64	0.00
Malaysia	0	0	0.00	-4.46	27	20	-12.96	-0.72	13	16	-5.85	0.73
Pakistan	0	0	0.00	-6.33	7	9	21.39	1.01	4	5	49.25	-1.00
Saudi Arabia	0	0	0.00	2.73	106	139	7.44	3.72	16	8	-5.35	-3.58
Turkey	0	0	0.00	-1.06	0	1	-51.66	0.41	1	0	9.38	-0.41
LEAST DEVELOPED COUNTRIES (LDC)	0	0	0.02	-7.18	185	244	0.07	2.28	10	5	12.24	-1.29
OECD[3]	2 357	2 852	3.34	1.63	80	67	-8.09	-0.99	1 640	2 070	4.45	1.88
BRICS	1 756	2 453	2.28	3.41	508	687	21.87	0.55	12	34	-20.46	15.09

.. Not available

Note: Calendar year: Year ending 30 June for Australia and 31 May for New Zealand.

Average 2011-13est: Data for 2013 are estimated.

1. Includes Israel and also transition economies: Kazakhstan, Kyrgyzstan, Tajikistan, Turkmenistan, Uzbekistan, Armenia, Azerbaijan and Georgia.
2. Refers to mainland only. The economies of Chinese Taipei, Hong Kong (China) and Macau (China) are included in the Other Asia Pacific aggregate.
3. Excludes Iceland but includes all EU28 member countries.
4. Least-squares growth rate (see glossary).

Source: OECD and FAO Secretariats.

StatLink ᘰ️ *http://dx.doi.org/10.1787/888933102240*

Table A.31.2. Whole milk powder projections: Consumption, per capita
Calendar year

	CONSUMPTION (kt)		Growth (%)[1]		PER CAPITA (kg)		Growth (%)[1]	
	Average 2011-13est	2023	2004-13	2014-23	Average 2011-13est	2023	2004-13	2014-23
WORLD	**4 717**	**6 040**	**3.37**	**2.23**	**0.7**	**0.8**	**2.15**	**1.20**
DEVELOPED COUNTRIES	**527**	**562**	**-2.76**	**0.99**	**0.4**	**0.4**	**-3.22**	**0.69**
NORTH AMERICA	38	36	-5.68	-0.05	0.1	0.1	-6.54	-0.83
Canada	14	13	-14.23	-0.43	0.4	0.3	-15.17	-1.34
United States	24	23	6.08	0.17	0.1	0.1	5.14	-0.60
EUROPE	386	417	-2.22	0.78	0.5	0.6	-2.39	0.79
European Union	289	293	-0.76	0.08	0.6	0.6	-1.08	-0.06
Russian Federation	62	92	-7.75	3.84	0.4	0.7	-7.67	4.18
Ukraine	8	12	5.98	1.38	0.2	0.3	6.51	2.08
OCEANIA DEVELOPED	47	46	-7.80	3.71	1.7	1.5	-9.22	2.51
Australia	44	43	-8.07	3.86	1.9	1.6	-9.57	2.61
New Zealand	3	4	-3.44	2.12	0.6	0.7	-4.49	1.20
OTHER DEVELOPED[2]	56	62	1.56	1.21	0.2	0.2	0.91	0.83
Japan	12	12	-2.48	1.56	0.1	0.1	-2.51	1.81
South Africa	15	17	4.07	1.36	0.3	0.3	2.86	0.76
DEVELOPING COUNTRIES	**4 189**	**5 479**	**4.38**	**2.37**	**0.7**	**0.8**	**2.96**	**1.16**
AFRICA	486	625	3.24	2.53	0.5	0.5	0.67	0.09
NORTH AFRICA	232	283	4.37	1.80	1.4	1.4	2.78	0.46
Algeria	180	202	2.59	1.19	4.7	4.4	0.78	-0.27
Egypt	35	59	16.72	3.89	0.4	0.6	14.78	2.44
SUB-SAHARAN AFRICA	254	343	2.27	3.18	0.3	0.3	-0.47	0.52
LATIN AMERICA and CARIBBEAN	1 461	1 670	2.85	1.36	2.4	2.5	1.67	0.40
Argentina	78	47	0.48	-3.59	1.9	1.0	-0.40	-4.33
Brazil	598	705	3.81	1.48	3.0	3.3	2.84	0.78
Chile	80	93	2.49	0.86	4.6	4.9	1.52	0.09
Mexico	302	344	2.53	1.21	2.5	2.5	1.26	0.18
Uruguay	21	31	19.35	3.10	6.2	9.0	19.00	2.79
ASIA and PACIFIC	2 243	3 183	5.75	2.90	0.6	0.7	4.57	2.01
Bangladesh	33	52	6.02	4.02	0.2	0.3	4.84	2.90
China[3]	1 576	2 289	6.95	2.99	1.1	1.6	6.29	2.58
India	1	2	6.47	5.17	0.0	0.0	5.07	4.07
Indonesia	119	171	11.26	3.03	0.5	0.6	9.76	1.98
Iran, Islamic Republic of	5	6	4.54	2.05	0.1	0.1	3.27	0.94
Korea	6	7	-0.78	2.20	0.1	0.1	-1.35	1.80
Malaysia	10	4	-17.58	-5.04	0.4	0.1	-19.02	-6.33
Pakistan	3	5	0.36	3.55	0.0	0.0	-1.43	1.99
Saudi Arabia	78	131	9.21	4.38	2.8	3.9	7.06	2.85
Turkey	1	0	-44.61	1.23	0.0	0.0	-45.35	0.25
LEAST DEVELOPED COUNTRIES (LDC)	**193**	**238**	**2.85**	**2.38**	**0.2**	**0.2**	**0.55**	**0.17**
OECD[4]	**796**	**849**	**-0.24**	**0.82**	**0.6**	**0.6**	**-0.90**	**0.34**
BRICS	**2 253**	**3 106**	**5.33**	**2.64**	**0.7**	**1.0**	**4.38**	**1.96**

Note: Calendar year: Year ending 30 June for Australia and 31 May for New Zealand.
Average 2011-13est: Data for 2013 are estimated.
1. Least-squares growth rate (see glossary).
2. Includes Israel and also transition economies: Kazakhstan, Kyrgyzstan, Tajikistan, Turkmenistan, Uzbekistan, Armenia, Azerbaijan and Georgia.
3. Refers to mainland only. The economies of Chinese Taipei, Hong Kong (China) and Macau (China) are included in the Other Asia Pacific aggregate.
4. Excludes Iceland but includes all EU28 member countries.
Source: OECD and FAO Secretariats.

StatLink ⟪⟫ http://dx.doi.org/10.1787/888933102259

Table A.32. Fresh dairy products projections: Production and consumption per capita

Calendar year

	PRODUCTION (kt)		Growth (%)[4]		CONSUMPTION PER CAPITA (kg)		Growth (%)[4]	
	Average 2011-13est	2023	2004-13	2014-23	Average 2011-13est	2023	2004-13	2014-23
WORLD	**502 551**	**658 602**	**2.95**	**2.37**	**71.1**	**83.1**	**1.73**	**1.33**
DEVELOPED COUNTRIES	**141 291**	**151 291**	**0.32**	**0.59**	**101.7**	**105.2**	**-0.15**	**0.29**
NORTH AMERICA	27 933	27 963	-0.30	0.03	79.3	72.8	-1.21	-0.75
Canada	2 896	2 905	0.03	0.00	83.1	75.3	-1.07	-0.91
United States	25 037	25 058	-0.34	0.04	78.9	72.5	-1.23	-0.73
EUROPE	82 783	84 896	-0.23	0.20	111.5	114.2	-0.40	0.20
European Union	46 769	48 230	-0.17	0.30	92.0	93.3	-0.49	0.16
Russian Federation	18 309	18 715	0.28	0.20	127.9	135.4	0.36	0.53
Ukraine	9 321	9 668	-1.52	-0.22	204.8	229.0	-1.02	0.47
OCEANIA DEVELOPED	2 876	3 176	1.74	1.00	104.6	101.5	0.18	-0.16
Australia	2 419	2 749	2.10	1.21	105.0	104.4	0.44	-0.01
New Zealand	456	427	0.00	-0.21	102.3	86.5	-1.08	-1.12
OTHER DEVELOPED[1]	27 700	35 256	2.75	2.11	103.6	126.3	2.09	1.73
Japan	4 317	4 323	-2.18	-0.32	33.9	34.8	-2.21	-0.07
South Africa	2 986	3 433	2.65	1.27	57.0	61.2	1.45	0.67
DEVELOPING COUNTRIES	**361 259**	**507 311**	**4.15**	**2.96**	**63.6**	**78.2**	**2.73**	**1.75**
AFRICA	35 445	51 393	2.69	3.25	34.7	38.5	0.14	0.79
NORTH AFRICA	9 655	12 980	7.12	2.07	57.2	66.1	5.49	0.72
Algeria	3 634	5 197	8.31	2.05	94.4	114.2	6.40	0.59
Egypt	2 997	3 546	8.97	1.31	37.1	37.5	7.16	-0.11
SUB-SAHARAN AFRICA	25 790	38 413	1.39	3.68	30.3	33.8	-1.33	1.01
LATIN AMERICA and CARIBBEAN	46 611	58 117	3.49	1.69	76.5	85.5	2.31	0.72
Argentina	1 835	2 104	2.10	1.14	44.4	46.8	1.19	0.38
Brazil	14 984	17 352	4.87	1.27	75.5	80.7	3.90	0.55
Chile	1 276	1 399	0.07	1.49	73.1	73.5	-0.87	0.72
Mexico	5 330	6 753	3.13	2.34	44.1	49.7	1.85	1.30
Uruguay	962	1 550	3.49	2.75	283.3	441.1	3.19	2.44
ASIA and PACIFIC	279 203	397 802	4.46	3.13	68.9	88.9	3.30	2.23
Bangladesh	3 012	4 240	3.99	3.31	19.5	24.3	2.84	2.20
China[2]	30 042	37 608	3.72	2.22	21.8	26.0	3.08	1.82
India	157 503	238 524	5.17	3.72	127.3	171.2	3.79	2.64
Indonesia	1 069	1 496	2.94	2.52	4.3	5.4	1.55	1.48
Iran, Islamic Republic of	2 861	3 503	6.41	1.14	37.4	40.5	5.12	0.04
Korea	1 352	1 359	-0.04	0.04	27.6	26.5	-0.62	-0.35
Malaysia	100	118	6.22	1.39	3.4	3.5	4.36	0.01
Pakistan	57 565	76 596	3.32	2.53	321.3	360.8	1.48	0.98
Saudi Arabia	618	1 008	-5.24	2.05	21.7	30.1	-7.10	0.56
Turkey	14 127	18 829	6.44	1.42	187.8	224.4	5.03	0.44
LEAST DEVELOPED COUNTRIES (LDC)	**28 291**	**42 955**	**1.65**	**3.80**	**32.6**	**38.9**	**-0.62**	**1.57**
OECD[3]	**105 305**	**113 532**	**0.66**	**0.53**	**81.1**	**82.9**	**0.01**	**0.06**
BRICS	**223 824**	**315 632**	**4.43**	**3.12**	**74.4**	**97.2**	**3.49**	**2.44**

Note: Calendar year: Year ending 30 June for Australia and 31 May for New Zealand.

Average 2011-13est: Data for 2013 are estimated.

1. Includes Israel and also transition economies: Kazakhstan, Kyrgyzstan, Tajikistan, Turkmenistan, Uzbekistan, Armenia, Azerbaijan and Georgia.
2. Refers to mainland only. The economies of Chinese Taipei, Hong Kong (China) and Macau (China) are included in the Other Asia Pacific aggregate.
3. Excludes Iceland but includes all EU28 member countries.
4. Least-squares growth rate (see glossary).

Source: OECD and FAO Secretariats.

StatLink ᴍᴤᴸ *http://dx.doi.org/10.1787/888933102278*

Table A.33. Milk projections: Production, inventories, yield

Calendar year

	PRODUCTION (kt)		Growth (%)[4]		INVENTORIES ('000 hd)		Growth (%)[4]		YIELD (T/head)		Growth (%)[4]	
	Average 2011-13est	2023	2004-13	2014-23	Average 2011-13est	2023	2004-13	2014-23	Average 2011-13est	2023	2004-13	2014-23
WORLD	**748 665**	**928 175**	**2.18**	**1.87**	**636 538**	**740 713**	**1.59**	**1.28**	**1.18**	**1.25**	**0.57**	**0.58**
DEVELOPED COUNTRIES	**371 884**	**411 620**	**0.90**	**0.80**	**77 783**	**78 539**	**-0.13**	**-0.04**	**4.78**	**5.24**	**1.03**	**0.84**
NORTH AMERICA	98 824	112 193	1.61	0.91	10 154	10 138	0.10	-0.11	9.73	11.07	1.51	1.02
Canada	8 722	9 355	0.74	0.56	962	954	-0.82	0.05	9.07	9.80	1.57	0.51
United States	90 102	102 837	1.70	0.94	9 193	9 184	0.20	-0.12	9.80	11.20	1.49	1.07
EUROPE	212 280	223 518	0.23	0.40	43 490	38 056	-1.41	-1.39	4.88	5.87	1.66	1.81
European Union	152 264	160 524	0.37	0.45	23 127	19 708	-0.95	-1.76	6.44	7.99	1.25	2.29
Russian Federation	31 660	33 497	0.07	0.42	8 961	8 170	-1.23	-0.80	3.53	4.10	1.31	1.23
Ukraine	11 379	12 011	-2.36	0.03	3 669	3 342	-3.68	-1.28	3.10	3.59	1.37	1.33
OCEANIA DEVELOPED	28 808	36 538	2.32	1.95	6 492	7 454	1.19	0.99	4.44	4.90	1.13	0.95
Australia	9 575	11 711	-1.13	2.02	1 656	1 785	-2.30	0.56	5.78	6.56	1.20	1.45
New Zealand	19 232	24 827	4.48	1.92	4 835	5 670	2.65	1.12	3.98	4.38	1.79	0.78
OTHER DEVELOPED[1]	31 972	39 372	2.20	1.86	17 647	22 890	2.98	2.33	1.81	1.72	-0.76	-0.46
Japan	7 542	7 467	-1.23	-0.10	926	883	-1.65	-0.37	8.14	8.46	0.43	0.27
South Africa	3 330	3 784	2.26	1.17	1 035	1 079	3.95	0.21	3.22	3.51	-1.63	0.96
DEVELOPING COUNTRIES	**376 781**	**516 555**	**3.58**	**2.81**	**573 936**	**688 631**	**2.05**	**1.56**	**0.66**	**0.75**	**1.50**	**1.23**
AFRICA	39 088	55 493	2.46	3.06	211 245	266 331	1.91	1.97	0.19	0.21	0.54	1.06
NORTH AFRICA	12 843	16 530	4.55	1.84	48 937	66 491	6.60	1.97	0.26	0.25	-1.93	-0.13
Algeria	3 166	4 525	8.17	2.04	18 316	23 324	7.93	0.29	0.17	0.19	0.22	1.74
Egypt	5 843	6 608	2.58	0.94	6 642	6 223	0.61	-0.54	0.88	1.06	1.96	1.48
SUB-SAHARAN AFRICA	26 245	38 963	1.55	3.62	162 308	199 840	0.79	1.98	0.16	0.19	0.76	1.61
LATIN AMERICA and CARIBBEAN	80 382	97 984	2.34	1.69	49 466	54 971	1.69	0.85	1.62	1.78	0.64	0.84
Argentina	11 638	15 899	2.86	2.61	2 352	2 549	1.47	0.87	4.95	6.24	1.37	1.72
Brazil	28 475	32 660	1.85	1.53	24 158	27 812	2.40	1.31	1.18	1.17	-0.54	0.22
Chile	2 692	3 077	2.02	1.45	1 323	993	-4.06	-1.96	2.04	3.10	6.33	3.47
Mexico	11 160	11 872	1.19	0.54	2 389	2 472	1.00	0.32	4.67	4.80	0.19	0.22
Uruguay	2 226	2 857	4.85	1.61	790	885	0.69	0.14	2.81	3.23	4.14	1.47
ASIA and PACIFIC	257 311	363 078	4.18	3.09	313 226	367 329	2.19	1.38	0.82	0.99	1.94	1.69
Bangladesh	3 455	4 885	4.10	3.30	36 736	42 560	4.95	1.19	0.09	0.11	-0.81	2.09
China[2]	40 382	52 085	3.50	2.65	11 847	13 379	1.57	1.37	3.12	3.60	2.25	1.37
India	133 818	202 201	4.87	3.73	117 890	142 741	2.51	1.69	1.13	1.42	2.30	2.00
Indonesia	1 396	1 960	7.11	2.47	11 906	14 089	3.94	0.96	0.12	0.14	3.06	1.50
Iran, Islamic Republic of	7 640	8 664	0.99	1.13	21 275	18 715	-3.21	-0.85	0.36	0.46	4.34	1.99
Korea	1 912	2 115	-2.00	0.89	227	246	-2.52	0.34	8.42	8.61	0.53	0.54
Malaysia	77	90	6.34	1.38	158	168	6.17	0.38	0.48	0.54	0.16	1.00
Pakistan	37 879	50 343	3.51	2.53	29 088	34 554	2.64	1.50	1.30	1.46	0.85	1.01
Saudi Arabia	2 013	2 692	7.19	2.65	4 070	3 659	-3.11	-0.29	0.50	0.74	10.63	2.94
Turkey	16 964	22 460	5.93	1.52	21 282	23 805	3.50	0.16	0.80	0.94	2.35	1.36
LEAST DEVELOPED COUNTRIES (LDC)	**29 321**	**44 216**	**1.72**	**3.72**	**210 103**	**264 912**	**1.93**	**2.11**	**0.14**	**0.17**	**-0.20**	**1.58**
OECD[3]	**327 214**	**363 435**	**1.14**	**0.79**	**67 082**	**66 798**	**0.65**	**-0.44**	**4.88**	**5.44**	**0.49**	**1.24**
BRICS	**237 664**	**324 227**	**3.47**	**2.89**	**163 892**	**193 182**	**2.19**	**1.48**	**1.45**	**1.68**	**1.25**	**1.39**

Note: Calendar year: Year ending 30 June for Australia and 31 May for New Zealand.
Average 2011-13est: Data for 2013 are estimated.

1. Includes Israel and also transition economies: Kazakhstan, Kyrgyzstan, Tajikistan, Turkmenistan, Uzbekistan, Armenia, Azerbaijan and Georgia.
2. Refers to mainland only. The economies of Chinese Taipei, Hong Kong (China) and Macau (China) are included in the Other Asia Pacific aggregate.
3. Excludes Iceland but includes all EU28 member countries.
4. Least-squares growth rate (see glossary).

Source: OECD and FAO Secretariats.

StatLink *http://dx.doi.org/10.1787/888933102297*

Table A.34. Whey powder and casein projections

Calendar year

		Average 2011-13est.	2023	Growth (%)[2]	
				2004-13	2014-23
AUSTRALIA					
Net trade, whey	kt pw	85.4	76.1	1.30	-1.06
Exports, casein	kt pw	4.4	5.6	-13.88	3.37
CANADA					
Net trade, whey	kt pw	21.0	22.7	25.58	0.56
EUROPEAN UNION					
Whey powder					
Production	kt pw	1 831.9	2 145.7	1.95	1.24
Consumption	kt pw	1 358.3	1 454.9	0.75	0.48
Net trade	kt pw	473.6	690.8	6.27	3.05
Casein					
Production	kt pw	131.8	156.5	-2.13	1.62
Consumption	kt pw	84.1	85.0	-4.45	-0.04
Net trade	kt pw	47.7	71.5	4.41	4.01
JAPAN					
Net trade, whey	kt pw	-51.6	-81.4	0.43	4.92
Casein imports	kt pw	13.6	13.3	-3.67	-0.02
KOREA					
Net trade, whey	kt pw	-27.5	-29.7	-4.12	1.94
MEXICO					
Net trade, whey	kt pw	-30.0	-26.6	-4.43	-1.07
NEW ZEALAND					
Net trade, whey	kt pw	7.5	11.7	17.28	3.78
Exports, casein	kt pw	150.5	200.5	-0.28	2.58
UNITED STATES					
Whey					
Production	kt pw	485.4	513.7	0.06	0.57
Consumption	kt pw	282.5	205.0	0.09	-2.74
Exports	kt pw	203.8	308.7	0.53	3.56
Imports, casein	kt pw	111.6	150.7	0.06	2.22
ARGENTINA					
Net trade, whey	kt pw	62.0	129.0	30.25	5.41
BRAZIL					
Net trade, whey	kt pw	-21.3	-32.1	-3.22	4.00
CHINA[1]					
Net trade, whey	kt pw	-373.6	-641.8	10.84	4.49
RUSSIAN FEDERATION					
Net trade, whey	kt pw	-55.7	-70.5	2.65	2.18

Note: Calendar year: Year ending 30 June for Australia and 31 May for New Zealand.

Average 2011-13est: Data for 2013 are estimated.

1. Refers to mainland only. The economies of Chinese Taipei, Hong Kong (China) and Macau (China) are included in the Other Asia Pacific aggregate.
2. Least-squares growth rate (see glossary).

Source: OECD and FAO Secretariats.

StatLink 🔗 http://dx.doi.org/10.1787/888933102316

Table A.35. Main policy assumptions for dairy markets

Calendar year

		Average 2011-13est	2014	2015	2016	2017	2018	2019	2020	2021	2022	2023
CANADA												
Milk target price[1]	CADc/litre	73.9	76.8	78.1	79.3	80.7	81.9	83.2	84.4	85.6	86.7	87.9
Butter support price	CAD/t	7 293.4	7 470.9	7 552.3	7 627.8	7 704.1	7 781.2	7 859.0	7 937.6	8 016.9	8 097.1	8 178.1
SMP support price	CAD/t	6 381.7	6 489.0	6 831.8	6 892.3	7 069.8	7 241.3	7 423.1	7 613.7	7 784.3	7 931.7	8 064.0
Cheese tariff-quota	kt pw	20.4	20.4	20.4	20.4	20.4	20.4	20.4	20.4	20.4	20.4	20.4
In-quota tariff	%	1.2	1.2	1.2	1.2	1.2	1.2	1.2	1.2	1.2	1.2	1.2
Out-of-quota tariff	%	245.6	245.6	245.6	245.6	245.6	245.6	245.6	245.6	245.6	245.6	245.6
Subsidised export limits (WTO)												
Cheese	kt pw	9.0	9.0	9.0	9.0	9.0	9.0	9.0	9.0	9.0	9.0	9.0
SMP	kt pw	45.0	45.0	45.0	45.0	45.0	45.0	45.0	45.0	45.0	45.0	45.0
EUROPEAN UNION[2]												
Milk quota	kt pw	149 203	150 446	0	0	0	0	0	0	0	0	0
Butter reference price[3]	EUR/t	2 463.9	2 463.9	2 463.9	2 463.9	2 463.9	2 463.9	2 463.9	2 463.9	2 463.9	2 463.9	2 463.9
SMP reference price	EUR/t	1 698.0	1 698.0	1 698.0	1 698.0	1 698.0	1 698.0	1 698.0	1 698.0	1 698.0	1 698.0	1 698.0
Butter tariff-quotas	kt pw	86.4	86.4	86.4	86.4	86.4	86.4	86.4	86.4	86.4	86.4	86.4
Cheese tariff-quotas	kt pw	107.0	107.0	107.0	107.0	107.0	107.0	107.0	107.0	107.0	107.0	107.0
SMP tariff-quota	kt pw	68.5	68.5	68.5	68.5	68.5	68.5	68.5	68.5	68.5	68.5	68.5
Subsidised export limits (WTO)												
Butter	kt pw	411.6	411.6	411.6	411.6	411.6	411.6	411.6	411.6	411.6	411.6	411.6
Cheese	kt pw	331.7	331.7	331.7	331.7	331.7	331.7	331.7	331.7	331.7	331.7	331.7
SMP	kt pw	323.4	323.4	323.4	323.4	323.4	323.4	323.4	323.4	323.4	323.4	323.4
JAPAN												
Direct payments	JPY/kg	12.2	12.6	12.6	12.6	12.6	12.6	12.6	12.6	12.6	12.6	12.6
Cheese tariff[4]	%	31.2	31.2	31.2	31.2	31.2	31.2	31.2	31.2	31.2	31.2	31.2
Tariff-quotas												
Butter	kt pw	1.9	1.9	1.9	1.9	1.9	1.9	1.9	1.9	1.9	1.9	1.9
In-quota tariff	%	35.0	35.0	35.0	35.0	35.0	35.0	35.0	35.0	35.0	35.0	35.0
Out-of-quota tariff	%	732.6	732.6	732.6	732.6	732.6	732.6	732.6	732.6	732.6	732.6	732.6
SMP	kt pw	115.7	115.7	115.7	115.7	115.7	115.7	115.7	115.7	115.7	115.7	115.7
In-quota tariff	%	15.8	15.8	15.8	15.8	15.8	15.8	15.8	15.8	15.8	15.8	15.8
Out-of-quota tariff	%	210.4	210.4	210.4	210.4	210.4	210.4	210.4	210.4	210.4	210.4	210.4
WMP	kt pw	0.0	0.0	0.0	0.0	0.0	0.0	0.0	0.0	0.0	0.0	0.0
In-quota tariff	%	24.0	24.0	24.0	24.0	24.0	24.0	24.0	24.0	24.0	24.0	24.0
Out-of-quota tariff	%	316.2	316.2	316.2	316.2	316.2	316.2	316.2	316.2	316.2	316.2	316.2
KOREA												
Tariff-quotas												
Butter	kt pw	0.4	0.4	0.4	0.4	0.4	0.4	0.4	0.4	0.4	0.4	0.4
In-quota tariff	%	40.0	40.0	40.0	40.0	40.0	40.0	40.0	40.0	40.0	40.0	40.0
Out-of-quota tariff	%	89.0	89.0	89.0	89.0	89.0	89.0	89.0	89.0	89.0	89.0	89.0
SMP	kt pw	1.0	1.0	1.0	1.0	1.0	1.0	1.0	1.0	1.0	1.0	1.0
In-quota tariff	%	20.0	20.0	20.0	20.0	20.0	20.0	20.0	20.0	20.0	20.0	20.0
Out-of-quota tariff	%	176.0	176.0	176.0	176.0	176.0	176.0	176.0	176.0	176.0	176.0	176.0
WMP	kt pw	0.6	0.6	0.6	0.6	0.6	0.6	0.6	0.6	0.6	0.6	0.6
In-quota tariff	%	40.0	40.0	40.0	40.0	40.0	40.0	40.0	40.0	40.0	40.0	40.0
Out-of-quota tariff	%	176.0	176.0	176.0	176.0	176.0	176.0	176.0	176.0	176.0	176.0	176.0

Table A.35. **Main policy assumptions for dairy markets** (cont.)

Calendar year

		Average 2011-13est	2014	2015	2016	2017	2018	2019	2020	2021	2022	2023
MEXICO												
Butter tariff	%	0.0	0.0	0.0	0.0	0.0	0.0	0.0	0.0	0.0	0.0	0.0
Tariff-quotas												
Cheese	kt pw	9.4	9.4	9.4	9.4	9.4	9.4	9.4	9.4	9.4	9.4	9.4
In-quota tariff	%	50.0	50.0	50.0	50.0	50.0	50.0	50.0	50.0	50.0	50.0	50.0
Out-of-quota tariff	%	116.7	75.0	60.0	45.0	45.0	45.0	45.0	45.0	45.0	45.0	45.0
SMP	kt pw	90.0	90.0	90.0	90.0	90.0	90.0	90.0	90.0	90.0	90.0	90.0
In-quota tariff	%	0.0	0.0	0.0	0.0	0.0	0.0	0.0	0.0	0.0	0.0	0.0
Out-of-quota tariff	%	83.7	60.0	60.0	50.0	45.0	45.0	45.0	45.0	45.0	45.0	45.0
Liconsa social program	Mn MXN	1 093.3	1 050.0	1 050.0	1 050.0	1 050.0	1 050.0	1 050.0	1 050.0	1 050.0	1 050.0	1 050.0
RUSSIAN FEDERATION												
Butter tariff	%	15.0	15.0	15.0	0.0	0.0	0.0	0.0	0.0	0.0	0.0	0.0
Cheese tariff	%	15.0	15.0	15.0	0.0	0.0	0.0	0.0	0.0	0.0	0.0	0.0
UNITED STATES												
Milk support price[1]	USDc/litre	22.5	22.5	22.5	22.5	22.5	22.5	22.5	22.5	22.5	22.5	22.5
Target price[5]	USDc/litre	37.3	37.3	37.3	37.3	37.3	37.3	37.3	37.3	37.3	37.3	37.3
Butter support price	USD/t	2 315.0	2 315.0	2 315.0	2 315.0	2 315.0	2 315.0	2 315.0	2 315.0	2 315.0	2 315.0	2 315.0
SMP support price	USD/t	1 763.7	1 763.7	1 763.7	1 763.7	1 763.7	1 763.7	1 763.7	1 763.7	1 763.7	1 763.7	1 763.7
Butter tariff-quota	kt pw	13.1	13.1	13.1	13.1	13.1	13.1	13.1	13.1	13.1	13.1	13.1
In-quota tariff	%	10.1	10.1	10.1	10.1	10.1	10.1	10.1	10.1	10.1	10.1	10.1
Out-of-quota tariff	%	112.0	112.0	112.0	112.0	112.0	112.0	112.0	112.0	112.0	112.0	112.0
Cheese tariff-quota	kt pw	135.0	135.0	135.0	135.0	135.0	135.0	135.0	135.0	135.0	135.0	135.0
In-quota tariff	%	12.3	12.3	12.3	12.3	12.3	12.3	12.3	12.3	12.3	12.3	12.3
Out-of-quota tariff	%	87.0	87.0	87.0	87.0	87.0	87.0	87.0	87.0	87.0	87.0	87.0
Subsidised export limits (WTO)												
Butter	kt pw	21.0	21.0	21.0	21.0	21.0	21.0	21.0	21.0	21.0	21.0	21.0
SMP	kt pw	68.0	68.0	68.0	68.0	68.0	68.0	68.0	68.0	68.0	68.0	68.0
INDIA												
Milk tariff	%	80.0	80.0	80.0	80.0	80.0	80.0	80.0	80.0	80.0	80.0	80.0
Butter tariff	%	40.0	40.0	40.0	40.0	40.0	40.0	40.0	40.0	40.0	40.0	40.0
Cheese tariff	%	40.0	40.0	40.0	40.0	40.0	40.0	40.0	40.0	40.0	40.0	40.0
Whole milk powder tariff	%	20.0	20.0	20.0	20.0	20.0	20.0	20.0	20.0	20.0	20.0	20.0
SOUTH AFRICA												
Milk powder tariff-quota	kt pw	4.5	4.5	4.5	4.5	4.5	4.5	4.5	4.5	4.5	4.5	4.5
In-quota tariff	%	20.0	20.0	20.0	20.0	20.0	20.0	20.0	20.0	20.0	20.0	20.0
Out-of-quota tariff	%	80.8	80.8	80.8	80.8	80.8	80.8	80.8	80.8	80.8	80.8	80.8

Note: Average 2011-13est: Data for 2013 are estimated.

The sources for tariffs and Tariff Rate Quotas are the national questionnaire reply, UNCTAD and WTO.

1. For manufacturing milk.
2. Till 2014, EU farmers can be granted the Single payment scheme (SPS) or the Single area payment scheme (SAPS), which provides flat-rate payments independent from current production decisions and market developments. From 2015, it becomes the Basic payment scheme (BPS) and it shall account for 68% maximum of the national direct payment envelopes. On top of this, from 2015 onwards, new compulsory policy instruments are introduced: the Green Payment (30%) and young farmer scheme (2%).
3. Buying-in when market prices go below the reference price for SMP and 90% of the reference price for butter is operable automatically for a maximum quantity of 109 000 tonnes for SMP and 50 000 tonnes for butter (before 2014, this ceiling was set at 30 000 tonnes). Above that ceiling intervention can take place only via tender.
4. Excludes processed cheese.
5. The counter-cyclical payment for milk is determined as a percentage difference between the target price and the Boston class I price. The difference is set at 34% in 2007 and 2008, at 45% in 2009-2012 and 34% thereafter. The target price is adjusted by 45% of the percentage difference between the National Average Dairy Feed Rations Cost and the target cost of feed rations of 16.20 USD/100kg between 2009 and 2012 and 20.94 USD/100kg thereafter.

Source: OECD and FAO Secretariats.

StatLink ⟶ http://dx.doi.org/10.1787/888933102335

Table A.36. World cotton projections

Crop year

		Average 2011-13est	2014	2015	2016	2017	2018	2019	2020	2021	2022	2023
WORLD												
Production	Mt	26.8	25.7	25.4	25.8	26.2	27.5	28.3	29.1	29.6	30.3	31.0
Area	Mha	33.1	33.6	32.9	33.3	33.8	34.9	35.8	36.3	36.8	37.1	37.8
Yield	t/ha	0.67	0.76	0.77	0.77	0.78	0.79	0.79	0.80	0.81	0.82	0.82
Consumption	Mt	23.3	25.0	26.3	27.3	27.4	28.0	28.1	29.5	29.8	30.4	30.8
Closing stocks	Mt	18.0	21.2	20.5	19.2	18.2	18.0	18.4	18.2	18.2	18.4	18.8
Price[1]	USD/t	2 005.4	1 681.9	1 641.3	1 607.1	1 744.9	1 747.0	1 803.1	1 913.7	2 000.6	2 084.1	2 131.2
DEVELOPED COUNTRIES												
Production	Mt	6.3	6.3	5.8	5.7	5.7	5.8	5.9	6.0	6.1	6.3	6.4
Consumption	Mt	1.6	1.7	1.8	1.8	1.9	1.9	1.9	1.9	1.9	1.9	1.9
Closing stocks	Mt	2.0	2.7	3.0	3.1	3.1	3.3	3.5	3.7	3.8	3.9	4.0
DEVELOPING COUNTRIES												
Production	Mt	20.5	19.5	19.5	20.1	20.5	21.6	22.4	23.1	23.5	24.1	24.6
Consumption	Mt	21.6	23.3	24.5	25.4	25.6	26.1	26.2	27.6	27.9	28.5	28.9
Closing stocks	Mt	16.0	18.5	17.4	16.1	15.1	14.6	14.9	14.5	14.4	14.5	14.8
OECD[2]												
Production	Mt	5.9	5.6	5.2	5.1	5.1	5.2	5.3	5.3	5.5	5.7	5.8
Consumption	Mt	3.0	3.4	3.5	3.6	3.5	3.6	3.6	3.6	3.6	3.7	3.7
Closing stocks	Mt	2.3	3.1	3.2	3.2	3.3	3.5	3.7	3.9	4.0	4.1	4.2

Note: Crop year: See Glossary of Terms for definitions.

Average 2011-13est: Data for 2013 are estimated.

1. Cotlook A index, Middling 1 3/32", c.f.r. far Eastern ports (August/July).
2. Excludes Iceland but includes all EU28 member countries.

Source: OECD and FAO Secretariats.

StatLink ᐧᐧᑕ *http://dx.doi.org/10.1787/888933102354*

Table A.37.1. Cotton projections: Production and trade

Crop year

	PRODUCTION (kt)		Growth (%)[4]		IMPORTS (kt)		Growth (%)[4]		EXPORTS (kt)		Growth (%)[4]	
	Average 2011-13est	2023	2004-13	2014-23	Average 2011-13est	2023	2004-13	2014-23	Average 2011-13est	2023	2004-13	2014-23
WORLD	**26 842**	**30 975**	**0.01**	**2.43**	**9 271**	**10 800**	**1.48**	**3.67**	**9 417**	**10 569**	**1.14**	**3.76**
DEVELOPED COUNTRIES	**6 276**	**6 390**	**-3.05**	**0.74**	**369**	**457**	**-14.35**	**1.30**	**5 007**	**4 843**	**-1.50**	**1.98**
NORTH AMERICA	3 344	3 513	-5.43	0.40	4	7	-29.73	11.48	2 557	2 568	-3.25	2.27
Canada	0	0	0.00	0.00	1	5	-40.20	19.76	0	0	0.00	0.00
United States	3 344	3 513	-5.43	0.40	3	1	..	-1.12	2 557	2 568	-3.25	2.27
EUROPE	324	314	-6.06	0.22	256	231	-15.49	-1.95	294	280	-4.07	0.41
European Union	322	312	-6.09	0.22	194	196	-13.58	-1.01	293	278	-4.08	0.42
Russian Federation	1	1	0.21	0.26	57	30	-20.65	-6.15	0	0	0.00	0.00
Ukraine	1	1	0.00	0.05	1	1	0.00	-0.12	1	1	0.00	0.12
OCEANIA DEVELOPED	1 065	1 047	13.11	3.25	1	1	-30.40	0.00	1 119	1 036	12.46	2.95
Australia	1 064	1 046	13.14	3.26	0	0	-52.88	-0.19	1 118	1 035	12.49	2.96
New Zealand	1	1	0.00	0.00	1	1	0.00	0.00	1	1	0.00	0.00
OTHER DEVELOPED[1]	1 543	1 515	-2.52	0.16	108	219	-8.18	6.75	1 037	959	-4.39	0.95
Japan	0	0	0.00	0.00	72	68	-9.64	-0.92	0	0	-16.84	0.00
South Africa	9	9	-6.44	-0.40	31	146	-2.82	16.62	11	151	46.11	22.96
DEVELOPING COUNTRIES	**20 544**	**24 586**	**1.13**	**2.92**	**8 894**	**10 343**	**3.08**	**3.78**	**4 426**	**5 726**	**5.39**	**5.53**
AFRICA	1 495	2 010	-2.52	4.18	96	97	-7.05	-5.22	1 219	1 717	-2.39	3.73
NORTH AFRICA	130	88	-9.36	-1.15	91	78	-6.08	-6.33	72	11	-5.63	-16.88
Algeria	0	0	-19.20	0.06	3	2	-21.09	-4.24	0	0	0.00	0.18
Egypt	130	88	-9.36	-1.15	54	45	-8.26	-9.01	72	11	-5.62	-16.90
SUB-SAHARAN AFRICA	1 365	1 922	-1.67	4.51	5	19	-17.16	1.28	1 147	1 706	-2.16	4.25
LATIN AMERICA and CARIBBEAN	2 118	2 939	2.59	4.90	382	615	-5.73	0.48	1 063	1 542	9.91	11.91
Argentina	192	252	4.86	3.89	7	8	-20.88	-12.22	55	179	21.12	217.05
Brazil	1 590	2 344	3.10	5.56	27	269	-10.19	9.08	929	1 284	12.30	11.15
Chile	0	0	0.00	0.37	0	0	-47.42	-0.33	0	0	0.00	0.46
Mexico	226	216	5.64	2.15	234	202	-5.90	-4.24	57	50	1.98	0.64
Uruguay	1	1	0.00	0.10	1	1	0.00	-0.14	1	1	0.00	0.14
ASIA and PACIFIC	16 930	19 636	1.32	2.54	8 416	9 630	3.92	4.19	2 144	2 467	12.58	4.09
Bangladesh	23	38	8.87	3.85	707	1 300	3.44	4.14	0	0	0.00	0.01
China[2]	7 133	6 371	-0.62	0.33	4 317	3 297	7.91	7.05	11	13	2.16	2.85
India	6 272	9 234	5.30	4.68	231	261	7.80	2.89	1 723	2 151	19.59	5.16
Indonesia	6	7	-0.34	0.32	629	943	3.62	4.97	2	0	22.41	0.20
Iran, Islamic Republic of	59	66	-8.75	0.54	61	67	17.58	-0.15	0	0	-48.50	0.03
Korea	0	0	0.00	0.00	278	280	1.55	0.78	0	0	20.46	0.00
Malaysia	0	0	0.00	0.08	182	188	19.66	1.76	178	173	174.45	1.94
Pakistan	2 180	2 939	-0.20	2.78	355	662	-3.21	2.45	143	74	7.13	-1.23
Saudi Arabia	1	1	0.00	0.10	1	1	0.00	-0.14	1	1	0.00	0.14
Turkey	898	677	0.79	-0.07	628	1 249	-2.44	3.58	50	41	6.96	0.89
LEAST DEVELOPED COUNTRIES (LDC)	**1 170**	**1 668**	**-0.73**	**4.06**	**709**	**1 330**	**3.46**	**4.09**	**796**	**1 241**	**-3.80**	**4.94**
OECD[3]	**5 870**	**5 781**	**-2.43**	**0.85**	**1 416**	**2 007**	**-5.67**	**1.42**	**4 092**	**3 988**	**-0.56**	**2.23**
BRICS	**15 006**	**17 959**	**1.98**	**3.02**	**4 663**	**4 004**	**5.87**	**6.78**	**2 674**	**3 599**	**14.85**	**7.29**

.. Not available

Note: Crop year: See Glossary of Terms for definitions.

Average 2011-13est: Data for 2013 are estimated.

1. Includes Israel and also transition economies: Kazakhstan, Kyrgyzstan, Tajikistan, Turkmenistan, Uzbekistan, Armenia, Azerbaijan and Georgia.
2. Refers to mainland only. The economies of Chinese Taipei, Hong Kong (China) and Macau (China) are included in the Other Asia Pacific aggregate.
3. Excludes Iceland but includes all EU28 member countries.
4. Least-squares growth rate (see glossary).

Source: OECD and FAO Secretariats.

StatLink ⟨⟩ *http://dx.doi.org/10.1787/888933102373*

Table A.37.2. Cotton projections: Consumption
Crop year

	CONSUMPTION (kt)		Growth (%)[1]	
	Average 2011-13est	2023	2004-13	2014-23
WORLD	**23 251**	**30 837**	**-0.77**	**2.18**
DEVELOPED COUNTRIES	**1 625**	**1 912**	**-7.29**	**0.91**
NORTH AMERICA	753	890	-7.29	1.21
Canada	1	5	-39.78	19.66
United States	752	885	-6.89	1.16
EUROPE	285	267	-15.49	-2.13
European Union	219	231	-14.31	-1.23
Russian Federation	61	31	-19.43	-6.73
Ukraine	1	1	0.00	-0.18
OCEANIA DEVELOPED	9	8	31.51	-0.13
Australia	8	7	133.28	-0.14
New Zealand	1	1	0.00	0.00
OTHER DEVELOPED[2]	578	746	1.07	1.91
Japan	69	68	-10.05	-1.00
South Africa	19	0	-11.98	-41.87
DEVELOPING COUNTRIES	**21 611**	**28 925**	**-0.08**	**2.27**
AFRICA	275	354	-7.51	0.80
NORTH AFRICA	146	155	-8.05	-1.12
Algeria	3	2	-20.94	-3.79
Egypt	108	121	-9.42	-1.27
SUB-SAHARAN AFRICA	129	200	-6.90	2.59
LATIN AMERICA and CARIBBEAN	1 592	1 930	-2.02	0.32
Argentina	149	45	-0.11	-10.75
Brazil	900	1 282	-0.74	2.23
Chile	0	0	-41.43	-0.33
Mexico	329	370	-4.59	-2.23
Uruguay	1	1	0.00	-0.18
ASIA and PACIFIC	19 743	26 641	0.23	2.44
Bangladesh	767	1 311	4.70	4.39
China[3]	8 322	9 742	-1.51	1.38
India	4 733	7 201	4.33	4.08
Indonesia	514	940	1.10	3.94
Iran, Islamic Republic of	117	133	-0.68	0.15
Korea	263	280	0.72	0.27
Malaysia	15	16	-13.39	1.35
Pakistan	2 374	3 495	-0.80	2.81
Saudi Arabia	1	1	0.00	-0.18
Turkey	1 351	1 855	-1.45	1.86
LEAST DEVELOPED COUNTRIES (LDC)	**1 064**	**1 706**	**5.64**	**3.65**
OECD[4]	**2 999**	**3 706**	**-5.05**	**0.82**
BRICS	**14 035**	**18 257**	**0.00**	**2.38**

Note: Crop year: See Glossary of Terms for definitions.
Average 2011-13est: Data for 2013 are estimated.
1. Least-squares growth rate (see glossary).
2. Includes Israel and also transition economies: Kazakhstan, Kyrgyzstan, Tajikistan, Turkmenistan, Uzbekistan, Armenia, Azerbaijan and Georgia.
3. Refers to mainland only. The economies of Chinese Taipei, Hong Kong (China) and Macau (China) are included in the Other Asia Pacific aggregate.
4. Excludes Iceland but includes all EU28 member countries.
Source: OECD and FAO Secretariats.

StatLink http://dx.doi.org/10.1787/888933102392

Table A.38. Main policy assumptions for cotton markets

Crop year

		Average 2011-13est	2014	2015	2016	2017	2018	2019	2020	2021	2022	2023
ARGENTINA												
Export tax equivalent of export barriers	%	5.0	5.0	5.0	5.0	5.0	5.0	5.0	5.0	5.0	5.0	5.0
Tariff equivalent of import barriers	%	7.5	7.5	7.5	7.5	7.5	7.5	7.5	7.5	7.5	7.5	7.5
BRAZIL												
Producer Minimum Price, lint cotton	BRL/t	2 973.3	2 973.3	2 973.3	2 973.3	2 973.3	2 973.3	2 973.3	2 973.3	2 973.3	2 973.3	2 974.3
Tariff equivalent of import barriers	%	8.0	8.0	8.0	8.0	8.0	8.0	8.0	8.0	8.0	8.0	8.0
EUROPEAN UNION												
Area for coupled payment	kha	301.7	301.7	301.7	301.7	301.7	301.7	301.7	301.7	301.7	301.7	301.7
Coupled payment per ha[1]	EUR/ha	900.0	900.0	830.0	830.0	830.0	830.0	830.0	830.0	830.0	830.0	830.0
Tariff equivalent of import barriers	%	0.0	0.0	0.0	0.0	0.0	0.0	0.0	0.0	0.0	0.0	0.0
INDIA												
Minimum support price	INR/t	36 166.7	38 500.0	38 500.0	40 271.1	41 452.8	43 061.4	44 677.5	46 327.2	48 169.3	51 031.4	51 031.4
Tariff equivalent of import barriers	%	0.0	0.0	0.0	0.0	0.0	0.0	0.0	0.0	0.0	0.0	0.0
JAPAN												
Tariff equivalent of import barriers	%	0.0	0.0	0.0	0.0	0.0	0.0	0.0	0.0	0.0	0.0	0.0
KOREA												
Tariff equivalent of import barriers	%	0.0	0.0	0.0	0.0	0.0	0.0	0.0	0.0	0.0	0.0	0.0
MEXICO												
Tariff equivalent of import barriers	%	0.0	0.0	0.0	0.0	0.0	0.0	0.0	0.0	0.0	0.0	0.0
RUSSIAN FEDERATION												
Tariff equivalent of import barriers	%	0.0	0.0	0.0	0.0	0.0	0.0	0.0	0.0	0.0	0.0	0.0
UNITED STATES												
ACRE participation rate	%	1.1	1.1	1.1	1.1	1.1	1.1	1.1	1.1	1.1	1.1	1.1
Loan rate, upland cotton	USD/t	1 146.4	1 146.4	1 146.4	1 146.4	1 146.4	1 146.4	1 146.4	1 146.4	1 146.4	1 146.4	1 146.4
Production flexibility contract payments	USD/t	147.0	147.0	147.0	147.0	147.0	147.0	147.0	147.0	147.0	147.0	147.0
CRP area	Mha	1.1	1.1	1.1	1.1	1.1	1.1	1.1	1.1	1.1	1.1	1.1
Economic Adjustment Assistance payment level	USD/t	73.5	66.1	66.1	66.1	66.1	66.1	66.1	66.1	66.1	66.1	66.1
TRQ	kt	73.2	73.2	73.2	73.2	73.2	73.2	73.2	73.2	73.2	73.2	73.2
In-quota tariff	USD/t	44.0	44.0	44.0	44.0	44.0	44.0	44.0	44.0	44.0	44.0	44.0
Out-of-quota tariff	USD/t	314.0	314.0	314.0	314.0	314.0	314.0	314.0	314.0	314.0	314.0	314.0
CHINA												
TRQ	kt	894.0	894.0	894.0	894.0	894.0	894.0	894.0	894.0	894.0	894.0	894.0
In-quota tariff	%	1.0	1.0	1.0	1.0	1.0	1.0	1.0	1.0	1.0	1.0	1.0
Out-of-quota tariff	%	40.0	40.0	40.0	40.0	40.0	40.0	40.0	40.0	40.0	40.0	40.0
TURKEY												
Tariff equivalent of import barriers	%	0.0	0.0	0.0	0.0	0.0	0.0	0.0	0.0	0.0	0.0	0.0

Note: Crop year: See Glossary of Terms for definitions.

Average 2011-13est: Data for 2013 are estimated.

1.   If the area is higher than the ceiling, the amount is proportionally reduced.

Source: OECD and FAO Secretariats.

StatLink ⬛⬛ *http://dx.doi.org/10.1787/888933102411*

Table B.1. Information on food price changes

	Total inflation % change (year-on-year)		Food inflation % change (year-on-year)[2]		Expenditure share of food		Food contribution to total change in inflation[3]	
	2013	2014	2013	2014	2013	2014	2013	2014
OECD								
Australia[1]	2.5	..	0.3	..	12.8	12.8	0.0	..
Austria	2.7	1.5	3.9	2.7	12.0	12.0	0.5	0.3
Belgium	1.5	1.1	3.7	1.9	17.4	17.4	0.6	0.3
Canada	0.5	1.5	0.6	1.0	11.5	11.5	0.1	0.1
Chile	1.6	3.0	5.3	4.4	18.9	18.9	1.0	0.8
Czech Republic	1.9	0.2	5.7	3.9	17.0	17.0	1.0	0.7
Denmark	1.3	1.0	2.3	-1.0	11.5	11.5	0.3	-0.1
Estonia	3.4	1.1	5.5	2.5	21.7	21.7	1.2	0.5
Finland	1.6	1.6	5.3	3.9	13.4	13.4	0.7	0.5
France	1.2	0.7	2.0	0.1	14.7	14.7	0.3	0.3
Germany	1.7	1.3	4.0	3.2	10.4	10.4	0.4	0.3
Greece	0.2	-1.5	0.2	-0.8	17.1	17.1	0.0	-0.1
Hungary	3.8	-0.1	6.1	-0.7	19.6	19.6	1.2	-0.1
Iceland	4.2	3.1	5.3	3.6	14.9	14.9	0.8	0.5
Ireland	1.2	0.2	2.4	-1.7	11.7	11.7	0.3	-0.2
Israel	1.5	1.4	3.0	2.8	14.3	14.3	0.4	0.4
Italy	2.2	0.7	3.1	1.3	16.3	16.3	0.5	0.2
Japan	-0.3	1.4	-0.8	1.5	19.0	19.0	-0.2	0.3
Korea	1.6	1.1	2.3	-1.8	14.4	14.4	0.3	-0.3
Luxembourg	2.1	1.5	4.1	3.1	11.1	11.1	0.5	0.3
Mexico	3.3	4.5	5.4	4.9	18.9	18.9	1.0	0.9
Netherlands	3.0	1.4	3.8	0.6	11.3	11.3	0.4	0.1
New Zealand[1]	1.1	..	0.5	..	17.4	17.4	0.1	..
Norway	1.3	2.3	0.0	3.1	13.3	13.3	0.0	0.4
Poland	1.7	0.7	3.6	2.4	24.1	24.1	0.9	0.6
Portugal	0.2	0.1	2.3	0.2	18.1	18.1	0.4	0.0
Slovak Republic	2.4	0.0	5.9	0.8	18.4	18.4	1.1	0.1
Slovenia	2.4	0.9	5.2	1.6	17.0	17.0	0.9	0.3
Spain	2.7	0.2	3.2	1.2	18.2	18.2	0.6	0.2
Sweden	0.0	-0.2	2.3	0.3	13.9	13.9	0.3	0.0
Switzerland	-0.3	0.1	1.0	1.1	10.8	10.8	0.1	0.1
Turkey	7.3	7.8	6.8	10.9	26.8	26.8	1.8	2.9
United Kingdom	2.7	1.9	4.2	2.0	11.8	11.8	0.5	0.2
United States	1.6	1.6	1.1	0.5	7.8	7.8	0.1	0.0
OECD Total	1.7	1.7	2.1	1.5	..	..	..	..
Enhanced Engagement								
Brazil	6.2	5.6	11.1	7.3	22.5	22.5	2.5	1.6
China	2.0	2.5	2.9	3.7	33.6	33.6	1.0	1.2
India	11.6	7.2	11.6	7.2	35.4	35.4	3.8	1.8
Indonesia	4.6	7.8	7.3	11.0	19.6	19.6	1.4	2.2
Russian Federation	7.1	6.1	6.3	4.3	32.8	32.8	2.1	1.4
South Africa	5.5	5.8	5.9	4.9	18.3	18.3	1.1	0.9

Table B.1. **Information on food price changes** (cont.)

	Total inflation % change (year-on-year)		Food inflation % change (year-on-year)[2]		Expenditure share of food		Food contribution to total change in inflation[3]	
	2013	2014	2013	2014	2013	2014	2013	2014
Non OECD								
Algeria	8.1	2.0	9.3	1.7	43.8	43.8	4.1	0.7
Argentina	11.1	13.8	9.5	12.6	20.3	20.3	1.9	2.6
Bangladesh	7.4	7.5	1.2	10.2	28.6	28.6	0.3	2.9
Bolivia	4.9	5.9	7.1	8.7	39.3	39.3	2.8	3.4
Botswana	7.5	4.4	7.5	3.6	23.7	23.7	1.8	0.9
Bulgaria	2.6	-1.3	6.6	4.7	37.2	37.2	2.5	1.7
Colombia	2.0	2.1	1.7	1.2	34.7	34.7	0.6	0.4
Costa Rica	5.7	3.1	3.9	2.2	25.7	25.7	1.0	0.6
Dominican Republic	4.7	2.8	6.6	0.7	29.2	29.2	1.9	0.2
Ecuador	4.1	2.9	5.1	3.1	31.7	31.7	1.6	1.0
Egypt	6.3	11.3	7.8	18.5	26.3	26.3	2.1	4.9
El Salvador	0.9	0.8	1.9	1.7	38.1	38.1	0.7	0.6
Ethiopia	12.7	7.8	12.7	5.1	57.0	57.0	7.2	2.9
Ghana	10.1	13.8	8.0	7.1	37.0	37.0	3.0	2.6
Guatelama	3.9	4.2	7.0	8.9	28.6	28.6	2.0	2.5
Haiti	7.2	3.4	7.8	3.2	50.4	50.4	3.9	1.6
Honduras	5.7	6.0	4.6	6.1	31.8	31.8	1.5	1.9
Hong Kong, China	3.8	3.9	3.8	4.2	16.1	16.1	0.6	0.7
Iraq	2.7	4.0	-0.4	10.2	35.0	35.0	-0.1	3.6
Jordan	6.7	3.3	3.8	3.0	35.2	35.2	1.3	1.1
Kenya	3.7	7.2	2.4	10.1	36.0	36.0	0.9	3.7
Madagascar	5.8	6.6	6.4	3.0	60.0	60.0	3.8	.8
Malawi	31.4	26.0	27.3	26.0	25.0	25.0	6.8	6.5
Malaysia	1.3	3.4	2.2	4.2	56.3	56.3	1.2	2.4
Moldavia	-2.0	0.4	1.7	0.5	60.0	60.0	1.0	0.3
Morocco	2.5	0.5	4.2	-0.2	40.4	40.4	1.7	-0.1
New Caledonia	1.9	0.0	2.6	-0.7	21.0	21.0	0.5	-0.1
Nicaragua	8.1	4.9	10.4	5.2	26.1	26.1	2.7	1.4
Niger	1.0	0.1	3.5	0.3	29.0	29.0	1.0	0.1
Nigeria	9.0	8.0	10.1	9.3	51.8	51.8	5.2	4.3
Pakistan	8.1	8.4	8.1	8.4	45.5	45.5	3.7	3.3
Panama	4.7	3.4	7.1	4.5	33.6	33.6	2.4	1.5
Paraguay	4.1	3.9	2.8	4.8	39.1	39.1	1.1	1.9
Peru	2.8	3.2	4.3	2.8	29.0	29.0	1.2	0.8
Philipinnes	3.1	4.2	2.4	5.5	39.0	39.0	0.9	2.1
Romania	6.0	1.1	7.2	-2.2	37.4	37.4	2.7	-0.8
Rwanda	5.7	3.7	8.3	4.2	48.4	48.4	4.0	2.0
Senegal	1.2	0.5	1.2	0.3	53.4	53.4	0.6	0.2
Singapore	3.6	1.4	1.0	3.0	8.5	8.5	0.1	0.3
Sri Lanka	9.8	4.4	10.8	1.3	41.0	41.0	4.4	0.5
Chinese Taipei	1.1	0.8	2.4	1.0	16.6	16.6	0.4	0.2
Tanzania	10.9	6.0	6.0	6.0	33.6	33.6	2.0	2.0
Thailand	3.4	1.9	4.3	3.6	33.0	33.0	1.4	1.2
Tunisia	6.0	5.8	8.7	7.6	33.8	33.8	2.9	2.6
Uganda	4.9	6.9	0.0	11.1	27.2	27.2	0.0	3.0
Uruguay	8.7	9.2	11.9	9.0	19.2	19.2	2.3	1.7
Zambia	7.0	7.3	7.6	5.9	52.5	52.5	4.0	3.1

.. Not available

1. No data available for January 2014 in Australia and New Zealand.
2. CPI food: definition based on national sources.
3. Contribution is food inflation multiplied by expenditure share, expressed in %.

Source: OECD and national sources (for details, see the online version of tables).

StatLink ⫘ *http://dx.doi.org/10.1787/888933102430*

ORGANISATION FOR ECONOMIC CO-OPERATION AND DEVELOPMENT

The OECD is a unique forum where governments work together to address the economic, social and environmental challenges of globalisation. The OECD is also at the forefront of efforts to understand and to help governments respond to new developments and concerns, such as corporate governance, the information economy and the challenges of an ageing population. The Organisation provides a setting where governments can compare policy experiences, seek answers to common problems, identify good practice and work to co-ordinate domestic and international policies.

The OECD member countries are: Australia, Austria, Belgium, Canada, Chile, the Czech Republic, Denmark, Estonia, Finland, France, Germany, Greece, Hungary, Iceland, Ireland, Israel, Italy, Japan, Korea, Luxembourg, Mexico, the Netherlands, New Zealand, Norway, Poland, Portugal, the Slovak Republic, Slovenia, Spain, Sweden, Switzerland, Turkey, the United Kingdom and the United States. The European Union takes part in the work of the OECD.

OECD Publishing disseminates widely the results of the Organisation's statistics gathering and research on economic, social and environmental issues, as well as the conventions, guidelines and standards agreed by its members.

OECD PUBLISHING, 2, rue André-Pascal, 75775 PARIS CEDEX 16
(51 2014 04 1 P) ISBN 978-92-64-21089-9 – 2014-02